A SURVEY OF
NORTH WEST AFRICA
(*THE MAGHRIB*)

A SURVEY OF
NORTH WEST AFRICA
(THE MAGHRIB)

Edited by
NEVILL BARBOUR

Issued under the auspices of the
Royal Institute of International Affairs

OXFORD UNIVERSITY PRESS
LONDON   NEW YORK   TORONTO
1959

Oxford University Press, Amen House, London E.C.4

GLASGOW NEW YORK TORONTO MELBOURNE WELLINGTON
BOMBAY CALCUTTA MADRAS KARACHI KUALA LUMPUR
CAPE TOWN IBADAN NAIROBI ACCRA

PRINTED IN GREAT BRITAIN

CONTENTS

COMMONLY USED ABBREVIATIONS

AEF   L'Afrique Équatoriale Française.

AML   Amis du Manifeste et de la Liberté (Algeria).

AOE   Africa Occidental Española.

AOF   L'Afrique Occidentale Française.

CCE   Comité de Coordination et d'Exécution.

CRUA   Comité Révolutionnaire d'Unité et d'Action (Algeria).

FLN   Front de Libération National (Algeria).

MNA   Mouvement National Algérien.

MTLD   Mouvement pour le Triomphe des Libertés Démocratiques (Algeria).

OCRS   Organisation Commune des Régions Sahariennes.

PCA   Parti Communiste Algérien.

PDI   Parti Démocratique de l'Indépendence (Morocco).

PPA   Parti Populaire Algérien.

UDMA   Union Démocratique du Manifeste Algérien.

UGTA   Union Générale des Travailleurs Algériens.

UMT   Union Marocaine de Travail.

UGTT   Union Générale des Travailleurs Tunisiens.

PREFACE

THE object of this Survey is to present the principal facts about North West Africa in as concise and yet readable a manner as possible. For this purpose a separate section has been devoted to each of the four major territories concerned and to each of those areas which were under a distinct administration on 1 January 1958—Mauritania, various portions of the Sahara, the Spanish *presidios* on or near the Mediterranean coast of Morocco, and the enclave of Ifni, recently constituted a Spanish province. The Cape Juby or Tarfaya district of Morocco also appears among the latter because it was still a Spanish protectorate at the time of writing, though it has since been reunited with the remainder of the Moroccan Kingdom. Notes have been included on the historical relations of Spain with Morocco and of Italy with the Eastern Maghrib. The regional chapters are completed by a general introduction which treats the area and its history as a whole.

North West Africa was chosen for the title rather than North Africa because the latter is often restricted to the area formerly under French control and suggests primarily the relatively well-watered and thickly-populated region of the three western countries only. The Survey on the contrary covers the whole of the area between the Atlantic and the western frontiers of Egypt and of the Republic of the Sudan. This region forms a linguistic, geographical, and sociological unit which makes it eminently suitable for treatment as a distinct section of the African continent.

It is an area which is evolving very rapidly. Libya, Tunisia, and Morocco have recently emerged from protected or colonial status and become independent and sovereign states. Algeria, by midsummer 1958, had been in a state of armed insurrection for nearly four years. The future status of Mauritania and the Saharan regions is a matter of dispute. Further important changes may well occur between the time when this book goes to press and the date of its publication. It has therefore to be made clear that the viewpoint is that of the beginning of 1958, though it has been possible to make mention of the more important later events such as the bombing of Sakiet Sidi Yusuf, the Maghrib Unity Conference in Tangier, and the dissidence in Algeria which led to the assumption of power by

General de Gaulle. The Survey can only be considered topical in the sense that it is designed to prepare the reader for whatever developments may occur in the next few years.

Contemporary Arab names, whether of people or places, are given in the spelling which readers are most likely to encounter in books and newspapers or on maps. The name of any given person or place is spelt in the same way throughout the book, but the same Arabic original, in the case of two people or places of the same name, may appear in more than one form. This is due to the influence of the European language predominant in the country concerned or, sometimes, in the case of personal names, simply to the preference or fancy of the owner of the name. Where a generally accepted English form exists, this has been preferred, e.g. Algiers, not the Arabic al-Jazair, the French Alger, the Spanish Argel, or the Italian Algeri. Shauen, not Xauen or Chauen; Wazzan and wadi, not Ouezzane and oued. Arabic personal names which have passed into history are transliterated on a uniform system.

In order to ensure unity of treatment, the editor was given entire responsibility for the choice and handling of the subjects, for the arrangement of the book, and for the opinions expressed. For this reason his name alone appears on the title-page. But in fact the work is the result of co-operation not only by British specialists but also by members of the other three European nations which have been directly concerned with the government of North Africa during the last hundred years. All of them have friends in the area concerned as well as an extensive knowledge of its affairs. Thus, though the picture has been painted from the outside, it is hoped that citizens of the Maghrib will recognize it as a fair portrait.

In conclusion, the editor wishes to convey his warmest thanks to all those who have contributed material for the various sections, particularly M. André Adam, Director of the École d'Administration Marocaine, Rabat; Professor Francesco Gabrieli, Professor of Arabic, University of Rome; Mr. Thomas Hodgkin, writer and traveller; Señorita Carmen Martín de la Escalera, of the Centro de Estúdios Políticos, Madrid; M. le Commandant Vincent Monteil, Director of the Centre d'Études Pratiques d'Arabe Moderne, Bikfaya, Lebanon; M. Henri de Montéty, formerly *Contrôleur Civil*, Tunis; Mr. J. S. Trimingham, Head of the Arabic Department, Glasgow University; and Lieut. Colonel P. Sandison, OBE, formerly of the British Military Administration, Libya.

His best thanks are also due to those members of a Chatham House committee who kindly read the book in typescript and made a number of valuable suggestions; and to Miss H. Oliver whose devoted work as sub-editor eliminated a number of errors and contributed greatly to the final form of the book.

NEVILL BARBOUR

November 1958

INTRODUCTION

NORTH WEST AFRICA (*AL-MAGHRIB AL-ARABI*) AND ITS PEOPLE

APART from the Sahara, North West Africa is today divided into four main territories; Morocco, Algeria, Tunisia, and Libya. Their present frontiers date from the Turkish conquest of the three eastern areas rather more than 400 years ago. Before the recent French and Spanish protectorates, however, Morocco had existed as an independent state for 1,000 years; while Tunisia with certain interruptions—principally the 600 years of Roman rule—had been the seat of independent or virtually independent governments for the greater part of the time since the establishment of Carthage in the first millennium before Christ.

Geography

For political reasons, and for the purposes of this book, the eastern limit of North West Africa can be taken as the Libyan-Egyptian and Libyan-Sudanese frontiers. Geographically, however, and to some extent historically, it is more correct to define it as the 300 miles of desert, running right down to the sea, which separate the Libyan coastal province of Tripolitania from the other Libyan coastal province, Cyrenaica.

In the north the area is limited by the Mediterranean sea; and in the west by the Atlantic. Only in the south is there any uncertainty. Clearly some portion of the Sahara should be included in North West Africa, but it does not necessarily follow that the whole of it should be. In fact, however, the people of the Sahara, with few exceptions, are Arabic or Berber-speaking, just as are the people of the coastal states; they derived their religion from the north, not from the south; their way of life has been determined by insufficiency of water, just as that of the people of the countries on their north. Racially the Saharans belong mostly to the white north, not to the black south. While, therefore, the country adjoining the Niger and the Senegal is obviously a border land between black and white, the Sahara as a whole should be included with North West and not with Central Africa. The logic of this was recently recognized by the

1

French Government and they therefore formed the *Organisation Commune des Régions Sahariennes* by adding territories formerly attached to French West and Equatorial Africa to the much larger Algerian and Moroccan Saharas formerly known as the Southern Areas.

Language

Roughly three-quarters of the population of the whole area speak Arabic as their mother-tongue, and one-quarter Berber. A knowledge of French is common among the Muslim upper and middle classes in Tunisia, Algeria, and the former French zone of Morocco, as well as among the Christian residents; Spanish in the northern zone of Morocco; Italian in Libya and, to a limited extent, in Tunisia; and English in Libya. This linguistic mosaic is of course the result of the period of European domination of which the first sign was the short-lived occupation of certain Tripolitanian and Tunisian coastal towns by the Norman rulers of Sicily in the twelfth century. It was resumed with the Portuguese and Spanish captures of African seaports in the late fifteenth and early sixteenth centuries; almost disappeared in the seventeenth and eighteenth centuries, but revived with the French capture of Algiers in 1830. It culminated with the occupation of the Anti-Atlas and the Moroccan Sahara in 1934, and began to pass away with the independence of Libya in 1951.

In Arabic, which is the mother-tongue of the people who are now resuming control of North West Africa, the area is known as the Maghrib or 'west'. The portion of the world throughout which Arabic is spoken is in fact divided into three parts, roughly equal in population. The Arab world, as it is often called, can be thought of as a bird with outstretched wings. Egypt and the Nile valley including the Sudan represent the body; Arab Asia forms one wing, and the Maghrib the other. During the period of European control of the southern shore of the Mediterranean, we have been accustomed to think of the Arab world and the problems belonging to it as confined to the area which begins at Alexandria, at the far end of the Mediterranean, and extends north, south, and east from that point. We have now to get accustomed to the idea, familiar enough to our ancestors, that what we call the east begins for us at Tangier, only eight miles beyond south Spain and no farther from America than we are ourselves. It was thus through Morocco, Algeria, and Tunisia that American troops approached Europe in 1942. Gibraltar and Trafalgar are Arabic names and at least 700 other place-names in Spain can be definitely identified as

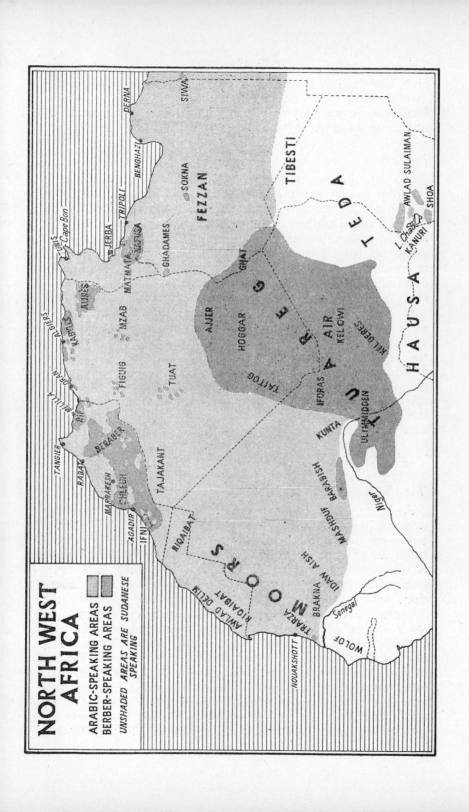

NORTH WEST AFRICA

ARABIC-SPEAKING AREAS

BERBER-SPEAKING AREAS

UNSHADED AREAS ARE SUDANESE SPEAKING

TUNIS
Cape Bon
ALGIERS
ORAN
TANGIER
MELILLA
RIF
RABAT
MARRAKESH
AGADIR
IFNI
CHLEUH
BERABER
KABELIA
AURES
MZAB
FIGUIG
TAJAKANT
RIQAIBAT
AWLAD DELIM
TRARZA
RIGAIBAT
NOUAKSHOTT
BRAKNA
IDAW AISH
Senegal
WOLOF
MASHDUF
BARABISH
KUNTA
IFORAS
TAITOG
TUAT
AJER
HOGGAR
GHAT
AIR
KELOWI
KEL GERES
ULIMMIDDEN
Niger
GHADAMES
MATMATA
JERBA
TRIPOLI
BENGHAZI
DERNA
SIWA
SOKNA
FEZZAN
TIBESTI
TEDA
AWLAD SULAIMAN
SHOA
L. Chad
KANURI
HAUSA
TARGUI

of Arabic origin. So can a number of important words in our
own language, for example, admiral and arsenal. Arabic
civilization came very close to us once and it is a mistake to
underrate it today.

Population

The population of the Maghrib is about 26 million, of whom
1 million live in the Sahara. Of the remaining 25 million about
10 million live in each of Morocco and Algeria; 4 million in
Tunisia, and 1 million in Libya. About 1½ million of the total
are European Christians; these immigrated during the last 130
years and two-thirds of them have settled in Algeria. Most of
them came from South Europe: people of French origin predominate in the central portion of Algeria, in Tunisia, and in
the main zone of Morocco; people of Spanish origin in the
northern zone of Morocco and in the Oran province of Algeria; people of Italian and Maltese origin in the east. With the
exception of about 500,000 Jews, the remainder of the population are arabized Berbers or North African Arabs. These, however, have distinct national characteristics in the various territories concerned. In late Roman times, Christianity was widespread and there were very many African bishoprics; unlike
the Middle East, however, where indigenous Christian groups
survived, indigenous Christianity in North Africa died out in
the eleventh century and for the common people the words
'Arab' and 'Muslim,' are more or less synonymous.

The Habitat

As in the rest of the Arab world, the fertile, thickly inhabited
areas of North West Africa are really islands, set not in the sea
but in the desert or between the desert and the sea. Apart from
the scattered oases of the south, the population of the Maghrib
is thus concentrated in the west and the north in a long,
narrow coastal strip, about 2,600 miles long and rarely more
than 50–100 miles deep, though it widens out a little on the
Atlantic coast where the Moroccan plains are cut off from the
desert by the lofty ranges of the Atlas Mountains. In so far as it
is a thickly populated land, the Maghrib is shaped like Chile,
but it differs from that country in running east and west instead
of north and south, and in backing on to a desert through
which caravans used to conduct trade from north to south, and
vice versa, until European development diverted traffic to the
sea ports of West Africa. The desert area is now known to contain immense resources of oil and iron which could be profitably

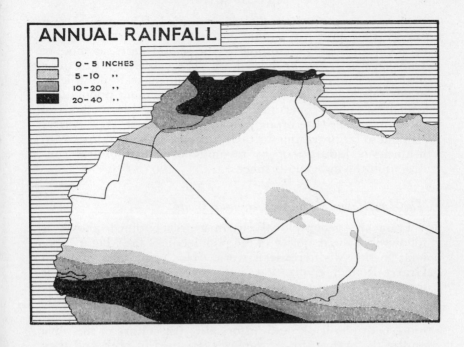

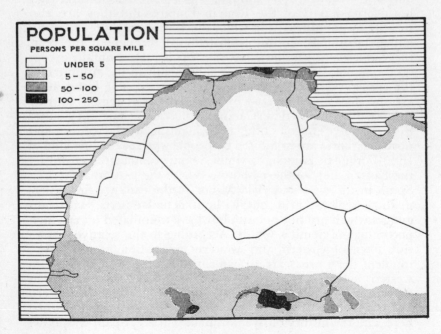

B

exploited if political conditions permitted. The capital and energy thus provided would be sufficient to transform the economy and living conditions of the coastal states, as those of Iraq have been by the Kirkuk oil. The employment of these natural resources for this purpose would make it possible to create tolerable living conditions for the teeming populations which European government, by introducing the methods of modern hygiene, has brought into being in North West Africa, without so far providing for their sustenance through the establishment of industry or by revolutionizing agricultural conditions in the indigenous sphere.

The Two Halves of the Mediterranean World

From the geographical circumstances outlined above, it follows that the majority of the population of the Maghrib belong to the Mediterranean world. This world, the home of Graeco-Roman civilization, has two distinct halves. One is formed by the western and northern shores, and is European; the other by the eastern and southern shores, which are Asiatic and African respectively. The two halves have much in common, both physically and historically; the culture of the olive and of the orange, for example, is practised in both and they both formed part of the Roman Empire. But they are also sharply distinguished; for while the European shores have an adequate rainfall, equitably distributed throughout the year, the eastern and southern have an inadequate rainfall, except on the actual coast, and the rain falls mainly in the autumn and the spring, often in great momentary excess. The latter areas are therefore characterized by extensive desert regions and by the presence of the desert animal, the camel; and they suffer from extensive erosion of the soil. Linguistically the western and northern shores are inhabited by people who speak some kind of Indo-European language; while Semitic languages prevail on the eastern and southern shores. Where the two areas join, in Spain in the west and Asia Minor in the east, we find intermediate regions, arid but without actual deserts, with languages which are not Semitic but have assimilated a very high percentage of Semitic words. According to the relative attractive force of eastern and western civilization at any given moment these areas are drawn into the orbit of eastern or of western culture. Thus both Spain and Asia Minor have had periods of greatness as representatives at one time of western and at another of eastern civilization. We are not concerned here with the history of Byzantium or Turkey; Spain was, however, at one time an extension of the Arab Maghrib, sometimes described as 'the second Maghrib',[1] and calls for special consideration because it was a centre from which Muslim civilization and Arab culture spread to the southern shores of the Straits of Gibraltar.

The Autochthonous People

Remains of primitive man have been found in Morocco, Algeria, and Tunisia, but the first inhabitants of whom we have historical knowledge were the people whom the Arabs and we ourselves, copying them, call Berbers. The Berbers have formed the basis of the population of the Maghrib since at least the second millennium B.C. and are the origin of the name 'Barbary' which was commonly used by Europeans to describe the North African states during the period of the Turkish domination. In all probability the word is simply an adaptation of the Greek word for barbarians, applied by the Greeks and Romans to any people who did not speak their own languages or share the culture which the use of those languages implied. In the New Testament the word is used of the people of the island of Malta which, like Tunisia, had been colonized by the Phoenicians and was no doubt Punic-speaking. The Berbers include different physical types but, like Arabs, they belong to the white races and cannot be distinguished from Europeans when they dress and live like them. Their ultimate origin is shrouded in mystery but it is generally held that they came originally from the east, like the Carthaginians and the Arabs. A learned Jew of Tangier has sought to demonstrate that the superstitious and magical practices of Moroccan Berbers have much in common with those of the Canaanite inhabitants of Palestine, and so to confirm a tradition, based on the statement of a Roman author, that the Berbers were originally Canaanites who were driven out by Joshua the son of Nun. This is, however, in the highest degree speculative and all that can be said with some assurance is that they probably arrived as invaders at some remote period and pushed westward until they reached the Atlantic. This they penetrated as far as the Canary Islands whose primitive inhabitants spoke a form of Berber, known as Guanche. The Berber language is classed by philologists as Hamitic; this implies that it is related to ancient Egyptian but does not tell us much more than that it is probably more akin to the Semitic languages than to the Indo-European. One of the most striking

[1] e.g. by the Almohad Sultan Muhammad al-Nasir in a letter of 1204 (*Hesperis* (Rabat), 1928).

things about it is that in spite of its diffusion over a vast area, it has virtually never been written. In consequence it is broken up into a number of dialects which are mutually intelligible only with difficulty and there is no literature to create a standard. The Berber-speaking groups today form islands of population all the way from the Siwa oasis in Egypt to the Atlantic coast. There are some in Libya and a good many in the central and southern Sahara; but very few in Tunisia. There are big groups in the Kabyle country and in the Aurès mountains of Algeria, while the largest concentrations are found in Morocco, the main body being in the central and southern Atlas and a smaller group in the Rif. The position of the Berber language in North West Africa is thus rather like that of the Celtic languages in Britain; it has often survived in place-names after it has ceased to be the locally spoken language. It has in fact provided some of the most characteristic and romantic-sounding names of the Maghrib—Agadir (the fortress), Azrou (the rock), Ifni (the rocky desert), Taourirt (the round peak), Tizi Ouzou (the rainy mountain pass), Tsettauen (Tetuan, the springs). Since ancient Egyptian times, the Berbers have called themselves *Imazighen*, which means the free men; and in fact they are distinguished by a great love of personal and group liberty. So intense was this feeling that it rendered the creation of a centralized authority very difficult, unless it was based on the fellow feeling and domination of some particular clan or tribe. As soon as this cohesive force disappeared, the state organization dissolved with it unless it was replaced by the domination of a different clan. It is perhaps for this reason that the Berbers are almost the only people who have inhabited a given area for so many hundred years without ever forming a state with a culture of their own, but only states with the culture of some dominant people, Carthaginian, Roman, or Arab. The last example of a Berber state, formed in the traditional manner, was the short-lived Republic of the Rif, created by Abdelkrim al-Khattabi from 1922–6. Abdelkrim was himself the leader of a Berber clan, the Beni Uriaghel, and it was on their support that his Government depended; nevertheless he was an Arabic scholar and the language of his administration was Arabic. Modern thinkers of the Maghrib, such as Allal al-Fasi, acknowledge that the Berbers are the basis of the population of the Maghrib today, particularly in Morocco; but of course the majority have been profoundly arabized and are Muslims. Though there are important nomad branches, Berbers are for the most part settled agricultural people, living in solidly-built villages. In the coastal areas, and particularly in Tunisia, there is a considerable admixture of other stock, Carthaginian, Roman, Vandal, Arab, Turkish, and modern European. There has also been intermarriage with negroes.

1. IN ANTIQUITY

Foreign Influences

The original Berber population has, through the centuries, been subjected to five principal foreign influences. The first was Phoenician and Carthaginian, and lasted for some 1,000 years from about 1200 B.C. The second was the period of Roman domination which was firmly established with the destruction of Carthage in 146 B.C. and lasted for about 650 years. There followed the interlude of the Vandals and the Byzantine restoration (429–642). This was succeeded by 1,200 years of Arab predominance in Morocco; and by about 800 in the rest of North Africa, where a Turkish régime established itself at the beginning of the sixteenth century and continued in a modified form until the European occupation in the nineteenth century.

The Carthaginians

The Carthaginians profoundly influenced the whole African shore of the Mediterranean from Tripolitania westwards, and also Sicily, Sardinia, Malta, the Balearic Islands, and south Spain. Carthage, situated on the coast a few miles from the present city of Tunis, was originally a Phoenician colony of Tyre and is reputed to have been founded about 800 B.C. by Queen Elisa (Dido), whom Virgil anachronistically makes a contemporary of the Trojan War.[1] The Carthaginians were distinguished as sailors, as merchants, and as miners. They founded trading settlements at many points of the south Mediterranean and are believed to have explored the coast of West Africa at least as far as the Gulf of Guinea. Their typical settlements were on small and easily defensible peninsulas, such as the hill on which the old Melilla, originally the Carthaginian settlement of Rusadir (Rosh-adir, the Great Cape), is built. The obvious modern parallel is a British settlement such as Hong Kong. The Carthaginian state included the northern portion of modern Tunisia, but extended westward like medieval Tunisia to include the region from Bône to Constantine and

[1] *Adrian*: Widow Dido, said you? You make me study of that:
    She was of Carthage; not of Tunis.
Gonzalo: This Tunis, Sir, was Carthage.
Adrian: Carthage?
Gonzalo: I assure you, Carthage.

Shakespeare, *The Tempest*, II 1.

eastward to include the Tripolitanian coast. Being interested
in trade rather than in imperial expansion or colonization, the
Carthaginians appear to have maintained friendly relations
with the Berbers (at that time known in general as Libyans; as
Numidians in eastern Algeria; and as Mauri in the west)
though there was a serious rebellion of those whom they employed as mercenary troops.

Carthaginians and Numidians

Educated Numidians seem to have adopted Carthaginian
names, and there was intermarriage between Carthaginians
and Numidians, as between Carthaginians and other peoples—
the famous Hannibal, for example, had a Spanish wife. Indeed,
as a distinguished French historian writes:

> For centuries Carthage alone represented civilization in the eyes
> of the Berbers. Thus all the Numidian and Moorish (*Maures*) Kings
> who ruled outside the Carthaginian territory adopted the civiliza-
> tion and often the language of their neighbour. . . . Far from
> becoming fixed as a foreign rule, Punic civilization was, as it were,
> naturalized and spread by a spontaneous movement in the more
> evolved portions of the Berber world.[1]

This is illustrated by a well-known story recounted by the
Roman historian, Livy. Towards the end of the long struggle
between Rome and Carthage, the Romans succeeded in making
allies of two related Numidian princes, Massinissa, ruler of east
Numidia, and Siphax, ruler of west Numidia. The latter displaced Massinissa and occupied his capital Cirta, the modern
Constantine. Siphax, however, then married the beautiful
Sophoniba (or Sophonisbe), daughter of the Carthaginian
Hasdrubal. The Princess, who was a skilled musician and well
versed in literature, as well as beautiful, used her influence over
her husband to set him against the Romans. Massinissa hoped to
take advantage of these circumstances and make himself King
of all Numidia. Siphax was in fact defeated outside Cirta by
the combined forces of Massinissa and the Romans, after which
Massinissa succeeded in persuading his allies to allow him to
enter Cirta ahead of the Roman troops, in order to strengthen
his claim to repossess the kingdom, rather like Colonel Lawrence
and King Faisal at Damascus. On entering the capital, Massinissa was met by Sophoniba—the name in Phoenician means

---

[1] The passage continues: 'The Roman conquest, far from stopping this tendency,
accelerated it. . . . In fact most of the evidence for this penetration is subsequent to
B.C. 146. . . . When one observes how naturally and indeed inevitably the French
occupation of Morocco spread the religion and Arabic language of the towns
throughout the countryside, the apparent paradox becomes perfectly intelligible'
(H. Terasse, *Histoire du Maroc* (Casablanca, 1949), i. 44).

'she who is my treasure'. Flinging herself down before him, she clasped his knees and kissed his hands, begging him not to allow the Romans, her country's enemies, to take her to Italy to make a Roman triumph.

If she had to die, she said, then let Massinissa kill her himself. 'If only as the wife of Siphax' she said, 'I prefer to trust the word of a Numidian, a man born in the same Africa as myself rather than that of a foreigner by birth and nationality' (*alienigenae et externi*).[1] Greatly taken with the queen, Massinissa resolved on the desperate step of facing the Roman commander with a *fait accompli* and therefore married her immediately. This device failed, and in view of Roman insistence that he must either give Sophoniba up or resign the kingship, Massinissa sent the Queen a bowl of poison, saying that this was not the wedding gift that he would have wished to offer but that in view of her feelings he saw no alternative. The Queen returned word that if her husband could do no more for her, she would accept this wedding present with gratitude; after which she drank the poison and died. Massinissa duly became King of all Numidia and, according to the Roman historians, did a great deal to develop his kingdom and render it prosperous. Finally he died at the age of 90, a disappointed man because the Romans had not allowed him to add portions of the territory of Carthage, as they conquered it, to his own realm and so create a united, autochthonous North African kingdom. A subsequent member of the family, Massinissa's grandson Jugurtha, was involved in a long struggle with Rome in which he was finally defeated, taken to Rome, and left to die of cold and hunger in the prison of the Capitol. It was he who once described Rome as 'a town for sale, which would soon perish if anyone offered a good enough price'.[2] The last member of the dynasty was Juba II, King of Mauritania, an area corresponding to the province of Oran, and not to be confused with the modern Mauritania, south of Morocco. He is known chiefly for his literary activities, including an account of the Canary Islands, and for his marriage to Cleopatra Silene, the daughter of Antony and Cleopatra (p. 82). These stories have their relevance today since the Berbers of the Kabyle country,

---

[1] Livy. 30 xii. 15–17 &c. The story was made famous in France by the play of Jean de Mairet, the predecessor of Racine, and in English by James Thomson, author of *The Seasons*, in a play of the same name. The latter contained the line 'Oh Sophonisbe, Sophonisbe, oh!' which some critics have quoted as an example of bathos. It is said that a member of the audience on hearing the line called out 'Oh, Jamie Thomson! Jamie Thomson, oh!'

[2] 'Urbem venalem et mature perituram, si emptorem invenerit.'
(Sallust, *Jugurtha*, xxxv)

in their struggle against the French, took these kings of antiquity as national heroes, having perhaps learned about them from a French school book, and put their names into a doggerel verse in Berber which runs:—

> Jugurtha, hear, your children are awake;
> Tell Massinissa, now his vengeance he shall take.
> Algeria's sons, we'll set our country free.
> Frenchmen? No. Frenchmen we will never be.

Since the rising of 1954 has further brought Arabs and Berbers together with a common Algerian sentiment, this song, with its emphasis on Berber nationalism, is no longer in favour and has been supplanted by others of a nature to appeal to Arabs and Berbers alike.

Punic as a Forerunner of Arabic

Apart from these evidences of Berber or, if you like, Algerian nationalism in antiquity, the chief interest of the Carthaginian period today is the extent to which it may have prepared the way for the future Arab conquest. The Carthaginian language, known as Punic, was developed from Phoenician. It is very closely related to Hebrew, and is as near to Arabic as Spanish is to French. The very name of the city of Carthage—*Qart Hadasha* or new city—would be in Arabic *Qariat Haditha*; and the pre-Islamic Arab personal name *Abdshams* was as common in Carthage as in Arabic. The name of the original Phoenician settlement, *Utica*, meaning 'old town', has also precisely the same meaning in Arabic. This linguistic similarity was probably paralleled by many other characteristics. The Spanish Roman poet, Martial, when inviting a friend to a quiet dinner and assuring him that there would be none of those irritating distractions, which for the Romans were the equivalent of the modern television, assured him that there would be no dancing girls from Cadiz.

> Nec de Gadibus improbis puellae
> vibrabunt sine fine prurientes
> lascivos docili tremore lumbos.[1]

Since Cadiz was a very ancient Carthaginian settlement it is hardly possible to doubt that these dances were an eastern art which the Carthaginians had brought with them from Syria.

It is certain from the writings of St. Augustine of Hippo (Bône) that Punic was still spoken in the fifth century A.D. in the eastern portion of what is today Algeria. For the Saint, in

[1] Martial, v. 78.

his capacity as Bishop, sought to ensure that Punic-speaking Bishops, who would be intelligible to the people, should be appointed in the dioceses concerned. It is true that this still leaves a gap of 200 years till the arrival of the Arabs, but if the language survived the pressure of Roman culture for 600 years, it may well have lasted another 200 after that pressure had been removed and replaced only by the temporary presence of Vandal or Byzantine governors. A more serious objection is that no Punic elements have been found in the modern Arabic dialects of North Africa, but our knowledge of Punic is not so extensive that there may not be traces which have escaped the notice of the philologists.[1] However this may be, it is much easier to understand the speed with which Arabic spread in Tunisia and with which a flourishing local Arabic culture came into being, if we can assume that the process was facilitated by the fact that the people were talking a kindred language at the time of the Arab invasion and were already impregnated with a Semitic culture. The process would then be exactly parallel to what happened in the Aramaic-speaking territories of Syria and Iraq. It would also help to explain why Berber has disappeared so much more completely from Tunisia than it has from Algeria or Morocco.[2]

The Romans

Six hundred years of Roman domination and an interregnum of 200 intervened between the fall of Carthage and the coming of the Arabs. The Roman period is familiar to all travellers from the magnificent remains of Roman cities which are to be found from Cyrene in Libya to Volubilis near Meknes in Morocco. It was a time of tremendous material development, inspired and directed from Rome as it was throughout the rest of the Empire. Agriculture and forestry, already highly developed by the Carthaginians, were maintained and extended. In addition to the great material monuments, cities, roads, dams, and country houses, whose mosaics are magnificently represented in the Bardo Museum in Tunis, the period of Roman rule left the world a great intellectual monument in the works of St. Augustine, Bishop of Hippo. What St. Augustine was by

[1] In the field of anthropology, there seems no doubt that the so-called 'hand of Fatima', universally used in North Africa as a protective device against the evil-eye, is derived from the emblem of a hand which is frequently to be found on Punic funeral monuments.

[2] It has recently been suggested, e.g. by the late Charles Courtois, that when St. Augustine spoke of Punic, he really meant Libyan or Berber. Seeing that St. Augustine knew at least some Punic and was aware of the close relationship of Punic with Hebrew, this supposition cannot be accepted without the production of evidence which has not so far been forthcoming.

race is uncertain, though we know that his opponents described him as 'Punic'. Roman rule in North Africa also produced a great Emperor in Septimius Severus, who was born in 146 A.D. near the city of Leptis Magna, for whose monumental character he is responsible, and who died at York in 211. Septimius Severus was certainly African, probably Punic and not Berber. He had to learn Latin as a boy; when his sister came to visit him, as Emperor, in Rome, she made him blush by her inability to speak the language and he persuaded her to return to Africa.

His example proves that at least a minority of Africans were completely assimilated into Roman life, though they may have had a disintegrating influence on it,[1] but we have little direct evidence of how Roman civilization was regarded by the population of North Africa as a whole. A number of writers consider that Christianity in Africa was a religion of the masses and essentially opposed to the influence of Roman civilization. The episode of Tacfarinas the Numidian (p. 208), who after serving in the Roman legion deserted and became the leader of a rising which went on for years in the Aurès district of Algeria, certainly reminds us of the beginning of the present rising in that country; for the latter had its origin in the same area, under the leadership of an Algerian who, like Tacfarinas, had previously had a distinguished record in the army of the ruling power. We may be sure also that a certain nationalist sentiment lay behind the activities of the Numidian kings Massinissa and Jugurtha, though this is not brought out in our historical sources; being entirely Roman, these credit the Numidian kings with no motive other than personal ambition.

The Province of Africa

During the whole of the Roman period and indeed also during the two following centuries, when first the Vandals and then the Byzantines dominated, the centre of power in North Africa remained the former domain of Carthage. The Romans named it the Province of Africa, and this name has been perpetuated in Arabic by the use of the word 'Ifriqiya' to denote the same area. It thus continued to be the most highly civilized portion of North Africa, though Roman rule at its widest extension included the country as far as Volubilis and Salé in Morocco.

---

[1] According to a modern Spanish historian, 'Septimius Severus remained an African throughout his life. In his heart of hearts, he always felt—unlike Hadrian—that the two victorious civilizations of the Mediterranean were something alien, and himself adhered to the vanquished civilization of Carthage, a greater admirer of Hannibal than of Scipio. In consequence he had no scruples in doing violence to the prerogatives of Rome' (R. Menéndez Pidal, ed., *Historia de España* (Madrid, 1947–56), ii. xx).

2. THE MIDDLE AGES

The Coming of the Arabs

The next fundamental change was brought about by the coming of the Arabs; these first appeared in Libya in 642 A.D., only nine years after the death of the Prophet Muhammad. It took them very little time to overthrow the Byzantine régime, but about a century more to subdue the resistance of the Berbers. When they had done so they had established not so much the rule of Arabs in North Africa as the rule of the Arab spirit and of the religion of Islam or, if you prefer, of the Arabic language and of Islamic culture. The administration which was established was in the material sense inferior to that of the Romans; but it had a quality which Roman civilization had lacked in Africa (though not in Gaul)—that of being assimilable by the mass of the population. The Arab achievement in this respect, described in the words of a French scholar in the section devoted to Algeria (p. 209), was very remarkable, and even if we accept the theory of the persistence of Carthaginian influences, remains almost inexplicable unless there was in fact some sort of natural affinity between the Berber and the Arab way of life and thought which did not exist between Berbers and Romans. Much also must be attributed to the effect of the intense religious faith of the Arabs in the years which immediately followed the prophetic revelation. The sincerity, passionate belief, and rough and ready honesty of many of the early Muslim leaders no doubt had a great effect upon the uncultivated Berber population, even where it was superficially Christian.[1]

The tremendous transformation wrought by Islam in the condition and status of the Arabs themselves can hardly have failed to make a great impression on all who saw it. The change has been described in striking phrases by Ibn Khaldun, the great fourteenth-century North African Arab historian who was of Andalusian origin, though born and brought up in Tunis.

The Arabs [in their primitive state, he wrote] are the least adapted of all people for empire-building. Their wild disposition makes them intolerant of subordination, while their pride, touchiness and intense

---

[1] The second of the Prophet's successors has thus been described by a great Italian historian: 'Caliph by election, not by hereditary right; living as frugally as the humblest Muslim; without display, without civil list, without guards, personally haranguing the assembled people, tolerating patiently the reproaches of the humblest as of the greatest, consulting in every circumstance the other Companions of the Prophet, who like himself were the depositaries of the latter's words, that is those sparks of the eternal wisdom which God had not thought fit to include in the Quran' (M. Amari, *Storia dei Musulmani di Sicilia* (Florence, 1854–72), I. 70).

jealousy of power render it impossible for them to agree. . . . Only when their nature has been permeated by a religious impulse are they transformed, so that the tendency to anarchy is replaced by a spirit of mutual defence. Consider the moment when religion dominated their policy and led them to observe a religious law designed to promote the moral and materal interests of civilization. Under a series of successors to the Prophet, how vast their empire became and how strongly it was established!

Ibn Khaldun goes on to describe how a proud Persian, Rustum, amazed at the sight of the serried ranks of Arabs prostrating themselves in prayer behind the Caliph Omar, exclaimed that he could do nothing against a man 'who can turn dogs into civilized beings'.[1]

Arab Imperialism

As the Carthaginians and the Romans, so the Arabs made the former realm of Carthage their base, founding a new capital at Kairouan. Now Arab imperialism in the west (for imperialism it was) differs in certain essentials from Roman imperialism and from the European imperialism which was in time to succeed it in North Africa. There was no settling of colonists who possessed an advanced civilization of their own. We find indeed the establishment of an Arab ruling class; this, however, consisted of the descendants of Arabs whose wives might have been non-Arabs from the moment of the conquest. Thus an 'Arab' of the third generation might already have one only grandparent of pure Arab blood; his father might be only half Arab and his grandmother and mother completely non-Arab. In the case of a great ruling family, the Beni Umayya Caliphs of Córdoba, whose marital connexions are known to us, it has been mentioned by an Arab writer that they had a marked natural preference for blondes, and that the mothers of the rulers were almost invariably Christian slaves from the north of Spain.[2] The Spanish orientalist Ribera worked out mathematically that the percentage of Arab ancestry in the Caliph Abd al-Rahman III (912–61) was 0·39 per cent., the remaining 99·61 per cent. being Spanish.[3]

In this way, and by large-scale conversion, new civilizations were rapidly produced whose cultural level depended largely

---

[1] Ibn Khaldun, *Muqaddima* (Beirut, 1900), p. 152.

[2] 'Kulluhum majbuluna ala tafdil ash-shaqra' (Ibn Hazm, *Tauq al-Hamama* (Algiers, 1949; Bibliothèque Arabo-française), viii. 72).

[3] Julian Ribera, *Disertaciones y Opusculos* (Madrid, 1928), p. 16. It has, however, to be noted that intermarriage must have become the exception, except for those rich enough to own slaves, once a large distinct Muslim community had been established.

upon the contribution made by the original inhabitants of the country, either directly as converts or through the mothers of the ruling classes; for the Arabs themselves brought little in the way of material civilization, but only their language, with all that that involves in ways of thought, and their religion. Thus we find that in Tunisia, where there was an old-established tradition of civilized living, a highly-developed Arab civilization came into being almost at once; whereas in Morocco, which was relatively barbarous in the seventh century, a high level of civilization took much longer to appear. It has to be noted too that in addition to the ruling and assimilating Arabs the conquest also brought with it Arab tribes who might remain in compact masses. These sometimes amalgamated with an existing population, but sometimes remained purely Arab, often constituting a backward and retrograde element. The ruling classes, proud themselves of being Arabs, often refer disparagingly to such tribes as 'Arabs' (as they do at other times to corresponding Berbers) using 'Arab' in the sense of beduin, or primitive Arabs—a double use of the word which can be highly confusing. Taking North Africa as a whole, the effect of the creation of an Arab empire was very rapidly to turn the area into the *Maghrib* or western portion of the Arab world, giving it that typical Arabo-Berber aspect which it has retained ever since. Still basically Berber, its individuality was expressed henceforth through the medium of Islamic civilization and the Arabic language.

Within a century or so the process was so complete that Arab rule was no longer felt as foreign rule. Local princes appeared, who may have been Arab or Berber by race, but whose ways of thought, and language and methods of administration were Arab. Meanwhile the Arab and Berber dislike of central control soon reasserted itself and after a period during which governors were appointed and deposed by the imperial authority in Damascus local dynasties were established. Largely independent, they still sought recognition from the east, however, for reasons of religious or worldly prestige and for the practical assistance which it might bring.

During the whole of this period, until the Turkish predominance in the sixteenth century, Arab culture and political power tended to radiate from two centres. One was in the east, in Ifriqiya; and the other in the west, where it was first situated in southern Spain and later in Morocco. The rulers in Tunisia generally controlled eastern Algeria and Tripolitania, either directly or through tributary rulers in Constantine and Bougie, or in Tripoli, as the case might be. The capital was at first the newly-founded city of Kairouan; then another new city, Mahdiya, on the east coast, and finally Tunis. Western Algeria tended to be subordinate to Morocco.

Ifriqiya

During 800 years of Arab rule, four dynasties succeeded one another in Ifriqiya. The first were the Aghlabids (800–909) with their capital in Kairouan. This dynasty conquered Sicily in the ninth century and made it a Muslim state. The Muslim rulers of the island soon became independent but were themselves driven out by the Normans in the eleventh century. It was at this time also that Malta was first captured and then freed from the Muslims. The next dynasty, the Fatimids (909–69), propagated a heretical form of Islam. After establishing themselves in Tunisia, where they created the new capital, Mahdiya, they moved east, conquered Egypt, and founded Cairo. They then made this their capital, leaving Tunisia to be administered by their tributaries, the Zirids. When the latter became independent, the Fatimid Caliph in Cairo authorized two large and troublesome nomad Arab tribes, who were at the time in Upper Egypt, to attack them and establish themselves in Ifriqiya. These two tribes, the Beni Hilal and the Beni Sulaim, can be taken as typical of the non-assimilating Arab; and their misdeeds will be found mentioned in the articles on individual countries. They are generally held responsible for causing immense destruction in Ifriqiya, provoking disturbances, and serving as mercenaries in any local fighting. Certainly they caused the ruin of Kairouan, which indeed continued to exist as a holy city, but only—to this day—as a profoundly 'depressed area'. Some scholars attribute a large part in the arabization of the Maghrib to the two tribes. They can, however, have hardly numbered more than 150,000, and appear to have had none of the religious fervour of the original invaders. While, therefore, they no doubt increased the proportion of Arab inhabitants by settling in Libya and in the Moroccan plains (pp. 84, 348), it does not appear that they can have made any cultural contribution. Ifriqiya itself had clearly been arabized, as far as culture and administration were concerned, long before their arrival which simply inaugurated a period of anarchy, further increased by the Norman capture of a number of coast towns during the twelfth century. This was ended by the arrival of Almohad forces from Morocco. In the thirteenth century a new dynasty, the Hafsids, arose through the transformation of the Almohad viceroys into an independent reigning family. This family, who were Berber in origin, had been intimately connected with the beginnings of the Almohad movement in Morocco; and they ruled Ifriqiya for over 250 years. Their capital was Tunis and in their time we can discern the rudiments of a Tunisian nationality which can be considered as the forerunner of the present Tunisian state.

Islam on the Defensive

Though the Christian advance in Spain, which had resulted in the capture of Toledo in 1085, was then held up for two centuries; and though the Almohads drove the Normans from Ifriqiya, Islam in the west was on the defensive from the eleventh century onwards. The Hafsid period was itself one of relative peace and of extensive trade relations with Christian Europe (p. 285). It is true that raids on one another's shipping were not infrequent on the part of Tunis and the Italian maritime republics such as Pisa and Genoa; but there was no serious attempt to change the general balance of power. When the Genoese in 1390 persuaded the Duc de Bourbon and many French knights to lead an expedition against Mahdiya in Tunisia (known at that time to Europeans as 'Africa'), the Muslims were astonished.

We have nothing trespassed them [they said in discussion among themselves]. Of a truth there hath been war between us and the Genoways, but that war ought not to touch Christian men of countries far off. As for the Genoways, they are our neighbours; they take of us and we take of them; we have been ancient enemies and shall be, except when truce is between us.[1]

This state of affairs was brought to an end about the beginning of the sixteenth century by the Christian Spanish onslaught which had been directed against Ifriqiya as well as against the last Muslim state of Spain, Granada, and against Morocco. In desperation the Arabs of Ifriqiya turned to the Turks, now powerful in the eastern Mediterranean. The latter thereupon drove off the Spanish, whose main efforts were already being diverted to Europe and America; but they then made themselves masters of the territories which they had liberated from the Christians.

But before we consider the Turkish irruption in the east, we must look briefly at the course of events in the west.

[1] The Christians replied that they considered all Saracens to be their enemies because they had killed the Messiah and did despite to the Christian faith. At which 'the Saracens did nothing but laugh', saying that it was the Jews and not themselves who had judged the Messiah and put him to death (*The Chronicles of Froissart*, Globe ed. (London, 1895), p. 402).

Islam in the West

In the early days of the conquest, the chief significance of Morocco (in Arabic geography *al-Maghrib al-Aqsa* or the 'Far West'), was as the starting point for the Arab invasion of Spain. That enterprise, however, cannot be considered as in any way a Moroccan undertaking, even if a number of Moroccan Berbers participated in it, any more than the Allied invasion of Italy during the last war could be called an Algerian or Tunisian undertaking on the ground that it started from Tunisia and a considerable number of Algerian troops took part in it. The invasion of Spain was an Arab enterprise, part of the whole great conquest which was at that time still being directed from Damascus; as a result of it Muslim Spain, *al-Andalus*, came to play such an outstanding part in the history of Islam in the west that it cannot be omitted from a survey of the history of the Maghrib.

The Conquest of Spain

Though the early Caliphs had been much alarmed at the idea of occupying territory across the sea, the Straits of Gibraltar appear never to have constituted in themselves a very serious obstacle between the countries to the north and south of them. It is difficult, perhaps impossible, to find any moment in history when all the territory to the north of the straits was in the power of one government and all the territory to the south in the power of another; almost invariably some portion of territory on the one side has been in the power of a government on the other. Climatically, too, there is a close resemblance between northern Morocco and the Iberian peninsula. In fact the French witticism that Africa begins at the Pyrenees can only be held valid if we balance it by saying that Europe begins at the Atlas.

As in North Africa, the invading Arabs put an end to the existing (in this case Visigothic) government with extraordinary ease. They were assisted in this by their fellow orientals, the Jews, who had recently suffered severe persecution at the hands of the Visigothic government, and Jewish garrisons were put in charge of various towns during the advance. Unlike North Africa, however, there was no prolonged resistance to be overcome on the part of the local population, except for the tiny unassimilable area in the extreme northwest which in the course of centuries gave rise to the Christian reconquest. A great number of Spanish were rapidly converted to Islam. The remainder often received extremely favourable terms; and many of the former Gothic rulers retained the greater portions of their estates and privileges, some as converts but others still as Christians. The Arabs at first intermarried freely with the Spanish, the example being set by the Arab ruling classes. Thus the son of the first Arab Governor of Muslim Spain married Egilona, the widow of the last Visigothic king, who was known in Arabic as Um Asim. The lady was shocked that her Arab husband had no such emblem of authority as her former husband had done, and urged him to wear a crown. Unconvinced by his explanation that such a proceeding would be deeply offensive to the democratic spirit of Islam she persuaded him to put on, when at home, a diadem which she had ordered to be made for him. The news got abroad, suspicion was aroused, and the governor assassinated.

Splendour of Muslim Civilization in Córdoba

The population with which the Arabs were mingling in Andalusia had an incomparably higher standard of civilization than the Berbers of Morocco, higher probably than that of the people of Ifriqiya, though they resembled the latter in being the product of Carthaginian and Roman culture. Andalusia had produced one of the greatest of Roman Emperors, Trajan, who was succeeded by another Spaniard, Hadrian. Apart from another great Emperor, Theodosius, Roman Spain was the home of a host of soldiers, poets, bishops, and philosophers. It was therefore not surprising that it should be in Spain, and particularly in Andalusia, that the Arab imperial system yielded some of its most remarkable results. From about 800 to 1000 A.D., and indeed until 200 years later, *al-Andalus*, or Muslim Spain, was the most civilized area of western Europe, as is shown by a number of picturesque stories recorded by Arab historians or medieval European chroniclers. The Christian King Sancho the Fat of Castile (955–67), who was deposed by his subjects on the grounds of his obesity, was advised by his grandmother Queen Toda of Navarre to go to a Muslim doctor in Córdoba for treatment; rather as a Persian Gulf Shaikh today might be recommended to go to London or Paris. The Caliph Abd al-Rahman III put at his service his best physician, the Jew Hasdai ben Shaprut, who was also his Secretary for Foreign Affairs (958). The treatment was successful, for Sancho recovered both his figure and his throne; but it also proved expensive, since he had to hand over several frontier fortresses in payment. Pope Sylvester II (Gerbert of Aurillac 999–1003) was able to introduce a great advance in

c

western mathematics because as a young man he went to study
with the Muslims (it is said at Córdoba), in spite of the opposition of his relations who considered Muslim learning as witch-
craft.[1] A couple of centuries later the English King John is recorded to have sent an Embassy to an Almohad Sultan of
Morocco asking for his aid and, it is said, offering to do allegiance to him and adopt the Muslim faith. On this occasion the
English Ambassadors, we are told, found the Sultan refreshing
his knowledge of Christianity by reading the letters of St. Paul.[2]
These stories, of which there is no reason to doubt the substantial truth, serve to give an idea of the remarkable development of science and learning which took place in the Amirate
of Córdoba and was commended by an Arab poet in the
following verse:—

In four things Córdoba surpasses the capitals of the world—
Among them are the bridge over the river and the mosque.
These are the first two; the third is Madinat al-Zahra;
But the greatest of all things is knowledge—and that is the
    fourth.[3]

The bridge over the Guadalquiver at Córdoba was built by
the Romans and restored by the Arabs; the Great Mosque,
still known today as the *Mezquita* (Mosque), was an essentially
Arab creation in which much classical material, including many
columns from Carthage, was used; while Madinat al-Zahra
was the famous complex of palace and government offices constructed for Abd al-Rahman III (912–61), who of all the Beni
Umayya princes was most consciously the creator of a synthesis

[1] *William of Malmesbury's Chronicle of the Kings of England* (Bohn ed., 1883), p. 172.
From 967–970 Gerbert was assistant to Hatto, Archbishop of Vich in Catalonia.
According to Ademar de Chabannes, Gerbert 'visited Córdoba for the sake of
wisdom' (*causa sophiae lustrans Cordubam*) (R. Menéndez Pidal, *España, eslabón entre
la Cristianidad y el Islam*, Madrid, 1956).
[2] Matthew of Paris in Roger of Wendover, *Flowers of History* (Bohn, 1849), ii.
283. King John's connexion with Muslim Spain was probably through his ally,
King Sancho of Navarre, whose sister had married John's brother, Richard Coeur-
de-Lion. Sancho is known to have spent three years in Muslim territory. Four
hundred years later another Moroccan Sultan, Maulay Ismail, addressed a long
letter to James II, then in exile, explaining the merits of Islam. In conclusion he
urged him either to adopt that faith or at least return to Protestantism which
Maulay Ismail regarded as less idolatrous than Catholicism. He added that if he
and his people had not been 'Arabs and ignorant of nautical matters' he would,
if James became Protestant, have sent an expedition to assist him to regain his
throne (H. de Castries, *Maulay Ismael*, Paris, 1903).
[3] *Bi arbain faqat al-amsara qurtabatu;*
    Minhuna qantaratu'l-wadi wa jami'uha,
    Hatan ithnatan, wa'z-zahra-u thalithatu;
    Wa'l 'ilmu a'athamu shai-in, wa hua rab'iuha.
              (Al-Maqqari, *Nafh al-Tib* (Cairo, 1338/1920), i. 84.)

of Muslim, Christian, and Jewish cultures. The four lines thus introduce the essential elements of the great Muslim capital.[1]

The Muslim City States

Fifty |years after Abd 'al-Rahman III's death the Cordoban state collapsed, for reasons which are not altogether clear, and Muslim Spain broke up into a galaxy of twenty-six little city states. 'Galaxy' seems the appropriate word since some of these little states—Seville, Córdoba, Badajoz, Granada, Almeria, Murcia, Valencia, Mallorca, Saragossa—shone in the medieval darkness with the brilliance of the little Italian states of the Renaissance. In their divided condition, however, they were no match for the less civilized but virile little Christian states of the north. In 1085 Toledo was captured from the Muslims by Alfonso VI of Castile, and in the following year al-Mutamid, the brilliant soldier-poet-king of Seville, decided to invoke the help of the Almoravid Sultan, Yusuf ibn Tashufin, who had made himself ruler of Morocco and of much of the rest of the Maghrib.

Al-Mutamid did not take this decision lightly, nor without long and anxious consultation with his advisers and particularly with his son and heir who was opposed to seeking African aid. Finally, however, his sentiment as a Muslim overcame his doubts as a Spaniard. 'I do not want my name to be remembered for evil in the pulpits of al-Andalus, as certain others have been', he said. 'I would sooner be a camel-herd in Africa than a swine-herd in Castile.'

The Moroccan Intervention in Spain

A very clear view of the cultural and political relations between Morocco and Muslim Spain at this period can be gathered from the writings of Arab historians and men of letters. The Moroccan Sultan whom al-Mutamid invited to Spain was Yusuf ibn Tashufin, the first of the Almoravid Sultans. The latter were Berbers from Mauritania, a territory which lies to the south of Morocco. As their name implies, they had been inmates of fortified convents (*ribat*) and came to power as the

---

[1] A Spanish poet, Manuel Machado, about 1,000 years later, described the Córdoba of his day as 'romana y mora, Córdoba callada' (quiet Córdoba, Roman and Moorish). This marked a revival of Spanish interest in the Muslim past, for the great sixteenth-century poet of Córdoba, Luis de Góngora, in his famous sonnet to the city which ends with the lines 'O patria, O flor de España', makes no reference to its Moorish characteristics. It should be noted that the word 'Moorish' in such connexions is generally the equivalent of 'Muslim' and only occasionally has the connotation 'Moroccan'. Shakespeare's Moor of Venice was probably either a black slave from Morocco, named 'Utail' or 'Atallah', or else a dusky Moor from Mauritania. Madinat al-Zahra, whose very site was lost for centuries, is now being excavated and patiently and brilliantly reconstructed.

result of a movement to restore Islam to its primitive simplicity. Yusuf ibn Tashufin himself was a fighting monarch and an administrator whose life was based on the simple and austere morals of the early Muslims. Nomad by origin, his principal food was camel milk, camel flesh, and barley bread; his garments were always of wool. His mother-tongue was Berber; although he knew some Arabic, and his correspondence was conducted in that language, he was not able to appreciate the subtleties of the Arabic tongue as it was spoken and written in al-Andalus. His outlook, at once primitive and austere, did not appeal to the cultivated rulers of Muslim Spain, for whom his assistance was a necessary evil; but they had a strong attraction for some of the Spanish men of religion and for those of the masses who disliked the luxurious living, the scientific and artistic pursuits, the wine-drinking and the hedonism of their upper classes; and, perhaps even more, the taxation which the satisfaction of these tastes involved.

The Moorish intervention completely changed the military position, for the allies inflicted a resounding defeat on the King of Castile near Badajoz. The Court poets set themselves to flatter Yusuf as they had been accustomed to do their own kings. The Almoravids belonged to the Berber tribe of Sanhaja, which had appropriated an Arab genealogy and claimed descent from the Arabs of Himyar; they also observed the habit, still in force today among the Tuareg, of wearing a face-veil.[1] An Andalusian poet utilized these characteristics for a panegyric in which he wrote:—

A king who has the high honour to descend from Himyar.
If there are tongues which challenge this and whisper 'Berbers',
Yet they are the people that they are—such people that they first united every virtue in their persons, and then, in modesty, veiled themselves.

It was not long, however, before the poet changed his tone and added a further couplet:

The Almoravid is not open handed—except to his own relations; His features are as ugly as his actions; and therefore he veiled himself.[2]

These verbal pinpricks were the prelude to more serious events. On Yusuf's third visit to Spain, he first secured a *fetwa* from the Muftis (religious consultants) condemning the irreligious taxation and practices of the princes and then put an end to the princedoms, taking al-Mutamid to Morocco as a

[1] More properly a mouth-muffler.
[2] Rawd al-Qirtas al-Shaqundi, *Risala fi fadl al-Andalus.*

prisoner. The deposed king finished his days in captivity at
Aghmat, in the foothills of the Atlas, a few miles outside the
Almoravid capital, Marrakesh. Here, where a river runs out
into the plain, amid walnut trees and green vegetation, behind
which the high snow peaks rise into the blue sky, al-Mutamid
continued to write poems, as moving and melancholy as they
had once been gay and vainglorious.

Out of this Moroccan intervention Muslim Spain gained two
centuries of reprieve, shielded by the power of Africa. Neither
the Almoravids, however, nor their successors, the Almohads,
ever made the necessary sustained effort to tackle the Christian
menace at its source.

Islam in Morocco

When the Arabs first reached the 'far west', at the beginning
of the eighth century, their governors followed the Byzantine
practice of making their headquarters in Ceuta or Tangier.
Civilization had not spread very far beyond these cities, though
the Phoenicians had apparently once had trading posts as far
down the coast as Wadi Nun, a few miles short of the present
southern frontier of Morocco, and traces of Punic influence
and inscriptions have been found at various points of Roman
Morocco. The work of introducing civilization into the farther
portions of the country was left for the Arab or Arabo-Berber
rulers to accomplish. It was not, however, until the coming of
the Almoravids in the eleventh century that Morocco acquired
a real measure of unity and began to play a part on the stage of
world affairs. These rulers united Morocco itself and, besides
making themselves rulers of Muslim Spain, also controlled the
whole of western Algeria. The next dynasty, the Almohads, annexed also Tunisia, later to become an independent kingdom
under the Hafsids who were originally Almohad viceroys.

The Influence of Muslim Spain on Morocco

The Moroccan conquerors of Spain were very rapidly taken
captive by the civilization of the people whom they now ruled.
Architects and engineers were transferred from Spain to the
south of the Straits. The architect who built the Giralda tower
in Seville had first been brought to Morocco to build the
Kutubia tower in Marrakesh and returned later to plan the
Hasan tower at Rabat. The extension of Andalusian civilization to Morocco had in fact begun earlier; for in the last days of
the Caliphate of Córdoba the rulers of Morocco had owed
allegiance to the Caliph. The troubles accompanying the end
of the Caliphate intensified the process.

North Africa [says an Arab historian of the twelfth century] may be said to have derived its present wealth and important commerce from Spanish Muslims settling in it. When God was pleased to afflict Spain with the recent disastrous civil war [following the fall of the Caliphate] thousands of Spanish Muslims of all classes and all professions sought refuge on these shores. . . . Agriculture was developed by newly arrived farmers, springs were discovered and used for irrigation; trees were planted; watermills and other useful machinery constructed. . . . Large numbers of educated towns-people did useful work in the administration. The numerous artisans and workmen were particularly valuable. Before their arrival many crafts which are now flourishing were hardly known and it is generally admitted that the immigrants ranked far above the natives in energy and skill.[1]

Influence of Muslim Spain on Christian Europe

Though rather beyond the scope of this survey, it is perhaps worth noticing here that another current of migration, that of the arabized Christians, or Mozarabs [2] was at the same time beginning to move north into the Christian Spanish kingdoms, which were growing in extension and in power as the Muslim power decreased. These arabized Spaniards carried Andalusian civilization with them into northern Spain and it was probably they who were responsible for introducing so many words and terms of Arabic origin into modern Spanish, particularly in the spheres of agriculture and administration, as for example, *alcalde* (*al-qadi*) for the town mayor. Through the great school of translators set up in Toledo by Alfonso X, Muslim science and learning and Greek scientific works which had been preserved in Arabic were made available to European scholars. The prestige of Arabic as a language of science and administration remained so great that when Toledo was settled with arabized Spanish Christians from the south, after the Christian conquest in 1085, these Mozarabic Spaniards preserved the use of Arabic for legal purposes, such as marriage settlements and the transfer of property, for another 250 years, right into the fourteenth century.

3. THE END OF THE MIDDLE AGES

The Segregation of Christians and Muslims

These migrations were, however, also having another effect. Spain was ceasing to be an area consisting of a number of kingdoms, some Christian and some Muslim, in which

---

[1] Quoted in al-Maqqari, *Nafh al-Tib.*
[2] Arabic, *must'arab* (meaning 'arabized').

Christians and Muslims lived together. Fanaticism was increasing. On the Muslim side, this was due to the arrival of the Africans, for whom the sight of a Christian was a novelty and who had no sympathy for them as fellow Spaniards. On the Christian side it was fomented by the crusading spirit which came with the monks of Cluny and the warriors from the north of the Pyrenees. Christians and Muslims were being increasingly sifted out, with all the Christians collected on one side of the frontier and all the Muslims on the other.

By the middle of the thirteenth century the Kingdom of Granada was the only Spanish state still under Muslim rule. During the 250 years which it survived there was a slow but steady pressure on Muslims remaining in the Christian states of Spain to abandon their faith, emigrate to Granada, or leave Spain altogether.

Granada

The Muslim state of Granada, in spite of being Muslim, was in a sense still accepted as being natural to Spain, though only on conditions of armed coexistence. Periods of peace alternated with periods of war; periods when Granada paid tribute to Castile with periods when it felt strong enough to refuse tribute. On occasions very remarkable treaty arrangements illustrated the nature of this coexistence. In 1456 a general truce was agreed between Castile and Granada with the proviso that fighting was nevertheless permissible on one particular stretch of country—the frontier of the province of Jaen. In 1481 another truce extended to the entire frontier, but fighting was nevertheless declared permissible in the form of operations which must be completed within three days, during which no trumpets must be blown, no flags flown, and no permanent headquarters set up. Under this arrangement the Castilians were able to capture the town of Villaluenga, massacre the inhabitants, do damage in the neighbourhood of Ronda and burn an isolated fortress, all within three days and so without violating the truce. The Muslims for their part retaliated by capturing a town called Zahara and enslaving its inhabitants, also without breaking the truce. This limited degree of tolerance came to an end with the fall of Granada on 2 January 1492. The pressure on the two or three million Muslims remaining in Spain to choose the alternative of conversion or emigration became overwhelming and in 1610 the remaining Moriscos, or forcibly converted Muslims, were simply expelled.[1]

---

[1] These expulsions led to further settlements by Spanish Moriscos on the North African coast, from Morocco to Tripoli.

This brought into being a new state of armed coexistence in which all the Muslims were to the south of the Straits and all the Christians to the north. It was, however, a long time before this state of affairs was stabilized. In the first flush of the conquest Portuguese and Spanish carried the war on into Africa and early in the sixteenth century we find the Portuguese in possession of Mazagan, Tangier, and Ceuta, and the Spanish of Melilla, Oran, Algiers, Tunis, and Tripoli. The main Iberian effort was, however, diverted elsewhere and the Moroccan dynasties managed, during the late sixteenth and seventeenth centuries to regain all that they had lost, with the exception of Ceuta and Melilla, which remained Spanish, and Mazagan, which was only recovered from the Portuguese in 1790.

4. THE BARBARY STATES

The Western Corsairs

Three centuries of raiding by corsairs was the price for the expulsion of the Muslims and for the transference of the war into Africa—justification for which could be found at least in the sixteenth century in Spanish fears of a Muslim counter-attack, backed by the growing power of the Ottoman Turks. The raiding had, however, originally been provoked by the Portuguese policy of carrying the war on into Africa, inaugurated with the unprovoked attack on Ceuta in 1415. In the discussions which preceded the attack, the Portuguese King, John I, pointed out to his impatient, half-English sons that an attack on the Muslims in Africa would be certain to expose south Portugal to constant raids and would also cause the closing of the Straits and the interruption of the valuable Portuguese trade with the Mediterranean in wine, oil, and fruit. The Muslims, far from being aggressors on this occasion, contributed to the success of the unexpected attack by the friendly and unsuspecting welcome which they gave to a spying expedition which was presented to them as a Portuguese Embassy on its way to and from Sicily. The assault was followed by the merciless sack of the city and by the slaughter or enslavement of its inhabitants.[1] The later Portuguese attack on

---

[1] Oliveira Martins, *Los Hijos de Don Juan*, based on Eannes de Zarura, *Chronica de D. João I*, Spanish trans. (Buenos Aires, 1946), iii. 7–12. King John married Philippa, daughter of the Duke of Lancaster; their sons included his successor King Duarte, Prince Henry the Navigator, and Prince Fernando, 'el Príncipe Constante' (p. 182). When Queen Philippa, in view of the King's age, endeavoured to dissuade him from taking part himself, he replied that he had shed much Christian blood in his youth and that his conscience would not be at rest until he had atoned for this by shedding a corresponding quantity of the blood of the infidels.

Tangier was carried out against the recommendation of the Pope, who was consulted by King Duarte in 1437. War should not be made, the Pope said, against countries which were not Christian but at the same time not idolatrous, unless they were aggressive. A king should not expose his people to unnecessary dangers and the proposed war was not one for whose success prayer could be ordered.[1] The consequence of these attacks was that the North African states for centuries waged a war of privateers against any Christian state which had not made a special arrangement with them: this generally involved a cash payment. In the west, the warfare was carried on mainly by Muslim refugees from Spain; they settled in Tetuan and Salé, bringing with them a knowledge of seamanship, which they had acquired in the great days of the Spanish fleets, as well as an intense hatred for the Christian government which had expelled them. Those who settled in Tetuan rapidly became assimilated to the Moroccans; but the 4,000 or more in Salé seem to have been largely Spanish-speaking, with a strong Spanish sentiment, and from 1627 for some time they maintained themselves as an autonomous maritime republic governed by two Alcaldes, one for the town and one for the fortress, who were elected annually. In 1631 those settled in Rabat made approaches to the Spanish King. They were, they said, genuine Christians and had been persecuted for that reason by their Muslim neighbours. If the King would permit them to return to Spain, they would undertake to deliver the place up to him and he could be sure that Moriscos elsewhere would follow their example.[2] The proposal was not accepted, and the use of Spanish by the Muslims died out fairly soon, though many Spanish words passed into the local Arabic dialect. The language is, however, still spoken by Jews in the coast towns. Many Muslims as well as Jews have retained names denoting their Spanish origin—such as Ronda, Mulin, Castillo, Torres, Denia, Bargash (Vargas).

With some difficulty Morocco itself managed to retain its independence at the expense of almost entirely losing contact with the outer world. The result was that its civilization remained medieval, in an ever-increasing state of degeneration.

The practice of privateering was, however, suspended by Sultan Muhammad ibn Abdullah at the end of the eighteenth century and he also released European captives. Raiding was, however, only definitely brought to an end by Maulay

[1] Martins, Los Hijos de Don Juan, p. 166.
[2] H. Terrasse, Islam d'Espagne (Paris, 1958), p. 262.

Sulaiman in 1817, about the same time as Muslim slavery was abolished in the Kingdom of the Two Sicilies (1815).

The Turks and the Eastern Corsairs

In the central and eastern portions of the Mediterranean the Muslim reaction to Spanish attacks took a similar form to that in the west. Diego de Haedo, Spanish Archbishop of Palermo during the second half of the sixteenth century, in his history of Algeria, notes that a great development of privateering followed the capture of Granada in 1492.[1] In the eastern states, however, the course of events developed differently from Morocco, which always remained primarily a land power. When the Algerians, Tunisians, and Tripolitanians appealed to their co-religionists for help against the Spanish, the people who were in a position to assist them were the commanders of Turkish naval forces in the eastern Mediterranean.

When these had accomplished the task of driving out the Spanish, they established a Turkish régime with themselves as rulers and seem to have thought of their prizes in the first place as naval bases. Thus the ports of Tripoli, Tunis, and above all Algiers, the capital of the richest of the three Ojaks or Regencies into which Turkish North Africa was divided, began to specialize in privateering, while continuing to be centres of trade. 'Privateers' are defined by experts in naval law as 'vessels owned and manned by private persons, but furnished with the authority of their Government to carry on hostilities; they were used to increase the naval forces of a State "by causing vessels to be equipped from private cupidity, which a minister might not be able to obtain by general taxation without much difficulty".' [2] In other words, individuals received authorization, known in England as Letters of Marque, to equip warships which were then free to attack shipping of any state with which the parent state was at war—a stipulation which seems often to have been interpreted very freely. Thus Sir Francis Drake 'set out on one of his famous voyages to the new world in his "good ship well equipped for war" without a commission of any kind, since "as England and Spain were not then in the best terms of friendship, he thought the general Licence of the Times would be his justification." ' [3]

As was to be expected in these circumstances, endless corre-

---

[1] Diego de Haedo, *Topografía e Historia General de Argel* (Valladolid 1612; Madrid, 1927) i. 26. Ibn Khaldun, the fourteenth-century Arab historian, notes that in his day Bougie was a great centre of privateering.

[2] A. P. Higgins and C. J. Colombos, *The International Law of the Sea*. 3rd ed. (London, 1954), p. 389.

[3] Quoted in G. Fisher, *Barbary Legend* (Oxford, 1957), p. 140.

spondence passed between the chancelleries of the various governments about the rights and wrongs of individual captures and about whether the ships and their passengers had or had not fulfilled the necessary formalities to ensure them the right of unmolested passage. It was equally natural that those who suffered on these occasions rarely hesitated to accuse their aggressors of piracy, though the chancelleries concerned always discussed cases on the basis of the accepted law and practice.[1] The real grievance against the Barbary states was not piracy but the fact that they constantly used small pretexts to threaten a declaration of war. By this means they hoped either to extort monetary concessions, or, if war ensued, to make a profit by privateering.

Any proceeds of such warfare were divided in a legally fixed proportion between the owner, the captain, the crew, and the government. In the sixteenth century English privateers were notorious and much resented by the more organized Spanish navy, just as the Barbary corsairs were later by the European powers. A scene in Shakespeare's *Twelfth Night* is illustrative of this. The Duke, having had the ship's captain presented to him with the words, 'Orsino, this is that Antonio that took the Phoenix and her fraught from Candy and . . . did the Tiger board, when your young nephew Titus lost his leg', addresses him as 'Notable pirate! thou salt water thief!' This it has been suggested may be the echo of some Spanish grandee's words to a captured English privateer.[2] Certainly privateering was in no sense a monopoly of the Muslims.

In 1518 or 1520, for example, it was in a Muslim ship off Jerba that a young Muslim afterwards known as Leo Africanus was captured by a Christian, probably Maltese, corsair; owing to his exceptional intelligence and wide travels, his captors, instead of selling him in the great slave markets of Pisa and Genoa, presented him to Pope Leo X.[3] Malta was in fact a great centre

---

[1] 'Although the Algerian corsairs were not in general particularly scrupulous, the instructions which they received from their Government were regularly based on the principles of international law. They could only legally capture vessels of states with whom the Regency was at war' (E. Pellissier de Reynaud, *Annales algériennes* (Paris, 1854), i. 15).

[2] *Twelfth Night*, Act V, Scene 1. There was an actual *Tiger* which sailed the Mediterranean from 1583 till 1614, when she was captured in Tunis harbour by French ships variously described as men-of-war, Marseilles pirates, or as an official peace mission. In 1587 the *Tiger* on her way to Alexandria put in at Algiers from 6 January–1 March and at Tunis from 8 March–3 April; on her return journey she again called at Algiers. John Evesham who has left an account of this journey describes Algiers as 'well-victualled with all manner of fruits, bread and fish, good store and very cheap' (Hakluyt, *Principal Navigations* &c. (Glasgow, 1906), vi. 35–38; Fisher, *Barbary Legend*, p. 131).

[3] E. W. Bovill, *The Golden Trade of the Moors* (London, 1958), p. 121.

for preying on the shipping of Tunis and Tripoli; in the year
1720 there were 10,000 Muslim slaves held in the island.[1]

European Organization of Privateering

An interesting feature of the corsair period is the very considerable extent to which those concerned were Muslims of
European origin. The brothers Barbarossa, who expelled the
Spaniards and founded the Algerian state, came from the island
of Mitylene and are believed to have been of Albanian origin.
The four Turkish Governors of Algiers who held office from
1574 to 1586 were all European—a Sardinian, an Albanian, a
Hungarian, and a Venetian. When Cervantes was captured in
1575 the privateer Captain was a Greek Muslim. In the west,
we have seen already that the corsairs were mainly Muslim
Spanish.

The Three Regencies

It was in this Turkish period of rule, dating from early in
the first half of the sixteenth century, that we first find eastern
and central Maghrib divided into three distinct areas, Tripolitania, Tunisia, and Algeria, with the frontiers which exist today.
The importance acquired by Algeria at this period was due to
the fact that the Barbarossas made it their headquarters and
then succeeded in adding the former territories of Tlemsen,
Bougie, and Constantine to their domain.[2] For a century or so
Governors were directly appointed or removed by Istanbul,
but later all three Regencies acquired a degree of independence,
though they always recognized the suzerainty of the Sublime
Porte in some form and contributed naval and military forces
when the Government in Istanbul required them. In Tripoli
and Tunisia hereditary dynasties were founded. That in Tunis
originated with a Cretan Muslim, Husain Bey, in 1705 and
members of the family continued to reign for 252 years until the

[1] J. Godechot, 'La Course Maltaise', *Revue Africaine*, 1952. Goods captured from
Muslim ships during six years of the eighteenth century included: barley, wheat,
maize, bread and French beans, raisins, honey, salt, melons, wool, cotton, silk
cloth, woollen cloth, carpets, sacks, cinders, saffron, iron goods, firewood, tobacco,
wax, skins, soap, sheep, camels, silver. Under the Knights of St. John, Malta played
a part in the naval warfare of Christendom which has many analogies with the part
played by Algiers in the naval warfare of the Muslims. The name 'the ships of
religion' given to the fleet of the Order itself seems an echo of ideas related to the
Jihad, or Holy War, of the Muslims. See also Addenda, p. 382 below.

[2] 'Kheir-ed-Din Barbarossa', writes the most recent historian of the naval
activities of the Barbary States, 'who has . . . come to be depicted in our latest
histories as an "infamous character" and "professional pirate", was in his own age
reputed by Christians generally to be a wise statesman, an able administrator, and
a great soldier, noted for his orderly and civilized conduct of war' (Fisher, *Barbary
Legend*, p. 9).

last Bey, Amin, was deposed on the proclamation of the Tunisian Republic on 25 July 1957. Though both the Tunisian and Tripolitanian reigning families became largely arabized, the Tunisian court retained to the end a Turkish rather than an Arab aspect in ceremonial and costume. This lingering air of foreign domination was no doubt one factor which enabled the dynasty to be finally removed without raising a ripple on the surface of Tunisian public opinion. Within the Ottoman Empire, the Regencies can in fact be considered self-governing colonies; and their fleets were at the service of the mother country. In Algeria the native population was excluded from the central Government, but in general left to go its own way, provided taxes were paid and communications not interfered with. An English visitor in the 1730's remarked that 'the natives of Algiers live extremely happy; for though the government is nominally despotic it is not so in reality'.[1]

In a sense Turkish rule was a westernizing influence, whether direct as in Tripoli or indirect as in Tunisia. The latter country before the French occupation was one of the more advanced Arab countries and was the first Arab state to experiment with a constitution.[2] This was, however, no doubt primarily due to its ancient traditions and connexions.

Algiers

The most original as well as the most powerful of the three Regencies was Algeria.[3] It was here that maritime activity reached its greatest development and in the sixteenth century the Algerian fleet operated against the Spanish possessions in Italy in direct alliance with the French fleet.[4] In the winter of 1543 King Francis I of France handed Toulon city and harbour over to the Algerian fleet as winter quarters. Though Algiers is connected primarily with the corsairs in the memory of Europeans, thanks to the description of the captivity there of Cervantes and to similar narratives, there was in fact a considerable commercial activity. Several powers, including France, who was interested in the coral fisheries, and England,

---

[1] Thomas Shaw, *Travels or Observations relating to Barbary*, in Pinkerton, *Voyages*, xv. 499–680.
[2] F. Prévost, *La Tunisie* (1862); Émile Cardon, *Étude sur le progrès de la civilisation dans la Régence de Tunis* (1861).
[3] Officially styled in treaties with the United States as 'the warlike city and kingdom of Algiers' (W. Shaler, *Sketches of Algiers*, Boston, 1826).
[4] 'Voyages accomplished in common on the coasts of Italy; adventurous expeditions, where French and Barbaresques rivalled one another in planting the fleur-de-lys standard of the Kings of France and the green standard with the golden crescent of the Deys of Algiers on the walls of enemy cities' (P. Heinrich, *L'Alliance franco-algérienne*, 1898).

maintained Consuls for the purpose of facilitating trade. Wheat was the principal export and went through Bône and Oran as well as Algiers. There were also exports of raisins, figs, dates, woven stuffs, tobacco, leather, and wax. At one period Gibraltar was largely supplied from Algiers. Flourishing local crafts and industries catered for the internal market. The nature of the imports denotes the luxurious life led by the notables in the state's heyday. They consisted mainly of Dutch tiles, Italian marble, silk and velvet from Genoa and Lyons, Venetian mirrors, Bohemian glass, and English clocks; in primary necessities the state was self-supporting.

Unlike the two other Regencies, Algiers became an oligarchic republic. The ruler of the state, the Dey, was elected for life, like the Doge of Venice—the electors in the Dey's case being the Diwan or principal officers of state. Though nominally absolute, his powers were greatly restricted by the insubordination of the ships' captains and the army officers. In fact of 28 Deys no less than 14 died violent deaths—as opposed to one Venetian doge who was executed. The language spoken in the Diwan was Turkish, and the ruling class consisted of some 20,000 Turkish-speaking people, divided between soldiers and civilians. Here again the European element was prominent and a number of rulers were of known European origin, among them a Venetian.

A very unfavourable picture of the state is given in the mass of tendentious, or as we should say, propaganda literature about Algiers. This was, however, largely inspired, according to a French resident in Algiers in the eighteenth century, by the desire of redemptionist Spanish monks to raise funds to ransom captives. Certainly there exist also a number of much more favourable references, particularly concerning the sixteenth and early seventeenth centuries. A French traveller in 1551 speaks of the good arrangement of the city, of the pleasant private houses, and of the number of baths and eating-houses. The city, he said, was 'very merchant-like' and surprisingly thickly populated for its size. Food was good and cheap, particularly partridges; and he admired the oven-incubators used for hatching chickens.[1] A hundred years later Francis Knight, an Englishman who was there as a prisoner for seven years, describes the city as 'built on the side of a hill . . . in form of a top-sail hoised; her houses built stair-like one over the other . . .; scarce any house of the city but hath the prospect of the sea; there are in her many stupendious [sic] and sumptuous edifices,

[1] N. N. Daulphinois, in T. Osborne, Collection of Voyages and Travels (London, 1745), ii. 559.

though outwardly for the major part present themselves but simple and rude'. He too remarks on the teeming population, and also on the great wealth of 'gold, plate [silver], and household furniture' and on the beauty of the women.[1] The gardens around the city were commented on favourably throughout all the three centuries of the regency. Thus Dr. T. Shaw of St. Edmund's Hall, Oxford, in the early eighteenth century, wrote:

The hills and vallies round about Algiers are all over beautified with gardens and country-seats, whither the inhabitants of better fashion retire, during the heats of the summer season. They are little white houses, shaded with a variety of fruit-trees and ever-greens; which, besides the shade and retirement, afford a gay and delightful prospect towards the sea. The gardens are all of them well stocked with melons, fruit, and pot-herbs of all kinds.[2]

Another traveller considered the melons to be of 'marvellous goodness and incomparable sweetness'.

No doubt much of the wealth of the city came from privateering but, as has been mentioned, this was at the worst an abuse of a legitimate form of warfare, not given up by England and France until the Conference of Paris in 1856, though fallen out of general use long before that time. At the moment of the conquest the administration of justice was said by an Austrian officer who accompanied the French expedition to have been swift, fair, and efficient; [3] and most observers speak well of the character of the last Dey, Husain.

When the foreign invasion came, it was provoked by the episode when the Dey struck the French Consul with a fly-whisk; but the Dey appears to have been greatly provoked. The British Consul reported the occurrence as follows: 'It appears that a warm discussion had arisen . . . Expressions of a very gross and irritating nature were said to have been indulged in by the Consul, which after being tolerated for a time, excited the Dey's indignation to a degree which caused him to forget his own dignity.' In reporting the matter to the Sultan in Istanbul the Dey remarked that the Consul first said in an insulting manner that the Dey could not expect the French Government to reply to his letters, and then added insulting remarks about the Muslim religion and 'the honour of Your

---

[1] Francis Knight, *A Relation of Seven Years Slavery under the Turks of Algier* (London, 1646; in Harleian Collection of Voyages, vol. 2). If we are to believe the stories told by captives, many of them seem to have enjoyed surprising opportunities of meeting Muslim women. It is, however, clear that many of these narratives were written to rouse sympathy or to entertain and have very little connexion with reality.

[2] Shaw, *Travels and Observations relating to Barbary* (Pinkerton's *Voyages*, xv. 533).

[3] *Ruckblick auf Algier* (Vienna, 1837), p. 51. Cf. Shaler, *Sketches of Algiers*, p. 23.

Majesty, the protector of the world'. Whereupon 'unable to bear this affront which passed all tolerable limits, listening only to the natural impulse of a Muslim, I struck him two or three light blows with the fly-whisk which I was holding in my humble hand'.[1]

The Decay of the Corsairs

The great days of the corsair states were the sixteenth and seventeenth centuries. By the eighteenth the growing technical superiority of the European fleets was already reducing the profits from captures. The population of Algiers city diminished and the number of captives fell from 30,000 to a mere hundred at the time of the French attack in 1830.

Islam in the West

When we survey the history of Islam in the west over the eleven centuries from the eighth to the nineteenth, it falls into three clearly marked periods. The first extends from the seventh to the beginning of the eleventh century and is the period of extension and consolidation. Islam comes to be established in nearly the whole of Spain, Sicily, and Malta.

The second period runs from the later part of the eleventh until the beginning of the sixteenth century; this is marked by the advance of the Christian reconquest, first in Sicily and Malta, then in Spain, and finally in Africa. The third is the long period of armed coexistence, in separate continents, which lasted from the beginning of the sixteenth until the beginning of the nineteenth century.

European historians have usually taken a very unfavourable view of the North African or as they called them the 'Barbary' states during this period. It was in fact a time of slow decay for Islam, in the west just as in the east; and it cannot be said that the Barbary states in the Turkish period made any particular contribution to civilization. Still the same could be said of many other countries; the bad reputation of North Africa was primarily a reaction to the privateering. This is often spoken of as mere piracy, and the impression is given that the Barbary states consisted exclusively of pirates living off the proceeds of their ill-gotten gains. This is a very misleading picture; privateering was 'legal'; but the geographical position of the Muslim states and the tradition of enmity between them and the Christian maritime states enabled them to abuse the practice and turn it into a lucrative national profession—as, it is only fair to add, the Elizabethan English did also. The capital cities

[1] 'La Lettre du Dey', *Revue Africaine*, 1952.

benefited from this, but the proceeds cannot have affected the economy of the population in the interior.

In so far as Muslim policy was aggressive it was due to the growth of the power of the Turks, and their establishment in the Maghrib which was itself brought about by the Spanish attacks. No doubt the feeling persisted in North Africa that in attacking Christian shipping a blow was being struck in the Holy War, as well as an opportunity for enrichment being seized. On the whole, however, the North African attitude at this time was defensive, as it had been ever since the loss of Sicily. Privateering was in part a reaction to the declared intention of Christian states to possess themselves of North Africa, and in part to the treatment inflicted on Muslims by the Christian government of Spain. For the west, we have the evidence of an authoritative Spanish writer. 'The people of the Canary Islands [i.e. the Spaniards]', he writes, 'continued their raids on the neighbouring Moroccan coasts throughout the whole sixteenth century; only when the Muslim piracy [sic] began to develop, creating a certain danger for them, did they find it necessary to suspend these raids or make them less frequently.' [1] Certainly the accounts of their sufferings, written by Christian captives, are often heart-rending, but if we had accounts written by the Muslim captives in Malta, who were sold in large numbers to the French Government as galley slaves, we should no doubt find them just as moving as those of the prisoners in Algiers.

Even the evidence for the ill-treatment of the Christian captives, however, is much less convincing than might be supposed by those who know only the literature circulated by the Christian agencies concerned with the redemption of slaves and the voluminous literature based on them. A French Marine Commissary who lived in Algiers in the first half of the eighteenth century and dedicated his book on Algiers to the French Consul in that city, while recognizing the relatively 'uncivilized' or unpolished character of life in Algiers, flatly denied that Christian captives were in general badly treated. Having himself been a prisoner of war of the Spanish in 1706, he says that he 'would prefer ten years of slavery in Algiers to one in Spain'. [2] For the period after 1775, when slaves were held only by the state and not by private individuals, we have the testimony of the United States Consul, General W. Shaler.

[1] T. García Figueras, *Marruecos* (Madrid, 1944), p. 303.
[2] Laugier de Tassy, *Histoire du royaume d'Alger* (Amsterdam, 1725), p. 329. It may, of course, be the case that conditions in the eighteenth century were more humane than in the sixteenth, as they were also in Europe.

D

It is no more than justice [he wrote] to say that their condition was not generally worse than that of prisoners of war in many civilized, Christian countries. Female captives were always treated with the respect due to their sex; the labour required of the men was not excessive; those who could find security that they would not escape, were allowed to go at large on the payment of about 75 cents per month; there were a number of lucrative offices that were always occupied by slaves, in which many enriched themselves; those who were employed in the palace, or attached to the great officers of state, were treated with the greatest mildness; and generally all those who were industriously disposed easily found the means of profiting by it. In short there were slaves who left Algiers with regret, and it is believed that, in the aggregate, they carried away vast sums at their embarkation. That they suffered occasional cruelty and hardship from the caprice or brutality of their keepers and overseers cannot be doubted, for such are inseparable from the unprotected situation of captives of any description.[1]

With regard to the character of the Algerian people, Shaler remarks 'they are a people of very insinuating address, and in the common relations of life, I have found them civil, courteous and humane. Neither have I ever remarked anything in the character of the people that discovers extraordinary bigotry, fanaticism or hatred of those who profess a different religion.'[2] The captives who suffered worst seem to have been the prisoners who were taken to row in the galleys; but this applied equally to the Muslim and the Christian fleets.

In the first part of the period, the Muslim raids on Christian territory were replies to Christian attempts to invade and occupy Muslim territory; in the latter half the Muslim attacks against shipping were their reply to attacks on their own territory, as well as on their shipping. As a student of the subject has written, 'While the Barbary danger had disappeared on the European coast for more than a hundred years the Christian danger existed on the African shores until the end of the eighteenth century.'[3] Nor apparently is it true that the original provocation in the periodical disputes with the Algerian Government came normally from the Muslims.

It is too readily assumed [wrote de Grammont, the French historian of Turkish rule in Algiers] that the Pashas and Deys always acted in bad faith in their relations with the Christians. It is very convenient to explain the incidents which brought the European fleets before Algiers in this way; but it is not in accord with the truth. Careful examination of the facts produces overwhelming evidence

---

[1] Shaler, *Sketches of Algiers*, p. 76. [2] Ibid., p. 55.
[3] Godechot, 'La Course Maltaise', *Revue Africaine*, 1952.

that in the majority of occasions the first wrongs were committed by the westerners, though it can certainly be granted that the Dey's government was always quick to profit from circumstances where he had any excuse, however small, to break the peace and to begin hostilities which were certain to be profitable to him.[1]

Napoleon Ends a Period

In 1798, when Napoleon captured Malta, he released the 2,000 Muslim slaves whom he found there. In gratitude for this the Dey of Algiers renewed relations with France, and it might have been thought that an era of peaceful Christian and Muslim coexistence, each in their own territory, was about to begin. In fact, however, neither side was ready for such a state of affairs. The technical disparity between Muslims and Europeans was perhaps too great for such a thing to be practicable. The Muslims were still situated, intellectually, in the Middle Ages and it was impossible for them to live in harmony with a post-Renaissance world on the eve of the scientific discoveries of the nineteenth and twentieth centuries. There had to be a further period in which the modern world totally overran Islam (or perhaps we should rather say 'overran the countries which were still medieval') before there could be created the conditions for a future of mutual respect and comprehension.

5. THE EUROPEAN OCCUPATION

The Assault on Algiers

The launching of the assault on Algiers in 1830 was presented to Europe by the French Government as an operation to put an end to piracy. By this time Muslim naval activity from the Barbary states was simply an irritating survival. The forces of the Christian powers were by now so superior that Barbary privateering was regarded in Europe as a provocation by states too weak to defend themselves. In this respect the relations of the newly independent United States of America with the Regency are so instructive that it is worth while to outline them at some length.

The American Colonies had established a certain trade with the Levant. Since their shipping was regarded as British, it benefited from the security afforded by British treaties with the Barbary states, and American people and ships were always well received. When the United States became independent, British treaties ceased to apply to American shipping, and the Barbary states in due course let it be known that they would

[1] H. D. de Grammont, *Histoire du massacre des turcs à Marseille en 1620* (Paris, 1879), p. 6.

consider themselves free to attack United States shipping (on the grounds of alleged Muslim or Turkish rights in the Mediterranean) unless treaties were negotiated. The United States, which at that time possessed no navy, approached French and other European powers in the hope of getting coverage for American shipping with theirs. The powers concerned, though sympathetic, did not consider this practicable; it would obviously rouse protests and a demand for compensation. The United States then decided to negotiate treaties of their own and a committee was formed for this purpose, composed of John Adams, Benjamin Franklin, and Thomas Jefferson; this was allotted the sum of $80,000 with which to negotiate. In the case of Morocco, which had been the first country to recognize American independence, a treaty was successfully negotiated in 1786, with the assistance of the Spanish Government. It was initialed by Thomas Barclay in Marrakesh; the monetary consideration involved, which did not form part of the actual treaty, was agreed in the following year at $10,000. Apart from occasional demands for increased payments, notably in the time of Sultan Maulay Sulaiman, which were successfully resisted, the arrangement worked well and American shipping was not molested in the Atlantic approaches.

The demands of the three Turkish Regencies were very much higher. Negotiations were moreover delayed by the death of Thomas Barclay and then by that of the negotiator appointed to succeed him. Meanwhile Algerian privateers captured two American ships, the *Maria* and the *Dauphin*, in the Straits of Gibraltar (1785) and took twenty-one prisoners. Jefferson tried unsuccessfully to organize a combined front with the European powers; the formation of a small American navy was also authorized, though the construction of the ships was to be suspended if in the meanwhile a treaty were signed with Algiers. The matter became urgent when the Portuguese, who had been at war with the Regency, made peace in 1793; after this the Algerians captured further American ships and took 117 more prisoners. In their indignation, the Americans accused the British of encouraging the Portuguese to make peace and of instigating the Algerians to attack American shipping in order to rid themselves of unwelcome competition. This charge was based on some unhappy remarks made by a Member of Parliament.[1] Benjamin Franklin went further and attributed to

---

[1] John Holroyd, first Earl of Sheffield (in Irish peerage). He was M.P. for Bristol. The remarks occur in a pamphlet attacking a proposal for free trade between the United States and Great Britain. He said that the Barbary states would be 'useful' in limiting American competition.

British statesmen a remark, which had been attributed some decades earlier, in corresponding circumstances, by Spanish statesmen to Louis XIV, to the effect that if Algiers had not existed, it would have been desirable to create it. It was also suggested that the British Consul in Algiers had urged the Dey to ill-treat American prisoners.

It was not in fact until the original captives had spent over ten years in Algiers that a treaty was finally signed. This and the accompanying ransom of the captives cost the United States $642,500 in cash and the promise of an annual delivery of $21,600 worth of stores. In 1798 treaties were signed also with Tunis and Tripoli, and Consuls proceeded to take up appointments in all three Regencies. One of the former American prisoners, S. L. Cathcart, who had during his captivity been employed as Secretary by the Dey, was made Consul in Tunis. Another former captive, R. O'Brien, became Consul in Algiers and Consul-General for the Barbary coast, while the post in Tripoli was given to the fiery William Eaton (p. 350) who had no previous experience of the Mediterranean world. On his way through Algiers to take up his post, Eaton was presented to the Dey by Consul-General O'Brien, and emerged in a rage because he had been expected to remove his shoes, according to the Muslim habit on entering a house, and to kiss the Dey's hand. 'Is it not unbelievable', he said, 'that this elevated brute has seven kings of Europe, two republics, and a continent [*sic*] tributary to him, when his whole naval force is not equal to two line-of-battle ships?' [1]

Unfortunately relations with the Regencies rapidly deteriorated again, mainly owing to the failure of the United States to make payments and deliver the stores on the appointed dates. In excuse the United States Government pleaded their limited resources and difficulties caused for them by French privateers (1799).

Eaton now became the principal advocate of a policy of force.[2] He was infuriated that the European powers should still

[1] J. L. Cathcart, *Tripoli; First War with the United States, Inner History* &c (La Porte, Ind., 1901). Modern American writers echo his protest. 'That Europeans for generations suffered the depredations and insults of these gangs of petty sea-rovers is a scandalous indictment of the mutual jealousy and selfishness of the maritime nations' (L. B. Wright and J. H. Macleod, *First Americans in North Africa* (Princeton Univ. Press, 1945), p. 14). In fact, however, the United States had no choice but to follow example. Apart from Spanish attacks in the sixteenth century, operations were undertaken against Algiers by France in 1661, 1665, 1682, 1683, and 1688, and a number of naval demonstrations in the eighteenth century; by the United States in 1815; by Spain in 1775, 1783, and 1790; by Britain in 1622, 1635, 1672, and 1825; and by British and Dutch in 1816.

[2] General William Eaton, whose rank of 'general' was conferred on him only by the pretender whom he unsuccessfully tried to make ruler of Tripoli, was a valiant

put up with arrangements which had been accepted at a time when the relative strength of the Muslims was very much greater—an historical fact which he ignored. 'Shall America', he asked, 'who, when in an infant state, destitute of all apparatus of war, without discipline and without funds, dared to resist the whole force of the lion's den of Great Britain to establish her freedom, now that she has acquired manhood [sic], resources and experience, bring her humiliation to the basest dog kennel of Barbary.' [1]

In 1801 the newly formed American navy was brought into operation against Tripoli (p. 350) and in 1815 against Algiers; in the latter operations the squadron was commanded by Commodore Stephen Decatur who had distinguished himself twelve years earlier in the Tripolitanian operations. American diplomacy, backed by this naval force, was able to secure new treaties. Thereafter relations with Algiers remained undisturbed until the loss of the latter's independence in 1830, thirty-three years after the destruction of the Venetian Republic by Napoleon had shown that the days of small maritime republics were drawing to a close.[2]

In the official 'statement of grievances', which was issued by the French Government on the occasion of the invasion of 1830, however, references to piracy occupied a singularly small place. The major grievance was quite clearly the Dey's refusal to continue to allow the French a privileged trading position, based on a fortified *enceinte* ('the Bastion', near Bône), and the serious loss of trade which its loss might involve.[3] In the audience which ended with the blow of the fly-whisk, the Dey had in fact affirmed that he would no longer allow a single French cannon to remain on Algerian soil and that French merchants could for the future only enjoy the same rights as other merchants.

---

but extravagant character. When it suited his purpose, he claimed that there was an affinity between the Muslim religion and that of the Americans. 'Varying a little the subject', he writes, in describing an interview with the ruler of Egypt, 'I touched on the affinity of principle between the Islam [sic] and American religion.' God, he told some Arab Shaikhs, in the course of his expedition to Derna, had promised a separate heaven to Americans; in this, however, they would be free, if they wished, to make up parties and visit the paradise of Muhammad or the heaven of the Papists. His Arab listeners laughed and said they doubted if it would be possible for him to visit the paradise of Muhammad unless he had in his lifetime become a 'sincere Muslim' (Cathcart, *Tripoli*).

[1] Ibid.

[2] After the bombardment of Algiers by Lord Exmouth in 1815, British payments had been confined to a sum of £600 for renewal of consular privileges on the occasion of the appointment of a new Consul (E. Dupuy, *Américains et Barbaresques* (Paris, 1910), p. 5). Receipts from privateering appear to have ceased from this date.

[3] H. Garrot, *Histoire générale d'Algérie* (Algiers, 1910), p. 665.

In reality, there is little doubt that the basic motive of the French Government was its desire to restore the tottering credit of the régime by a military success; and to win for the restoration Government the credit which Napoleon had lost by the evacuation of Egypt. In the event Algiers was duly captured and the achievement inspired a number of laudatory poems throughout Europe including one in the dialect of Genoa, that ancient rival of the Barbary states; [1] but Charles X was nevertheless dethroned. In any case neither his nor the succeeding Government was at all clear how to follow their victory up.

The expedition had been accompanied by propaganda to the effect that the French were coming to liberate the Algerians from their Turkish tyrants.

We French, your friends [said one document], are leaving for Algiers. We are going to drive out your tyrants, the Turks who persecute you, who steal your goods, and never cease menacing your lives . . . our presence on your territory is not to make war on you but only on the person of your Pasha. Abandon your Pasha; follow our advice; it is good advice and can only make you happy.[2]

This propaganda had not been entirely insincere; there was a proposal to set up an Arab prince and administration. The age, however, was the age of imperialism and after months and years of indecision it was decided to conquer and colonize the whole country in the high Roman style. According to the standards of today the times were still barbarous and the operation itself was infinitely harder than had been anticipated. In consequence, the sufferings imposed on the Algerian people were very great. Some of their best mosques were taken for churches; Muslim feast-days ceased to be legal holidays; tribal lands were confiscated, and every sort of national symbol was destroyed. The policy of colonization was accompanied by announcements which indicated a changed attitude to the Arab population. 'Soldiers', said General Bugeaud in 1841, 'you have often beaten the Arabs. You will beat them again, but to rout them is a small thing; they must be subdued.' To civilians he added: 'The Arabs must be reduced to submission so that only the French flag stands up on this African soil.' [3]

The First Pacification

Much of the severity employed was no doubt essential to the success of the military operations; but there was wanton cruelty also, and accounts given in the works of French

---

[1] *A Spedizion d'Argê* (Genoa, 1834). Cf. p. 19 above.
[2] Baudicourt, *La Guerre et le gouvernement de l'Algérie* (Paris, 1853), p. 160.
[3] Rousset *La Conquête de l'Algérie* 1889.

historians go far to explain the subsequent difficulties of France in Algeria. Examples have been given in the section on Algeria; the following is one which deals with the operations in the Kabyle country, which is once again today a centre of resistance.

Our soldiers returning from the expedition were themselves ashamed . . . about 18,000 trees had been cut down; houses had been burnt; women, children, and old men had been killed. The unfortunate women particularly excited cupidity by the habit of wearing silver ear-rings, leg-rings, and arm-rings. These rings have no catches like French bracelets. Fastened in youth to the limbs of girls they cannot be removed when they are grown up. To get them off, our soldiers used to cut off their limbs and leave them alive in this mutilated condition.[1]

It is distressing to have to dwell on such episodes of the past; yet it is impossible to understand the present rising unless one does. After 1880 when the Algerians had been cowed and Algiers became the favourite winter resort for wealthy Englishmen, a book was written about Algeria, entitled *The New Playground*. It may have seemed such to the casual English visitor in search of a pleasant winter climate with an exotic background; but it was full of underlying discontent. In 1905 Budgett Meakin, an Englishman who had an unrivalled knowledge of Muslim life in Morocco a full decade before the occupation and was fully aware of the unfavourable aspects of independent Muslim rule, visited Algeria and Tunisia. He had much good to say of French administration in Algeria, but certain aspects of the régime horrified him. The natives, he wrote,

are despised, if not hated, and despise and hate in return. The conquerors have repeated in Algeria the old mistake which has brought about such dire results in other lands, of always retaining the position of conquerors, and never unbending to the conquered, or encouraging friendship with them. . . . There is actual hatred in Algeria, fostered by the foreigner far more than by the smouldering bigotry of Islam. They do not seem to intermingle even as oil and water, but to follow each a separate independent course.[2]

Of course there was a different side to the picture. There was the comradeship of Frenchmen and Algerians fighting side by side in war; the devotion of doctors to their patients; the affection between teachers and their pupils. A limited number of Algerians undoubtedly absorbed more of the French outlook than those of any other of the North African countries. The

[1] Baudicourt, *La Guerre* &c., p. 372.
[2] Budgett Meakin, *Life in Morocco* (London, 1905), pp. 308–9.

leaders of the present revolution are themselves mostly the product of French schools or have gained their military experience with the French army in the Second World War or in Indo-China, often with high commendation. The Front of National Liberation, as a result of French teaching, stands for a lay state which will admit any existing resident of Algeria to citizenship on equal terms. Yet all this cannot cancel the memory of the past, the invasion, the series of 'pacifications', the hopes of equal citizenship which were never fulfilled, the galling contrast in the standards of living of European and of Muslim communities, and the absence of Algerians from any position of high responsibility.

The Extension of European Rule

Once French rule was established in Algeria, it was only a matter of time and diplomacy before France extended her control to the countries on either side. In fact in 1881 a second Arab country, Tunisia, lost its independence; followed, in the east, by Egypt in 1882. By now times had changed; though there was an element of force in the occupation of Tunisia, the operation was more diplomatic than military. The country was not conquered but became a protectorate, retaining its monarchy and something of its former administration, though in practice all authority was soon in the hands of French officials. Budgett Meakin, pursuing his travels to Tunisia, considered the system to be in every respect an improvement on that in force in Algeria even if, as he impishly added, 'the result is a nominally native administration which takes the blame for failures and a French direction which takes the credit for successes'.[1] Though much land passed to the colonists, there was no downright confiscation; mosques were not converted into churches and there were no memories of suffering connected with a long and bitter struggle.

Italy and Libya

The third stage in the European occupation of North Africa was the Italian invasion of Libya in 1911. This was presented to the Libyans in the same way as the attack on Algiers had been to the Algerians, namely as liberation from Turkish government. The policy had the same result; after disposing of Turkish resistance quite easily, the Italians found themselves involved in a long and bitter struggle with the Arab inhabitants, particularly in Cyrenaica. Under Fascism, the subjugation of

[1] Budgett Meakin, *Life in Morocco* (London, 1905), pp. 308–9.

the Sanusi was achieved by very harsh measures against non-combatants, who were enclosed in concentration camps with a terrible loss of human life. After this operation was completed, the régime took on a distinctly racialist aspect, though in its material aspects it was highly efficient. However, the Second World War intervened, bringing the experiment to an end before it was possible to judge how Italian-Arab relations were ultimately going to develop.

Marshal Lyautey in Morocco

Finally, in 1912, Morocco was occupied jointly by France and Spain. By this time ideas concerning the government of subject peoples as a sacred trust for humanity were already in the air. As in the case of Tunisia, the occupation was brought about by diplomatic as much as by military means. Moreover the first French Resident General, Marshal Lyautey, was a man of genius, very humane as well as a great soldier and administrator, a man who appreciated the millennary civilization of Morocco and loved the country and the people. Though just as persuaded as any other Frenchman that the future of Morocco was henceforth to be indissolubly linked with that of France, he worked with an understanding and sympathy which gave the French régime in Morocco a send-off much more auspicious than that in Tunisia, just as the latter had been more auspicious than that in Algeria. In the incredibly short space of forty-four years, Morocco was brought out of its isolation and freed from the medieval fetters of the spirit in which it had been bound.

Morocco Before the Occupation

It is difficult to realize how great was this transformation unless we first form an idea of what Morocco was like in the first years of the twentieth century. Travellers and residents of several nationalities have left excellent descriptions of the country at the beginning of the century. None failed to be touched with a sense of romance. The long journeys on horseback or mule-back over almost virgin soil covered in the spring with carpets of wild flowers; the medieval cities with their bustling brightly-coloured markets within the walls, contrasting with the immediate transition to the country outside the city gates; the houses of the rich merchants with their blank walls outside and their tiled courtyards, their fountains and their orange gardens inside—all these made an unforgettable impression on European travellers. Here is a description by a French writer, Eugène Aubin, written in 1903.

Our stay in Fez was long enough to enable us to enter Moorish society. I cannot express the pleasure which I experienced in a form of living which, however degenerate, was once so glorious and still remains so impervious to European influences and so distinct from our own. I have spent most agreeable hours in very fine houses, where I have been invited to an excellent dinner accompanied by the strangest music. I have shared in the refined life of the Fasis. I have received information about details of dress from men reserved and cultured, whose flowing garments enhance their dignity, who enjoy the pleasures of music and good cheer without ostentation, who are attentive and polite, leave their slippers at the door to avoid soiling the carpet with the mud of the street, come in softly, exchange some polite formula with their host or kiss him on the shoulder, and, if they have something to say, enter into conversation in a low tone to avoid disturbing the general quiet. . . . The patio is lighted by several lanterns, placed on the ground, while tapers in a room at the other end produce an effect of indefinite depth in the obscurity of the night. From a neighbouring room comes the sound of music softened by the distance, as it mingles with the splash of the water that falls from the fountain or bubbles within the basin in the centre of the court.[1]

But other aspects of life in the Morocco of that time were less agreeable. The country entered the twentieth century without one engineer, doctor, or chemist; virtually without a road or any wheeled traffic. Indifference to physical suffering in man or beast; inhuman punishments; ignorance of the first notions of modern science; the gory heads of decapitated rebels or criminals nailed over the city gates, these were medieval features which were horrifying to European visitors. In 1909, when the rebel leader Bu Hamara was captured and exhibited in an iron cage (made by the Italian armourer to the Sultan) before the eyes of the European diplomats, while his followers were submitted to amputations and other barbarous punishments, it was clear that intervention would not long be delayed; three years later, in 1912, Sultan Maulay Abd al-Hafidh signed the Treaty of Fez.

6. THE STRUGGLE FOR INDEPENDENCE

The Completion of European Control

Though Morocco had been occupied by diplomatic methods and the protectorate established by a treaty signed with the reigning Sultan, there were areas in which only the most powerful rulers had been able to exert their authority and where no recognition would be paid to the word of a Sultan who

[1] E. Aubin, *Le Maroc d'Aujourd'hui* (Paris, 1904), pp. 335–6.

48   INTRODUCTION

entrusted the government of the country to the Christian foreigner.

Two regions, both of them primarily Berber, were particularly involved; one was the Rif, the other the Anti-Atlas. The history of the rising in the Rif is given elsewhere (p. 149). It was a traditional Moroccan reaction to a weak ruler, such as in the past had often led to the accession of a new dynasty. Taking place when it did, under a leader who had an intimate knowledge of Spain and Spanish administration, it marked a transitional stage on the way to modern nationalism. In the Anti-Atlas, on the other hand, the fighting was never more than the reduction of outlying and stubbornly independent tribes. In 1934 the process was completed and the whole of south Morocco with the Moroccan Sahara beyond it was brought under French (or, in the case of Ifni, Spanish) administration. Since General Graziani had reduced the Sanusi to submission two years earlier, the whole Maghrib had at last been brought under the rule of France, Italy, and Spain, except for Tangier in whose government eight European countries were to participate.

Nature of European Rule in the Maghrib

European rule, thus established in North West Africa, naturally varied according to whether the rulers were French, Italian, or Spanish; according to the time when the occupation took place; and according to the nature of the country or the portion of the country occupied. If one surveys the picture as a whole, however, it is fair to say that the fundamental conception of both French and Italians was that they were the heirs of Rome, and that they were taking up and carrying on a task which had been interrupted some 1,200 years before. It is true that the Italian Government had at first the idea of establishing local parliamentary government; but soon, with the advent of the Fascist régime, ancient Rome became very consciously the model. French methods varied very greatly between Algeria and the two protectorates; but if the method was different, the goal appeared the same. One may go further and say that French and, for the short time that it lasted, Italian rule had the same general effect as Roman rule. The civilization of the metropolis was implanted by administrators and colonists; the latter were backed by armed force, remained 'aliens', and enjoyed a privileged position with regard to the indigenous population. So far as an ultimate end was ever envisaged by the French rulers, it appeared to be not the revival of Arab states in a modernized form but the creation of neo-French states whose civilization would, in some remote future, bear the same relation to French civilization as that of France itself bears to Roman civilization.

The main difference was perhaps that ancient Rome gave the impression of building for eternity, while there was a certain air of improvisation about the French and Italian constructions, as if they had an uneasy awareness that their domination was not to last very long. The work done was, nevertheless, comparable with that of the Romans.

Certain special problems arose connected with the period in which the colonization took place. The world was being revolutionized by modern science and by its application to human health and industry. Modern hygiene soon produced an enormous growth of the population, just as it had already done in the previous century in Europe. Industry, on the other hand, apart from some mining and a tremendous development in building, remained limited, and thus failed to provide a livelihood for the rapidly expanding population. This did not, however, prevent a repetition of some of the industrial evils of the nineteenth century in Europe, particularly in the creation of enormous *bidonvilles*, or shanty-towns, on the outskirts of every city. In Morocco, in particular, where industry was more developed than in the other areas, its economic basis was the abundant supply of inefficient but cheap labour. Though European experience acquired in the previous decades enabled some remedial measures to be taken, the position was inevitably made worse than in Europe by the fact that the employers were for the most part of a dominant, and the workers of a subject, race. Administrative attempts at improvement came up against local opposition inspired by economic interests. It can hardly be doubted that higher taxation on the employers and industrialists of Casablanca, and the investment of the proceeds in the education and housing of the workers, would in the long run have been advantageous for both Moroccan and French interests, even if it had acted as a considerable brake on industrial development. The *laissez-faire* system which prevailed left the successor governments with problems which make exceedingly difficult both their task within the country and their relations with the former protectors.

In the Spanish zone of Morocco a certain difference was to be noted. Spain had had its own tradition of imperialism, and this had been markedly different from the European imperialism of the nineteenth century. In some respects it was nearer to Arab imperialism. Its essential characteristics had been conquest, followed by an assimilation based primarily on the implantation of the religion and language of the conquerors, assisted by intermarriage.[1] Spanish expansion in Africa in the nineteenth and twentieth centuries, however, came after the 'europeanization' of Spain during the centuries following the Reconquista and its methods were copied from those of France. The Spanish never seemed completely at ease with these. Unable to hope for the assimilation that can only be brought about by religious unity they preferred to adopt a non-assimilationist policy more like the British practice in Arab countries. Influenced by historical memories, the protectorate authorities seemed to be feeling their way toward some cultural ideal which was not entirely Christian Spanish. Thus Tomás García Figueras, a very experienced protectorate official, in his book *Marruecos* claimed that Spain envisaged as the goal of the protectorate 'a free and great Moroccan people who will be united with Spain. . . . A people who will collaborate with her in a magnificent renaissance of hispano-arabic culture.' [2] The precise implications of this ideal are extremely obscure, but it appears to imply a cultural partnership of some sort, not the complete absorption of Morocco into Spanish civilization. It would not be easy to find any parallel French or Italian statement of intention, for which indeed no historical background exists.

The differences which resulted in practice in the Spanish area are described later (p. 67). Superficially the administration did not appear very different. In fact it can be said that throughout the whole of North West Africa the most significant result of European occupation in the long run has been the creation of a modern-minded Muslim *élite*. It is on the qualities of this *élite* that the future of the area, and of the masses who inhabit it, now depends.

The Growth of Nationalism

Most observers in 1934 must have supposed that European government had been established more or less permanently over all North West Africa. In fact, however, the last resistance of the old type had no sooner been overcome than a new type

---

[1] In Mexico, one of Montezuma's daughters, for example, married three Castilian noblemen consecutively, forming illustrious Spanish families by two of them. Another daughter became the ancestress of the family of Sotelos de Montezuma. One of Montezuma's sons also married into the nobility, and a descendant became Viceroy of Mexico from 1697–1701. Marina, the Aztec girl whose assistance was invaluable to Cortes, later became the legitimate wife of Don Juan Xamarillo (Prescott, *Conquest of Mexico*, ii. 301).

[2] García Figueras, *Marruecos*, p. 290.

of nationalism began to develop. The same year 1934, which saw the completion of the occupation, was marked in Tunisia by the birth of a dynamic new nationalist party, the Neo-Destour, under the leadership of the future President of independent Tunisia, Habib Bourguiba; while in Morocco on 8 May 1934 a visit by Mohammed V to Fez was the occasion of a significant nationalist demonstration which prepared the way for co-operation between the nationalists and the monarch and so led to the termination of the French protectorate within twenty-five years. The actual origin of the nationalist movement in Morocco can, however, be dated from eight years earlier, 1926, the year of Abdelkrim's surrender and of Marshal Lyautey's departure. On the night of 1 August 1926 eight young men from Rabat and two from Tetuan met in a garden outside Rabat. Sitting in the shelter of a mulberry tree and sipping the mint tea which is the national beverage of Morocco, they listened to what one of the party, Mohammed Bennouna of Tetuan, back from the University at Cairo, had to tell them of the growth of the nationalist movement in Egypt. They then went on to draw up plans for a movement of their own. The oldest member of the party was 36, while the youngest but one of them, Ahmed Balafrej, later to be the first Foreign Minister of independent Morocco, was 18. So quickly did things go that the first generation of western-educated young Moroccans were to provide most of the ministers for the first Moroccan cabinet. In the same period, other young men were holding similar meetings in other cities, notably in Fez, the former political capital and centre of Muslim tradition. Among them was the 18-year-old Allal al-Fasi, later President of the Istiqlal Party and the most original thinker of the movement. Three years before, he had composed a poem entitled 'My people will know me'. It began

> Am I still a child, at fifteen years old, and playing,
> While my people, with their hands bound,
> cannot find the way to their desire?[1]

The nationalist movements in Tunisia and Morocco were not very different from those which we have seen develop elsewhere. Their first requests—in Morocco, for example, for the abolition of direct French administration, for equality between Frenchmen and Moroccans, and for the creation of elected municipalities—do not at this distance of time appear so unreasonable and dangerous as to justify treating those who put them forward as agitators, or calling them Communists, and

[1] *Al-Adab al-Arabi fi'l Maghrib* (Rabat, 1929).

eventually imprisoning or banishing them.[1] It is interesting to speculate what would have happened if they had been more sympathetically handled, given by degrees posts of responsibility and allowed to work for the political and technical preparation of their country for renewed independence. It may well be that it would have made little difference to the outcome, but the goal would surely have been reached with less sterile controversy by the way, and without leaving such a heritage of unsettled problems for the newly independent states and between them and their former protectors.

French Policy before 1954

In fact, however, the furthest that the French Government before 1954 would ever go in recognizing the goal of independence was to concede that the more advanced of the two protectorates, Tunisia, might eventually enjoy some form of internal autonomy. Of any modification of the protectorate treaties there was no word.

The rising in the Aurès on 1 November 1954 brought a fundamental change. Until that moment successive French Governments had persuaded themselves that the promulgation of the Statute of 1947 had ensured the tranquillity of Algeria, whatever might be the case elsewhere. In this idea they were encouraged by one of their greatest Arab experts, the late Robert Montagne. In his *Révolution au Maroc*, published in 1953, the year before the outbreak, he had written:—

> In Africa only Algeria, thanks to the Statute of 1947, seems to have found a solution leading the various ethnic and religious groups to co-operate in a semi-autonomous regime. . . . Today, in the tempestuous east, only Algeria appears like a rock, from end to end, above which the French flag flies freely, while the troubled seas surge round it.[2]

The shots which shattered the silence of the night of All Saints, 1954, shattered these illusions also and led to a reappraisal of the French position in North Africa which has not yet been completed. In Morocco the policy initiated by General Juin and carried on by his successor, General Guillaume, had culminated a year earlier in the forcible deposition and banishment of the Sultan. Mohammed V had succeeded to the throne as a young man of 18, twenty-five years before, and

---

[1] The case of Allal al-Fasi, who was first known as a poet, is an illustration of a saying of Maulay Ahmad al-Raisuni, the adventurer of the early days of the century. 'In prison', he said, 'poets die—and politicians are born' (quoted in García Figueras, *Marruecos*, p. 123).

[2] *Révolution au Maroc* (Paris, 1952), pp. 407, 412.

thus belonged to the same generation as the members of the Rabat tea-party. With the years he had developed great diplomatic talents, showing himself persevering, patient, modernminded, and determined. During the war he had assisted the French, but after the Armistice of 1940 had also protected his Jewish subjects against an attempt to introduce anti-Jewish racial legislation. General Juin, himself of Christian Algerian origin and in some respects the leader of the French North Africans, on becoming Resident General in 1947, decided that the combination of nationalists and Sultan must at all costs be broken up; if need be, the Sultan must be eliminated. Since the whole system of government in Morocco had been built up on a measure of co-operation between the Sultan and the Resident General (officially his Foreign Minister) this was not an operation to be lightly undertaken. Finally, however, in August 1953, in the time of General Juin's successor, it was put into effect, without the acknowledged or fully conscious approval of the Government in Paris, being arranged to appear as far as possible the work of a spontaneous Moroccan movement. By November 1954 it was already clear that the result was not what had been hoped for. The Sultan who replaced Mohammed V proved totally ineffective, nor did the administration do anything to reconcile Moroccan opinion by the introduction of genuine reforms. The country began to be plagued with terrorism, a thing which had hitherto been unknown in Morocco; and an armed outbreak appeared likely. In Tunisia, it is true, the position had recently been greatly eased by the promise of internal autonomy, publicly announced by the Prime Minister, M. Mendès-France, in person at Carthage on 31 July, but negotiations on the terms of the new régime, which it was intended to make extremely restrictive, were going very slowly. There had been fighting once; there might be again. Now fighting had begun in Algeria.

A New Policy

It was only after a bewildering series of deliberations and changes in policy, lasting for over a year, that the decision was finally reached to give independence to Morocco, and in its wake to Tunisia, and then to try and hold on to Algeria at all costs. These decisions seemed in the end to be arrived at independently and almost by accident, yet the reasons for them are clear. It was desired to retain as much of France's position in the Maghrib as possible, both for its own sake, for the sake of the mineral wealth in the Sahara, and on account of the increased political demands that independence throughout North

E

Africa would provoke in black Africa. If the whole area could not be held, then it would be best to let the two protectorates go and to stand firm in the central key position, to which France had a better right juridically, as well as by the number of her subjects settled there and by length of possession. The drawback was that independence granted to the two sister countries must give moral encouragement to Algerian nationalism, while at the same time making it very much harder to control the passage of men and arms across at least Algeria's eastern and western frontiers. It could also be said that it was illogical, and even impracticable, to apply one type of policy on the two flanks of Algeria and a different one in Algeria itself. If there were good reasons for granting independence to Tunisia and Morocco there was logically no reason to deny it to Algeria, even if it were theoretically an integral portion of France.

Some liberal-minded Frenchmen would have replied to this that the two countries would have such a feeling of gratitude to France that they would preserve a state of genuine neutrality with regard to Algeria. This point of view ignored the strength of the sentiment of solidarity among three neighbouring and related peoples. As a Moroccan delegate said at the United Nations, 'When three houses in a row are inhabited by three brothers and the centre house is on fire, it is not much use expecting the brothers on either side not to interest themselves in what is happening in the centre, whatever the legal position may be.' There were, however, other arguments which probably carried greater weight with French ministers.

First, as organized under the French régime, the economies of all three territories were dependent on subsidies from the French Government to the extent of about a third of their total budget; without these subsidies they would find it very hard to maintain their existing level of activities, and they all had such a problem of under-employment that they could not afford to take big risks. Though the adjustment could be made by degrees, by no manner of means could it be achieved for at least several years.

Secondly, under the French system something like two-thirds of all officials and practically all the technicians were French. In Tunisia, for example, out of 600 doctors, only about 200 were Tunisians.[1] In the very much larger Morocco, there were less than 50 Moroccan doctors. Difficulties of expense and language would make it impossible to replace these by foreigners and there were no native substitutes.

Thirdly, the French forces in the country would remain until

---

[1] Egypt with a population five times larger has not 1,000, but over 3,000.

a new agreement was reached. Thus though there were no formal reservations attached to Tunisian or Moroccan independence, as there had been to Egyptian independence after the declaration of independence of 1922, and the French Residents General were to be replaced by Ambassadors, yet in fact the liberty of action of the two countries would inevitably be almost as restricted as that of Egypt had been before the signing of the Anglo-Egyptian Treaty of 1936.

These arguments have in fact proved to some extent to be valid; but the continuance of the fighting in Algeria and the necessity to be constantly bringing these means of influence to bear has embittered relations, in spite of excellent Franco-Moroccan co-operation in certain spheres. Their employment has made the prospects of a permanent and genuine Franco-Moroccan and Franco-Tunisian co-operation, on a basis of friendship and free consent, increasingly unfavourable. The existing Governments in both countries were anxious to collaborate with France and the west. If, however, the Algerian issue continues to act as an irritant, there is undoubtedly a prospect of their either themselves being forced into extremism or replaced by more extreme elements, and of the two countries finally drifting towards Russia at least as far as certain Middle Eastern states have shown signs of doing.

Tunisia and Morocco Compared

While Tunisia and Morocco have much in common, there are profound differences between them. Tunisia is a relatively small but culturally advanced republic, with markedly bourgeois and possibly socialist tendencies. It has a strongly centralized Government, with power in the hands of the Neo-Destour Party and its leader, who is at once President of the Republic and Prime Minister. Morocco on the other hand is a spacious land, far from homogeneous but with a certain air of empire about it. The main factor of unity is the monarchy; this is an indigenous institution deeply rooted in the life and traditions of the country. There is a huge Berber-speaking area, which the new rulers are confident that they can manage, but which was very independent of the central authority before the French and Spanish occupation and which must still give some cause for anxiety. The seat of power is by no means so clearly defined as in Tunisia. The personality and prestige of the reigning Sultan makes him the main source of authority and the symbol of national unity. Beside the royal authority, however, there is also that of the Istiqlal Party who are the driving force in the Government. A further distinction has to be made between the Istiqlal ministers in the Government and other Istiqlal leaders such as Allal al-Fasi, the President of the party, who remain outside. Al-Fasi, a thinker and academic student rather than a politician in the normal sense of the word, stands for modernization as the other elements do, but with a more traditional, more puritanical, and more Islamic colouring. The Istiqlal Party itself contains a conservative and an activist left wing. Outside the official sphere altogether there are the irregular forces of the former Liberation Army. Located in the south of the country and suspected of being behind the Ifni rising and the raids on Spanish and French posts in Mauritania, no outsider knows by whom they are controlled. There is further the huge proletariat of the Casablanca and other *bidonvilles*, and the important labour unions which represent them. Outside this, and yet intimately bound up with it, there is the great semi-American, semi-Oriental, city of Casablanca with its important European population, economy, and industry. Finally there is the northern zone with its tough mountaineers and an urban population which has received a Spanish intellectual and cultural formation, in some ways nearer to Moroccan culture than the French culture of the south. This division is reflected in the new Royal Army, a serious fighting force, composed of troops who formerly formed parts of the French and Spanish forces; at the beginning of 1958 they still contained a high proportion of French and Spanish officers. There are regiments from both the southern and the northern zones, and it has 400 cadets training in Europe, half of them in St. Cyr and half in Toledo. Larger, richer, with much greater natural potentialities than Tunisia, Morocco has a long way to go before it can achieve the homogeneity of the sister Maghrib state.

Even the capital of Morocco poses a problem. Before the occupation there were four imperial cities, Fez, Marrakesh, Meknes, and Rabat, in any of which the Sultan and his ministers might take up their residence. Though King Mohammed has since independence revived this practice to a limited extent by spending a considerable time in Marrakesh with his principal ministers in the early summer of 1957, such migrations as a regular practice are excluded by the complexity of modern administration. On the other hand it has to be recognized that the present location of the capital in Rabat was a matter of French convenience and security. It is true that in consequence of the creation of the port of Casablanca and European development in general, the coastal area has a far greater relative importance now than it formerly had. Yet Morocco is a large country, whose traditional capitals were well in the interior. This was the case even in the Almohad period in which Rabat first became important on account of its central position in a Moroccan kingdom extending to Castile in the north and to Tunis in the east. No immediate change is likely, but it would seem that geography must exert a pull towards the interior.

The Maghrib and the Arab League

While the differences are important, they should not be allowed to obscure what the two countries have in common. A certain fellow feeling springs in the first place from their common Maghribi, that is to say western Arab, experience. This distinguishes them to some extent from the eastern Arabs, whose common background has been very different. It gives them a certain spirit of emulation with regard to the eastern Arabs, a determination to show that the west can do as well as, or better than, the east. In the second place, there is the common experience of French rule. Beyond this there is also, however, a very powerful bond of sentiment which binds them to the Arab world in general; this makes it certain that they will share the general Arab view in all matters where that exists, though not of course necessarily with the same intensity. Thus the place held by the Palestine question in the east is taken by that of Algeria in the west. It may then be asked why both Tunisia and Morocco were slow in joining the Arab League. The answer is that the Arab League is itself divided and indeed in a state of suspended animation. Morocco and Tunisia had urgent problems of their own with which to deal; it was not in their interest to complicate the position further by joining a body which would compel them to take sides in the disputes which were rending the eastern Arab world and might well make their own relations with France and other western powers more difficult than they are already. In so far as they manifested a preference it was for the Iraqi point of view represented by the former régime there, which did not despair of furthering Arab interests by co-operation with the west; but the feeling was not so strong as to take priority over the consolidation of their own independence. Libya is in an intermediate position. On first achieving independence, she was naturally attracted to the eastern bloc of Arab states, who alone were independent at that time. When an independent Arab bloc came into being in the west, Libya tended to move away from the east and towards the west. Historically Tripolitania was always closely linked to Tunisia, while Cyrenaica generally led a more or less distinct existence in the shadow of some larger body.

The Jewish Communities of the Maghrib

These tendencies can be illustrated also in the attitude of the Maghrib states towards their Jewish communities and to Zionism. Libya shared very fully the eastern resentment against Jews at the time of the Partition Resolution of the United Nations and a number of Jews were killed. In consequence there has been a massive Jewish emigration. In Tunisia and Morocco circumstances have been different. Certainly the two states share the general Arab view of Zionism and will no doubt increasingly participate in the Arab blockade of Israel and similar measures. But the question is not felt with such intensity as in the east. Palestine is of less immediate importance to them than the strengthening of their own economy and the increase of their technical competence. In both of these matters, the local Jewish communities can be of the greatest assistance. In Tunisia and Morocco, therefore, the emphasis is less on opposition to Israel and more on the need for the complete assimilation of the Jewish population and its integration into the national life. This was symbolized in both countries by the presence of a Jewish minister in the first Governments, though not in a policy-making department or as a representative of Jewish interests. As we pass westward, we find that in Tunisia emigration has only reduced the Jewish population by a third, as opposed to four-fifths in Libya, while in Morocco it has perhaps fallen to the same extent but is being largely made up by the general population increase which is particularly high among Jews. In fact the farther west one goes the more Jewish emigration is motivated by economic factors and less by Zionist sentiment. The Jewish community of the Spanish town of Melilla is interesting in this respect. The community came into being when the city expanded in 1909, and it rose to the figure of 4,000, always enjoying excellent relations with the Spanish authorities. In the last ten years the Jewish population has diminished to 2,000 owing to emigration for economic reasons. This has been directed principally to Venezuela and the sums sent back have been sufficient to eliminate the worst features of poverty in the Melilla Jewish community.

Morocco and Tunisia in 1957

During 1957 it was noticeable that Franco-Moroccan relations were generally more friendly than Franco-Tunisian relations, in spite of the more flexible and more compromising nature of Tunisian nationalism in the past. In part this may no doubt have been due to the much greater impact which the

Algerian fighting had on Tunisia as compared with Morocco. Tunisia is a small country so that the Algerian frontier, the fighting, and the presence of Algerian refugees provoke immediate reactions as far as the capital. Unlike Morocco, which has a substantial and moderately well-equipped fighting force, formed out of former Moroccan forces serving with the French and Spanish armies, Tunisia, which provided only one regiment under the protectorate, has forces far smaller and less well equipped than those of the Algerian rebels. Tunisia is thus directly caught in the overspill of the Algerian war and is involved in disagreeable frontier incidents for which the Tunisian Government is blamed by the French press and politicians. On the other hand Tunisia also enjoys more independence of political action because she is better equipped professionally and technically (as the relative number of Tunisian and Moroccan doctors shows) and has fewer internal problems. She has only one ex-protector to deal with, not two; she has no southern frontier problem; no unabsorbed Liberation Army, and no great city such as Casablanca with its American-style development to keep going. For these reasons Tunisia, in spite of her smaller size and lack of military potential, is yet able to take a more independent line *vis-à-vis* France, thus producing more strained relations.

The Algerian Rising

Support given by Morocco and Tunisia to the Algerian nationalists would matter less to any French Government if it could feel sure of bringing the rising in Algeria to an end. This, however, is by no means certain. The movement, which is different in origin from the Tunisian and Moroccan nationalist parties, is run by very determined people. The *Front de Libération Nationale* came into being as a resistance movement, organized by men who had decided that political agitation was never going to get them anywhere. The FLN has no one outstanding leader; it was not founded by intellectuals but by practical men and men of action, people whose experience of life had been as n.c.o's in the French army, during the Second World War or in the fighting in Indo-China, and who are mainly mechanics, small farmers, and the like. Only after some eighteen months of fighting did the movement absorb into itself virtually every political intellectual leader of standing. By 1957, however, the only exception was the old chief, Missali Hajj, and those of his followers who had not been able to bring themselves to sink their identity in a united new movement, even if its objective were the same as their own. The movement is more than

merely military; it is a revolution affecting every branch of life
and is quite likely to result, for example, in the more rapid
emancipation of Algerian women. The leaders, as is to be expected in a country which has been brought into close contact
with Europe for so long, are deeply impregnated with modern
thought, sharing the American and European scorn of people
who seem old-fashioned. A journalist who visited the Algerian
fighting units in 1957 mentioned their criticism of the King of
Morocco for continuing to wear traditional Moroccan costume
and of Bourguiba for his theatricality.[1] If an independent Algeria comes into being, it is likely to carry out westernizing reforms more drastically than Tunisia has done, possibly in the
style of Kemalist Turkey. Whatever the position may have been
before 1954, there is no doubt that today a highly developed
national consciousness exists in Muslim Algeria, a sense of pride
in what has been endured and achieved, and some impatience
with the neighbouring states whose independence was won more
easily—thanks, as the Algerians say, to 'our rising'.

Position in Algeria at the Beginning of 1958

At the end of 1957 the French Government, and particularly
the Minister for Algeria, were expressing unbounded confidence that the military rising was coming to an end. They had,
it is true, made similar optimistic statements previously, which
events had falsified; but it could be pointed out at that moment
that terrorism in Algiers city had been greatly reduced (though
at the cost of wholesale arrests and the use of torture to extract
information); that very heavy punishment had been inflicted
on the rebel forces; and that the electrified fence along the
Tunisian frontier had reduced the movement of arms and men
in that area. On the other hand the rebel recruitment was fully
maintained and their armament seemed to be improving. The
leaders showed no signs whatever of yielding. Even if the
military rising were to die away, it was hard to see any body of
Algerian Muslims other than the FLN with whom the French
Government could negotiate; or how elections which were in
any sense free could yield anything but a body overwhelmingly
and perhaps unanimously in favour of independence. This position was not fundamentally altered even by the settler and army
rising of May 1958.

Problems of Franco-Maghribi Relations: (1) Algeria

It does not seem in the least likely that Tunisian or Moroccan
support for Algerian independence will diminish; on the con-

[1] *The Observer*, 26 January 1958.

trary, as the two states consolidate their own position they will undoubtedly feel impelled to take a stronger line in favour of their fellow North Africans. The probability is that they will be forced into an ever-increasing hostility towards France; and towards the other western powers, in so far as these are closely associated with France in the matter of Algeria. The former Governor-General Jacques Soustelle has suggested that the choice for the future is between an Algeria integrated with France and an Algeria partitioned among the settlers, who would occupy all the richer parts of the country, and the Muslims, who would be left with the rest. Since it seems unlikely that the settlers could bring this about by their own efforts, it appeared that M. Soustelle envisaged the use of the French army to impose and maintain partition. It was, however, possible that the choice had been wrongly stated by him. One alternative might be an independent Algeria, in which those Europeans who are willing to take Algerian citizenship would co-operate in the Government, in proportion to their numbers and capacities, to form a state which would work with France and with French aid, and might even exert an influence over her more purely Muslim neighbours in this sense; while the other alternative would be a purely Muslim Algeria, dominated by extreme elements, for whom the remaining Europeans would be unwanted aliens, to be removed more or less gently as time passes. The longer the war continues, the more probable the latter alternative becomes.

Problems of Franco-Maghribi Relations: (2) The Sahara

It would be a mistake to suppose that the denial of independence to Algeria is the only obstacle to Franco-Muslim co-operation in North Africa. There is also the question of the Sahara. The occupation of the Algerian Sahara was the consequence of the French occupation of Algeria, and the occupation of the Moroccan Sahara was the result of the French occupation of Morocco. If both countries regain their independence, it is hard to see what claim France would have on their hinterland. An independent Algeria would undoubtedly consider that the mineral wealth of the Sahara should provide the capital and the energy necessary to revolutionize the Algerian economy, as the oil of Kirkuk has Iraq's. Moroccans feel the same about the area south of Morocco. Until 1900 the Sultan exerted influence as far as Tuat through a Khalifa (lieutenant) at Tafilalet and as far as Saguiat al-Hamra and the far south through his Khalifa at Marrakesh. Foreigners clearly regarded the regions south of the Dra as a Moroccan sphere of influence. Since they wanted to secure concessions there, they sought them from the Sultan. It is true that in 1767 a Sultan stated that an area near Cape Juby was not part of his domains, meaning that he was not in a position to guarantee security there.[1] When any foreigner sought to establish himself independently, however, the Sultan would make every effort to bring the concession to an end. This was the case of the factory which a Scot, D. Mackenzie, established at Tarfaya in 1876; in 1895 he was bought out by the Sultan for £50,000.

On this occasion, moreover, the British Government specifically recognized that after the sale 'no one will have any claim to the lands that are between Wad Draa and Cape Bojador, and which are called Terfaya above named, and all the land behind it, because all this belongs to the territory of Morocco'. (Anglo-Moroccan Agreement, 13 March 1895.) [2]

E. F. Gautier in his book *Sahara the Great Desert*, published in 1928 (with an authorized English version in 1935), wrote:

The extreme occidental portion of the Sahara, westward from the Saura and the Niger, is an immense country of which there is very little for us to say. A considerable part of the coast is Spanish territory and still unexplored; while the interior is Moroccan not Algerian territory, and the French occupation of Morocco has hardly more than succeeded in crossing the Atlas.[3]

In fact from the seventeenth century, when the Moroccans captured Timbuktu, they controlled the entire western Sahara for a quarter of a century, and after the accession of the Alawite dynasty maintained Governors in Tuat, in the central Sahara, all through the eighteenth century, and again from 1892 to 1900.[4] The same seems to have been true of Mauritania during the eighteenth century. Thomas Pellow, an English captive who was in the service of the Moroccan Government for twenty-three years, records finding that a Moroccan Governor was regularly resident in Shinqit (Chinguetti) in 1727.[5] As regards the twentieth century, an interesting piece of evidence as to the generally accepted view is contained in letters exchanged by the French and German Governments on the occasion of the signing of the agreement of 4 November 1911. In these it is

---

[1] See below, p. 190.
[2] *State Papers*, vol. 87, p. 972.
[3] *Sahara the Great Desert*, trans. by D. F. Mayhew (New York, 1935), p. 211.
[4] R. le Tourneau, 'Maroc et Sahara Occidental,' *Le Monde*, 18 June 1956.
[5] *Adventures of Thomas Pellow* (London, 1890). Pellow, who disliked intensely both Moors and Mauritanians (whom he calls *Laurbs*, presumably *al-Arab* or *al-Urb*, the beduin) says 'in the original I take them to be all one and the same people, yet is there here always a Moorish governor residing'.

stated to 'be understood that Morocco includes all of North Africa comprised between Algeria, French West Africa, and the Spanish colony of Río de Oro'.[1]

The existing southern frontier of Morocco in fact represents the limit of more or less effective Moroccan administration at the moment of the inauguration of the protectorate, that is at the time of Morocco's greatest weakness. It was primarily a line agreed by the French and Spanish protectors for the purpose of settling their own disagreements over the division of Moroccan territory; it has never been acknowledged by an independent Moroccan Government. Indeed the Franco-Spanish Convention of 1912, in delimiting the area of the Spanish protectorate south of the Dra, implied that the area outside that line was also the territory of the Sharifian Empire for some undetermined distance.[2]

During 1957 it was announced that Franco-Moroccan discussions were to be held on the subject of the frontier, but these had not been held by November 1958. On the other hand the Istiqlal Party and its President Allal al-Fasi carried on a campaign for a greater Morocco which was to include not only the whole area described as Moroccan in the Franco-German exchange of letters on the occasion of the signing of the agreement in 1911, but also the Spanish colony of Río de Oro. This campaign, supported by an Arabic weekly, *Sahra al-Maghrib* (The Moroccan Sahara) specially founded for the purpose by Allal al-Fasi, no doubt played a part in stimulating the attacks made in the autumn of 1957 by bands of irregulars in Río de Oro and in French Mauritania as well as the rising of the Ba Amran in Ifni. Co-ordinated Franco-Spanish reaction to these attacks in its turn provoked a greater activity on the part of the Moroccan Government. In February 1958 the King visited Zagora near the existing southern limits of Moroccan territory. Speaking to representatives of the Riqaibat and other Saharan tribes he reminded them that his grandfather, Sultan Maulay al-Hasan, had made two expeditions to the Sahara 'in order to consolidate the unity of Morocco and its sovereignty over the whole of the national territory, at a moment when it was the object of foreign covetousness'. 'We proclaim solemnly', he went on, 'that we shall continue our action for the return of the Sahara in

---

[1] Quoted in H. Marchat, 'La Frontière Saharienne du Maroc', *Politique Étrangère*, 1957, vi. 655.

[2] See below, p. 75. The pre-occupation position is best studied in A. J. P. Martin, *Quatre siècles d'histoire marocaine* (Paris, 1923). Martin was a military interpreter who used Arabic documents which he collected. He encountered official opposition in publishing his book.

accordance with respect for our historic rights and the will of its inhabitants.' [1]

From the point of view of geography and population, greater Mauritania or Shinqit comprises the present French Mauritania, which now possesses a degree of autonomy and an embryonic national sentiment, the Río de Oro, and the territory lying between these two areas and Morocco, including Tinduf and the iron ore of Gara Jbilet. It is a vast, sparsely-populated area, with no urban settlement of any size. A descendant of the Mauritanian leader Ma al-Ainen sits in the Moroccan National Assembly, in which he is treated as representative of Mauritania. In the spring of 1958 two members of the Government of Mauritania left the country and established themselves in Rabat. There is now a group of Mauritanian notables there, under the leadership of Horma ould Babana, who are conducting propaganda for the incorporation of Mauritania as a province of Morocco.[2]

Problems of Franco-Maghribi Relations: (3) French Troops in Morocco and Tunisia

The third problem still outstanding is that of the French troops in Tunisia and Morocco. Even where no 'colonial' issues arise it is hard to know whether the presence of foreign bases in a country will be regarded as of such potential assistance to it as to outweigh the increased danger of involvement in a conflict with which it is not directly concerned. In the case of Tunisia the French position was rendered untenable by a series of incidents of which the bombing of Sakiet Sidi Yusuf was the most dramatic and in July 1958 the outlying garrisons were withdrawn or concentrated in Bizerta. This reacted on the Moroccan Government, in spite of its undoubted pro-western and anti-Communist sentiment and of its urgent need for western aid, both technical and financial. On the other hand facilities for NATO troops might have been negotiable, provided they were justified by a considered plan for western defence. The issue was, however, bound up with the solution of the Algerian problem and the question of the southern frontiers.

The question of French troops in Morocco, like that of the frontier, was scheduled for discussion in 1957, but was also allowed to wait. It appeared that for the time being the Moroccan Government would be content with some regrouping of the forces which would render them less conspicuous. In March

---

[1] *Le Monde*, 27 February 1958.
[2] For Mauritanian affairs see also pp. 109, 197, and 270 below.

1958 the French Government announced its intention of transferring 10,000 men to Algeria; this would, however, still have left some 30,000–40,000 in Morocco.

United States Airfields in Morocco

The present United States bases in Morocco were granted by the protectorate authorities without any reference to the Sultan or any Moroccan authorities. Negotiations between the United States and the Moroccan Government were carried on in the latter half of 1957 and it was expected that a process of bargaining would finally produce an agreement, analogous to that between the United States and the Libyan Government. This had, however, not been reached by July 1958, and after the Conference of Tangier agitation for the removal of United States troops was intensified.

Prospects of Federation or a Mediterranean Bloc

After the declaration of independence of Tunisia and Morocco there was much speculation concerning a federation of the Maghrib and of the possibility of such a federation forming some sort of economic unity with France; there was also talk of the possibility of an allied bloc to be formed by western Mediterranean states, to include France, Spain, and Italy. On the whole it seemed unlikely that the newly emancipated states would wish to create any new bonds linking them exclusively to France. As regards a federation of the two, or eventually three, Maghrib states, with or without Libya, their very markedly different outlook and characteristics rendered unlikely any very close bond; but a measure of cultural, political, and economic co-operation might be given a framework of confederation, especially if this seemed likely to promote the independence of Algeria. The interdependence of the three countries was in fact solemnly proclaimed in the resolutions of the Conference for Maghrib Unity, held in Tangier from 27–30 April 1958. This meeting was organized by the Istiqlal Party of Morocco and attended also by representatives of the Neo-Destour Party of Tunisia and of the Algerian FLN. The delegates included the Foreign Minister (now Premier) of Morocco and the Vice-Premier of Tunisia, who attended in their capacity as members of the Istiqlal and Neo-Destour parties. The resolutions were later presented to, and accepted by, the King of Morocco and the President of Tunisia, and also to the King of Libya. These resolutions recognized the FLN as the only representatives of the Algerian people; declared the right of Algeria to independence; demanded the evacuation of foreign troops, incompatible with independence, from Tunisia and Morocco; and expressed sympathy with the 'profound longing of the Mauritanians for union with Morocco'. The formation of an Algerian Government was recommended, after consultation with the Tunisian and Moroccan Governments; in the meanwhile it was proposed to set up a Consultative Assembly drawn from members of the National Assemblies of the two independent states and from the Council of the Algerian Revolution; a secretariat would be formed with two members from each of the three countries. The hope was expressed that Libya, invited too late to participate in the Conference, would nevertheless adhere in due course. A bloc of western Mediterranean states was also a possibility, though the idea was encouraged by France and the Maghrib states for opposite reasons and its significance would in any case be symbolic rather than practical. It is at any rate certain that the independence of two of the three North African states has set a limit to the period of the overwhelming French, or in the northern zone Spanish, share of trade with them, which the protectorate period brought about in spite of the provisions of the Act of Algeciras. The Moroccan import of British cotton goods, for example, which had been sufficiently extensive before the protectorate to lead to the establishment of a small Moroccan colony of merchants in Manchester, completely disappeared.

Morocco and Tunisia will now certainly wish to extend their relations with the rest of the world; and both states have already certain important links with the United States. Very shortly after independence American missions made careful studies of the economies of the two countries and, on the strength of their reports, substantial aid was granted. Since the war America has been fully aware of Morocco's potentialities and American business interests have shown considerable activity. Trade relations are also being developed with a number of other countries.

Attitude of the Soviet Union

Russia for the first two years kept herself in the background, apart from establishing an Embassy in Libya and directing Arabic broadcasts to North Africa, from the satellite states as well as from Moscow; the latter enterprises have had little success since the opening days of a broadcast from Budapest in 1955 when some North Africans supposed it to be a genuine 'free Algerian' transmission. Possibly Russia believed that an expenditure of effort on her part was unnecessary. If the leaders of the western nations played their cards well, she would have difficulty in displacing them; while if they did not, the Maghrib would automatically slide in her direction at least to the extent that Egypt did. During 1958 she established trade and diplomatic relations with Morocco.

The Role of Spain

After the end of the war in the Rif very little was heard in Europe about the Spanish protectorate in Morocco. Only in 1953, when Spain refused to endorse the French deposition of the Sultan, was some notice taken in the European press; most of this was highly critical of the action of the Spanish authorities. Superficially Spain appeared in Morocco as an inconspicuous second fiddle to France, modelling her system on the French system; in January 1958 she again copied a French precedent by declaring Ifni and the Spanish Sahara to be two Spanish provinces. In fact, however, there were very important differences. First, as is recorded elsewhere (pp. 137–43), Spain's historical relations with Morocco are much more complex than those of France, extending as they have done over more than 1,000 years. A Spanish-Moroccan war seems almost to have something of a civil war about it; violent antagonisms are matched by a certain store of common experience and even outlook. Moroccans who have worked in both the former French and the former Spanish zones remark on the insignificance of the Spanish achievement, compared with the French achievement, even allowing for the relative poverty of the area involved; on the other hand they find no trace in the Spanish of something which they feel in the French as 'racialism'. In the Spanish zone, at least after the period of the Spanish Civil War, there was no attempt to assimilate Moroccans by insisting on educating them in Spanish rather than in Arabic. There was never any attempt to divide Berber from Arab. At one time contact with eastern Arab states was actually encouraged; Egyptian schoolmasters were brought to Tetuan, and Moroccan students were sent to the east with protectorate scholarships. An attempt was made to establish a curriculum based on specially prepared Arabic textbooks. After the early days, there was little Spanish settlement on the land and at times considerable difficulties were put in the way of Spanish who wished to settle in Moroccan towns. Moroccans born in the *presidios* enjoyed the full advantage of Spanish citizenship, and a Muslim officer from Melilla became a Lieutenant-General in the Spanish army and Military Governor of two Spanish provinces successively. With regard to the Arab world in general, Spain went out of her way to cultivate friendly relations. A number of

Arab rulers and the Secretary-General of the Arab League were invited to visit Spain, while several leaders of the nationalist movement who were refugees or exiles from the French zone were able to make their home in Madrid, among them Allal al-Fasi and Ahmed Balafrej. The result was that there was less tension and less violence in the northern zone than in the south, though of course there was not the startling social and economic development either. In the last years of the protectorate, however, a great deal was done to construct an extensive and well-planned educational centre in Tetuan, making provision for primary and secondary education for both sexes; and to provide housing both for officials and for the working class. Readers of the section on the Spanish protectorate will see that in general life ran on in the northern zone with something of the leisureliness and charm of a Spanish provincial capital.

On the other hand Franco-Spanish relations added a great deal to the complexity of the international relations of Morocco. Only during the Rif war and again in the winter of 1957–8 was there any close co-operation between the two protectors; more often there seemed to be a policy of mutual pin-pricks. Spain, twice herself occupied by France during the nineteenth century, was not very happy at being encircled on the south. There was a moment early in the present century when France had offered to recognize the whole northern half of Morocco as a sphere of Spanish influence. The suggestion lapsed because the Spanish Government of the day did not ratify the agreement. The reason given was the desire not to act against a previous understanding with Britain; but it is hard to avoid the impression that in fact the Spanish Government did not feel capable of taking on such a large commitment.

As long as France remains in Morocco and continues to exert a great influence, Spain will desire to retain her own corresponding positions. Probably this Spanish counterweight is not unwelcome to the Moroccan Government.[1] Naturally the same sort of problems are, however, pending between the Moroccans and the Spanish as between the Moroccans and the French. Agreement was reached in 1957 for the withdrawal of the peseta currency from the northern zone and this was carried out early in 1958; but there is also the question of the ultimate withdrawal of Spanish troops, of the Moroccan request for the return of Ifni, and of possible Moroccan claims on the Spanish

[1] The Sharif Ahmad al-Raisuni once remarked that Spain was 'strong enough to help the Arabs, but not strong enough to oppress them', and on another occasion that 'French bayonets will press hard upon the heels of Spain's departure'. The argument retains its force. (Rosita Forbes, *El Raisuni* (London, 1924), pp. 16 and 186.)

Sahara. Moreover Spain is deeply attached to the two *presidios* of Ceuta and Melilla which have been Spanish for hundreds of years, in which many generations of Spaniards have been born, lived, and died, and which are now Spanish towns in every sense of the word except the geographical. Their status, in an age where the self-determination of definite geographical areas is the rule, is undoubtedly anomalous; they have few resources and are dependent on neighbouring Moroccan territory for their water supplies.[1] All these considerations must play their part in the formation of Spanish policy, as well as the fact mentioned in the Spanish communiqué of 6 December 1957 (p. 196) that there were forces in south Morocco which did not obey the order of the Moroccan Government and which stood for reuniting all geographical Morocco, including the Sahara, with the independent kingdom. Moreover Spain, like other countries, is not free to consider her Moroccan policy in isolation; France is a neighbour with whom good relations are no less important than with Morocco. At the beginning of 1958 the Spanish Government gave the impression of hoping to remain on friendly terms with the Moroccan Government while co-operating with the French Government to resist Moroccan claims in the south and to eliminate, or at least reduce to ineffectiveness, the forces of the so-called Liberation Army in the areas outside the present limits of the Kingdom of Morocco.

European Residents

During the struggle for Moroccan and Tunisian independence, it was often claimed that nationalist governments would introduce legislation or take administrative steps to make life impossible for European residents. The first two years of independence did not justify this fear. Though a few individuals were required to leave, the independent Governments were anxious in their own interest that there should be no large-scale emigration. Under the French régime a very high percentage of official and administrative posts were filled by Europeans; and though the new Governments were anxious to retain the services of a third or a half of these, the departure of those officials who were being replaced has led, with that of their families, to an emigration of many thousand people. Departures on this scale removed an appreciable part of the clientele of the establishments which served their needs; the ultimate withdrawal of French troops would remove a great many more. For this reason a number of tradespeople sold their

[1] The two cities have been compared to the children of divorced parents, brought up by one parent against the will of the other.

F

businesses, if they were able to secure a reasonable price, and also departed. To this has to be added the business recession caused by the apprehension of industrialists on the grounds of security, of possible measures of nationalization or of exaggerated labour demands. In Morocco the Meknes massacre in the autumn of 1956, after the kidnapping of the five Algerian leaders, accelerated the movement of emigration. In February 1958 the French bombing of Sakiet Sidi Yusuf, in Tunisia, and the subsequent tension, had a similar effect in stimulating French emigration from that country. These factors combined were responsible, it is estimated, for the departure of some 165,000 Europeans from the two countries. Early in 1957 the Moroccan Government became seriously alarmed at the possible economic and social results of emigration on this scale and in the summer of that year the Palace, the Government, and independent Istiqlal leaders made a concerted effort to reassure European residents. Verbal assurances were reinforced by the complete restoration of security and by measures taken to punish the Meknes ringleaders, with the result that many Europeans reconsidered their provisional decision to leave. Against this there has to be set, particularly in Tunisia, the constant sense of uncertainty produced by the Algerian war, by the unsettled question of the evacuation of French troops, and, in Morocco, by that of the southern frontier.

It is noteworthy that in Libya, where no questions remained outstanding between the new state and the former ruling power, the vast majority of resident Italian shop-keepers, skilled workers, and settlers have remained and are able to gain their livelihood in peace and security, though of course they have had to accept the status of resident foreigners with the obligations which that implies.

Position at the Beginning of 1958

A survey of the scene as a whole at midsummer 1958 showed that the political situation was still very fluid. The attitude which Morocco and Tunisia would adopt, as their independence was consolidated, was still uncertain. It was impossible to say how the two fundamental issues of Algeria and the Sahara would evolve or what effect they would have on the general situation. The future of French policy was also unclear; it seemed doubtful whether the *loi-cadre* for Algeria would ever be applied and almost certain that it would not in any case provide a sure base for the future of Algerian-French relations. An effort certainly was being made to introduce reforms and improve the status of the Algerian Muslim people. This, however, is a regular feature of colonial rule when it encounters a strong nationalist challenge. Experience elsewhere suggests that while such reforms can be most beneficial to the country concerned, they do nothing to reduce nationalist sentiment, rather the contrary. It looked therefore as if, in the long run, the function of the *loi-cadre*, like that of the formula of inter-dependence in the case of Morocco and Tunisia, might be that of a face-saving device by which negotiations could be discreetly initiated. Meanwhile the sentiment of Algerian nationality had taken concrete form. If an Algerian state came into being it would have the solidity given to it by having been forged the hard way in a long struggle. Since Algeria had in the past had no possibility of showing what characteristics it would possess as an independent nation, it might yet surprise the world. If the co-operation of the European population could be secured, the state so formed might have a unique character in bringing together not only Muslims and Christians but also Europeans and Arabs. Such an outcome would of course depend on the willingness of European Algerians to take Algerian nationality; the prolongation of the war made a solution of this nature seem increasingly improbable.

Conclusion

Viewed in the light of 1,300 years of Muslim-Christian relations in the western Mediterranean, it looks very much as if a new phase of coexistence is being born, a phase in which Islam will be as predominant on the south of the sea as Christianity is on the north. The outlook of the new rulers of the Maghrib will be that of the twentieth century. Since the basis of civilization in both areas will be the common stock of ideas of the modern world, to which Christianity and Islam will now hardly do more than give a different colouring, it may be that for the first time an era not merely of coexistence but also of peaceful coexistence is possible between them. Even at the end of 1958, however, it did not appear that France was willing to make the voluntary sacrifice of political control which was the necessary prerequisite of such a new relationship.

PART ONE

THE WESTERN MAGHRIB

(*AL-MAGHRIB AL-AQSA*)

I

THE KINGDOM OF MOROCCO
(*AL-MAMLAKAT AL-MAGHRIBIYA*)

FROM MEDIEVAL EMPIRE TO MODERN KINGDOM

GEOGRAPHY AND POPULATION

SITUATED at the north-west corner of the African continent, the present kingdom of Morocco is shaped like an irregular quadrilateral. Its sides are formed by 620 miles of Atlantic coast, by 290 miles in the Straits of Gibraltar and on the Mediterranean, 310 miles of frontier with Algeria, and 680 miles of frontier with the Sahara. Morocco falls within latitudes 28 and 36 north and between the 2nd and 11th longitudes west of Greenwich. Its area is about 190,000 square miles.

Geography

The land frontiers are not indicated by definite geographical features such as mountain ranges or rivers. They have, therefore, remained indeterminate and have been the subject of disputes which are not yet settled. On the east an Algerian-Moroccan frontier was laid down by the Convention of Lalla-Marnia, in 1845, following the Franco-Moroccan conflict which resulted in the Moroccan defeat at Isly. But though the delimitation is clear in the zone of the Tell, from the mouth of the river Kiss to Teniet Sassi, this is not the case either in the High Plateaux, where the Convention merely gave a list of tribes which were administered by each of the two countries, or farther to the south where it merely mentions that Figuig is Moroccan. After the difficulties which followed the French occupation of the Saura, the limit was given as a line west of Jbel Gruz, which joined the river Guir and followed it all the way to Igli. Farther south, in the western Sahara, the frontier is even vaguer. By virtue of the Franco-Spanish Convention of 1912, Spain was to exercise her protectorate in that part of the Sharifian Empire comprised between the lower course of the Dra, latitude 27.40 north and meridian 11 west of Paris. Between Igli and the point of intersection of these two co-ordinates, the limit is not defined in any text. This is the legal basis of claims put forward by certain Moroccan political parties to Mauritania and to the Río de Oro, and the cause of the disagreement which has arisen between France and Spain on the one hand, and Morocco on the other over the delimitation of the southern frontier of independent Morocco.

Morocco's geographical position gives her a special and privileged place among the countries of North Africa, to which she definitely belongs since there is no break in continuity between Morocco and Algeria in the spheres of geography, climate, botany, or the human way of life. Morocco's strong individuality comes from her being the only country in North Africa which has an Atlantic façade and is thus at the same time oceanic and Mediterranean. When the Algerian ranges reach Morocco their east–west alignment is interrupted; the Atlas bends to the south-west and opens out like a fan towards the ocean, thus winning from the desert a wide belt of land; for Marrakesh is on the same parallel as the Algerian oasis of Wargla.

In fact, however, this vast maritime façade has played a less significant role in the life of the country than might have been expected. This is due to both natural and human factors. The Mediterranean shores, as well as the Atlantic, are inhospitable. The former are lined by the Rif mountains which drop sheer to the sea; the latter are rendered dangerous to navigation by the 'bar'. Add to this that Moroccan Berbers are not a people who have ever taken to maritime activities, and we understand why the sea has generally held a secondary place in Morocco's relations with the rest of the world. This is, however, no longer the case, now that modern techniques have made possible the construction of artificial ports such as Casablanca.

In the north, Morocco projects in the form of the Tangier peninsula as if reaching out to meet Europe and the Iberian peninsula at the point of Tarifa, only nine miles away across the sea. This double role, as the southern shore of Straits which form one of the most important and frequented waterways of the world, and as an outpost of Africa at the gateway of Europe, marks Morocco out as an intermediary and as a point of union. A bridge between two continents, situated between the main continent of Africa and a headland of Europe, she forms a junction where their two civilizations can meet; while her position at the extreme west of the Muslim world, of which she was once an outpost, looking across at Christendom, make her one of the possible junctions of east and west.

This privileged position is also one of strategic importance, a quality which can bring danger with it. In the case of Morocco, it was responsible for the establishment of Portuguese and Spanish outposts on her shores when the Reconquista was nearing completion. The shores of the Straits have provoked the coveteousness of great powers with the result that Tangier has often been in the hands of strangers, and Ceuta still is. In modern times they made the entire country the stakes of a great international power struggle. The protectorate of 1912 was the final outcome of the triangular rivalry of England, Germany, and France. In 1942 the Americans made Morocco their springboard for the liberation of Europe. Today the country is an 'aircraft carrier' for the defence of the free world.

Geologically, the soil of Morocco can be divided into three principal zones; these differ in age and structure. Northern Morocco is a detached fragment of Europe, and the Rif an Alpine range which prolongs the Andalusian Cordillera. The extreme south belongs to the ancient primary continent known as the 'Saharan shield'. Central Morocco is intermediary in age as well as in position. The Hercynian fold constituted the base on which deposits settled during the secondary and the beginning of the tertiary eras, while folds of jurassic type were added later in the tertiary.

The country has a strongly marked relief. Several peaks in the High Atlas reach 13,000 feet while Tubkal (13,694) is the highest in all North Africa. It has been pointed out that if the level of the sea were to be raised by 1,000 feet the general outline of the country would still be the same. High plains and plateaux work their way into the heart of the main ranges.

The latter are like a jaw, opening towards the west. The more northerly branch, the Rif, which is prolonged by the Beni Snassen mountains to the east of the Muluya, runs along the Mediterranean. The lower branch is separated from the former on the east by the narrow Taza corridor, forms the circle of an arc, north-east and south-west, and ends at the edge of the Atlantic. This branch is more complex than the other. Three ranges can be distinguished: the High Atlas, which runs beside and then accompanies the Middle Atlas range to the north, beyond the valley of the upper Muluya; and in the south the Anti-Atlas, which is joined to the High Atlas by the footbridge-like Sirua mountain.

This mountain framework has had important consequences— some of them happy, others less so. As has been mentioned, Morocco lies wide open to the ocean to whose beneficent influences she is subject. The two arms of the pincers enfold the fertile plains of the Gharb, the Chaouia, and the Sus, which are the heart and the wealth of the country. Almost all the great cities are to be found there: Fez, Meknes, Rabat, Casablanca, Marrakesh. The Rif on the other hand cuts Morocco off from the Mediterranean, which has only played a substantial part in the life of the country by means of the Straits. In the north, Tangier and Tetuan are the only large cities. The High and Middle Atlas themselves cut off a vast zone from the Atlantic plain and bring it under the influence of the desert, all the way from the mouth of the Dra on the Atlantic to that of the Muluya on the Mediterranean. This is the Morocco of the pre-Saharan steppes, and of the High Plateaux of eastern Morocco, the domain of nomads and of extensive stock-breeding. This outer Morocco, as we may call it, has always been incompletely connected with the other Morocco, but it has nevertheless weighed upon it very heavily in the course of the centuries, periodically casting out hungry warriors to seek their destiny in the rich plains of the north-west. It is no accident that the majority of the great movements which have convulsed the country, as well as the majority of the dynasties which have ruled over it, have emerged from this arid Morocco of the deep south.

The High and Middle Atlas form a true central mountain block, difficult to penetrate, where sturdy mountaineers were long able to defy the central power and to threaten communications between the provinces.

They are also the reservoir of Morocco. From them, a number of vigorous watercourses emerge in various directions: the Muluya, which empties itself into the Mediterranean; the Sebu and the Um er-Rebia, which run towards the Atlantic; and the Saharan wadis—the Dra, which the breath of the desert dries up before it can reach the ocean; the Ziz and the Gheris, which lose themselves in the sands of the Sahara after watering the palm groves of Tafilalet. The Sebu and the Um er-Rebia, both more than 300 miles long, are the most important rivers of North Africa. The Dra with its 745 miles would rank as the longest, if it were not intermittent in its lower course.

The presence of this compact mountain block in the centre of Morocco renders communications between certain regions difficult. The prolongation of the Middle Atlas towards the ocean causes the main road from Fez to Marrakesh to pass by the coast. This is the line followed by the principal railway, connecting Marrakesh with Casablanca, Rabat, Kenitra (Port Lyautey), Meknes, Fez, and Ujda and continuing beyond that to Algiers and Tunis, with its 1,860 miles of permanent way. From this principal axis there branch off the Tangier–Fez line (which is the oldest of them); a line joining Casablanca to Wadi Zem, whose principal function is to serve the phosphate deposits of Khouribga; and a line Safi–Louis Gentil which carries the phosphates from the latter centre. The total length of the railway network is 1,150 miles.

The principal road axis follows much the same route as the railway, though since the completion of the occupation, a direct road has joined Fez with Marrakesh, crossing the Middle Atlas and running along the foot of the High Atlas. The cities of the plain are connected across the Atlas with the oases of Tafilalet (Erfoud), of the Dra (Goulimin), and of south-east Morocco (Figuig). The existing road network extends over 28,000 miles in the former southern zone, 1,520 in the former northern zone, and 102 in the province of Tangier.

There are connexions with the exterior by land (railway and road to Algeria), by sea, and by air. Regular lines of steamships connect Casablanca with Marseilles and Bordeaux in one direction and with Dakar and black Africa in the other. Interior air lines serve Agadir, Marrakesh, Casablanca, Tangier, Meknes, Fez, and Ujda; while there are exterior services connecting Morocco with Paris and various lesser French towns, and also with Madrid, Lisbon, Oran, Algiers, Dakar, and South America.

Population

The vast majority of the Moroccan population belong to the white race; on a linguistic basis, which does not necessarily correspond with their racial origin, they can be divided into those who speak Arabic and those who speak Berber.

The Berbers formed the population of all North Africa at the dawn of history and are the oldest-established inhabitants of Morocco. As in Algeria and the Sahara, Berber is still spoken in Morocco, and by a higher percentage (35 per cent). The Arabs arrived later, in two main waves; the first, at the time of the Muslim conquest in the eighth century; the second during the twelfth and thirteenth centuries with the coming of the Beni Hilal and the Maaqil. Many tribes which are today Arabic-speaking were not so originally, but are Berbers who have been arabized. The process of arabization, which is not yet complete, has continued at an increased rate during the last forty years.

Generally speaking, the process has gone farthest in the towns, the plains and plateaux, and in the pre-Saharan regions. The mountain areas have remained Berber-speaking except for the Jebala, east of Tangier, which has long been arabized through its position as a much frequented passage between Muslim Spain and Morocco.

Apart from the Arab and Berber majority, the population of Morocco contains a large foreign minority of Christians, chiefly French in the southern zone and Spanish in the north. Native Moroccans, in addition to the linguistic distinction, can be divided racially into white and black, and by religion into Muslims and Jews.

The blacks are a small minority, for whom no statistics exist, and are of diverse origin. In the towns their presence can be explained by the former existence of slavery, particularly of black concubines who were very popular with the well-to-do citizens of the towns. In the southern oases, however, all along the edge of the Sahara, there is a particular type of black population known as *Haratin* (in the singular *hartani*). Some of them are no doubt the result of a crossing of Berbers with Sudanese blacks, imported by the nomads to cultivate the oases. But it is possible that as a whole they represent a former black population of the Sahara whom the *periplus* of Hanno calls Ethiopians and describes as existing at the mouth of the Dra.

The Jewish population are in part the descendants of Jews expelled from Spain after the Reconquista; these settled by preference in the coastal towns. But the majority, who call themselves *Plishtim* (Palestinians), claim that their forbears came directly from Palestine. History, however, has nothing to tell us of mass Jewish migration from Palestine to North Africa. It is more probable that the 'Palestinians' are the remnants of former Berber tribes converted to Judaism and then conquered and dispersed by the Muslim conquest, which they resisted desperately.

The statistics of the Moroccan population are imperfectly known. Registration was established only in 1950 and has not yet extended to the whole population. Counts made before the pacification, from 1921 on, are very unreliable as far as concerns regions not then occupied. The only more recent censuses in which some confidence may be placed are those of 1936 and 1951-2. So far only the foreigners and the Jews have been enumerated by means of sheets distributed to householders. The count of the Muslim population was made verbally, because of the great number of illiterates, and has only yielded summary and imprecise results.

The census of 1951-2 gave a total of 8,003,985 inhabitants against 6,245,222 in 1936, an increase of 1,758,763. To this figure must be added 1,054,978 for the northern zone (1955); 172,000 for the Tangier zone; and 21,000 in the Tarfaya province in the south—a total of 9,251,963. Allowing for the probable increase in the southern zone since 1952, we may put the total figure for all Morocco at about 10 million.

The non-Moroccan, or foreign, population had reached 362,814 persons in 1951 in the southern zone, as compared with 202,594 in 1936. It was overwhelmingly urban—288,000 out of the total. French subjects accounted for 83·7 per cent. The Spanish colony came next with 26,100 members; then the Italian with 13,550. Of the foreign population 83 per cent. are less than 40 years old; 51 per cent. less than 20; they are native to the country to the extent that 36 per cent. were born there. In the years preceding independence their numbers rose to 400,000, but since 1956 have been reduced by about 100,000 owing to many French departures, especially of officials.

The non-European population reached 7,641,171 in 1951–2 as compared with 6,042,628 in 1936, an increase of 1,578,543. Of this total, 7,442,015 were Muslims, an increase of 1,541,543 on 1936. The mean annual increase, namely the excess of births over deaths, is 1·5 per cent., a rate which would, if it were maintained, result in doubling the population in forty years. This rapid increase obviously raises a serious economic problem, all the more so on account of the youth of the population, of whom 41 per cent. are less than 15 years old and about half less than 20, while only 7 per cent. are over 60. Though 80 per cent. are rural, the urbanization of the population is increasing rapidly; between 1936 and 1952 the annual increase of the urban population was 4·3 per cent., while that of the rural population was only 1 per cent. In the same period the Muslim population of Casablanca rose from 146,000 to 472,000, a mean annual increase of 7·6 per cent.

The Jewish population rose from 161,942 in 1936 to 199,156 in 1951. The mean annual increase was therefore 1·4 per cent., which appears rather less than that of the Muslims, but was accounted for by emigration to Israel and elsewhere, which deprived Morocco of 40,000 souls since 1947. The Jewish population is essentially urban, exactly in inverse proportion to the Muslims (80 per cent.). It is moreover concentrated in towns where there is a rapid economic development, more particularly in Casablanca which includes 75,000 Jews or 37 per cent. of all those in Morocco. In certain cities such as Marrakesh, which traditionally had large Jewish populations, the Jewish element had diminished since 1936. Many of the Jewish quarters and country villages (*mellahs*) have disappeared as the result of migration. The Jewish population is even younger than the Muslim, having 52 per cent. less than 20 years old.

Five towns in the southern zone had more than 100,000 inhabitants in 1957—Casablanca, Marrakesh, Fez, Rabat, and Meknes. Casablanca was a long way ahead with 682,388 inhabitants; its population which was 257,000 in 1936 more than doubled in seventeen years. It is the Moroccan town with the greatest number of Muslims, Europeans, and Jews.

HISTORY

From the Earliest Times to the Death of Maulay al-Hasan (1894)

The prehistory of Morocco is only just coming to be known. Man seems to have been present in Morocco from the chellean age. Many traces of his activities remain from the palaeolithic and neolithic eras, principally chipped or polished stones and rough pottery.

When the curtain rises on history, the country was inhabited by Berbers. All that we know of the history of ancient Morocco, however, is that of the foreign settlements. The Phoenicians were the first to land on the coasts of Morocco; in the twelfth century B.C. Rusadir (Melilla) was a staging post for them on the way towards Gadir (Cadiz) and Tartessos. Carthage followed and had a chain of trading factories on the Moroccan coast, of which the principal were Lixus (opposite the modern Larache), Thymiaterion (Mahdiya), Sala (Salé), and Karikon Teichos (Mogador). Punic civilization had, however, only a limited influence on Morocco in general.

In the Roman period 'Moorish' princes (*Mauri*) enter history. We learn that during the Jugurthan war the Moorish prince Bocchus abandoned Jugurtha to become the ally of Rome; but we still hear nothing about the life of Morocco. The Romans themselves did not penetrate western Mauritania until the time of Augustus. Juba II, though a faithful vassal of Rome, was killed by order of Caligula, and the annexation of his kingdom proclaimed in 40 A.D. The province called Mauritania Tingitana was not very extensive; the *limes* passed a few kilometres south of Rabat, and a little to the south of Meknes and Fez. The Governor generally resided at Volubilis, whose ruins have been excavated and have revealed noteworthy monuments. In 285 B.C. the province was reduced in size; Diocletian ordered the evacuation of the southern portion and attached the rest to the Spanish dioceses. Christian evangelization began in the third century and there were sufficient Christians to justify the creation of four bishoprics.

In some cities the Latin and Christian way of life survived the fall of the western empire. In the eighth century the Arab conquerors found some Christian tribes still existing and certain Latin inscriptions in Volubilis are dated as late as the seventh century. As far as we are concerned, however, Morocco during this interregnum is lost in almost complete obscurity.

Muslim armies raided Tunisia in 647 and are commonly held to have reached Morocco in 684. But the expedition of Sidi Uqba, the founder of Kairouan, was not followed up and it was Musa ibn Nusair who reduced Morocco to the allegiance of the Umayyad Caliph in Damascus at the beginning of the eighth century. The Berbers who were mostly pagans rallied readily to Islam and took part in the conquest of Spain and the invasion of Gaul. Morocco was not, however, destined to remain long within the empire of the Caliphs. With the rest of the Berber lands, it participated in the Kharijite schismatical revolt of the eighth century and in consequence became for ever detached from any political allegiance to the east.

Islamization, at first superficial, soon spread and strengthened its hold in the course of a confused and little-known history. Heretical kingdoms, for the most part Kharijite, divided the country among them, until an Oriental prince, Idris, a descendant of the Prophet, fleeing from the Abbasids, found refuge at Oualili, the former Volubilis. Chosen by Berber tribes as their leader, he was able to establish a kingdom whose religion conformed with orthodoxy. His son founded the city of Fez, which was destined to play a leading role in the diffusion of Islamic religion and culture.

Morocco was nevertheless unable to escape the backwash of the struggles between two great Berber tribes, the Sanhaja and the Zenata. The nomad Zenata, repelled by their opponents, penetrated Morocco by the Taza corridor and founded a number of principalities, without succeeding in forming an empire.

This was to be the work of their rivals the Moroccan Sanhaja, true nomads from the western Sahara. Converted to the austere Islamic rite of Malikism by a Muslim religious lawyer, they hurled themselves on Morocco to spread their doctrine. Emerging from a fortified monastery (*ribat*) on the Mauritanian coast, their rulers were destined to found Marrakesh and create the first great Moroccan dynasty, that of the Almurabitun or Almoravids—'the people of the *ribat*'—who reigned for a century from 1053 to 1147. Their power spread beyond Morocco and the first Sultan, Yusuf ibn Tashufin, ruled as far as Algiers. Summoned by the Spanish Muslims to put a stop to the reconquest he halted it effectively, but followed this success up by deposing the Spanish princelets and annexing their territories, while Andalusian civilization began at the same time to dominate the cities of Morocco.

Exhausted by the effort which they had made, the Sanhaja succumbed, after three generations, before the mounting force of another race, the Masmuda, long-established sedentary people from western Morocco. Once again, it was a religious impulse—the preaching of the unitarianism taught by a clerkly Berber, Ibn Tumart, whence the name al-Muwahiddun or Unitarians—which inspired these mountaineers. It was, however, an outsider, a Berber from the neighbourhood of Tlemsen, by name Abd al-Mumin, who succeeded Ibn Tumart as leader, struck down the Almoravids, and captured Marrakesh in 1147. He took over the task of the Almoravids and further enlarged their empire, making it stretch from the frontiers of Castile to Tripoli. In 1162 he assumed the title of Caliph.

His religious reform, however, did not prove durable and the Malikism of the Almoravids survived. The Christian reconquest, too, resumed its progress and finally Almohad princes, divided among themselves, succumbed to a new invasion by the Zenata.

The hour had come for the appearance of the third great Berber clan, led by the Beni Merin. Coming from eastern Morocco they first conquered the north, then took Marrakesh in 1269, and finally made their capital in Fez. They were unable to hold the former Almohad empire together. Several attempts to reconquer the eastern Maghrib failed; for a few years they retained Ifriqiya but could not permanently hold even Tlemsen on the threshold of Morocco.

Meanwhile the consequences of a new factor, the arrival of the beduin Arabs, had begun to make themselves felt. Certain tribes of purely nomadic camel-owners, the Beni Hilal, who had left Arabia and been settled for some time in Upper Egypt, reached Ifriqiya in the eleventh century. They continued their progress towards the west in the following century, only to be totally defeated by Abd al-Mumin at the battle of Sétif. The Almohad Sultan, Yaacub al-Mansur, deported some of the more turbulent and, in order to have them more under control, settled them in the Gharb plain in the north, in the Haouz near Marrakesh, and in the Tamesna around Casablanca. In the thirteenth century other beduins, the Maaqil, who came originally from south Arabia, reached Morocco along the northern border of the Sahara. Spreading through the pre-Saharan Moroccan steppes, from the mouth of the Dra to that of the Muluya, they subdued the Berber nomads. With the decadence of the Merinid power, they crossed the passes of the

Atlas and began a long odyssey, which finally brought some of them, the Zaer, up to the gates of Rabat. These beduin migrations were responsible for the arabization of the countryside.

The efforts of the Merinids on behalf of religion gave the Moroccan towns a delicate adornment of mosques and *madrasas* (colleges), which they still possess, but did not prevent the implantation in the countryside of a rather degraded form of sufism, or mysticism, which gave rise to an astonishing cult of holy men (marabouts).

In the fifteenth century a new peril threatened Morocco. As the Christian reconquest of the Iberian peninsula drew to its end, the Spanish and Portuguese began to assault the coast, establishing themselves at a number of points. By the beginning of the sixteenth century the Portuguese were masters of Ceuta, Tangier, and Arcila, had founded Agadir and Mazagan, and had captured Safi and Azemmour on the Atlantic.

The Merinids had meanwhile been succeeded by a related Zenata family, the Beni Wattas (1465–1549). When these proved impotent to check the Portuguese, resistance to the infidels was organized out of the popular depths by heads of confraternities, marabouts, or *shorfa* (descendants of the Prophet) who became leaders in the Holy War. With this multiplication of little local chiefs, characteristic of Berber individualism, the state itself disappeared until new leaders, the Saadian Sharifs, arose and favoured by fortune had little difficulty in disposing of the last Beni Wattas and their anaemic Makhzen, as the Moroccan state organization is called.

This was the end of the Berber dynasties; and, as we bid them farewell, it is just to pay them their due tribute of praise. They had not only lived their hours of glory, and decorated the cities of Morocco with grandiose or delicate and subtle monuments. They had also created the framework of the state, known henceforth as the Makhzen. This framework was solid enough to maintain itself through all the vicissitudes of fate and to surmount the most dangerous moments of decadence.

The Saadians (1549–1654) won their prestige through their successes against the Portuguese, whom they drove from Agadir, Safi, and Azemmour, and through their quality as *shorfa*. But they had no such strong tribal basis as the preceding dynasties and they had therefore to rely on a military force which was principally composed of outsiders. A bold military expedition across the Sahara reduced Timbuktu and Gao and drained the gold of the Sudan towards Morocco. This won them prestige in the eyes of the European powers, with whom they entertained fairly active diplomatic relations. They even took the Spanish

G

as allies in order to counter the Turks who were threatening their eastern frontier. In their day Marrakesh regained its former splendour and was adorned with a new series of decorative monuments.

The maraboutic crisis from which the Saadians emerged was also the cause of their disappearance. While the Moriscos expelled from Spain and installed at Rabat and Salé were creating a veritable corsair republic, holy men like al-Ayashi in the north and Bu Hasan in the Sus were busy carving out fiefs for themselves in the rest of the country. The most powerful of them were the holy men of Dila, a *zawiya* [1] in the Middle Atlas, who captured Fez and Salé and at one moment had the whole of north Morocco under their domination. It looked as if the Sanhaja of central Morocco might be going to repeat the achievement of the Almoravids.

For a moment it seemed so; but then the prospects of the Dilaids were ruined by the extraordinary career of Maulay Rashid (1660-72), a Sharif from Tafilalet who belonged to the Alawite family, that is to say a descendant of Ali ibn Abi Talib, the son-in-law of the Prophet. A new Sharifian dynasty had come into existence, that which is still reigning over Morocco today. Maulay Rashid's successor, Maulay Ismail (1672-1729), displayed enormous energy in the struggle against the Christians and against the Turks. He organized a corps of black troops and held the country with a network of fortresses. But the greatest danger which he had to face was the pressure of the Sanhaja Berbers from the Middle Atlas who were beginning to come down from their mountains and attempting to establish themselves in the Atlantic plains. During his lifetime he held them, but his immediate successors did not have the same energy as himself and his death was the beginning of a long period of anarchy.

Sultans of merit, such as Sidi Muhammad ibn Abdullah (1757-92), Maulay Sulaiman (1792-1822), and Maulay Abd al-Rahman (1822-59) made a sustained effort to keep the country under control and to ward off foreign intervention. Though they could not avert the French irruption of 1844 or the Spanish of 1860, they made skilful use of the rivalries which divided the powers and successfully neutralized England, Spain, France, and later Germany, by playing them off one against the other.

Internally they relied on the Arab tribes; these were treated as *gaish* (army) tribes and exempted from taxation, in return for which they provided the most effective contingents of the

---

[1] Small mosque or convent.

army. Conscious of their role as religious chiefs, the Alawite Sultans endeavoured to reduce the field of Berber customary law and to replace it by the Quranic law or Sharia; to repress the excesses of maraboutism and saint worship, and to establish a purified Islamic worship. The individualism of the tribes nevertheless persisted, and every time that there was a fresh manifestation the dissidence (*siba*) began to spread. One of their greatest weaknesses, as of preceding dynasties, was the difficulty of the succession. No simple and regular rule governed this and in consequence the death of the sovereign was almost invariably the signal for a struggle among the members of the reigning family which gave rise to a serious political crisis.

The last great Sultan before the occupation was Maulay al-Hasan (1873–94). More than any of his predecessors, he reduced the area of the *bled es-siba* (country in dissidence). He was also able to make himself respected abroad where he secured the summoning of a Convention of Madrid in 1880 in the hope of regulating the excesses of the system by which foreign 'protection' was given to Moroccan subjects, thus virtually withdrawing them from the operation of Moroccan law. He also endeavoured to modernize the country by sending missions of students to study abroad. The change from Moroccan to foreign conditions was, however, so abrupt and the training which the students acquired abroad was so alien to the ways of thought of their environment that when they returned they were unable to apply the knowledge which they had acquired. Morocco's fundamental problem was not solved. The outside world was evolving at an ever-increasing speed; new techniques were being adapted in the immediate vicinity of Morocco. Europe was in the full spate of expansion; its economic and military power and its corresponding demands were growing from day to day. Meanwhile Morocco remained as it had been for centuries, displaying indeed a noble devotion to its traditions, but with its organs of government and its customs suffering a fossilization which rendered them incapable of fulfilling the tasks required of them in the modern world. Maulay al-Hasan was thus unable to accomplish in Morocco the renovation which Peter the Great worked in the somewhat similarly-situated Muscovy of his day.

From the Death of Maulay al-Hasan to the Present Time

On the death of Maulay al-Hasan the Empire was fated to pass into weaker hands. His son and successor, Maulay Abd al-Aziz, was only 14 years old and for six years he remained the ward of a former slave of his father, Ba Ahmad ou Musa.[1] The latter took the title of Wazir and ruled with a rod of iron, in the old traditional way but without introducing new methods or any material reforms. When he died, in 1901, the young Sultan decided to govern himself. He was intelligent and anxious to modernize his empire, but did not have a strong will. He made light of the long-established etiquette of the court and surrounded himself with Europeans among whom there were a number of adventurers and salesmen. Fascinated by the products of modern science, he encumbered his palace at Fez with miscellaneous and highly expensive objects. As he was also genuinely trying to reform the state administration, disgruntled conservative circles had no difficulty in discrediting him in the eyes of the public. The discontent, heightened by dislike of the foreigners, began to spread to the tribes.

Agitation was set off by a financial reform which was excellent in principle but unskilfully carried out. The old Quranic taxes, *zaqat* and *ashur*, which gave rise to abuses in their collection and to excessive exemptions, were replaced in 1901 by a single tax, the *tertib*; this was calculated on income derived from land and livestock. All those who had been benefiting from the former state of affairs leagued themselves against this reform. When the mistake was made of abolishing the former system before the new one was ready to take its place, many tribes took the chance and paid nothing at all. Morocco entered on the fatal round of deficits and loans, debts and guarantees, which was to deliver its public finances over to the total control of the foreigner.

The tribes of the region of Taza, to the east of Fez, rose at the summons of the Rogui (pretender) Bu Hamara ('the man of the she-ass'), who passed himself off as the Sharif Mohammed, elder brother of the Sultan, and as some sort of inspired person. Having raised eastern Morocco, he captured Ujda in 1903. He then marched on Fez with the intention of dethroning Maulay Abd al-Aziz and having himself proclaimed Sultan. Though he failed, the troops of the Makhzen were equally unable to dislodge him from Taza. He was not defeated until several years later, by Sultan Maulay Abd al-Hafidh.

This state of affairs within the country was the more dangerous since Morocco, now almost the only African state to remain independent, was exciting the greed of the outside world. Her geographical and strategical position made her an important stake. It is true that mutually contradictory ambitions could to some extent be made to cancel one another out.

[1] 'Ou' is the Berber equivalent of the Arabic 'ibn', meaning 'son'.

Maulay al-Hasan had been very successful at this diplomatic game but when his successor tried to continue it the weakening of the central power made it much harder. Moreover competition among the great powers was becoming keener. France, having succeeded in covering her Algerian conquest on the east with a protectorate over Tunisia, wanted to cover it on the west also. In particular she feared the installation or preponderance of the Germans in Morocco; for Germany, having regarded the colonial expansion of France with a favourable eye as calculated to avert her thoughts from the 'blue line of the Vosges', was now becoming disturbed at a partition of Africa in which she had no part and at a French expansion which now appeared to her more dangerous than she had expected.

Great Britain, anxious for the security of the Straits, wished to prevent the southern shores from falling into over-powerful hands. Spain did not want to be overlooked in a competition which was being pursued on her doorstep and for a country in which she already had sovereign possessions. Other powers, less directly interested, supported their respective allies.

Morocco thus found herself involved in the major diplomatic crises of the beginning of the twentieth century and her fate bound up with European politics. In 1904 France succeeded in obtaining the recognition by Great Britain and Italy of her preponderance in Morocco, granting them in return a free hand in Egypt and Libya respectively. In the same year she concluded a secret agreement with Spain which delimited two zones of influence, one in the north and one in the south. Germany's opposition, however, still remained and set off three successive crises.

The first was provoked in 1905 by a spectacular visit of the German Emperor William II to Tangier. It brought about the resignation of the French Foreign Minister, Delcassé, and resulted in the Conference of Algeciras in 1906. The final Act of the Conference (7 April 1906) proclaimed the independence and integrity of the Sharifian Empire and the economic equality of the powers. French preponderance was rather vaguely recognized, as well as a certain Spanish participation, while Morocco became more than ever an international problem. The agreements of 1904 were not affected.

In eastern Morocco, incidents on the very vaguely defined frontier led to the intervention of French troops; these occupied Ujda on 29 March 1907 and the mountains of Beni Snassen in December 1907 and January 1908. At Casablanca the massacre of European workers who were engaged on the construction of a port and the disturbances which followed brought about the landing of a French expeditionary force. Attacks by the neighbouring tribes led little by little to the occupation of the whole of the Chaouia, in spite of the hesitations of the French Government at Paris.

The inability of Sultan Abd al-Aziz to prevent these foreign interventions finally discredited him with public opinion. In August his brother Maulay Abd al-Hafidh was proclaimed Sultan at Marrakesh. The French expeditionary force which at first resisted the new claimant was later ordered to remain neutral. Maulay Abd al-Aziz's forces were defeated and Maulay Abd al-Hafidh was proclaimed at Fez on 7 June 1908 and recognized by the powers on 5 January 1909.

A second Franco-German diplomatic crisis arose over deserters from the French Foreign Legion at Casablanca in 1908. It was solved by an agreement in 1909 in which Germany recognized 'France's special interests'. Franco-Moroccan agreements, concluded in March 1910, accentuated the French grip on the finances and administration. Further tribal disorder led to new interventions by French troops; and in 1910 the proclamation at Meknes of another pretender led Maulay Abd al-Hafidh to ask for help, whereupon Fez was relieved by a column under General Moinier. In 1911 Spain in application of the 1904 agreement occupied Larache and Alcazarquivir (al-Ksar al-Kebir).

Meanwhile the annoyance caused in Germany by the French advance was manifested in a third diplomatic crisis of which the culmination was the dispatch of a German gunboat to Agadir. Agreement was reached on 4 November 1911. In return for 'compensation' in equatorial Africa, Germany agreed to allow France, who had been supported by her British ally, to undertake the pacification and organization of Morocco, on condition that economic liberty was preserved. Maulay Abd al-Hafidh, now face to face with France alone, had no alternative but to sign, on 30 March 1912, the Treaty of Fez by which a French protectorate was established over Morocco. In a convention with France, signed on 27 November 1912, Spain agreed the limits of her zone. Though both zones were nominally under the sovereignty of the Sultan, the Spanish zone became virtually autonomous as the result of a permanent delegation of the Sultan's power to his Lord Lieutenant or Khalifa in that region. In principle it was agreed that Tangier should have an international régime but, as the powers had not yet agreed on the terms of this, the Statute of Tangier was not established until the Convention of Paris in 1923.

Though Morocco had lost her independence, her personality

survived as well as the theoretical sovereignty of the Sultan over the whole territory. French action remained subject to a number of international commitments which, for the most part, had their origin in the Act of Algeciras. On the other hand the Treaty of Fez was a supple instrument whose efficacy could be made to depend on the interpretation which was given to it.

In the beginning, the interpretation adopted was that evolved by the first French Resident General, Marshal Lyautey. A disciple of Galliéni, whose methods he had studied in Tonkin and Madagascar, this great soldier, aristocrat, and statesman of genius in his own way, was endowed with a remarkable gift for dealing with men, and he left an indelible personal impress on the protectorate system. His first task was to pacify the country. When he assumed his duties in Fez in April, riots had ravaged the city and it was besieged by the Berber tribes.[1] In the course of the summer Marrakesh had to be delivered from a holy man from Saguiat al-Hamra, al-Hiba, who had raised the south by preaching a Holy War. Al-Hiba's defeat brought about the adhesion of the Grand Caids of the Atlas, of whom the most powerful was the Glawi. Apart from the High Atlas of Marrakesh, however, the whole mountain area was in dissidence; the Zaer were threatening Rabat, and the Zemmour cutting the communications between Fez and the coast. The work was to take a long time. Lyautey himself did not see the end of it, for it was not completed till 1934. The task was delayed by two events: one external, the war of 1914–18, and the other internal, the extension of Abdelkrim's rising to the French zone in 1925. In 1914, in order to face the German invasion, the French Government ordered Lyautey to send the greater part of his troops back to France and to fall back on the coast. Lyautey sent the troops for which he was asked, but retained all occupied Morocco as well. By this brilliant and bold decision he saved the protectorate.

Resumed in 1920, the pacification was interrupted by another grave crisis, the rising in the Rif, which threatened Lyautey's work as well as that of the Spaniards. In the northern area the Spanish occupation had come up against a very stubborn and warlike mountain population. A Cadi of the Beni Uriaghel, Abdelkrim, proved himself to have remarkable military as well as political talent. In 1921 he inflicted a bloody disaster on the column of the Spanish General Silvestre, near Anual. Three

---

[1] He gratefully acknowledged the assistance which he received on this occasion from the British Consul, Mr. (later Sir) James MacLeod, whose advice saved the people of Fez from unnecessary reprisals. Cf. G. H. Selous, *Appointment to Fez* (London, 1956), p. 149.

years later, after the Spanish dictator General Primo de Rivera had carried out a strategic withdrawal from the interior, Abdelkrim, whose successes had won him great credit with the Rif tribes and who was now regarded as a liberator and religious and patriotic hero, launched an attack on the French zone. The frontier tribes made common cause with him. Lyautey, who had foreseen the danger and vainly asked for reinforcements, faced the attack with the insufficient forces at his disposal. In 1925 Fez was in danger, and only reinforcements brought from France and co-operation with the Spanish forces finally made it possible to throw Abdelkrim's forces back and force him to surrender. But Lyautey, who had prepared the way for the recovery, was no longer there to gather the fruits of the surrender. In 1926 he had been replaced by a civilian Resident, M. Steeg, while the responsibility for the military operations had been entrusted to Marshal Pétain. After the conclusion of the Rif war, operations against the dissidents went on slowly, since the French Government and Parliament were unwilling to devote large sums to them. They were terminated by the submission of the Anti-Atlas and the north of Mauritania in 1934.

The technique of the pacification had been determined by Lyautey, and it bore the stamp of his method. This was to show force so that it need not be used; to prepare the military advance by methods of persuasion; to economize means, by only acting at the appropriate moment and at the weak point, and by remembering that today's opponents should be tomorrow's allies.

His conception of the protectorate proceeded from the same order of ideas. He did not intend that it should become the shield for a colonial domination. He genuinely wanted to respect Moroccan sovereignty, to act in the name of the Sultan, to modernize the Moroccan Government rather than substitute a French administration for it, to train Moroccan officials and to associate them with the work of reform. Respecting the Muslim and Moroccan way of life, he preferred evolution to revolution, as the means of enabling this ancient country to fit itself into the modern world without denying its past and without undergoing the crises which are the inevitable accompaniment of abrupt social upheavals. His desire to modernize without destroying can be seen in his town planning. He created new European towns at some distance from the Moroccan towns whose style and ancestral ways of life he wished to respect. In fact, however, this was possibly an unhappy idea, since it tended to segregate the two populations and gave

Moroccans who wished to become modern the impression that it was desired to keep them from any real development.

For all this, the French administration loomed very large even in Lyautey's day. No doubt this was difficult to avoid, in view of the lack of qualified Moroccans. Lyautey saw the danger; realizing the movement of ideas which the mere presence of the French was certain to provoke, he laid down, in a famous report, addressed to the French Government in 1920, the broad lines on which the protectorate ought to develop—the formation of a Moroccan *élite*; their ever-increasing association with the administration; their training to manage their own affairs. His successors were less perceptive of future developments. The habit of direct administration became ever more deeply implanted. French teachers did indeed train a Moroccan *élite*, but French administrators did not employ them, or at least not sufficiently. Out of this was born Moroccan nationalism.

It was born just as soon as the first Moroccan generation came out from the schools and colleges which Lyautey founded. While Abdelkrim's successes had found an echo among the tribes, they had on the contrary been rather a cause of anxiety to the well-to-do citizens of such towns as Fez. It was not till 1931 that the Berber *Dahir* (decree) produced the first public manifestation of nationalism. This relied largely on the exploitation of Islamic sentiment. The promulgation of the Berber *Dahir* caused the protectorate to be accused of wishing to withdraw a section of the population from the influence of Muslim law.[1] Islamic solidarity was fully brought into play and demonstrations took place not only in Fez but also in Damascus and most of the great cities of the Muslim world.

Two influences worked on Moroccan nationalism—western ideas such as liberty, democracy, and the right of peoples to dispose of themselves; and those of the Arab east where several states had been modernized and were acceding to independence. According to whether Moroccan intellectuals had studied in France or in the east, they tended to be more responsive to one group of ideas or the other. Hence the connexions which they formed on the one hand with the politicians and

---

[1] Lyautey himself had written: 'It is not our business to teach Arabic to populations which have hitherto got on without it. Arabic is a factor of Islamization, because it is acquired with the Quran. It is our interest to make the Berbers develop outside the framework of Islam' (quoted in P. Marty, *Le Maroc de Demain*, p. 228). On the other hand Sultan Maulay Hasan had years ago promised the tribes to respect Berber law. The promise was repeated by protectorate officials and the *Dahir*, they said, simply gave it legal effect.

parties of the French Left and on the other with theoreticians and men of action such as Shakib Arslan.

The Moroccan nationalist movement was in the beginning a movement of reform. It was not until 1944 that the claim to independence was advanced. In 1934 a plan of reforms was presented to the French Government. The gist of this was that the spirit of the Treaty of Fez should be respected and that the protectorate should take the form of control, not of direct administration. In 1937 an economic crisis which raged for some years gave a new impulse to an agitation which had by now reached the man in the street. The town of Fez was occupied by the army, the principal leaders were arrested, the parties dissolved, and the papers forbidden. The nationalist movement, known as the *Kutlat al-Amal al-Watani* (National Action Bloc), was itself split by a division. The main body, of which Allal al-Fasi remained the uncontested chief, took the name of *al-Hizb al-Watani* (National Party) while Mohammed ibn al-Hasan al-Wazzani founded *al-Harakat al-Qaumiya* (Popular Movement). This division, which still exists under the names of *Hizb al-Istiqlal* (Independence Party) and *Hizb al-Shura wa'l-Istiqlal* (Party of Democratic Independence or PDI), was due much more to a clash of temperament than to any doctrinal opposition. Allal al-Fasi, whose powerful personality was a cause of offence to the protectorate authorities, was exiled to Gabon where he was to remain for nine years.

From this time on the history of Morocco is dominated by the figure of the young Sultan, Sidi Mohammed ibn Yusuf. When Maulay Abd al-Hafidh had abdicated after the signing of the Treaty of Fez he was succeeded by his youngest brother, Maulay Yusuf. On the latter's death in 1927 the protectorate authorities put forward his youngest son, a youth of 17, who had not been educated with a view to the succession, but whose inexperience would, it was thought, make him easy to control. Those who made the choice on these considerations were not to know that they were selecting for the throne a prince who was to be the principal architect of Moroccan independence. Intelligent, industrious, with a high sense of duty and responsibility, open to modern ideas though profoundly attached to Islam, an enemy of all violence, but patient, tenacious, and a skilful negotiator, the young sovereign soon began to win popularity and embody the hopes of the patriots.

In the bad days of 1940 he and his people with him supported France, but in spite of the bonds of confidence and sympathy by which he was attached to General Noguès, then Resident General, he refused to follow him when the latter left

Rabat in November 1942 to organize resistance to the American forces. An interview with President Roosevelt at Casablanca in January 1943 opened his eyes to the profound changes which the war was going to bring about in the equilibrium of world forces and in the ideas by which the peoples of the world were moved. In a resounding speech at Tangier, in 1947, he proclaimed the affiliation of Morocco with the Arab world and demanded that its legitimate national aspirations should be satisfied.

The nationalist claims were defined in 1944. No doubt the crisis of November 1943 in the Lebanon, resulting in the termination of the French Mandate, was a factor in this. On 11 January 1944 a manifesto signed by members of the National Party and by independent personalities was handed to the Sultan, to the Residency, and to the Consuls General of the Allies. This asked the Sovereign to begin negotiations with France for the abrogation of the protectorate treaty and for the recognition of the independence of Morocco. It was the first time that the word *istiqlal* (independence) had been formally advanced. The arrest of a nationalist leader, Ahmed Balafrej, fifteen days later, caused serious outbreaks in Rabat and Fez.

The nationalist parties had increased their audience and their influence. They now dominated the bourgeoisie and a great part of the intellectuals. Two important elements of the population were, however, still beyond their reach; these were the new proletariat in the cities and the masses in the countryside. They also encountered an increasingly violent opposition from certain traditionalist elements who were afraid of losing the power which their support of the protectorate had brought them; these were the big families in the provinces, who controlled certain tribes, and the heads of religious confraternities. Influential circles among the protectorate authorities were naturally led to the idea of making use of these to contain the progress of nationalism. After the speech at Tangier the Sultan appeared to them to be the real leader of Moroccan nationalism, so that henceforth the struggle between the Residency and the Nationalists was transformed into a struggle between the Residency and the Palace. General Juin, who succeeded M. Erik Labonne in 1947, after the stir caused by the Sultan's Tangier speech, began to exercise strong pressure on the Sultan from 1951 to induce him to disavow the Istiqlal Party, as the former National Party was now called. The difference between towns and countryside was utilized on this occasion; and armed horsemen, led by their Caids, appeared and camped under the walls of Fez and Rabat. The operation did not have the desired effect, since the Sultan merely withdrew a little, without yielding completely, and the Resident General was not fully supported by the French Government. From this distance the movement gives the impression of a rehearsal for that which was to be carried out in 1953.

Nationalism consolidated and extended its position. The working classes were now affected, as was shown by incidents in Casablanca in 1952. The tribes, who had been made use of for political purposes in 1951, were no longer so indifferent to political developments as they had been. The small rural centres became efficient relay posts for propaganda. International opinion began to take notice, and the United Nations was notified by the independent Arab countries. A part of French public opinion considered the policy of the Residency as reactionary and dangerous, and refused to accept the suggestion that the Sultan and the nationalists were 'anti-French' or 'crypto-Communists'.

Among French circles in Morocco, however, the partisans of a policy of force prevailed. Two influential Moroccans were put forward whose personal resentment made them enemies of the Sultan. One was Thami al-Glawi, Pasha (Governor) of Marrakesh and master of a great part of the Moroccan south; the other Abd al-Hai al-Kittani, chief of an important religious confraternity. They rallied a great part of the Caids and rural notables; these then took an oath on the tomb of Maulay Idris and demanded the deposition of Mohammed V. This menace was supported by a new 'march of the tribes'. On 20 August 1953 Resident-General Guillaume accordingly deposed the Sultan, who was transported with his family first to Corsica and then to Madagascar. Another member of the Alawite family, Sidi Mohammed ibn Arafa, 60 years old, was put on the throne and received the homage of the conspirators and the investiture of the Ulama.

Moroccan opinion was dumbfounded. The nationalists, whose leaders were for the most part in forced residence, did not respond with any immediate action. But Mohammed V was at once regarded as a martyr, and became the object of what was almost a religious cult. The nationalist idea found in him precisely the symbol which was necessary to sweep the masses. In place of the political parties which the authorities had destroyed, a clandestine organization grew up and set terrorism in action. French liberal opinion condemned the action of 20 August severely, and sought a means of escaping from what was regarded as a dead end.

Changes of Resident General failed to affirm the authority

of a Sultan whom the majority of Moroccans refused to recognize. After several attempts on his life, the attempt to make him appear in public was abandoned. In 1955, on the second anniversary of the deposition, serious troubles occurred at Wadi Zem (Tadla) and among the Berber Zayans. Many French people were massacred and there were severe reprisals. On 1 November 1955 a Moroccan 'Army of Liberation' attacked French posts in the Rif and in the Middle Atlas. The French Government, reluctant to go completely in reverse and recall Mohammed V, began to consider setting up a Council of Regency and negotiating with the exiled monarch. Realizing that he had lost all chance of winning, the old Berber leader Thami al-Glawi, repeating a gesture which men of his race had often made in the past, rallied to the exiled Sultan, and later made a humble act of public contrition before him in the hope of safeguarding that which was most essential in his eyes—the future of his family.

There was now nothing to be done but to restore the legitimate Sultan. By this time, however, there could be no question of his returning as a protected sovereign. By the Declaration of La Celle St. Cloud on 6 November 1955 France undertook to terminate the protectorate and recognize the independence of Morocco. The Sultan would reciprocate by recognizing French interests in Morocco and accept 'independence within interdependence'. Freely-negotiated agreements were to define the application of these principles.

On 18 November 1955, the twenty-ninth anniversary of his accession to the throne, Mohammed V returned amid indescribable scenes of popular enthusiasm which no disorder marred. For months thousands of Moroccans flowed into the capital from every corner of the country in order to greet the liberator.

A Government was formed under the Presidency of Si Bekkai, an army colonel who had served with distinction in the war, and an independent in politics, with ministers chosen from both nationalist parties, the Istiqlal and the Democratic Party of Independence, and from independents. The Istiqlal ministers were in the majority, as the importance of their party merited. The first task of the Government was to negotiate the terms of the independence which had been agreed in principle. The negotiations were completed on 2 March 1956 and power was rapidly transferred. Morocco thus recovered not only internal autonomy but also the full attributes of sovereignty, in particular foreign affairs and the army. On 7 April 1956 a corresponding agreement was reached with the Spanish

Government, and the way prepared for the reintegration of the northern zone. Later in the year the incorporation of the Tangier zone was agreed by the various powers concerned.

The problems facing independent Morocco were enormous. In the first place Moroccan officials had to be found to fill the places left vacant both by former Moroccan officials, who had practically all been discredited by their participation in the events accompanying or following the Sultan's deposition, and by French officials who had been withdrawn.[1] Order had to be restored, and the mass of the population brought back to habits of discipline which had inevitably been relaxed, as in all periods of revolution. A national economy, which the troubles had slowed down and the massive departure of French capital severely shaken, had to be re-established. The 'Army of Liberation' which was still functioning in the Rif had to be absorbed. The three zones of the country had to be integrated and a programme of arabization and moroccanization, which the nationalist parties had promised, had to be put through without prejudice to the working of the administration.

Several of these tasks were successfully accomplished by the end of a year. Both town and country had received a framework of officials, and security was complete. The administration functioned normally. Part of the Liberation Army had been absorbed, while the rest was located in the far south. Diplomatic relations had been established with the principal foreign powers and with the Muslim countries of the east. The unification of the country was proceeding, as administration was taken over from the Spanish in the north, and a new Statute for Tangier was issued. Agreements for co-operation with France were signed, covering the administrative, judicial, and cultural spheres. England and Spain resigned rights which they had enjoyed under the treaties of 1856 and 1860 respectively and which had been extended to other countries by the Act of Algeciras; the country thus recovered its tariff liberty and a new scale of customs dues was introduced which became applicable to all parts of the country.

Many problems, however, still remained unsettled at the beginning of 1958. It had not been possible for Morocco in such a short time to produce all the officials necessary to fill the gaps left by French departures. The economy had not yet recovered; capital which departed had not returned, though

---

[1] French officials were estimated to number 23,200 on 1 May 1955; 19,600 on 31 August 1957; and 16,500 on 31 December 1957. Many more were expected to leave on 1 July 1958, since many had signed a year's contract in 1957 which they were not expected to renew.

the country, like all other backward countries, requires heavy capital investments. Future financial aid from France was dependent on the signature of a Convention of Establishment, guaranteeing the rights of French residents, both as to their persons and their property. This was not concluded owing to disagreement over the question of certain lands, affecting about 700 settlers, which had been taken for colonization during the protectorate; and negotiations were interrupted in February 1958, after the bombing of Sakiet Sidi Yusuf in Tunisia. Most serious of all, it could not be said that relations with France had been stabilized. The French army was still stationed in the country and a number of incidents had occurred. The southern frontier, which had never been clearly delimited, was the subject of claims which had been made more pressing by the discovery of important mineral resources in the western Sahara. More acute than these was the situation in Algeria. Arab and Muslim solidarity made it inevitable that public opinion and the Moroccan Government should show sympathy for the Algerian nationalists whom France was fighting. In October 1956 the diversion of the aeroplane which was taking ben Bella and other Algerian leaders to Tunis, as guests of the Sultan, provoked the recall of the Moroccan Ambassador from Paris and created a grave state of tension between the two countries. In Morocco itself popular demonstrations degenerated at Meknes into disorders which cost the lives of many French people. For a moment it seemed that Franco-Moroccan relations were definitely compromised. But a remarkable improvement followed, and by January 1958 there was for a time hope of a speedy settlement of the principal issues in dispute.

Internally, the figure of Mohammed V continued to dominate political life. Within the Government, the co-operation of the two political parties did not prove lasting. In November 1956 a ministerial shuffle eliminated the ministers of the Democratic Party of Independence; the new Ministry consisted of an Istiqlal majority with a few independents. The drawing up of a constitution was under discussion, but it was too early to prophecy whether this would produce a constitutional monarchy after the British fashion or a presidential régime of the American type, with the monarch taking the place of a permanent president. Meanwhile a Consultative Assembly had been formed, with a majority belonging to the Istiqlal in alliance with the powerful Labour Federation (*Union Marocaine de Travail*). The delimitation of rural communes and of constituencies was under study. But no one could foretell how the political forces of the country were likely to develop as the influence of the common struggle for independence became blurred by the passage of time.

In May 1958 a new Government was formed with Ahmed Balafrej as Prime Minister. This marked a further step towards a homogeneous Istiqlal Government, though the cabinet, now reduced to ten members, contained three ministers whose appointment was criticized by the organ of the Istiqlal Party as the choice of the Palace rather than of the Prime Minister. At the same time the King, in a broadcast address, announced the granting of a Royal Charter. This declared that the national sovereignty was embodied in the person of the King, and that the form of government would be a constitutional monarchy. Ministers would be individually and collectively responsible to the King, but the sphere of action of the Prime Minister and of each minister as well as those of the cabinet as a whole would be defined. There would be a distinction between legislative and executive power. Liberty of opinion, expression, assembly and association would be guaranteed within the limit of respect for the monarchical régime, the security of the state, and the needs of public welfare. Municipal and local councils would be formed, on a communal (regional), not a tribal basis. When these councils had been established a National Deliberative Assembly would be created, having the right of discussion and of voting the budget. The members of the Assembly would be elected by the municipal and local councils. In a final stage this Assembly would be replaced by a National Assembly elected by universal suffrage.

GOVERNMENT AND POLITICAL LIFE

Government and Administration

Before the protectorate, Morocco was an absolute monarchy, only very slightly tempered by the ancient tradition of *mushawwara* or 'consultation' with the notables. All power, whether executive, legislative, or judicial, was concentrated in the hands of the Sultan. A degree of religious authority should be added to these, since Muslim tradition makes no definite division between spiritual and temporal. As head and Imam of the Moroccan Muslim community, the Sultan disposed, within his own empire, of all those powers which the Caliphs had exercised over the totality of the lands of Islam.

The protectorate brought this system under foreign control, while leaving it theoretically intact. The Sultan remained the official source of all power and all law. A *Conseil du Gouvernement* was indeed created, but this body which contained French as well as Moroccan members was nominated by the Resident and had only a consultative status. The members of municipal commissions were also nominated. It was only at the end of the protectorate that any steps were taken to separate judicial from executive authority or to create district councils on an elective basis.

The achievement of independence, by removing the control of the protecting state, may be said to have re-created the former situation. The King not only reigned, but also governed and legislated. He remained the religious head of the community, the Imam. His quality as Sharif (descendant of the Prophet) added to the religious quality of his power and gave the Sovereign a special position in the eyes of the masses. Every Friday he attended the midday prayer in great pomp, supported by court dignitaries and the members of the Government. On the other hand the significance of the change in style, announced in 1957, from Sharifian Empire and Sultan to Kingdom and King of Morocco should not be overlooked.

It is generally recognized that the uncertainty of the succession was a cause of weakness in medieval Muslim states. The Prophet himself died without having named a successor or fixed any rules for the succession. The first Caliphs were chosen by the Companions of the Prophet, with the assent of the faithful, not without dissensions which degenerated into civil war under Ali. Though the Umayyads gave the Caliphate a monarchical aspect which it never afterwards lost, Muslim jurisprudence, based on the practice of the earliest times, prevented hereditary succession from being ever accepted as a principle. Accession always remained theoretically subject to the *baiya* or taking of allegiance and to investiture by the doctors of the law. The only way for a Sultan of Morocco to ensure the succession of a son, not necessarily the eldest, was by having him recognized in his own lifetime and by associating him with himself in the exercise of sovereignty. This by no means always prevented other claimants from arising and putting the issue to the arbitrament of arms, the Ulama almost invariably ratifying the successful pretender.

In 1957 Mohammed V took the step of having his eldest son, Prince Maulay Hasan, officially and solemnly proclaimed as Heir to the Throne, though the principle of hereditary succession would have to be ratified in the constitution. The King also instituted a Council of the Throne, composed of three members nominated by himself. The choice of members demonstrated the desire to rely on the religious and traditional forces of the country.

H

Under the protectorate there was properly speaking no 'government'. Certain Wazirates such as those of Justice and of Habous (Religious Endowments) did indeed survive. But most of the departments were headed by French directors, in theory appointed by the Sultan but in fact chosen by the Resident. On the return of the Sultan from exile a Government properly so-called was constituted, having a President of the Council at its head. After the reshuffle of November 1956 the following ministries existed: Minister of State in charge of the Civil Service; Minister of the Royal Household; of Justice; of Foreign Affairs; of Defence; of Economy (with a State Under-Secretariat for Finance); of the Interior (with a Directorate General of Public Security); of Education; of Agriculture; of Public Works; of Labour; of Health; and of Posts, Telegraphs, and Telephones. The former Ministry of Habous has become a Directorate General. In the ministry of May 1958, the Prime Minister became responsible also for the Foreign Office, and the Minister of Economy for the Ministry of Agriculture.

A Council of Ministers met periodically under the Presidency of the King and there was a weekly Cabinet Council at which the President of the Council presided. The ministers were nominated by the King and responsible to him. The first ministry to be constituted after independence included Istiqlal ministers in a majority, with some ministers from the PDI, and some independents. In the Government, as it existed in 1957, there were nine ministers belonging to the Istiqlal Party while the remainder, including the President of the Council, were independent or belonged to minor parties. The PDI was no longer represented. In the Government of May 1958 all ministers except one were members of the Istiqlal.

The national territory was divided into seventeen provinces and five prefectures (the large cities), at the head of which are governors (*Amil*, pl. *Umala*), appointed by the King. Local administration was still in the hands of Caids or tribal leaders, also appointed by the Sovereign. The former apparatus of control, exercised through *Contrôleurs Civils* or *Officiers des Affaires Indigènes* disappeared. But the new régime kept the former *cercles*, at the head of which were officials known as *supercaids*.

The principle of the separation of executive and judicial powers was announced and the movement adumbrated in the last years of the protectorate greatly accelerated. Caids lost all judicial attributions and these were handed over to judges-delegate. The reform was carried out as fast as qualified magistrates became available.

The ministries were the heirs of the Directorates under the protectorate and in general kept the same structure. The achievement of independence, however, involved the creation of two entirely new ministries—the Ministry of Foreign Affairs and that of National Defence—since both these functions had been exercised exclusively by the protecting power. By January 1958 Morocco had exchanged Ambassadors with most of the great powers (with the exception of the Soviet Union and the Chinese People's Republic) and with the states of western Europe, as well as with the Arab and Muslim states of the east. A diplomatic convention signed with France provided for the latter exercising the representation of Moroccan interests in countries where Morocco had no representation of her own, except for Latin America where a convention with Spain accorded the latter country a similar privilege. Morocco had been admitted to the United Nations, to UNESCO, and to most of the big international organizations.

The political system was of course provisional. The first Government was formed primarily to negotiate independence. Though the latter now officially existed, by no means all its implications had yet been implemented. Conventions had been signed with France concerning diplomacy, judicial affairs, technical and administrative assistance, and also a cultural and university agreement, but it remained to sign the Convention of Establishment, of which the terms were still under discussion, and to come to an agreement about the presence of French troops in Morocco. Constitutional reforms outlined by the King in May 1958 had to be made a reality. Statements from all responsible sources, beginning with the monarch, forecast a democratic régime, with a constitutional monarchy. But these terms admitted of widely divergent interpretations. Such matters were the subject of discussion, not in public but within the political parties and among all those who were interested in public affairs. It was impossible to foretell what would emerge, particularly as the external situation, both in North Africa and the east, could not fail to affect developments within the country, where the left-wing, activist element in the Istiqlal Party was becoming increasingly vocal.

Hitherto cautious progress seemed to be preferred. Granted that there should be popular consultation, it was yet felt important to avoid the inconveniences which a number of new countries had encountered as the result of imitating the political institutions of western Europe, without discrimination. The Moroccan people were without experience in the working of democratic institutions and it was hoped to lead them to it by degrees. For this purpose the King in 1956 had created the Consultative Assembly. Though nominated by the monarch, membership was arranged to reflect the political and social forces of the country as fully as possible. Not only the political parties were represented but also agricultural interests, the liberal professions, commerce, industry, the trade unions, and so on. In spite of the fact that the political parties were not largely represented, the Assembly had a political colouring and sympathizers with the Istiqlal were in a clear majority. The Assembly discussed whatever questions were submitted to it by the Government, and more particularly the budget, and expressed its opinions and wishes. It was, however, a consultative body whose resolutions did not bind the Government. In the debates, it appeared that the position of many delegates was more radical than that of the Government.

Municipal elections were promised, and should have taken place before the end of 1957. The preliminary studies were, however, not completed in time. The limits of the future districts are being fixed in such a way as is hoped will dislocate the tribal organization and accelerate its disappearance. The electoral system was also under discussion. The principle of universal suffrage seemed likely to prevail, and there was support for the inclusion of women voters. The next stage would be the establishment of provincial councils. Only after that would there be elections for a National Assembly.

The essential prerogative of such a National Assembly would, as in all countries, be the voting of the budget. Meanwhile this was drawn up in the Under-Secretariat of State for Finance, approved by the Council of Ministers, and submitted to the King, whose signature gave it the force of law.

The Army

A national army was constituted out of the former Moroccan troops, once known as *supplétives*, composed of *goums* from the French southern zone and *mehallas* from the former Spanish zone. The basis of an officer corps was formed by Moroccan officers who were serving in the French or Spanish armies and was completed for the moment with French and Spanish officers and n.c.o.'s. The formation of Moroccan officers was entrusted in part to a Military School at Meknes, which was created under the protectorate and from which the southern zone Moroccan officers of today have graduated, and in part to the French military college at St. Cyr and to the Spanish military academy at Toledo. For n.c.o.'s a school was established at Ahermoumou near Fez. The King was Commander-in-Chief of the army which was officially designated as the Royal Moroccan Forces, while the Crown Prince was Chief of the General Staff. The effectives, which were 15,000 at the moment of formation in May 1956, were to be raised progressively to 30,000. A great part of the Liberation Army which operated in the Rif in 1955–6 was integrated into the Royal Moroccan Forces. Equipment, mostly of American or French origin, was furnished in general by France; while the French troops in Morocco provided a certain number of auxiliary services, such as intendance, health services, and maintenance. The Royal Forces included infantry, cavalry, artillery, engineering units, and a few tanks. There was no navy or air force, except for a few liaison planes.

Justice

The organization of justice at the beginning of 1958 was complicated. Certain elements still persisted from before the occupation; others had been inherited from the protectorate and had not yet been modified; while others again had been reformed or created after the coming of independence.

In the early days of Islam the Cadi was judge for all purposes. Very soon, however, the executive power withdrew from him what appeared to it to be an essential element of authority, the repression of crime. Penal and civil justice were thus separated, the first becoming an attribute of the executive and its representatives. In Morocco Pashas or Governors administered penal and to some extent civil justice in the towns, and the tribal Caids in the country, while the Cadi was concerned only with matters affecting personal status and inheritance, which were governed by the Sharia, or Quranic, law. Under the protectorate, however, a High Sharifian Court was created, with its seat at Rabat, which dealt with crimes.

Moroccan justice was not applicable in the case of foreigners. French courts similar to those in metropolitan France were created by the protectorate, with a court of appeal at Rabat. These administered justice not only in the case of French and foreign subjects in general (with the exception of the United States, which had not resigned its capitulatory privileges, including the right to trial by consular court), but also of Moroccans where the crime or the dispute involved a non-Moroccan. The process of land registration was also a function of the French courts.

In the matter of personal status, the situation was equally complicated. In towns and in Arabic-speaking areas of the countryside, the Cadi judged according to the Sharia; but in

Berber tribes which still clung to their customary law courts composed of notables or clerkly persons judged according to a custom which varied from district to district. To this there had to be added rabbinic courts which applied, and still apply, Mosaic law in the case of Moroccan Jews. The latter was a highly developed code, based on the 'Custom of Castile' of the sixteenth century, modified by *takanot* (improvements) of the twentieth century which approximated to modern law.

Towards the end of the protectorate there was a move in favour of the separation of powers. Judges-delegate were instituted in the cities and in certain tribes, while regional courts judged more serious cases and heard appeals from the lower courts. But the protectorate authorities were unwilling to deprive the Caids of all their powers of inflicting punishment and at the moment of independence the reform had not yet been applied universally or in all its implications.

One of the first cares of the new Government was to decree the principle of the separation of powers and to name judges-delegate in all areas. Though it was impossible to find an adequate number of qualified judges, those now responsible for Government had suffered so much from the former system that they preferred to appoint a less qualified but independent judge to the old-style caid-judge. Customary justice was connected in the minds of nationalists with the memory of the ill-fated Berber *Dahir* of 1930 and was therefore condemned. Cadis were named everywhere. Though in principle they apply Quranic law, they appear to have been recommended not to go too fast where the population is still strongly attached to customary law.

French justice could no longer exist as such. The judicial convention signed with France turned the former French courts into Moroccan courts, new style. French judges continued to sit, together with Moroccan judges who had acquired the necessary diplomas. French subjects had the right to be judged by these courts, which applied French law though they delivered judgment in the name of His Majesty the King of Morocco.

At the summit, a Supreme Court was constituted. Under the protectorate appeals against the sentences of French courts in Morocco were heard by the Appeal Court in Paris, while appeals against administrative decisions were heard by the French *Conseil d'État*. Since this procedure was unsuitable in an independent state, the Moroccan Supreme Court was given an administrative section which played the part of *Conseil d'État* and one or more judicial sections which dealt with appeals. There was a French majority among the judges and state councillors, but the first President and the *Procureur Général* were Moroccan.

Foreign Policy

Morocco's foreign policy like that of other countries is determined by her natural affinities, modified by considerations of what is in fact practicable and possible. Natural affinity binds Morocco closely to the other North African countries and less directly to the eastern Arab states and the Muslim world in general. Inevitably the effect of the Algerian question on Moroccan relations with France was the most pressing problem of the country's foreign policy. Though not so directly involved as Tunisia, Morocco could not be indifferent to the struggle for independence of a sister North African and Muslim country. In spite of this difficulty she nevertheless managed to maintain friendly diplomatic relations with France (except at the moment of the arrest of the five Algerian leaders), and not to give offence by ostentatious displays of aid to Algerian nationalism. This did not, however, mean that Moroccan public opinion was not profoundly disturbed by the continuance of the fighting; for it was bound to provoke increasing anxiety and to exacerbate the situation to a point where it became a danger for the whole of North Africa. These considerations were the determining factor in various negotiations with Tunisia and with the FLN; these culminated in the offer of good services jointly made by King Mohammed and President Bourguiba at the end of 1957.

During the same period Morocco adopted a cautious attitude towards the Arab League. Not only did she postpone adherence, but she was also careful not to become involved in the quarrels of the existing members. Steps towards achieving the unity of the North African countries, which were to make a notable advance at the Conference of Tangier in April 1958, both held out hope of increasing the power of resistance of the three countries towards French domination and also had the secondary advantage of creating a western group strong enough to treat on terms of equality with the Arab groups of the east.

The statement that Moroccan policy has to take into consideration what is practical and possible implies that account has to be taken of the extent of technical and cultural assistance which the young state has been receiving from France and which it would have been very hard to do without or to replace at short notice. Inevitably relations between the former protecting power and the former ward have been delicate and difficult. This was more because certain traces of the former

protectorate status had not yet been eliminated, and because
the Algerian war kept alive the fear of an imperialist counter-
attack, than because of any resentment from the past on the
part of the Moroccan *élite* or of any lack of appreciation of
certain cultural and intellectual values of which France has
been the chief exponent in the world. But in some quarters
there was apparent the fear that an attempt might be made to
regain in the economic and perhaps in the cultural field those
positions which had been lost politically, and so establish a
type of 'neo-colonialism'. The possibility of such a development
in Moroccan-French relations is certainly present also in the
thinking of the Spanish Government; and the idea that Spanish
withdrawals might lead to the extension of French influence in
zones where Spanish influence was before predominant has
sometimes acted as a brake on Spanish readiness to meet
Moroccan desires for the elimination of the remaining traces of
the Spanish protectorate.

Two years after independence, the other most pressing
problems were the continued presence of foreign troops and the
delimitation of the frontiers. Both of them affect Spain as well
as France. The strained relations between the two former protecting powers and their disagreement with regard to Moroccan
policy in 1953 were factors which facilitated the task first of the
nationalist movement and then of the diplomacy of independent Morocco. The approximation of the French and
Spanish points of view which was indicated by the meeting of
the Foreign Ministers of the two countries in San Sebastian in
the summer of 1957, and later by a similarity of views and
action with regard to events at Ifni and in the Sahara, was a
cause of anxiety to the Moroccan Government which was
fully aware of the difficulties which concerted Franco-Spanish
action could create for it.

The continued presence of French troops in Morocco was
bound up with the desire of the French Government to maintain military bases in the country, but was also regarded by a
section of French opinion as important for another reason. The
incidents at Meknes at the end of 1956, which resulted from the
arrest of the five Algerian leaders and led to the death of a
number of French residents, created a sense of insecurity
among their compatriots which tended to make them look on
the continued presence of French troops as a guarantee of their
security, though in fact the opposite could be argued and in any
case troops were not present in adequate numbers for their
defence. As far as the French Government was concerned, it
would probably have been satisfied if it could have reached an

arrangement for the maintenance of bases, primarily for naval and air purposes. This, however, it wished to make a condition of withdrawal, while the Moroccan Government regarded the latter action as the preliminary to free negotiations.

The formula 'evacuation of foreign troops' applies not only to the French and Spanish garrisons but also to the American naval and air bases which were established under the protectorate. While not recognizing the validity of the latter concession, the Moroccan Government has not refused to negotiate on the subject. Conducted in a desultory manner, and no doubt brought into relation with the question of American financial aid, these negotiations had not resulted in an agreement by November 1958, though talks had begun months earlier. This did not, however, prevent Moroccan relations with the United States from being very friendly and further strengthened by the visit made by King Mohammed to America at the end of 1956. It was, however, also an undoubted fact that the doctrine of neutralism preached by India, and later adopted by Egypt, had gained some ground with Moroccan public opinion.

Since Morocco's land frontiers had never been clearly defined on the east and still less in the south (p. 75), it was never doubted that some adjustment would be necessary. The question acquired much greater importance, however, when the Istiqlal leader, Allal al-Fasi, put forward a claim to what he described as 'Morocco's natural and historical frontiers', meaning by this the inclusion in Morocco of the western Sahara as far as the Senegal river. After considerable hesitations, this point of view was officially adopted by the Moroccan Government and supported by the King himself towards the end of 1957.

This claim, besides affecting France in Mauritania, affects Spain in the Spanish Sahara. This question is treated in detail in the section on Spanish West Africa (p. 197). Here it should perhaps be noted that though the Moroccan Government did not raise any simultaneous claim to the Spanish territories (the *presidios*) in the north, it did not think fit to establish consulates in either Ceuta or Melilla, an action which would have implied official recognition of Spanish sovereignty over those cities.

Political Life and Parties

The political life of contemporary Morocco has original and complex characteristics which cannot be fitted into any of the existing categories of twentieth-century political science. Morocco cannot be called a democracy, since all power is legally concentrated in the hands of the King. But neither is it an absolute monarchy since political parties play a significant role. Nor is it a dictatorship since it is not a one-party régime. A specialist in constitutional law has suggested that it might be called the 'régime of a dominant party'.

The party concerned is of course the Istiqlal or Independence Party, the heir and successor of *al-Hizb al-Watani*, or National Party, of 1937. It is opposed by the PDI, itself the heir of *al-Harakat al-Qaumiya* which was formed by secession in 1937.

There was little difference in the attitude of the two parties during the crisis of 1953–5. The Residency did indeed try to play the PDI off against the Istiqlal, but in order to succeed it would have had to grant to the former precisely what it would not grant the latter. Both parties had clandestine branches which employed violence. Both were represented in the Army of Liberation. While they both participated in the first Government of Premier Bekkai, formed on the return of Mohammed V, the PDI had no share in the second which was formed in November 1956. Since then the PDI has been in opposition, while the Istiqlal, after the formation of a new cabinet in May 1958, formed the Government. The two big parties attack one another vigorously in the press and at public meetings. Like all opposition parties, the PDI is not always able to resist the temptation to go one better than the Government. It is, however, hard to find any real difference of doctrine or of programme between them. At most, it can be said that the PDI, like the independents and minor parties, puts greater stress on democratic liberties, while the Istiqlal insists on the need for national discipline and a strong state. But it would be a mistake to conclude that one party is democratic and the other totalitarian. If they were to change places, no doubt they would change their language also, as is the habit of governments and oppositions in all countries and ages.

There is no means of estimating the number of adherents of either party, though the Istiqlal is obviously far the more numerous. The entry of the PDI into opposition at the end of 1956 brought it a number of new adherents, but this tendency seemed rapidly to reach its limit. The Istiqlal on the other hand has an expansive quality derived from the number and quality of its members, and from its organization. The party is structurally strong, with cells at the base, regional councils in the middle, and a National Council at the summit. The secrecy in which it had to exist during the years from 1937 to 1946 and again from 1952 to 1955 resulted in the organization becoming more supple as well as stronger. Originally a party of middle-class intellectuals, from 1947 onwards it became increasingly a party of the people also, capable of mobilizing the urban masses and exercising an effective influence in the country districts.

In the latter direction, however, it still has its limits and its potential rivals. Its action is limited partly by rural particularism, partly by the difficulty which town dwellers have in making themselves understood by peasantry, and partly by the suspicions of the tribal authorities whose inveterate tendency to mistrust the towns has not altogether been removed even by the renovation brought about by the liberation. For this reason the tribal masses remain outside political life, though the more mixed and more responsive city population and also the smaller centres have been won over. Stirred for a moment out of their habitual apathy by the great crises of 1953-5, the rural masses seem to have fallen back into indifference, entirely absorbed in the problem of winning their daily bread. It may be that here there is a position to be occupied and scope for political activity on rather different lines. This seems to have been the view of Ahardan, a former officer in the French army and Governor of Rabat province, who in the summer of 1957 took a prominent part in trying to create a new popular party. This was forbidden and when the Governor protested he was dismissed on the grounds that serving officials should keep clear of political activities. Discontent in certain Berber areas, notably the Rif, gave rise to incidents towards the end of 1958. Meanwhile legislation to regulate associations and political parties was finally issued in November 1958.

The Istiqlal and the PDI are not the only parties in Morocco. The Party of Independent Liberals provided two ministers, Rashid Moulin, Minister of State, and Rida Guedira, Minister of Information, in the second Government. This is a party of middle-class intellectuals, much attached to liberal ideas on the one hand and to the person of the King on the other. The Unity and Independence Party of Mekki Nasiri has a membership limited to Tangier and the northern zone. The former Reform Party (*Hizb al-Islah*) of Abdel Khalek Torres used to be the counterpart in the northern zone of the Istiqlal in the south; and since the independence it has fused with the latter. The Moroccan Communist Party was at one time exceptional in containing both European and Moroccan adherents. Its tactics were those of Communist parties everywhere—unconditional support for nationalist movements, and an attempt to form a common front of all those who oppose 'colonialism'. Its offers of co-operation were, however, always met with reserve on the part of the nationalists whose general staff and the mass of whose adherents were very hostile to Communism. The Moroccan Communist Party has no newspaper and cannot indulge in public manifestations, and at the moment its influence cannot be measured by the number of its adherents. It works by spreading slogans and by exploiting the economic difficulties of the masses, with whom it keeps in close touch. There is no doubt that Marxist theories exert a certain power of attraction on a growing number of students and young intellectuals, though this cannot be attributed to the action of the party as such.

Among the political forces of the new Morocco, King Mohammed V remains the prime factor. After 1947, and above all after 1953–5, he personified the national struggle for independence. His prestige achieved legendary proportions and he became the idol of an entire people. If the exaltation of the 'Glorious Three Days' of the return could not be entirely maintained, yet the authority and prestige of the Sovereign has persisted. His wisdom and political sense make him an arbitrator whose voice is always heard. None of those who do not share his point of view dared to come out in the open during the first two years of independence. When the constitution finally appears in the form of a legal text, there can be no doubt that the weight of his personality will be reflected in it. If there are republican tendencies anywhere in Morocco, it is unlikely that they will prevail as long as Mohammed V is on the throne.

SOCIAL CONDITIONS [1]

Health

There was a time when Arab civilization was famous for the study and practice of medicine; and until today bearers of Arab names such as Ibn Sina (Avicenna) are still honoured beside Hippocrates and Galen as heroes of the medical art of the past. This tradition was, however, lost; in the nineteenth century medicine was not even a subject of study in the venerable Qarawiyin university mosque in Fez, capital of the country which was formerly the home of the famous Ibn Rushd (Averroës), at once physician, mathematician, and philosopher. At the time of the European occupation, Morocco did not possess a single doctor in the modern sense of the word. The mass of the people, believing that disorders of the body were primarily due to supernatural causes, such as possession by evil spirits or the influence of the evil eye, had resort to magico-religious rites, of which black slaves or ex-slaves were the chief exponents and in

[1] Excluding northern provinces.

which the influence of beliefs and practices from south of the Sahara were very obvious. Only the imperial court and the notables of certain towns such as Tangier were able to call on the services of trained doctors.

In the work of modernization undertaken by the protectorate, medicine was expected to play a leading part. The first Resident General, Marshal Lyautey, thought of 'pacification' as primarily a political task in which force should be used as little as possible. For reasons of policy, therefore, as well as of humanity, he relied largely on the benefits of medical science to gain the sympathy of the populations which were to be brought under control; one doctor, he was fond of declaring, was worth as much to him as several battalions. In addition to the duty of looking after the health of the troops in the field, army doctors were expected to give consultations in the villages and markets, to deal with epidemics, and to vaccinate the villagers. As the frontiers of uncontrolled country receded, civilian doctors took over from their army colleagues. These services, being intended for the necessitous, whose goodwill it was sought to gain, consultations of this nature as well as treatment in dispensaries and hospitals were given free. This has remained the case until today.

Since independence the Directorate of Public Health and of the Family has been transformed into the Ministry of Health. Its three divisions deal with curative and preventive medicine, and with administration. Each province and municipal area has at its head a Doctor in Charge, assisted by one or more doctors responsible for preventive medicine and by a senior woman social assistant. In 1957 the budget of the Ministry amounted to 7,522 million francs, as opposed to 1,794 million in 1950. The increase corresponded to the budgetary increase in general and was due in part to the construction during the last few years of several big new hospitals, the cost of maintaining which has now reached the maximum.

The hospital services dispose of 16,873 beds; of which 2,319 are intended for surgical, 2,757 for tubercular, 1,353 for ophthalmological, and 2,023 for psychiatrical cases. Naturally, the towns are better supplied than the country; while the rural population forms 80 per cent. of the total, the beds available in rural areas amount to 2,437 compared with 2,462 in the cities.

The total number of doctors in the health service and in private practice amounts to about 1,200 in all Morocco, including 72 in the former northern zone. They are, however, very unequally distributed, particularly in the case of the doctors in private practice; these are in fact to be found only in the towns. One city, Casablanca, has 300 doctors. The rural districts are thus compelled to rely entirely on the doctors of the Public Health service; these numbered 398 at the end of 1957, while 30 new posts were to be created in 1958. The official objective was to provide one public health doctor for every 10,000 inhabitants.

The overwhelming majority of doctors in Morocco are still Europeans and the number of sixty to seventy Moroccans practising the art of medicine has actually been reduced since independence, because some of them have been taken to fill political, administrative, or diplomatic posts. It is, however, to be noted that students of medicine form the largest group of young people now taking higher studies.

The activity of the Ministry of Health is directed as much to the prevention of disease as to its cure. Among a population which is still largely ignorant of the elementary rules of hygiene, the former task assumes great importance. Special campaigns have been undertaken to deal with prevalent complaints such as eye-disease, malaria, tuberculosis, and venereal disease; and also with epidemics of which three—smallpox, tuberculosis, and diphtheria—can be controlled by vaccination. In these campaigns Morocco has been helped by the World Health Organization and by the United Nations Infant Welfare Fund.

In the field of social assistance Centres for the Protection of Mothers and Infants take charge of expectant mothers during pregnancy and childbirth, and give instruction in the care of health to married women and girls. There is also a special health service for schools and universities, and a corps of female social assistants who work among the poorer classes.

A great effort has been made to provide an adequate material basis for the health services. This has come up against two obstacles, one financial and the other human. The former is the fact that money can only be found for them at the expense of capital investment; the second a lack of staff which makes itself felt not so much in the category of doctors as in that of nurses, social assistants, and laboratory personnel; this latter problem is, of course, only one aspect of the more general problem of education.

Education

As in all underdeveloped countries, the problem of illiteracy is very great. There are estimated to be about 1½ million children of school age. Of these, 287,000 were actually receiving education in 1955, 204,000 being boys and 83,000 girls. Of them 40,000 were Jewish (equally divided between boys and girls); a figure which means that the entire Jewish child population was receiving education. This result was due to the efforts of the *Alliance Israélite Universelle*, founded in Paris under the Second Empire; this had already opened schools in Morocco before the protectorate and has since taken almost complete charge of the education of young Jews, with the help of important subsidies from the Government.

The work of the protectorate in the field of education was violently criticized by the nationalists, while the French authorities claimed that their action was highly creditable. The latter emphasized that what existed had been created out of nothing; while the former were moved by the consideration that even in the later years of the protectorate, when the annual increase in the numbers of children receiving education amounted to 15,000–20,000, this was only just sufficient to maintain the percentage of children receiving education at the existing very low level, without holding out any hope of improvement. While it is no doubt too soon to express a final judgement, certain factors have to be taken into consideration. The French educational authorities, for example, always gave great importance to the quality of education; the fact that studies were of the same length and of the same standards as in France had the effect of excluding a rapid and extensive increase in the numbers taught. While money was one limiting factor, lack of teachers was even more serious. These could not all be supplied by France, and for a long time the educated youth of Morocco was more attracted to careers other than that of teaching. One aspect of nationalist criticism, however, which appeared of undoubted validity was the fact that such an immense task could not be carried through without the enthusiastic co-operation of the people as a whole, and that such enthusiasm could not be generated under the protectorate régime or without the stimulus of independence.

In fact a private system of Muslim education, inspired by national sentiment, came into being under the protectorate; it was regarded with considerable suspicion by the authorities, who completely ignored it in official reports and kept it from the notice of foreign visitors. Before the Second World War permission was secured from the Residency for the establishment of such schools and several were founded in which the same programme of instruction was followed as in the government schools, though instruction was in general given through Arabic instead of French. The most important of these institutions was the Guessous College at Rabat, directed by Ahmed Balafrej, afterwards first Foreign Minister, and in 1958 Prime Minister, of independent Morocco.

From 1943, with the active encouragement of the Sultan, many such private schools were established throughout the country. The buildings were erected with funds raised by voluntary subscriptions, but having little official support fees were charged to contribute towards the cost of salaries and maintenance. These were, however, often inadequate and led to the transference of certain schools to the Directorate of Education, while others were assisted by a small government subsidy. The schools often had a markedly political tone, mostly being of Istiqlal inspiration, while a few were of PDI allegiance. They prepared for an Arab diploma, parallel to the primary Franco-Arab diploma. The Mohammed V College at Rabat created a secondary education in Arabic, with syllabuses similar to those of the corresponding protectorate schools.

With the coming of independence these schools kept their private character, but received more generous government assistance. At the beginning of 1958 they contained 72,000 pupils, equal to more than a quarter of the total number of pupils in the former protectorate schools; 42,000 were boys and 30,000 girls, the percentage of the latter being much higher than in the protectorate schools. This educational venture was one of the most constructive achievements of any Arab country under foreign control.

The effect of patriotic stimulus was shown clearly during the first two years of independence. School attendance rose from 287,000 in 1955 to 415,000 in 1956 and to 625,000 in November 1957, apart from 38,000 in the northern zone. These figures are impressive, even if it be true that they have involved giving every teacher far more pupils than is normal in a class, as well as creating half-time classes, and engaging teachers with only rudimentary qualifications. The authorities are perfectly aware of the dangers of such conditions, but they hold that attendance at school has the great social advantage of taking children off the streets; that it is essential to profit from the enthusiasm which independence has created before it dies away; and that the quality of the teaching can be progressively raised.

One great weakness was the insufficiency of technical training. Out of the total of 32,000 Muslims in secondary schools, there are no more than 10,000 Muslims in technical schools, of whom only 1,600 (as opposed to 4,000 French) are in the secondary stage. Even if we add to this a few schools which do not come under the Ministry of Education, such as the School of Agriculture, the number is quite insufficient. The explanation of the fact is probably to be found in a traditional outlook towards study which has not yet entirely disappeared from the more backward parts of Europe. Science and culture were regarded as being something quite apart from man's economic activities or the practice of a craft. They applied only to the abstract world of the intelligence and had no connexion with the task of gaining a living. Hitherto the Moroccan young man who regards himself as educated has generally been unwilling to adopt a way of life which involves working with his hands; and in this he has the sympathy and support of his parents. The Government which was formed in May 1958 has included the extension of technical education as a major item in its programmes.

A cultural convention signed by France and Morocco authorizes the former to maintain a 'cultural and university mission' in Morocco in order to provide instruction for French children and adolescents; to this, however, all classes of the Moroccan population can also be admitted. Until the mission should be able to construct the buildings which it needed, the Moroccan Government ceded it the use of eight establishments of European secondary education, situated in Rabat, Casablanca, Marrakesh, Meknes, Fez, Ujda, and Tangier, and also a certain number of primary schools. In November 1957 this French mission was providing instruction for 9,045 secondary students of whom 2,261 were Moroccans, Muslims, and Jews in equal proportion, and for 38,431 primary students of whom 5,337 were Moroccan Muslims and 2,654 Moroccan Jews.

Not all French students are looked after by the mission. The Moroccan Ministry of National Education maintains a 'European' section at both the primary and secondary stages. Under the terms of the convention, its syllabus is the same as that in the corresponding establishments in France and the courses are open to all, whether they are Europeans or Moroccans.

This implies that there were in 1958 8,997 French students in Moroccan secondary and 12,737 in Moroccan primary schools. There are also a certain number of European children in private schools, mostly Catholic, to which Muslims are also admitted.

A traditional form of higher education is given in the ancient and famous Qarawiyin University of Fez, and in the Yusufiya College at Marrakesh. These establishments give education at all levels, and there are about 300 students in the highest grade. Young Moroccans who wanted higher education on modern lines were, until independence, obliged to seek it abroad,

I

principally in France. In this they were assisted by a liberal distribution of scholarships. In 1957 there were some 400 Moroccan students in France, 250 in the Middle East (Egypt, Syria, Iraq, and Kuwait), 20 in German-speaking countries (Germany, Austria, and Switzerland), 10 in Great Britain, and 10 in the United States. In Morocco itself three institutions which were originally designed for scientific research only have been gradually transformed into establishments of higher education, more particularly since 1940. These are the *Institut des Hautes Études Marocaines* (arts); the *Centre d'Études Juridiques* and the *Centre d'Études Supérieures Scientifiques*; they prepare for French higher diplomas. About 300 Moroccan students are enrolled in them.

In December 1957 three establishments were constituted—Faculties of Letters, Law, and Science—and a Moroccan University was inaugurated with due solemnity. This continues to prepare for French degrees with the assistance of French professors; but a Moroccan degree of Moroccan law has also been established, which can be taken in French and Arabic, or in Arabic only. An Arabic degree will certainly also be constituted for arts. In the field of science, the use of Arabic is impossible in the immediate future, and French will no doubt remain the language of instruction for a considerable time.

The problem of language affects education at all stages, and not only in the higher ranges. Modern education as organized under the protectorate was given almost entirely with French as the language of instruction. In the form of primary instruction, known as Franco-Musulman, 20 hours weekly (out of 30) were devoted to instruction with French as the medium of instruction (French language, science, and geography) and 10 hours to teaching with Arabic as the language of instruction (Arabic language, religion, history). In secondary colleges teaching was given entirely in French, including the period given to the study of Arabic. The time devoted to the latter subject was considerable in the earlier stages but diminished as the student approached his final examinations for which the syllabus was the same as in France.

This process of de-arabization was a basic grievance in nationalist criticism of education under the French protectorate. The independent Government, as was to be expected, proclaimed Arabic as the national language and began to introduce Arabic as the language of instruction. The governing class, however, had no intention of cutting the country off from western culture. French retained an extensive place in primary instruction; the former proportion was simply reversed, so that there are now 20 hours in Arabic and 10 in French during the first year, or 15 of each in the later years of the primary first two years. In secondary education the reform has so far only affected the first year, 13 hours out of a total of 33 being devoted to Arabic. These measures were provisional and do not mean that further adjustments will not be made. For the moment, however, the further process of arabization is hindered by the lack of teaching staff.

The Press and Broadcasting

Under the protectorate a considerable number of French and Arabic papers came into existence. The press code was liberal in theory but the state of siege, originally justified on grounds of insecurity, then continued through the war, and never terminated, made it possible in practice to suspend or suppress papers at will. The nationalist papers, of which the first began to appear after the issue of the Berber *Dahir*, were often suppressed and suffered long periods of eclipse.

Eighteen months after the end of the protectorate, the French-language papers remained the same as before and with the same staff, though ownership had changed as had the policy followed. They now avoided political comment, limiting themselves to information, for which they were read as much by the Moroccan as by the French public. For political comment, French residents relied on papers from France which arrived by air a few hours after their publication while Moroccans depended on the Moroccan national press in Arabic and French. At the beginning of 1958 the Arab press included two principal dailies: *al-Alam* (The Standard), the organ of the Istiqlal Party, and *al-Rai al-Am* (Public Opinion), the organ of the PDI. The latter was suppressed a little later in the year. *al-Alam* was the most widely studied, its public not being confined to the literate. Those who cannot read had it read to them and, in so far as they failed to understand journalistic Arabic, explained to them by others. During the troubled times which preceded independence it was quite common to see a circle of listeners in the popular quarters seated around a public newspaper reader whom they remunerated with a small sum. The UMT has a weekly, *al-Talia* (The Vanguard).

Each of the two parties publishes also a weekly in French intended to reach the French and general European public, but also read by the Moroccan educated classes. The Istiqlal weekly is called *L'Istiqlal* (*Indépendence*) and that of the PDI *Démocratie*. The contributors include French as well as Moroccans. The radio has a far wider appeal, the habit of radio listening having become very widely spread during the crisis when the nationalist papers were forbidden. Cairo, the BBC, and an Arabic broadcast from Budapest were the transmissions most listened to. The women, in particular, who went out very little and were often illiterate, had a passion for this means of information which brought the echoes of the outer world to them in their homes. The importance of the radio in a country like Morocco is something difficult for the untravelled European to realize. It is not only an instrument for the propagation of ideas but also of education in general. Understanding this very well the new rulers of Morocco gave great attention to the Moroccan National Radio which has both Arabic and French transmissions, and also minor services in Spanish and English. While transmissions were given in Moroccan dialectal Arabic and in Berber, in order to reach all sections of the nation, the majority of transmissions were in standard modern Arabic which made the radio a factor of first importance in spreading a knowledge of the Arabic language as it is understood throughout the Arab world.

ECONOMIC CONDITIONS

Agriculture

Agriculture is the country's principal resource, and the basic activity of the Moroccan population. If we adopt the classic division into primary, secondary, and tertiary activities, then primary activities, meaning production through agriculture and mining, occupy 72 per cent. of the population; this figure is equal to that of Egypt and compares with 36 per cent. in France and 16 per cent. in the United States. Agricultural income represents more than 40 per cent. of the national revenue. In exports agriculture leads with 39·8 per cent., followed by mining with 32·3 per cent., and by the products of industry and the crafts with 27·4 per cent.

Mountains and arid zones occupy much of the area of the country. Cultivated land, which is of the order of 12½ million acres, is worked by about a million people. Though this figure looks satisfactory, it is misleading since many estates are large and the majority of cultivators have insufficient land.

In Morocco two distinct types of agriculture exist side by side: one is agriculture of a modern type, as practised by the European settlers and by a certain number of Moroccan land-owners. This is a mechanized agriculture which uses the rotation of crops and mineral fertilizers, and forms part of an exchange economy. The other is archaic, with highly subdivided holdings partly individual and partly collective; it knows nothing of the rotation of crops or of artificial fertilizers but relies almost entirely on the cultivation of cereals. It is a subsistence agriculture, producing no income and yielding very poor crops of not more than 6 quintals[1] of hard wheat per acre.

European colonization, which is eight-ninths French, controls 4,000 farms or about 1½ million acres of cultivated land. It is located principally in the Atlantic plains of the Gharb, Chaouia, Doukkala, Abda, the environs of Fez and Meknes, and the valley of the Sus; little land is devoted to cereals (2·6 per cent. of the total barley and 13 per cent. of the total hard wheat). On the other hand, it produces 85 per cent. of the total citrus, 80 per cent. of the total tobacco, and 75 per cent. of the total grape crop. Half of the farms have from 250 to 1,250 acres.

Traditional agriculture, practised on nine-tenths of the cultivated land, is almost completely at the mercy of natural conditions. The soils are very varied, ranging from light sandy soils (*rmel*) to strong dark clayey soils (*tirs*), passing through pebbly (*harrouchas*), sticky (*dess*), and red (*hamri*) soils. Though the fertility of certain soils is remarkable, particularly the *tirs*, rainfall is the determining factor in agricultural production, not so much by its quantity as by its distribution through the seasons. For in Morocco rainfall is irregular and if rain comes too late the wooden ploughs of the fellahin cannot penetrate the soil, hardened by four or five months of summer dryness, and they are not able to plough at the proper time. There are drying winds, such as the sirocco or *shergui*, which are particularly deadly in those areas which are far from the coast. Lastly there is that ancient plague, the locust, which can consume the entire vegetation at the spot where its hordes settle. Fortunately modern anti-locust services possess powerful and efficient means of dealing with them.

In comparison with other North African countries, Morocco is blessed with a wealth of surface and subsoil water, and with reserves formed by the snows which fall in the high mountains in the winter. At the foot of the mountain masses the water which springs from the valleys is utilized by means of little channels (*seguia*); when the water-table is not far below the surface, it is also possible to dig wells and pump very economically. The Moroccan peasant has always shown ingenuity in making use of water resources, as is proved by the methods of irrigating the palm groves and the valleys of the High Atlas. The *ghettara* of Marrakesh and the *foggara* of Tafilalet are more remarkable still; they are subterranean channels which lead

[1] The French hundredweight (quintal) equals 100 kilos.

the waters to the surface after a long journey down a slope less steep than that of the ground above; their flow remains approximately the same in summer and winter. Relatively, however, irrigated land is not very extensive. The greater part of the surface is dry (*bour*), entirely at the mercy of climatic risks, particularly in the southern half of the country.

During the last twenty-five years immense works have been constructed to capture and utilize the waters which pour from the Atlas; for example, the great dam at Bin al-Widan (Ouidane) whose cement wall is more than 300 feet high and creates a lake as large as the Lake of Annecy, supplying electric power and making it possible to create irrigated perimeters, with an effectively cultivated area of 90,000 acres. The area affected by the work, in its present state, is 167,000 acres while the area theoretically irrigable amounts to nearly a million.

Methods of land tenure are not as different from those of Europe as might have been expected. Apart from direct exploitation by the owner, the fellahin largely work on contracts of partnership. The practice varies from region to region and from tribe to tribe. The commonest form of contract is the *khammes* (fifth part); the owner provides the land and the seed, sometimes the tools also; the *khammes* provides the labour and receives one-fifth of the produce. But the term *khammes* covers also contracts under which the proprietor gives more, sometimes as much as a third or a half. The fact remains, however, that in most cases the *khammes* does not make enough to provide a decent living—on an average, less than £30 per year and per person. In case of drought he has nothing to eat and has no alternative but to leave and swell the numbers of the urban proletariat.

Native agriculture produces chiefly cereals. Barley, an inferior cereal, predominates: in 1955 15½ million quintals were produced as against 6½ millions of hard, and 3½ of soft, wheat. In 1958, which was a year of good crops, 755,000 tons of wheat were reported; in 1957 only 160,000. The export of fresh vegetables amounted to 85,000 tons in 1956 and to 88,000 in 1957.

The rearing of stock also holds an important place in Moroccan economy. Goats and sheep predominate, amounting to 20 million head out of a total of about 25 million. Sheep abound everywhere and form the sole capital in the high plateaux and the Berber mountains. In the Middle Atlas and the central High Atlas entire tribes devote themselves almost exclusively to sheep rearing; they are migratory, moving from lower to higher pastures and vice versa. But any increase of cultivation in the lower zones reduces the area available for pasturage and can make migration impossible. The higher pastures then become overcrowded. The only remedy for this is the cultivation of fodder. At present this is quite insufficient, not more than 50,000–60,000 acres being devoted to it. As a result the meat supply is barely adequate. Drought produces a catastrophic mortality among the animals; in particularly bad years some regions may see their flocks reduced by nine-tenths.

Various measures have been taken to remedy the insufficiency of Moroccan agriculture and to meet the rapid growth of the population. Increasing the cultivated area is a process which cannot be continued indefinitely and it is therefore on productivity that efforts have been concentrated. In a dry climate, irrigation is evidently one of the most hopeful means. The big dams mentioned above have made possible the irrigation of large areas. Below Bin al-Widane in the Tadla there has been created the irrigated perimeter of Beni Amer Moussa, managed by a special office. The peasants are not free to cultivate what they like or how they like. The Office imposes a rotation of crops; and the arrangements of the lots, formed so as to constitute wide lands of homogeneous crops, makes mechanized cultivation possible and also the growing of commercial crops such as cotton.

Though all the water which flows from the Atlas has not so far been utilized, a number of reasons (of which finance is not the least) make it impossible to continue development at the same rate. It is more important, and less costly, to modernize the traditional methods of agriculture. Benevolent societies with the loan of selected seeds and various types of co-operatives such as joint oil mills have done something to improve the peasant's lot. In 1945 the protectorate made a great effort with the *Secteurs de Modernisation du Paysannat* which gave rise to great hopes. In view of their limited number, however, their chief value in the end was as models. A great difficulty for the Moroccan fellah is that his minute income does not permit him to modernize his equipment. He must therefore have state help. In autumn 1957 the independent Moroccan Government organized what the papers named 'operation ploughing'. A thousand tractors ploughed or were to plough 375,000 acres, on which artificial manure was to be applied and the exploitation be compulsorily divided into two rotations, one for cereals and one for a root break.

There is a double obstacle to rational cultivation. One aspect is the subdivision of land holdings. This can only be remedied by reassembling; this is a complicated and lengthy process. The other is the inherited mentality of the peasants, which is perhaps most important of all. It is no good saying that it is the fault of ignorance. There is a second problem behind it. The inhabitants of the Moroccan plains are not an old-established sedentary population with deeply-rooted peasant traditions like those who are found, for example, in the western High Atlas. They are for the most part former nomads whose migration has been gradually limited and who now combine agriculture with the rearing of animals. Their hereditary disposition indisposes them to become real peasants. There have thus been great difficulties with the Beni Amer, semi-nomads of the Tadla region, whom it was sought to convert suddenly into workers on irrigated land. Sometimes they watered so thoroughly that they 'scoured' their land and made it sterile. The primary problem is to instruct, organize, and advise these rural masses. It is thus a problem of providing staff—and that is the problem which meets us in the new Morocco at every turn.

Industry and Mines

The legal basis of mining was governed until 1929 by the liberal principle of attributing each mining location to the first properly registered applicant. This principle, however, already suffered a great derogation by Lyautey's creation in 1920 of the Sharifian Phosphates Office. At the end of 1928 a special organization called the *Bureau de Recherches et de Participations Minières* was created to specialize in the study of mineral resources of first importance and to participate in enterprises of extraction which called for financial and technical assistance from the state. The collaboration of public and private interests gave a considerable impulse to the Moroccan mining industry which has since become the principal wealth of the country after agriculture.

The great phosphate deposits of Khouribga and of Louis Gentil saw their output rise by 220,000 tons in the one year 1955–6. During the first three-quarters of 1957 output reached $4\frac{1}{2}$ million tons. The importance of phosphates to the Moroccan economy is considerable; they constitute the largest tonnage item in the exports from Casablanca, they are the reason for the existence of the port of Safi; they ensure the profitability of the railway administration; they are the largest clients of electric energy, and the principal providers of foreign exchange for the Moroccan treasury.

Eastern Morocco, formerly a poor relation among the various regions, is on the way to becoming one of the richest of them, thanks to its deposits of coal, lead, and zinc. The anthracite deposits at Djerada produced 381,000 tons in the first nine months of 1957. Reserves are estimated at approximately 100 million tons. The lead of Zellija and of Touissit, near the Algerian frontier, exploited by the most modern means, together with various mines in the Atlas, furnished 76,500 tons of concentrate for export in the first three-quarters of 1957.

The Moroccan subsoil also produces metallurgic manganese with an export of 258,000 tons, cobalt with 2,820, iron with 395,000, and zinc with 68,600.

Oil has been found in the Gharb near Port Lyautey and Petit Jean. A refinery for catalytic cracking was established at Petit Jean some years ago. The production of crude oil is about 100,000 tons annually. Prospecting continues and has been extended to the Mogador area where borings have been begun.

Insufficiency of natural sources of energy is a weak point in Morocco's economy. The three primary sources—coal, oil, and water, are only sufficient to cover about one-half the energy needs—13·2 per cent. through coal, 7·8 per cent. through oil, and 27·4 per cent. through hydro-electric power. Thanks to a very considerable effort in providing hydro-electric equipment during the last few years the former French zone of Morocco now has a productivity of 1,300 million kilowatt hours, which will enable it to supply requirements for some years. But these are expected to double in a decade; and on account of the large investments necessary this energy is expensive.

This lack constitutes a serious handicap for Moroccan industry which provides one-third of the national income, a proportion almost equal to that of agriculture. Since January 1956 and the coming of independence, building and public works have suffered from a severe recession involving a 20 per cent. reduction in labour, owing to the cessation of foreign investments. The processing industries on the other hand have more or less maintained the level of preceding years.

Moroccan industry can be considered in two categories. The first is composed of industries complementary to the natural resources. Some of these produce for the internal market, such as those which treat cereals—flour mills, macaroni products; milk products, which are concerned with only 5 per cent. of the total milk output; tinned meat (60,000 quintals); shoes (1 million leather pairs); cement and building material (700,000 tons of cement in 1956); chemical industries (superphosphates); steelworks and foundries (500 tons at Skrirat near Rabat). Others produce principally for export; canned fish (9 milliard francs' worth in 1956); vegetables and fruit juice; leather and skins (over 1 milliard francs' worth); vegetable fibre (73,000 tons, worth 2 milliard francs); cork (3 milliard francs); cellulose (Gharb factory, 15,000 tons of paste anticipated in 1958); aromatic plants (450 tons treated in 1956); treated mining products (Pena Pennaroya Zellija foundry); in 1956 26,700 tons of soft lead and 21 tons of silver.

The second category are industries using imported raw materials with a view to satisfying local needs. The Casablanca sugar refinery produced 210,000 tons in 1956, out of a local consumption of 300,000. There are 10 refineries for cooking oils; these have a capacity of 100,000 tons, of which only one-fifth is of local origin. In 1956 the 10 soap factories produced 24,000 tons. The needs of Morocco in manufactured textiles amount to 43,500 tons, of which local industry only supplies 25 per cent., though it represents an investment of 8 milliards and employs 8,600 workers; the protective tariff which this industry was granted in 1957 give it hope of important development. A few metal industries manufactured principally packings such as tins for conserves. A sulphuric acid factory may also be mentioned (20,000 tons in 1956); 3 glass works (7,100 tons in 1956); a paper and cardboard industry (28,500 tons); 2 wax vesta factories; and 3 tobacco factories which process nearly 4,000 tons annually.

Two features are typical of Moroccan industry. One is the primary importance of foreign participation, both in capital and staff; the other the concentration of industrial establishments in Casablanca and its annexe, Fedala.

Under the protectorate another characteristic was the absence of protective tariffs, resulting from the Act of Algeciras. Morocco has now recovered her liberty in this respect and the régime of the 'open door' is a thing of the past.

Labour and Trade Unions

As we have seen, the greater part of the Moroccan population is occupied in agriculture. A few work on large estates, but the mass is formed of fellahin with small holdings or working as khammes.

Secondary activities occupy 18 per cent. of the working population, as compared with 8·5 per cent. in Egypt, 33 per cent. in France, and 27 per cent. in the United States. Labour in industry, mines, building, and public works is estimated at 250,000 wage-earners (excluding the ex-Spanish zone); 70,000 are employed in processing industries.

In the higher posts staff are almost all Europeans, overwhelmingly French. There are still very few Moroccan engineers, since Moroccan intellectuals have not hitherto been much attracted by scientific studies apart from medicine. Moroccan business men are still unwilling to embark on activities whose technique is unfamiliar to them and they are only found at the head of enterprises which are not too remote from those traditional in Morocco, such as flour-milling, oil-pressing, or refineries and tanning. Foremen and skilled workmen are also for the most part European and very often Spanish. Education for the masses is quite inadequate, and it is almost impossible to make qualified workers out of the illiterate.

The Moroccans provide the great mass of unskilled and semi-skilled workers. They have the reputation of being mediocre workers, irregular and careless. In so far as this judgement is correct, it can be explained by their conditions of life. For the most part they are uprooted peasants, driven from their homes by drought and drawn to the towns by wages which, if not high, are generally superior to the average earnings of a *khammes*. Torn from their tribal background, bewildered by the life of a great city, generally lodged in a tintown shack, knowing no urban skill, ready to try anything but expert at nothing, working when work offers, habitually undernourished, they neither know how to settle to a job or how to take an interest in it. On the other hand when they have acquired a skill and are in regular employment, so that they can get enough to eat, they can make excellent workmen. In France, where Moroccan workers are a small minority in comparison with the Algerians, they are highly esteemed, not only in the building trade but also in much more technical occupations such as rubber manufacture. Technical education and craft training are among the greatest social needs of Morocco today.

Among these transplanted peasants one category requires special mention. These are the Chleuh, or Berbers, from the south-west and from the High and Anti-Atlas. Very much attached to their poverty-stricken country, where they live under a patriarchal family régime, the men migrate alone, when need forces them to do so, leaving their wives and children at home. The women carry on with the ploughing while the men work in Casablanca or in the mines in order to earn money to send to them. Living a celibate life, they keep together in groups from the same village or tribe; sleep in a communal bedroom; do their cooking jointly, and talk about home. When one of them returns to his family, after a year or more, a brother or cousin practically always comes to take his place and his job. They thus form real colonies in certain enterprises and monopolize certain occupations, not by virtue of any special aptitude but thanks to the solidarity which binds men of the same tribe together.

Such social legislation as exists in Morocco has been inspired by that of France, but it is of course far less developed. The main provisions relating to the hours of work, to safety measures, and to the employment of women and children exist, and are applied in modern enterprises which are examined by a corps of labour inspectors. They are much more difficult to enforce in traditional occupations. Minimum wages are fixed by law (76 francs an hour, at the beginning of 1958) and provision is made for bonuses for long service, skill, and production. A Social Assistance Fund, to which employers contribute, makes it possible to pay family allowances. The state has encouraged the creation of Benevolent Funds in big enterprises. These are managed by the workers on mutualist principles and enable help to be given in case of sickness. So far, the system of social insurance has been considered too expensive and too complicated for the Moroccan economy, but it is being again studied since the achievement of independence. The principle of collective bargaining has been recognized by recent legislation; and discussions between associations of employers and the trade unions were in progress at the beginning of 1958.

The first trade unions to exist in Morocco were formed by Europeans during the protectorate. As a consequence of incidents at the Khouribga mines in 1936, Moroccans were forbidden to join unions. From 1943 onward, various projects for Moroccan unions were examined but none was adopted. However, after the reconstitution of the CGT in 1943 the latter enrolled a considerable number of Moroccan workers, including office staff, without the authorities raising difficulties. The extent of Communist influence in some of the CGT unions alarmed the nationalists who in any case, on principle as well as for tactical reasons, were demanding the right for their compatriots to form purely Moroccan unions which could be united in a national confederation, independent of metropolitan France. In the last period of the protectorate the CGT leaders had been instructed by their leaders to make room for Moroccans in responsible positions.

In 1955 a *Union Marocaine de Travail* (UMT) was constituted without the protectorate authorities venturing to forbid it. After the return of Sultan Mohammed V, practically all Moroccan wage-earners were enrolled, at least as far as concerned the cities and small urban centres, and it thus achieved a figure of about 600,000–700,000 adherents. Such an expansion was too rapid; many of the workers had only the vaguest idea what a trade union was though they naïvely expected that it would solve all their problems and make them rich as well. Here, as in other spheres, there were nothing like sufficient trained officials. Disillusion was inevitable and a great many members did not renew their cards. The result was, it is said, the reduction by half of the number of registered members. This was not a misfortune, since it is far better that the new unions should be composed of workers who understand what a union is and that recruitment should not exceed the supply of trained managers.

The UMT has close links with the Istiqlal Party, as the *Union Générale des Travailleurs Tunisiens* does with the Destour in Tunisia. An attempt at secession, which originated in Rabat, did not meet with the approval of the Palace and was a failure.

The leaders of the UMT during the first two years of independence showed much discretion and restraint. They were able to resist demagogic excesses and it is in part thanks to this that the upheaval which followed the achievement of independence did not have more alarming consequences. At the beginning of 1958 their demands were still being kept within reasonable limits and had not created the embarrassment to their friends in the Government which a different attitude might have done. Their position will, however, become very difficult, if the economic recession becomes worse or is prolonged for too long.

Hitherto, though anxious to improve the standards of the workers, the UMT has been influenced by nationalist doctrine in the first place and by economic and social doctrine in the second place. Nationalism rather than doctrinaire socialism lies behind certain talk of nationalizing key industries which are in foreign hands and some of the lands of European colonization. In this age nationalist and socialist ideas are natural allies in countries which are emerging from a colonial status. It is an open question whether Communism will develop an appeal to militant labour leaders. A UMT delegation which visited the Chinese People's Republic in 1957 was very much interested in what they saw, preferring it apparently to what they had heard of Russia. Some considered that the Chinese experiment was highly significant for their own problem, and it is thus possible that there will at some time emerge a cleavage between the nationalism of the bourgeoisie and that of the workers.

The Budget

The ordinary budget for 1957 was for 118·4 milliard francs, as compared with 28·9 milliards for 1950. The largest single item in the increase has been that for personnel, which rose in seven years from 16·6 to 67·5 milliards, 25 per cent. of which occurred in 1956 and 1957, due largely to the charges involved in sovereignty, more particularly the army and diplomacy which were previously met by France. Expenses for material and maintenance have also increased and amount to 39·8 milliards. The public debt rose from 2·6 to 11·1 milliards between 1950 and 1957. It is in fact to foreign aid that Morocco has to look for funds for its development budget, which as in all developing countries is constantly growing. Foreign aid, supplied before 1957 by France, in the form of long-term loans, amounted to 13·7 milliards in 1950; by 1955 it had exceeded 20 milliards. For 1957 Morocco received 16 milliard francs from France and the equivalent of 7 milliards in aid from the United States; the latter was doubled for 1958 and will probably be increased further.

Out of receipts amounting to 110 milliards, 81 come from taxes which are mostly indirect—33 per cent. of them from indirect taxes properly so-called, and 24 from customs. Six milliards come from registration dues. Direct taxation produces 18 milliards only, of which 5·5 from the *tertib* or land tax, which has dropped since 1956; 2·4 milliards are raised by income tax on salaries, 9·1 by tax on professional earnings. It was estimated that in 1955 taxation represented 15 per cent. of the national income as compared with 19 per cent. in Algeria and 33 per cent. in France. The national income cannot be precisely evaluated but is probably about 500 milliards.

As an underdeveloped country, Morocco has to face a rapid increase in population, more rapid at present than the increase in resources. A big effort of equipment and therefore of investment is necessary merely to maintain the existing standard of living and a still bigger one to raise it. As things are there does not seem any source for such investments except foreign aid.

The budgetary payments of the Moroccan state are accounted for in the first part of the budget, known as the 'ordinary budget', which covers recurrent annual expenses; and in the second part, or 'extraordinary budget', which covers expenses incurred in capital investment.

The total budgetary expenses rose from 56·7 milliard francs in 1950 to 145·2 milliards in 1957. Details of this increase are shown in the following table.

(*milliard francs*)

	1950	1951	1952	1953	1954	1955	1956	1957
Recurrent expenses .	28·9	38·8	48·8	55·8	66·3	82·4	110·0	118·4
Capital expenditure	27·8	28·0	32·8	36·3	37·7	34·5	30·8	26·8
Total . .	56·7	66·9	81·6	92·2	99·0	111·9	141·8	145·2

The rise in the figures is due in part to monetary depreciation, resulting in an increase in prices and in salaries; in part to the repercussion of capital expenditure on the ordinary budget —a factor which is very significant in the case of expenditure on social welfare in such forms as hospitals and schools; and in part to new charges, arising from the status of independence, in connexion with national defence, foreign affairs, and justice.

The following table shows the principal headings of expenditure in the ordinary budget.

(*milliard francs*)

	1950	1951	1952	1953	1954	1955	1956	1957
Public debt . .	2·6	3·9	5·5	7·0	8·4	9·2	9·8	11·1
Personnel . .	16·6	23·4	27·7	30·1	35·7	42·7	63·5	67·5
Materials . .	7·3	8·9	12·2	14·7	18·1	26·9	33·8	35·9
Maintenance . .	2·2	2·6	3·2	3·9	3·9	3·6	3·9	3·9

The principal items of expenditure can also be classified under departmental headings as follows: Education in 1957 accounted for 18·75 milliards against 4·02 in 1950; Interior and Public Security 21 milliards in 1957 against 6 milliards in 1950; Public Works 6·43 milliards in 1957 against 2·17 milliards in 1950; Agriculture 5·94 milliards in 1957 against 2·11 milliards in 1950; Post Office 7·52 milliards in 1957 against 2·20 in 1950; Health 7·52 milliards in 1957 against 1·79 in 1950.

The accession to independence has involved the following additional charges in the ordinary budget: Ministry of Foreign Affairs 0·46 milliards in 1956, the year of its creation, and 1·33 for 1957; Ministry of Defence 1·2 milliards in 1955 when it covered only the Gendarmerie and the Military Schools, 11·58 milliards in 1956, and 16·39 in 1957. Reforms in the administration of justice have involved a rise in expenditure from 2·31 milliards in 1955 to 4·44 in 1957.

The capital investment budget was apportioned in 1957 among economic and social investments as follows.

(*milliard francs*)

Agriculture	3·8
Hydraulic works	5·3
Communications	5·4
Social and cultural equipment	10·6

Movement of Capital

This cannot be evaluated with precision, but the following may be taken as a reasonably reliable estimate.

At the end of the Second World War Morocco served as a refuge for much capital, predominantly French. This was inspired by the desire to avoid taxation and by the fear of nationalization in France. The outbreak of the Korean War produced a fresh influx, due to fear of the war spreading to Europe and to the expansion of mineral output in Morocco, stimulated by the rise in world prices. From 1953 till 1955, when the Sultan returned from exile, the level of capital remained virtually unchanged.

From 1955 to October 1957, with the coming of independence, there was an exodus of capital. While in 1954 the balance of capital exports and imports had been favourable to Morocco by some 20 milliards, this fell to 7 milliards in 1955. In 1956 the movement was accentuated, but in the second half of 1957 a movement began in the opposite direction; this was inspired by the possibility that the French franc might be devalued, while the Moroccan franc retained its value. Some 20 milliards returned in this way during the last three months of 1957.

Foreign Trade and Tariffs

The foreign trade of Morocco corresponds to her status as an underdeveloped country. She exports mainly raw materials, without adding to them the results of the work of her abundant labour force; and she imports manufactured articles. Her exports are cheap and her imports costly, and the latter include goods necessary for the subsistence of the nation. For example, Morocco exports minerals, barley, and skins in their natural state, and imports American cars, household goods, sugar, and tea, as is shown in the table below.

Until 1957 Morocco was the slave of that relic of international rivalry, the Act of Algeciras, which had established an *ad valorem* duty of 12 per cent. on all imported goods without regard to their place of origin or their nature. It was impossible to protect a local industry, put a heavier tax on unnecessary imports, or lower the tax on a matter of prime necessity such as sugar. Moreover, French-protected Morocco was not only incorporated into the franc zone but had all its supplies of foreign currency controlled by France.

The deficit in the commercial balance was 49 milliards in 1950; 85 in 1952 and 37 in 1956. In the latter year exports amounted to 119 milliards and imports to 155. The diminution in the deficit was due to a reduction in imports rather than to an increase in exports.

Principal Imports and Exports

(milliard francs)

IMPORTS				EXPORTS			
	1953	1954	1955		1953	1954	1955
Sugar . .	14·4	13·6	16·5	Phosphates .	17·3	20·1	21·3
Motor cars .	8·6	8·7	8·8	Wheat . .	1·2	5·1	7·6
Petrol . .	6·4	6·0	6·6	Citrus fruits .	4·8	3·5	6·8
Tea . .	7·0	6·7	7·6	Barley . .	7·0	8·7	6·7
Iron and steel *	3·1	3·2	3·7	Fish: preserved .	8·4	6·2	6·3
Cotton fabrics .	6·6	6·1	4·7	Lead . .	3·2	3·3	4·7
Printed fabrics .	2·9	2·4	3·3	Manganese ore .	6·3	4·9	4·6
Commercial				Wine . .	1·0	1·9	4·2
vehicles .	3·3	3·5	3·3				
All imports .	171·2	167·9	173·9	All exports .	93·8	100·5	114·2

* Wire, bars, and shapes.

Note: The data refer to the area of the former French Protectorate and exclude trade with the former Spanish Protectorate and with Tangier.

Source: UN, *Yearbook of International Trade Statistics, 1956,* vol. 1.

France holds the predominant place—more than half—in Moroccan external trade. This is the result not only of the importance of French capital and personnel in Morocco but also, and indeed principally, to the existence of quotas for the admission to France of duty-free goods. This has the result of reducing the shortage of francs, while maintaining that of other currencies. The franc deficit for 1950 was 47 milliards; in 1952, 62, but only 9·5 in 1956. For the same years the dollar deficit was 15, 22, and 16·7 milliards. With Great Britain on the other hand there is a favourable balance.

In August 1957, when the French Government took measures which were the equivalent of a devaluation of 20 per cent., Morocco necessarily followed suit. Goods considered not to be of first necessity were exempted from the 20 per cent. charge. In consequence the effect on the cost of living was limited. When France later suppressed these exemptions vigorous agitation

K

ensued in Morocco. A current of opinion favoured detaching the Moroccan from the French franc, while remaining if necessary within the franc area, and revaluing it by 20 per cent. in relation to the French currency. Non-experts were probably influenced as much by the desire to assert the independence of the Moroccan currency, and its superior value, as by an exact understanding of the advantages or disadvantages of such action. The Moroccan Government took an informed and realist point of view and accepted instead a number of compensatory measures which gave it satisfaction on the material issues.

In the matter of tariffs, conversations had been held with Great Britain in 1937 with the object of securing the abrogation of the Anglo-Moroccan Treaty of 1856 which was the juridical basis of the Algeciras tariff. These had not been brought to a conclusion by the beginning of the Second World War. In 1957 the renewed independence of Morocco enabled agreement to be reached with Great Britain and Spain by which the two countries renounced the rights acquired by them in the treaties of 1856 and 1861 respectively. Morocco thus recovered economic liberty and on 24 May 1957 a new tariff was published which came into force throughout the country from 4 June. Henceforth raw materials necessary for agriculture and industry were to be taxed at 0–10 per cent.; half-finished products at 5–20 per cent., according to whether there existed or not an industry capable of providing them locally; and finished products from 10–15 per cent. if they were capital goods and from 15–35 per cent. if they were consumer goods. In certain cases, such as carpets and cigarettes, where it was desired to discourage imports the tax might be as high as 50 per cent.

Government circles anticipated a rise in the cost of living of the order of 1·7 per cent. for the working-class budget and 4·6 per cent. for the westernized classes. The effect of momentum might it was thought bring these as high as 8 and 10 per cent. respectively. In fact the tendency was for prices to rise even higher and the Government was forced to take counter measures.

Art, Architecture, and Tourism

Moroccan art has a glorious past whose remains are the adornment of ancient cities such as Fez, Marrakesh, and Rabat. The famous Moroccan dynasties were great builders and their architecture has left a heritage of splendid monuments.

While this art has obvious affinities with that of the east, it has an originality of its own and it is to Muslim Spain that one must look in so far as its origin is to be sought outside the country. It is customary to talk of Hispano-Moorish art, and in fact certain famous monuments of the two countries are due to one and the same architect, not merely to a common style. The Giralda of Seville is the sister of the Kutubia of Marrakesh.

Almoravid art left few traces, though it was then that Andalusian artists were first brought to Morocco. In the time of their successors, on the contrary, the Almohads (1129–68), Moroccan art reached its highest point, 'uniting Andalusian subtlety with Moroccan strength', in the words of a French archaeologist and historian. The Kutubia at Marrakesh and the mosque at Tinmel in the Atlas were due to Abd al-Mumin, the first sovereign of the dynasty. Abu Yaacub Yusuf, who began the Giralda, also had the great mosque of Salé built. Yaacub al-Mansur ordered the building of the walls of Rabat and began the immense Hasan Mosque with the massive stone tower which still dominates the banks of the Bu Regreg at Rabat.

The Merinids were also great builders and Morocco is indebted to them in particular for some charming *madrasas* (colleges) at Fez and at Salé. These are masterpieces of subtle decoration, in which delicate contrasts take the place of grandeur. The Saadians built monuments all over Morocco, and especially in Marrakesh; these are often very rich but are nevertheless imitations of the great styles of the past. After their time the creative impulse gradually died away. The Spanish stimulus was no longer operative and Morocco, withdrawn into herself, took pleasure in the endless repetition of the gestures and ideas of former times, in art as in other spheres.

There is also a Berber architecture in Morocco, equally original in character and often grandiose. The *tighremt* (fortified houses or villages) of the south are entirely different from the architecture of the towns. Built in *pisé* (beaten earth, often mixed with straw), their square towers thickening at the base, they raise the sober, geometric patterns of their decoration towards the firmament. From a comparison with architecture in the Sudan, it has been suggested that Moroccan Berber architecture has been influenced by negro art. It appears, however, that the contrary is true, and that nomad Berbers carried with them the eagle's-nest style of buildings in which they stored their grain right across to the other shore of the desert. For many of these fortress-like buildings are in fact *agadir* or fortified collective granaries. There are also minor Berber arts, principally pottery and carpets, whose decorative motifs recall the arts of the civilization of the Aegean or of civilizations on the very threshold of history.

It is quite different with the pottery of Fez, the carpets of Rabat, and in general with all the decorative urban arts, where one finds again the influence of Muslim Spain, as with the architecture. The prototypes of the rich compositions of Fez ceramics, for example, are to be found in the ceramics of Paterna (thirteenth–fourteenth century). Only the book-binders go their own way by choosing Syro-Egyptian rather than Hispano-Moorish models.

The classical music of Morocco is also Andalusian. Today its creative period is over and it is not being renewed. The younger generation tend to forsake this old-fashioned but charming art, preferring the Oriental and particularly the Egyptian style. While there are many competent executants, there are today few creative artists in either style.

It is interesting to speculate whether contemporary art will bring about a rebirth of Moroccan art. Recently there has been a flowering of young Moroccan painters whose pictures, if sometimes clumsy, reveal an interesting personality and an original sense of colour. European music has not yet found adepts in Morocco. A few theatrical troupes have come into being, some of which have shown remarkable talent. So far as modern architecture is concerned, the new towns contain some very fine examples, but these are all the work of Europeans.

Tourism. Morocco has attractions beyond those of its monuments. The old Moroccan towns (*medinas*) are intensely picturesque and one can still feel oneself transported to the Arab middle ages, with their clashing colours and the perfume of their spices. The *qisaria* of Fez and the *suqs* of Marrakesh transport the visitor from Europe into an entirely different world from that of European life. There are also magnificent natural sites, notably in the Atlas, where winter sports can now be practised (as at Ifran in the Middle Atlas and Oukaimeden in the western High Atlas), and also in the far south. The latter areas with their fortified villages, their oases, their desolate steppes, and their valleys enclosed between twin walls of sunburnt rock offer a strong foretaste of Saharan Africa.

The network of hotels in which tourists can be accommodated is extensive and well organized: 303 hotels with 9,444 rooms of which 7 are luxury hotels with a total of 1,747 rooms. Everywhere the traveller can find ultra-modern hotels, some of which are former Arab palaces where the water still sings among the flowers; while others are 'road houses' where the latest modern comfort has been installed in the midst of the oases or in the heart of a Berber Casbah.

MOROCCAN RELATIONS WITH SPAIN FROM ANTIQUITY TILL 1912

In 1898, after the Spanish-American War, Spain lost Cuba and the Philippines, the two last substantial portions of her empire. The shock was great and an influential school of thought favoured 'bolting and barring the door' and devoting all the national energies to internal reform. Nevertheless fourteen years later Spain accepted the responsibility of a protectorate over a mountainous and economically unrewarding area of Morocco, inhabited by a notoriously warlike and independent-minded population. Geography and history had in fact made it inevitable that Spain should wish to participate in any European control to be exercised in Morocco—especially since France, who had twice invaded Spanish soil in the preceding century, was now to become the predominant power to the south as well as to the north of the Iberian peninsula.

Relations from Antiquity to 1912

The connexion of Spain with Morocco, only eight miles away across the Straits of Gibraltar, probably goes back far into prehistory. It is at least arguable that the first known inhabitants of Spain, the Iberians, were organically connected with the first known inhabitants of Morocco, the Berbers, or that the two peoples had common ancestors in the neolithic age.

It is fairly certain that the influence of the Tartessian kingdom, founded on the banks of the Guadalquivir (al-Wadi al-Kabir) about 2000 B.C., extended over some part of Moroccan territory also, just as did the later Phoenician and Carthaginian domination. In the year 69 Rome united Baetica—the region of Seville—with the Moroccan province of Tingitanis (Tangier) on the south of the Straits. We are told by Roman historians that in 172 A.D. the Moors (Mauri) overran much of Spain and that Marcus Aurelius dispatched Septimius Severus, himself an African from Libya, and later Emperor, to restore order.[1] In 711 Tariq who was himself a Berber, or possibly a Persian, invaded Spain with 7,000 troops, mostly Berbers, under Arab command. The subsequent conquest, carried out by the Arab Musa ibn Nusair, resulted in wholesale conversions to Islam, leading to intermarriage and to the creation of all sorts of links of convenience and interest which brought Arabs, Berbers, and native Spanish together for generation after generation. In fact, during the independent Amirate of Córdoba (756-1031), a new

[1] Spartianus, Lives of Marcus Aurelius and Septimius Severus.

people was formed out of the amalgam of Arabs, Berbers, and Muslim Spanish, among whom a large Christian Spanish population continued to live. The latter helped to form, and participated in, a civilization which was at that time the most advanced in the western world.

In 917 Morocco came within the sphere of influence of Abd al-Rahman III, founder of the western Caliphate, a state just as Spanish as the little Christian states of the north, at that time confined to León, Navarre, and Catalonia. The Spanish-Muslim civilization of Andalusia, which was the product of Spanish, Arab, and Berber interpenetration, began to spread south of the Straits and to bear fruit in customs, habits, architecture, music, and indeed types of religious sentiment, which were common to both sides of the Straits.

Sixty years after the fall of the Caliphate in 1031, a Moroccan Sultan, Yusuf ibn Tashufin, became master of Muslim Spain. His successor, Ali ibn Yusuf, whose mother is said to have been a Christian slave, was strongly influenced by Spanish civilization and recruited a Christian Spanish foreign legion. This body, commanded by a Catalan named Reverter, had its headquarters in Marrakesh, the new capital which the Almoravids had created in south Morocco. It was presumably recruited either from north Spanish Christians who had been captured, or from arabized Christians (Mozarabs) from south Spain who were either volunteers or had been deported south of the Straits for security reasons. In 1137 in fact we hear of a Mozarab bishop, Miguel Abd al-Aziz, being permitted to return to Spain. These Christian troops had chaplains and were permitted to maintain a church in Marrakesh.

The next Moroccan dynasty, the Almohads (1147–1269), retained Spain and promoted a notable migration of Andalusian men of learning and craftsmen to the south of the Straits. One of the last members of this dynasty, al-Mamun, owed his succession in 1229 to the aid of 15,000 Christian soldiers who were loaned to him (in return for the surrender of two fortresses) by the King of Castile, St. Ferdinand, who later conquered Córdoba (1236) and Seville (1248). The Castilian King made the condition that no conversion to Islam on the part of the Christian soldiers would be recognized as valid, though conversions of Muslims to Christianity would be. The members of this force were permitted the public exercise of their faith, including the ringing of church bells, though nine years earlier the fanaticism of another Sultan and the mystic enthusiasm of five Franciscan missionaries sent to Marrakesh by St. Francis himself had provoked their martyrdom in that city.

The next Moroccan dynasty, the Beni Merin, were never able to establish themselves permanently in Spain, though one Sultan, Abu Yaacub ibn Abd al-Haqq, twice crossed the Straits with an army, making a loan to the King of Castile, Alfonso X, in the interval. Their efforts, which included the capture of Gibraltar in 1333, did, however, have the effect of delaying the Christian advance and enabling the little Kingdom of Granada, now the only Spanish territory under Muslim rule, to strengthen its position and so maintain itself during its 250 years of armed coexistence with Christian Spain. When Granada finally fell in January 1492 its suppression marked the culminating point of the mutual incomprehension of Muslims and Christians. This had been steadily growing since the Almoravids had crossed into Spain from Africa at the end of the eleventh century, and since the Christian reconquest had been stimulated by the Crusading spirit injected into it from north of the Pyrenees. This crisis in the relations of the two types of Spaniard was symbolized by the forcible conversion and wholesale expulsions of Spanish Muslims. But though Spanish-Muslim civilization thus ceased to have any independent existence, it continued to live a vicarious life both as an essential element in Muslim civilization south of the Straits and as an unacknowledged but undoubtedly powerful element in the Christian Spanish civilization north of the Straits.

Even after the Catholic Kings had achieved the unity of Spain as a Christian state, influences from north of the Straits continued to reach the Maghrib by means of Muslim refugees, principally in 1492 and 1501 after the risings in the former Kingdom of Granada, and in 1610 with the final expulsion of the Moriscos or forcibly-converted Muslims. Some of the results of this policy have been described in the Introduction (p. 29).

As is well-known, the resentment of the refugees against the Christian Government which had expelled them created an almost insurmountable barrier between Spain and Morocco. First Portuguese, and then Spanish, attempts to carry the war on into Africa made matters worse, and in the case of Spain, turned relations with Morocco into a secondary aspect of Spanish relations with the Muslim countries of North Africa in general. These in their turn provoked Muslim reaction in the form of attacks on Spanish shipping and raids on the Spanish coast. Contacts were nevertheless still made in the course of this bellicose coexistence. They generally resulted from the efforts of semi-official intermediaries such as the Franciscans, established in Morocco since the time of the Almohads, rather than from those of professional diplomats. Philip II maintained friendly relations with Ahmad ibn Muhammad who became Sultan after the Battle of Wadi Makhazin (Alcazarquivir) in 1578, in which King Sebastian of Portugal as well as the reigning Sultan was killed. In the following year a Spanish Embassy took delivery of the body of the dead King. Subsequently for several decades Spain was too much occupied with her European wars to pay more than desultory attention to Morocco, apart from military raids which resulted in the capture of La Maamora and Larache (1610). In 1613 the Sultan offered 60,000 ducats for 5,000 Arabic volumes treating of poetry, medicine, philosophy, politics, and religion, which had been captured while being transported by sea. As the King demanded also the release of all the Christian prisoners then in Morocco and the Sultan was not willing to grant this, the books remained in Spain and were deposited in the Escorial, where the greater part were destroyed by fire in 1671.[1]

The accession of the present Alawite dynasty in 1659 inaugurated a fresh era. The powerful and despotic Maulay Ismail (1672–1729) recaptured La Maamora (1681) and Larache (1689); but rather surprisingly showed great friendliness to the Spanish Franciscans who ministered to the Christian captives. During this reign they possessed a convent and a parish church in Meknes, as well as two of four chapels in that city, the Portuguese maintaining the other two. They were also able to found a second convent in Fez, and had chapels in Tetuan and Salé. In all these they were able to 'exercise the Catholic rites with the same correctness and liberty that they could in Spain'.[2]

In the following century, the eighteenth, embassies were exchanged between Charles III and Sultan Muhammad ibn Abdullah, both Governments being anxious to find a formula which would permit friendly relations. There resulted the treaty of peace and commerce signed in Marrakesh in 1767. This treaty, which was far-reaching in its provisions for mutual trade and for the security of the shipping of both states, served as the basis of later treaties. Towards the end of his reign the Sultan, who had a number of European advisers as well as European craftsmen in his service, declared privateering to be abolished. On the other hand, after recapturing Mazagan from the Portuguese in 1769, he put forward a demand for the return of Ceuta, Melilla, and the Peñons, on the ground that the treaty was concerned exclusively with maritime matters and that there was nothing in it authorizing the Spanish to exercise

[1] M. P. Castellanos, *Historia de Marruecos*, 3rd ed. (Tangier, 1898), p. 403.
[2] Ibid., pp. 452–3.

rule over any portion of Moroccan territory. This provoked Spain into a declaration of war in 1774, which was followed by a Moroccan attack on the various *presidios*. These failed, in part owing to the Spanish fleet successfully preventing a British squadron from delivering arms and munitions to the besieging Moroccan forces. This quarrel was, however, soon forgotten again and a new treaty of friendship and commerce was signed in Aranjuez in 1780 by the Count of Floridablanca and the Moroccan delegate Muhammad Uthman. This resulted a year later in the peaceful settlement of one of the recurrent disputes concerning the limits of the Spanish enclave of Ceuta.[1] Important assistance was also rendered by the Sultan to Spain during the great siege of Gibraltar (1779–83), during which he expelled the British Consul and 108 other British subjects who had been supplying the garrison with information from Tangier and Tetuan.[2]

Four years later, in 1786, the Sultan sought Spanish assistance in arranging a commercial convention with the Kingdom of the Two Sicilies, and also a treaty with the United States in the same year. He also had money coined in Seville. In the two years' reign of his successor, al-Yazid, who through his mother was the grandson of an English renegade, there took place an exchange of Embassies, a declaration of war on Spain by Morocco, two attacks on Ceuta, and a declaration of war by Spain on Morocco. Al-Yazid's brother and successor, Sulaiman, maintained relations with Spain at a quieter rhythm. Godoy took the opportunity to plan an invasion of Morocco; this was, however, rejected by the King, Charles IV, primarily on moral grounds. It was a wise decision, for Sulaiman took Spain's part against Napoleon, maintaining friendly relations with her, and with her English ally, throughout the period of French invasion. This provoked the dispatch of a French mission which threatened the Sultan with a French disembarkation if he persisted in his attitude. Sulaiman ignored the threat; and also an

---

[1] It is stated in García Figueras, *Marruecos* (p. 69) that there was an attack on Ceuta in 1782. This seems to be based on a statement to the same effect in Castellanos's *Historia de Marruecos*, p. 468. The context, however, shows without the least doubt that the date is a misprint for 1732.

[2] The Spanish Government having made a tempting offer to the Sultan, the latter, who was on friendly terms with Britain informed the Governor of Gibraltar, General Eliott, suggesting that he would refuse it if the British Government would supply him with stores for three new vessels in order to deal with possible Spanish attacks. The Governor, who estimated the value of the stores at not more than £1,500, recommended the British Government to give double this sum, as the proposition seemed to him reasonable and moderate. When, however, the British Government did not so much as reply, the Sultan concluded the bargain with the Spanish (Capt. J. Drinkwater, *A History of the Siege of Gibraltar* (London, 1905), p. 133).

offer by Joseph Bonaparte to cede Ceuta and Melilla, if the
Sultan would recognize him as King of Spain. In 1810 Sulaiman received an Embassy from the Junta of Cadiz.

The occupation of Algiers by France in 1830, and the subsequent pressure on the Moroccan frontier, provoked great
diplomatic activity on the part of his successor, Maulay Abd
al-Rahman, to secure Spanish support. But Spain, reeling under
the loss of almost the whole of her vast empire and involved in
sordid internal struggles, would or could do nothing to answer
this appeal. After the defeat of Abd al-Rahman at Wadi Isly,
in 1844, the independence of Morocco was clearly passing away
and there was thus brought to a close a period in which by a
sort of natural law Morocco and Spain had on occasions overcome their quarrels with one another in order to give each other
support in their relations with other Christian and Muslim
powers.

It was thus left to an Englishman, Sir John Drummond-Hay,
to mediate between Spain and Morocco in 1845. The relations
of the two countries during the rest of the century were concerned exclusively with their own disputes; the most serious of
these led to the war of 1860 and the temporary occupation of
Tetuan. Thus the ensuing treaties of 1860 and 1861 though
excellent in intention remained completely inoperative. In 1880
the Conference of Madrid was assembled to limit the right of
foreign protection of Moroccan subjects; in this Spain and
England supported the Sultan, but the outcome was a failure
and merely emphasized the extent to which Morocco was
becoming an international question. From that time forward
Spain, weakened by the internal struggles of the nineteenth
century, supported the thesis of the inviolability of the Sultan's
sovereignty and the integrity of his domains; in this she was
backed by England and Germany in so far as this was a hind-
rance to French ambitions in Morocco.

Meanwhile the current of European expansionism in Africa
found an echo in Spain and was expressed by the formation of
a number of societies interested in colonization in that continent. In another sphere, the creation of a fine school of
Arabic studies in Spain, after a long period of neglect, began to
bring about a new attitude towards Arab and Muslim civilization. These two developments helped to prepare the way, one
for limited Spanish intervention in North West Africa, and the
other for the friendly policy towards the Arab world in general
which was to be a feature of Spanish policy after the Civil War.

The Franco-Spanish agreement of October 1904, which was
the complement of the Franco-British agreement of April of the

same year, in fixing limits of French and Spanish influence in Morocco, implied that the Sharifian Empire was doomed. The theatrical gesture of William II at Tangier hastened the calling of the Conference of Algeciras in 1906. Its ambiguous conclusions satisfied no one, but prepared the way for a protectorate which was already creating difficulties between the future protecting powers before it actually came into being. In the negotiation of these agreements the Sharifian Empire had no share.

Little by little Morocco was losing the power of independent action, except for such feverish outbursts as the troubles in Casablanca in 1907. From the conclusion of the Act of Algeciras, she was increasingly becoming the passive object of other people's decisions.

THE SPANISH PROTECTORATE IN THE NORTHERN ZONE, 1912–56

Area and Population

The legal basis of the Spanish protectorate in Morocco was the Franco-Spanish agreement of 27 November 1912; this regulated the position of the two nations with regard to the protected territory.

The area of the zone which was entrusted to Spain was 8,500 square miles, as compared with 157,000 in the French and 283 in the Tangier zone.

The population, which was estimated—probably underestimated—in 1917 as 404,000 reached 700,000 in 1930. In 1955 the final statistics of the protectorate gave a total of 1,054,978 inhabitants of whom 955,403 were Muslims; 8,217 Jewish; 90,939 Spanish; and 419 of various nationality. In 1955 the rural population formed 77·06 of the total.

In 1954 the population of the towns was as follows.

	Muslims	Spanish *
Tetuan	83,302	31,445
Larache	42,370	13,193
Alcazarquivir	32,242	3,680
Nador	23,115	9,025
Shauen	14,175	2,569
Arcila	13,650	2,541
Villa Sanjurjo (now Alhucemas) .	11,251	7,591
	220,105	70,044

* Including officials and the wives and families of officers and soldiers but not the armed forces themselves.

HISTORY

The Beginning of the Protectorate

The first Article of the Treaty of Fez of 1912, by its reference to Spanish interests, implicitly provided for the administration by Spain of a zone in northern Morocco. It thus gave legal sanction to the partition of a country the integrity of whose territory, and the independence of whose sovereign, had been solemnly affirmed in 1906 by the signatories of the Act of Algeciras. In fact, however, various districts of the now decrepit empire had long been escaping the control of the Sultan and, in this respect, events in the north had been typical.

In 1889, for example, Sultan Maulay al-Hasan had directed one of his many punitive expeditions against rebellious tribes in the western half of the future Spanish protectorate—Jebala, Gomara, and the Atlantic zone, around the cities of Tetuan, Shauen, Tangier (Tanja), Arcila (Asila), Alcazarquivir, and Larache (al-Araish). A few years later the Jebala tribal area, east of Tangier, and the near-by Atlantic coast had been involved in the struggle of the Sharif Maulay Ahmad al-Raisuni to create an autonomous fief for himself in those regions. Among the many outrages of this half-feudal and half-religious adventurer were the kidnapping of foreigners, among them the American millionaire, Perdicaris; the well-known English traveller and writer, Walter Harris; and the Scot, Caid Sir Harry Maclean, who was military adviser to the Sultan. Having failed to reduce Raisuni by force, Sultan Maulay Abd al-Aziz decided to conciliate where he could not command and appointed him Governor of Tangier. A little later Raisuni transferred his allegiance to Maulay Abd al-Hafidh when the latter rose against his brother, Maulay Abd al-Aziz; and he was in consequence confirmed as Governor of the Jebala and of the adjacent Atlantic coast when Maulay Abd al-Hafidh became Sultan in 1908. His authority was, however, never firmly established over the whole area; at the moment of the signature of the Treaty of Fez many tribes still ignored the Sultan's authority and that of his representative.

Nor was the imperial authority more firmly established in the eastern half of the northern zone, known as the Rif. Expeditions of Sultan Maulay al-Hasan in 1874 and 1876 against the Rif and Garet had only a temporary effect. Thus the picturesque pretender, or 'Rogui', Bu Hamara, easily found supporters among the Rifi tribes when he raised the standard of revolt in Taza, in 1902, passing himself off as the one-eyed Prince Mohammed,

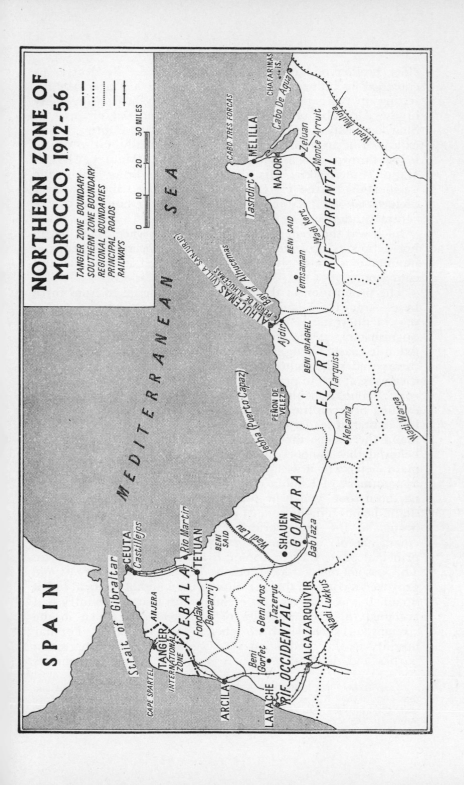

NORTHERN ZONE OF
MOROCCO, 1912–56

TANGIER ZONE BOUNDARY
SOUTHERN ZONE BOUNDARY
REGIONAL BOUNDARIES
PRINCIPAL ROADS
RAILWAYS

0   10   20   30 MILES

SPAIN

Strait of Gibraltar

MEDITERRANEAN SEA

CAPE SPARTEL

TANGIER
INTERNATIONAL
ZONE

ANJERA

JEBALA

Fondak
Bencarrij

Beni
Gorfet

Beni Aros

Tazerut

ARCILA

LARACHE

RIF OCCIDENTAL

ALCAZARQUIVIR

Wadi Lukkus

CEUTA
Castillejos

Rio Martin
TETUAN

BENI
SAID

Wadi Lau

SHAUEN
Bab Taza

GOMARA

Jebha (Puerto Capaz)

PEÑON DE
VELEZ

EL RIF

Targuist

Ketama

CABO TRES FORCAS

MELILLA

CHAFARINAS
IS.
Cabo De Agua

Zeluan
Monte Arruit

NADOR

Tashdirt

BENI SAID

Wadi Kert

Temsaman

RIF ORIENTAL

Wadi Warga

Wadi Muluya

ALHUCEMAS (VILLA SANJURJO)

Bay of Alhucemas
(PEÑON DE ALHUCEMAS)

Ajdir

BENI URIAGHEL

elder brother of Sultan Maulay Abd al-Aziz. By degrees he
extended his influence to Ujda and to the tribes near Melilla,
setting up the capital of his romantic story-book principality
in the Alcazaba of Zeluan, where he held out against the
Sharifian expeditionary forces until 1909. Captured and
exhibited in an iron cage in Fez, he was finally put to death,
being thrown, it was said, to the lions of Maulay Abd al-
Hafidh's menagerie. His death failed to bring about the
pacification of the eastern zone where the tribes, however
divided among themselves, were united in hostility to the
central authority.

Such was the scene in the northern zone when Spain began
her action as protector of a singularly poverty-stricken and
mountainous zone, given over to perpetual indiscipline and
confusion.

The penetration of the country was undertaken from three
bases—from the Spanish city of Melilla, at the eastern end of
the Mediterranean coast of Morocco; from Ceuta, also a
Spanish city, at the western end; and from Larache on the
Atlantic coast. Though these three zones were soon brought in
theory under the control of the High Commissioner in Tetuan,
they were at first in practice independent fronts. In the Atlantic
coastal zone, difficulties were aggravated by the bad relations
existing between the masterful adventurer Raisuni and the no
less masterful leader Colonel Silvestre who had been in command there since the original landing in June 1911. Raisuni
believed that Colonel Silvestre's doubts about him were the
main factor which was preventing him from being offered the
appointment of Khalifa (Lord Lieutenant or Viceroy) of the
northern zone, which he passionately desired.[1] Furious at the
slight, he put himself from March 1913 at the head of the forces
hostile to the protectorate. From that moment until the
emergence of Abdelkrim, eight years later, Raisuni was the
principal anxiety of the Spanish administration in Morocco.
This was not only for local reasons, but also because his attitude
provoked a considerable reaction in the internal political life of
Spain. It was with very little enthusiasm that the country had
accepted the responsibilities of a protectorate which in the
circumstances she had no choice but to accept. Popular
hostility to the occupation was organized by the opposition
parties and used as a weapon against the last governments

---

[1] Later Raisuni told Rosita Forbes that he had been mistaken in this belief and
that other factors had prevented his appointment. Personally he seems to have
quite liked Silvestre but, as he said, 'There cannot be two lions in one forest' (*El
Raisuni*, p. 117).

under the monarchy, and against the monarchy itself. For this reason the history of the Spanish protectorate is so mingled with that of Spain herself that the two subjects cannot be considered independently.

The Treaty of Fez had been signed by representatives of the French Republic and of the Sultan only. In order, however, that Spain should enjoy full liberty in the administration of the zone accorded to her by the treaty, it was arranged that the Sultan should make a full delegation of his powers, as far as these affected the northern zone, to his Khalifa or Lord Lieutenant in Tetuan. The latter thus became a sort of viceroy, nominally subject to the imperial power but in fact acting with complete independence. The first Khalifa to be appointed, Maulay el-Mahdi, a cousin of the Sultan, arrived in Tetuan in April 1913 and was received by the first High Commissioner, General Alfau. Superficially conditions were quiet but in fact the tribes were restless. Opposition to the foreigner, at first ill-defined, was soon crystallized by the insubordination of Raisuni into the form of clear-cut, armed resistance. This did not for the moment prevent General Alfau from continuing his policy of trying to persuade Raisuni to accept the Sharifian authority and so achieving the penetration of the country by peaceful means. As the situation became increasingly critical, however, he undertook punitive operations against certain tribes who periodically cut vital communications between Tetuan and Ceuta and against others who were creating trouble in the neighbourhood of Larache. Deceived by the tactics of the Moroccans, whose armed groups came together and then separated again according to the circumstances of what was really guerrilla warfare, General Alfau broke off military operations and began negotiations for peace. The tribesmen, interpreting this as a sign of weakness, demanded the abandonment of Tetuan by the Spanish forces as a preliminary to negotiation. This claim brought about the resignation of General Alfau, who was succeeded by General Marina. The latter followed the line traced by his predecessor and attempted to renew relations with Raisuni. This policy was, however, brought to an end by the assassination of Raisuni's emissary while travelling with a Spanish safe-conduct. Since a junior officer of the Spanish forces was implicated, General Marina felt it his duty to resign, while Colonel Silvestre was relieved of his post.

During his period of office General Marina had begun to organize the administration of the pacified regions on lines which were subsequently formulated by royal decree of

January 1916. It is to be noted that the protecting power respected the outward forms of Moroccan rule as was done in the neighbouring zone, and did not attempt to make revolutionary and spectacular changes. As far as the general pacification of the zone was concerned, little progress was made during General Marina's period of office as High Commissioner.

The next holder of the post, General Gómez Jordana, did not make any great changes, since the First World War had come by then and had indirectly complicated Spanish policy. The Spanish Government, officially neutral, thought it best to adopt a waiting attitude and to continue conciliating Raisuni. The Sharif was very skilful in exploiting these pacific intentions to the full, particularly as they were reinforced by the way in which the opposition in Spain presented the Government's action in Morocco as the basic factor of every economic and social problem of the Spanish people.

In October 1915 an agreement was reached by which Raisuni was recognized as Governor of the tribes over which he had previously been appointed by Maulay Abd al-Hafidh. After the submission of a number of tribes at the beginning of 1916, the Fonduk of Ain Jedida, half-way between Tetuan and Tangier, was occupied without fighting and communications were thus secured between Tetuan, Tangier, and Larache. This success was more spectacular than substantial. As Raisuni's pride and ambition grew, his pretensions became limitless, and it took all General Gómez Jordana's skill and patience to carry out the Government's order to maintain the *status quo* until after the Armistice of 1919. A few months later, the High Commissioner died, while still in office in Tetuan.

The European war having ended, the Government reconsidered its policy in agreement with the new High Commissioner, General Berenguer, who knew the country well.

Operations in the summer of 1919 were markedly successful and resulted in the submission of various tribes. At the same time, in the region of Larache, Raisuni's communications were cut between Tazerut, where he had established himself since the new break with Spain, and Tangier whence he was being supplied with arms. The penetration continued throughout 1920 and culminated in October with the occupation of Shauen, while the ring round Tazerut was being steadily tightened by operations in the mountainous zone of Beni Gorfet. When operations were begun, in July 1921, in Beni Aros, nearer Raisuni's stronghold, the pacification of the western zone as a whole appeared to be in sight. They were, however, interrupted and the hopes roused by General Berenguer's political and military successes brought to nought by an unexpected event in the eastern end of the zone—the disaster of Anual.

In spite of this setback in the east, the position in the western zone was maintained; though men and supplies, already limited by considerations of policy at home, had to be further reduced in order to send help to Melilla. The advance had had to be arrested, and Raisuni remained unbeaten in his mountain stronghold. From this time on, however, he was to play only a secondary part on the Moroccan stage, and the principal role was taken over by Abdelkrim al-Khattabi.

Abdelkrim and the Rif War

For a number of years Mohammed Abdelkrim had been known as a friend of Spain. Berber in origin but a good Arabic scholar, he had been *Qadi al-Qudat* (chief judge) of the region of Melilla and editor of the Melilla newspaper, *el Telegrama del Rif*. Outspokenly anti-French, his attitude had provoked protests from the French authorities. Though other reasons have been suggested, it was probably on account of these protests that Abdelkrim was imprisoned by the authorities of Melilla at the end of the war. This piece of tactlessness converted him into an implacable opponent of Spain and of all foreign influence. Having unsuccessfully tried to escape, he was transferred at the beginning of 1919 to Ajdir, where he began to plan vengeance by raising the Rif. His experience of Spanish administration and his understanding of the political position in Spain were factors in his success; the inveterate tendency of General (former Colonel) Silvestre, now commanding in the east, to take independent action was another.

In fact, while General Berenguer was preparing the operations designed to liquidate the rising organized by Raisuni, General Silvestre, who was in theory subordinate to him, embarked on a series of rash operations, advancing like an arrow without securing either his flanks or his rear. All of a sudden, the advanced post at Igueriben was besieged and the danger of the situation became apparent. From his headquarters at Anual, General Silvestre asked for reinforcements. The night of 21–22 July 1921 was dramatic. By now the enemy were everywhere and the entire region in arms. The order was given to retire —an operation of extreme difficulty, in view of the nature of the ground and the tactics of the Moroccans. General Silvestre's suicide completed the disorganization and the collapse of the fighting spirit. The native troops went over to the enemy, increasing the panic. In the first days of August Zeluan and

L

Nador, 24 and 9 kilometres from Melilla respectively, fell to Abdelkrim, and his forces flushed with success reached the racecourse in the immediate outskirts of the city. For a few days longer Monte Arruit, about 30 kilometres away, held out in isolation. Finally this too fell, the survivors being made prisoner. In the following months Abdelkrim, now abundantly supplied with captured arms and ammunition, organized a simple but effective form of government over the region which he now controlled; to this he gave the name of the Republic of the Rif.

In Spain this disaster, in its day as notorious as the fall of Dien Bien Phu in 1954, brought to the boil the emotion roused by previous reverses. Grief at the disaster was exacerbated by the opposition who exploited the situation for party purposes. The strong feelings aroused made it difficult for the Government to produce the men and the means for a vigorous counter-action. Nevertheless the situation in the eastern section gradually improved. By December 1921 Spanish troops were again established on the river Kert and by March 1922 they had mastered the Beni Said tribes after some hard fighting.

In summer 1922 General Berenguer was succeeded as High Commissioner by General Burguete. The latter's first care was to seek a new agreement with Raisuni; this was achieved in October and agitation in the western zone was brought to an end, as far as he was concerned. Very soon, however, Abdelkrim, by infiltration through non-occupied territory, succeeded in stirring it up afresh. Meanwhile in the eastern zone the Spanish front was progressing towards Tizi Azza and Azib al-Midar. Once again, however, the Government, under opposition pressure, suspended operations which had begun successfully. The appointment of a civilian, Señor Silvela, as High Commissioner, in December 1922, had little effect on the military situation which was again becoming acute in the western region.

On 13 September 1923 a dictatorship was established in Spain by General Primo de Rivera. On assuming power, he promised to produce a solution in Morocco, and meanwhile named General Aizpuru as High Commissioner; the latter confirmed the agreement with Raisuni and so maintained peace in the western zone while devoting his attention to the east. Raisuni was, however, now no more than the ghost of the formidable chieftain of earlier times. His hour of history had already passed. Abdelkrim, on the other hand, who had now appointed himself President of the Republic of the Rif, was firmly established both in the Rif proper and in Gomara and

Lau, quite close to Tetuan. The title which he assumed expressed a form of regional patriotism which had not yet reached the stage of a modern nationalist movement.

By 1924 agitation had recommenced everywhere. This was not a war in the proper sense of the word; but rather an exhausting and bloody Ibero-Berber guerrilla, a nightmare for any regular army which has to deal with it. In May Abdelkrim launched simultaneous attacks in the eastern region and on the Wadi Lau, west of Tetuan. Although repulsed, he renewed the attack in July. This reawoke the restlessness in Spain. General Primo de Rivera could no longer defer the decision which was expected of him and which he had so far been putting off.

Contrary to what might have been expected of a soldier who had all power in his hands, General Primo de Rivera opted for tactics of semi-abandonment. His plan was to establish and fall back on a line against which the enemy would wear himself out, and meanwhile to intensify the action of the protectorate in the areas under control. In view of the greatness of the responsibility, in case the enemy should advance like an avalanche when the retreat began, General Primo de Rivera in October 1924 himself took over command of the armed forces and the High Commissionership.

In the long run, this methodical withdrawal proved a success. The rebel attacks broke against the well-garrisoned and well-defended Primo de Rivera line. Beyond it, however, Abdelkrim moved on towards Jebala, occupying Shauen, which the Spanish army had evacuated in a very difficult and dangerous operation, and in January 1925 he attacked Raisuni in Tazerut. Rather than avail himself of the refuge which Spain offered him, the old Sharif preferred to be taken prisoner by his own people; three months later he died obscurely.

Meanwhile Abdelkrim, supported by various foreign elements and more particularly by the French Communist Party, became more ambitious or more desperate. After the French had occupied the Warga valley, from which he had drawn much of his provisions, he launched an attack against the French forces in April 1925. This was a whirlwind assault along the line of the river Warga and it brought isolated bands of his troops within 20 kilometres of Fez where he may have dreamed of being proclaimed Sultan. The French hold on the whole interior of Morocco was threatened, and while Marshal Lyautey remained Resident General, his post as Commander-in-Chief was transferred to Marshal Pétain.

Common misfortune now brought Spain and France

together and led to the holding of a Conference in Madrid in June and July 1925. The purpose of the Conference was to concert political and military measures to put an end to the rising. Since, however, Abdelkrim's stand had by now aroused a great deal of sympathy in circles opposed to the forcible imposition of colonial rule, references were made by both French and Spanish representatives to a generous 'guarantee of administrative, economic, and political autonomy for the Rif and Jebala tribes'. At the same time they laid it down that the initiative must come from Abdelkrim; and since the latter, either from pride or over-confidence, was unwilling to make a public approach, he missed his opportunity of seeking favourable terms, and of profiting from a certain divergence of views between the two Governments, of which the French was thought to be more willing than the Spanish to grant autonomy in an area over which it would not in any case have any control.

The basic element of the joint operations which were finally agreed on was to be a Spanish disembarkation at Alhucemas. This was successfully effected by the Spanish troops on 8 September 1925. Abdelkrim reacted violently with a diversionary attack at Kudia Tahar in Gomara, but could not hinder the development of the operations which were taking place in the very heart of the Rif; and at the end of September Ajdir, the leader's birthplace, was captured. Meanwhile Spanish and French troops were undertaking co-ordinated action in the Melilla sector.

The campaign was now going so well that the accession of a new Khalifa, Maulay Hassan ben el-Mehdi, the son of the former Khalifa, could be celebrated in Tetuan with a grandiose display. General Primo de Rivera took the opportunity to return to Spain leaving General Sanjurjo as High Commissioner.

By now Abdelkrim was heading straight for defeat and he therefore initiated negotiations for peace. Since, however, he was still unwilling to accept terms which, in return for his own exile and the disarmament of the tribes, would produce only the promise of a very limited autonomy of a vague character for the Rif, a conference at Ujda between representatives of Spain and France and three Rifi representatives was broken off in April 1926. Combined operations were resumed at the beginning of May and, after a brief further struggle which involved attacks on convoys and other incidents in the region of Tetuan, Abdelkrim surrendered to the French on 27 May 1926. It was then learned that almost all the Spanish prisoners, including every officer, had succumbed to ill-treatment or the hardships of life in captivity in the Rif.[1]

Though the rebellion was now beheaded, there remained substantial rebel centres to be reduced by mopping-up operations, by peaceful expeditions, or by political negotiations. On 25 August Shauen was peacefully reoccupied. By the end of 1926 30,000 rifles, 135 cannon, 8 mortars, and 199 machine guns had been collected in the Khalifan zone. The great majority of these had been originally captured either from the Spanish or from the French armies. Abdelkrim had finally been overcome by combined Spanish and French forces amounting to about 250,000 men equipped with every type of modern arm.

During 1927 mopping-up operations continued successfully. The most difficult were those in March, in the Temsamani area of the eastern Rif, when snow storms augmented the difficulties of manoeuvre in a district of high mountains. These troubles were, however, soon overcome. In April there were a number of engagements in the Gomara and Jebala areas in the west where the mountains rise to 4,800 and 5,200 feet. By 10 July, however, General Sanjurjo was able to announce that peace reigned throughout the Khalifan zone. In October of the same year King Alfonso and Queen Victoria Eugenia paid a visit to Morocco; this marked the termination of the long period of struggle. In the course of 1928 General Sanjurjo handed over the office of High Commissioner to General Jordana, who some years later became Minister of Foreign Affairs.

The Organization of the Protectorate

The organization of the zone now became the main preoccupation of the authorities and the difficulties of the transitional period were overcome without any serious setback. The religious beliefs and the traditions of the country were respected. So far as human fallibility permitted, it was sought to improve the working of its social institutions. The result was an association of Spaniards and Moroccans, and a mixed system of administration, partly direct and partly indirect, which was

[1] In May 1947, twenty-one years later, the French Government permitted Abdelkrim to leave the island of Réunion where he had been exiled in order to take up residence in France. As the ship bringing him passed through the Suez Canal, King Faruq of Egypt, at the request of the North African leaders in Cairo, offered him asylum in Egypt, which he accepted. He then became head of the newly-formed Maghrib Office in Cairo which served as a co-ordinating point for the various nationalist movements. He was, however, out of sympathy with the political activities of the Istiqlal movement and with its leader, Allal al-Fasi. In April 1958 it was announced that he had been offered a pension from the King of Morocco but had maintained his refusal to return to Morocco until all of North Africa had been freed.

designed to promote the evolution of the country while preserving its individuality.

One of the principal instruments of action was the *Servicio de
Intervenciones*; in this the *Interventores* corresponded to District
Commissioners in former British mandated territories, such as
Palestine, or to the *Contrôleurs Civils* in the French zone. Their
first task was to complete disarming the tribes, with the aid of
the *Makhazniya*, or Moroccan constabulary, under Spanish
command. Some order was brought into the chaos of land
tenure (*habous*, state domains, collective lands, &c.) and the
collection of taxes was put on a firm basis. At the same time
health control was improved and a campaign begun against
endemic diseases such as malaria, syphilis, and trachoma, while
attention was given to the spread of education. During this
period the Agricultural, Forest (in Spanish *Servicio de Montes*),
and Veterinary services were established. The Public Works
Department drew up a plan for roads and tracks; these were
the first to be constructed in a hitherto roadless land.

New official and private buildings increased the size of
Tetuan, supplying it with amenities which it had not before
possessed, and new urban centres began to be formed beside
the military encampments at Alhucemas (Villa Sanjurjo) and
Puerto Capaz.

During the four brief years which passed between the
restoration of peace and the fall of the Spanish monarchy there
was great activity in the Khalifan zone which prevented its
suffering economically from the great reduction in Spanish
forces in the territory. In the international field, Holland gave
up her right to Capitulations in 1929, while in June 1930
France and Spain signed an agreement for the working of the
Moroccan telephonic and telegraphic services. These were the
only occurrences of significance in the Khalifan zone from 1927
to 1931; nor was there any marked Moroccan reaction to the
important events which preceded the Spanish elections of
13 April 1931, and prepared the way for the fall of a monarchy
whose foundations the Moroccan problem had helped to
undermine.

The Period of the Republic

The establishment of the Second Republic in Spain was
marked in Morocco by violent incidents, provoked by Spanish
nationals in front of the offices of the High Commission in
Tetuan. The High Commissioner himself, General Jordana,
had to escape secretly from Tetuan, like a fugitive from justice;
while the capable Colonel Capaz, Head (*Delegado*) of the Native

Affairs Department, was set upon in the streets. Very soon the political and administrative structure of the Khalifan zone was being put to a severe strain through the lack of a considered policy on the part of the provisional Government. An alarming state of unrest manifested itself, to put an end to which General Sanjurjo was temporarily appointed High Commissioner. On 5 May a disorderly demonstration of Moroccan workers, demanding an eight-hour working day and equality of wages with Spanish workers, was firmly suppressed by General Sanjurjo; but was followed by signs of disaffection in the Foreign Legion which were similarly dealt with. After a few weeks of office, General Sanjurjo was replaced by Señor López Ferrer, the considered choice of the provisional Government.

This civilian High Commissioner endeavoured to apply in Morocco the basic principles of the new Spanish régime. Since one of these was the reduction of the influence of the military element in public life, he began to restaff the *Servicio de Intervenciones* with civilians. The proposal in itself was unobjectionable, but unfortunately party interests in these appointments often prevailed over the need to choose the best man for the fulfilment of the purposes of the protectorate. A number of unsuitable appointments resulted, while in Spain at the same time the strife of ideas created a background most unfavourable for constructive action.

In these circumstances there took place in December at Bab Taza an incident promoted by the Derkawa confraternity of Tangier. This small movement of rebellion had no great importance in itself, except as a symbol of general unrest; it was settled by the arrest of some members of the confraternity. It was, however, made a pretext by a portion of the Spanish press for instigating an absurd campaign against the Spanish Franciscans of Tangier, who were accused of instigating the affair in the hope of discrediting the republican régime. At the same time there occurred in Tetuan the first signs of a modern nationalist movement; this was led by Abdel Khalek Torres, and was the counterpart in the Khalifan zone of the western type of nationalism which the first generation of French educated young Moroccans had begun to organize in the Sharifian zone (*Kutlat al-Amal al-Watani* or National Action Bloc) as a reaction to the Berber *Dahir* of May 1930.[1]

In May 1933 Señor López Ferrer was replaced by Señor Moles. The latter set himself to draw up a considered plan for the zone. When the budget was presented to the Directorate General of Morocco and Colonies, the scheme was rejected,

[1] See above, p. 93.

provoking the resignation of Señor Moles in January 1934. His brief period of office left no trace and the only occurrences of importance which took place during it were the visit of the President of the Republic, at his suggestion, and a noticeable growth of nationalist sentiment in the urban centres.

The succession fell to Señor Rico Avello. The latter's first achievement was to persuade Colonel Capaz to return to Morocco and resume the work which he had abandoned as the result of disagreement with Señor López Ferrer's attitude towards appointments to the *Servicio de Intervenciones*. During Señor Rico Avello's two years as High Commissioner he made a careful and valuable study of agricultural problems. He also carried out a useful work in co-ordinating the administrative services, undeterred by the political difficulties which the situation in Spain inevitably brought to Morocco. In spite of the background of trouble the protectorate remained free from the violence and disorders which were increasingly frequent in Spain. There was, however, a sense of uneasy expectation.

In March 1936 Señor Moles was again sent to Tetuan, in replacement of Señor Rico Avello. Spaniards influential in the régime made his brief stay difficult by pressing him to promote in Morocco tendencies which had been set in motion by the triumph of the Popular Front in Spain in February 1936. He also came into conflict with the nationalists with whom he had already had difficulties during his first period of office. In the course of an interview with reporters he told them that he had found that a soft policy merely played into the hands of agitators. He was therefore determined, he said, to carry out a firm policy similar to that which had recently been inaugurated by Resident-General Peyrouton in the French zone. Being very soon appointed Minister of the Interior, he was temporarily replaced by Señor Alvarez Buylla, who was himself overtaken by the emergence of the national movement of 18 July 1936.

Looking at the action of the Second Spanish Republic in Morocco as a whole (1931–6), it is clear that it suffered from the confusion reigning in Spain itself. Nevertheless, having come into power, the former opposition could not disinterest themselves of the task, as they had formerly claimed they could; nor did they show themselves at all more liberal with regard to nationalist claims.[1] The fact was that with regard to Morocco

---

[1] Shakib Arslan, the pan-Arab nationalist from Syria who took an active interest in North African Arab nationalism, wrote in his review *La Nation Arabe*, published in Geneva, in September 1936, 'for six years during which Spain has been governed by a Republican régime, self-styled liberal, going by its liberalism very near to anarchy, the zone which Spain occupied in Morocco has in no way differed, in its arbitrary administration, from what it was under the monarchy'.

there was a Spanish attitude which was neither monarchical, republican, nor peculiar to the régime of General Franco, but simply Spanish.

The Spanish Nationalist Régime

The rising in Spain of 18 July 1936 initiated a new chapter of Spanish history; and this brought with it a change of emphasis in Spanish action in Morocco. Though this looked like a new development it was in reality simply the application of directives which had been formulated at the time of the Madrid Conference of 1881.

Contrary to what might have been expected, the rising against the constituted authority of the state did not give rise to any disorder among the Moroccan population. On the contrary it brought about a degree of co-operation between the Moroccan nationalists and the authorities which may have been influenced to some extent by the denomination of 'nationalist' common to both, in spite of its very different significance in the two cases. At the same time it produced a temporary divergence between the outlook of the Moroccan nationalists in the Spanish and in the French zones, between which a further barrier was now created by the distaste which the French Government felt for the new Spanish régime.

In the period between the formation of the Popular Front in Spain and the nationalist rising, two emissaries of Moroccan nationalism in the northern zone had gone to Madrid in the hope of securing a promise of independence from the Popular Front Government. They were warmly received; but when no action was seen to follow from these fair words the disillusion which Señor Moles had already caused set in all the more strongly. Thus although the Khalifa protested on the day after the rising at the extension of Spanish internal differences to Moroccan soil, and though General Franco confined the nationalist leader Abdel Khalek Torres to his house for a few days as a precautionary measure, Moroccan sympathies in the northern zone were on the whole with the nationalist Spanish who were now themselves promising to 'offer Morocco the most resplendent roses when the blossoms of peace unfold'.[1] Many Moroccans in the zone felt that the Spanish nationalists were justified in claiming that the action which they had taken was the only alternative to submitting to Communist rule.[2]

In the southern zone, on the other hand, where the nationalists regarded the French Left as their allies, the reaction was

[1] Mahdi Bennouna, *Our Morocco* (1951), p. 49. Printed in Morocco.
[2] Ibid.

different. For Allal al-Fasi, the leader of the nationalists in the south, the Spanish rising was a 'Fascist rebellion'.[1] A delegation from the southern zone was sent to Madrid in the hope that the leftist principles and the military difficulties of the Republican Government would produce a promise of independence. The latter was, however, more interested in maintaining good relations with the French Government than in conciliating Moroccan nationalism. After consulting the French Government, therefore, it merely informed the delegation that the Republic would make an effort for the well-being of Morocco when victory had been attained, and in the meanwhile offered them 40 million pesetas to carry on publicity for Spanish democracy. This offer was rejected with scorn. On the other hand the Catalan authorities in Barcelona who were also approached are said to have signed a document promising their support for Moroccan independence; this was, however, a document which remained completely inoperative.

The result in the northern zone was thus a measure of co-operation between the Moroccan nationalists and the Spanish authorities which was regarded with a certain suspicion by Moroccan nationalists in the southern zone. Northern sympathies had been further stimulated on the day after the rising by the action of the Republican air force in bombing Tetuan. By the autumn, adherence to the Spanish nationalist movement was general in the northern zone, as was demonstrated by a celebration in Beni Aros at which the Khalifa, in the presence of thousands of assembled tribesmen, expressed his wishes for the success of the movement. It was also shown by the massive participation of the latter in the ranks of the nationalist forces and the very substantial contribution which they thus made to the eventual victory.

The policy of collaboration with the Moroccan nationalists was considerably developed by General Beigbeder when he became High Commissioner in August 1937, in succession to General Orgaz who had occupied the post since the departure of General Franco for Spain a month after the beginning of the rising.

From the outset, the Spanish national movement claimed that its policy was based on two principles; the first was that Morocco was one and indivisible, and the other that the purpose of the protectorate was to restore the country's historic personality. Though allegiance to such principles may sound commonplace, it was in fact a sign of originality at a moment

---

[1] Allal al-Fasi, *The Independence Movements in North Africa* (Washington, 1954, p. 149; originally published in Arabic, Cairo, 1948).

when there was a tendency to convert protectorates into colonies in neighbouring areas.

In application of the two principles, considerable freedom was allowed to the Arabic press. The first paper to appear was *al-Hurriya* (Freedom), edited by Abdel Khalek Torres, who had recently founded the first Moroccan political party, al-Islah (Reform).[1] A little later one of his former assistants, Mekki al-Nasiri, founded a second party and paper to which he gave the name *al-Wahda al-Maghribiya* (Moroccan Unity). One or other, or both, of these parties was favoured by the High Commissioner according to the circumstances of the moment. The parties were also authorized to found free schools. Direct Spanish control over Muslim Justice, Education, and Religious Endowments was relaxed, the post of Minister of Habous being accepted by Abdel Khalek Torres and that of Inspector of Education by Mohammed Daud, a nationalist sympathizer. The latter visited Egypt and on his return was able to introduce a number of reforms acceptable to nationalist opinion. Six Egyptian professors were brought to teach in Tetuan, while a number of students were sent to study in Madrid and Cairo with scholarships from the administration. Thus in 1938 the Khalifa told a Syrian journalist that 'Spain, far from persecuting the natural and healthy nationalist movement, welcomes it warmly and gives it constant proofs of its sympathy'. Though both Torres and Daud later resigned as a protest against restrictions placed on their liberty of action, this liberalization of the régime resulted in the complete tranquillity of the zone throughout all the vicissitudes of the Civil War. Nationalist Spaniards on their side felt a sense of gratitude for this participation in their eventual triumph on the part of those whose fate had been linked by destiny with their own. It was indeed noteworthy occurring, as it did, only ten years after the end of the Rif war.

At the end of the civil conflict, Spain was a wreck. The Second World War made it more than ever difficult to remedy the shortage of supplies and foodstuffs. At the expense of considerable effort, priority was given to the Moroccan protectorate during the world conflict, at the cost of making the zone appear privileged in comparison with Spain itself and with the rest of Morocco.

Giving as the reason the state of war prevailing between the co-protectors of the international zone of Tangier, Spanish forces in June, 1940 occupied the city and zone in the name of

---

[1] Previously there had existed only a loose organization common to both zones and known as the *Kutlat al-Amal al-Watani* or National Action Bloc.

the Khalifa. The decision provoked no reaction from Moroccans, but was greatly resented by the Allies, though in fact it was of no benefit to the Axis. In her own interest, Spain discouraged propaganda destined to favour a change of protectors. In 1941 General Orgaz took over the High Commissionership from General Asensio, who had succeeded General Beigbeder in 1939, and he was still in office at the time of the Allied landings in November 1942. These had a decisive influence in the acceleration of the movement for Moroccan independence.

The nationalist Moroccan scene at once began to change very perceptibly. Independence was no longer a remote goal to be reached by progressive stages; it became an immediate demand which accentuated the division between the older generation and the younger. One result of this was a clash between the nationalists and the Spanish authorities, a situation which became acute when the High Commissionership was taken over by Lieut. General Varela in 1945. On the economic side, the position in the zone was made very difficult by a severe drought in the year 1945–6 which resulted in actual famine. The nationalists, who were now working in close co-operation with those in the French zone, inaugurated a period of open opposition and came into conflict with the police during meetings held in Tetuan. This conflict did not, however, mean that the principle that Morocco should in time recover her independence was denied. The trouble was confined to Tetuan and to the adherents of the Islah Party; it did not seriously affect the general development of the zone. In 1946, however, Abdel Khalek Torres retired to Egypt, where he made contact with other North African leaders and helped to lay the bases of co-ordinated action throughout the Maghrib. In June 1947 another nationalist, Mehdi Bennouna, was sent to New York to carry on propaganda at the United Nations.

In the beginning of 1948 a meeting took place in Tangier between General Juin, Resident General in the French zone, and General Varela. When various nationalist leaders from the Spanish zone arrived shortly afterwards from Cairo and from New York, they were forbidden to enter the Spanish zone. Protest demonstrations which took place in Tetuan on 8 February resulted in loss of life both among the demonstrators and the police. This led to the arrest of the committee of the Islah Party.

Meanwhile, however, the inhabitants of the Khalifan zone continued to acquire the skills necessary for self-government, even though advance was far slower than they wished. In 1948 a Ministry of Public Instruction was created. Modifications were also made in the structure of the Khalifan Makhzen, while five-year plans were drawn up for economic development.

The Coming of Independence

On the death of Lieut. General Varela in 1951, he was succeeded by Lieut. General García Valiño. The latter released the political detainees and in 1952 Abdel Khalek Torres returned from Egypt; once again there began to be at least a limited degree of co-operation with the authorities. A new Arabic paper, *al-Umma* (The Nation), was founded and was allowed to express the ideas of the nationalists with great freedom, at least as far as concerned the French-controlled zone. Meanwhile the violent state of tension there continued to increase without having serious repercussions in the Khalifan zone, though it did unite the whole Moroccan population in a great and growing longing for independence. The nationalists in the northern zone began to criticize with increasing violence the restrictions placed on political activity outside the towns and the slowness of the advance towards self-government. General García Valiño replied by undertaking that Spaniards should be replaced in administrative posts by Moroccans as fast as the latter should become available. He also persuaded Abdel Khalek Torres and another nationalist to accept posts as ministers. The deposition of Sultan Mohammed V on 20 August 1953 finally produced a complete unanimity of feeling in zones whose circumstances were by no means the same. The favourable attitude adopted by Spain towards the exiled monarch was due partly to respect for the obligations undertaken in the Treaty of Fez but also to her understanding of the political background and her regard for the feelings of the Moroccan people. At a mass meeting in Tetuan in January 1954 the High Commissioner gave spectacular support to Moroccan protests at the deposition of the Sultan and undertook to forward them to the Head of State in Madrid. This action was appreciated by the Moroccan population, and the inhabitants of the zone manifested very emphatically their fidelity to their Sultan and their patriotic ardour.

When the latter returned from exile in October 1955 Moroccan national sentiment was grateful for the Spanish attitude during the dramatic and anxious moments through which the nationalist movement had been passing. Nevertheless a certain caution and reserve marked Spanish policy towards Morocco after the sudden change in the French attitude which had found expression in the declaration of La Celle St. Cloud on

6 November 1955. This disconcerted and irritated Moroccans, notably the political leaders, and was misunderstood in foreign countries. In its declaration the French Government had spoken of independence, but also of interdependence. The Spanish Government sought to find out whether this ambiguous term concealed an intention to maintain French influence in a new form and indeed extend it to the rest of Morocco from which Spain would meanwhile have been excluded. Until this point had been cleared up, the Spanish Government was not willing to take the course of endorsing the declaration of independence.

Exploratory conversations between Madrid and Rabat, lasting for some months, enabled the immediate difficulties to be surmounted. At the invitation of General Franco, the Sultan then visited Madrid; and on 7 April 1956 the two Heads of State signed a joint declaration by which Spain recognized the independence and the unity of Morocco. Practical effect was given to the new position in two ways. The northern zone was reintegrated administratively with the rest of Morocco; and further negotiations were arranged to clarify Spanish-Moroccan relations in general.

It was clear that these negotiations would often be difficult, since there are many matters still outstanding between the two countries. In the northern zone the question of the withdrawal of the Spanish troops would arise in time, just as it did immediately with the French troops in the south. As is described elsewhere (p. 196), the position of the Spanish and Spanish-controlled territories in the south-west of Morocco and in the Sahara was necessarily affected by the renewed independence of Morocco. In the north itself the status of the cities of Ceuta and Melilla, which have been under Spanish sovereignty for centuries, had been queried by political parties and individuals in Morocco and could become a source of misunderstanding.

Nevertheless Spanish-Moroccan relations entered the new era under a happy star, even if they were very soon to be embittered by the insurrection in Ifni. Historically speaking, Spain is the European country with most Islamic affinities, while Morocco is the Islamic country most akin geographically to Europe. The consequent physical and spiritual propinquity has often been accompanied by bitter warfare between them, or rather between the various Christian and Muslim governments which have ruled on either side of the Straits of Gibraltar. But it has also created a store of common experience and interests which can be turned to the uses of friendly relationship. During twenty years Spain consistently adopted a more sympathetic attitude towards the Arab world than any other European power, and she gained credit with the Muslim peoples of North Africa for her refusal to associate herself with the French deposition of Mohammed V. The nationalists of the northern zone were just as resentful of Spanish control as the southerners were of French; but from the end of the war in the Rif the material clash was never so violent nor bitter feeling so widespread as in the neighbouring zone. The fact that no Spaniard was assaulted or in any way molested during the whole of the troubled period which preceded the declaration of independence is a matter of pride to those Spanish who had made their homes in Morocco; and it will no doubt be claimed by them as favourable evidence when history comes to give its verdict on Spanish conduct during their protectorate of the northern zone.

ADMINISTRATION AND POLITICAL LIFE

Administrative Organization

A decree of 24 January 1916 regulated the administrative organization of the Khalifan zone. Though subsequently much modified, two principles persisted throughout. The first was to respect the personality of Morocco by maintaining its characteristic organs of authority and administration. The second was to make the High Commission the corner-stone of an administration which was either parallel, or superior, to the Moroccan administration. In matters, which were within the sole competence of the protector, there was no parallel Moroccan body.

At the time of the declaration of independence, there existed three types of government organism, each with its own officials: Moroccan; mixed Spanish-Moroccan; and purely Spanish.

Under the authority of the Khalifa or Viceroy, who was assisted by a Privy Council, composed of twelve Moroccans and advised by the High Commissioner, there existed a Council of Ministers presided over by a Grand Wazir who was at the same time Minister of the Interior. These ministers had as little authority in matters of policy as those in the neighbouring French zone.

Under this Council was a Ministry of Justice and Habous, which was purely Moroccan, as well as Ministries of Agriculture and Production, of Economics and Trade, and of Social Affairs and Public Instruction. These had mixed Spanish and Moroccan staffs and were parallel with bodies within the High Commission.

Each of the 69 tribal areas (*kabila*) was administered by a Caid. These were subdivided into 307 districts (*fracciones*), and 3,663 villages (*aduares*); the latter contained an average of 218 inhabitants each. In 1935 rural councils (*jamaas*) were formed; in the tribal areas these were presided over by a Caid; in the districts by a Shaikh. The cities had town councils (*Juntas de Servicios Municipales*) which were presided over by the *Basha* (Mayor or Governor) and had Spanish and Moroccan staffs.

The High Commission was the depository of the powers of the protecting state. It contained all the services of a modern administration and was staffed by Spaniards. It worked in direct contact with the central Makhzen of the Khalifa, and through the District Commissioners (*Interventores*) in the case of the local Moroccan authorities. The *Interventores* themselves worked to the Native Affairs Office (*Delegación de Asuntos Indigenas*) which was linked to the High Commission. The High Commission reserved to itself diplomatic representation and defence and security.

Armed Forces

The armed forces included:

Moroccan units (Khalifan troops): five *mehallas* of infantry (total 5,000) and one of cavalry. In these all the private soldiers, n.c.o.'s, and some commissioned officers were Moroccan, commanded by Spanish officers and with Spanish instructors.

The *Makhazniya*. This was a Constabulary composed of Moroccans, with a Spanish command.

All the above units have now been incorporated into the Royal Moroccan Army.

The '*Regulares*' or mixed units. Five Tabors (total 1,500) including both Moroccan and Spanish soldiers. The officers were Spanish and Moroccan; the command Spanish.

The Spanish Army in Morocco. This had all the units and services of a modern army and was composed exclusively of Spaniards.

The existence of the various forces detailed above was compatible with real unity, thanks to a unified high command. Modifications in the organization of the protectorate, as far as the armed forces were concerned, were virtually limited to their subordination, or otherwise, to the High Commissioner. At the time of the declaration of independence, the High Commissioner was also Commander-in-Chief of the armed forces in Morocco.

Justice

In organizing the legal system, a Moroccan jurisdiction was preserved. The Spanish-Khalifan tribunals, created in 1914, dealt with needs which arose from the circumstances of the protectorate.

Muslim Courts. Sharia Courts depended from the Ministry of Justice. Their procedure remained unchanged. Little by little their attributions were limited to questions of personal status and inheritance; these were decided according to the Maliki rite.

In 1935 the Makhzen Courts were transformed into courts independent of the governmental authorities such as the town governors (*bashas*). They dealt with civil and criminal cases.

Jewish Courts. The Jewish community possessed Rabbinic courts and its own notarial service. These were governed by juridical principles of Spanish-Jewish origin—the so-called 'Custom of Castile' (*Costumbre de Castilla*).

Spanish-Khalifan Courts. Justices of the Peace and Courts of First Instance, with a Court of Appeal in Tetuan. Final appeal to the Spanish Supreme Court.

There were also military courts and a British Consular Court.

Relations between the two zones were regulated according to an agreement of 1916.

Political Parties

The earliest activities which can be properly described as nationalist, or at least as proto-nationalist, are connected in the northern zone with the name of Abd al-Salam Bennouna, who has been called the 'father of Moroccan nationalism'. A former Minister of Justice, he founded a free school in Tetuan in 1923. Wishing to secure a good independent Arabic education for his sons he sent them to the Najah School at Nablus in mandated Palestine, an example which was followed by a number of other parents in Tetuan. Here they acquired a familiarity with the English language and with the politically more advanced Arab world of the east. One of them, Mehdi Bennouna, later wrote an account of the nationalist movement which has been quoted in the present work; the eldest brother, Taieb, was to become the first Governor of Tetuan after the achievement of independence and later Ambassador to Spain. Abd al-Salam Bennouna also endeavoured to interest his compatriots in industrial enterprises, and successfully founded the Spanish-Moroccan Electricity Company, with predominantly Moroccan capital. He died, while visiting Ronda in Spain, in January

M

1935 and a detailed obituary by the pan-Arab Syrian leader Shakib Arslan, appeared in the subsequent number of *La Nation Arabe*, published in Geneva.

Moroccan nationalism, western in sentiment and methods, became evident in the Khalifan zone about 1931 and found expression in a committee of young men which was linked with the National Action Bloc in the French zone. In 1936, a year after the death of Abd al-Salam Bennouna, Abdel Khalek Torres founded the Islah or Reform Party. This maintained contact with the corresponding movement in the south and, with the coming of independence was merged into the Istiqlal Party. Chronologically it had been the first nationalist group in Morocco to be constituted as a political party. Torres himself became first Moroccan Ambassador to Spain, and subsequently to Egypt.

At the beginning of 1937 Mekki Nasiri, seconded by the Temsamani brothers from the Rif, founded the Moroccan Unity Party (*al-Wahda al-Maghribiya*) which functioned principally in Tangier. Some analogy can be seen between this party and the splinter party of Mohammed al-Wazzani in the southern zone.

In 1938 a so-called Liberal Party was founded whose action was limited to Moroccan officialdom. It was headed by the *Basha* of Larache, Khalid Raisuni, eldest son of the Sharif Raisuni of the early days of the protectorate. Married to a Spanish wife he became a leading supporter of the Spanish connexion. In the early days of the independence, after an attack on himself and his followers, he took refuge in Spain. The party dissolved, without ever attracting much notice, during the High Commissionership of General Orgaz.

In 1952 a party, *al-Maghrib-al Hurr* (Free Morocco), directed by Mohammed Zeriouh, came into being, with its headquarters at Nador, near Melilla. It published a paper of the same name. In November of the same year its activities were greatly reduced by the intervention of the authorities.

SOCIAL CONDITIONS

Health

At the beginning of the protectorate, health measures were a function of the army medical service. Later they were regulated by the *Instrucción General de Sanidad* (Public Health Decree) of 1921, which was applied and developed through successive vizirial decrees.

Service was given in 5 general hospitals, one for each territory (Lucus, Jebala, Gomara, Rif, and Kert), with attached pharmacies; 2 sanatoriums; 2 maternity homes (Tetuan, Alcazarquivir); 3 children's clinics; a nursing home at Arcila; a tuberculosis sanatorium; a leper colony at Larache; a lunatic asylum; and special dispensaries for trachoma, venereal diseases, malaria, and tuberculosis, established in the various towns. In the country there were 44 clinics, 18 rural medical centres, and 30 dispensaries. Consultations and advice on infant welfare were frequently available in the weekly markets.

In 1955 the number of sick treated in civil hospitals and of consultations in dispensaries and other centres amounted to 374,055.

The health services were backed by the Social Welfare Service supported by funds produced by *beneficenza* taxes, such as the stamps attached to hotel and restaurant bills. It gave special attention to the welfare of infants under 3 years old (care and feeding) and subsidized meals for necessitous children in the schools; the daily attendance in the dining rooms amounted to 5,300 children.

Education

There were two distinct periods in the organization of public instruction. In the first, assimilation was the guiding principle and was achieved through Spanish-Arab schools. In 1938, however, it was decided that Morocco should acquire modern culture without abandoning its own roots and language; a Moroccan school system was, therefore, created which was administered by the Ministry of Public Instruction, advised (*asesorado*) by the Delegation of Education and Culture attached to the High Commission.

Primary Education. A syllabus was drawn up adapted to the conditions of Morocco in respect of geography, history, grammar, religion, &c. There were Moroccan head and assistant masters, who were advised (*asesorado*) by Spanish teachers. Instruction was given through Arabic in so far as Moroccan staff was adequate to meet the increasing number of pupils.

Matriculation 1944–5 . . . 4,070
1954–5 . . . 13,206

Secondary Education. A Moroccan course for both boys and girls, covering four years, had 3,295 pupils in the school year 1954–5, of whom 1,181 were girls. This gave access (1) to the Spanish-Moroccan degree admitting to Middle Eastern universities; 541 entrants in 1954–5. (2) To Spanish degrees (5th to 7th year) admitting to Spanish universities and specialist schools; 92 entrants in 1954–5. (3) To a Polytechnic which gave agricultural and commercial training; degrees in administration; and prepared foremen, medical assistants, and midwives. Students (1954–5) 188. (4) Training schools for teachers. In 1954–5 these had 202 students of whom 136 were girls.

Religious Teaching. This was under exclusively Moroccan control and included primary, secondary, and advanced teaching. There were some 200 schools of this type.

Free Schools (Enseñanza Libre). With the permission of the authorities the Islah (Reform) and Moroccan Unity parties organized primary and secondary schools. These followed similar courses to the government schools but were more closely modelled on the system followed in Egypt and laid a greater stress on Moroccan patriotism.

Jewish Schools. The Jewish community possessed schools of its own; these were reorganized in 1938. They consisted of classes covering the entire period of primary instruction (*grupos escolares*) and were maintained by the Makhzen budget. There were also independent schools belonging to the *Alliance Israélite.*

Spanish Schools and Institutes. These came under the Delegation of Education and Culture and followed the programme of the corresponding schools in Spain. There were also two conservatoires of music, as well as industrial and labour schools, and a school of Moroccan arts and crafts. There were five libraries and five museums.

Some of the Spanish school-age population attended primary and secondary Spanish schools and colleges for both sexes which were maintained by the religious orders. These were attended also by a certain number of Moroccan pupils, both Muslim and Jewish.

ECONOMIC CONDITIONS

Agriculture

Agriculture is the basis of the economy of the northern zone. Though the total area of theoretically cultivable land is 1,700,000 acres, half of this is arid since the rainfall varies from 24–32 inches in Tetuan in the north-west to 8–12 inches in the south-east. For this reason the agricultural land does not amount to more than 940,000 acres, with an average of 1·1 inhabitants per cultivated acre as opposed to 0·5 in the southern area.

Efforts to improve cultivation and increase productivity come up against the nature of the soil, the doubtful rainfall, and the minute land holdings. Nevertheless the area in which cereals are cultivated, forming 86·6 of the total, has been increased, though the harvest remains at the mercy of the rains. The zone is in deficit in the production of grain for bread-making.

The culture of trees, fostered by nurseries, has increased considerably, there being 371,649 trees in 1955. Thanks to reafforestation, notably in the dunes of Tashdirt and Larache and in the plain of Ajdir, and to forest conservation, there are estimated to be 1,210,000 acres of wooded areas (including shrubland) mainly of cork trees, cedars (in Gomara and Ketama), oaks, and pines. Esparto grass is found in some areas. The quantities of wood produced are subject to great annual variation, according to the cutting permitted, and oscillate between 1,046,400 and 49,088 cubic yards of planks and between 82,000 and 70,000 tons of firewood.

Livestock suffers from the difficulty of inadequate pasturage and fodder crops, though the animal population has been slowly increasing since 1936. In 1955 there were 22,400 horses, 22,200 mules, 64,000 donkeys, 339,900 cattle, 734,000 sheep, 1,059,100 goats, 2,982 camels, and 4,269 pigs. The density of stock per square kilometre is 24 for cattle; 33·8 for sheep; and 52 for goats.

The fishing industry, which is almost entirely Spanish, is tending to increase. In 1956 the weight of fish caught was 9,000 tons; this compares with 90,000 tons in the rest of Morocco.

Mines

Practical experience soon destroyed the legend of the vast riches of the subsoil of the northern zone. The only really important industry is that of the iron ore of Kelata near Melilla which is exploited by three Spanish companies; of these the best-known, the Minas del Rif, had an output of 1,380,000 tons in 1956. There are also eight mining concessions for small industries, mining copper, lead, antimony, and bentonita. No oil, coal, or radio-active minerals have been found.

Industry

The limited viability of the zone, considered as an economic unit cut off from the whole, the scarcity of Moroccan capital, and the lack of interest on the part of Spanish financial groups are the causes for which little consideration was given under the protectorate to the possibility of industrialization. Existing industry is, therefore, confined to goods for local consumption, and has been created with a modest outlay. The principal industries are seventeen modern cement and tile-making installations; four foundries; the beginnings of a shipbuilding yard at

Larache; tanneries; sawmills, match, furniture, and canning factories.

On the eve of independence the construction of a fertilizer and chemical products factory was under consideration; and another for explosives, which is in course of construction.

There are 3 hydro-electric power stations, 32 thermal power stations, and 10 transformers. The output of 1955 was 66,800,000 kwh. and the consumption 56,900,000 kwh.; the potentiality of the installation 21,889 kva.

The Budget and the Moroccan Public Debt

Throughout the period of the protectorate, Spain covered the deficit in the budget of the Khalifan zone. From 1950 to 1955 this was established as follows:

(million pesetas)

Year	Total Budget	Local Resources	Advances and Grants-in-Aid at the charge of the Spanish Budget
1950 . .	280·4	138·9	141·5
1951 . .	280·4	138·9	141·5
1952 . .	378·8	168·8	210·0
1953 . .	378·8	165·1	213·8
1954 . .	470·2	220·2	250·0
1955 . .	470·2	220·2	250·0

In 1955 the Moroccan debt to Spain amounted to the following:

Advances from the Spanish state, theoretically repayable, to cover the zone's budget deficit from 1916 to 1955 inclusive. . 2,897,720,985 pesetas
(For 1916 the advance was 6,730,000 pesetas; in 1955, 250 million pesetas).
Value of loans (without counting the Imperial loan of 1910, at 5 per cent.) . 1,252,764,500

4,140,485,485

By the Spanish-Moroccan agreement of July 1957 the debt was written down to 2,300 million pesetas. It was considered as repaid by the transaction in which the peseta currency was withdrawn in January 1958.

The credits shown in the general State Budget of Spain (*Presupuestos Generales del Estado*) under the heading 'Spanish Action in Morocco' from 1913 to 1955 amount to 15,803 million pesetas.

Trade

The trade balance of the zone was in permanent disequilibrium; during the period 1951–5 there was an average of 100 pesetas of exports to 193·3 pesetas of imports.

(*million pesetas*)

Year	Total Imports	Total Exports	Relative Balance (*pesetas of imports for each hundred of exports*)
1951	808·4	300·5	269·0
1952	933·9	571·5	163·4
1953	950·7	627·5	151·5
1954	915·8	622·2	147·2
1955	984·2	748·7	135·5

During 1955 imports from Spain amounted to 519·4 million pesetas, and exports to Spain to 159·9, giving a relative balance of 324·8.

The countries to which the northern zone exported most were Great Britain (iron, vegetable fibres, and some cork) and Germany (iron, to a lesser extent than Britain; vegetable fibres and cork, to a greater extent than to Britain).

Imports came principally from Spain (all kinds of consumer goods such as foodstuffs, textiles, shoes, medicines, and light machinery); from Holland (radios and spare parts, electrical material, and the material for the narrow-gauge railway from Ceuta to Tetuan); from Cuba (sugar and tobacco), and from Belgium (iron for construction purposes and equipment material).

The economic pattern of the northern zone was radically changed by the withdrawal of the peseta currency and its transference to the franc area in January 1958.

Exports, e.g. cement, which had gone largely to Spain, were interrupted by the establishment of import and export quotas by both countries and by the need for payment in hard currencies. Similarly merchants supplying the internal market had to look for fresh sources of supply. The result was a growth of unemployment, at least for the time being, and a substantial rise in the cost of living. At the same time wages were more than doubled, as the result of the introduction of southern labour legislation; since these were now higher than the economy could support, this led to dismissals and short-time working. On the other hand horizons have been widened and when traders have adjusted themselves to the new conditions both they and the population as a whole should be able to profit from the new opportunities open. For example, a steel industry may be created using iron from the Rif mines and anthracite from Djerada in the former southern zone near-by.

THE TANGIER INTERNATIONAL ZONE, 1912–57

History

Tangier, situated at the western entrance of the Straits of Gibraltar, at the point where Africa most nearly approaches Europe, has always seemed a desirable prize to foreign powers and its history has therefore been eventful.

As long ago as fifteen centuries before Christ, Phoenician mariners seem to have established a trading post here corresponding to Gades (Cadiz) on the European shore. This post was later taken over by the Tyrian colony, Carthage, as were other such posts on the African coast. In the year 38 B.C. the Roman legions of Sertorius, lieutenant of Octavius, occupied the town then known as Tingis, in the course of their pursuit of King Bocchus of Mauritania who had been the ally of Mark Antony. In 42 the city became the capital of the Roman province of Mauritania Tingitana, with the name of Tingis Colonia Julia Traducta; and it continued to be the commercial capital even when Volubilis succeeded it as the political capital. The Romans remained for five centuries. After the dislocation of the western Empire, Roman rule was re-established by Byzantium in the course of Justinian's desperate attempt to restore the unity of the empire, and the Arabs found a Byzantine governor there at the end of the seventh century. After a resistance which lasted for years, the city was captured by Musa ibn Nusair in 707 and became a base for the Arab invasion of Spain. In the twelfth century, when the Almohads undertook the defence of Muslim Spain against the Christian reconquest, they turned Tangier into a busy port and equipped it with an arsenal. In the fifteenth century, when the tables had been turned and Morocco had to defend herself against invasion, the Portuguese got possession of Tangier, in 1471, in the course of their systematic acquisition of Moroccan ports. They can be said to have remained for two centuries, if we ignore the fact that from 1581 to 1643 the Spanish flag flew over Tangier since Portugal herself formed part of the Spanish domains for that period. In 1661 Catherine of Braganza by her marriage to Charles II of England brought Tangier with her as her dowry and the city thus became a possession of the British crown. The

English improved the port and fortified it, but were not able to prevent the people of the Rif from harassing the city, which in 1678 was moreover besieged by the reigning Sultan, Maulay Ismail. Parliament in London having decided that continued occupation was not worth while, the British troops in 1684 evacuated the city after demolishing the citadel and destroying the harbour mole. The town thus returned to Moroccan sovereignty under which it has since remained. While a number of Moroccan cities used to be virtually closed to unbelievers, Tangier was always open to them and many European merchants established themselves in it. At the end of the eighteenth century, the powers transferred their Consulates to the city and after the Spanish-Moroccan War of 1860 raised them to the rank of Legations. The presence of a diplomatic corps, around which a considerable European colony revolved, helped to give Tangier an international air and to establish important foreign interests in it. This situation was destined to give rise, when circumstances were propitious, to an international régime. Even before, while the town was still administered by a Pasha as were other Moroccan towns, the Makhzen delegated its attributes in sanitary matters to the diplomatic corps. A Sanitary Council thus came to be created in 1872; this had the duty of watching over the health conditions of the town and port. It was followed in 1892 by a Health Commission formed from members of the various foreign colonies.

Tangier played its part in the various conflicts and agreements on the subject of Morocco which marked the harmony or discord of the powers during the first decade of the twentieth century. The Anglo-French Agreement of 8 April 1904, in which a special position was recognized to France in Morocco, specified that Tangier and the surrounding country should be given a régime of its own, in recognition of the presence of the diplomatic corps and of the city's municipal and sanitary institutions.

The secret Franco-Spanish agreement of 3 October 1904 similarly respected the special status of Tangier. This was not, however, specified in the Act of Algeciras of 1906; it was merely decided that the policing of the city should be entrusted to two Moroccan tabors (companies), commanded in the one case by French and the other by Spanish officers, under the command of a Swiss colonel. The Treaty of Fez of 1912, which established the French protectorate over Morocco, specified in Article I that 'the town of Tangier will retain the special character which it has been recognized to possess and this will determine its municipal organization'. The agreement of 27 November 1912 between France and Spain excluded Tangier from the Spanish zone and reaffirmed the necessity of a 'special régime'.

The establishment of this régime was delayed by the war of 1914–18. It was thus not until 18 December 1923 that an agreement was signed at Paris between France, Spain, and Great Britain, establishing what was known as the 'Statute of Tangier'. The Sultan (which in practice meant the French authorities) was represented by a Mendub who was nominally responsible for the administration of the Moroccan population. A permanent delegation of powers of legislation and administration was granted to a Legislative Assembly; this was presided over by the Mendub and was composed of 17 Europeans and of 6 Muslim and 3 Jewish Moroccans. A Committee of Control, composed of Consuls of the powers which had signed the Act of Algeciras (excluding Germany and Austria, who had been defeated in the war), had the duty of seeing that the Statute was carried out. The zone was neutralized for military purposes; economic equality was guaranteed; capitulations were suppressed and a Mixed Court created, composed of European judges. The post of administrator, allotted to a French subject for the opening period of six years, was in fact retained by a Frenchman until 1940. In 1928 representatives of Italy and Portugal joined the Committee of Control, while certain modifications were introduced in order to meet the wishes of the Spanish Government.

The latter had always held that Tangier should form part of the Spanish zone, in which it formed a small enclave. In 1940 the collapse of France in the Second World War enabled Spain to realize this wish. Giving as justification the need to preserve the neutrality of the zone, she occupied it militarily on 14 July of that year. The international régime was abolished and the functions of the Mendub suppressed. Tangier and its zone were thereby assimilated to the territory in which the Sultan had delegated his powers to the Khalifa of Tetuan. This annexation lasted no longer than the war. After the Allied victory in 1945 Great Britain, the United States, and France determined on the immediate re-establishment of an international régime. A conference held at Paris in August 1945 was attended by their representatives and those of the Soviet Union. This decided provisionally to restore the Statute of 1923. The United States and the Soviet Union each acquired the right to send three representatives to the Committee of Control. The Soviet Union, however, declared that she would not use the right as long as the Franco régime continued in Spain. The forces of the latter country were to evacuate the zone by 11 October 1945, and it was agreed that the Chief Administrator should be Belgian, Portuguese, Dutch, or Swedish. A conference to be convoked within six months after the establishment of the provisional régime was to draw up a definitive Statute. This conference, however, never met.

On 30 March 1952, which was the fortieth anniversary of the signing of the Treaty of Fez, demonstrations occurred in Tangier which were directed primarily against the French. Spain thereupon proposed that the meeting foreseen in 1945 should now be held. The other powers did not agree to this, but consented to adjustments decided on by the Committee of Control. Thus two police forces were created, one urban and the other rural; the former having a Spanish commandant with a French assistant and the latter a French commandant with a Spanish assistant. Great Britain, Italy, and Spain each had their representation in the Committee of Control enlarged. This arrangement was initialed on 10 November 1952.

In 1953 the Mendub of Tangier, being subject to French influence, recognized the accession of Mohammed ibn Arafa as Sultan, while the Khalifa in the Spanish zone remained faithful to the exiled monarch.

In 1956 agreements between Morocco and France on the one hand and between Spain and Morocco on the other, by giving official recognition to the independence of the latter country, presaged the abolition of the zones and the unification of the country. The question of Tangier, with its international régime and problems of its own, called for special negotiations.

On the basis of the Protocol of 5 July 1956, which recognized the authority of the Sultan as alone valid in the administrative and legislative field, the former international zone was formed into a province and a Governor named on 10 July. In October of the same year representatives of Morocco, France, Spain, Great Britain, the United States, Italy, Belgium, the Netherlands, and Portugal met first in Fedala, and then in Tangier. A final declaration signed on 29 October 1956 abolished the international statute and completely integrated the former zone with the rest of Morocco. For the moment, however, no alteration was made in the economic and financial régime which was to be regulated later by a Royal Charter. Direct agreements were to be reached with France, Spain, Great Britain, and Italy in order to fix the status of health and educational institutions belonging to them or to their nationals.

The economic system established under the former statute

was of extreme liberalism. Capital could enter or leave without any control and all kinds of national currencies circulated freely, their rates of exchange being fixed by supply and demand. Taxation, which was very low, was almost entirely indirect, being derived to the extent of 80 per cent. from customs dues. There was no profit or income tax, and no death duties; nor were there any social welfare charges. Limited liability companies were not liable to taxation, nor did they have to produce accounts or a balance sheet. The result was that they abounded; the year 1951 alone saw 708 come into existence, representing a capital of a milliard francs. Trade was completely free with foreign countries, but restricted to products of Moroccan origin as far as the rest of Morocco was concerned.

The Royal Charter envisaged by the final declaration of the Conference of Fedala was promulgated on 26 August 1957. In general it maintained the former economic and financial system, including the free money market, quota-free trade with foreign countries, and low taxation. The exchange of goods between Tangier and the rest of the kingdom was to be regulated by subsequent order. The Charter was silent concerning other aspects of the Tangier régime, for which reference must be made to the Protocol of 29 October 1956 which stipulated that laws and regulations in force at Tangier would continue to be applicable as long as they had not been abolished or modified. A final article in the Charter fixed six months' notice for any proposed modification of the Charter.

Population

The population of the former Tangier zone has never been determined by census; but it can be taken as being about 120,000 Moroccans, of whom 15,000 are Jews, and about 52,000 foreigners.

The Moroccans are entirely Arabic-speaking, as they have been for a long time past, like the remaining population of the neighbouring areas. Owing to its troubled history, the city has a population of very mixed origins. After the departure of the English in 1684 mountaineers from the Rif occupied the town and divided the properties which had been abandoned among themselves and to a large extent settled on them. This is the origin of most inhabitants of the Fahs or area around the city. The big Muslim families of the city are mainly descended from Rifi chieftains of the reconquest.

The Jews seem to have disappeared from the city before the Muslim reoccupation as the result of persecution on the part of Christians as well as of Muslims. Those who live there today come for the most part from Tetuan, and often have Spanish names.

The most important of the foreign colonies was the Spanish, who formed about a third of the total European population. This was due to the proximity of Spain and to the attraction exercised on Spanish workers by rates of wages which were higher than in the neighbouring portion of the peninsula or in the surrounding Spanish-protected zone. Spanish was used more than any other European language in Tangier, and was followed by French. In the same way the peseta was the most used currency, though the legal tender was the Moroccan franc. The Spanish paper *España* was the most important of the city, and had a considerable circulation in Spain also.

The French colony did not amount to more than about 3,000 in 1940 but has almost trebled in the last few years. Its influence was always greater than its numbers suggested, partly because a French controller advised the Mendub and partly because there were many French officials in various branches of the administrations. French influence made itself strongly felt in the cultural field though the existence of two Lycées, of which one has now been allotted to the French cultural mission, and of five primary schools as well as eight 'Franco-Musulman' schools in which instruction was and is given in Arabic and French. French investments in Tangier were particularly important in the fields of banking and construction. Real estate belonging to French subjects formed 40 per cent. of the total in the period immediately preceding independence. This compared with 20 per cent. Spanish and 25 per cent. Moroccan. The Banque d'État du Maroc, which is five-sevenths French held, and other French banks, are together responsible for 80 per cent. of the total of business transactions. There is a French daily newspaper, the *Dépêche Marocaine*.

The British colony is estimated at 1,300, many of whom are Gibraltarians. It had its own post office, closed since independence, and in 1958 still had a weekly paper, the *Tangier Gazette*. Its activities were latterly doubled by those of the Americans who were less numerous but had more organs by which they could make their influence felt. After them, there come Italian, Portuguese, Belgian, Dutch, Swiss, and Hindu colonies, each having a few hundred members.

Economic Conditions

The natural resources of the former zone are limited. Its little territory, covering about 400 square kilometres, has no riches. Water is barely sufficient, and agriculture and stock-raising are not very prosperous. There is enough fishing to supply the local market. The only fortune of Tangier is in its situation which is one of great beauty.

The port, recently enlarged and modernized, has hitherto suffered from competition by Casablanca, Ceuta, and Gibraltar. Thanks to the unification of the country, it should now become the normal outlet for much of northern Morocco. A recent decree (3 August 1957) may have happy results in this sphere since it sanctions the grant of Moroccan nationality to shipping registered in Tangier, provided that it calls there at least once in every three months and is the property of 'persons domiciled in Morocco or of societies having their headquarters in Tangier or a branch with its headquarters in this port'. Regular sailings connect Tangier with Algeciras, Gibraltar, Casablanca, and Marseilles. The number of ships using the harbour was 2,507 in 1956, with a tonnage of 2,664,000. Tangier thus comes fourth in rank of Moroccan ports, following Fedala.

The airport, which is the property of Air France, is served by Moroccan, French, Spanish, Portuguese, and British lines.

Tangier is linked with the rest of Morocco by the Tangier-Fez railway and by roads leading through Tetuan to Wazzan and Melilla and through Larache to Rabat. It is also an important centre of broadcasting and telecommunications, having five transmitting stations.

Tourism plays an important part in the economy of the town, which has 2,700 hotel bedrooms and 128 restaurants. In 1956 346,000 travellers visited the town and 44,000 cars were embarked or disembarked in the port. Many of these 'visitors', however, are French residents from the southern zone who are returning from or going on holiday to France through Spain.

Industry in Tangier is not so unimportant as is ordinarily supposed. The building industry at the end of the Second World War gave employment to thousands of workers and involved an investment of millions of pounds. Later, however, this activity came to an end; at the end of the international régime there was no housing shortage in Tangier, except for the most necessitous class who were lodged in *bidonvilles* which were small compared with those of towns in the southern zone. A cement factory, employing 200 workers, produces 50,000 tons annually. Two textile factories handle in the one case jute, in the other cotton. Twenty shirt and similar establishments produce almost exclusively for the southern zone.

The trade balance has always been in deficit. Imports which diminished from 1953 onwards recovered in 1956, reaching nearly 12·5 milliard francs, while exports were a little less than 3 milliards, leaving a deficit of about 9·5 milliards.

Tangier sold between a half and two-thirds of its products to the rest of Morocco, particularly the northern zone, while it purchased from it only about 15 per cent. of its total. The principal suppliers in descending scale of importance were France, Spain, the United States, the rest of Morocco, Japan, and Great Britain. The principal purchasers were the rest of Morocco, the United States, Germany, the Netherlands, Gibraltar, Spain, Benelux, and Italy. Half these imports consisted of articles of food and clothing. Exports are of Tangerine origin to the extent of 35 per cent.; re-exports from the northern zone account for 15 per cent. and re-exports of foreign goods for 50 per cent. The trade deficit by monetary zones was distributed in 1956 as follows: franc zone 20·2 per cent.; peseta zone 11·59 per cent.; sterling zone 8·2 per cent.; U.S. dollar zone 18·7 per cent.; and other countries, particularly dollars and Swiss francs, 41·1 per cent.

This deficit obviously ignores the 'invisible exports' which have also to be taken into account. Here Tangier's position as a financial centre enters into the picture, thanks to the freedom of exchange and exemption from taxation, supported by an imposing banking structure. It is impossible to estimate the value of commissions, custody charges, and interest, or of speculative gains. The prosperity of Tangier in this financial aspect is subject to great variation. In the immediate post-war period and in moments of international tension the city has been a place of refuge for capital. With the coming of independence, however, it lost a great deal of its capital and practically all its gold deposits, which left for other financial centres such as Switzerland, Portugal, and South America. In any case the economy of Tangier never derived any great benefit either from the capital or from the gold deposits, since these were inspired by speculative motives and were rarely invested in productive enterprises.

The working class in particular derived no benefit at all from this state of affairs. On the contrary it suffered from the extreme liberalism of the economy and the lack of social legislation. It was not until March 1956 that a minimum wage of 34 pesetas a day was fixed by law, equal at that time to 290 francs and comparing to the Casablanca minimum wage of 536. The cost of living was it is true also very much lower than in the southern zone, though a good deal higher than in the northern.

In view of these facts, it cannot be assumed, in spite of

appearances, that Tangier's prosperity is dependent on the former monetary and fiscal régime. The future of the port and the economic activity of the province is bound up with that of the rest of the country, since its principal outlet for goods is the Moroccan market and the development of the port has hitherto been checked if not entirely prevented by the division of the national territory into zones. The new customs tariffs apply in Tangier as in other parts of the country.[1]

[1] For political developments in Morocco to the end of November 1958 see Addenda, p. 380 below.

II

THE GARRISON TOWNS (*PRESIDIOS*) OF CEUTA AND MELILLA, THE CHAFARINAS ISLANDS, AND THE PEÑONS OF ALHUCEMAS AND GOMERA

THE two towns of Ceuta and Melilla, and these various small islands, are situated on or just off the northern coast of Morocco. In Spanish terminology they are known as *Plazas de Soberanía* or fortified places of Spanish sovereignty. Children born there are Spanish citizens and apart from small minorities the inhabitants are Christians of peninsular origin. Administratively they depend either from the central Government directly or from one of the mainland provinces.

CEUTA AND MELILLA

Mythology relates that it was in Ceuta (Arabic *Sibta*, from Latin *Ad Septem Fratres*) and Gibraltar that Hercules set up the columns which he had split asunder in order to form the Straits dividing Africa from Europe. In historical times Ceuta was in turn a trading and political base of the Phoenicians, the Carthaginians, the Romans, and the Byzantines. It was there that the Vandals disembarked to conquer North Africa. Later, in the time of the Visigoths, the Byzantine Governor Count Julian, being determined to avenge the seduction of his daughter by the Gothic King Roderick, assisted the passage of the first Muslim troops into Spain, by himself conducting a trial raid in the month of October 709. It was from Ceuta in 741 that an Arab army which had been defeated by the Berbers in Africa passed over into Spain to rescue the recently established Arab Amirate of Córdoba from being overwhelmed by the Berbers in Spain. In 931 Abd al-Rahman III annexed Ceuta to the Amirate of Córdoba which he had recently declared a Caliphate. After the fall of the Caliphate in 1031, Ceuta shared the vicissitudes of the rest of Morocco. In 1084 it was captured by the Almoravids and it was thence that Yusuf ibn Tashufin embarked in 1086 to come to the help of the Muslims of Spain. The Almohad leader Abd al-Mumin occupied it in 1148; 125 years later it passed into the power of the rising Beni Merin dynasty. They kept it until 1305 when they lost it for a period of four years, after which it passed back into their power when a King of Castile, Ferdinand IV, failed in an attempt to seize it and so secure control of the Straits.

Before the end of the prolonged agony of the Muslim Kingdom of Granada, Ceuta entered the sphere of the now almost entirely Christian peninsula when it was captured by John I of Portugal, with the help of a number of British ships, in 1415.[1] Twenty-two years later the Moroccan Sultan received the person of the Portuguese Infante, Don Fernando, who had participated in a disastrous expedition against Tangier, as security for the handing over of Ceuta, the Prince refused to accept his freedom at the price of the abandonment of the highly-prized fortress and died in Fez, still a prisoner, six years later. This story is the theme of Calderón de la Barca's play *El Príncipe Constante*. Ceuta has another link with world literature in that Luis de Camoens, author of *The Lusiads*, lost an eye while taking part in an attack upon the city.

When the crowns of Spain and Portugal were united in 1580, Ceuta passed to Philip II, now king of both realms. When the two states were again separated in 1649, the people of Ceuta asked to remain with Spain from which the city has never since been separated.

During the sixteenth, seventeenth, and eighteenth centuries, when Spanish foreign policy was centred on Europe, Ceuta was only of secondary consideration. It did, however, serve as a point of observation and support—or as we should say today, base—in the lawless naval warfare that prevailed in the Mediterranean of that age.

At that time Ceuta was a little city-fortress, huddled on a narrow stretch of land, on the edge of a country whose relations with Spain and whose internal stability varied enormously according to the disposition of the reigning monarch. Since eighteen of these succeeded one another, with a greater or less degree of violence or order, between 1636 and the end of the eighteenth century, it can be understood how much conditions varied.

From 1648 to 1655 Ceuta was besieged by Ahmad Gailan, a north Moroccan chieftain in rebellion against the Sultan. When Maulay Ismail had defeated him, the King himself attacked the city in 1674, and again in 1680 and 1694 when he was assisted by France. Failing to capture it by storm, he blockaded it until 1720.

[1] Fisher, *Barbary Legend*, p. 22.

In 1727 it was assaulted unsuccessfully by another north Moroccan leader, Ahmad Ali al-Rifi. Instigated by the Baron de Ripperdá, a Dutch adventurer who first became a Catholic and a Spanish duke, and then a Muslim and adviser to the Sultan of Morocco, Sultan Maulay Ismail proposed to capture it in October 1732, but also without success. This attack was no doubt conceived as a reprisal for the capture of Oran by the Spanish in April of the same year, during which Ripperdá had been in command of Moroccan forces.

In 1780 a treaty of friendship and commerce was signed by Morocco and Spain; and in the following year a peaceful adjustment of the limits of Ceuta was agreed with the Sultan Muhammed ibn Abdullah. Though his violent and irresponsible son, al-Yazid, declared war on Spain in 1790, good relations were re-established when his death occurred in a civil war two years after his accession, and a further treaty of peace, trade, navigation, and fishing was signed in 1799.

This marked the end of the long period of sieges and assaults during which Ceuta had sheltered behind walls, of which some remains still exist, and behind a moat which converted the isthmus into an island.

Until 1844 Ceuta lived in peace with its neighbours. There then, however, arose a bitter wrangle concerning the limits of its territory. This was settled in the following year through the intervention of the active British representative in Tangier, Sir John Drummond-Hay. In 1859 the tribesmen of Anjera, as on other occasions, destroyed the boundary marks. Owing to reasons of Spanish internal politics, connected with the consolidation of the throne of Isabella II, Spain was led to declare war on Morocco. The ensuing operations, begun on 1 January, were known as the Campaign of 1860. After a battle at Los Castillejos, Tetuan was captured. On 23 March the battle of Wadi Ras, between Tetuan and Tangier, brought the fighting to a close. A treaty of peace and friendship was subsequently signed by which the limits of Ceuta were enlarged and an indemnity of 100 million pesetas was paid by the Moroccan Government; the latter also agreed to hand over to Spain a small enclave on the southern Atlantic coast opposite the Canary Islands (Santa Cruz de Mar Pequeña, now Ifni). After this, there were no further armed conflicts over Ceuta, and in 1874 the city was constituted the seat of the *Capitanía General de Africa*.

Melilla

Like Ceuta, Melilla played a part in the history of the Mediterranean peoples in antiquity. The Phoenicians established a factory there in order to trade with the inhabitants of the region, and this passed later to the Carthaginians. The Romans made a colony of it, preserving the Carthaginian name, Rusadir. By the Berbers it seems always to have been known as Mlilia, from which the present name is derived.

On account of its less significant geographical position and its lack of a good port, Melilla played a smaller part in history than Ceuta. However, it was probably thence that Abd al-Rahman the Umayyad embarked for Spain, with the result that he became the founder of the Amirate of Córdoba; and it was certainly in Melilla that Boabdil (Abu Abdullah), the last King of Granada, disembarked after being exiled from his former kingdom, lost in 1492. At this time Melilla formed part of the Kingdom of Tlemsen, and was partially abandoned. This circumstance encouraged the Catholic Kings Ferdinand and Isabella to authorize the ducal house of Medina Sidonia to capture it, which they did in 1496.

From that time, for several centuries, Melilla's history is similar to that of Ceuta, though its remoteness from the centres of Moroccan life made it less coveted by the Sultans. It was, nevertheless, repeatedly attacked by the neighbouring tribes. Apart from a more or less continuous blockade, it suffered a siege and several fierce onslaughts by the Rifis from 1562 to 1564. These were repeated in 1687, 1696, and 1697, when the city successfully resisted the attempts of Maulay Ismail to take it by assault.

There followed three-quarters of a century of relative peace. In 1771, however, in spite of a treaty of friendship and commerce signed in 1767, Sultan Muhammad besieged Melilla; and, when he failed in this, he repeated the attempt in 1774. In view of these circumstances, Spain declared war on Morocco. This was terminated by a treaty of peace and friendship which was signed in Aranjuez in 1780 and defined the limits of the two garrison towns.

In 1844 a further dispute over boundaries resulted in an attack by local elements. In connexion with this episode Sultan Abd al-Rahman, fifteen years later, signed an agreement by which the legal limits of the fortress were extended and measures were taken for the security of both towns; this agreement was subsequently incorporated in the Treaty of Madrid of 1861.

In 1893 an extension of the fortifications was repeatedly obstructed by the Rifis, giving rise to the so-called War of Melilla. This was ended by the Agreement of Marrakesh in 1894, which gave satisfaction to Spain.

A somewhat similar episode—the attack on the workers in the Rif mines, exploited under a concession granted to a Spanish company by the Moroccan Pretender, Bu Hamara—gave rise to the campaign of 1909. Involving an expeditionary force of 90,000 men and carried out in stages at a very fluid moment in Moroccan history, it is part of the history of the establishment of the protectorate almost as much as the threat of Abdelkrim to the city in 1921. It was in 1909 that the limits of Melilla were enlarged; from that date instead of being a little fortress perched behind its walls on a precipitous hill overlooking the sea, it began to expand into the large city of today.

On 17 July 1936 Melilla was the first Spanish city to rise against the Government of the Popular Front, its example being emulated by other cities on the following day.

The name of *presidio*, given to Ceuta and Melilla, is a Spanish word meaning a city, or fortified *enceinte*, which can be garrisoned by troops. It has also been extended to mean a 'penitentiary', because it was the practice to send convicted criminals to the *presidios* (as to a prison) in order to help in the work of fortification and supply. The walls of old Melilla which were built by the forced labour of these prisoners are still intact.

Area and Population

Ceuta and its hinterland cover an area of 19·36 square kilometres with a population of 59,936 according to the census of 1950.

Melilla covers 12·3 square kilometres with a population of 81,182. The latter includes a Jewish community which arose after the expansion of Melilla in 1909 as an offshoot of the Jewish community of Tetuan. Amounting at one time to 4,000, it has since been reduced to 2,000 by emigration for economic reasons, mostly to Venezuela. The community, probably the largest Jewish community on Spanish soil, enjoys excellent relations with the Spanish authorities.

Administration and Justice

The children of Spaniards born in Ceuta and Melilla are automatically Spanish subjects, as are also the children of the Muslim minorities in the two cities. The latter (in 1950, 4,710 in Ceuta; 6,277 in Melilla) have complete religious liberty and form Muslim communities. They have their own Statute by which their personal affairs, marriage, divorce, succession, and so on, are regulated. Spanish law is applied in civil and criminal cases and the Muslims are liable for military service. The same applies to the Jewish community, which is entirely assimilated to the uses and customs of Spanish life.

Children born in the minute islands of Spanish sovereignty— Peñon de Alhucemas off the Moroccan coast at Alhucemas; Peñon de la Gomera, a little farther west; and the Chafarinas Islands, off the mouth of the Muluya near the Algerian frontier —are also automatically Spanish.

Under the protectorate the political and administrative status of Ceuta and Melilla became very complex. Territories of full Spanish sovereignty, they yet were subject in certain respects to the High Commissioner who was also their Governor and was represented by a Delegate. In other respects, they were governed like a mainland Spanish province by dispositions emanating from the central Spanish Government. Strictly speaking, however, they are not provinces, since they have no provincial Assembly (*Diputación*) or Court of Appeal (*Audiencia*).

A Muslim from Melilla, General Mizzian, rose to the rank of Lieutenant General in the Spanish army and was at one time Military Governor of Galicia and later of the Canary Islands. He has now taken Moroccan nationality and is military adviser to King Mohammed.

Ceuta and Melilla both have city councils (*ayuntamientos*), governed by the Spanish Law of Local Administration. The relationship between these city councils and the High Commissioner was the same as that between any other *ayuntamiento* and the civil Governor of the corresponding province. Since the declaration of Moroccan independence the functions normal to a civil Governor are exercised by the Governor-General of the Spanish Places of Sovereignty (*Plazas de Soberanía*), except that he comes under the Directorate General of African Possessions and Provinces instead of the Ministry of the Interior (*Gobernación*).

Ecclesiastically and for the purpose of justice, Ceuta and Melilla come under Cadiz and Málaga respectively, as do also the naval Commands. Education and the teaching institutions on the other hand are linked with the University of Granada.

Units of the Spanish army stationed in the Places of Sovereignty used to form part of the armed forces in Morocco, whose Commander-in-Chief, at the time of the Declaration of Independence, was the High Commissioner, though each garrison had its own military command. Now that the Moroccan units have been integrated into the new royal army, Spanish forces still in the northern zone and those of Ceuta and Melilla have a common command.

All regulations in force in Spain with regard to social affairs, labour conditions, and political matters are applicable in the Places of Sovereignty, as are regulations governing the press, the cinema, associations, &c.

Trade and Industry

As a result of difficult conditions arising from the Second World War, Ceuta and Melilla, which had been free ports since 1860, were linked for economic purposes with the Department (*Delegación*) of Economy of Tetuan, that is of the protectorate, and this handled and dealt with all their commercial affairs. There was thus constituted in fact, though not in theory, a sort of partnership between the two cities and the Khalifan zone, within the framework of an economic liberty which implied almost complete freedom of trade. Since independence, the means of tying up these loose links in the Spanish economy has not yet been determined.

There is virtually no industry in Melilla and such as exists in Ceuta is on a very small scale, with the exception of a recently installed brewery which has hopes of exporting. Only the canning factories, exporting a proportion of their output, show signs of development; and fishing is virtually their only natural resource. The two cities depend even for their drinking water on sources outside their own territories.

	Fish landed in 1954	Crustaceans
Ceuta . . .	3,866 tons	10 tons
Melilla . . .	6,777 tons	197 tons

Canned and salted fish exported amounted to 930 tons from Ceuta in 1954 and 863 from Melilla.

Apart from this, commercial activity depends on shipping using the ports; this is very large in Ceuta and considerable in Melilla.

Ceuta port extends over an area of 310 acres; the covered quays amount to 9,600 square yards and the uncovered to 323,000. During 1954 2,348 ships were supplied with oil fuel; 537 with coal; 4,057 with ice; and 2,220 with drinking water.

During 1955 10,060 ships, Spanish and foreign in about equal proportions, entered the port of Ceuta, which thus holds the third place for traffic among Spanish ports (Gijón 10,720, Las Palmas 10,166, Barcelona 7,838). The number of passengers embarked and disembarked was 178,977; many of these were French residents in the southern zone returning to or from France. Merchandise discharged and loaded amounted to 936,589 tons.

Compared with Ceuta the importance of the port of Melilla is relatively small, both in the case of Spanish and foreign traffic. It is nevertheless of significance both locally and as the point of departure for the iron ore from the Rif. Statistics for 1955 showed 2,639 ships entering and leaving Melilla, of which 1,320 were Spanish; 74,594 passengers embarked and disembarked, of whom many were French on their way to or from Algeria by car through Spain. Merchandise loaded and unloaded totalled 1,133,577 tons, virtually all iron.

THE ISLAND *PRESIDIOS* AND PEÑONS

The Islas Chafarinas include three small islands, Congreso, Rey, and Isabel II. They lie about two and a half miles off the coast opposite Cabo de Agua, about twelve miles west of the Algerian frontier and were occupied in 1847 in order to forestall a French occupation. Congreso, which is a half a mile long and 500 yards across, and Rey, which has an area of 15 acres, are both uninhabited. Isabel II, with a perimeter of about a mile and a quarter, is inhabited by some 500 fisher-folk and has a small garrison.

Peñon de Alhucemas, which lies three-quarters of a mile from the coast opposite Ajdir, was occupied by the Príncipe de Monte Sacro in 1673. Crowned with fortified buildings, it is exceedingly picturesque when seen from the shore. There is a civil population of about 400. Until recently it had no garrison. It is connected by cable with Melilla, Ceuta, and Peñon de Vélez de la Gomera.

Peñon de la Gomera, fifty miles farther west, is barely separated from the mainland and is also very picturesque; it was occupied by Pedro de Navarro in 1508, but lost again shortly afterwards. In 1560 it was ceded to Spain by Sultan Abdullah al-Shaikh, though in fact it was at the time in the possession of the Turks. Four years later, in 1564, it was re-captured by the Spanish. There are about 500 inhabitants.

III

SPANISH WEST AFRICA AND TARFAYA

Spanish West Africa (*Africa Occidental Española*, as it is officially called) comprises two geographically distinct sections, Ifni and the Spanish Sahara. The northern section, Ifni, is a small enclave, approximately 40 miles long and 15 deep, carved out of the territory of the Kingdom of Morocco. It lies on the Atlantic coast, just north of the Wadi Nun, about 60 miles short of the present southern frontier. The population is believed to be about 40,000, including temporary absentees seeking work outside the enclave. The southern section, known as the Spanish Sahara, extended till April 1958 along the coast south-westwards for about 700 miles from the Wadi Dra to Cape Blanco. It had an area of about 110,000 miles and an estimated population of 60,000, of whom half are present only in the rainy season when they come to pasture their flocks. For administrative purposes it was divided until 1958 into three distinct territories. The most northerly, known as Cape Juby, Tarfaya, or Tekna, with its capital in Villa Bens, stretches from the Wadi Dra to 27° 40' N. and was acquired under the Franco-Spanish Convention of 1912 as the southern zone of the Spanish protectorate in Morocco. This was handed back to the Moroccan Government in April 1958. The central section, known as Saguiat al-Hamra or the Zone of Occupation, with its capital at al-Aiun, extends from a little south of Cape Juby to a little south of Cape Bojador. The most southerly and largest section, known as the Río de Oro, with its capital at Villa Cisneros, lies between Cape Bojador and Cape Blanco.

From 1934 until January 1958 the two territories which together constituted the Spanish Sahara were linked with Tarfaya and Ifni in a single centralized administration, with a military Governor resident in the capital of the Ifni enclave, Sidi Ifni. The Governor was represented by Delegates in the three southern territories; local administration was in the hands of military *interventores*. In spite, however, of this administrative unification, Ifni and the Spanish Saharan complex were always

189

sufficiently different, as regards their histories and problems, to deserve separate consideration.

On 14 January 1958 a Decree of the Presidency of the Council formed the area into two provinces, Ifni and the Spanish Sahara. Supreme military command was entrusted to the Captain General of the Canary Islands, but separate military Governors-General were appointed to each province, with headquarters in Sidi Ifni and al-Aiun respectively, each being responsible for military command and administration in his own area.

Ifni

The occupation of Ifni, in April 1934, was a renewed attempt to realize a Spanish imperial dream of the fifteenth century which had been revived by nineteenth-century European expansion in Africa. In the initial phase of colonization Spain had annexed the Canary Islands and for a time sought (with Portugal as a rival) to establish herself along the Barbary coast and far down the Saharan shore. One short-lived fruit of this period was the establishment by Diego García de Herrera, lord of the Canary Islands, of a fishing, slaving, and trading post, somewhere on the southern Moroccan mainland, which came to be known as Santa Cruz de Mar Pequeña. This Spanish settlement seems to have endured from 1476 until 1524, when it was finally abandoned owing to disease and 'the hostility of the Sharif'.[1] In the course of the next three centuries the site of Santa Cruz de Mar Pequeña was lost, though the memory remained, as is shown by intermittent references in Spanish-Moroccan treaties. Thus in the treaty of 1767 between Spain and Morocco the reigning Sultan excused himself from discussing the matter of 'the establishment which His Catholic Majesty wished to set up near the Wadi Nun' on the grounds that the area lay outside his dominions and was inhabited by fierce nomads. In that of 1799 he undertook nevertheless to take appropriate measures to rescue sailors and other persons who might have the misfortune to be shipwrecked there or made captives by the natives of those regions. After Morocco's defeat in the African War of 1860, however, Sultan Sidi Muhammad was obliged by the Treaty of Tetuan to concede in perpetuity to her Catholic Majesty, Isabella II of Spain, sufficient territory adjoining Santa Cruz de Mar Pequeña to establish a fishery like that which Spain formerly had there. The phrasing of this concession was different from that of the same treaty referring to certain territory near Ceuta; this was to be conceded to Spain 'in full dominion and sovereignty', while in the case of

[1] T. García Figueras, *Santa Cruz de Mar Pequeña–Ifni–Sahara* (1941), p. 34.

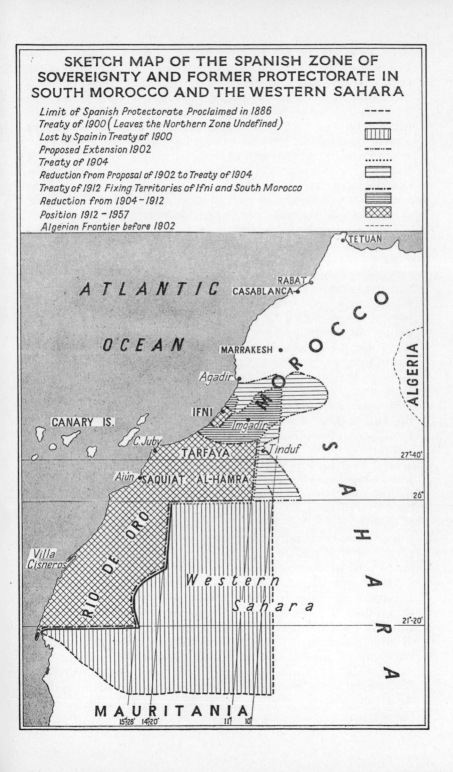

SKETCH MAP OF THE SPANISH ZONE OF SOVEREIGNTY AND FORMER PROTECTORATE IN SOUTH MOROCCO AND THE WESTERN SAHARA

Limit of Spanish Protectorate Proclaimed in 1886   ----

Treaty of 1900 (Leaves the Northern Zone Undefined)

Lost by Spain in Treaty of 1900

Proposed Extension 1902   --·--·--

Treaty of 1904   ··········

Reduction from Proposal of 1902 to Treaty of 1904

Treaty of 1912 Fixing Territories of Ifni and South Morocco

Reduction from 1904–1912

Position 1912–1957

Algerian Frontier before 1902   ------

ATLANTIC

OCEAN

TETUAN

RABAT

CASABLANCA

MOROCCO

MARRAKESH

ALGERIA

Agadir

IFNI

CANARY IS.

Imgadir

C.Juby

Tinduf

TARFAYA

27°40'

Aiün SAQUIAT AL-HAMRA

26°

RIO DE ORO

SAHARA

Villa Cisneros

Western Sahara

21°20'

MAURITANIA

15°28'   14°20'   11°   10°

Ifni no mention was made of any such condition. However, after obtaining permission to reoccupy the post, the Spanish Government was unable to identify it. In 1878 a mixed Spanish-Moroccan commission suggested Ifni, but doubts were raised in the Cortes concerning this identification and a subsequent mixed commission in 1883 failed to agree, the Moroccan members insisting on Puerto Cansado, farther south. Thus the Santa Cruz de Mar Pequeña question remained under discussion for a further fifty years; and became increasingly involved with the wider issue of competing European claims for spheres of influence and control in Morocco.

In the event Spanish ambitions to establish a protectorate over a large slice of southern Morocco and the western Sahara were gradually whittled down by French diplomacy and military power (see map p. 191). The territorial rights finally accorded to Spain by the Franco-Spanish Convention of 1912, after France had already occupied the main Moroccan centres of population, were substantially less than those which had been defined in the Franco-Spanish Conventions of 1900 and 1904. But they did include recognition of Spanish sovereignty over Santa Cruz de Mar Pequeña, now formally identified with Ifni. Even so, it was not until twenty-two years later, after several false starts, partly due to French requests for co-ordination with their own occupation of the neighbouring territory, that the Ifni enclave was actually occupied, immediately after the remainder of southern Morocco was brought under French military control. Thereafter problems of frontier definition arose; for Ifni's northern boundary was described in the Franco-Spanish Convention of 1912 as lying along the Wadi Bu Sedra, a *wadi* of which no one on the spot had ever heard; and its southern boundary was defined by reference to the Wadi Nun, 'which is not a *wadi*, but a vast alluvial plain'.[1] In fact the frontiers, as eventually established, include two administrative posts—Bifurna and Id Aisa—which lie outside the boundaries authorized by the Convention of 1912.

Geographically and historically Ifni belongs to southern Morocco: its constitutional attachment to Spain, for less than a generation, is in the nature of a curiosity. The enclave does not constitute a unity. The mountain ridge, rising to 4,000 feet and dropping to a narrow strip of coastal plain, which forms the backbone of the enclave, is a prolongation of the Anti-Atlas range. The principal inhabitants of the territory, the Ait Ba-Amran, are a group of six, predominantly settled, Berber-

---

[1] V. Monteil, 'Notes sur les Ifni et les Ait Ba-Amran', Institut des Hautes Études Marocaines, *Notes et Documents*, vol. 2 (1948), pp. 6-8.

speaking tribes; while a seventh tribe, the Sbuya, is semi-nomadic and mainly Arabic-speaking. 'Their mode of life, their customs, their language, do not differ from those of their Chleuh brothers' in the neighbouring region of southern Morocco.[1] There has been no effective hispanization; and though the European population has been estimated as 4,000, these are almost entirely short-term residents, military and civilian officials. The economic resources of the territory—rain-cultivation of wheat and barley; limited stock-raising of sheep, goats, cattle, donkeys, and camels; Barbary figs, honey; and some fishing—are insufficient to maintain the population which looks, commercially, to the neighbouring southern Moroccan market, Goulimin. Sidi Ifni itself provides a limited amount of employment of the usual colonial type—police, clerical work, domestic service, building, road-making, and retail trade. But the fact that in the past between a third and a half of the male population has normally been absent, working in Morocco, is an index of the extent of unemployment and under-employment in the enclave. There is a limited import trade, mainly with the Canaries; but virtually no exports: and the Sidi Ifni bar causes serious difficulties and delays for shipping. Plans exist, however, for the construction of a harbour, towards which $7\frac{1}{2}$ million pesetas were voted in 1954. Sidi Ifni itself, where before 1934 there was nothing but a marabout's tomb, has become a sizeable township. There is now a modern hospital, a well-equipped secondary school (where the pupils are almost all Spanish), public gardens including a zoo, a cinema, a local news-paper, and an airport which connects Ifni by a regular weekly service with Cape Juby and Las Palmas. The budget for recurrent expenses was fixed for the year 1958 at 40,108,735 pesetas.

The Spanish Sahara and Tarfaya

European connexions with the Río de Oro, the 'River of Gold', date back even before the fifteenth century. Cape Bojador is marked on the 'Catalan Map' of 1375 which was made for Charles V of France by a Jew, Abraham Cresques of Majorca; and thirty years earlier a Catalan expedition had set out to seek the 'River of Gold', believed to lie 150 leagues farther south. Cape Bojador was first rounded by Gil Eannes, com-manding one of Henry the Navigator's ships, in 1434; on a later voyage in the same year, in company with Afonso Gonçalves Baldaia, the King's cupbearer, Eannes returned with reports of footprints of men and camels found fifty leagues beyond the Cape. Revisiting the coast in 1436, Baldaia discovered an inlet

[1] Ibid.

which he took to be the mouth of the 'River of Gold'; since when this part of the coast has been known as Rio do Ouro in Portuguese, or Río de Oro in Spanish.[1] According to some authorities it was so named because the first gold dust from West Africa was obtained here; according to others, the Portuguese called it after the river Duero which the Spanish, not understanding, converted into d'Oro. This voyage of Baldaia's was the first occasion on which negro slaves, acquired from the Sanhaja Berbers, known to the Portuguese as 'Azanegays', were brought back to Europe: 'a estes Reynos foram trazidos os primeiros negroes'.[2] In 1445 a remarkable character, João Fernandes, who had learned Arabic as a slave in Barbary, volunteered to be left behind in Río de Oro, in order to learn what he could of the country and its inhabitants. Seven months later he was picked up again by Antão Gonçalves somewhat farther down the coast, having been well treated by the Sanhaja, and acquired valuable geographical and anthropological information. Thus European field studies in western Africa had their beginning at about the same time as the European slave-trade.

During this early phase it was the Portuguese rather than the Spaniards who explored the Saharan coast and penetrated into the hinterland: a Portuguese factory was established at Wadan, not far from Atar, in 1487. Early Spanish attempts to use the Canary Islands as a base for the extension of colonial power on the African mainland were not followed up, though the idea was canvassed from time to time, until the epoch of late nineteenth-century imperial expansion. Organizations with African interests (scientific, commercial, fishing, or some combination of the three)—the *Sociedad Geográfica de Madrid*, the *Sociedad de Pesquerías Canário-Africanas*, the *Sociedad Española de Africanistas y Colonistas*—were founded in the 1870's and 1880's. In 1884 Río de Oro itself, the site of the future Villa Cisneros, was occupied by Emilio Bonelli; and the Spanish Government officially staked its claim to a protectorate over a large area of the western Sahara between Cape Bojador and Cape Blanco. The further extension of Spanish power was checked for a generation, partly by French claims to Mauritania, partly by tribal

---

[1] Bovill, *Golden Trade of the Moors*, pp. 141–2. The term 'Río de Oro' can be used in at least four senses: (*a*) in the medieval sense, referring to the gold-bearing region known as 'Wangara', associated vaguely with the Senegal–Niger complex; (*b*) as used from Baldaia on, to refer to the inlet beside Cape Durnford, the site of the modern Villa Cisneros; (*c*) by extension, to refer to the Spanish colony on this Saharan coast; (*d*) by further extension, to refer in general to the Spanish Sahara. Here the term is normally used in sense (*c*), occasionally in sense (*b*). See Duarte Pacheco Perera, *Esmeraldo de Situ Orbis*, ed. by R. Mauny (Bissau, Centro de Estudos da Guiné Portuguesa, No. 19, 1956), p. 165, n. 33.

[2] Ibid. p. 20. [3] For Camoens' description of the coast see below p. 382.

resistance: Cape Juby was occupied by Colonel Bens in 1916; La Guëra in the far south in 1920; and Smara in the interior of Saguiat al-Hamra not until 1934.

Geographically and historically the Spanish Sahara is almost as artificial a political unit as Ifni; but, whereas the links of the latter are with southern Morocco, the former belongs, with French Mauritania, to the region long known in Arabic as Shinqit. 'Between Río de Oro and Mauritania the frontier, to the south of Saguiat al-Hamra, follows the 12th meridian west of Greenwich, cutting in two the Zemmour *massif*, the most clearly defined physical feature in the western Sahara.' [1] The spread of Islam throughout the region dates back to the proselytizing work of the Almoravids in the eleventh century. And, though certain basically Berber institutions, such as the prominent role of women in politics and education, have been preserved, the dominance of Arabic in its Hassaniya form is almost as complete as that of Islam. The nomadic Shanaqta, or *Maures* as the French call them, of the Spanish Sahara possess the same type of hierarchical social structure as is described below in the account of Mauritania. Indeed, many of the main tribal groupings—the Tekna, the Regeibat (Riqaibat), the Arusiyin —are found on both sides of the Franco-Spanish frontier, and continue to move, with relative freedom, across it. The development of what are in effect international markets at Atar in Mauritania, Goulimin in southern Morocco, and Villa Cisneros in the Spanish Sahara, as well as of lorry transport, has tended to stimulate an interterritorial exchange economy, based on the sale of camels and other livestock, and the purchase of essential imports—tea, sugar, rice, cotton goods. Along the coast, as far south as Villa Cisneros, are the nomadic groups of fishers, known as *Shnāgla* (*Imrāgen* in Mauritania), whose movements depend partly upon the movements of fish and partly on water supplies, paying tribute in kind to their superiors in the social hierarchy. Farther south, as in Mauritania, the proportion of negroes and mulattos (*porognes*), who are settled fishermen and cultivators, increases. A generation of Spanish occupation has had little material effect on *Shinqiti* society outside the partly Europeanized towns, Villa Cisneros, Cape Juby, La Guëra. The relatively highly developed system of traditional Quranic education survives; though a few public elementary schools have been established, in Tantan, al-Aiun, and Smara, as well as Villa Cisneros and Cape Juby, where the teaching of the Quran is combined with instruction in Spanish. Traditional medicine has likewise been supplemented by a public health

---

[1] R. Capot-Rey, *Le Sahara français* (Paris, 1953), pp. 368–9.

service, based upon mobile medical assistants and travelling dispensaries. There is an excellent *parador* (government hotel) in Villa Cisneros built when it was expected that the town would be an important air stage. A rudimentary road system links the main centres of population.

The Present Phase

The central question arising throughout AOE is whether, and in what form, Spanish influence can be maintained, confronted by the pressure of a nationalism which, though encouraged from Morocco and immensely stimulated by the recovery of Moroccan independence, is, so far as the Spanish Sahara is concerned, essentially *Shinqiti* in quality, with certain pan-Maghrib overtones. Here it is necessary to distinguish between the constitutional status of the various territories concerned. In the case of Ifni, Spain's case is based on the fact that successive international agreements have recognized Spanish sovereignty; and Morocco, it is contended, has now assumed the obligations resulting from them. The Moroccan view is that the vital 1860 treaty referred to fisheries, not to sovereignty; and that the recent 1956 agreement, by which Spain recognized Moroccan independence, effectively cancelled the Franco-Spanish Convention of 1912. In any case the situation is essentially unstable, since Ifni, from every point of view except the legal, is evidently Moroccan territory. The leaders of the Ait Ba-Amran have made clear that their loyalty is to the King of Morocco and his Government rather than to the Spanish administration, and have demanded the reincorporation of the enclave in Morocco. The Spanish Government before the rising of November 1957 declared its willingness to submit the dispute to some form of international arbitration. The fact is that Ifni is bound to be regarded as *terra irredenta*, and the tension which produced the rising of November 1957 to recur.

The position in regard to the southern zone of the former Spanish protectorate was different, since the Spanish Government never challenged the principle of the transfer of this territory as part of the general transfer to the Moroccan Government of the powers previously exercised by the Spanish authorities in their Moroccan protectorate. In a statement on 10 November 1957, explaining why the southern zone had not as yet been transferred to the Moroccan authorities, M. Balafrej, the Moroccan Foreign Minister, said that conditions imposed by the Spanish Government were unacceptable. According to the Spanish communiqué of 6 December 1957 this transfer, though never refused in principle by the Spanish

Government, was not requested by the Moroccan authorities until September 1957. If so this may have been due to the Moroccan desire at the time of the transfer not to complicate relations with the French who are very sensitive to any changes affecting the question of the southern frontiers of Morocco. After heavy surprise attacks by irregulars on garrisons in Ifni and the Sahara in the winter of 1957-8, the Spanish Government stated that it could not discuss Ifni or hand over the Juby zone as long as the Moroccan Government failed to exercise adequate authority in the regions south of the Atlas. In April 1958, when the Moroccan army had moved south, the Juby area was in fact handed over. In Ifni and the Spanish Sahara proper the Spanish intention seemed to be to hold the principal centres strongly while abandoning the outlying posts. In his New Year address for 1958 General Franco drew a sharp, though somewhat misleading, distinction between what he called 'the treacherous aggression on Ifni, a land of Spanish sovereignty' and 'the simple and noble people of Morocco' who had nothing to do with these irregular armed bands. About the same time there was a definite Franco-Spanish alignment to resist Moroccan claims in the Sahara south of Morocco, probably dating from the meeting of French and Spanish Foreign Ministers in the summer of 1957. This itself appeared to be the result of the change in Spanish Foreign Ministers.

In the case of the 'Zone of Occupation' and Río de Oro itself, the question is bound up with the wider problem of incipient Shinqiti nationalist as well as Moroccan territorial claims. From an historical, cultural, religious, and economic point of view, there is no doubt that the Shanaqta of the Spanish Sahara and of French Mauritania constitute a genuine community. The importance of the links between Shinqit and the Maghrib have been demonstrated by a succession of politico-religious revivalist movements, from the Almoravids to Ma al-Ainen, the learned and saintly Qadiri leader, who established himself in Smara and organized resistance to European, and particularly French, penetration during the early years of this century. In this he was supported by a succession of Sultans—Maulay Abd al-Rahman in 1857, Sidi Muhammad in 1873, Maulay al-Hasan in 1887 and, with troops and materials, by Maulay Abd al-Aziz in 1896 and 1906. Since 1956 a Mauritanian of a similar name has been admitted as a member of the Moroccan Consultative Assembly (see pp. 64, 271). During the recent colonial epoch the importance of the Spanish Sahara has lain partly in the fact that it provided at times an asylum for political exiles and refugees from French Mauritania. In 1957 the new factor in the situation was that

o

there existed in the western Sahara a political-military organization, known as the Southern Army of Liberation, or *Armée de
Libération du Grand Sahara*, with an estimated strength of at least
2,000, having some connexion with the Istiqlal Party in southern
Morocco, which—as its adherents claim—has its own underground branches in Shinqit, as far south as the Senegal river.

It is natural to ask why the Spanish Government, which has
sought to develop friendly relations with the Arab states,
should apparently wish to maintain, by force if necessary, a
colonial system in Ifni and the Spanish Sahara—since these
territories are economically a liability, and have only a slender
strategic value *vis-à-vis* the Canary Islands to recommend them.
Ever since the eruption of November 1957 Allal al-Fasi, as
well as General Franco, have taken pains to stress the ties of
sympathy and mutual respect which have traditionally linked
the Moroccan and Spanish peoples. So far it has been the
strategic argument for empire that has been mainly emphasized
by the Spanish Government in its public statements. For
example, General Barroso, the Spanish Minister of War,
addressing the Cortes on 21 December 1957, insisted that the
loss of the African coastal zone would leave the Canary Islands
'at the mercy of tactical aircraft, guided missiles, and other
powerful engines of destruction', which an enemy might
eventually install in the Sahara. It is also possible that control
of the Spanish Sahara might be turned to economic advantage,
either through the development of its own resources—particularly oil, if this is forthcoming—or by the building of the
projected railway linking the rich iron-ore deposits at Fort
Gouraud, in French Mauritania, with the sea at Villa Cisneros;
this would otherwise have to be transported by a much longer
line to be constructed through French-controlled territory to
Port Étienne. Another consideration, above all in the case of
Ifni, is the importance, from the standpoint of Spanish ruling
groups, especially the army, of preserving the *presidios* of Ceuta
and Melilla; and the fear that, if once Ifni were surrendered,
this might be treated as a precedent, justifying Moroccan claims
to the *presidios* at a later stage. Indeed, the 'African memories'
of the army, and its attachment to these vestiges of Empire, are
perhaps a sufficient reason why Spain, like other European
colonial powers, finds difficulty in meeting African nationalist
demands and so avoiding the risk of having them extorted later,
with consequent loss of goodwill. It is hard to give up imperial
status even on the most lilliputian scale.[1]

---

[1] On Mauritania and the problem of the southern limits of the Kingdom of
Morocco see also above, pp. 61, 75, and below, p. 270.

PART TWO

ALGERIA (*AL-JAZAIR*) AND THE SAHARA (*AL-SAHRA*)

IV

ALGERIA
(*AL-JAZAIR*)

GEOGRAPHY AND POPULATION

ALGERIA (in French *l'Algérie*, in Spanish *Argel*) takes its name from the Arabic words *Al-Jazair*, meaning the 'islands', in this case the little islands in the roadstead of Algiers, the capital city.

Geography

Apart from some three-quarter million square miles of desert, Algeria occupies an area of 125,000 square miles lying, between Morocco and Tunisia, in the centre of that stretch of the North African coast which lies between Tangier and Cape Bon. Its coastline is about 600 miles long while the depth of the country varies from about 220 miles at the Moroccan end to about 150 at the Tunisian frontier; the inland cities of Tlemsen and Biskra are on roughly the same latitude. Algeria lies high, having an average altitude of 3,000 feet.

From north to south, the country is divided into two natural regions. These run parallel to the sea; one is the Tell (an Arabic word meaning 'hill', but here perhaps rather a survival from the Latin *tellus*, 'the fruitful earth') and the other the Steppes of the High Plateaux. The latter lie between two parallel folds, one known as the Atlas of the Tell, the other as the Atlas of the Sahara, both running from east to west. The great desert, the Sahara, extends southwards from the foot of the Saharan Atlas.

In western Algeria the High Plateaux project to the north; while in eastern Algeria the Tell, in the form of two mountainous masses, the Constantine area and the Aurès, projects almost into the desert. These differences in the configuration of eastern and western Algeria were reflected in the Middle Ages by a political division, the Constantine area going with Tunisia in the east (Ifriqiya) and the Tlemsen area with Morocco in the west.

The Tell is a Mediterranean land; it has a regular annual rainfall of over 16 inches, which is the minimum necessary for growing cereal crops, but this is very irregularly divided between autumn and spring. The total rainfall is actually

201

greater in Algiers city than in Paris; and the occasional flood waters cause an erosion of soil which, on an average, costs Algeria 250 acres of cultivable land every day of the year. The mean annual temperature at Algiers is 64° F. Though its former forests have largely been destroyed, the Tell is naturally a land of trees and of jujube scrub. Except for the Chélif, the water-courses are no more than periodical torrents, the Arab *wadis*, which nevertheless carry away water capable of irrigating a million acres.

The steppes of the High Plateaux, at a greater altitude, have a more continental and a drier climate. When rain falls, it covers the soil with a thin layer of flood water, similar to the sheet-flood of the south-west of the United States. Esparto grass (*stipa tenacissima*), which is commercially exploited, extends over 10 million acres. The High Plateaux also contain immense basins of salt marsh, known as *shott* or *sebkha*.

Algeria, properly so-called, thus forms a narrow and moun-tainous rectangular pad which rises to 7,500 feet in the Jurjura of the Kabyle country and in the Aurès. Its landscapes re-semble those of the south of France, in Provence or Languedoc, at least in the neighbourhood of the sea. This resemblance, aided by proximity and ready access, made it easy to establish settlers of Mediterranean origin.

Communications

Algeria was first divided into three provinces by the Turks and after them by the French. Each of these provinces possesses a north–south route leading to the interior from one of the country's three principal ports—Oran, Algiers, Bône. Under the French occupation a network of roads, 50,000 miles in length, was created, based on three parallel west–east axes—a coastal route from Nemours to La Calle; a northern transversal from Ujda to the Tunisian frontier, and a southern transversal from Berguent to Tebessa.

The 2,800 miles of railway, of which half are normal gauge, are similarly disposed in the style of a herring-bone, with a long spine running from Morocco to Tunisia, from which lines diverge north to the ports or south towards the desert.

The harbours necessarily face north; there are twenty-one of them, of which the principal are Algiers, Bône, and Oran; they are served by a dozen shipping companies which are all French.

Air communications are important. There is an axis Casa-blanca–Algiers–Tunis; the capital is also linked both with Paris (three hours) and Madrid, and with the principal cities and centres of black Africa. Every year 400,000 passengers pass through Maison Blanche, the airport of Algiers.

Strategic Position

Algeria is a centrally situated 'turn-table' for North West Africa; and a junction between the countries of white man and black. It lies open to the teeming world of the Mediterranean as well as to the immense spaces of the Sahara with the mineral riches which these are now known to contain. From its ports on the north an active sea and air traffic connects it with France; from the desert ports on the south five 'imperial tracks' cross the desert, soon to be flanked by oil pipelines.

Algeria's strategic importance became very clear at the moment of the Allied landing of 8 November 1942, when the naval base at Mersa el-Kebir, near Oran, played an important role. After the war Algeria was expressly included in the area of the North Atlantic Treaty Organization, being attached to the regional group of South Europe and the western Mediterranean.

Population

The present population of Algeria is of the order of 10 million. Of these a little more than 1 million are European, if we accept the legal formula which classes Algerian Jews with Europeans.

Muslims. Nine-tenths of the population are Muslim; their number has now reached about 9 million; in 1830 it was estimated as 3 million. This fell to $2\frac{1}{2}$ million between 1851 and 1877, owing to fighting and to epidemics. Since then it has increased steadily. Muslim Algerians are in general of the white Arabo-Berber race, with a certain degree of cross-breeding owing to former black slavery. Except for 40,000 Kharijites (Ibadis) in the Mzab, they are practically all Sunni. The language of the majority is Arabic, with much dialectal variation, though nearly 30 per cent. speak Berber as their mother tongue, particularly in the Kabyle country and in the Aurès. The Muslims are a young population, since there are 125 infants and adolescents for every 100 adults. Generally speaking families have 3-4 children. The number of women is roughly equal to that of men. Polygamy is too costly to be frequent and in 1948 there were less than 40,000 cases of men having more than one wife at a time; a succession of wives is, however, frequent. Girls marry young, between puberty and 20 years.

Europeans. The word 'Europeans' is used in Algeria to mean all non-Muslim inhabitants, Christian or Jewish. Christians may be of French origin, naturalized, or aliens. The proportion of 'aliens' has diminished greatly since 1876; at the present time it can be said that about 50 per cent. of the European population is of French stock. In 1948 only 105,000 of the Frenchmen living in Algeria had been born in France. For the most part those of French origin have come from the south of France or Corsica, though there was an appreciable influx from Alsace and Lorraine after the war of 1870. Among the non-French, Spanish is the dominant stock, followed by Italian and Maltese. In the province of Oran, in 1911, there were two Europeans of Spanish origin for every one of French. This Christian population has rather more women than men. The girls marry between 25 and 30. Except in the Oran province marriages are less fertile than formerly.

The Europeans have many characteristics in common with the Muslim inhabitants. They have the same virtues of courage, generosity, and tenacity, and the same faults of violence, touchiness, and rivalry. This is not surprising when one considers their racial composition. Among themselves they talk a rather odd French, known as le *pataouète*, which they pronounce in a characteristic manner.

The two groups, European and Muslim, live side by side without fusing. By 1948 not more than 10,000 Muslims had been naturalized; these were mostly officials from the Kabyle country. Mixed marriages are rare; it is calculated that not more than about 75 a year are celebrated in Algeria, and about 400 in France itself; to this perhaps 5,000 cases of concubinage should be added. The only social mixing is where some hundreds of European settlers live among tens of thousands of Muslims.

Jews. Algerian Jews were naturalized *en masse* as French subjects by the *Décret Crémieux* of 24 October 1870. For many of the young people the Jewish faith is little more than a memory. On the lips of the grandchildren Arabic, which was the daily tongue of the grandparents, has been displaced by French. Strongly Europeanized for the most part, Algerian Jews, of whom there are about 140,000, are classified as Europeans, though it is believed that about half the members of the Jewish community in North Africa are descended from converted Berbers; more than 45 per cent. of them have Arabo-Berber family names. The remainder are mainly descendants of Spanish Jews expelled from Spain in 1492. Algerian Jews are firmly rooted in the country and emigration to Israel has so far been insignificant.

Density of Population. The cultivable area of the north, excluding the Southern Territories, is known to French writers as *l'Algérie utile* and has a density of about 40 persons per square kilometre. This population is mainly concentrated in the Tell, where three inhabitants out of every four have their home; it is thick on the coast, in the hills, in the zones of colonization, and in the east of the country. The Muslims are most numerous in the east; the Europeans in the centre and west and, to the extent of 80 per cent., in the towns.

The density of population in the department of Algiers, rising to 325 inhabitants to the square kilometre, is comparable with that of the department of the Rhône; in the department of Tizi Ouzou, with 140 inhabitants to the square kilometre, to that of Seine Maritime. This implies that the number of people to be supported in the Great Kabylia is as great as that in Seine Maritime with its cities of Rouen and Le Havre; and in the department of Constantine one and a half times as many as in the rich Gironde including Bordeaux. Nowhere in France is there a mountain area, without industry, which is as thickly populated as the Kabyle country.

The Towns. In 1957 there were four cities with more than 100,000 inhabitants. Algiers has a sea front of 12 kilometres and the urban area contains about 700,000 inhabitants. Oran has 300,000; Constantine 150,000, and Bône nearly 120,000. There are 56 localities with over 10,000 inhabitants.

The towns are becoming more and more the habitat of peasants who have left the countryside and formed proletarian settlements, known as *bidonvilles* or shanty towns; these shelter 40,000 people in Algiers and 43,000 in Oran. In the Casbah of Algiers about 80,000 people are crowded into an area of 75 acres.

Demographic Growth. Population increase is slight among the Europeans, whose mortality-rate is higher and birth-rate lower than in France, but is very high among the Muslims. The excess of births over deaths in 1955 was probably about 270,000. Statisticians calculate that at the present rate the Muslim Algerian population will amount to 18 million souls by 1980. It will certainly be a young population, since there will then be as many 'under 20's' in Algeria as there were in 1957 Muslims altogether, namely more than 9 million.

This rate of increase, which may well be called fantastic, originates in a high birth-rate, 47 per 1,000 in 1954, and a low death-rate which was 17 per 1,000 in the same year. Certainly Muslim infant mortality is still far too high—91 per 1,000 in the first year of life, due above all to the ignorance of the mothers. In spite of this Algeria has less coffins than cradles, because the Muslim population, which is unadapted to industrial life, is a backward group juxtaposed to a highly developed technical civilization.

In such circumstances, it is usual that the reproduction rate should approach a maximum, namely the biological rhythm of one baby every year. Certain social usages, such as early marriage and easy repudiation of the sterile or elderly wife, accentuate the tendency. Observation shows moreover that below a certain standard of income and culture the birth-rate rises. Contrary to a widespread belief, fecundity in a population is no proof of its prosperity, rather the reverse. According to Dr. Josué de Castro 'when the table is bare, the bed is fruitful'. On this basis, if the living standards of Muslim Algeria were to be further depressed, the birth-rate might rise even more than is expected.

The spread of hygiene and preventive medicine promotes this trend. The mortality in a backward group tends to approximate to that of an advanced group, in this case the Europeans; at the same time antibiotics, now available to the former, eliminate cases of sterility due to gonorrhoea and of abortion due to syphilis. Meanwhile the intermingling of the population due to the development of trade, internal migration, and the relaxation of tribal bonds, facilitates the forming of casual unions and hence increases the number of births.

In a country which cannot from its own soil support more than 3 million inhabitants without the aid of agrarian reform and the creation of industry this rate of increase can be a catastrophe, though the fact is quite unrealized by the Muslim masses. The children of the poor are their only wealth. It is they who personify hope for them. There are districts of Algeria, in the Kabyle country and elsewhere, in which the woman who has no son, or the daughter who has no brother, runs the risk of being turned out of the husband's or brother's house when he dies. In these conditions the preaching of birth control is as little likely to be effective as would be a campaign to induce Swedish couples to produce a baby every year.

HISTORY

From Antiquity to the Seventh Century A.D.

The prehistoric period of Algeria remains a mystery. All that we learn from the discovery of stone tools is that there were men in Algeria between the tenth and fifth centuries B.C. It would appear that the Berbers of today are the product of a complicated racial mixture due to a succession of invasions and cross-breedings.

From the twelfth century B.C. the Phoenicians used ports on
the Algerian coast as staging posts on the route from Carthage
to their distant trading establishments; Bône and Philippeville
were among their ports of call, and also Algiers, known to them
as 'Ikosim', which could mean in Punic 'Owl Island' or perhaps
'Thorn Island'. In this remote period the village seems to have
been the unit of settled, as the tribe was of nomadic, life.

After the overthrow of Carthage in 146 B.C. the Romans
formed a province of Africa corresponding, more or less, to
present-day Tunisia. Simultaneously a Numidian kingdom controlled by the great Berber chiefs Massinissa and Jugurtha for
the first time constituted a united and independent realm
corresponding to modern Algeria. A little later this was delivered into the hands of Rome through the agency of a more
westerly Berber realm, Mauritania.

During the following three centuries Roman provinces in
North Africa seem to have coexisted with native monarchies.
After that period Roman Algeria no longer included the western
High Plateaux. In normal times 30,000 men sufficed to maintain order, and a single Legion, the Third Augusta, was
stationed at Lambèse, about 120 kilometres south of Constantine. The *pax romana* was, however, punctuated by revolts
and in any case hardly affected the people in the mountain
country. The Romans built cities of their own; Caesarea, the
modern Cherchell, may have had 40,000 inhabitants. At the
eastern end of the country the Romans penetrated as far as the
desert. The cultivation of cereals became a source of revenue for
the Numidians. In the towns the current speech was Latin.
The existence of some twenty Bishops in Numidia in the middle
of the third century shows that Christianity was widespread and
flourishing.

In spite of all this, Berber tribal life continued its separate
existence in the High Plateaux of the south-west even in the
Empire's greatest days. With the decline of the Empire, the
Roman advance was followed by a withdrawal. Meanwhile
Roman legionaries had often turned into farmers; the fact that
some of them were Gauls could perhaps be quoted as the
justification for making Algerian schoolboys study textbooks
which begin with the phrase 'our ancestors the Gauls'.

Berber dislike of Roman authority often showed itself in the
form of revolts and tribal incursions, and perhaps most strongly
of all in the century of Donatist religious schism. In the territories which were evacuated by Diocletian a certain survival of
municipal institutions is discernible (though these may be
simply an early form of the Berber councils known in modern

times by the Arabic name of *jamaa*), and Christianity lingered on in the form of isolated churches. Africa was however already rapidly losing its Roman character when 80,000 Vandals arrived during the fifth century. Though they did no more than establish a number of coastal garrisons for a period of about a century or so, they cut Africa off from the imperial and pontifical authority. A number of Christian Berber kingdoms took their place. At the beginning of the sixth century the Byzantines drove out the Vandals but took over only eastern Algeria, leaving the rest in the power of the Berbers.

Though the pagan and Christian civilizations of Rome were at work in the Berber lands of North Africa for nearly 800 years, they have left few traces, apart from the ruins of their cities. There survived the use of the Julian calendar for agricultural purposes, a few Latin words, perhaps a few customs, and the plan of the Roman house adapted to Berber use. The last surviving Christian communities disappeared from Bougie and from Tlemsen in the eleventh century.

Throughout these centuries the love of liberty, indeed the anarchical tendencies, of the Berber population were very evident. At the beginning of the first century A.D. a legionary of Berber origin, called Tacfarinas, deserted from Roman service and summoned the tribes of the Aurès to arms; and was soon joined by people from the south and from the east. For seven years Tacfarinas and his bands held the Romans in check. When in danger, he would retire into the mountains or the desert. When left alone, he would fall upon villages and farms or assault a strongpoint. Finally surrounded near the present Aumale, 124 kilometres south-east of Algiers, he and a great number of his people died fighting.

It may well be asked whether the mass conversion to Christianity, followed by the speedy adoption of heresies, was not as much a political as a religious phenomenon. Impatient of the burden of Roman civilization and discontented with their existence on great estates (*latifundia*), poverty-stricken peasants may well have welcomed a revolutionary religion which appealed to the weak and the oppressed and undermined the foundations of the old Roman society.

The Middle Ages, from the Eighth to the Fifteenth Century

For 800 years, from the seventh to the fifteenth century, Algeria was no longer a separate land. As its geographical name in Arabic, *al-Maghrib al-Ausat*, or Middle West, indicates, it was the central portion of the Maghrib or Arab west. Its limit on the west was, roughly speaking, the Moroccan frontier of today, but the present eastern province, Constantine, was then normally part of Tunisia. Closely associated with its neighbours, Algeria regarded them with suspicion but bowed to their authority.

The country was at that time a great rural region, with little in the way of towns, inhabited by nomadic shepherds in the west and by peasants, either settled, or semi-nomadic, in the east. The names of two big Berber groups have survived; the Zenata who were mainly nomadic, except in the Aurès; and the Sanhaja who were mainly settled except for the notable exception of the Almoravids. The small Spanish horse known in English as a jennet possibly derives its name from the Zenata horsemen.

In the middle of the seventh century, fifteen years after the death of the Prophet of Islam, Arab horsemen appeared in the Berber lands for the first time. They soon put the Byzantine military forces out of action; but the Berbers gave them much trouble. The first centre of resistance was in the region of Tlemsen, not far from the Moroccan border, where they were led by a Christian chief, Kusayla; the next was near Biskra, where the Arab conqueror, Uqba ibn Nafi, died fighting. The natural fortress formed by the Aurès mountains held out for three years under a legendary Queen known as al-Kahina or 'the prophetess' who was apparently, like her subjects, a judaized Berber. Her defeat involved submission and the loss of independence; having submitted, the Berbers accepted Islam. Those Berbers who were Christians do not seem to have clung to their faith. They were, moreover, to be arabized, as well as made Muslims.

A French Orientalist, William Marçais, has thus described this event.

In the seventh century, the Berber country broke with the west and attached itself to the east, totally and irremediably, without it seems suffering any interior conflict or any qualm of conscience. Their new lords, the Arabs, soon had no need to exercise power directly. But though they now left the country to itself, they had marked it indelibly. It had been made so thoroughly Arab that the Maghrib, or Arab west, can today be considered almost in its entirety as a distant province of the Arab world, somewhat out of the general orbit.[1]

What is meant by 'making it Arab' has been admirably defined by the same writer. It implied he says, the adoption of Arabic as the language of civilization and of conversation, and pride in

[1] W. Marçais, 'Comment l'Afrique du Nord s'est Arabisée', *Annales de l'Institut d'Études Orientales de la Faculté des Lettres d'Alger*, iv, 1938.

membership of the civilization of which that language is the expression. It implied considering the literary monuments of the Arabs as a glorious inheritance, and taking their master-pieces as examples. In short, it meant wishing to belong to the Arab world and modelling oneself as far as possible upon its standards. In other words it could be defined as 'the intimate association of a certain linguistic condition with a whole body of aesthetic tastes, emotional aspirations and intellectual habits'.[1] For the purpose of daily speech, the Berber language has nevertheless remained the mother tongue of nearly a third of the population in certain mountain areas (p. 203).

A second Arab invasion, that of the Beni Hilal, who came from Upper Egypt in the middle of the eleventh century, devastated the Maghrib. 'Like an army of locusts', wrote the Arab historian Ibn Khaldun three centuries later, 'they destroyed everything in their path'. This invasion, like the first, failed to turn the Berbers of present-day Algeria into Arabs by race. The invasion of the seventh century (according to Mar-çais) involved about 150,000 fighting men, from which number some must be deducted as casualties but others added in the way of families, merchants, and officials. The second, in the eleventh century, consisted of two big tribes which it would be an exaggeration to estimate at 200,000 souls. Thus the inhabitants of Algeria today, as of the rest of North Africa, are more or less arabized Berbers. Other racial elements must have entered into their composition too—Phoenician, Roman, Vandal, Byzan-tine, together with an admixture of Iranians from Khorasan who were dispatched to North Africa as reinforcements by a Caliph of Baghdad, and of Persians who formed a kingdom in Tihert, near Tiaret, in the province of Oran in the eleventh century.

In the tenth century the Berbers adhered *en masse* to the egalitarian puritanism of Kharijite Islam; it was among the people of the Little Kabylia that there then arose the power of the Shiite Fatimids who subsequently conquered Egypt. A century later the Almoravids coming from Morocco took pos-session of the country as far as Algiers; they were succeeded by the Almohads who controlled Tunis also. Tlemsen, the Treme-sen of the medieval chronicles, profiting by an influx of refugees from the brilliant civilization of Muslim Spain, became capital of a prosperous Zenata kingdom, which was periodically menaced by its Moroccan neighbours, the Almohads and the Beni Merin, until it was finally annexed by the Turks in the beginning of the sixteenth century.

[1] Ibid.

Algeria under the Turks (Sixteenth to Nineteenth Century)

The three centuries of Turkish domination in Algeria have been little studied by historians. Yet the period was important, for it was then that Algeria received its present frontiers. It was also a time of fusion of the Arab and Berber elements of the population and, by no means least important, it was the moment when Algeria entered history as a distinct entity.

The Turkish arrival in Algiers was not the result of a plan thought out in Istanbul. At least at the start it was a private enterprise on the part of two corsairs, the Barbarossa brothers, Aruj and Khair al-Din. They had first become famous for harassing Christian shipping and for the help which they gave Spanish Muslims expelled from Spain who wished to cross to the shores of Barbary. At the beginning of the sixteenth century the Spaniards occupied several Algerian ports, including Mersa el-Kebir, Oran, and Bougie, and besieged Algiers itself. The inhabitants invoked the aid of Aruj who subsequently made himself ruler and began to carve out a kingdom, which soon stretched as far as Tlemsen. His brother and successor, Khair al-Din, did homage to the Sultan in Istanbul and was appointed Pasha, extending his rule to Bône and Constantine. In the south, he subdued Biskra, Touggourt, and Wargla. Tlemsen, which was for some time disputed between the Spaniards and the Moroccans, finally fell to the Turks also.

Political control was at first in the hands of Pashas appointed for three-year periods, and then of Aghas of whom there were four, all of whom were assassinated, and finally of Deys. Of the latter, who were addressed by foreign powers as 'Very Illustrious and Magnificent Sir', there were twenty-eight. They ruled absolutely, but fourteen of them died a violent death. They had to reckon with two rival powers; on the one hand the corps of Janissaries, called the militia (*ojaq*), who were recruited from the towns and islands of Anatolia and whose numbers fell from 20,000 at the end of the seventeenth century to 5,000 in 1830; and on the other with the Corporation of Corsair Captains (*taifat er-rais*), whose privateering was a principal resource of the Dey's treasury.

No full account exists of the internal organization of the Algerian state. It was divided into three provinces which were the origin of the later French departments—Oran in the west, Médéa or Titteri in the centre, and Constantine in the east. These were governed by Beys, while the district of Algiers formed a separate unit. The three Beys were responsible for the collection of taxes in their respective provinces. All public offices were farmed out by the state. Since the Turkish garrisons were inadequate to maintain order by themselves, the Turkish Government ruled by dividing. They relied on certain 'integrated' tribes—like the Makhzen tribes of Morocco or Tunisia—who were used to bring pressure on the remainder. Military colonies around the Kabyle country, for example, ensured the safety of travel. The Turkish Government of the Deys appears to have taken little interest in the interior of Algeria. Having arrived by sea, their principal interest was in that element, and the profits from privateering in the Mediterranean became a prime source of revenue. In the seventeenth century there were nearly 35,000 Christian captives in the prisons of Algiers. Military and naval action by Spain, followed by French and British and finally American naval demonstrations and, later, the great advance in European naval construction led to the decline of the corsairs who, in the early seventeenth century, had raided as far afield as Iceland and caused a scare on the coasts of Devon and Cornwall. From the middle of the eighteenth century the population of Algiers city began to fall. In 1816, when Lord Exmouth bombarded it, there were no more than 1,200 captives left in its prisons. By 1830 the population of Algiers, estimated in the seventeenth century at 100,000, had sunk to 40,000.

The immediate pretext for the French expedition of 1830 was the celebrated blow with his fly whisk which Dey Husain gave the French Consul Deval, in an altercation over the unpaid debt of two Algerian Jews who had furnished the French Government with large quantities of wheat years before under the Directorate. A more substantial reason was the desire of Charles X's Government to win credit by putting an end to the interference with maritime trade which the Barbary states were still capable of causing in spite of their decay. It appears, however, that there was one occasion on which Algeria herself sought French protection, in the middle of the sixteenth century. Simultaneously threatened by Muslim Turks and Spanish Christians after the Battle of Lepanto, certain Algerians (ceulx d'Alger) wrote to Charles IX (according to a letter which he sent to the French Ambassador in Istanbul) asking him 'to take and receive them into his protection'. In fact for many years there was a definite alliance between France and Algeria under which French and Algerian fleets jointly attacked the possessions of their common enemy, Spain. A French Consul was established in Algiers from 1581 and diplomatic relations continued between the two countries, except in time of war, from that time until 1830. Algeria exchanged diplomatic missions with a number of other countries including England, who also maintained a Consul in Algiers. The state coined its own money and the Dey had a Council consisting of a Foreign Minister and Minister of Marine (*Wakil al-Kharg*), a Minister of War (*Agha*), and a Minister of the Treasury and Interior (*Khaznagi*).

Algeria under the French, 1830–1957

On 25 May 1830 a French fleet, carrying an expeditionary force of 37,000 men, sailed from Toulon. Disembarkation began on 14 June, at Sidi Farruj. On 5 July Dey Husain signed an act of capitulation with General de Bourmont. Article 5 stated: 'The exercise of the Muslim religion will remain free; neither the liberty of any class of the inhabitants nor their religion, nor their property, nor their commerce and industry will be impaired in any way. Their women will be respected. The Commander-in-Chief gives this undertaking on his honour.' The evening before, Article 2 of the Convention presented to the Dey had declared that 'the religion and the customs of the Algerians will be respected. No soldier of the army will be permitted to enter a mosque.' The word of France was thus pledged, from 1830, to maintain Islam and the customs of the people of Algeria, which must presumably have included their language. These two points were to be specifically reproduced, more than a century later, in the Statute of Algeria of 1947, but were not, even then, to be completely applied.

On the financial side, the Algiers expedition was a rare example of an enterprise entirely covered by the sums 're-covered' on the spot. The Casbah treasury was found to contain 15,500 lb. of gold, worth 25 million francs of the epoch, and 220,000 lb. of silver, worth 24 million francs—in total 49 million francs, of which 43 million were dispatched to France. With other booty, the entire sum captured was 55 million francs. This covered the 48 million francs which the venture had cost, and left a profit of some 7 millions.

At the time when the decision to send the expedition was taken, very little was known in France about Algeria. It was appreciated vaguely that there was a Muslim population, of Arabic speech, ruled by a Turkish minority. After the capture of the city, the experience of the Regency administration could have been utilized. The official proclamation had, however, announced that the force was coming to liberate the Algerians from their oppressive (Turkish) tyrant. The former Turkish officials were not informed what their lot was to be but were deported or simply ignored. They therefore abandoned their

P

offices without passing the records to anyone and, for the most part, either carried off or destroyed their documents. By a mistake in the official proclamation in Arabic, drawn up by the illustrious orientalist Silvestre de Sacy, the Algerians had been addressed as *Maghariba* or Moroccans; and the lack of interpreters was a cause of difficulty. To crown all, the French Government had no idea what it wanted to do with Algeria. From 9 July until the fall of the Bourbon Government, the Commander-in-Chief received only two messages from France; one asked for the dispatch of 60 camels, to be acclimatized in the Landes, and the other for the making of collections of herbs and insects for the museum. In Paris seven possibilities had been laid before the cabinet. The first was to maintain the Dey, having extracted guarantees against slavery and an indemnity of 50 million francs. The second was to destroy the fortifications and port of Algiers and then retire. The third was to set up an Arab prince to rule Algiers, with an Arab administration. The fourth was to ask the Sublime Porte to take over and to appoint a Pasha. The fifth was to hand the city over to the Knights of Malta. The sixth to retain Algiers and to colonize the coastal areas. The seventh was to invite other European powers to join in. Spain was to take Oran; Britain, Arzew; the Austrians, Bône; Sardinia, Stura; the Grand Duchy of Tuscany, Djidjelli; and the Kingdom of Naples, Bougie.

In considering the subsequent history of Algeria, there are two methods of approach. The first, which has been that generally practised, consists in treating Algeria as an object, the object which the conquest set out to acquire; and then to enumerate the actions carried out by the occupying power, without attempting to find out what the occupied felt or thought about it. The second has been practised only by a few nationalist Algerian writers, such as Mustafa Lacheref (al-Ashraf); his method is to recount the history of the Algerian people as a community or, if you like, of Algeria as a living entity. The assertion that there never was such a thing as an Algerian nation or nationality is often advanced today as a reason for rejecting modern nationalist claims. Yet these two expressions recur in the works of French writers, both military and civilian, during the nineteenth century, that is to say precisely at the time when in the case of other nationalities the idea of statehood was crystallizing out of the ferment of ideas and becoming a reality.

In 1883 Paul Gaffarel, in his book *L'Algérie*, wrote: 'the Arabs . . . had on several occasions tried to throw off the yoke of the Turks and to claim their national independence; for they

ALGERIA 215

considered themselves the legitimate owners of the country, though in fact they were themselves conquerors. But then their conquest was ancient and had so to speak been legalized by long possession.' He adds that whereas 'in 1830 we presented ourselves to the Algerians in the light of liberators, we learned little by little to imitate the proceedings of the oppressors'. An anonymous English writer, in a pamphlet, published in Paris in 1833, under the title *Appel en faveur d'Alger et de l'Afrique du Nord, par un anglais*, quotes the following passage from an Arabic leaflet which, he says, was distributed by the French forces in Algiers: 'We are going to drive out the Turks. We are not conquering the town to remain its masters. We swear this by our blood. Join us, be worthy of our protection, and you will rule your country again, independent and masters of your native soil.'

From the standpoint of the Muslim inhabitants, the history of Algeria since the occupation of the capital can be divided into three periods. The first lasted forty years, from 1832 to 1871, with sporadic extensions until 1884; was marked by continuous fighting, and was the period of active resistance and local and rural patriotism. The second, which covered about fifty years, ended in the 1920's, and was the period of silence. The fact that during this second period Algeria enjoyed that kind of happiness which is denoted by an absence of 'history' was probably due in part to the physical and spiritual exhaustion of the Muslim people for whom it was a period of convalescence after the struggles of the preceding years. But there was also a mood of expectancy. An educated minority came into existence and were attracted by the benefits of French civilization. These saw the remedy for the troubles of their people in an extension to them of the French education and civilization from which they themselves had profited. It was only by degrees that they realized that the path to wholesale assimilation was blocked, politically by the incomprehension and opposition, inspired by fear, of the politically active members of the European minority and economically by the immensity of the financial effort which such a policy would have entailed for the French authorities. For this reason the second period, the period of silence, during which the Algerian Muslims slowly recovered their strength and self-confidence, though it did create a minority who felt themselves to be Frenchmen of the Muslim faith, did not end in an epoch of integration and co-operation. The third period, which has now lasted for more than thirty years, proved on the contrary to be the period of assertion by the Algerians of the claim to be a nation, in the twentieth-century meaning of the word.

Such a presentation of the course of events is not that set out in official textbooks. It is nevertheless an honest way of presenting the history of Algeria and, without doubt, a fruitful one.

Without the adoption of a guiding principle—which was precisely what was lacking to the original expeditionary corps—the description of events and particularly of their military aspects yields at best a disconnected narrative and at worst a complete tangle. After the capture of Algiers, Bourmont so deceived himself as to believe 'that the Regency would probably submit within fifteen days'. This remark showed complete ignorance of the structure of the Algerian state, by assessing its power of resistance as that of the 5,000 janissaries, or the 15,000 representatives of the Turkish ruling class. It ignored the tribes, some of them owing allegiance to the Turks, others theoretically integrated, and the rest independent. It forgot the unifying force of Islam and the interest which the Muslim neighbours of Algeria could not fail to take in its affairs.

In fact the French conquest of the Algiers area cannot be said to have been complete until 1834 and then only to the extent of a 'restricted occupation', which applied the principles of a protectorate without using the word itself. It was only later, in 1840, that the conquest of Algeria as a whole was undertaken. On the fall of Algiers, two out of the three Beys, those of Oran and Médéa, rallied to the French; but Ahmad Bey of Constantine did not submit until 1848. In the west, at Mascara, the Amir Abdelkader personified the danger to the French occupation from 1832 until his submission in December 1847. His influence extended far into the east of Algeria and General Changarnier wrote that 'as long as Abdelkader had forces and a regular government, the resources, stores and water courses which he controlled compelled us to make the same sort of strategic calculations as in Europe'.[1] To conclude the war, Bugeaud had to increase his force to 100,000 men and in 1844 to defeat the army of the Sultan of Morocco.

Judgements expressed by the Amir's enemies do as much credit to them as to him. After the successful operation against him at Sikak in 1836, the Duc d'Orléans wrote: 'The Arab army had been scattered, but the people remained intact, thanks to their unity, their morale and their elusiveness.' [2] In 1842 General Duvivier expressed himself in these terms:—

The real strength of Abdelkader, the force which is resisting us, has its origin in an idea . . . Abdelkader was Amir because Liberty

---

[1] Général C. A. T. Changarnier, *Campagnes d'Afrique; mémoires du Général Changarnier* (Paris, 1930), p. 316.
[2] Duc d'Orléans, *Campagnes de l'Armée d'Afrique, 1835–9* (Paris, 1870).

had entrusted him with her sword. . . . He was the man of history; she will never forget him; she will repeat his name. . . . History will excuse his rigorous death sentences; have not people who are fighting for liberty always put deserters to death? . . . Unhappy son of the desert, future generations will honour your name. Woe to him who will not say a blessing over those who are the martyrs of liberty.[1]

In 1883 the historian Gaffarel wrote: '[The Amir Abdelkader] hero of the Arab resistance knew how to concentrate around himself the scattered forces of Arab nationality.' He adds that in 1845 'it was against an entire nation, inspired by the double fanaticism of patriotism and religion, that the war had to be waged'.[2] In 1862 France herself, grateful for the gesture by which Abdelkader in Damascus in 1860 had saved the lives of some thousands of Christians, presented her former adversary with a medal bearing these words: 'Amir of North Africa, Defender of Arab nationality, Protector of oppressed Christians'.

The support given to the Amir by the Kabyle country, and by his representative there, Ibn Salim, is one of the many features which suggest that the resistance of the peasants was nation-wide. Little as the history of these events is known, certain essential facts must be given their due, as, for example, the congress of the united Algerian delegations in 1838 at the camp of Bu Khorshfa, near Miliana, in the presence of Abdelkader. Unity was proclaimed in the sacred names of the Faith, of the defence of human liberties and of a rural patriotism based on community spirit and the instinct of self-preservation.

In fact, European colonization was threatening the peasants' lands and even their existence. By 1846 there were already 100,000 settlers and Martimprey was preaching the necessity of the 'deportation of the Muslim population to other selected areas in order to dispose of the land freely'. In 1847 Lamoricière asserted that 'colonization and the exigencies which it implies will be the proof that submission is genuine'.[3] It was, however, the Senatus-Consultus of 1863 which 'sealed the final fate of native property'. Till then the basis of the patriarchal system of Algerian land-holding was the 'tribal holding'—land held collectively. The law of 1863 caused this to be broken up by constituting individual holdings and leaving the individual free to sell the land which he received from the distribution. In the conditions of the time this entailed dismemberment for the

[1] Général F. F. Duvivier, *Quatorze observations sur le dernier mémoire du général Bugeaud* (Paris, 1842).
[2] *L'Algérie*.
[3] Général de Martimprey and Général de Lamoricière, *Projets de colonisation pour es provinces d'Oran et de Constantine* (Paris, 1847).

benefit of the speculator. Fifty years later Raymond Aynard was speaking of the 'agrarian obsession of the Muslim Algerians. In their eyes', he says, 'colonization appears primarily as the deduction of some 2,000,000 hectares, the equivalent of one-fifth of the area available for cultivation in the Tell and on the High Plateaux'.[1] When account is taken of the sequestration of forests, water-courses, mines, common lands, and pasturage, it will be found that Mustafa Lacheref's estimate of 8–9 million hectares for this 'deduction' is substantially correct.

Insurrections provoked by peasant patriotism were repressed with extreme rigour. On his return from an expedition in the Kabyle country in 1846, Bugeaud declared to settlers in Algiers: 'We have burnt a great deal and destroyed a great deal. It may be that I shall be called a barbarian, but as I have the conviction that I have done something useful for my country, I consider myself as above the reproaches of the press.' [2] The historian Gaffarel wrote, with reference to the revolt of Bu Baghla in 1851:

More than 300 villages were burnt. War was waged also on plantations and on trees. In the basin of the Sahel several thousand olive trees were destroyed . . . Friendly tribes had their throats cut as if they had been enemies . . . The consequence of these useless atrocities was that the Kabyle people were the more obstinate in their resistance and that the cause of Bu Baghla became a national one.[3]

The centre of Ichirriden was the high place of this Kabyle resistance and the historian C. Rousset compared their resistance with that of Vercingetorix at Alesia. An even more famous case was the sacrifice of 157 *musabbalin* (devotees) at Tishkert on 17 June 1857. Inspired by a woman, Lalla Fatima of Soumer, who can be considered a sort of Kabyle Joan of Arc, they fastened themselves together by the knees, at the entrance to the village, and so caused themselves to be massacred on the spot in one body.

The Aurès had already witnessed the 'terrible fate' of the oases of Zaatcha (1849) and Nara (1850), which were burnt and laid waste and had their thousands of palm trees cut down by the Canrobert expedition. The rising of 1871, during which there were more than 300 engagements, held 80,000 soldiers in check for an entire year. The chastisement of the rebels was intended to serve as an example; animals and land were seized; a fine of 60 million gold francs was imposed and 180,000 rifles confiscated; there were executions, deportations, and the transfer to France of hundreds of hostages. Yet, in spite

[1] Raymond Aynard, *L'Oeuvre française en Algérie* (Paris, 1913).
[2] Gaffarel, *L'Algérie*.   [3] Ibid.

of this, eight years later, in 1879, another nine battalions and eight squadrons were needed before an end could be put to another rising. It is understandable that the Duc d'Orléans, always remarkable for his objectivity, should have written in 1870 in his *Campagnes de l'armée d'Afrique (1835–1839)* with reference to the poet, Bu Thelja, who belonged to the Hajoute tribe in the Mitidja, 'A simple soldier he died like Koerner (the German patriot poet, killed fighting against Napoleon) at the hand of a Frenchman; both of them fought for countries which they dreamed to see great but which neither of them ever saw other than unhappy.'

It is impossible to deny that an Algerian fatherland existed and that it was an ideal for which many thousand Algerians gave their lives. If, in 1936, Ferhat Abbas, then the Algerian assimilationist leader, declared that he had tried in vain to find an Algerian nation in history, it was because the centres of Arabic culture had been destroyed and his French upbringing had confined his education to textbooks used in the French schools. The long years of the silence separated him from the memory of the great peasant risings in which his compatriots expressed their patriotism in the only way that was open to them. Subsequent experience led him to become one of the principal spokesmen of the FLN and, in 1958, Prime Minister of the self-constituted Algerian Provisional Government.

The first expression of a new stirring of Algerian sentiment was the ephemeral but symbolic action of the grandson of Abdelkader, the Amir Khalid, in 1921 and the founding of the movement *Étoile Nord Africaine* in 1923. This time an urban nationalism came into being among Algerian workers in Paris; here they were stimulated by mixing with the French proletariat and were brought into contact with the stirring world events of the moment—the birth of Communism, the class struggle, the French Mandate in Syria, the Turkish revolution of Mustafa Kemal, the war in the Rif. With the founding of the *Parti Populaire Algérien* in 1936, a specifically nationalist activity took shape. During the Second World War under the Vichy régime racialism led to criminal excesses in Algeria. On 1 August 1942 the French Mayor of Zeralda, on a flimsy pretext, assassinated twenty-seven innocent Muslims by asphyxia in the municipal prison.[1] Though the Muslims of Algeria, after the Allied disembarkation in Africa, had taken a glorious part

---

[1] *Communauté Algérienne* No. 8 (Algiers, 1955). He was sentenced in Oran to two years' imprisonment. Muslims in Zeralda, according to a statement by an eyewitness, were forbidden to market at the same time as Europeans or to sit beside them. They were not admitted to cinemas frequented by Europeans or to the beach where Europeans bathed.

in the liberation of France, a demonstration at Sétif, in the department of Constantine, carrying Algerian flags on the occasion of the celebration of the victory in Europe in May 1945, was broken up by the police. An incipient rising followed in which about 100 Europeans were killed. This provoked reprisals in the course of which some 10,000 Muslim villagers were massacred. The final rising was that which began on 1 November 1954, and is still continuing. The appointment of Jacques Soustelle, who had played a considerable part in the Free French movement, as Governor General in 1955 appeared to offer a chance for a real 'new deal'; but the opportunity was allowed to pass and the rising grew into what is virtually a state of war.

The ideological and revolutionary character of the present rising has at least one precedent in Algeria, as has been pointed out by Mustafa Lacheref. In 1871 committees of ten to twelve elected members, known as Shartiya, were formed to administer large areas in parallel to the official administration. According to Colonel Rinn, who wrote an account of the rising, their task was to supervise the Caids, inflict fines, seize the property of recalcitrant persons or those who refused to make common cause with them, to buy horses, arms, and ammunition, and to act as a court of appeal from decisions of the Cadi and of the disciplinary commissions. [These illegal] 'bodies of peasants and proletarians were a danger to the very principle of action of the French government'.[1]

GOVERNMENT AND POLITICAL LIFE

Government and Administration

The political and administrative organization of Algeria is the result of a long period of groping and of modifications which were, as often as not, made in response to the pressure of events. The same is true also of the legal status given to the Muslims, for the two questions were intimately linked. For obvious reasons, the settlers have always insisted that no difference should be made between Algeria and France as far as they were concerned. In this they saw the guarantee for their security, their rights, and their property. But as for the Muslims, so different in language, culture, religion, race, and customs, what was to be done? Were they to be treated as aliens, as protected persons, or as citizens?

The Ordinance of 22 July 1834 provided for a military régime, directed by a Governor-General, himself a soldier,

[1] Colonel Louis Rinn, *Histoire de l'insurrection de 1871 en Algérie* (Algiers, 1891).

having at his disposal a *Service des Bureaux Arabes* in each of the three divisions, Algiers, Oran, and Constantine. In his circular of 17 September 1844 Bugeaud recalled that 'we have always presented ourselves to the Muslims as more just and more capable of governing than their former masters and have promised to treat them as children of France. We have given them formal assurances that we would preserve their laws, their property, their religion, and their customs. We owe it to them, and to ourselves, to keep our word in every respect.' Bugeaud thus renewed the Bourmont–Husain Pact of 1830 and assumed the attitude of a father towards the Muslims. He left them to be administered by their own chiefs, though these were appointed and supervised by officers of the Arab Bureaux, according to a system which was to be taken up again, and adapted to the use of Morocco, as the *Service des Affaires Indigènes*.

The Second Republic practised a policy of encouraging French settlement and Muslim assimilation. In each of the three provinces a civil territory was constituted; in 1848 these became departments, at the head of which were prefects to administer the settlers. For all other purposes, the military organization was preserved.

The Second Empire was a period of confusion. From 1858 to 1860 Algeria was governed from Paris by a Minister for the Colonies; it then reverted to a military Government. Meanwhile Napoleon III, in face of the opposition of the settlers, made the assertion that 'Algeria is not a colony, properly so-called, but an Arab kingdom. The natives, like the settlers, have a right to my protection, and I am just as much Emperor of the Arabs as I am Emperor of the French. . . . We must convince the Arabs that we are not here to despoil them, but to bring them the benefits of civilization.' [1] The preamble of the Senatus Consultus of 14 July 1865 declares that 'there is no purpose in recounting the insurrections of the natives whose affronted national sentiment is immediately awakened. Separated from their new masters by their preconceptions, their beliefs, their laws, and their very virtues, they were always delighted to oppose every kind of passive and active resistance to the rights of their conquerors.' Having thus admitted that an Algerian national sentiment had existed for thirty-five years, the law of 1865 went on indirectly to proclaim the annexation of Algeria. The imperial champion of the 'Principle of Nationalities' did not see fit to hold a plebiscite in Algeria as he had in Nice and Savoy.

In 1865 the rapporteur of the Senatus Consultus declared that henceforth 'the Muslim native is a Frenchman. This

[1] Letter to General Macmahon (Gaffarel, *L'Algérie*).

declaration puts an end to all doubt and uncertainty and needs no interpretation.' In reality the Muslims thus became French subjects, but not French citizens; for they retained their personal status, had no political rights, and continued to be subject to special police regulations. When, in 1903, one of them became a convert to Catholicism and claimed that he thereby ceased to be subject to the *Code de l'Indigénat* (established by law in 1881, modified in 1914, and finally abolished in 1944), his plea was rejected by an Algiers court on the grounds that 'the term *Muslim* had no confessional connotation; it denoted any person of Muslim origin who, not having been admitted a citizen, necessarily kept his Muslim status even though he might adhere to the Catholic faith'.

In 1870 the settlers, having expelled the officials of the Empire, tried to govern as a revolutionary authority through the Commune d'Alger. On assuming power Thiers decided to establish a civil régime in Algeria. The scope of the civil territories was expanded, while the *Bureaux Arabes*, which were military, were relegated to the south. Where the settlers were numerous, *Communes de Plein Exercice* or 'Fully-empowered Localities' were established and administered as in France by a Mayor and Municipal Council; where the settlers were few, the community was called a *Commune Mixte* and directed by civil administrators who were the successors of the officers of the *Bureaux Arabes*. The administrative and financial autonomy of Algeria was made complete in 1900. The budget was voted by *Délégations Financières* in which the Muslims participated to the extent of one-third; and in 1919 Clemenceau gave them the right of participating in the elections to the *Délégations Financières*. By now, the Governor-General had become a high official with far-reaching powers. As representative of the Government in the region, he exercised the right of sovereignty; as representative of a decentralized local administration, he supervised Algerian affairs in general. From 1881 to 1896 the administrative services were placed under the direct authority of the relevant ministries in Paris. At the end of this 'period of attachment', far-reaching powers were again conferred on the Governor-General. The legal position of the Muslims, however, remained unchanged. In 1936 the proposed Blum–Violette reforms which would have given French citizenship to 30,000 Muslims were brought to nought by the resignation of the Algerian Mayors; meanwhile the project had, it seems, raised real enthusiasm among the Muslims for acquiring French citizenship. Its rejection was the final death-blow to assimilation.

It is true that in the eyes of Algerian nationalists assimilation must have seemed a one-way process. The complete attachment of the Algerian departments to France was an operation from which only the European settlers seemed likely to benefit, since the Muslims were still held in the grip of the *Code de l'Indigénat*; from this they could only escape by naturalization, that is to say by renouncing their personality as Muslims, a step which only about 2,500 chose to take between 1866 and 1934. And then the land problem would have remained precisely as it had been. As Raymond Aynard wrote in 1913, 'in a conquered country, almost the only sort of co-operation possible between the two races is one in which the conquered work for the conquerors as tenants or wage-earners'.[1]

The Second World War provided another opportunity to cut the knot. At Constantine on 12 December 1943 a new prospect was opened up by General de Gaulle. 'The territories of the French imperial community', he said, 'have all of them shown that they have put their trust in France. And when they say France they mean the gospel of the brotherhood of peoples, of the equality of men, and of the constant maintenance of order so that the liberty of all may be protected.' [2] He went on to say that France must honour her contract and that the loyalty of which she had been the object had 'put her under an obligation, particularly in the case of the Muslims of North Africa'. In fulfilment of this view the Ordinance of 7 March 1944 extended citizenship to certain categories of Muslims, while the Law of 1946 accorded them 15 deputies in the National Assembly and 7 senators in the Council of the Republic.

But the blood-stained days of May 1945 had meanwhile opened a new gulf between the two Algerian communities. On 2 August 1946 Ferhat Abbas, leader of the *Union Démocratique du Manifeste Algérien* (UDMA), laid before the National Constituent Assembly in Paris a 'draft law designed to prepare the way for the constitution of an Algerian Republic, as a federated unit of the French Union'. There was at that moment a favourable feeling towards federal solutions of this nature but, notwithstanding, the proposal was never taken into consideration, owing to the pressure brought to bear by the settlers and to sentimental attachment to the classical schoolroom catchword 'Algeria is part of France'. Seeing that assimilation was getting nowhere, the organic law of 20 September 1947, known as the Statute of Algeria, adopted a related formula, integration, the significance of which was not very clear. Its purpose was to be all things to all men, by maintaining strict institutional bonds

[1] *L'Oeuvre française en Algérie.*   [2] *France,* 13 December 1943.

with the metropolis while at the same time recognizing that Algeria was something different, with a 'personality' of its own.

The essence of the new Statute was the creation of an Algerian Assembly, having wide powers in financial matters and some influence over administration. It was composed of 120 deputies, elected in equal numbers by two electoral colleges. The first was composed of Europeans and assimilated Muslims, numbering 370,000 and 60,000 respectively, and the second of 1,300,000 Muslim voters, from which women were for the time being excluded, though the Statute decreed their inclusion. The Algerian Muslims were to become real French citizens, with the title of Muslim French, while keeping their personal Quranic status. The Statute provided also for the progressive disappearance of the military territories of the south, and of the *Communes Mixtes* which were to be assimilated to the *Communes de Plein Exercice*. The Statute in fact returned to the original pact of 1830, reaffirming the independence of the Muslim religion *vis-à-vis* the state and arranging for the teaching of Arabic at all levels.

The debate in the French Parliament was long drawn out, and the discussions heated. Finally the Statute obtained 320 votes out of 624, with the fifteen Muslim deputies abstaining. France had set out along the path of integration, that is to say of absorbing 8 million Muslims. The logical consequence of the Statute would have been the election to the French Parliament in Paris of 100 Muslim French deputies. Yet for all its shortcomings, the Statute of 1947 did offer hope of a peaceful solution. Through the Algerian Assembly, it provided the Muslims with a legal means of expressing their views and of taking a part in the direction of their own affairs. Unfortunately, it was never sincerely or completely applied. The elections of 1948 were 'managed' by the administration, the apparent intention being to avoid the election of 'extremists'. The result was a crisis of mistrust which has never subsequently been overcome. It was accentuated by the fact that the remaining provisions of the Statute, regarding the mixed communes, the teaching of Arabic, and the independence of the Muslim religion from state interference remained a dead letter. It was here that the immediate cause of the rising of 1 November 1954 is to be found; the Muslims rebelled in desperation.

After the systematic sabotage of the Statute, one last chance occurred in the governorship of Jacques Soustelle, in whom great hopes had been placed. At the end of June 1955 he explained his plan for the gradual integration of Algeria with metropolitan France; it was too little, and too late. Soon afterwards, General de Gaulle took up the theme of integration, but added that it must be 'in a community which is larger than France' and repeated that 'no policy which does not envisage the replacement of domination in North Africa by association is either worthy of France or has any chance of being useful'.[1] Soon, however, the rebel attack of 20 August 1955, with its extensive slaughter of French non-combatants, opened the way to the policy of 'pacification', and this in its turn was to bring the use of torture to extract information, and the slaughter of innocent populations. In the atmosphere of hate and terror, subsequent reforms came to nothing, without being as much as heard of—the dissolution of the Algerian Assembly at the beginning of 1956; the nomination of a Resident Minister in 1956, turned into a Minister for Algeria in 1957; the creation of a whole twelve new departments; and a rearrangement of municipalities so that at the end of January 1957 Algeria had 1,438 municipal areas of which 333 enjoyed *plein exercice*. Since it was difficult to find willing Muslims capable of occupying public appointments, Special Administrative Sections (*Sections Administratives Spéciales-S.A.S.*) had to be set up. These were run by officers who were the latter-day heirs of the *Bureaux Arabes* and had the task of regaining contact with the people. An effort was also made to increase the number of Muslims in the administration; in 1955, out of 26,000 government posts held by appointed officials, only 4,600 were held by Muslims, that is to say 17·5 per cent., a figure lower than that in pre-independence Tunisia or Morocco. At the end of 1957 the Government in Paris prepared a *loi-cadre* concerning a régime to be bestowed on Algeria. The purpose of this was to create a number of separate regions, each with its own local council. These would, after two years, be represented in a federative council, the word 'federative' being chosen as less suggestive of a sovereign body than 'federal' would have been. The powers to be given to these bodies appeared to be less than those of an English County Council. They were, however, to have been elected on a common electoral roll and most of them would presumably have had Muslim majorities. The thought of this was sufficient to cause the French political parties, which lend an ear to the settlers and were now inspired by M. Soustelle, to engineer the rejection of the draft law in October 1957. Since the preamble specifically declared Algeria to be an integral part of the French Republic, it was unlikely that this project for splitting the country up would appeal to the Muslims. A modified text was finally voted in November 1957.

[1] Press Conference, 30 June 1955.

Hitherto social relations between Europeans and Muslims have not extended much beyond those of settlers with their labourers or employers with their employees, to which can be added occasional friendly relations which persist between former school-fellows or between neighbouring European and Muslim farmers. In certain remote corners of the Aurès no non-Muslim Frenchman had ever been seen by the Muslim French since 1830. It was chiefly in France itself that the two kinds of Frenchmen had a chance of getting to know one another, in factory, street, or regiment. In 1954 a high official of the Government General found it necessary to issue instructions 'for a more humane administration'. Since 'Algeria is part of France', Muslims, who have little in the way of schooling, have to manage as best they can with innumerable regulations in French which they are very rarely able to read; the Algiers prefecture in 1954 no longer thought it necessary to keep an Arabic interpreter.[1] Since the rising of 1954, the relations of Muslims with Europeans have been more and more confined to those which the army thinks suitable. Very few French people are on terms of friendly confidence with Muslims. If, one day, something of Franco-Muslim friendship is saved, it will be due mainly to the self-sacrifice of those women and men who have worked together, for example in the Social Centres (pp. 237, 238–9) for an Algeria where brotherliness and justice have more chance of prevailing. It would be wrong to think that all

---

[1] The difficulty of translation seems to reach even to the Governor-General's office. In his book *Aimée et souffrante Algérie* M. Jacques Soustelle, Governor-General 1955–6, quotes a captured document in Arabic (p. 219) which he forwarded to Paris and regards as conclusive. The document concerned is a receipt for arms, issued by a commander in the Army of National Liberation. In the translation given by M. Soustelle the final sentence appears as follows:—'Il [the FLN leader] en remercie vivement les membres du comité du Maghreb et son chef, le commandant de la révolution, Bikbashi Gamal Abdel Nasser' ('he thanks the members of the Maghrib Committee warmly for them, and its chief, the leader of the revolution, Colonel Gamal Abdel Nasser'). At the end of the book however a photostatic copy of the Arabic original is printed, with the statement above it in French that it was addressed to Colonel Abdel Nasser. The Arabic text does not agree with the translation, and indeed makes it seem impossible that the letter should have been addressed to Colonel Abdel Nasser. The Arabic says: 'He also sends his warmest and best greetings [not 'thanks'] to all the members of the Arab League [not 'the Maghrib Committee'] and especially [not 'and its chief'] to the leader of the revolution, Colonel Gamal Abdel Nasser.' There is also an error in the translation of the preceding sentence, where the Arabic *Trablus al-Gharb*, meaning 'Tripoli of Africa', is rendered by 'western Tripolitania'. The mistranslation is the more remarkable because the earlier paragraphs dealing with the quantity of arms delivered, which are much more difficult to decipher, are rendered accurately. In the circumstances, it seems hard to avoid the suspicion of a deliberate falsification at some stage. M. Soustelle refers again to the letter in his *Le Drame algérien* (Paris, 1957) in the following words: 'nous n'avons pas forgé de toutes pièces l'accusé de réception d'armes addressé par Chihani Bachir au même Nasser' (p. 54). It was, however, certainly mistranslated.

French residents shared the views of the politically active settler leaders who were opposed to all reforms tending to equality of status.

The part played by Muslim Algerians serving in the army in the three national French wars, 1870, 1914–18, and 1939–45, was considerable. Algerian contingents served also in the Indo-Chinese war, and in 1957 20,000 Algerian Muslims were serving as regular soldiers and 35,000 as partisans (*harkas*) with the French forces. From the end of 1956 450,000 young French national service men have been serving in Algeria to maintain order which is menaced by about 65,000 armed Muslims of whom 35,000 are 'regulars' and 30,000 'partisans'. Between 1 November 1954 and 1 October 1957 French troops lost 4,750 killed.[1] Technically, the problem is that of the 'revolutionary war' in which the clandestine establishment of a political authority is just as important as the guerrilla fighting. It is the type of war about which the Chinese leader, Mao Tse-tung, remarked that 'the population supports its army, as the sea supports its fish'.

Justice

The judicial organization of Algeria is based, more or less, on that of France. There are 17 Tribunals of First Instance, the same number of Assize Courts, and a Court of Appeal in Algiers. Matters of personal status and succession are dealt with in the case of Muslims by 84 religious judges, or cadis, and 23 subsidiaries. Their jurisdiction is however optional, while in the Kabyle country it does not exist at all and Muslims can always address themselves to *Juges de Paix* who apply Muslim law, or to the French courts. Since 1955 provisions of the law concerning the 'State of Emergency' have permitted the internment of about 5,000 suspects in *Centres d'Hébergement* where they have no means of appeal. In July 1957 Algeria was visited by a delegation of the International Committee Against Concentration Camps. After investigation this body of highly qualified investigators declared itself convinced that ill-treatment and torture had been inflicted on arrested persons by various members of the security forces. These measures did not seem to it to 'conform with the principles of respect for human rights to which the French Government and all democratic nations have adhered'.

---

[1] In the spring of 1958 the French authorities ceased publishing the figures for French losses. For April and May 1958, they gave the figure of 3,803 and 3,393 rebels killed respectively; and 663 and 672 captured. In general French losses can be assumed to be 1 in 8 or 10 of the Algerian losses (*Figaro*, 7 June 1958).

Political Life

Frenchmen in Algeria belong to the same political parties as in France. A few Muslims also do so and have been elected as Radicals, SFIO,[1] or MRP. The Algerian Communist Party (PCA) has very few adherents among the Muslims, partly because of its changes of policy and partly because of its inability to find a suitable formula for the local problem, which is a matter of racial hostility rather than class struggle. The two main tendencies which divided Muslim opinion until 1954 corresponded to two conceptions of progress—one of direct action and social agitation; the other of evolution by stages.

The first tendency was represented by the *Parti Populaire Algérien* (PPA). This was founded in 1936 by Missali Hajj, on his return from France, to replace the *Étoile Nord Africaine* movement born in 1923 among Algerian workers in France. Dissolved in 1939, the PPA continued to develop clandestinely until the amnesty of 1946. Little by little the PPA acquired a hard core among the students; these created in it a hierarchy of control organized like a pyramid. At the base, there were cells of four militants; at all levels, a distinction was drawn between militants, or shock troops, and elements of infiltration. At the top there were clandestine nerve centres at which decisions were taken unanimously.

In the general elections of 1 November 1946 the clandestine PPA, camouflaged under the label MTLD (*Mouvement pour le Triomphe des Libertés Démocratiques*) obtained five of the fifteen seats in the National Assembly in spite of administrative 'obstruction'. Its programme was somewhat indefinite; its essential demand was 'the return of the Algerian people to national sovereignty', by means of an 'Algerian constituent assembly, sovereign, elected by universal suffrage, without distinction of race or religion'. In April 1948 the 'arranged' elections for the Algerian Assembly reduced the MTLD to a condition of semi-illegality. In 1950 the police made much of the discovery of a plot organized by an *Organisation Secrète* (OS) of the illegal PPA. In 1951 the MTLD formed a joint Algerian front with the UDMA, the PCA, and the Association of Ulama; but this dissolved a year later. The party was moreover weakened internally by three conflicting trends. One group believed in the revolutionary, messianic views of Missali Hajj; others preferred the constructive activity of the Central Committee whose members were elected to Municipal Councils where they co-operated loyally with their European col-

---

[1] *Section Française de l'Internationale Ouvrière.*

leagues; while a third group, small but active, preached resort to violence pure and simple. In July 1954 a Congress was held in Belgium. This confirmed the division of the MTLD–PPA into three conflicting groups—Missalists, who considered themselves the only orthodox body; Centralists, now excluded by the Missalists but still controlling the machine, the staff, and the funds; and the activists, who were now to form a *Comité Révolutionnaire d'Unité et d'Action* (CRUA) in Cairo. It was the latter which was directly concerned in the outbreak of trouble in November 1954, that is to say, of the present rising. Failing to grasp what was happening, the French Government, in a gesture of blind reaction, decided to dissolve the MTLD as a whole.

The other main political tendency among the Algerian Muslims is symbolized in the career of its leader, Ferhat Abbas. Originally assimilationist to the point of writing, in 1936, that 'France means myself', this Sétif pharmacist, married to a Frenchwoman, as is also Missali, was disillusioned by the persistently colonial outlook of the administration, and on 10 February 1943 issued his Manifesto of the Algerian People; as a result, he was kept under house observation. After the Ordinance of 7 March 1944, he founded the party of the *Amis du Manifeste et de la Liberté* (AML) which secured half a million cards of membership within a year. The party was blamed for the demonstration of 8 May 1945 in Sétif; this was, however, rather the work of the PPA who had moved in, with quite peaceful intentions, and then been overtaken by events. In 1946 Ferhat Abbas founded the UDMA; this was less intransigent than the MTLD had been, but envisaged as its ultimate objective the achievement of an Algerian Republic, democratic and freely associated with the French Republic. In the general elections of 1946 the UDMA obtained 11 seats out of 13 in the Constituent Assembly and 10 out of 15 in the National Assembly. When the project put forward by Ferhat Abbas was not even discussed, the UDMA tried to secure the settlement of various problems which fell within the framework of the Statute of 1947. In the general election of 1951 the big Algerian families had the backing of the administration and so secured most of the seats. Early in the rising, at the time of the appointment of M. Soustelle as Governor-General, the UDMA, which had been losing ground, might have come to the fore again in support of a real new deal—had any such new deal been forthcoming.

The same is true of the Association of Ulama, founded in 1935, under the inspiration of Shaikh Brahimi. This was a movement of Arabic-speaking intellectuals whose object was to purify Islam from popular superstition, to fight for the independence of the Muslim religion from official interference, and to spread the teaching of the Arabic language. In theory the Statute of 1947 should have been satisfactory to them on the two latter points, and the Ulama led by Shaikh Brahimi and the well-known writer and speaker, Tewfik Medani, might have quitted the political field if the Statute had been fully applied. But this was not the case; the project for the teaching of Arabic, not finally produced until 1955 (that is, after the outbreak of the rising) used the word 'optional' instead of 'obligatory' and excluded the Kabyle country, on the grounds of Berber 'particularism', from the area to which it was applicable.

Finally, in desperation, nearly all leading Algerian personalities in the spring of 1956 began to join the *Front de Libération Nationale* (FLN), which had formed its headquarters in Cairo for the time being, and to participate either as representatives abroad, or in the directing body within Algeria (the Committee of Co-ordination and Executive, CCE), or in fighting posts with the Army of National Liberation. The only exceptions were the Missalists, found chiefly among the Algerian workers in France and grouped in the *Mouvement National Algérien* (MNA); some of their members took part in the guerrilla fighting in Algeria but had bloody settlings of accounts with the Front. It is very difficult to give any accurate figures, but there is no doubt that the FLN is the most truly representative body of Algerian nationalism and that it contains practically all the *interlocuteurs valables*, or leaders worth negotiating with, and certainly the only political brains and responsible spokesmen capable of ordering a cease fire and seeing that it is carried out. Some people have claimed to see Soviet influence in the 'collective leadership' of the five, and later nine, members of the CCE; but this supposition is fanciful for it might just as well be the influence of the old Kabyle custom of the *kharrouba* or family groups (pictured as seeds in a carob pod). There has been no true political life in Algeria since the dissolution of the Algerian Assembly in 1956 and the French general elections, since which no Algerian representatives, either Muslim or Christian, have sat in the French Assembly but only in the *Conseil de la République*.

The Course of the Algerian Rising

On 1 November 1954, the night of All Saints, armed groups made concerted attacks, principally in the Constantine department, on key points, such as police and gendarmerie posts and forest guards. The action was sharpest at Batna, the administrative centre of the Aurès, and the death of ten Europeans was sufficient to set off a strong emotional reaction. The Government, attacked in Parliament and harassed by the settlers, reacted brutally and without discrimination. The MTLD, though in fact divided into three sections of which one only believed in direct and violent action, was held responsible and dissolved. No less than 2,000 members of the two sections, Missalists and Centralists, who at that time were still in favour of political action only, were arrested; indiscriminate reprisals were carried out in the Aurès, entailing military action and *ratissages*.[1]

In mid-February of the following year Jacques Soustelle, appointed Governor-General with a special mission but delayed by a ministerial crisis, arrived in Algiers to take up his post. At that time there were not more than 500 rebels under arms in all Algeria; 350 in the Aurès and 150 in Kabylia. The chief of the Aurès section, ben Boulaid, was arrested in Tunisia on his way to Egypt. The rebellion was in the doldrums. The immediate and integral application of the Statute of 1947 accompanied by the release of innocent detainees and the restoration of public liberties could hardly have failed to win over many waverers. Instead a State of Emergency was voted by Parliament; this reinforced the powers of the police and set on foot the wholesale arrest of suspects who were sent to 'Lodging Camps' (*camps d'hébergement*). In June 1955 a Soustelle Plan was announced but failed to produce an alternative to the dead-end of assimilation. After this disappointment, a mood of desperation prevailed among Algerians and the revolt spread. On 20 August 1955 a wide extension of the rising failed to secure the large-scale capture of arms for which the insurgents had hoped, but degenerated into the massacre of Europeans at Ain Abid and the mine of al-Halia. These were countered by summary executions of Muslims in the stadium at Philippeville. A moat of blood was thus dug between the two communities. The French elections of 19 January 1956 brought into power the Republican Front which had fought the electoral campaign on a platform of 'peace in Algeria'. The new Prime Minister, Guy Mollet, a Socialist, appointed General Catroux to Algeria and himself visited Algiers on 6 February. Bombarded with harmless missiles by the Europeans, he yielded to their pressure. General Catroux withdrew, without ever having taken up his appointment, and Robert Lacoste was appointed Minister

---

[1] Searching of villages, generally accompanied by destruction of property and rough treatment—'beating-up'.

Resident in Algeria. Little by little the policy of Mollet and Lacoste deviated farther and farther from the electoral aims of the Republican Front, and came to favour a solution in three stages—a cease-fire with the insurgents, free elections after the restoration of calm, and finally negotiations with the Muslim representatives whom the elections would produce. Meanwhile terrorism developed and 'pacification' assumed the shape already familiar in Indo-China.

In November 1956 a meeting was due to be held in Tunis between Tunisian, Moroccan, and Algerian leaders. Five of the latter were to come from Rabat in a plane chartered by the Moroccan Government but piloted by a French crew. Its captain, with whom the French intelligence service communicated by wireless while the plane was in Mallorca was induced to alter course without the knowledge of his passengers and to take them to Algiers where they were arrested. The prisoners included ben Bella, whose capture was hailed as that of the real leader of the military rebellion; and its forthcoming collapse was foretold. In fact, however, it continued and the most tangible result of the kidnapping was a savage popular reaction in the Meknes area of Morocco where forty French settlers were massacred.

The year 1957 was marked by the passage through Parliament of a law granting the Government special powers to deal with the rebellion; these were to some extent applicable also in metropolitan France, to which terrorism among Muslims had by now spread. When terrorist activities were organized on a large scale in Algiers city, parachute troops were made responsible for their suppression. This put a stop to most of the outrages, but the success was achieved by measures which led the Government to appoint a Committee for the Safeguarding of the Liberties of the Individual. The report of this body was not published until some months after it had been delivered to the Government and then only after the Government's hand had been forced by its unauthorized publication in *Le Monde*. By now the insurgents were not only indulging in random terrorism but also employing most brutal measures against any Muslims suspected of treachery, of collaboration, or even of merely helping the authorities by not actively opposing them; but an increasing volume of liberal and Christian opinion in all classes of French society nevertheless began to show its disapproval of the use of torture by the French authorities and of the treatment of the civil population.

At the end of 1957, a series of attacks were made upon the military and upon oil prospecting teams in the Sahara, near

Timimoun, creating a fresh zone of insecurity. The FLN talked of a Saharan front, and though the attacks were speedily brought to an end a protective organization had to be set up which took some of the parachutists from Algiers.

Also at the end of the year the Minister for Algeria and those around him were once again expressing a high degree of optimism about the forthcoming collapse of the rising. Yet it was becoming increasingly clear that no progress was possible without someone to negotiate with. This was shown by the discussions at the United Nations, by the laborious elaboration of an Enabling Act for Algeria (which was rejected by the insurgents out of hand), and by the joint offer of mediation by the President of Tunisia and the King of Morocco, together with the growing disquiet of France's allies which showed itself in a statement made by the Leader of the Opposition in Great Britain, Mr. Hugh Gaitskell, on 20 November, to the effect that negotiations would have to be undertaken on the basis of the eventual independence of Algeria. And if negotiators were necessary, it was impossible to see any such person or body other than the FLN.

In the first months of 1958 it became apparent that the forces of the Army of National Liberation were more numerous and better armed than before. Casualties inflicted on the nationalists rose on occasion as high as 1,000 in a single week, while the French casualties rose correspondingly, maintaining the customary proportion of one French to eight or ten Algerian casualties. In April M. Gaillard's Government fell, whereupon the Socialist Party were unwilling to allow the Socialist minister M. Lacoste to remain longer in Algeria. The new Prime Minister, M. Pflimlin, in his investiture speech, after insisting on the need of defeating the armed resistance, referred to future 'negotiations'. This combination of circumstances was sufficient to set off in Algeria on 13 May 1958 a revolutionary movement which was initiated by politically active settlers. The offices of the Government General were sacked, several prefects were chased from office, and Committees of Public Safety, in which the military leaders participated, were formed. Essentially a protest against the alleged mishandling of the Algerian situation by successive French Governments, the movement had a striking resemblance to similar movements which had occurred in 1848, 1870, and 1898.[1] In 1958 it had the support of the army leaders in Algeria, who definitely assumed its leadership; the outcome was the assumption of power in France by General de Gaulle, with a programme of reforming the constitution. In

[1] Charles-André Julien, *Le Monde*, 12 June 1958.

spite of allegedly widespread fraternization of Muslims and Europeans during the demonstrations which led to the establishment of the new régime, the main factors of the problem which faced the new Prime Minister had not essentially altered since the end of April when French difficulties had been increased by the resolutions of the Conference of Tangier (p. 65). These involved much closer co-operation between the Tunisian and Moroccan Governments and the Algerian FLN, so that France was now faced by a co-ordinated North African bloc. General de Gaulle's first statements on the Algerian problem were highly ambiguous, but it soon became clear that there was a wide difference between his views and those of the settler leaders. In the demonstrations which began on 13 May 1958 the principle of 'integration' had been a rallying cry. It soon became apparent, however, that the revolutionary element among the settlers thought of this as the final elimination of any separate Algerian 'personality'. General de Gaulle on the other hand was thinking rather of complete equality of rights between Muslims and Europeans. It was also the latter conception which had inspired whatever was genuine in the 'fraternization' by the Muslims. Externally the first action of General de Gaulle's Government was to make an agreement with the Tunisian Government for the withdrawal of French troops in that country from outlying posts to the fortified base of Bizerta. This was precisely the measure which had led the political parties supporting the settlers to bring about the fall of M. Gaillard's Government and so provoked the long political crisis which followed. It appeared that the General's intention was to try and draw the Tunisian and Moroccan Governments towards France by a number of concessions, while at the same time appealing to those Algerian Muslims who were still attracted by the idea of French citizenship. In this way, it was hoped, the FLN would be increasingly isolated. The idea of a semi-autonomous Algeria within a French federation or Commonwealth did not appear to be excluded.

The Front directs the fighting through armed groups of the Army of National Liberation. According to its own statement, it disposed in 1957 of 100,000 fighters (though according to the French General Staff not more than 25,000–35,000) divided by provinces (*wilayat*). There appeared to be no difficulty in securing recruits; arms were acquired by means of ambushes and by smuggling them across the frontiers, particularly by sea. The movement was financed by contributions and forced levies. In its civilian aspect, the politico-administrative organization of the Front extended throughout Algeria and metropolitan France right down to the humblest levels. Fifty-four members were delegated by the *militants de base* to the *Comité National de la Résistance Algérien* (CNRA). The general direction of the rising was assured by a War Council, known as the CCE (Committee of Co-ordination and Executive), consisting of 9 members, 4 civilians and 5 military. It included two members of the former moderate Manifesto Party, one of whom was Ferhat Abbas. The Front always declared that it rejected Communism and was fighting for a lay republic of a democratic and socialist nature, with an Islamic and North African background.

SOCIAL CONDITIONS

Health

In considering social and economic aspects of Algeria, the student has at his disposal a great quantity of official publications. This literature, informative as it is in many respects, tends by its nature to dwell on the positive achievements of French rule, and it produces abundant evidence that these were great in many fields. Most remarkable of all was the creation of a second Algerian people of European origin. A million strong, this people, with standards of living approximately equal to those of their countries of origin, had developed specific national characteristics of their own. But official literature gives us little assistance in detecting the background causes of the present rising. For this purpose it is necessary to consider Algeria not as a homogeneous administrative unit, but as a composite structure in which the circumstances of two non-assimilated and in many respects disparate bodies are treated separately. The results of this investigation yield a much less favourable picture. This does not imply the denial of achievements which have been amply and frequently demonstrated but demonstrates the defects of a system, stemming from the time and circumstances of the original occupation of Algeria, with which neither the French Government nor the European Algerians (not to speak of the Muslim Algerians) have ever felt satisfied.

In the case of health and education, for example, official statistics are no great help. In the first place, they do not generally reveal whether those who benefit from public health and educational institutions are Europeans or Muslims, whereas for our purpose it is essential to know to what degree Muslims are, or are not, medically treated or educated in school. In fact the realities of the Algerian situation, as far as the rural population and the urban proletariat are concerned are not a matter of statistics at all.

The first of these realities, and the grimmest, is hunger. Germaine Tillion, in her book (so excellent in its descriptions, though so questionable in its conclusions) *L'Algérie en 1957*, distinguishes between 'primary hunger'—the need of anything to fill one's belly with, and 'secondary' hunger, which is the need for a certain amount of meat, fat, and fruit. Hunger of the first type still exists in Algeria, for example at the moment of 'junction' between two years (falling in January and February) when people live off acorn cake in the Kabyle country and off boiled juniper berries in the Aurès. On an average, according to the calculations of the *Institut de Conjuncture*, the Muslim Algerian can only reckon on 1,250 calories per day (the administration says it is 2,100) instead of the 2,400 considered necessary for light work or the 4,500 indispensable for heavy work.

In 1952 Dr. Venezia published a study of the 'influences which affect physiological and psychological development in early infancy among the Muslims'. In the first place he notes that deliberate abortion is virtually unknown. Before conception, he notes the prevalence of 'Mediterranean anaemia'. During gestation the calory intake of the expectant mother is 1,250 instead of 3,200, and her diet is unbalanced, being too rich in carbohydrates. Difficult child-birth is frequent—seven cases out of ten—in the Kabyle country, generally as the result of the youth of the mothers (12–15) and the absolute lack of hygiene at birth. Total dependence on breast-feeding continues for too long—up to two years for boys—while the mother's milk is lacking in vitamin A. Upon weaning, the child frequently develops a deadly oedema, due to lack of proteins. There is no bodily hygiene; the child is neither washed nor bathed. On top of this there are the primitive living conditions; the promiscuity; and the congestion and unhealthiness of the working-class dwellings. The Casbah of Algiers, where 80,000 Muslims are packed into the square kilometre, is a breeding ground of tuberculosis; in 1951 a systematic investigation made in the schools of Algiers showed that 30 per cent. of Muslim children were tuberculous, as opposed to 8 per cent. of Europeans, and that 40 per cent. of the tuberculous cases came from the Casbah.

Of course there are hospitals and busy doctors. Even in the remotest parts of the Aurès malaria, typhus, and typhoid, which as lately as 1942 were still devastating the area, have almost disappeared, just as cholera and plague did before them.

Specialists marked out the malarial areas and DDT did the rest. The elimination of epidemics has greatly lowered mortality, and antibiotics are having the same effect. But no one should be deceived; outside the areas of Algiers and Oran, the medical staff serving 7½ million Muslims number less than 2,000. According to Germaine Tillion, certain districts in the Aurès had, up to 1954, never been visited by any doctor or nurse. It required an armed rebellion to get tracks made, up which the sanitary jeeps of the medical service could climb, to get urgent cases removed by helicopter, and to improvise the military medical aid of the Special Administrative Services. Only in 1955 were Social Centres organized, with the task, among others, of spreading the teaching of elementary hygiene to the Muslim population. A Muslim doctor, himself a Kabyle, living in the Kabyle region where he was related or known to every-body, acknowledged that he was only consulted as doctor as third or fourth choice, after the local marabout, the healer, and the wise woman. In 1939 one of his Kabyle colleagues estab-lished that in the case of 28,000 births a doctor had only been summoned in 7 per cent. of cases. The basic problem remains that of the education of Muslim Algerians of both sexes.

Education

Many Europeans in Algeria are still to be heard condemning education for Muslims as 'not likely to make them happy'. Have such people ever considered the results of ignorance? We have seen what it means in the matter of health. Apart from this, the child who does not go to school is abandoned to the streets. In 1952, in Algiers, 32 per cent. of delinquent children were completely illiterate, 50 per cent. went to school for a certain period, and only 10 per cent. had enjoyed a normal school life. The illiterate person is the ready prey of inter-mediaries, translators, and interpreters who take for them-selves, according to the relevant government department, no less than 4 out of the 14 milliard francs of pension money paid to Muslim ex-servicemen (*anciens combattants*). It is safe to say that a male or female Algerian who is married, poor, and illiterate has no prospect of doing anything but live in destitu-tion. Unless he has a basic minimum of education or some pro-fessional training the young Algerian can only become a day-labourer or unskilled workman; no other work is available to him. And how can he fail to notice that every young European Algerian gets to school?

How can schooling be provided for all children from 6 to 14 years old? The present position is that the potential Muslim school population in Algeria is estimated at 2½ million children. There is a schools plan, dated 27 November 1944, but it has long been overtaken by the growth of population, since it provides for the education of only 1 million children by 1965. In fact, however, only about 317,000 little Muslims were being educated in government schools on 1 October 1957, about one-eighth of the total, for the official figure of one in four is arrived at by calculating the Muslims jointly with the Europeans. A distinction must be drawn between the sexes. In 1954 only one girl out of sixteen went to school. Of the total population only 6 per cent. of men and 2 per cent. of women were literate in French. It is also necessary to take into account the difference between town and country. In Algiers city, 13 out of 18 Muslim boys go to school; whereas in 1954 in the Commune of Braz, in the valley of the Chélif, only 300 out of 14,900 children of school age or 1 in 49 attended school and in the Commune of Teniet al-Had, fifty miles south of Cherchel, only 150 out of 9,500, or 1 in 70. On top of this, most of the classes in the countryside only work part time, or half time, owing to lack of space to accommodate two classes simultaneously. It is safe to say that there are at least 2 million Muslim children still at large in the streets.

Of course there is a financial difficulty, and also, though to a less degree, one of finding staff. Public expenditure on education, including that of the Europeans, amounted to 30 milliard francs in 1956. Schooling for all, maintaining the present standards, would require 100 milliards a year today and 200 milliards by 1980. These figures are based on buildings of the standards which prevail in France and on teachers with diplomas, paid at the Algerian rate for 'expatriates' from France. It would seem reasonable to abandon the idea of luxurious schools and highly trained teachers and return to the ideas of Jules Ferry (1882) about 'a school in every hamlet': a modest hut, mats, no tables or chairs, a blackboard and slates; and as teachers 'monitors', some of whom might be volunteers. The reason this cannot be done at present is that since 'Algeria is France', the laws governing education in France must be applied in Algeria too, and nobody is bold enough to alter them. Germaine Tillion considered that at a reasonable calculation, primary education per child from 6–14 years would cost 300,000 francs, and the teaching of a trade per adolescent and per year 600,000 francs. In the latter respect, the current plan provides for the training of 7,000 skilled workers each year. In fact, in 1957, there were 6,500 Muslims in technical schools. Meanwhile the Social Centres and the SAS are doing what

they can to spread rudimentary education. Algerian mothers
are anxious to get education for their children and cases are
quoted where they have managed to teach themselves in order
to teach their children.

At the time of the conquest of Algeria by France, General
Valze, presenting the conclusions of the *Commission d'Afrique,*
recognized that 'practically all Arabs know how to read and
write. There are two schools in each village' (January 1834). In
1850 General d'Hautpoul recognized that twenty years earlier
'Muslim studies had been relatively flourishing'; and according
to General Bedeau 'there existed about 1837 in Constantine
ninety Muslim primary [presumably Quranic] schools, attended by 1,300 to 1,400 pupils'. Little by little, the teaching of
Arabic was limited to three *madrasas,* in Algiers, Tlemsen, and
Constantine, which were transformed in 1951 into *Lycées
Franco-Musulmans,* with 430 pupils. 'Free' education on a confessional basis, was organized in rivalry with the official
institutions, and had about 150,000 pupils in 1951; the majority
of these (136,000) were in rudimentary Quranic schools and
the remaining 14,000 in *madrasas,* which are a kind of primary
school for teaching written Arabic and giving religious instruction. Fifty-five out of eighty such schools are maintained by the
reformist Ulama; but all of them are 'illegal' in the eyes of the
administration.[1] A number of Algerian students make their way
to the Middle East; and by an arrangement made by Shaikh
Brahimi with the Ruler of Kuwait some dozen Algerian boys
receive a free secondary education in that city at the expense
of the Kuwait Government. 'You see', they tell visitors, 'French
colonization forces us to go 3,000 miles to get education in our
mother-tongue.'

The Statute of 1947 laid it down in Article 57 that the teaching of Arabic should be organized at all levels; hitherto it has
been taught like any foreign language for two hours a week in
certain government primary schools, by a corps of 168 *mudar-
risun* or Arab teachers; even so it was optional. A new scheme
was prepared but remained a dead letter; in any case it marked
a final abandonment of the idea of making Arabic a 'second
national language', or compulsory in the schools, or of extending
it to the predominantly Berber-speaking Kabyle country.

Settler opposition to the teaching of Arabic used as a pretext
the existence of a difference between the spoken and written

---

[1] In North Africa under French rule the existence of a number of parties and
institutions was tolerated though technically illegal. The threat of suppression
which hung over them very materially increased the difficulties of maintaining
them.

languages. 'There is a spoken language which is not written and a written language which is not spoken'. Thus certain Inspectors of Primary Education of the Algiers department laid it down that 'neither dialectal Arabic, which has only the value of a patois, nor grammatical Arabic, which is a dead language, nor modern Arabic which is a foreign language, can constitute a compulsory subject of primary education'.[1]

The difficulty created for teachers and pupils by the existence of written and spoken languages is real enough; but it is overcome in all the Arab countries of the east, and the problem is no different in the west. Nor indeed is Arabic the only language with which the difficulty arises. As things stand a minority of Europeans lay down the law about a language of which they know little—as is shown by the odd remark that 'modern Arabic is a foreign language'—and then proceed to impose their views upon the remaining nine-tenths of their countrymen whose language it is.

Secondary education is provided in 30 boys' schools and 18 girls' schools which had 6,500 Muslim pupils in 1957. The University of Algiers had only 500 Muslims among its 5,000 students in 1953 while in 1954 1,100 Muslim and Algerian students were studying in French universities. In 1956 the FLN ordered a general strike of students; the order was unpopular with parents and after a period of effectiveness was ended in October 1957.

The Press, Broadcasting, and Literature

The press, since the establishment of 'special powers' in 1956, has been reduced to five or six French dailies of which the three principal, published in Algiers, are organs of big colonial capitalists. The *Dépêche Quotidienne* belongs to Senator Borgeaud, the *Écho d'Alger* to Alain de Sérigny, and the *Journal d'Alger* to G. Blachette. The Communist *Alger Républicain* has ceased to appear since the Communist Party was declared illegal in Algeria in 1955. The Muslims have had no regular organ of expression since the disappearance during the rising of the *République Algérienne* of the UDMA and *al-Basair* of the Ulama. Nationalist tracts, however, are distributed from time to time and there is a paper *al-Moudjahid* (*Résistance Algérienne*) which is published clandestinely or abroad. *L'Espoir*, a liberal weekly, found it impossible to continue publication in the conditions created by the restrictions on freedom of expression. Radio Algiers broadcasts in French and in Arabic, but mainly in

[1] *L'École Républicaine*, 5 March 1954.

dialect, which it tends to standardize; the output is strongly coloured by official directives.

Literature has produced no modern Arabic writer of distinction with the exception of Tewfik al-Madani and the poet Mohammed al-Id. There is a considerable Arab and Berber folklore, particularly in the Kabyle country; this has been in part collected, recorded in Latin script, and translated, principally by the White Fathers. Europeans writing in French include such considerable names as Camus, Emmanuel Robles, Jules Roy, and Gabriel Audisio. Muslim writers in French include Mouloud Faraoun, Mouloud Mammeri, Mohammed Dib, and above all Katib Yacine. The latter, with his play *Le Cadavre Encerclé* and his novel *Nedjma*, can be considered as one of the greatest living writers of the French language.

ECONOMIC CONDITIONS

Agriculture

Agriculture and stock-breeding are the principal industries of Algeria; they produce one-third of the income of the territory and support two-thirds of the inhabitants. The total area of northern Algeria without the Sahara is 52 million acres. Of these 32 million acres are cultivable, of which however only 17·5 million are actually cultivated in the sense of being ploughed or planted. In 1951 about one-third of the cultivated land, or more than 5 million acres, was in the hands of some 21,650 European settlers. The Muslim peasant population, who amounted to 6,300,000 persons in 1954, lived on the rest, namely about 10 million acres.

It must be added that the lands held by the Europeans are the best lands—the most fertile—and that in 1925 the average value of their land per acre was calculated at three times the average value of the Muslim-owned acres. The European holdings are highly concentrated. The number of settlers, which was 25,000 in 1940, dropped to 21,650 by 1951 and in 1957 was not more than 19,400. Of the latter, 7,400 own less than 25 acres. The real 'settlers' are about 12,000 in number, of whom 300 are rich and a dozen excessively rich. With their families, these 12,000 form a population of about 45,000 people. The biggest estates belong either to individuals [1] or to limited companies such as the *Fermes Françaises de Tunisie* which has 15,000 acres in the plain of Bône, the *Compagnie Génévoise* with

[1] Borgeaud, with domain of la Trappe at Staoueli, 2,500 acres; Germain; Gratien Faure, &c.

37,500 acres around Sétif, and the *Compagnie Algérienne* with 155,000 acres in the department of Constantine.

All these estates have passed into the hands of Europeans thanks to legal proceedings of more or less debatable equity. Of the four types of landed property that existed in Algeria in 1830, the state lands and *habous* were confiscated in 1843; the collective or tribal lands (*arsh*) were declared 'vacant and ownerless'; individual freeholdings (*melk*) were 'bought', sequestrated, or dismantled. In the beginning the plots made available for colonization were from 10 to 30 acres; after 1870, big societies and big settlers began to acquire and regroup them. At the present time 8 per cent. of European holdings are in the hands of big colonization ventures.

Among the Muslims, 10,250,000 acres of cultivated land are divided into approximately 600,000 holdings of which 70 per cent. consist on an average of 10–12½ acres. A handful of Muslim landowners have big estates; these have, however, a poor yield. The majority of Muslims have not sufficient land off which to live as the necessary minimum is 50 acres of unirrigated land. Finally, more than 600,000 peasant families, implying a population of over 3 million, are completely landless and constitute an agricultural proletariat who have work only for a few days every year.

Erosion at present robs Algeria of 250 acres of topsoil daily. So far the preservation and restoration of surfaces attacked has not covered more than half the total affected. Moreover the thousands of terraces constructed, at great expense, do not arouse the interest of the Muslim population which is instinctively hostile to any activity connected with 'colonialism'. The co-operation of the population, even in its own interest, could be won only in an atmosphere of confidence, and indeed enthusiasm, which is entirely lacking at present. Irrigation too produces problems of its own. Twelve big barrages have been built since 1920, capable of holding 1,000 million cubic yards, and having the capacity to irrigate 500,000 acres of which 100,000 are already receiving water. Only one-quarter of them, however, belong to Muslims, the rest have gone to the big colonization ventures. Moreover, silting threatens the big barrages, which will require to be doubled every fifty years. A policy of small waterworks appears better adapted to the country and to the needs of a peasant population; the catchment of water at the source; the drilling of wells; small dams to catch flood water, and so on.

Mechanization is general on the big estates, where the first harvesters appeared after the Exhibition of 1878 and where there are at present about 4,000 of them, and more than 20,000 tractors. Their use has, however, the effect of reducing still further the employment of agricultural labourers and thereby increasing the number of workless. After the Second World War the institution of the *paysannat* developed some hundred Sectors of Rural Amelioration (SAR) which affect about 200,000 Muslim peasants (fellahin). In 1953 the organs of agricultural credit devoted more than 45 milliard francs to short-term agricultural loans, but of these only 5·5 milliards have gone to the fellahin through the Agricultural Providence Societies (SAP).

The products of agriculture, amounting to 200 milliards a year, represent 35–40 per cent. of the national income of Algeria. For crops, excluding stock-breeding, the share of the settlers (100 milliards in 1955) was double that of the Muslim cultivators (45 milliards). In fact, 6,000 big European land-owners dispose of more than half the entire crop production of Algeria. The principal element consists of crops for export which fetch as much as 350,000 francs the acre for certain citrus fruits. Cereals have diminished to make place for vines, which occupy 1 million acres; three-quarters of the vintage is concentrated in the hands of 13 per cent. of the European owners. Cereal areas cultivated by Europeans occupy 2,150,000 acres, with a yield of 8 cwt.[1] per acre, while the Muslims, driven back towards the south, have less than 5 million acres with a yield of 2 cwt. per acre.

The main problem, that of feeding the Algerians, is in the main a matter of cereals. Only on fourteen occasions in the fifty years 1901–50 did the mean annual production of these exceed 20 million cwt. In order to live, the Algerians need, at 1 lb. 5 oz. a day per person, a total of 17 million cwt. of cereals annually for their own consumption, plus 3·5 million cwt. for sowing and 4 million for their animals—a total of 23·5 million. In order to settle the 600,000 landless families, even with as little as 25 acres of unirrigated land each, it would be necessary to find 15 million more acres—or the equivalent of the total area of cultivated land. Certainly the better feeling which would follow from a just political settlement of the Algerian question would facilitate the struggle against erosion; at present the annual area of soil removed is the equivalent of a loss of 200,000 cwt. of cereals. Irrigation, for example in the Shott al-Shergui in the High Plateaux south of Oran, would produce another 250,000 acres of good land. The reconquest by cultivation of the former Roman *limes* south of the Aurès should be

---

[1] The French hundredweight (quintal) equals 100 kilos.

possible. Crops could be improved by modern techniques and mechanization. This is in fact what the SAR are attempting to do, but the total funds of which they disposed for the period 1947–54 were less than 2½ per cent. of the capital investment budget for all Algeria. All these improvements call for an enormous capital outlay. Even with this, the task of keeping pace with the growth of the population would be immense.

Since 1935 Algeria has not been able unaided to assure the subsistence of the whole of the population. In 1936 400,000 cwt. of flour were distributed to the needy, and in recent years 17 per cent. of the commercial harvest of cereals has had to be retained against possible emergencies. On account of the growth of population, for every inhabitant of Algeria for whom there were 5 cwt. of cereals available in 1871 there are now only 2.

Can agrarian reform save the situation? The Government General issued a certain number of decrees in March and April 1956. These proposed to limit the area of irrigated holdings to 125 acres, thus permitting the redistribution of about 100,000 acres and the resettlement of 5,000 fellahin; 75,000 more acres of land were to be irrigated, and those owners who had more than 2,500 acres or who left their land uncultivated were to be expropriated. The redistribution of land was to be entrusted to a Fund of Accession to Land Holding and Rural Development, which was to be charged with distributing state domains and common lands (650,000 acres) and with redeeming the 155,000 acres of the *Compagnie Algérienne* and the 37,500 acres of the *Compagnie Génévoise*. One year after the issue of this decree, however, the intention seemed to be to recover only 100,000 acres and to resettle 5,000 peasants. Any real agricultural reform would involve undertaking an accurate cadastral survey and entirely re-casting the legal basis of land tenure in Algeria. In Berber country the rule of inheritance is to share, so that a fig tree may be shared among several families. In Arab country, on the contrary, maintenance without division is the rule and it is difficult to ascertain to whom a particular piece of land belongs. After this, there would come the task of regrouping, of improving output, of introducing new crops and fertilizers, and of supervising markets. All this would require a legion of supervisors and the whole-hearted co-operation of the peasantry. It could be carried out only by a political régime which could rouse the enthusiasm of the masses and carry them with it.

The remaining agricultural resources of Algeria are its forests and stock-breeding. Since 1830 the forest areas have diminished by 2·5 million acres, on account of random clearing by army engineers and by settlers to whom 1½ million acres were allotted, and also on account of the failure adequately to replant. To make up the loss, it would be necessary to replant 250,000 acres annually; in the best year so far, 1950, 25,000 acres were planted. The Cork Company of Hamendas and of the Lesser Kabylia exploits 125,000 acres of cork trees and export 4 milliard francs' worth of untreated wood annually. Esparto grass, the raw material of high-class paper, is a monopoly of the well-known capitalist, Georges Blachette. He works 1,722,000 acres of concessions; 150,000–200,000 tons are exported annually to Great Britain, a ton fetching 17,500 francs in 1956, less a tax of 15–25 centimes taken by the Treasury. Stock-breeding produces 1 million cows, 3 million goats, and 6 million sheep. The latter numbered 8 million in 1880 but had dropped to 4 million by 1946 to 1953, partly on account of restrictions on the right to lead the flocks in the south seasonally across the mountains in search of pasture.

Menaced by famine, Algeria appears to many people a poor country. 'As long as exploitation remains archaic', wrote Germaine Tillion, 'this country can nourish only two to three million people'.[1] Others, such as Marcel Egretaud, think that 'it is not so much natural conditions which are the cause of the present and future misery as the harm done to these conditions by colonization itself'.[2] Many place their hopes of improvement in the creation of Algerian industries.

Industry

The existence of mines appears at first sight to favour the creation of industries. Iron ore is rich and abundant, particularly at Ouenza near the Tunisian frontier. Algeria produces 3 million tons annually and could produce 4 million; a steel industry seems a possibility. The *Houillères du Sud-Oranais*, in the neighbourhood of Colomb-Béchar, nationalized in 1947, have increased their production to 300,000 tons; but the coal is poor, a long way from the coast, and insufficient for even half of Algeria's present needs. Moreover the 3,000 workers employed cost France an annual subsidy of a milliard francs, namely more than 300,000 francs per worker of whom more than two-thirds are Arab.

Phosphates are not of good enough quality to be worth exploiting in the Jbel Ouk, where they would provide work for 2,000, or elsewhere in Algeria except at Jbel Kouif, near Tebessa, where the mines are nearly worked out. Almost

---

[1] *L'Algérie en 1957*, p. 15.
[2] M. Egretaud, *Réalité de la nation algérienne* (Paris, 1957).

R

700,000 tons a year are still being extracted, thanks entirely to the aid of the North African Office of Phosphates. The remaining minerals are hardly more than samples: 55,000 tons of zinc ore; 15,000 tons of lead ore; 25,000 tons of iron pyrites; 100,000 tons of rock-salt, and so on. Other subsoil resources have been investigated, but appear to be small and not worth exploiting.

One-third of the electric energy is furnished by water power and an effort is being made to build hydro-electric power stations in order to reduce the imports of coal for the thermal power centres. But the kilowatt hour is 35–80 per cent. dearer than in France which is an obvious handicap for the creation of an Algerian industry. On the other hand petrol and diesel oil are 30–50 per cent. cheaper than in France.

Since 1940, and particularly since 1946, a certain industrial activity has been noticeable in Algeria, though not sufficient to make much impression on local unemployment; in 1942 the inadequacy of local industry was painfully evident. Such industry as the country possesses is concentrated near the ports. In 1949 there were reckoned to be 800 factories or workshops. A Plan for Industrialization, drawn up in 1946, merely consisted in a list of projects which the Government General has agreed should benefit from certain statutory financial and fiscal advantages. For the most part, it concerned branches of French or foreign establishments. Certain industrial circles in France are in any case not favourable to the idea of thus promoting competition. Some settlers do not like the idea of losing agricultural labour. Existing industries for the treatment of local products are unimportant; 50,000 tons of esparto grass are treated locally; 2 milliard francs' worth of cork is worked up or pressed for export. The output of cement has roughly doubled in the last ten years and amounted to 670,000 tons in 1956. Generally speaking, factories do not employ more than some hundreds of workers. In 1955 the *Manufacture des Textiles Oranais* had to close down at the demand of the big French textile manufacturers.

The total industrial output represents only 28 per cent. of Algerian production, or 15 per cent. if we exclude mines, power, building, and public works. In this connexion, the disappearance of rural and urban production by craftsmen is a factor of which note should be taken. Formerly clothes, tents, bedspreads, and carpets used to be spun and woven. Today, as Germaine Tillion remarks, 'it requires weeks of work and seven fleeces to weave one burnous—a fleece costing from 500–1,000 francs; it would be absurd for people who only eat meat four times in the year to spend this amount of money and time on a garment, when they can for practically nothing acquire a cast off garment which may be repellent but at any rate protects from the cold'.[1]

Given this background, what are the present prospects of creating a substantial degree of industry in Algeria? Views on this subject vary very greatly. There is a general recognition that technical conditions are unfavourable. Though local oil may now become available, power has hitherto been scarce or expensive; so is skilled labour; construction costs are high. A joint inquiry, undertaken in France in 1952, recommended decentralizing French industry and encouraging the establishment of branches in Algeria by the offer of financial and tax inducements; it was, however, recognized that commercial outlets would be small and that the iron and steel and sugar industries were reluctant to co-operate. In June 1957 a strictly technical, semi-official memorandum stressed three major obstacles to the establishment of industry in Algeria. First, the peculiar shape of the country, nearly 1,000 kilometres long, which involves difficult transport problems. Second, the limited internal market, so long as the income of the vast majority of the population remains low. Third, the customs union with France, which prompts French competitors to resist any change. As it is, their opposition recently brought about the failure of the *Manufacture des Tapis d'Oran* and the *Manufacture Nord Africaine des Faiences*. An independent tariff system is in fact an indispensable prerequisite of industrial independence in an underdeveloped country. The authors of the memorandum came to the conclusion 'that the industrialization of Algeria is a myth, in so far as it is proposed to realize it within the framework of a Franco-Algerian symbiosis'. From another point of view, Germaine Tillion believes it 'unhealthy to create an industry where the population has not yet reached the level of industrial civilization'.

The external trade of Algeria is typically colonial. The trade balance was in deficit to the extent of 78 milliards in 1954; in 1957 this deficit rose to 211 milliards, mainly because of the heavy requirements of the armed forces and the considerable imports of consumer and capital goods by the oil companies operating in the Sahara.[2] Imports (272·7 milliards in 1956) consist of industrial products and foodstuffs. Of the exports to France and elsewhere wine represents half and iron more than a third. France is Algeria's principal client and third in the list of her suppliers. France controls more than three-quarters (in

---

[1] *L'Algérie en 1957*, p. 32.
[2] Board of Trade, *Special Register Information Service*, 9 July 1958.

value) of all Algerian trade. Algeria is kept as a preserve of metropolitan France by means of a customs union, which benefits chiefly big exporters among the settlers and big capitalists among the importers, and of a 'monopoly of the flag' whereby almost the entire maritime traffic is reserved to big French and Algerian companies. This situation may of course change as the result of the establishment of a European Common Market.

Principal Imports and Exports
(milliard francs)

IMPORTS				EXPORTS			
	1954	*1955*	*1956*		*1954*	*1955*	*1956*
Metal manufac-				Wine . .	56·9	62·6	57·3
tures . .	7·2	8·4	12·7	Iron ore . .	10·9	12·8	9·2
Sugar . .	11·4	12·3	12·5	Citrus fruits .	7·6	10·6	9·1
Electrical appa-				Vegetables §	3·3	3·8	5·7
ratus * . .	6·7	8·4	9·3	Cork . .	3·6	4·2	3·2
Motor cars .	8·1	9·4	8·9	Vegetable oils .	0·9	2·6	3·0
Machinery † .	9·4	9·5	8·4	Potatoes . .	2·5	2·0	2·9
Wood and pro-				Esparto grass .	1·8	2·9	2·5
ducts ‡ .	6·3	7·7	7·4				
Coffee . .	9·0	6·9	7·3				
All imports .	217·7	244·0	272·7	All exports .	140·3	162·1	150·1

* Excluding wire and cable.   † Excluding electrical.
‡ Excluding furniture.   § Excluding potatoes.

Source: UN, *Yearbook of International Trade Statistics, 1956*, vol. 1.

It is often claimed that the political severance from Algeria would entail a grave loss of profit to France and that French industry is kept 'working one day a week by Algeria'. In fact exports from France to Algeria in 1954 amounted to less than a fortieth of the 9,000 milliard francs of potential French exports; in other words the Algerian market was only one-fiftieth of the internal French market. Take sugar; Algeria, as an importer, attracts only one-thirtieth of France's total business; as regards lime and cement, one-seventeenth. Moreover Algerian exports to France, citrus and early vegetables, could be replaced advantageously from the French point of view by similar imports from Spain or Italy who would then become a more profitable market for French exports than Algeria. As for Algerian wine, of which 40–60 milliard francs' worth is imported into France annually, this is surely a burden for France, whose own production is generally in excess of requirements so that 30 milliards have to be spent most years to put things right by converting the wine into alcohol. It is in fact French and Algerian consumers who really pay for the maintenance of Franco-Algerian colonial trade; and France has to make up the deficit in the balance of Algerian trade to the extent of 56 milliards and that of foreign exchange for Algerian imports to the value of 20 milliards. Algeria may be France's principal customer, but she is certainly not the most paying; one-third of her purchases are paid for with money furnished by her supplier. It is therefore not the political status of Algeria which determines the size of the Algerian market for French goods, but the amount of money which France spends there. From the economic point of view, the present state of affairs rather implies that it is Algeria who needs France; though in time Algeria would certainly benefit from the ability to organize trade in her own interest. If the demand for consumer goods in Algeria increased greatly in 1956–7, this was due to the presence on Algerian soil of nearly half a million soldiers whose purchasing power was relatively high and who wanted wine, tobacco, and preserved foodstuffs. Meanwhile the purchase of capital goods or durable goods such as tractors has practically come to a standstill.

Income and Labour

The national income of Algeria was estimated for 1954 at 600 milliard francs for $9\frac{1}{2}$ million inhabitants. The mean income of an Algerian was thus 60,000 francs a year. But this figure in itself tells us nothing, since everything depends on the distribution of the income. A recent objective study, the *Rapport Maspétiol* of 1955,[1] classifies the Algerian population under five headings.

1. Traditional cultivators (all Muslim) . . . 5,840,000
2. Muslims in urban areas 1,600,000
3. Wage-earners, artisans, and commercial employees,
   of whom 510,000 are Muslim 950,000
4. Middle class, of whom 50,000 are Muslim . . 595,000
5. Well-to-do (exclusively European) . . . 15,000

According to this report, the annual income of the middle class—category 4—is 227,000 francs per head as compared with 250,000 for France. The well-to-do European class disposes of about $1\frac{1}{2}$ million francs per head annually, while the traditional Muslim cultivator in 1955 had 19,200 to live on per person, per year. This is on paper the same figure as that for 1936,

[1] France, Groupe d'Étude des Relations Financières entre la Métropole et l'Algérie, *Rapport* (Algiers, 1955).

though in fact it is lower by 5,000 francs, since the figure for the later date includes remittances from France. Thus the Minister Resident, Robert Lacoste, stated in the Algerian Assembly on 21 February 1956 that in Algeria 'five million people live with the utmost precariousness, on an average income which, when account has been taken of what they consume themselves, does not exceed 16,000 francs per head per year'. Lower than the Egyptian figure (40,000) and the Indian (25,000), this figure is only slightly above that of the Arab of the Yemen (14,000).[1] This deplorable standard suggested to Germaine Tillion the term *clochardisation* which evokes the disastrous condition of paupers.

How many Algerians can find work? According to statistics for 1954, barely 570,000 men and women are effectively employed in industrial, commercial, and administrative occupations. Adding to this figure 200,000, who are held to have regular employment in agriculture on the ground that they work for at least 90 days in the year, we arrive at a figure of 770,000 wage-earners, of whom a part are not full-time. The total number of unemployed can thus be estimated at about 2 million, of both sexes, as under:

150,000 totally unemployed in the cities
370,000 totally unemployed in the countryside
480,000 surplus family 'hands' practically unemployed (men)
960,000 surplus family 'hands' unemployed (female)

When the families are added, the victims of pauperization amount to about 5 million.

The development of mechanization has had serious repercussions. One bulldozer replaces 500 workmen and one combine harvester, manned by four or five men, does the work of 100. Industrialization is apt to work in the same direction. Nearly 100,000 workers have found employment in factories, but machines are fast replacing workmen. Wages in industry are lower than in France; the minimum inter-trade guaranteed wage varies from 79.50 to 95 francs per hour. Agricultural wages are officially fixed at from 440 to 525 francs a day, but these rates are not always observed. At the beginning of 1955 250,000 partially employed had registered themselves at work centres (*chantiers de chômage*); these institutions at that time had at their disposal 800 million francs, which is less than 800 francs per unemployed man per year.

Social insurance (*securité sociale*) applies only to workers who

[1] U.N. estimate, quoted by Germaine Tillion, *L'Algérie en 1957*, p. 70 n.

can prove that they have regular employment. Family allowances are available only to wage-earners in commerce and
industry, that is to about 300,000 Muslims in 1954. Contrary
to the egalitarian provisions of the 1947 Statute, rates are only
about one-third of those in metropolitan France. Moreover the
allowances given to parents of two or three children are actually
less than the deduction made from their wages to provide
allowances for the fathers of large families, so that the system
actually deprives them of a small margin which might otherwise
enable them to keep themselves alive.

Apart from these factors the problem of under-employment is
aggravated by the growth of population. In the coming decades
several million extra jobs will have to be found. So far, the only
outlet has been emigration to France. At first clandestine, but
legal since the 1947 Statute, a completely accurate figure for
the number of Algerian workers in France cannot be given, but
it is certainly above 300,000. Only half of these are in work.
Few arrive with a contract. At the beginning most were
Berbers from the Kabyle country. At the present time a third
come from the Constantine district and from other Arabic-
speaking areas of the Oran and Algiers provinces. Lacking professional training, they are mostly employed as unskilled workers
in the mines, in iron foundries, in chemical factories, and in
building. About 50 per cent. are concentrated in the Paris area;
other centres exist at Lyons and Marseilles, on the Loire, in the
north and in the east. For a long time exclusively male and
adult, the flow has brought over about 10,000 women and
11,000 children since 1954. Their living conditions in France
are for the most part precarious; they are exploited by un-
scrupulous lodging-house keepers and are a prey to tuberculosis.
They are blamed for acts of violence which more often than
not have hunger as their motive. A horrifying picture of their
life in Paris is given by the Moroccan writer Dris Chraibi in his
novel *Les Boucs*.

The sums which they remit to Algeria from their wages
amounted to 35 milliard francs in 1955, say an average of
100,000 francs per worker. This sum has been saved at the cost
of great privations, some of the men eating nothing but bread
and coffee; but it is precisely this supply of cash which has
hitherto saved from total indigence the families which they have
left behind in Algeria, say 1½ million people. Indeed, it may
well be that as many as 3–4 million people are dependent on the
enterprise of these emigrants. Calculations suggest that the
sum remitted is the equivalent of the entire agricultural wages
paid in Algeria, or one-quarter of the wages paid in the

industrial sector. It also appears approximately equal to the sum spent by Europeans from Algeria during their summer holidays in France or elsewhere abroad; in 1952, for example, this last figure was more than 20 milliards, which was the precise equivalent of the remittances sent by the emigrants through the post to Algeria in 1951.

Emigration has had important social results in Algeria. It has caused the system of share-cropping to evolve; in many places half, instead of a fifth, of the harvest now goes to the relative charged with looking after the property during the owner's absence. Life in France has led to a notable improvement in local housing. It has educated the emigrants politically, enabling them to play an active part in municipal activities on their return. On the other hand it has also created new problems: mixed marriages, concubinage, criminality. In the trade union field, it has brought French workers into contact with the Algerian proletariat. Two changes stand out; on the one hand the awaking of a vague racial feeling, and on the other a self-withdrawal and a tendency to accentuate an Algerian individuality which originally was a matter of religion.

This 'hunger' emigration remains the only outlet for the growing Algerian population. Between 1951 and 1954 600,000 emigrants left for France, while 500,000 emigrants returned to Algeria. This represents an annual outflow from Algeria and influx into France of more than 100,000 souls, and the establishment in France of about 25,000 people a year. If the Algerian population continues to increase as it has been doing, and it remains impossible to provide work for them within the country, the rate of emigration is likely to increase; while from 1965 France will have to find a great deal of extra employment for the large number of young people, born in France at the end of the war, who will then be growing up. At that moment Algerian immigration will come to be regarded as a serious social and economic menace. In any case, it is quite possible that in the meanwhile French employers may prefer to employ Spaniards, Italians, or Poles, who are already very numerous and do not raise the same social problems. For people who are seeking work in France as 'handymen' a French identity card is the best recommendation, and it is the possession of this which is the chief advantage which the Algerian at present possesses. Germaine Tillion claims that it increases the chance of finding work tenfold—as is suggested by the fact that Tunisia and Morocco together have sent to France not more than 30,000 workers, though they too have a rapidly increasing population and much unemployment.

Trade Unions

The trade union position in Algeria is in process of evolution. The two big French organizations, *Force Ouvrière* (FO), of socialist tendencies with 25,000 members, and the Christian Trade Unions (CFTC), with 35,000 members are almost exclusively European. The former CGT, which has now become the *Union Générale des Syndicats Algériens*, lost three-quarters of its Muslim members after 1954 and in 1957 had barely 15,000 adherents. In the trade union world, Muslim workers at the same period were separated from their European colleagues and their interests are represented in two new organizations, which, in practice if not in theory, are 'confessional' in basis. They are attached respectively to the two national political movements, the FLN and the Missalists or MNA. The *Union Générale des Travailleurs Algériens* (UGTA), founded in 1956 and sympathizing with the FLN, claims at least 100,000 adherents, particularly among the workers in government and industrial enterprises. It seems to be developing more slowly in France and in the agricultural sector, but it has also a parallel employers' association, the *Union Générale des Commerçants Algériens*. It adheres to the International Confédération of Free Trade Unions (ICFTU) and is, in principle, affiliated with the corresponding organizations in Tunisia and Morocco. The Missalist organization, linked to the MNA, was also founded in 1956 and is known as the *Union des Syndicats de Travailleurs Algériens* (USTA). Weak in Algeria, where it has hardly 5,000 adherents, mainly among the Algiers tramwaymen, it claims nearly 100,000 members in France where it held a congress in 1957.

The Budget

The Algerian budget for 1955–6 amounted to 150 milliard francs, of which two-thirds were for ordinary expenses and the rest for development. It is only balanced with the help of massive aid from France; for 1956–7 this last amounted to nearly 100 milliards: 21 towards ordinary expenses, 57 for development, and 20 milliards for loans for the benefit of French and mixed societies and credit institutions. This is a very considerable commitment, larger than the total aid earmarked by the United States for all the Arab countries put together. Unfortunately, according to Jacques Peyrega, Director of the *Institut de Recherches Économiques et Sociales d'Alger*, 'a policy of massive investment in Algeria, even if its general effects appear favourable, might, instead of reducing actually increase the economic distortion and so the social inequalities and political ferment'. The present fighting makes the danger more acute, since it causes the flight of private capital to France. The 'pacification' itself was costing France 700 milliards a year in 1957, according to the United Nations *Economic Survey of Europe*—170 milliards of normal military expenditure, 390 milliards of extraordinary military expenditure, and 140 milliards in loss of production due to the calling up of labour for the armed forces.

An attempt has been made to establish what capital sum would have to be invested regularly in Algeria to maintain or improve the actual standard of living. To raise it by 4 per cent. in the case of this rapidly growing population would call for an increase of the annual investment to 800 milliard francs in 1980. At this rate it would require fifty years to bring the income per head to 160,000 francs, that is to half the rate in France. But it is to be feared that Algeria could not absorb such a massive investment, which France in any case would not be willing to provide. A less ambitious plan of 'first aid', limited to creating a minimum of 300,000 new jobs, with the provision of universal schooling and the indispensable agrarian reform, would require an investment of about 2,000 milliards, spread over four or five years at the rate of 400 milliards annually, roughly equal to the cost of the present exceptional military expenditure.

Tourism

In times of peace, tourism was highly developed and there is an adequate provision of hotels, guides, and means of transport. Scenery offers varied landscapes on the coast, among the mountains, and in the desert. There are some remarkable remains of Roman cities. Fine examples of the traditional type of house with an interior court or patio can still be seen; from the Arab point of view, Tlemsen is the town of most interest. Feminine costumes still sometimes have fine embroidery and there is interesting silver and gold jewellery. The rhythmical music, and the cooking with its strong contrasts, are similar to those of the eastern Mediterranean. Well-known dishes, provided also in many Algerian restaurants in Paris, are *couscous* (steamed semolina), *kebab* (brochettes), *meshwi* (roast meat—sometimes a whole lamb roasted in the open air). The four types of carpet seem to have been borrowed respectively from Turkish Anatolia, Baluchistan or Afghanistan, and Hispano-Moorish art. In general, northern Algeria, in spite of its natural beauty, cannot rival Morocco in artistic native craftsmanship or in the splendour of traditional costume.

CONCLUSION: PROPOSED SOLUTIONS

A number of fundamental solutions have been proposed in France, by Frenchmen, for the problem set by the Algerian tragedy. The first is that of abandonment, recommended on grounds of material advantage. 'Germany is astonishingly prosperous without colonies', it is said; 'we should do better to colonize our own Lozère.' A solution by force has also its defenders; but it is difficult to see, even if all moral considerations are ignored, how France could keep up her present military effort indefinitely and how she could face the ensuing international isolation. Integration pure and simple is a thing of the past and ignores the growing national sentiment. Partition into hostile zones is a counsel of despair. Algeria is not as easily divisible as Ireland; partition would mean, as in Palestine, the dispossession of the Arabs from the best land and from nearly all the sources of wealth, and it might also well leave equally thorny problems of irredentism. The other alternative seems to be the grant of the largest possible measure of autonomy, if necessary an independent Algerian republic. From the French point of view it would be essential that this republic should not only respect the rights of the European minority but also fall within the framework of a French federation. Only an independent Algeria could spread the practice of birth-control, introduce a real agrarian reform, restore the soil, establish universal elementary education, and create industry. For years the political problem seemed insoluble, but if it could be solved France, thanks to her long connexion with Algeria, would be the country best adapted to invest largely, to subsidize five-year plans, to provide work for emigrants, to provide technicians, and to organize professional training. Compelled to seek aid elsewhere, Algeria could hardly fail to undergo a period of extreme hardship. The former colonial system has clearly gone for ever; but if France is to subsidize Algeria and accept Algerian workers on French soil, French public opinion will certainly insist that the new state permit certain limitations of its sovereignty in favour of a larger confederation in which France participates and to which Morocco and Tunisia would also be welcomed.

Since the rising began Muslim opinion within Algeria has been canalized by the FLN. This stands for an independent Algeria of which European residents can become citizens with the same rights and duties as other citizens, provided they are willing to take Algerian nationality. On the economic issue it maintains that the problem is due to the system of government established by France; the remedy therefore lies in abolishing that system and establishing an independent Algerian Government which will reorganize the economy in the interests of the population as a whole. It looks to the mineral resources of the Sahara to supply the necessary funds.[1]

[1] For political developments to the end of November 1958 see Addenda, p. 379 below.

V

THE SAHARA

(*ORGANISATION COMMUNE DES RÉGIONS SAHARIENNES*—OCRS)

THE Algerian Sahara covers almost 750,000 square miles. Its frontiers are artificial, due to military advances and diplomatic agreements. On the north it extends to cultivated Algeria; on the west to Morocco, the Spanish Sahara, and Mauritania; on the south to the Sudan, Niger, and Chad; on the east to Libya and Tunisia.

Some oases in the Sahara such as Laghouat and Wargla were occupied as early as 1844 and 1852 respectively, but it was not till 1900 that French troops entered Tuat and Gourara and occupied Colomb-Béchar. Communication with the Chad area was also made effective about 1900. A law of 1902 created a special 'Organization of the Southern Territories'.

On the other hand that part of the area which was previously known as the Moroccan Sahara was not occupied until the whole of Morocco had been 'pacified'; thus it was only in 1934 that French troops entered Tinduf. For this reason the western area remained under Ain Safra for administrative purposes, though from the military point of view it depended on the *Commandement Militaire des Confins Algéro-Marocains* whose headquarters were first at Tiznit in south Morocco and later at Agadir, rather farther north.

Geography

The landscape of the Sahara has often been described in books, while photographs and the cinema have made the vast arid stretches of stone or of sand familiar to viewers. The *reg* is a continuous horizontal surface, strewn with sand, pebbles, or gravel. Heaped-up dunes constitute the sea of sand known as the *erg*. The desert also has its highlands or *hamadas*, and in the south-east an imposing mountain range, the Hoggar, which rises to 9,843 feet. There are very great differences of temperature at different seasons, so that it may freeze in the winter while at Tinduf in the summer the thermometer may record 57° C. (135° F.); there are also big variations of temperature between day and night. The dryness is extreme, the rainfall

257

irregular and insufficient. The wind piles up sand and models it into strange shapes which stand out in the landscape. Vegetation is scarce, being dependent on subterranean water or appearing for brief periods with the rain.

Population

The population is relatively small: rather more than 800,000 people, entirely Muslim except for the few European officials, traders, and technicians. This population is largely sedentary, concentrated in oases of palm groves which shelter cultivation and villages known as *ksours*; for example, the seven towns of the Mzab of which the best known is Ghardaia. The remainder are nomads, mostly camel owners, of whom the Tuareg are celebrated for their face-veil or muffler, their lance, their shield, and the cross-shaped pommel of their saddles. Like many of the settled Saharans, they too are Berber-speaking. The Tuareg have kept a social structure in which the woman plays an outstanding part, perhaps as the survival of a matriarchal stage, and they have an archaic alphabet akin to that of the Libyan inscriptions. They call it *tifinagh*, which is perhaps a Berber derivation from the word 'punic'. A whole romantic literature, written and on the screen, has grown up around these 'People of the Veil', most of it showing little critical judgement. It nevertheless remains true that the traditional type of Saharan life, like that of the Eskimos, is a most remarkable achievement denoting an extraordinary power of adaptation on the part of the human species in a hostile and almost entirely bare universe.

Administration

Administratively the Algerian Sahara used to be divided into four military territories: Ain Safra, Ghardaia, Touggourt, and Oasis. In August 1957 it was regrouped into two departments—Oasis in the east, with the capital at Laghouat; and Saoura in the west, with its capital at Colomb-Béchar. Five 'imperial tracks' cross it from north to south: Tinduf–Senegal (No. 1, through Mauritania); Colomb-Béchar–Gao (No. 2); El Golea–Tahoua (No. 3); Wargla–Tahoua (No. 4, rejoining No. 3 north of Tamanghasset; (Tunis)–Fort Saint Bilma (No. 5).

Mineral Resources

The mineral resources of the region of Colomb-Béchar, near the Moroccan frontier, have enabled the *Bureau d'organisation des Ensembles Industriels Africains* (BIA), created in 1952, to bring into production *Zone d'Organisation Africaine* No. 1 (ZOIA 1) of which the coalfields of Kenadsa produce 300,000 tons. The strategic importance of this zone consists in the existence of a *Centre d'Essai d'Engins Spéciaux* which has collected a group of more than 1,000 technicians. Other and more recent discoveries have, however, completely changed the prospects for industry in the Sahara.

These are in the first place the iron at Gara Jbilet to the south-west of Tinduf, close to the Moroccan frontier. Deposits of a mineral akin to the Kiruna 11 in Sweden show a reserve of 3,000 million tons, at surface level. The transport of this would most naturally be by a railway, 500 kilometres long, terminating near the mouth of the river Dra. The necessary work would cost 85 milliard francs and the minimum annual tonnage would be in the order of 5 million tons. Petroleum has given rise to even greater hopes. The deposits at Hassi Messaoud to the south-west of Wargla show a reserve of at least 300 million tons, about 150 metres broad and more than 3,000 metres deep. A 6-inch pipeline from Hassi Messaoud to Touggourt and the railway began delivery at the Algerian port of Philippeville in January 1958; work on a 24-inch pipeline from Hassi Messaoud to Bougie was to begin shortly. On the Libyan frontier deposits at Edjelé and Tinguentourine are already yielding powerful gushers and it is hoped to be able to transport 4 million tons by pipeline annually from 1959. South of In-Salah, in the very centre of the Sahara, an enormous pocket of natural gas was found three years ago; it appears to contain about 100,000 million cubic metres of gas (equivalent to 100 million tons of petroleum), namely one-quarter (according to Andre Labarthe) of the basin of Lacq in the French Landes, but twice as much as that in the valley of the Po. This gas could be decisive for the creation of industry in Algeria, as the methane has been for the economy of Italy. A pipeline to the coast will cost 35 milliard francs; on account of its remoteness the gas has not so far been utilized and the taps are closed. Finally at Hassi Rmel in the region of Laghouat, only 450 kilometres from Algiers, in 1957 boring indicated a reserve of 100 million tons of petroleum or its equivalent in gas. Altogether the Saharan reservoir already prospected and the borings indicate a minimum reserve of 500 million tons which, exploited on the standard methods, would yield 25 million tons annually.

It can be understood that these prospects should have led an engineer, Émile Belime, as early as 1951, to launch the idea of nationalizing the Sahara. Disturbed at seeing its immense riches distributed between two Algerian departments, the two protectorates of Tunisia and Morocco which have subsequently gained their independence, and the territories of black Africa, the promoters of the project of a French Sahara undertook a campaign which resulted, in January 1957, in the voting by Parliament of a law creating an *Organisation Commune des Régions Sahariennes* (OCRS). This new entity embraces a vast territory and adds to the Sahara a part of the French Sudan, Niger, and Chad, though Mauritania, relatively inhabited and having a regional government of its own, was not willing to be included in OCRS.

Altogether OCRS deals with a vast area of about 4 million square kilometres, with rather more than a million inhabitants. The programme of the Organization will be laid down by a High Commission of 32 members, one-half of whom will represent the population of the Sahara and the other the Constituent Assemblies of the French Republic. Executive power is entrusted to a Delegate General who is charged with applying the decisions of the High Commission, of representing the Republic, and of assuring the good order and the security of the Saharan territories. OCRS can also seek the adhesion of neighbouring territories and make agreements with them.

Since 1953 prospecting has been undertaken by four societies: the *Société Nationale des Recherches et d'Exploitation de Pétroles en Algérie* (SN–REPAL), the *Compagnie Française des Pétroles d'Algérie* (CFPA), the *Compagnie des Pétroles d'Algérie* (CPA), 65 per cent. of whose shares are controlled by the Royal Dutch Shell, and the *Compagnie de Recherches et d'Exploitation des Pétroles au Sahara* (CREPS). The permits, which expired in the autumn of 1957, were renewable. Independent American companies have lately been competing with French interests and the first French company for petroleum has been negotiating with the Standard Oil of New York. Precedent shows that technical difficulties will be overcome; in this case they are principally lack of water, the climate, transport, and to some extent labour. The security problem is obviously bound up with the progress of 'pacification' in Algeria. The transport of oil to the coast implies that the entire length of the pipeline or railway must be protected from sabotage. In the present state of hostilities, this means policing the whole area. Transport can only be secure if peace is restored.

The discovery of important sources of energy in the Sahara is regarded by the French Government as a great opportunity to make France independent in respect of oil; French consumption, amounting in 1957 to 24 million tons, is less than the anticipated annual output from the desert. Certainly atomic energy must now be taken into account also, but oil will surely long remain irreplaceable, at least for light industry. As far as

Algeria is concerned, projects for the creation of industry could at the same time be greatly facilitated by the discovery of oil, provided that French finances did not have to face excessive charges, as would be the case if the exploitation of the Sahara took place in a hostile environment which had to be held in check by a formidable military force, or if it was complicated by being combined with an attempt to produce a marked rise in the standard of living. The attitude of the neighbouring countries, Tunisia and Morocco, has also to be taken into account—the former because it is the natural terminus of the Edjelé pipeline, and the latter for the export of the iron of Tinduf. Their geographical situation, commanding the approaches to the Sahara, would enable them totally to defeat any attempt which was made without their agreement. In the summer of 1958 a new development of this issue was raised when the Tunisian Government gave its sanction to the construction of a pipeline from Edjelé, with an outlet at the Tunisian port of Skhira. This news provoked a strong protest from the FLN who claimed that it was a violation of the resolution of the Conference of Tangier which provided for the co-ordination of foreign policy between Morocco, Tunisia, and the FLN. They requested an urgent meeting of the permanent secretariat of the assembly which the two countries and the FLN were to set up in accordance with another resolution of the Conference. A little earlier in the year the Moroccan Government was reported to have warned foreign companies interested in exploiting the iron of Fort Gouraud in Mauritania that they would be doing so at their own risk in regard to Moroccan claims to this territory. Presumably the Moroccan Government would hold the same views more strongly about the iron of Tinduf to which district their claim is very much easier to substantiate. The outlook was therefore not very favourable to an agreement. On the other hand in favourable circumstances the Sahara, instead of being an apple of discord, might perhaps become a cause of reconciliation and the centre of a common French-North African Organization which would extend also to certain territories of black Africa. Instead of being a last redoubt of old-time colonialism, the great desert could serve the gradual and experimental construction of a sort of Commonwealth of which France was the focus.

Whatever happens, there should be no question of keeping the benefits of the exploitation of the Sahara from those who have been inhabiting it from time immemorial, cultivating its dates and breeding its camels. The Sahara is not an empty world; nor is it a world altogether apart. It is inseparable from

s

its shores; it and its confines are complementary. The nomads have always needed to exchange their salt and their animals for the dates and grain of the settled peoples. The problem of using the maximum water possible for agricultural purposes has not been solved. The settled population are 90 per cent. indigent for lack of cultivable soil; and the nomads with their superior ethnic qualities are victims of the lack of water, losing for example 4 out of 5 million sheep between 1940 and 1945. In an average year (1946) in Hoggar the budget of a settled Saharan amounted to 105 kilogrammes of grain and 600 francs in cash per head; and of a nomad 145 kilogrammes of grain and 1,200 francs. The traditional society of the Sahara is in course of disintegration. The appearance of industry will hasten its destruction. The local labour force is, however, the only one adapted to the climate at all seasons; it is easy to recruit on the spot and it is stable and not expensive. Of 3,000 workers in the *Houillères du Sud Oranais* 2,200 have come from the nomads. OCRS will have the task of feeding the Saharan populations and this presupposes a policy of finding water supplies, of leaving to the people the enjoyment of the space necessary for the life of their flocks, and of undertaking a substantial development of medical assistance. Elementary education will also have to be provided; up to 1954 there were less than 20,000 children in the schools of the Algerian territories of the south. It should not be forgotten that one-twentieth part of the milliards engaged in prospecting and boring would be sufficient to supply the daily bread of all the inhabitants of the Saharan oases and to assure the nomads against famine. The Saharans ought to be associated in the exploitation itself, as well as in the indirect benefits of any future industry. Those most concerned should be consulted; they have a right to cast their vote.

VI

MAURITANIA (*SHINQIT*) AND
THE FAR SOUTH

FOR the purpose of this survey the Southern Sahara may be defined roughly as the vast region lying between the 25th and 15th parallels of latitude. It is limited in the west by the Atlantic, in the north by the southern frontiers of the Algerian and Libyan Saharan areas, in the east by that of the Republic of the Sudan, and in the south by no administrative boundary but by the human borderland where white and black Africa (*bilad al-bidan* and *bilad as-sudan*) intermingle. The region embraces the whole of Mauritania, together with the northern, triangular portion of the Sudan, most of the Niger Colony, and the northern portion of the Chad Territory—in other words, the Saharan sections of French West and Equatorial Africa of which the remaining and much larger sections are negro.

Geography

The region is one of vast plains which, however, present varied characteristics: steppes covered here and there with a meagre vegetation of stunted shrubs and tufts of harsh grass, sandy wastes called *regs* which, if hard, are ideal for camel travel but are devoid of water and plant life. These must be differentiated from those agglomerations called *ergs*, composed largely of shifting dunes. The monotony of these plains is relieved by dried-up river valleys, rocky plateaux, and by rare oases formed where underground water is accessible. The character of the meagre vegetation reflects these topographical differences. The most important of the high plateaux and mountain masses (*adrar*) which divide the plains are, from west to east, Adrar Tmar in the north and Tagant in the south-east of Mauritania; Iforas in the Sudan; Air in the Niger Colony; and Tibesti in Chad. Their relief assures them a regular season of rains and, possessing permanent water and pasture grounds, they are among the more favoured regions. The principal villages, such as Shinqit and Atar in the west and Agades in the centre (Air), owe their existence to relatively good pastures, date-palm groves, or importance in trans-Saharan traffic. The

263

first mentioned, Shinqit (of Soninke origin), is the Arabic name of the area, possessing a certain linguistic and racial unity, to which Europeans have, in modern times, confusingly given the name Mauritania, so that its inhabitants, the Shanaqta, are known in French as *Maures* (Moors). It is a *zawiya* centre, now decadent, which earned a certain reputation in the Islamic world because of the frequent pilgrimages of its inhabitants.

The desert character of the region, the extreme poverty of vegetation, and the rarity of animal life are due not to the nature of the soil but to the aridity of the climate, marked by the irregularity or absence of rain, aided by high temperatures and intense evaporation. Two climatic bands may be distinguished: the south-Saharan proper from approximately 25° to 18° N.; and the Sahilian from 18° to 14° N. As will be seen from a climatic map these divides are wavy and variable; for instance, in the plain (*tenere*) between Tibesti and Air the Sahara advances southwards to 16°. These areas belong to the southern watershed in that the rains fall during the summer and not, as in the northern Sahara, during the winter. The southern Sahara is much less desolate than the northern portion; most years it rains nearly everywhere, though irregularly, and great herds of camels and sheep can find pasturage, even if oases are rare and poor compared with those of the north. The Sahilian (Ar. *sahil*, 'borderland') is distinguished from the Saharan climate in that it rains regularly to the extent of 8–20 inches each year between July and September. The feature which distinguishes it from the Sudanese climatic band, which follows it, is that the rains are insufficient to allow for cultivation without irrigation. The Niger itself flows through 300 miles of desert in the big sweep, the so-called Niger bend, which it makes to the north, reaching its apex at the caravan port of Timbuktu. Though there are a few negro villages in the dry valleys, the area is Saharan rather than Nigerian. The Sahara is traversed from north to south by caravan routes which avoid the *ergs* and keep to the rocky or gravel desert.

Population

In spite of its aridity human beings can live in parts of these wastes. The population of the definitely Saharan area is about 320,000 of whom some 140,000 are Mauritanians; but it must be remembered that white Saharans also inhabit the Sahil. Mauritania proper has a population of about half a million of whom the majority are white. Similarly the majority of the Tuareg are located in parts of the Sahil because any increase in population is impelled there by the barren nature of their homeland. Apart from French officials, the dominant inhabitants, all Muslim, are Moors in the west, Tuareg in the centre, and Teda in the east. At the beginning of the Christian era negroes were the dominant race in the southern Sahara and they still form an important part of the population; they are scattered all over the region but are now subordinate to new dominant groups. Speaking either Arabic or Tamahaqq, they belong culturally more to the Saharan than to the negro world. Their former culture, however, reveals itself in their superstitions and in their enjoyment of drum and dance rhythms. They are an important element in the life of the Sahara, because its agricultural economy is wholly dependent upon them, and they have made a deep racial imprint upon many groups of whites. There are two types of blacks: oasis cultivators (Arab. *harratin*, Tam. *ikawaren*), to be clearly differentiated from the descendants of slaves (Arab. *abid*, Tam. *iklan*), who cultivate favourable valleys, tend herds, and act as servants of the whites.

The Teda (or Tubu) form a distinct and homogeneous people; though dark and speaking a Sudanese language, they are not negroes but probably an old Saharan race. They number about 100,000 (44,000 in Niger and 56,000 in Chad Territories) and are scattered over a vast area of the eastern Sahara from Hoggar in the west to the Libyan desert in the east, and from Fezzan in the north to the Chad in the south. Their main groups live in the mountainous regions of Tibesti, Borku, and Ennedi, the Kawar group of oases, and parts of Kanem and Waday.

In the west the Moors are the dominant people; in the centre, the Tuareg. The Moors (450,000 in Mauritania, 12,000 in the Senegal, 175,000 in Sudan) occupy all habitable country between the Atlantic and the Iforas mountains. Of Berber origin, they are now Arabic-speaking and call themselves 'whites' (Ar. *bidan*) as opposed to the 'blacks' (*sudan*). In the south of Mauritania, the Trarza, Brakna, and Kunta are the most important tribes; in the north the great nomadic tribe of Riqaibat, part of whom are in Río de Oro; in the Saharan parts of the Sudan such as Hawd and Azawad we find smaller tribes including the Barabish, Kunta, Idaw Aish, Ahl Tishit, Awlad Mubarak, Mashduf, and Awlad Delim. The ruling clans of Arab origin such as the Beni Hassan are sometimes mixed with and sometimes juxtaposed to their Berber tributaries or *zanaga*. Arabization has had a variable effect upon the social organization of the Moorish groups but nowhere has it obliterated the Berber foundation. Thus the Riqaibat speak pure Hassaniya Arabic with Berber admixtures, but their social organization is basically Berber. Women, as with all Saharan nomads, play an important role. Monogamy is universal. Women are masters of the tent, receiving and entertaining visitors. The assembly (*jamaa*) is the governing body; cadis are tolerated, but only as advisors if someone invokes Islamic law, not as judges.

The Tuareg domain stretches from In-Salah in the northern Algerian Sahara to Hombori within the Niger bend in the south, and from Iforas in the west to Tahoua in Niger Territory. They speak a particular Berber dialect, known as Tamahaqq, and have preserved a Libyan script called *tifinagh*. The northern group, who live in the mountainous area of the central Sahara beyond the limits of the area we are considering, are small in numbers. The main groups live north and south of the Niger bend and in Air, and these through living in a different physical environment and in contact with negroes have been modified in physical characteristics, mode of life, and customs. Most of them have lost their camels, which could not stand the change of climate. Noble clans have sometimes retained their racial purity owing to the matrilineal reckoning of descent; thus the son of a noble and a serf woman would not be a noble but belongs to his mother's class. In fact the Tuareg display every gradation of type from Berber to negro. The southern Tuareg have increased in numbers, whereas the pure nomads are kept at a constant level by a lower birth-rate and by migration.

Saharan society is divided into classes, whose interests are, however, closely linked. At the summit of the Moorish hierarchy are the Hassan Arabs who constitute the noble warrior class. Next come the clerical or maraboutic class (Ar. *zwaya*) of arabized Berbers who, as tributaries of the nobles, do not bear arms but tend the herds of Arab clans and perform religious duties. Many of these are now free from Arab tutelage. Another class of Berber origin are the Zanaga (Berb. *idnagen*) who also are tributaries and pay dues to the Arabs. Below them come sedentary black peoples (*harratin* and *abid*). There are also rigid caste groups of smiths, hunters, and bards (Hassani Arabic *igiu*; in French *griots*). Tuareg and Teda society is divided on similar lines.

Besides the above there are in the Chad district Arab tribes known as the Shoa or Shuwa who have penetrated from the east. Some are camel-nomads (*abbala*), but the majority are semi-nomadic cattle-breeders (*baqqara*) who occupy fixed villages during part of the year. They speak their own Arabic dialect, their social organization is quite different from that of Saharans, and they belong more properly to the Sudan. A distinct Arab group of camel nomads are the Awlad Sulaiman who migrated from the Fezzan after expulsion by the Turks in 1842 into the Teda area north-west of the Chad. They live and speak like Tripolitanian Arabs.

It is difficult to assess the population figures, not only because it is hard to take a census in the desert but also because the areas concerned, with the exception of Mauritania, form only portions of the provinces of French West and Equatorial Africa. The following table is therefore only approximate except for Mauritania:

	Area (km)	Population	Approximate Saharan Population
Mauritania . .	1,165,000	546,400	140,000
Sudan . . .	1,221,000	3,445,000	35,000
Niger . . .	1,256,000	2,165,000	100,000
Chad . . .	1,284,000	2,249,400	45,000

It will be realized that more Moors, Tuareg, and Teda inhabit the Sahil than the Sahara proper.

History

The history of the south Sahara during the past 2,000 years is composed of three interwoven strands: the migrations and struggles of nomad tribes, the control of the routes and tribes by negro states in the Sahil and Sudan, and, throughout the whole period, the steady pressure of the white Saharans upon its negro inhabitants. From the fourth century A.D. the multiplication of the camel resulted in the formation of powerful Berber groups and the gradual reduction of Sahara blacks to the status of slave cultivators. Nevertheless the great negro empires of the Sudan continued to dominate the southern Sahara, controlling its trade routes and exploiting deposits of salt, which is not found in negroland, until the Moroccans conquered the Songhay state in 1591. This intervention was exceptional; in general, relations with North African states were almost entirely economic, apart from the occasional exchange of a diplomatic mission. Arab geographers and historians, our chief source for this period, testify both to the security of the trade routes under the negro empires and to the accompanying spread of Islam. The rise of the Almoravid dynasty in the wastes of Mauritania in the eleventh century and its conquest of the Maghrib and Muslim Spain had as an offshoot the conquest of the capital of the Ghana empire in 1076. But though Almoravid rule strengthened the hold of

Islam over the western Berbers, its major effort was directed towards the north. It never gained control of the Sahil and its influence as an islamizing factor can be exaggerated.

In the fourteenth–fifteenth centuries an Arab tribe, the Maaqil, advanced into Mauritania. They were a branch of the Beni Hilal whose unleashing upon North Africa by the Fatimids in the middle of the eleventh century was a cause of its further arabization. Their dominion led to a transformation in the life of the western Berbers and to their adopting the Arabic language. They gave up the custom of wearing the mouth-muffler (Ar. *litham*, Tam. *taghelmuzt*), a characteristic feature of all Saharan Berbers which is still retained by the Tuareg. Many arabized Berbers had regained their independence by the nineteenth century. Arab tribes also pressed on the Berbers of the Hawd (Sudan) but were repelled, though Arab sections like the Kunta established themselves peacefully, and these tribes also became arabized. In the central Sahara the Tuareg resisted both Arab penetration and arabization. The destruction of the Songhay state by the Moroccans led to Tuareg expansion and control over the Niger bend (completed by 1770) and finally the whole Sahil from Timbuktu to the Chad. This Tuareg supremacy lasted until the French conquest. On the other hand the Teda in the Sahara north of Lake Chad resisted Tuareg pressure and remained independent.

The French Occupation. The present French control of the whole area grew out of their occupation of the negro Sudan at the end of the nineteenth century. The nomads remained undisputed masters of the southern Sahara up to 1900. In 1890 the French and British agreed that the region situated south of Algeria and Tunisia should be regarded as a French sphere of influence as far as a line running from Say on the Niger to Baroua on Lake Chad. Modifications were made in 1898, 1904, and 1906. After Kitchener's conquest of the Eastern Sudan in 1898 another agreement defined the boundary with that country and brought Tibesti, Borku, and Waday into the French sphere. Farther west, Senegal was first relieved from the pressure of the Moors by Governor Faidherbe (1851–65). After he left further expansion was not encouraged from Paris and it was only in the present century, after the occupation of negro Sudan, that the western caravan routes and south Mauritania were brought under control through operations which were completed in 1934 when the assumption of the protectorate over Morocco enabled expeditions from the south to be joined by others from the north.

After posts were established along the Niger bend (1899)

control was gained over the Ullemmeden Tuareg and the Moorish tribes of the Sudan. Farther east, after the defeat of Rabih in the Chad region (1900), action was taken against the Sanusi, leading to the establishment of control over Waday, Borku, and, finally (1914), Tibesti. The position was not changed by the important Sanusi rising of 1916–17.

Government and Administration

When the French gained control of the southern Sahara they attached most of the region to the northern provinces of French West Africa (AOF), while that situated north-west of the Chad was included in the Chad Province of French Equatorial Africa (AEF) by an anomaly due to the peculiarities of the conquest. In contrast, therefore, to the other sections of this Survey, the region does not form an administrative unit, but is simply the northern march of black Africa from which it is administered. In the early days of the occupation administration was military. The former province of Haut Sénégal–Niger formed a vast military province stretching from the Senegal to the Chad. As things settled down modifications were made, e.g. a decree of 1911 detached the *Territoire militaire du Niger* which then included Tibesti. The various territories took their present shape on 1 January 1921, with subsequent minor modifications such as a shift in the boundary between Mauritania and the Sudan whereby the first received an additional population of 188,500.

The eight territories of the AOF form a federation administered by a High Commissioner. Each territory has at the head a Governor, assisted by an elected *conseil général*; and is subdivided into *cercles* under French administrators (Mauritania has ten *cercles*). Within each *cercle* chiefs of tribes and villages are designated by the administration following local custom. Administration is therefore direct. The *commandants de cercle* were civilian except in the Saharan territories which for long remained military. The *chef-lieu* in the desert *cercles* was not a civilian headquarters as elsewhere, but a military base. Today, however, only two military *cercles* remain.

Since the reforms of 1946 each territory elects representatives (17 in 1946, increased to 21 in 1951), representing the 17 million people of the AOF, to the three Assemblies in Paris, and each has an elected assembly. An enabling bill (*loi-cadre*) passed in 1956 permits the introduction by decree of sweeping constitutional reforms in the AOF and AEF. These aim at the gradual transfer of political power from Paris, and from the local French administrations, to responsible African Governments.

Mauritania

The people of the southern Saharan regions under the French administration looked south rather than north, in so far as they were politically conscious. Only the one unified Saharan province, Mauritania, whose people are predominantly white, looked north as well as south. The uncertainty to which area it really belongs is illustrated by a story in Ahmad ash-Shinqiti's well-known book on the scholars and saints of the region (*al-Wasit fi tarajim udaba ash-Shinqit*, Cairo 1329/1911). He records the decision of a mufti in Medina who, on the matter being raised by an Algerian, ruled that Mauritanians should, for the purpose of charitable grants, be considered Sudanese, not North Africans. Shinqiti himself naturally controverts this view since the Moors are whites not blacks. Mauritania already possesses a very distinct political personality and appears likely to emerge as a significant unit. The first proposals (1951) to form a 'French Sahara' involved the partition of Mauritania and evoked strong local reactions. In the scheme finally approved (28 December 1956) Mauritania was only to be 'associated' with the new organization.

The double outlook of Mauritania is reflected in its politics. As shown elsewhere the leader of the Moroccan Istiqlal Party has advocated union with Morocco and in this is supported by some Mauritanians including the *Entente Mauritanienne*. Others claim that it can become a significant political unit, and this claim has been strengthened by the discovery of mineral resources. The present deputy, Sidi al-Mukhtar N'Diaye, as the spokesman of the *Union Progressiste Mauritanienne*, points out that after the bitter rivalries between tribes began to smooth out under the French peace the idea of a homogeneous Mauritania acquired substance when its assembly was set up in 1946, and would be strengthened when the new constitutional reforms were brought into effect. Whilst it is true that ties of kinship, language, culture, and religion constitute an important link between Mauritanians and Moroccans it is uncertain whether the tribes as a whole would desire to become part of Morocco. Equally, however, Sidi al-Mukhtar is opposed to the inclusion of Mauritania in a French Sahara since this would be directly contrary to the proposed policy of devolution of power in French Africa. Independent of direct external control throughout almost the whole of their history, the dominant party in

Mauritania has hitherto been no more willing to be under the Moroccans than the French, though prepared to be associated both with Morocco and with the French Community.

In February 1958 Moktar ould Daddah, the young Vice-President of the Mauritanian Government, declared that the Mauritanians were determined to resist the activities of un-controlled bands coming from the north which had been cutting the country off from the markets of south Morocco and so causing complete stagnation in northern Mauritania. He had, he said, asked for French action on the borders of the Río de Oro. But he added that the Mauritanian population were entirely Muslim and, to the extent of four-fifths, Arabo-Berbers. Since 1951 they had been torn between their sincere attachment to France and the Islamic and Arab solidarity which bound them to their brethren in North Africa. Things would be much easier if the Algerian problem were solved in a way acceptable to the nationalists as well as to the French. He then deplored the recent bombing of Sakiet in Tunisia. This he described as the latest of a series of headstrong actions which had settled nothing, but put France in a very difficult position, morally and diplomatically, and one which was above all very painful for members of the Franco-Arab community.[1]

Meanwhile the movement for unification with Morocco, initiated by Horma ould Babana, had taken on a considerable extension. In the spring of 1958, Mauritanians who had sought refuge in Rabat included, in addition to Horma ould Babana himself and Mohamed el Haiba ould Shaikh Malainine, also Mohamed Fall ould Oumeir, Amir of Trarza; Dey ould Sidi Baba, former Minister of Commerce, Industry and Mines; Mohamed el Moktar ould Bah, former Education Minister; Shaikh Ahmedou, leader of the Mauritanian Youth Move-ment, and a number of others. They claimed that the here-ditary chiefs of Mauritania had always acknowledged the supremacy of the Sultan of Morocco, rendering him assistance and being helped by him in time of need, and that prayer had always been offered for him in the mosques. As long as the whole area had been equally under French control, they had had no complaint against French administration. Now, how-ever, Morocco was again an independent country, while they themselves were invited either to join a federation of black states in which they would be a minority element or to adhere to the French-controlled OCRS. In the circumstances their choice must be to become part of Morocco. They asked for no special position within the country and had no aspirations for

[1] *Le Monde*, 15 February 1958.

independence, since they did not constitute a unit capable of separate existence and 'had no desire to become a second Jordan'.

In July 1958 these Mauritanian leaders were all granted advisory posts in the Moroccan Government.

One of the first actions of the Mauritanian Government after achieving a degree of autonomy was the decision to move the capital from St. Louis on the Senegal into Mauritanian territory proper. A site has been chosen at Nouakshott, four miles from the coast, half-way between the Senegal and the southern frontier of the Spanish Sahara. The project was estimated to cost £4 million, and it was hoped that the Mauritanian Assembly would be able to meet there in December 1958.[1]

SOCIAL AND ECONOMIC CONDITIONS

French administration has led to an economic and social revolution. Raiding and the slave-trade have been suppressed and the status of slavery officially abolished. Trade has been directed to West African seaports, with the result that the caravan routes across the Sahara have lost their importance. Though the latter are now quite secure, traffic along them has been reduced to a trickle. The salt-caravan still plays an important part in Saharan trade, but it is not a trans-Saharan traffic and has not prevented the decay of the caravan ports of Timbuktu, Zinder, and Air.[2] Motor traffic follows roughly the old Saharan routes, but this mode of transport by-passes the nomads and is an expensive mode of carrying goods. The nomads, whose future here as everywhere in the modern world has become a difficult problem, have had their normal poverty and insecurity increased by the reduction of their functions as carriers and controllers of trade routes. The economic future of those nomads, such as the Riqaibat and the unmodified

---

[1] For Mauritanian affairs see also above, pp. 61, 75, and 198.

[2] Salt has always been the principal factor in the relationship of Saharan whites with Sudanese blacks, and it still holds first place in south Saharan commerce. It is important in providing nomads possessing few other resources with money exchange. The total value of salt exports from the Sahara into Negroland is estimated at about 200 million francs. The principal places of extraction are:

(a) Idjil in the N.W. of Mauritanian Adrar. The principal market in the Sudan for this salt is Nioro: 3,446 camel-loads in 1950.

(b) Tawdeni (Taoudeni), 700 km. north of Timbuktu, exploited from 1585 when the Moroccans took control of the salt-pans of Taghaza which was still farther to the north. Two *azalay* (November and March) form at Timbuktu (20,000 to 30,000 camels), under the control of the Kunta, with which the Barabish of Azawad are especially concerned.

(c) Kawar and Agram. This holds the place in the Tuareg world that the other two hold in the Moorish world. The principal centres are Bilma, Seguedine, and Fachi. Two caravans a year (20,000 camel-loads) in October and February.

Tuareg, who are dependent on one animal, the camel, is precarious. Their finely-poised economy has been upset, they tend to move south and it is there that their greatest concentrations are to be found today. Another development affecting the Tuareg, who had always been rather uncertain Muslims, derives from the revival of Arab civilization and the increased facility of communications. They are thus, as a result of the spread of the Arabic language, acquiring from the marabouts a greater knowledge of Islam and of its rules of life while losing the use of the *tifinagh* script. On the other hand contact with negroes is also affecting their way of life, so that the lower grades of their society have taken to living in villages. Some have so changed physically that they can now hardly be distinguished from Songhay and Hausa; yet the majority of Ullemmeden and Kel Air remain Tuareg in customs, retaining the traditional dress and mouth-muffler.

Health

That a large part of the Saharan population is under-nourished will be obvious from what has been said about its resources. This applies to sedentaries as well as to nomads, and the former are also subject to many more diseases. Even when the total calories seem sufficient, at favourable times of the year, their food is unbalanced owing to the insufficiency of animal protein and the consequences of malnutrition are seen in the number of blind, cripples, and idiots among the sedentaries. The French administration has been able to do little to help the situation, for complete pacification only dates from 1934 and agriculture can be extended but little. What medical resources are available are found in the Sahil and a few administrative posts.

Religion and Education

The Islam of the region belongs to the North African religious cycle and is to be distinguished from that of the negro Muslims to the south, though its leaders have strongly influenced negroes in the Sahil. The North African religious revolution of the fifteenth–sixteenth centuries was essentially a matter of the tribes and countryside, rather than of the towns, and it quickly affected Mauritania. It was characterized by the spread of belief in holy power (Ar. *baraka*) transmitted by heredity and initiation which is the foundation of the religious brotherhoods (Ar. *tariqa*) and is accompanied by saint and tomb reverence. It also led to the formation of clerical or maraboutic tribes (*zwaya*) which were the primary factor in the emancipation of the Moorish tribes from Arab tutelage. In North Africa the *tariqas* are in decline in consequence of secularist and reforming movements, but in Mauritania and Sudan and in the settled parts of Niger territory their leaders still exert great influence. The Qadiriya, in a number of family branches, notably the Fadiliya, Kunta, and Sidya families, is the most widespread. The Tijaniya does not possess the influence it has in negro West Africa, but groups of adherents are found scattered throughout the south Sahara and Sahil. The strongest centre of Moorish Tijanism is in Tagant, especially among the Idaw Ali. The influence of the Sanusiya, once strong in Niger Territory and Chad, has weakened considerably.

Mauritania has a long tradition of Islamic learning centred on the personal renown of clerics belonging to traditional religious families scattered in the multi-function *zawiyas* to be found at well centres. A fair proportion of Moorish girls are to be found attending Quran schools along with their brothers. The conservatism of the teachers is very rigid and their teaching follows the traditional method of memorization of the Quran and legal texts. The Moors remain proud of their teachers and relatively few seem to go to North African centres of study like the Qarawiyin and Zaituna Mosques. Tijanis go on pilgrimage to the tomb of their founder in Fez. These traditionists are suspicious of reformers and modernists, like Allal al-Fasi, who have been influenced by the Egyptian Salafiya, because they advocate a reformed education and denounce as a corruption of pure Islam the superstitions upon which the old leaders thrive.

French education is centred in the Sahil. Little has been done in Mauritania since the few who desire its benefits can go to schools in the borderland and Senegal. The number of these seeking French education is, however, steadily increasing and we hear of leaders of Moorish and even Tuareg tribes asking for teachers to be sent to conduct schools in their encampments or nearby centres of settlement.

Pastoralism and Agriculture

Pastoralism is the characteristic economic activity of such a region. Vast areas are unsuitable even for the nomadic life and the nomads are compelled by the irregularity and meagreness of the rains to live in small and scattered groups. They own large numbers of animals but the latter are not of great economic value. The camels of northern Mauritania are taken to the north to be sold in the Moroccan markets near Wadi Nun and the Dra, whilst the sheep and goats of the south are taken to the Sudanese markets. Tuareg cattle are exported to the Gold Coast and Nigeria. Twenty thousand sheep a year are driven from the Tuareg Iforas region to the oases of southern Algeria.

No less important than the nomads are the industrious sedentary negroes and *harratin* tending date-palms and cultivating grains. Although the division between these two occupational groups is typical of Saharan society they are yet mutually interdependent. There has been an increase of population (for example, that of Mauritania is said to have increased by 48 per cent. between 1933 and 1949), but as Saharan agricultural resources have not increased in proportion, emigration continues. There is both a seasonal and a definitive emigration towards the south. Moors of Mauritania go into the Senegal every year to transport groundnuts, as do the Tuareg of Air into Nigeria, and their *harratin* tend more and more to settle in the region of the river and become cultivators, so that 30,000 Moors and their *harratin* are now living in Senegal Territory. Again Tuareg tribes, impelled to migrate by prolonged drought, tend more and more to remain in the Sahil where their black serfs take up agriculture.

The Saharan territories are not self-sufficient in grain but import large quantities of millet from the south where new barrages in Brakna, Assaba, and Hodh are enabling cultivation to be increased. To pay for this they have very limited resources: profits from the transport of salt and groundnuts, handicrafts, the sale of animals, some earnings from employment by the administration, and pay as soldiers and pensioners.

Date production is not as important as in the northern Sahara, but there are plantations in Moorish country in southern Adrar, Tagant, and Hodh, and in Borku and Tibesti. These, which had deteriorated greatly, more through the inertia of the people than through lack of water, have been developed since the war, though the new trees are not yet in production. The present date production of the AOF is about 11,660 tons of which four-fifths are from Mauritania and one-fifth from Kawar-Djado; while from Borku and Tibesti in the AEF it amounts to 5,000 tons. Very little is exported.

Fishing is carried on along the Mauritanian coast. French companies based on Port Étienne, the only Mauritanian port (if we exclude St. Louis, the capital, as really belonging to the Senegal), exported 860 tons of dried fish in 1950. One company has installed a factory-boat in the Bay of Levrier which dispatches fish-meal, oil, and tinned fish to France.

France can do little to alleviate the progressive economic paralysis which has overtaken south Saharan economy since her occupation, except in a few centres which are hardly noticeable in the Saharan immensities. She is, however, doing much to help agriculture in the sahilian borderlands, such as the fertile section of the Gorgol north of the Senegal river and in southern Niger and Chad Territories, by irrigation schemes and building dams, with the aid of the local development fund and public works authorities.

Industry

Until the last few years virtually the only industry was the extraction of salt, whose role in Saharan economy has already been stressed. Natron exists in Tibesti and Manga but it is not regularly exploited as in Fezzan. A certain amount of handicraft work is carried on in the oases and tents; sandals and saddles in Agades, and products made by Tuareg and Moorish women and by caste groups such as smiths.

In addition to the oil and iron mentioned in the section on the Sahara (OCRS), much attention has recently been given to the possibility of exploiting other mineral resources. Tin-bearing ores and wolfram have been found in southern Air. In Mauritania copper has been found in commercial quantities at Akjouit and a pilot plant for its exploitation was inaugurated in 1954. By far the greatest importance so far, however, is attached to the proved iron deposits of high quality near Fort Gouraud. An iron company MIFERMA (*Société des Mines de Fer de Mauritanie*) was formed in 1953, with 51 per cent. of the capital held by French interests and 34 per cent. by a Canadian group (Frobisher), and work was begun the same year. In southern Sahara Mauritania offers the best prospects for exploitation from the point of view of labour and for transport owing to its proximity to the Atlantic; if prospects are realized, the region may in the future undergo a great transformation (see p. 258).

PART THREE

THE EASTERN MAGHRIB
(*AL-MAGHRIB AL-ADNA*)

VII

RELATIONS OF ITALY WITH THE
EASTERN MAGHRIB[1]

In passing eastwards from Algeria, we finally leave the regions where the influence of the Atlantic as well as that of the Mediterranean makes itself felt, as in Morocco and Spain and even to some extent in Algeria. We approach an area which was the centre of the civilization of the ancient world. While the Muslim monuments of Andalusia, such as the Great Mosque of Córdoba and the Alhambra Palace at Granada, ensure that most people realize that Spain had a Muslim past, relatively few people recollect that there was a significant period of Muslim rule in Sicily and Malta also. Very few realize, for example, that the Maltese language, as spoken in the latter island today, is simply a dialect of North African Arabic which has been modified by various European influences. For this reason it is profitable, before passing on to consider the specific history and present conditions of the two eastern Maghrib states, Tunisia and Libya, to describe briefly the impact of Islam, in the heyday of its triumphant advance, upon the greatest of the Mediterranean islands and upon Italy herself.

The Arab Conquest, and Loss, of Sicily

Throughout the centuries, geography and the circumstances of history have constantly created close links between Italy and the North African countries situated to the south of her, on the farther shore of the Mediterranean. For antiquity, it is sufficient to mention the Punic Wars—the great duel between Rome and Carthage for the hegemony of the western Mediterranean. Similarly when Islam began to spread throughout the Mediterranean basin, Italy was situated in a forward position among the eddying currents of its advance. The new faith was soon established on her soil, with the result that Sicily became an Arab province from the ninth to the eleventh centuries.

After 150 years of intermittent raids which had no lasting

---

[1] *Al-Maghrib al-Adna* means literally 'the Near West'. This expression, which is similar in form (though in reverse) to our own phrase 'the Near East', denotes the eastern section of the Maghrib, viz. Libya and Tunisia; similarly Algeria is *al-Ma hrib al-Ausat*, or 'the Middle West', and Morocco *al-Maghrib al-Aqsa* or 'the Far West'.

consequences, the Arabs (coming from nearby Tunisia) disembarked in Sicily in the summer of A.D. 827—116 years after their descent upon Spain—with the intention of making a permanent conquest. The expedition, commanded by Asad ibn al-Furat, had been organized at Sousse—by order of the Aghlabid Amir Ziyadat Allah, in response to a request for aid from a Byzantine admiral, Eufemius, who had rebelled against the central Sicilian authorities. The Arabs disembarked on the north-west coast of the island, at Mazara; after defeating the Byzantine forces they advanced on Syracuse, the capital of Byzantine Sicily, which they were unable to capture. For a while the invaders were in serious difficulties, but soon overcame them, thanks to assistance from Muslim Spain. In 831 they made themselves masters of Palermo, which became their capital and headquarters for the rest of the conquest. Castrogiovanni, the former Enna, in the centre of the island, fell in 859; and Syracuse itself, after a terrible siege, in 878. With the capture of the latter city the conquest can be considered as complete, although certain isolated strong places still held out such as Taormina, for example, which was not taken until 902. The whole of Sicily thus became a province of the Aghlabid domain in Africa, and officials to govern it were appointed from Tunis. In the first years of the tenth century the Aghlabids were replaced by the Fatimids who also inherited the province of Sicily. The subsequent displacement of the Fatimid empire from Tunisia to Egypt, about 970, loosened the bonds by which the island was held in direct dependence on Africa; formal connexion was, however, maintained until the middle of the eleventh century and, as recent texts have shown, some of the Caliphs gave more attention to Sicily than had previously been supposed. It is, however, certain that direct authority in the island was in the hands of the Kalbid dynasty from the middle of the tenth century (948–1040). This family was descended from a Fatimid Governor, al-Hasan ibn Ali al-Kalbi, who succeeded in converting his post into what was for all practical purposes a hereditary principate. The Kalbid dynasty symbolized the golden age of Arab rule in Sicily. The island had already for some time become a base for sea and land expeditions against the Italian mainland; there, however, the Arabs never made durable conquests, except for two principates, at Bari and Taranto in Puglia; these endured for some decades during the ninth century. They seem to have been independent of Sicily and to have owed a nominal allegiance to the Caliph in Baghdad. Another settlement, which may have been subordinate to the Arabs of Sicily, was the military colony on the

Garigliano in Campania; this lasted from 882 to 915. Under the Kalbids raids on Calabria and the rest of southern Italy became more frequent, as is shown for example by the Battle of Stilo and the defeat of the Emperor Otto in 982. Meanwhile the island itself enjoyed a high degree of material prosperity and intellectual activity; the Arab traveller, Ibn Hawqal, who visited Palermo in 972, was able to describe the Sicilian capital as a metropolis of the Muslim world.

In 1040, however, as the result of a civil war, the Kalbid dynasty came to an end and its disappearance ushered in a period of anarchy which was the prelude to the Christian reconquest of the island. During this period the former capital, Palermo, was administered as a republic and governed by its municipal council (*jamaa*), while various other cities were ruled by minor princes. Fighting between two of these, Ibn al-Thumna, lord of Catania, and Ibn al-Hawwas, lord of Girgenti, was the occasion of the first Norman intervention. Count Roger, having got possession of Messina in 1061, was invited by Ibn al-Thumna to help him against his rival; having done so, he continued the conquest on his own account, together with his brother, Robert Guiscard. At the beginning of 1072, the two Norman adventurers entered Palermo, but had to struggle for another twenty years before they overcame the last centres of Muslim resistance in the island—the most memorable episode of this period being the struggle put up by the Amir of Syracuse, Ibn Abbad, known in Christian sources as Benavert, who fell in a naval engagement in 1086. Not till about 1091 could it be said that the Norman conquest of Sicily was complete. Even then, there remained a number of minor leaders in mountain strongholds, together with a large Muslim population which survived under Norman rule, in gradually diminishing numbers, throughout the following century—the twelfth—and even later. The last trace of Sicilian Muslims disappears only in the middle of the thirteenth century, when Frederick II deported the turbulent remnants to Lucera in the Capitanata (province of Foggia), where they formed an active Muslim colony under Swabian rule and at the beginning of the Angevin Kingdom.

Characteristics and Effect of Arab Rule

During their rule in Sicily, the Arabs put into force the civil and military ordinances of Muslim public law applicable to conquered countries. The Christian population had to pay tribute as *dhimmi*, though in certain areas, particularly in western Sicily, their numbers diminished rapidly through conversion to Islam. Estates were extensively broken up, being distributed very widely among the conquerors; this had favourable results for the development of agriculture, a sphere in which the Arabs introduced many new systems of cultivation and many new species, among them citrus fruits, flax, hemp, and cotton, as is attested by the nomenclature of Sicilian agriculture until today. The population of the island was composed in part of the former Graeco-Italic inhabitants, who were largely arabized and islamized, and in part of invaders, themselves divided into African Arabs, who arrived in several waves after the first conquest, and Berbers who were generally agriculturists. Indigenous Latin culture seems to have disappeared almost entirely during the Arab period though Greek culture, in the form of hagiography and edifying literature, held its own in the many surviving monasteries of eastern Sicily.

The dominant culture in these two centuries, and to some extent in those of the Norman domination which followed, was Arabo-Islamic, employing the language and the forms typical of medieval Arab culture. Although little has survived from that first period, we know that there was a great flowering of literary, poetical, grammatical, philological, and religious studies. The names at least of the most distinguished exponents of these arts in Sicily have survived. The most illustrious Sicilian Arab poet was Ibn Hamdis (c. 1055–1135), who was contemporary with the last days of Arab rule in the island. After fighting against the Norman invaders as a young man, he left the island and spent the rest of his life wandering through Spain and the Maghrib and often recalling his homeland in nostalgic and moving verse. Very many of the Sicilian-Arab intellectual and scientific *élite* emigrated with him, at the moment of the Christian reconquest, and were dispersed in Egypt and all along the coast of North Africa. Many, however, remained and, thanks to the enlightened tolerance of the Norman kings, kept alive in Sicily not only the Arab ethnic element but also Arabic culture and speech. Arab poets sang the praises of King Roger in their own language; Arab scientists, like Idrisi the geographer, worked for him. Both Roger himself and his successors regarded Arab culture as an indispensable element of their state and preserved certain Muslim Arab institutions of an administrative and financial nature such as the *Diwan at-Tahqiq* or *doana a secretis*, for the taxation of land and real estate, with its *defetarii* (Arabic *daftar*, register). The Norman kings assumed Arabic as well as Greek and Latin titles, minted money with Arabic inscriptions, and adorned their monuments with Arabic poetic epigraphs some of which have been preserved. Though no direct examples of Arab art (except the paintings on the wooden ceiling of the Cappella Palatina in Palermo, which were probably executed by Muslim artists from abroad) are to be found in Sicily today, elements derived from Arab art were combined with Greek and western elements to create a composite Norman-Arab art of which not only Sicily but also southern Italy has preserved some splendid examples. Sicily served as the meeting place of the traditions of oriental art, in its Maghribi form, with those of the west.

Literary connexions between east and west, owing to contacts with Arab Sicily are, on the other hand, uncertain and indefinite. There is an undoubted Arabic influence in the vocabulary of Sicilian and Italian, but apart from this it is uncertain whether possible traces of Arab thought and art in Italian culture and civilization can be attributed to a specifically Sicilian source. There can be no doubt that Spain was the principal channel through which a knowledge of Muslim thought and science passed to Italy. Only in a subsidiary way can one think of Sicily; and even for that there is no documentary proof. The theme of literary history most discussed in this connexion today is possible Arab influence on the metres, subjects, and spirit of the earliest romance poetry. On this question Sicily can throw no light, since all surviving Arab verse from Sicily is written in strictly classical metres and so far there is a total lack of any examples of Sicilian Arab strophic verse comparable to the Muslim Spanish *muwashshaha* or *zajal*. In the field of ideas, too, every influence on nascent Italian civilization which can be identified as Muslim seems to have come by way of Spain; for example, the eschatological *Book of the Stairway*, which Dante may have known, goes back to an Andalusian book of popular piety. For all that, there is no reason to exclude the possibility that contacts were also made between Arab and Italian culture, at moments and in ways which at present escape us; for the last voices of Arab poetry fall silent in Sicily only half a century before the appearance of the first documents of popular Italian poetry, such as the *Contrasto* of Celo d'Alcamo and the Sicilian poetic school.

The Motives of Muslim-Christian Warfare

The Muslims were led to invade Sicily and then to make repeated raids on southern Italy not only by the worldly desire for conquest and booty but also by the religious concept and duty of Holy War, taught in certain well-known Quranic passages. In the Italian reaction, on the other hand, and in the injuries inflicted by Italy on North African Islam, the religious motive was much vaguer, and often entirely lacking. These episodes had their origins almost entirely either in the principle of legitimate defence and economic and commercial interest or in certain cases in a conscious imperialistic desire for expansion. When fighting against Muslims took place on Italian soil, it must of course be considered as purely defensive—for example, the wars by which the Emperor Louis II, in Campania and in Apulia in the ninth century, put an end to the Muslim settlement at Bari; the naval battle of Ostia, won by the combined forces of Rome and Naples in 849; and the campaign which destroyed the colony on the Garigliano in 915. But the naval and land actions of the Tyrrhenian maritime republics against the Muslim menace were clearly offensive as well as defensive. Such was the war which Pisa waged in Sardinia in 1015–16 against Mugetto (al-Mujahid ibn Abdallah, Lord of Denia); he had seized possession of the island, from which he was then driven out again; or the attack which the Pisans and Genoese carried out jointly against al-Mahdiya in 1087, forcing the Zirid Amir Tamim to pay an indemnity, liberate prisoners, and grant them customs privileges. These were the years in which the Normans were completing the conquest of Sicily. For reasons of geography the defence of Islam in the island should certainly have been the task of the African Zirids rather than of the distant Fatimids, but in fact it was only undertaken by them half-heartedly, and in the end Tamim made an outright non-aggression pact with King Roger.

The Norman Invasion of the Maghrib

The Norman Kings, once their domination had been consolidated in Sicily, turned their eyes increasingly towards the North African coast from which, three centuries earlier, the Muslim invasion had originally been launched against the island. Under King Roger II, Christian Sicily began a counter-offensive against the neighbouring Maghrib. After a few initial failures, such as the Battle of Cape Dimas in 1137, this resulted in the founding of a veritable overseas Norman empire in Tripoli (1146), and on the coast of present-day Tunisia—in Mahdiya, Sousse, and Sfax, occupied in 1148, and in Bône, Gabes, and Jerba occupied in 1153. For a moment it appeared as if the direction of the invasion had been reversed and that a movement of conquest by the Christian west was going to engulf the Maghrib. This was, however, only a passing episode, dependent on the impulse given by the great Norman king and his minister of genius, Admiral George of Antioch. After their deaths, the African conquests were rapidly lost—Sfax already in

1156 and Tripoli in 1158, as the result of spontaneous internal revolts; while Mahdiya was occupied by the Almohads in 1160. Nothing but a memory then remained of the ephemeral Norman empire of the Maghrib. Apart from the Genoese expedition under the Duke of Bourbon against Mahdiya in 1390 there were no further attacks from Italy on the Maghrib in the grand style until the expedition of Charles V against Tunis in 1535, which contained contingents from Naples and Sicily, and the colonial enterprise of united Italy in 1911.

Trade Relations from the Eleventh to the Sixteenth Century

Apart from this episode of expansionism by the Norman Kingdom in North Africa, the policy of the medieval Italian states towards the Maghrib was essentially dictated by commercial interests, such as the desire to assure freedom of navigation and traffic in the western Mediterranean, access to the ports, and favourable tariff conditions for merchandise. There is no doubt that the Italian maritime republics maintained commercial and trading establishments (*fondachi commerciali*) in Egypt. For example, a recently published document demonstrates the existence in Alexandria in Fatimid times of a flourishing colony from Amalfi; in all probability similar establishments existed in the Maghrib also, though there is at present no certain evidence for this. Naval actions and demonstrations were undertaken from time to time in defence of trade interests, such, for example, as the operations carried out by Genoa against Ceuta in 1235–6; more often, however, the peaceful negotiation of commercial treaties with the Muslim states of Africa was preferred. The texts of many such treaties have survived until today, either in the original Arabic or in Latin or Italian versions; these were collected and published by Michele Amari in 1863. Although some of the documents are older, the majority of such treaties concern relations between the Hafsid dynasty of Tunis in the thirteenth and fourteenth centuries and the republics of Pisa and Genoa. We have, for example, two important commercial treaties of which one was made by Pisa with the founder of the dynasty, Abu Zakaria, in 1234, and the other with his son and successor, al-Muntasir billah, in 1264. Relations between the Hafsids and Genoa are illustrated principally by letters of a later period (also published by Amari), some with the Sultan Uthman in 1462 and some with the last independent Hafsid, Abu Abdullah Muhammad, in 1517. From these and similar documents, it can be seen that relations between the Hafsid state and the Italian maritime powers of the western Mediterranean were often very

far from hostile, being marked on the contrary by an appreciation of mutual interests and by a spirit of genuine collaboration
and cordiality.

The Barbary States and Modern Times

This pacific phase of the complicated relations between Italy
and the Maghrib lasted to the very end of the fifteenth century
and was followed by the painful period of the Barbary states.
On the Muslim side there was a recrudescence of the war of
privateering. The west chose to call this piracy, while for the
North Africans it was a legitimate application of the religious
laws of Islam and of the relevant jurisprudence. Meanwhile in
Italy maritime republics such as Pisa and Genoa had decayed
or disappeared; defence against the Barbary corsairs, apart
from the provision of a system of coastal towers, look-out posts,
and garrisons, was now conducted mainly by the naval forces
of essentially continental states, such as the two Spanish vice-
royalties in southern Italy, the Grand Duchy of Tuscany and
the Duchy, later Kingdom, of Sardinia. But in this period
the most notable part in the repression of Barbary privateering was played less by the regular forces of these states than
by the autonomous religious and knightly orders such as the
Order of Malta (formerly the Hospitallers or Knights of
Rhodes) and the Tuscan Order of Santo Stefano. But Italian
states also acted with their own forces as, for example, Venice,
in the last years of the Republic, with the action of Admiral
Emo against Tunis in 1769, and the kingdom of Sardinia with
the demonstration against Tripoli under the command of
Sivori in 1825.

The Barbary incursions finally ended in the first half of the
nineteenth century, when the French occupation of Algiers
eliminated the most dreaded centre of privateering and
European naval and military superiority had restored complete
security to the Mediterranean. In the years of the Italian
Risorgimento, the shores of North Africa frequently gave
shelter to Italian patriots and refugees, as for example Tunis
and Morocco to Garibaldi. When Italian unity had been won,
Italy began to look towards the 'fourth shore', where the
occupation of Algeria in 1830, and of Tunisia in 1881, had
already firmly established French rule. The occupation of the
latter state was the cause of great heart-burning in Italy on
account of the presence there of a numerous and active Italian
colony, in great part of Sicilian origin. Once the French occupation was an accomplished fact and had removed any possibility
of action on the nearby coast, Italian political and economic

interest was displaced to the remoter Tripoli, now the only North African zone open to Italian penetration. Italians had not forgotten the period of Sicilian domination there, even if it had been shortlived, nor the more recent occupation of the city (1530–51) by the Knights of Malta whose activity had always been considered as something specifically Italian, especially in the naval sphere. These memories were further stimulated by private initiatives of an economic and commercial nature such, for example, as the opening of a branch of the Bank of Rome in Tripoli in 1907, and above all by the desire that Italy should not remain entirely without a share in the Mediterranean expansion and colonization for which a number of European powers were now rivals. Italy was thus led into the Libyan expedition of 1911, little knowing that the foothold thus to be acquired on the coast of North Africa, so late and with so much difficulty, would be lost again within a few decades, to some extent in expiation of her own errors and to some extent as part of the general collapse of the European colonial system in the Maghrib.

VIII

THE REPUBLIC OF TUNISIA
(*AL-JUMHURIYAT AL-TUNISIYA*)

GEOGRAPHY AND POPULATION

The Geographical Setting

If the Maghrib, apart from Libya, is regarded as a quadrilateral of mountains, then Tunisia forms its eastern flank and marks the limit of the ranges which issue from the Atlas. Standing like a corner tower above the Sicilian Straits, at the point where the Italian peninsula projects farthest from Europe, Tunisia faces the east, as if in welcome.

No natural barrier separates Tunisia from Algeria of which it is in fact the prolongation. The only perennial watercourse in the country, the Majarda, rises in Algeria; the high lands of Tunisia are formed by the convergence of the twin mountain ranges of Algeria—the Atlas of the Sahara, and the Atlas of the Tell or fertile mountains of the north; in the south high steppes and sandy deserts are found on both sides of an arbitrary political frontier.

In spite of this, Tunisia is distinguished from Algeria by a geographical trait of her own. This is the long, flat, and smiling coast into which the steppes and mountain valleys of the Tell descend. This plain, known in Arabic as the Sahil, forms the core of Tunisia. By it the country has, from time immemorial, been laid open to influences coming from the east and from Europe. Unlike Algeria, its political personality has been determined by these influences.

Though Tunisia's backbone of mountain divides the Tell in the north from the Steppes in the south and makes them two distinct regions, the country is more significantly divided by a line which is invisible on the ground. This separates the long ribbon of coast, the Sahil, with its many cities, connecting Bizerta in the north with Zarzis in the south, from a hinterland of mountains and steppes which more closely resemble the rest of the Maghrib. This hinterland is nevertheless detached from Algeria and made tributary to the Sahil by political and economic influences which the latter exerts through its dense population and many cities.

288

MEDITERRANEAN SEA

SICILY

Bizerta

Gulf of Tunis

Tabarka

CAPE BON

Bône

Ain Draham

TUNIS

Kelibia

PANTELLERIA

TELL

Béja

Teburask

Zaghouan

Nabeul

Sakiet Sidi Yusuf

Le Kef

Gulf of Hammamet

Majarda

Kairouan

Sousse
Monastir

JEBEL SHAMBI
1544 FT.

Mahdiya

STEPPES

SAHIL

Sfax

Gafsa

Gulf of Gabes

Tozeur

Shott-
al-Jarid

Gabes

JERBA
ISLAND

Matmata

Zarzis

A L G E R I A

S a h a r a

LIBYA

TUNISIA

LAND ABOVE 1500 FT.
SALT MARSH

0   25   50   75 MILES

Four regions are to be distinguished in Tunisia: the Tell, the Steppes, the Sahil, and the Sahara.

The Tell is the mountainous region situated to the north of the dorsal chain. The Majarda which, with its tributaries, traverses it, carries towards the Gulf of Tunis the rain-water which falls on the high ground adjoining Algeria. Near the frontier the mountains of Khrumerie rise to 3,600 feet, forming precipices on the side of the sea. Only one port, Tabarka, a former Genoese settlement, has found a lodgement here. Running through the Tell from south-west to north-east the broad alluvial valleys of the Majarda, with the rich hill lands on either side, were selected as areas for large-scale European colonization and for the cultivation of cereals. They contain a number of old-established towns, such as Le Kef, Beja, Tebursuk, and Zaghouan, and some small modern centres which serve the needs of the colonists. The Tell, fertile and well watered, with an annual rainfall of 16–24 inches, is enclosed on the south by a continuous mountain barrier, running from south-west to north-east and terminating in Cape Bon: its culminating points are Jebel Shambi (5,000 ft.) near the Algerian frontier, and Jebel Zaghuan, near Tunis (4,260 ft.).

The Steppes are formed by the rising ground south of the Tell, mounting from the Sahil to the high tableland of Algeria, and they are divided into large basins by several rocky ridges. Consisting of vast stretches of esparto grass and of pasturage for sheep and camels, they are however gradually being transformed by the planting of olives and almonds. The climate of the steppe is characterized by great irregularity of rainfall (annual mean 6–12 inches) and of temperature; cereals can be grown only in the rare years of relatively plentiful rains.

The Sahil, spread along the whole east coast, is sometimes flat and sometimes undulating: it is widest opposite Tunis, Cape Bon, Sousse, and Sfax. The sandy coast forms large bays which at intervals are prolonged by lagoons as at Bizerta and Tunis. The climate is mild and regular; from north to south the rainfall varies from 20 to 8 inches. This area is famous for the cultivation of the olive, particularly in the stretch between Sousse and Sfax to which the term Sahil more particularly applies. Farther north, around Tunis and Bizerta and on Cape Bon, the cultivation of vines and fruit trees, principally citrus, is combined with market-gardening and the growing of cereals and fodder to provide a living for a considerable European colony. It is a zone of smallholdings as well as of ancient urban settlement, and innumerable big villages lurk among the gardens and olive orchards; larger towns, famous in history, line the coast—Tunis, Sousse, Monastir, Mahdiya, Sfax, and, finally, Gabes off which lies the island of Jerba.

The Tunisian Sahara projects like a wedge between Algeria and Libya. The immense Shott al-Jarid (50 feet below sea-level) which marks the northern limit of the Saharan region is circled by a string of oases, famous for their dates.

Communications

The natural lines of communication converge towards the east coast. This is itself a vast transversal line of transit from Bizerta in the north to the Libyan frontier in the south; at the same time its ports afford openings to the exterior. Several good roads assure the connexion of north with south; one of these joins up with the road to Tripoli. A railway runs from Bizerta to Gabes, of which the portion from Tunis to the south is narrow gauge.

In the north, communications between the region of Constantine in Algeria and that of Tunis and Bizerta are facilitated by the valley of the Majarda; this route is followed by a first-class road as well as by a normal gauge railway which forms the Tunisian section of the line to Algiers. There are two secondary roads—one in the north from Bizerta to Tabarka; the other in the south, from Tunis through Tebessa to Le Kef. The latter is flanked by a narrow-gauge railway.

In the centre of the country two channels of communication, a road and a narrow-gauge railway, descend the steppes, the former terminating at Sousse and the latter at Sfax. In the south, a track leads towards Ghadames in Tripolitania. The length of railway lines (860 miles) is proportionally half that of Spain but double that of Turkey. There are 9,000 miles of roads of which 6,000 are first-class.

The internal communications system serves four principal Tunisian ports: Bizerta, primarily military but exporting cereals, iron, and cement; Tunis, principally handling imports, but exporting cereals, iron, and phosphates; Sousse, exporting esparto grass and olive oil; Sfax, exporting phosphates and olive oil. The other ports, Tabarka, Kelibia, Monastir, Mahdiya, and Gabes are small; they live principally by fishing.

Tunis is the nodal point of the whole system: it is the only port served by passenger lines and the only one to possess an airfield of international importance. It has regular connexions with Algiers, Rome, Paris, Tripoli, and Cairo. Tunis is also the telecommunications centre.

Strategic Importance

By its position, protruding into the Mediterranean, by its welcoming shores, by its coastal roads connecting the Maghrib with the east, Tunisia has been throughout history a meeting place of peoples and a strategic point of permanent importance.

Situated at the cross-roads of all the rivalries of Europe and the east, Carthage had to be destroyed before the Roman Empire could be established. Vandals, Byzantines, and Normans all used Tunisia as a base; for the Arabs it was the starting-point of their conquest of the farther Maghrib and later of Sicily. In Tunisia the Spanish monarchy clashed with the Ottoman Empire. Only recently, Tunisia was the point from which the Allies began to throw the Nazi imperialists back in Europe. Tomorrow it could equally well be an outpost of the west, facing the eastern Mediterranean, or an outpost of the east facing the west.

In particular, the fortress of Bizerta with its deep-water lagoon surrounded by hills, where a whole fleet can shelter, with its arsenal at Menzel Bourguiba (formerly Ferryville), with its underground installations and its excellent military aerodromes, not only commands the Sicilian channel but can also control much of the central and western Mediterranean. In the south Gabes, at the narrow passage formed by the salt marshes (*shotts*) and the mountains of Matmata, holds a key position on the routes leading to the Sahara and to Libya.

Population

The population of Tunisia is more than 90 per cent. Muslim. For the most part they are natives of the country or immigrants from Algeria (many of whom arrived as refugees) or from elsewhere in North Africa. There is also a European minority, composed principally of French and Italians. The Jewish community under the protectorate was largely assimilated to the European minority; it is now adapting itself anew to an Arab régime.

At the census of 1956, the population of Tunisia was estimated at 3,782,209, composed of:

Tunisian Muslims	3,383,904 }	3,441,696
Jews	57,792 }	
Algerian Muslims	66,885 }	86,189
Other Muslims	19,304 }	
French	180,440 }	
Italians	66,910 }	255,324
Other Europeans	7,974 }	

THE REPUBLIC OF TUNISIA

Owing to a high birth-rate and a diminishing death-rate, the Muslim population is increasing at the rapid rate of 2 per cent. annually. In consequence the proportion of young people to old is very high; almost half the population is less than 20 years old, as compared with 30 per cent. in Europe.

The Tunisians are an old-established people, probably in essence the same Berber and Carthaginian population as inhabited the country in the time of the Romans. This population was arabized as the result of the Arab invasions of the seventh and subsequent centuries, while the Arab invaders themselves were eventually fused into the general mass. There must also be an appreciable intermixture of Europeans of Mediterranean origin who became Muslims after entering Tunisia individually, or who arrived as refugees from Muslim Sicily and Spain. By the fusion of all these elements a distinct state came into being during the rule of the Hafsid dynasty from the thirteenth to the sixteenth centuries, though it was only under subsequent Turkish rule that Tunisia acquired her present frontiers. Tunisians today possess a national unity and personality which distinguish them from the inhabitants of other Arabic-speaking countries in the Maghrib and in the east.

In Tunisia before the protectorate there was, it is true, a distinction between the citizens of the Sahil who formed the framework of the state and the beduin in the countryside. This contrast has, however, been blurred in the course of the present century; there has now been a fusion of the two groups, the townspeople penetrating the country and the beduin entering the towns. This has resulted in a rapid approximation of thought and manners.

The governing class, in the past a small and compact group, has recently been growing, owing to the spread of education, and has acquired a modern outlook. A middle class has come into being, whose standards of living are comparable to those of Europeans. The great majority of the Muslims, however, still live in a state not far removed from destitution; the contrast between the standards of rich and poor is very great.

Among the European minority, the standards of living are in general higher and the contrasts far less striking. As a group the Europeans form a social entity which is sharply distinguished from the Muslims. It is formed principally of two elements, the French and the Italian, of which the former are now the most numerous; many Tunisian Jews are assimilated to it. At the centre of this group, the French colony, virtually the sole possessors of political power under the protectorate, used to exert a force of attraction which enabled them to absorb by

U

naturalization a large part of the Italian, Maltese, and other communities. This minority long held a controlling position in the intellectual and political life of the country; their influence was far greater than that of the Muslim upper classes beside whom they lived without mingling. Its members considered themselves a ruling class and behaved accordingly.

Even before independence, a new directing class of a modern type had come into being among the Muslims and it was rapidly taking the place of the European staff in the administration and in the professions. This class has become increasingly European in outlook without, however, intermarrying or in other respects fusing with the Christians. Mixed marriages remain very exceptional.

The Jewish community of Tunisia, now a united body, has various origins: periodical immigration, of which the oldest occurrence is traditionally said to have taken place at the time of the first diaspora; the conversion of Berber tribes in Roman times; and, from the eleventh century, the influx of Jewish refugees from Muslim and Christian Spain. Some of the community have become French by naturalization; but the majority have remained Tunisian, and there is at the moment a swing back from French to Arab culture. Anti-Semitism was never strong in Tunisia and the new Government has affirmed its intention to treat Jews as citizens with the same rights and duties as any others. It has shown its goodwill repeatedly and the ministry formed after independence included a Jew as Minister of Reconstruction and Housing.

In Tunisia as in other countries there is a tendency for the urban population to increase disproportionately, in spite of the limited development of industry. The population of Tunis and

Population in Principal Cities

	1931	1946	1956
Tunis city	202,400	364,593	410,000 *
Tunis suburbs	61,000	99,000	151,000
Sfax	40,000	55,000	65,000
Sousse	25,324	36,566	48,172
Bizerta	23,206	39,327	44,681
Smaller towns forming municipalities .	—	—	530,000
Total urban population . .			1,250,257

* Tunisian Muslims 240,000; Tunisian Jews 32,000; other Muslims 18,500; Europeans 119,500.

its suburbs has risen from 313,000, in 1931, to 561,000 in 1956 of whom 120,000 are Europeans. In other towns, it has risen from 380,000 to 688,000. This implies that by 1956 over 30 per cent. of the population were urban, and that half of them were in the capital and its suburbs.

HISTORY

From Antiquity till the French Occupation

The history of Tunisia is closely bound up with that of North Africa as a whole, that is to say with the destiny of the Berbers who were the earliest-known inhabitants of the country, apart from the prehistoric peoples who have left traces of themselves in the settlements of Gafsa. It was mainly through Tunisia that other races penetrated into North West Africa and in Tunisia many decisive battles were fought. Though an integral part of Barbary, Tunisia has her own individuality and forms a distinct entity.

In antiquity, Carthage was the capital city for thirteen centuries under the Phoenicians, the Carthaginians, the Romans, the Vandals, and the Byzantines. Throughout this period it owed its prosperity and fame principally to the Carthaginians and the Romans. From time to time, however, the native, Berber, population asserted their independence and succeeded in forming ephemeral kingdoms, such as those of Massinissa, Jugurtha, and Juba.

Though Phoenician Carthage has completely perished, a number of grandiose ruins have survived from the period of Roman rule, notably the Colosseum at al-Djem, capable of holding 60,000 spectators; the exquisite temples of the Roman watering-place of Dougga, and the unrivalled collection of mosaics in the Bardo Museum. Most sites, in particular Carthage, have been used as a quarry by subsequent builders; and Roman columns and marbles are to be found built into the mosques of Kairouan, Tunis, and Córdoba.

The thirteen centuries of Arab rule resulted in the country becoming Muslim in religion and Arab in language and sentiment. Berber is now spoken only by some of the inhabitants of the island of Jerba, in the Matmata, and near Gafsa, while Christianity as an indigenous religion has disappeared for many centuries. Tunisian independence has nevertheless constantly been asserted—first in the resistance of the Berber heroine, al-Kahina, against the Arab invaders and then by the formation of independent dynasties of Arab culture. The first of these was the Aghlabids, who made their capital in Kairouan and who successfully undertook the conquest of Sicily. After them the Fatimids, heretical Muslims, made their capital in Mahdiya, later conquering Egypt and establishing a Shiah Caliphate in Cairo. During their rule they were faced by the formidable rising of another propagandist of local heresy, Abu Yazid, 'the man with the donkey'; he was, however, finally defeated.

In the middle of the eleventh century an Egyptian Fatimid Caliph retaliated on the now rebellious Tunisians by letting loose on them two Arab tribes, the Beni Hilal and the Beni Sulaim, brigand beduin, described two centuries later by the great Tunisian Arab historian Ibn Khaldun as 'an army of locusts'. These ravaged first Tunisia and then the rest of the Maghrib, often as allies of the local dynasties. In the twelfth century the Normans, having dispossessed the Arab Government of Sicily, established a short-lived outpost on the coast of the Sahil; while the Almohads, a Moroccan dynasty of arabized Berbers, made themselves masters of the interior.

In the thirteenth century the Hafsids, a dynasty established by a rebel Almohad governor, founded a Tunisian kingdom over which they ruled for two centuries. During this period Tunis first began to benefit from the arrival of refugees from Muslim Spain; they formed an intellectual and social *élite* and their skill as artisans contributed greatly to the prosperity of the capital. In 1270 Saint Louis of France died on the hill at Carthage during his abortive Crusade against the Hafsid rulers.

In general, the Hafsid kingdom seems to have had a more specifically Tunisian character than its predecessors and may be thought of as foreshadowing the Tunisian state of today, though the dynasty, and with it the independence of Tunisia, collapsed at the end of the fifteenth century under simultaneous blows from the Spaniards and the Ottoman Turks. When Charles V was unable to maintain the base which he had acquired in Tunis, Ottoman domination was extended as far as the Moroccan frontier.

Under the régime of Istanbul, Ifriqiya was divided into three *ojaks* or 'regencies'—Tripoli, Tunis, and Algiers; and it is from that time that the present frontiers of these three territories became more or less definite. Turkish rule was that of a military caste which resided in the country and administered it in a rudimentary fashion, enjoying a large measure of autonomy with regard to Constantinople. The Husainid dynasty which reigned until 1957, when Tunisia was declared a Republic, was founded by a Turkish Agha of the Janissaries, of Cretan origin, who made himself Bey in 1705. In spite of exercising absolute power within Tunisia, the country was still known as the Regency till the end of the protectorate. In 1848, however, a Tunisian mission which was sent to Queen Victoria received strict instructions from the Tunisian Government that it was on no account to allow any interposition on the part of the Turkish Ambassador in London.[1] If such an eventuality looked like becoming inevitable, the mission was to avoid it by returning to Tunis and leave its task unfulfilled. The beylical administration continued the Turkish politico-military framework of the state. Efforts by Tunisian liberals secured the issue of a constitution in 1856, the first of its kind in an Arab country. Though the experiment proved abortive, it is commemorated in the name *Destour*, or 'Constitution', in the title assumed by subsequent nationalist parties.

Certain facts stand out from this long history.

During the 2,500 years of her history Tunisia has twice been in the sphere of Semitic civilization. Once was under the Phoenicians and the Carthaginians, people who had been living in the Mediterranean basin for as long as we have knowledge of them, and once under the Arabs, people who only reached the Mediterranean from their previous desert environment a few years before they arrived in North Africa. Tunisia has also twice been in the sphere of western Mediterranean civilization, first under the Romans and then under the French. In our own times these Semitic and European influences are mingling, partly in opposition to one another, partly in fusion, within Tunisia herself. Such economic or other advantages as foreign rule may have been able to offer have never put an end to movements for independence.

Tunisia has always been a country of cities—Berber settlements, Phoenician colonies, Roman municipalities, Arab cities around their mosques. These cities have always been subordinate to the capital, to a greater extent than in the rest of the Maghrib. The individuality of Tunisia is largely the product of the city of Tunis which has given its name to the country as a whole.

Social conditions do not appear to have varied very greatly during the centuries. Citizens and nomads have always regarded one another askance. There have always been cultivated and powerful minorities and a wretched proletariat; governments

---

[1] By firman of 25 October 1871 the Sultan laid down the conditions of the suzerainty of the Sublime Porte and renounced the former tribute. According to the firman, the Bey received the investiture of Constantinople; he must not make war, conclude peace or cede territory without the authorization of the Sultan. He could negotiate with foreigners only on internal affairs. He must coin money in the name of the Sultan and put his troops at the disposal of the Sublime Porte in case of war. Internally the Bey's authority was absolute (*Almanach de Gotha*, 1881).

controlling the army have ruled over a long-suffering people. Economically there was a magnificent development in Carthaginian and Roman times and a considerable revival under Arab rule in the thirteenth and fourteenth centuries. Subsequently economic life withered until it barely sufficed to keep the population above starvation level.

The French Protectorate, 1881–1943

By the middle of the nineteenth century Tunisia, with her decayed economic life and her archaic political régime in acute financial difficulties, was an obvious field for European expansion. After a prolonged struggle for influence between Great Britain, Italy, and France, the latter, determined to prevent another great power from occupying a position on the flank of Algeria, decided on military intervention in order to bring Tunisia under her own control.

An incursion from Tunisia into Algeria by some mountain brigands, the Khrumirs, provided a pretext; two expeditionary columns, one coming from Algeria by Le Kef and the other disembarking at Bizerta, occupied the country without having to fight. As the result of an ultimatum, the Bey Mohamed Sadoq (al-Sadiq) on 12 May 1881 signed a treaty at Kassar Said (the Bardo) authorizing France to occupy Tunisia militarily and to take charge of foreign affairs and finance.

Two years later, on 8 June 1883, a further convention was signed at Mersa which placed the internal sovereignty of Tunisia also under French supervision. By virtue of the first article of this convention the Bey undertook to introduce such administrative, judicial, and financial reforms as the French Government should deem advisable. The protectorate thus became total and a French administration took over the management of the country.

Supervision very soon turned into more or less direct administration. The real possessor of power was the representative of France, who bore the title of Resident General. The sovereignty of the Bey and a Tunisian Government, reduced to two ministers—the Premier and the 'Minister of the Pen'—was preserved for form's sake. The traditional hierarchy of local administrative authorities such as Caids and Shaikhs was preserved, but placed under the strict control of a body of French officials, known as *Contrôleurs Civils*.

Large modern departments were created and directed by Frenchmen—Finance, Public Works, Public Instruction, Agriculture, Commerce, Health, and Justice. This administration, acting in the name of the Tunisian sovereign but in fact under the direction of the Resident General, legislated, created organs of government, and became all powerful. It gave Tunisia the framework of such public works as ports, roads, railways, schools, and hospitals and endowed the Tunisian state with the machinery of a modern administration.

France further succeeded in persuading other European powers to surrender their Capitulations in favour of French tribunals which were given competence in all cases in which a European was involved. At the same time Tunisian justice was reorganized and secular courts established; these were provided with modern codes while the Sharia courts retained competence only in matters of Muslim personal status. On top of this, a mixed court was set up for the registration of immovable property as part of a land legislation inspired by the Torrens Act in Australia.

The protectorate favoured the establishment of extensive European settlement and this gave an impetus to the development of the country. The French were particularly privileged; part of the state domains was earmarked for their benefit and they occupied two-thirds of the posts in the administration.

In order to satisfy the aspirations of this French community the principal human liberties, including the freedom of the press, the rights of meeting, of free speech, and of forming associations were guaranteed them, and they were granted certain representative institutions; these privileges were gradually extended to Tunisians as well. Municipal institutions were set up in the principal cities; though only that in Tunis was elective. An institution known as the *Grand Conseil*, formed of Tunisian and French sections, both of which were elected, was given the function of voting the budget.

By allowing the French colony to participate in the direction of public affairs, the French protectorate was tending to establish a joint Franco-Tunisian sovereignty. Tunisian public opinion, or at least the educated classes, reacted sharply against a state of affairs which threatened to reduce their country to the status of a French colony. Resistance to the increasingly French character being given to it became apparent at the beginning of the present century; in 1907 a 'Young Tunisian' party was founded which maintained the right of Tunisians to manage their affairs themselves.

In 1920, after the First World War, to which Tunisia made a contribution, and under the influence of the ideas of President Wilson, a party was formed for the purpose of securing the emancipation of Tunisia as a nation. This took the name of the Tunisian Party of the Constitution (Destour). Under the direction of Shaikh Thaalibi, it devoted itself to resisting those actions of the protectorate which were offensive to national sentiment, while at the same time carrying on propaganda to win the support of the masses. This policy produced a series of incidents. In 1922 the reigning Bey, Sidi Naceur (al-Nasir), threatened to abdicate in support of the claims of the Destour. The Resident General, Lucien Saint, thereupon initiated systematic measures of repression, while at the same time promoting liberal reforms.

In 1934 a group of young nationalists, led by Habib Bourguiba (Bu Ruqaiba), a lawyer, and by Mahmoud Materi, a doctor, broke away from the Destour and founded a new party, the Neo-Destour, which was more modern in outlook and more dynamic. Roughly handled by Resident General Peyrouton, who put the leaders in a concentration camp, the Neo-Destour were now enthusiastically supported by the masses who considered them martyrs, while the original party, now known as the Old Destour, was confined to old-fashioned bourgeois circles.

When the Popular Front Government came to power in France, a liberal policy was adopted in Tunisia. The deported members of the Neo-Destour recovered their liberty and initiated a vigorous propaganda campaign throughout the country. This provoked strong competition from the Old Destour Party who were able to make use of the prestige of Shaikh Thaalibi who had been permitted to return from exile. A short and sometimes bloody struggle resulted in the complete triumph of the Neo-Destour.

The latter then took the opportunity to organize an elaborate network of cells and local federations. Habib Bourguiba, sure of the support of Tunisian opinion, undertook a campaign in France to convince French opinion of the justice of Tunisian national demands; this campaign was characteristic of his policy of seeking to obtain the independence of Tunisia through persuasion and negotiation, while at the same time maintaining friendly relations with France. Meanwhile, however, the Popular Front Government fell, French policy towards the protectorates hardened and, as the result, Habib Bourguiba changed his tactics and launched a campaign of civil disobedience. Demonstration followed demonstration and police action followed. This terminated in a riot in Tunis accompanied by bloodshed on 9 April 1938. Habib Bourguiba and other principal Neo-Destour leaders were arrested and brought before courts martial; the party itself, though dissolved and disorganized, continued to work underground.

In 1939 the Second World War diverted Tunisian attention from the internal political situation. Opinion was preoccupied by Mussolini's designs on Tunisia and disturbed by the defeat of France. It was hoped that the policy of Marshal Pétain and of Germany would defeat the Italian plans. Nationalist hopes were revived by the accession of a new Bey, Moncef (al-Munsif), who belonged to a branch of the ruling family which sympathized with the Neo-Destour Party.

When the Axis troops entered Tunisia in November 1942, Moncef Bey formed a ministry of nationalist tendencies; but he took care not to claim independence *vis-à-vis* France or to throw himself into the arms of the Germans, in spite of their advances and the favourable light in which the public regarded them. The Tunisian campaign, the victory of the Allies and the liberation of Tunis, which caused immense joy to the French colony, were a source of consternation to the Tunisian people who foresaw the return of the French in force and the consolidation of their domination. Their consternation reached its height when they learned of the arrest and deportation of Moncef Bey on 10 May 1943. His successor, Lamine Bey (al-Amin), was badly received by Tunisian public opinion and the beginning of his reign was difficult. The nationalist ministry was replaced by a ministry presided over by Salah eddin Baccouche; it was entirely subservient to France.

The Path to Independence, 1944–56

In the days following the Allied victory the authority of the French protectorate was reaffirmed under the vigorous leadership of General Mast. Extensive public works were undertaken to repair the devastation caused by the war; large-scale barrages were constructed. Meanwhile the Tunisians retired into themselves and brooded over their disappointed hopes.

The Neo-Destour leader, Habib Bourguiba, had been detained in French prisons from his arrest in 1938 until he was released by the Nazis in December 1942, after they had occupied Vichy France. Handed over by them to the Italians, he resisted attempts to extract from him a statement of sympathy with Axis aims and was eventually allowed to return to Tunisia in March 1943. In 1945, finding that his offers of collaboration were not welcomed by the French authorities, he escaped from Tunis and took refuge in Cairo. With the acquiescence rather than the encouragement of the Arab League, who mistrusted his policy of compromise, he set himself to make the Tunisian issue an international question, interesting not only the Arab states and eastern states such as India, but also the great western powers. Meanwhile, in Tunisia, the Secretary-General of the Neo-Destour, Salah ben Youssef, was reorganizing the party; after the death of the exiled Moncef Bey he won the support of Lamine Bey who thus gained a relative popularity.

In another sphere Tahar ben Ammar, President of the Tunisian section of the *Grand Conseil*, gathered together eighty independent and Neo-Destour personalities; these drew up a minimum programme of demands designed to restore the 'internal autonomy' of Tunisia. When this was rejected by the Resident General, Destourians and moderates held a joint meeting in September 1946, on the night of the Id al-Saghir, and undertook to fight together until independence was obtained.

However a new Resident General, M. Jean Mons, adopted a more sympathetic spirit towards the national movement; he tried to canalize it by forming a ministry composed of moderate nationalists, under the Presidency of Mustafa Kaak, *batonnier* of the order of advocates. The Neo-Destour saw a trap in this and promoted popular agitation against the Kaak Government. In 1950 the French Government decided to promise the Tunisians, through the mouth of the Premier, Robert Schuman, the achievement of internal autonomy by negotiated stages. M. Perillier, who was appointed Resident General to carry out this programme, requested the Bey to form a ministry of negotiation. The latter responded by appointing Mohamed Chenik, who had been Prime Minister under Moncef Bey, as President of the Council, and by giving ministerial office to Salah ben Youssef, Secretary General of the Neo-Destour, and to Salah Farhat, Secretary General of the Old Destour.

The ensuing negotiations resulted in an extension of the powers of the Tunisian Government, by which French control was somewhat relaxed but not suppressed, and in a reform of civil service regulations which gave priority to the recruitment of Tunisians. However, the stubborn resistance of the French colony, unwilling to abandon the co-sovereignty which it in fact exercised, slowed down the implementation of the reforms and embittered Franco-Tunisian relations. The main nationalist demand was for the establishment of a Tunisian Parliament; the Bey formulated this in his speech from the throne on 12 May 1951, instructing his ministers to seek the agreement of the French Government.

Premier Chenik thereupon went to Paris, in October 1951, and began conversations. He was, however, badly received by the French Government, on whom the French colony had exerted great pressure, and on 15 December 1951 they informed him in writing that they were unwilling to proceed with further reforms. The brusquely worded letter made a violent impact on public opinion in Tunis. Bourguiba decided to resume the struggle, to rouse the country, and to bring the issue before the United Nations.

A new Resident General, de Hautecloque, charged with suppressing the nationalist drive, arrested Bourguiba on 18 January 1952; he placed him in forced residence first at Tabarka near the Algerian frontier and then in the island of Galite, otherwise used only for a lighthouse. His principal supporters in the Neo-Destour Party were interned in the far south; a few weeks later the members of the Chenik Government were arrested also, though Salah ben Youssef and another minister succeeded in escaping and finding refuge in Cairo. The Bey, under constraint, appointed a new Government, amenable to French purposes, under the Presidency of Salah eddin Baccouche, Prime Minister in the days of General Mast.

Agitation now became general throughout the country and acts of terrorism began to take place against French police and against Tunisian personalities who collaborated with the representatives of France. The limited reforms proposed were surreptitiously resisted by the Bey until the French Government finally decided to send a new representative, M. Pierre Voizard, with the mission of reconciling the Bey and forming a ministry capable of introducing progressive reforms, tending towards internal autonomy. This Government was, however, immediately and violently attacked by the Neo-Destour; the terrorist movement spread more widely, provoking a French counter-terrorist movement. Organized bands of fighters, called by the French *fellagha* (a local arabic word for bandits afterwards regarded as a title of honour by the rebels), appeared in the mountains.

This position was suddenly changed for the better by a solemn declaration made on 31 July 1954 before the Bey at Carthage by the French Premier Pierre Mendès-France, who was accompanied by Marshal Juin. France recognized the right of Tunisia to complete autonomy and proposed the immediate opening of negotiations for a convention which would confirm the new status and regulate French interests in Tunisia. The Tunisian question was at last released from the *cul-de-sac* in which it had been confined since the letter of 15 December 1951; and the Declaration of Carthage roused great enthusiasm in the Tunisian people.

A Tunisian Government, with a large participation of Neo-Destour ministers, was immediately formed under the Presidency of Tahar ben Ammar. Mr. Bourguiba, who had already been transferred to France, was freed a few months later and followed the course of the negotiations in Paris in a semi-official capacity. A new Resident General, General Boyer de la Tour, offered a pardon to those members of the armed bands who laid down their arms.

The Paris negotiations were laborious and prolonged, encountering continued resistance on the part of the French colony; though a few members of it conducted a campaign to create a French public opinion favourable to the emancipation of Tunisia. Franco-Tunisian conventions determining the conditions of internal autonomy for Tunisia were finally signed on 3 June 1955, while Mr. Bourguiba on 1 June had already made a triumphant return to Tunisia where he was welcomed by delirious crowds.

Three months later Salah ben Youssef returned from Cairo and immediately took up a position opposed to the conventions accepted by Mr. Bourguiba; he considered these as binding Tunisia too closely to France. However a national congress of the Neo-Destour, held in Sfax in November 1955, unanimously approved the Bourguiba policy, holding that the conclusion of the conventions constituted a decisive stage on the road to independence.

Salah ben Youssef refused to appear before the Congress, whereupon the latter dismissed him from the office of Secretary General. He then attempted to rally dissidents and discontented, and undertook a violent campaign against Mr. Bourguiba, going as far as the assassination of certain of his followers; armed bands raised by him gained the *maquis* near the Algerian frontier, making common cause with the rebels in Algeria. The Tunisian Government, at the instance of the Neo-Destour, took strong measures to suppress this rebellion; with the result that Salah ben Youssef fled and took refuge in Tripolitania.

In November 1955 the French Premier at La Celle St. Cloud promised the independence of Morocco to the Sultan. This made very difficult the position of Mr. Bourguiba and the Tunisian Government who had signed conventions imposing severe limitations on Tunisian sovereignty. Mr. Bourguiba and Premier Tahar ben Ammar thereupon urged the Socialist Government which was now in power in France to give Tunisia the same complete independence which it had given to Morocco. This was in due course proclaimed in a protocol signed in Paris on 20 March 1956, while it was left to later negotiations to establish a new basis for relations and links of 'interdependence' which should take the place of the conventions signed on 1 June 1955. The 20th of March was designated as National Day.

The Independent Government, 1956–8

In March 1956 the Government of Tahar ben Ammar organized elections for a Constituent Assembly which was to elaborate a constitution which the Bey undertook to ratify. The list of 'National Unity' sponsored by Mr. Bourguiba, which contained a majority of militant members of the Neo-Destour, with some independents and trade unionists, was elected without opposition.

As soon as the Assembly met, it acclaimed the results of Mr. Bourguiba's policy and charged him to form the first Government of independent Tunisia. The Government was entirely Neo-Destour, five of its members being also trade unionists and leaders of the powerful *Union Générale des Travailleurs Tunisiens* (UGTT).

The first care of Mr. Bourguiba's Government was the restoration of order; the security services which had been still in French hands were now handed over to the Tunisian authorities. The Youssefist bands were tracked down, the principal agitators arrested, brought before a special court of justice, and given exemplary sentences. An end was put to the threat of anarchy in the countryside which had been stimulated by economic distress.

At the same time the Bourguiba Government established the principal attributes of full sovereignty. The recognition of foreign powers was secured and Embassies were established in the principal western and Arab countries. A small Tunisian army was organized, with the aid of the French army; and, finally, Tunisia was admitted to the United Nations with French sponsorship.

Internally, the Government proceeded to purge the administration of elements which appeared to it as untrustworthy; in order to give it a more national character, French heads of services were rapidly replaced by Tunisians. As Tunisia lacked qualified staff, the change-over could not be total; but it was sufficient to disturb that section of the French population from which the officials were drawn and a movement of withdrawal to France began. An agreement with the French Government, signed on 9 March 1957, provided for the maintenance in Tunisia, under contract with the Tunisian Government, of 3,500 French officials and teachers—about one-third of the previous total.

In another sphere Mr. Bourguiba set himself to modernize

certain out-of-date traditional institutions. The control of *habous* or religious endowments, known in the east as *awqaf*, was transferred to the department of state domains; the importance of the Zaituna Mosque University was reduced by confining it to religious instruction; a code of personal status was promulgated which gave women a status equal to that of men and included the abolition of plural marriage. The Sharia courts were suppressed and the system of modern secular justice reorganized.

These judicial reforms involved the disappearance of French courts which had been rendering justice in cases concerning Europeans ever since the Capitulations had been abolished and whose maintenance for a certain period had been foreseen by the conventions of 1955. Agreement was reached with the French Government on 9 March 1957; French jurisdiction in Tunisia was abolished but provision was made for the secondment of a number of French judges to the Tunisian courts in the capacity of counsellors.

The powerful trade union federation, the UGTT, directed by the youthful but strong Ahmad ben Salah, had supported Mr. Bourguiba against Salah ben Youssef. As a partner in the Government, in which, however, Ahmad ben Salah personally had refused office, it appeared that the UGTT might exert a decisive influence in the formation of social and economic doctrine and impose views of socialist tendencies. These influences alarmed the bourgeoisie and appeared likely to be an obstacle in the path of the financial aid which Tunisia was seeking in France and in the west.

Disturbed by the position taken up by Ahmad ben Salah, who had manifested the intention of founding a socialist party, Mr. Bourguiba and the Neo-Destour Party took steps to remove him from the commanding position which he occupied. A new trade union federation, the UTT, was promoted as a rival to the UGTT and, under pressure from the Government and the executive of the Neo-Destour, Ahmad ben Salah agreed to withdraw and to hand over direction of the UGTT to Ahmad Tlilli, a member of the Neo-Destour executive. Some months later, at the suggestion of Mr. Bourguiba, the two trade union federations drew together, with a view to re-establishing trade union unity.

At the end of October 1956 Franco-Tunisian relations suddenly became tense in connexion with the problem of Algeria. The arrest of leaders of the Algerian FLN, at the moment when the Sultan of Morocco was expected in Tunis for a conference at which it was anticipated that the solution of the Algerian problem would be proposed and the foundations of a North West African confederation in union with France would be laid, provoked a violent agitation. Tunisia withdrew her Ambassador from Paris and a number of incidents took place between the population and French troops stationed in Tunisia. By the end of the year more confident relations had been restored.

These, however, again deteriorated in 1957, owing to incidents arising out of the fighting in Algeria, the French Government reproaching the Tunisian Government for support given to the insurgents. Thus the French delegation at the Independence Day celebrations on 20 March 1957 withdrew as a protest against the presence of a delegation from the Algerian FLN. A little later French troops began to claim and exercise the right of 'hot pursuit' in the case of Algerian bands crossing the Tunisian frontier and on 31 May the Secretary-General of the Tunisian Foreign Office who was investigating an earlier incident was severely wounded near the frontier. At the end of June the French Government decided to transfer the bulk of its troops to Algeria, maintaining garrisons in Bizerta, Tunis, Sfax, Gafsa, Gabes, and Remada.

On 21 May the French Government suspended financial aid, and no agreement had been reached on the subject by the end of the year. On 25 July 1957 Sidi Lamine Bey was deposed, the monarchy abolished, and a Republic proclaimed by the Constituent Assembly. The latter conferred the title of President of the Republic on Habib Bourguiba and endowed him with full authority, pending the issue of a constitution. The change of régime was carried out without the slightest disturbance of order. The beylical family was placed under surveillance in a Tunis suburb and certain personalities of the former régime were made subject to prosecution with a view to the recovery of doubtfully acquired property and declared guilty of 'national unworthiness'.

In the late autumn the refusal of the French Government to supply arms for the Tunisian army, unless the Tunisian Government undertook to accept them from no other source, led the United States and the British Governments to make token deliveries of arms which were delivered on 16 November. It was made clear that the purpose of this was to prevent the Tunisian Government, which had repeatedly declared its attachment to the western bloc, from turning for arms to the Communist countries. Preoccupied by these repercussions of the Algerian struggle and by the presence of over 100,000 Algerian refugees on Tunisian soil, Mr. Bourguiba on 28 November, at the end of a visit to the King of Morocco, issued jointly with the latter an offer to mediate between the French Government and the Algerian FLN.

This offer, though not rejected outright by the French Government, was ignored in practice. When the optimism expressed by the French Minister for Algeria at the end of 1957 was falsified by the recrudescence of fighting early in 1958, the French Government attributed this to the facilities enjoyed by the Algerian FLN in Tunisia. Accordingly in February 1958 French planes bombed the Tunisian border town of Sakiet Sidi Yusuf, choosing a market day, killing a number of women and children, and destroying Red Cross vehicles which were making a distribution to refugees. This action, presented as a reprisal for the firing of a machine-gun on a French plane from a Tunisian town, caused strong expressions of indignation throughout the world, and the French Government was constrained to accept an offer of Anglo-American good offices. A neutralist and pro-Soviet trend of feeling in Tunisia was held in check, at least for the time being, only by the use which the Tunisian Government was able to make of this Anglo-Saxon intervention.

Meanwhile Tunisia steadily worked her way out of the French orbit, not without encountering economic difficulties. After losing French financial aid, the agreement for a common cereals market with France seemed certain not to be renewed. Its termination would involve a drop in cereal prices of 50 per cent., unless some alternative market could be found; this would create serious difficulties for producers who had enjoyed a good harvest. A similar prospect faced the producers of wine and citrus.

The reorientation of the Tunisian economy thus began to take place at a speed which was bound to involve serious temporary hardship. The budget for the coming year, amounting to 46 milliard francs, showed signs of austerity, and no investment budget could be drawn up for lack of external aid. It was announced that the new Tunisian Bank of Emission which was to take over from the Bank of Algeria would issue a dinar currency.

GOVERNMENT AND POLITICAL LIFE

The State Organization

On accession to independence, the Tunisian state began to undergo a process of transformation. The actual administrative structure established under the protectorate was not greatly modified; but it was integrated into the framework of Tunisian sovereignty. The latter found expression in the creation of new organs—a diplomatic service, an army, and information services.

In May 1956 a Constituent Assembly was elected, to which the Bey gave authority to establish a constitution. As mentioned above, this Assembly on 25 July 1957 declared the Tunisian state to be a Republic. In this way legislative and executive authority were concentrated in the hands of the President of the Republic. He was assisted by Secretaries of State, chosen and appointed by him and responsible to him. The period of office of the President of the Republic was to be laid down in the constitution which would also decide the manner in which he would be designated, determine his relations with a Legislative Assembly, and define his responsibilities.

The constitution was in course of preparation for over a year; but the proclamation of the Republic involved far-reaching modifications of the draft which had been drawn up. It was expected that the Constituent Assembly would adopt a system inspired by the constitutions of the United States and of Egypt. The Head of State would be elected directly by the people, hold office for a determined period, and exercise executive power. A national assembly also elected by the people would control the budget and vote the laws. There would be an independent judiciary, controlled by a Judicial High Council which would be appointed by the President and the Assembly; and finally an Economic Council with advisory functions.

Administration (January 1958)

The Secretary of State at the Presidency of the Republic was charged with co-ordinating the other Secretariats of State and National Defence. He was assisted by an Under-Secretary of State for Planning and by another for Defence. Co-ordination was assured by the cabinet of the Presidency of the Republic, of which the principal Secretary of State was in charge; it specifically included the direction of the Information Services, of Control of Expenditure, of recruitment and organization of the civil service, and of Protocol. The office of Grand Mufti was also attached to the Presidential Cabinet.

The remaining Secretariats of State were Foreign Affairs, Interior, Justice, Finance, National Economics, National Education, Agriculture, Public Health, Town Planning and Public Works, Posts, Telegraphs, and Telephones, Social Affairs, Youth and Sport.

Security was maintained by two police forces. One consisted

x

of urban police. These, which included Commissioners of Police
and Inspectors as well as rank and file, numbered about 2,000
effectives. The other consisted of rural police, provided by the
National Guard; these also constituted a general security force
and numbered about 3,000 effectives. Both forces were under
the authority of the Director-General of Security and were at
the disposition of the Governors responsible for local security.

The units of Tunisian administration at the lower level were
the municipalities and the *shaikhats*. About 100 of the main
cities and townships had municipal organizations and were
administered by an elected town council, for which women as
well as men were entitled to vote. This council elected a mayor,
except in the case of Tunis, where the Mayor is an official
appointed by the Government. A number of French subjects
were summoned to sit in the town councils, on the designation
of the Government. In the rural districts, administration was
assured by a Shaikh who was chosen from among local residents
and appointed by the Government after consultation with the
Governor.

At the summit, there were fourteen provinces (*wilayat*), each
administered by a Governor (*wali*) who represented the central
authority. The Governor had an elected Governorate Council
which voted the provincial budget and he was assisted by a
Secretary-General for administrative questions and by Delegates (*mutamid*) who represented the Governor in the sub-
divisions (*mendubiyat*) of the Province. These high officials,
appointed by the Government, had functions comparable to
those of prefects and sub-prefects in France; they no longer
exercised the fiscal and judicial functions of the former Caids
and *khalifas* (deputies) whom they replaced.

Though the civil service would henceforth be exclusively
Tunisian, the state, for a transition period whose length had not
been determined, retained officials of French nationality in its
various services; these were recruited on individual contract,
within the framework of the agreement for technical assistance
concluded with France on 9 February 1957. The number of
French officials to be thus retained was fixed at 3,500, including
teaching staff. This compared with a figure of 12,000 French
officials in the last years of the protectorate. French officials who
were not retained were reabsorbed into the civil service in
France.

Justice

The French protectorate introduced French courts in
Tunisia; these, as heirs of the Capitulations, administered

justice in all civil or penal cases in which a European was involved. The jurisdiction of the Sharia or Muslim religious law was, however, allowed to remain in matters affecting the personal status of Tunisian Muslims and in matters affecting real estate such as unregistered house property. For all other civil cases secular Tunisian courts were organized, and also for criminal cases concerning Tunisians. A mixed Franco-Tunisian court dealt with the registration of house and landed property.

In the French courts French law was applied, subject to the provisions of international law in the case of non-French Europeans. Muslim law was applied in the Sharia courts; while secular Tunisian law was applied in the Tunisian courts, for which purpose appropriate modern codes were drawn up and promulgated, including a Code of Obligations and Contracts, a Penal Code, and a Code of Civil and Criminal Procedure. The Mixed Court and the various courts applied a special land law for the registration of property in houses and land.

The independent Tunisian Government, being anxious to unify justice within the framework of Tunisian sovereignty, prepared the way for this by promulgating a Nationality Law and a Code of Personal Status for Tunisian subjects; this was inspired by the Sharia, but with modern modifications such as the introduction of monogamy, civil marriage, and judicial divorce; it was accompanied by the suppression of the Sharia courts whose functions passed entirely to the secular Tunisian courts. The Government next reformed the Code of Criminal Procedure, in order to assure the accused all the guarantees of modern law. A Commercial Code was also being promulgated. After taking these preparatory measures, the Tunisian Government requested France to give up its jurisdictional privileges. These were abolished by the agreement reached in March 1957, which regulated the transfer of their functions to Tunisian courts. For the time being, French judges continued to sit with Tunisian judges in cases involving French subjects and the proceedings were to be held in French for their benefit.

At the same time the Tunisian Government reorganized its own judicial machinery, decentralizing and increasing the number of courts. The new organization consisted of a High Court of Appeal, a Court of Appeal in each of the three cities of Tunis, Sfax, and Sousse, 11 Courts of First Instance, and 40 cantonal Courts of Justice. Only one judge sat in the latter; in the other courts the bench was taken by three judges. Criminal justice was rendered by a special court which held one

or two sessions annually at the seat of each Court of First
Instance. This criminal court was composed of three judges and
four assessors or jurymen (*mahallef*) who deliberated jointly.
The President could exercise a right of pardon in the case of
death sentences.

The Tunisian Government was proposing to carry out a complete revision of the existing codes in order to establish a unified
modern code, capable of general application after submission
to a vote of the National Assembly. For the time being Tunisian
Jews were still subject to their religious courts and to Mosaic
law in matters of personal status, while the very few Christian
Tunisians were subject to the French civil code.

Finally, a general reform of civil status was in progress. This
would bring about the adoption of family names and of marriage certificates; a reform of the care of minors which would
include the creation of a Trustee of Wards in every court; and
also of an office of notaries and the institution of bailiffs for the
execution of justice. A legislative service within the Ministry of
Justice would supervise and co-ordinate the drafting of codes
and of legislation.

Defence

Immediately after the proclamation of independence, the
Tunisian Government began to organize a national army,
creating a Secretariat of State for National Defence which was
directly attached to the Presidency of the Council. A Chief of
the General Staff and a Commander-in-Chief were responsible
for command. Compulsory military service was decreed. In
theory it should have produced contingents of 40,000 men
annually, but in practice they were likely to be of the order of
15,000–20,000.

The Tunisian army for the time being consisted only of one
mixed regiment of 3,000 men and of the former Beylical Guard
which was created under the protectorate but has now been
absorbed into the rest of the armed forces. It was intended to
bring this force to the strength of one light division. Its development was, however, held up by lack of officers; 110 Tunisian
cadets were under training at the French military college at
St. Cyr, while a school for n.c.o.'s was formed at Tunis and
had 200 pupils in training.

The Tunisian army was being formed with the assistance of
the French army which was providing French equipment and
applying French methods of training. A French liaison unit was
established in the Secretariat of State for National Defence. The
Tunisian army had its own uniform, modelled on that of the

eastern Arab armies. Orders were given in Arabic, though the drill was French.

Relations between the Tunisian army and the French forces stationed in Tunisia were friendly, though no organizational link had been established between them. The question of the stationing of French troops in Tunisia was a matter of dispute between the French and Tunisian Governments. It was possible that the latter would negotiate a military alliance with France for the common defence of Tunisia, though this would be subject to the previous withdrawal of French troops. Military agreement, which was ruled out in 1957, was reached in June 1958, when all French troops were withdrawn to Bizerta. It was noteworthy that some 3,000–4,000 Tunisians were still serving as volunteers in the French army at the end of 1957, principally in Europe.

Foreign Policy

Before the establishment of the French protectorate Italian and British influence competed with that of France in Tunisia. During the protectorate Italy attempted to regain influence in the Regency, in which Italian immigrants had settled in considerable numbers. These activities were increased under the Fascist régime. Italian establishments soon multiplied; an Italian hospital was created, banks opened, and an intensive propaganda was carried on throughout the country. During the occupation by the Axis forces, an emissary arrived from Mussolini to propose a Franco-Italian condominium to Moncef Bey; the latter dismissed him curtly. Mr. Bourguiba, as we have seen, refused to become the tool of Italian intrigue, and the local Italians were not highly esteemed by Tunisian public opinion. After the collapse of the Axis, the Italians of Tunisia, reduced by measures of expulsion applied by the French authorities, retired again into the background.

The influence of the eastern Muslim states, while important on the plain of Muslim solidarity, was nevertheless not decisive. Until 1920 it was Turkey which exercised the greatest attraction for educated youth; later Egypt became their model. Though the Tunisian leaders looked to Egypt and the Arab League for support during their struggle, they never actively committed their nation to the pan-Arab movement. The Tunisian position with regard to Israel was not so intransigent as that of the eastern Arab states; nor was there any systematic anti-Semitism. Tunisian Jews were considered on the same footing as Muslims.

The foreign policy of Mr. Bourguiba during the first year and a half of independence was directed in the first place to securing liberty of action for Tunisia and a leading place among the neighbouring countries. He drew near to the United States in order to balance French influence; and he made approaches to Libya, with whom a treaty was signed, and to Iraq and Saudi Arabia in order to balance Egyptian influence. Tunisia also placed great hopes in the United Nations, where Mr. Bourguiba's intervention in a session of the General Assembly was much remarked. This policy of equilibrium was reflected in a certain mistrust of Egypt, which became apparent at the end of 1957. The sentiment of Muslim solidarity in Tunisians was modified by their feeling of belonging to the west and by their ambition to be a pilot nation, at the junction of the east with the west. Of all the western nations it is the United States which is the most highly appreciated. This is due to the understanding which she had from the beginning shown for the Tunisian national movement and to the support which some of her nationals gave the Neo-Destour. Her propaganda was active and her influence profound. An American mission made a study of the country's economy soon after independence and Tunisia has received not inconsiderable United States aid (p. 336). Germany, though never having an active policy in Tunisian affairs, always enjoyed a great reputation; this survived her defeat. France still had a special position after the abandonment of her political domination, in spite of the bitterness engendered by the struggle. The culture of the *élite* was still French; the economy of the country was still unable to do without French assistance, and until 1958 the French army still held strategic points from Bizerta to Gabes.

Beyond this policy of equilibrium, it would seem that M. Bourguiba pursued the larger design of the alliance of the North African people. At times it was suggested that this alliance or confederation might be in some sort of commonwealth or economic relationship with France and perhaps with other Mediterranean and African countries. The realization of such a plan was for the time being ruled out by the conflict in Algeria. In February 1958 the bombing of Sakiet Sidi Yusuf and the Tunisian reaction, which resulted in the confinement of French troops in the country to their quarters for a period of four months, put an end for the time being to the consideration of such projects, and led to the acceptance of an Anglo-American offer of good offices. The breach between Tunisia and France was further accentuated on the acceptance by the Tunisian Government of the resolutions of the Maghrib Unity Conference held in Tangier at the end of April (p. 65). In

June 1958, however, the accession to power of General de Gaulle was speedily followed by the announcement of agreement by the French Government to the withdrawal of all their troops in Tunisia to the fortress area of Bizerta within four months. At the same time the Tunisian Government undertook to negotiate an agreement concerning the future status of the Bizerta naval and air base, which France recognized as being under Tunisian sovereignty; it was envisaged that it would be maintained with the help of French technicians. With regard to the Algerian war, Mr. Bourguiba followed a flexible policy, supporting the national claims of the Algerians diplomatically to the brink of rupture with France by whom he would like to be accepted as mediator.

In general, Mr. Bourguiba's policy, named *bourguibisme* by the French press, consisted in seeking to attain his ends by persuasion and manoeuvre. It was exercised on two fronts—that of France, which he induced, little by little, to accept his views; and that of his own people, whose sometimes contradictory hopes he had to canalize and lead on the course which he considered best for his country.

Political Parties and Trends

Tunisian life was entirely dominated by strong national sentiment, but there were of course degrees in the intensity of this sentiment. In the case of the former protectorate officials, collectively known as the 'makhzen', nationalism went side by side with a profitable co-operation with the French authorities; in certain other cases, on the contrary, it was exaggerated to the extent of xenophobia. Generally speaking, while the Tunisian was patriotic and jealous of his independence, he was in no way hostile to strangers. He had usually shown sympathy rather than hostility towards individual Europeans.

Apart from this, Tunisian opinion had two aspects. One was its natural tendency towards a traditional Muslim and Arab way of life; the other the attraction towards a modern form of life for which it found its model in the west. There also existed a division between a bourgeois, conservative, tendency on the one hand and a progressive tendency towards social reform on the other; the latter tendency was strongly developed in the younger people.

These shades of national and social sentiment expressed themselves in delicate shades of political grouping. A noticeable reformist tendency had been expressed in a political party which later disappeared; its moderating influences still existed among the independent bourgeoisie of French culture. The revolutionary and nationalist tendency was expressed both in the intransigent and pan-Arab Old Destour and in the more flexible and westernizing Neo-Destour. The latter group contained both conservative and progressive tendencies in social affairs.

The Neo-Destour was the only important political party; it was highly organized, with a considerable number of active militants, to the point that it gave the impression of being the only party. It possessed big cultural and corporative institutions which were formed under its aegis and which participated in its activities with the title of 'national organizations'. The Old Destour by 1957 was no more than a fossilized general staff with neither troops nor function. Nevertheless the pan-Arab sentiment which it represented remained active in certain sections of society and it was this tendency which Salah ben Youssef tried to mobilize in order to displace Mr. Bourguiba.

The Tunisian Communist Party consisted only of a few hundred militants, of whom many were Jews; it made no attempt to proselytize, but cautiously awaited its time. There was no specifically socialist party, though the tendency was to be found in the younger people; the intention attributed to the trade union leader, Ahmad ben Salah, to create a socialist party was at once frustrated by the action of the Neo-Destour.

While the masses obediently followed the Neo-Destour, which embodied their feelings very accurately and had organized them systematically, there existed also an independent bourgeoisie, moderate in its nationalism and definitely conservative. Though this was not constituted into a party, it had leaders, such as Tahar ben Ammar who was the President of the Council in the negotiations leading to the declaration of independence. By giving representatives of this bourgeoisie a place in the list of the 'National Union' which it presented to the electors for the Constituent Assembly, the Neo-Destour linked the group to itself. While consisting mainly of militant Neo-Destour members, the list also included militant trade unionists from the industrial, craft, and agricultural unions, and independents. By means of this formula of national union, the Neo-Destour hoped to keep with it and to co-ordinate the various political tendencies among which public opinion was divided.

The Neo-Destour's organizational structure assured it a powerful hold on public opinion and the masses. At the base, the militants were grouped in 2,000 local cells, directed by an elected committee which received its instructions from the central organs and controlled all political activity in its own sector. These cells were grouped in thirty-six regional federations; the committee of each federation was elected by delegates from the various cells and served as a link between them and the central organization. The central organization itself was composed of three elements. First the National President of the party, namely Habib Bourguiba, elected directly by all party members. Secondly there was a Political Committee of 10 members, also elected by general vote, though it could be brought up to strength by co-option if certain members were prevented by circumstances from participating. Thirdly there was the National Council, composed of the 36 presidents of the federation together with 20 members elected by a general vote. The elections were supervised by a National Congress which laid down the principal party directives. This body was composed of one representative from every cell; it met at irregular intervals of two or three years when convoked by the Political Committee. The Political Committee was in fact the body in which power resided, the National Council serving as an advisory body when consulted by it. The National President had a preponderant voice only in the Political Committee whose decisions were by agreement. The work of the Political Committee was carried on by a Secretary-General, assisted by two assistant Secretaries, a Treasurer, and a Director of Administration. The Secretary-General enforced strict discipline in the party and was empowered to order expulsions.

The party had also organized 'Destour Youth Associations'. These had two purposes; the indoctrination of the young and the formation of social and political 'action groups'. Each cell had a youth association of about fifty members. There were also feminine groups for propaganda and social action. A school for training and propaganda was responsible for the formation of leaders.

The Neo-Destour Party drew its resources from the subscriptions of its adherents and from donations; its budget was important. Its headquarters were installed in a handsome building in the centre of Tunis; each federation and indeed each cell had its own rooms and services housed in well-furnished buildings. Finally, the party possessed a daily paper, *El Amal* (Action) which was entirely financed and managed by it.

Newspapers and Organs of Opinion

Liberty of opinion and expression were written into the draft constitution; they were, however, limited by press laws which gave the Government sufficient powers to enable it to forbid publications, foreign or Tunisian, which might be of a nature to obstruct its political or administrative actions. The press, therefore, whether in Arabic or French, took care to avoid violent attitudes.

The Government also controlled broadcasting, which had two parallel services, one in Arabic and one in French. While in the latter language news and commentaries were generally given with considerable objectivity, the Arabic transmissions were more directly coloured by government influence and propaganda. The Arabic service had a large audience in Tunisia and there was also a special transmission for Algeria in which nationalist Algerians co-operated. Some broadcasts were in dialect.

The Secretariat of State for Information, which was directly attached to the Presidency of the Council, directed this propaganda and co-ordinated the various means of influencing public opinion. These included broadcasting, the foreign and local press, for which the department was directly responsible, newsreels which a special branch supplied to all the Tunis cinemas, and the press, local and foreign. The department was responsible for the publication of documentation about the Government's activities. It also founded a school of journalism to train young Tunisians destined for this career. In general, the Government attached great importance to information and propaganda services.

The Tunisian press in Arabic until October 1957 had two daily papers—al-Sabah (Morning) and al-Amal (Action). Al-Sabah, founded in 1950, was originally the organ of the Neo-Destour. Financed largely by merchants from the island of Jerba, it took the side of Salah ben Youssef in the crisis of November 1955. For this reason the Neo-Destour founded a newspaper, al-Amal, run entirely by itself. This rapidly won an important place in Tunisian public opinion and has a circulation of 20,000. Meanwhile al-Sabah survived and retained a great portion of its readers and a circulation of 15,000 though it abandoned propaganda for Salah ben Youssef. It represented a pan-Arab tendency and continued a cautious opposition to the Government until its suppression in the autumn of 1957. It was permitted to resume publication in March 1958.

The former moderate organs, al-Zahra and al-Nahda, have disappeared and no other paper has taken their place in this respect. The Old Destour had a weekly, al-Istiqlal (Independence); this only reached a limited circle, having a circulation of 2,000–3,000. Each of the trade unions, the UGTT, the UTT, and the UNAT published a weekly. There were also a number of other more or less regular publications with small circulations: *al-Talia* (Vanguard) of the Communist Party (1,500); *al-Liwa al-Barlamani* (The Parliamentary Standard), independent and appearing irregularly; and *al-Shaab* (The People), pan-Arab (2,000–3,000). There was also an illustrated, *al-Lataif* (Novelties) which appeared under the auspices of the French Embassy.

The Tunisian press in the French language had two organs of political opinion; a daily, the *Petit Matin* and a weekly, *L'Action*. The *Petit Matin* belonged to a Tunisian Jew who was a member of the Government and it generally expresses a governmental point of view; it had a Neo-Destour outlook, but was more definitely western. It printed 12,000 copies; its readers included the best Tunisian intellectual circles and a certain number of liberal-minded French people. *L'Action* was a weekly, founded by a young and modern-minded group who took a view relatively independent of the Government in spite of belonging to the Neo-Destour. Enlivened with satirical cartoons it did not fear to tackle the problems of the day with objectivity and it had French contributors; it attracted many readers and its sphere of influence extended beyond Tunisia. Its circulation until its suppression in September 1958 was about 25,000.

The local French press, in the full sense of the term, had in 1956 and 1957 three dailies: two morning papers, *La Dépêche Tunisienne* and *La Presse*, and one evening paper, *Tunis-Soir*. *La Dépêche Tunisienne* was the organ of the French bourgeoisie of conservative tendencies and took a neutral attitude towards government policy; after independence its circulation soon dropped from 30,000 to 15,000. *La Presse*, which was linked with the Paris paper *Combat*, appealed to minor officials who were formerly of Gaullist sympathies and also had a circulation of 15,000. *Tunis-Soir*, a topical news-sheet without other appeal, ceased to appear in the autumn of 1957. A weekly, *Lundi-Matin*, published under the auspices of the French Embassy, followed a French official line and was little read. Most of the Paris papers were to be found in Tunis. *Le Monde* and *L'Express* were the most widely read, particularly by Tunisians. The Egyptian press had a significant appeal.

SOCIAL CONDITIONS

Education

The extension of education has been one of the most remarkable features of the last half-century in Tunisia and was a determining factor in the evolution of the country. The protectorate administration latterly achieved a spectacular success in this field. Schools were built all over the country, so that in 1955 there were 4,400 classes of which 2,000 had been added in the last ten years. The school population increased from a few hundreds in 1881 to 260,000 by the end of 1955; in 1957 it reached 316,000 with 5,500 classes. Teaching of a scholastic type, which was given in the Quranic schools, was replaced by a modern type of teaching in which the French language held a principal place.

Education, still far from reaching all the potential school-age population—amounting probably to 600,000–700,000—thus attained a school attendance of about 50 per cent., which compared favourably with many Muslim and other Arab countries. In 1957 it was estimated that all boys in the towns received some education, while in the countryside children, and more particularly girls, had as yet inadequate or no facilities for instruction. The current figures showed 217,000 boys receiving education as compared with 99,000 girls. The Tunisian state planned to continue this programme and extend education to all the population; since the latter was increasing at the rate of 120,000 annually, this would require a teaching staff and financial resources which Tunisia did not yet possess. The running of public instruction at the existing scale was already costing the state $7\frac{1}{2}$ milliard francs annually, the equivalent of 18 per cent. of the budget, while the cost of building new schools was another 1 milliard. If the cost of the French cultural mission, of private institutions, and of the youth associations is added to the expenditure by the state, it can be said that the education of the youth of Tunisia was costing more than 12 milliards annually; this equalled one-third of the ordinary state budget, or 4–5 per cent. of the national revenue.

Educational Policy. Immediately after the achievement of independence the educational policy of the Tunisian state began to be directed to the creation of a national culture, using the Arabic language. For the time being, however, the educational authorities were unable to dispense with French as a medium of education for modern science; this fact, together with the existing cultural and economic links created between Tunisia and France by the protectorate, made it necessary to use caution in carrying out their policy.

Reforms introduced so far have been designed, firstly, to make Arabic the basic language of instruction in the primary stage—the two first classes being entirely Arabic—and to enlarge the sphere of the Arabic language and culture in secondary education; secondly, to merge the different types of education (modern education in French; mixed Franco-Arab education; Muslim education in Arabic) into one unified national system. For this purpose the Ministry of Education instituted a Tunisian diploma of secondary studies. This scheme of study had two divisions, one a purely Arab curriculum, which would in time replace the teaching given in the Zaituna Mosque; the other a mixed Franco-Arab curriculum. Each of these sections had literary, modern, and technical branches. It was intended that this should eventually be the only system; for the time being, however, the establishments of the Ministry of Education continued to prepare for the traditional diplomas recognized in the French educational system.

The development of a unified type of education in Arabic, giving expression to the new sense of Tunisian nationality, would inevitably be slow. As a nation, Tunisia lacked the necessary educational resources, and though measures had been taken for the speedy formation of the necessary teaching staff, it would require at least ten years to train a sufficient number of Tunisians. Meanwhile, French would remain indispensable as the medium for teaching science, at least in the advanced stages, during the whole of this period and in all probability for a long time afterwards.

The establishments dependent on the Ministry of Education were classified as below:

1. *Primary and technical courses.* These were followed by 237,000 pupils of whom 10,000 were in technical schools. They involved five years of study. The programme was uniform, the two first years being given in Arabic and the other three partly in Arabic and partly in French. There were 6,000 teachers, of whom more than a third were French.

2. *Secondary courses.* These were followed by 11,341 pupils. They were of four types. Firstly, the so-called Zaituna type of instruction, given in the establishments formerly dependent on the Zaituna Mosque. These still prepared for a diploma given by the Mosque University, but would in time be integrated with the Arabic curriculum of the government schools. They already had the same entrance examination and the same curriculum. Secondly, the purely French and the Franco-Arab colleges, having 11,272 pupils. These included the former lycées and French secondary schools and the Sadiqi College, founded by the Bey Sadoq before the French occupation. These prepared for French diplomas, as well as for the Tunisian diploma which would become the rule in a few years time; the staff included 300 French teachers.

3. *Higher Education.* This had two distinct sections. The first was the University mosque of al-Zaituna. This kept its character as a University of Islamic sciences and had two sections, one of religious

sciences, properly so-called, the other of Arabic literature. The second was the *Institut des Hautes Études*, having 1,683 students. This functioned under the patronage, and technical direction, of the University of Paris which also supplied most of the teaching staff; it prepared for a certain number of higher degrees in the French faculties of arts, science, law, and medicine. Most of the students completed their studies in France.

4. *Training schools for teachers.* Hitherto a training school in Tunis had been preparing one hundred primary teachers, of both sexes annually. To this it was proposed to add three further training schools during 1958 while, for the time being, reliance was being placed on shortened training courses. It would, however, be difficult to meet the needs of the country for 500–600 new teachers every year. For secondary school teachers, intensive courses had been organized to provide more teachers of modern science and of the Arabic language.

French Educational Establishments. When responsibility for public instruction was transferred to the Tunisian state by the Franco-Tunisian Agreement of 3 June 1955, France retained the right to maintain a cultural mission at her own expense; this could own and manage primary, secondary, and technical schools; the latter had 40,000 pupils of whom 1,825 were Tunisians, and their working budget amounted to 1½ milliard francs. This French cultural mission provided Tunisia with an education having the standards of that of metropolitan France and it put this education at the service of the European population. The same task was also fulfilled by private educational institutions which were, for the most part, supported by Catholic congregations. They provided education for an important number of Tunisians, 5,366 out of a total of 14,000 pupils.

There existed also other foreign cultural institutions which were independent of the state. These included the *Alliance Israélite*, which maintained the Mosaic tradition; the *Alliance Française*, which propagated the higher intellectual and artistic culture of France, and the Information Centre of the United States which disseminated a knowledge of American thought. Mention should also be made of the *Institut des Belles Lettres Arabes*; this was founded by the White Fathers and brought Europeans and Muslims together for the study of the Arabic language and of Tunisian sociology, in an atmosphere of mutual understanding. There being as yet no modern university in Tunisia, a great many Tunisians completed their studies in France.

It seemed clear that Tunisian education, although nominally based on Arabic, would have in fact to continue for the time being to give a large place to the French elements with which it had been deeply impregnated under the protectorate. If students were to pass to advanced studies, they would require a solid grounding in French in the secondary stage and to have made a beginning in the primary stage. Tunisia would still have to rely on French teachers for a long time.

The mixed type of education, likely to prevail for a considerable period, had in fact already proved its serviceability. The present youthful governing class came largely from the Sadiqi College where they received this type of education under the protectorate and it had been increasingly adopted in the programme of all institutions of secondary education. The establishments of the French cultural mission, with their specifically French programmes and standards, could serve as a stimulus and pattern to the specifically Tunisian educational establishments of Tunisia, both public and private.

The extension of education to the whole school-age population must be a matter of many years, both because of the large capital sum which must be invested and because of the lack of teaching staff. During 1957 and 1958 600 classes have been added each year with an extra 25,000 pupils. This only equalled about a third of the growth in the population and it would seem difficult to increase an effort which already placed a heavy burden on the Tunisian budget.

Scientific institutes in Tunis included the Pasteur Institute, the Arloing Zootechnical Institute, and the Oceanographical Institute at Salambo. There was also a fine library, situated in the Suq al-Attarin.

Youth and Sport

In 1957 more than half the population of Tunisia were less than 20 years old; and young people played a big part in social life. The Neo-Destour had long realized that the future of the nation depended on these young people and had sought their support. The Bourguiba Government was particularly solicitous for their welfare and for this purpose established a Secretariat of State for Youth and Sport, coming directly under the Presidency of the Council; in the course of a year, it founded a number of new youth organizations.

Institutions for the protection of children included four main types of establishments. The first were infant welfare centres, dealing with children up to 4 years old. These functioned under the aegis of the Ministry of Health. The second were holiday and camping associations subsidized by the Government. The third were the children's homes, administered by the Secretariat of State for Youth. These took needy but not orphaned children, for whom there were no available places in the schools, looked after them during the daytime, and provided a simplified elementary education. There were 60 of these homes with 5,000 children. Fourthly, there were the children's villages. These collected and took complete charge of abandoned orphans, from 5 to 14 years old. This work, begun by a French philanthropist, was greatly extended by the Secretariat of State for Youth. Four villages housed 3,000 children; these received elementary education and instruction in scouting, and were taught a trade.

There were five principal youth movements. The first was the Association of Tunisian Boy Scouts, having 22,000 members affiliated to the world movement. Secondly, there were the Youth Work Groups. These were groups of unemployed, between the years of 20 and 30, who were given work for four hours a day and received a type of education designed to build character (3,000). Thirdly, there was the Destour youth movement, organized by the Neo-Destour cells. Members received training in scouting and in political ideas; they numbered 70,000–80,000. Fourthly, there were youth hostels and holiday travel. Fifthly, there was the organization known as the *Union Générale des Étudiants Tunisiens*.

The various sporting leagues and associations were given a specifically Tunisian character and were headed by the Higher Tunisian Sports Committee which supervised and subsidized French as well as Tunisian Sports Associations. A National Institute for Physical Education was also created in order to provide for the training of teachers and supervisors.

The Secretariat of State for Youth ran a National Centre for the training of officials for these organizations. It was very active and all these bodies were in course of rapid development. The budget for children and adolescents amounted to $1\frac{1}{2}$ milliard francs.

Health

The rapid growth of the population (2·0 per cent. per annum) was due not only to the high birth-rate but also to the steady lowering of the death-rate, particularly of infant mortality, as the result of the development of the medical services and the improvement in general hygiene.

The Public Health budget, which was only 2 per cent. of the total budget in 1920, had risen to 8 per cent. by 1955, and in 1957 amounted to 7 milliards. During the same period the number of hospital beds rose from 1,430 to 5,735, or to about 7,000 if nursing homes and other establishments not dependent on the Government were included. Measures undertaken by the Public Health services had succeeded in virtually eliminating the worst epidemics and in reducing endemic diseases such as malaria, syphilis, and trachoma.

The Public Health administration provided medical services in the cities, including six large hospitals in Tunis and five in the provinces; these facilities were augmented by private nursing homes and clinics, specialist institutes, and general and ophthalmic dispensaries. In rural districts the services included 40 dispensaries with nursing facilities and 177 rural dispensaries and consulting rooms. Each area had a doctor of the Public Health services attached and travelling male nurses. Centres and dispensaries of social hygiene and preventive medicine were directed by doctors who were on the staff of the Public Health services or on special contracts.

The staff running these services were 75 Public Health service doctors, 251 medical hospital assistants, 91 medical staff on contract, and 2,055 nurses and midwives. Including doctors in private practice, there were 600 doctors practising in Tunisia, that is to say 1 for every 55,000 inhabitants. About 400 of these were French.

The Pasteur Institute in Tunis had to its credit a number of discoveries of world importance in the investigation of typhus, recurrent fevers, and trachoma.

Town Planning

At the end of the Second World War the protectorate administration instituted a Commissariat of Reconstruction whose purpose was to repair war damage. Under its direction the European quarters of Sfax and of Sousse, which had been almost entirely destroyed, were replanned and rebuilt in modern style. The same service established plans for the main towns; in Tunis this took in an entirely new zone, where a complete new quarter has been built. The Tunisian Government made the service into a Secretariat of State of Town Planning and Housing. This Ministry continued to dispose of war damage payments provided by France but not yet expended. It continued the town-planning and housing schemes in a modified form. Its chief preoccupation was to provide adequate housing for the large, only semi-employed working-class population, which had been attracted to the larger towns and particularly to Tunis where it was lodged in miserable

Y

quarters composed of hovels, constructed by the inmates themselves, with no water supply or drains. The service was also endeavouring to improve rural housing which consisted for the most part of huts of beaten earth or of straw; well-planned villages were being created in the zones newly brought under cultivation.

ECONOMIC CONDITIONS

The economic life of Tunisia was characterized by a rapidly growing population which there were only limited resources to support. These resources were mainly agricultural, though agricultural productivity in Tunisia was very irregular on account of the climate. Mineral resources were limited and already very fully developed; extensive exploration had so far failed to discover oil. There was thus no apparent local source of energy and the prospects for an extension of industry were in consepuence very doubtful.

During the last twenty-five years agricultural productivity had increased only by 25 per cent., while the population had increased by 60 per cent. Meanwhile the needs of this population had themselves been growing, quite apart from its numerical increase. The growing number of young people constituted an extra charge, while modern progress created new needs. Employment had not kept pace with the population growth; unemployment was increasing and purchasing power remained low.

From these causes there ensued a general economic lack of balance which showed itself in three main features. Firstly, there was a lack of balance between production and consumption which climatic causes in any case caused to vary greatly from year to year; the deficit had to be made up by imports. Secondly, there was a permanent deficit in the balance of trade, on an average 30 per cent., which had hitherto been covered by a French grant. Thirdly, there had in recent years been a deficit in the budget, of which the expenditure column has trebled since the war; this had, however, been to some extent corrected since independence when the French Government became responsible for certain charges which formerly fell on the Tunisian Government.

This position had been summed up in the phrase that 'population and public expenditure are developing more rapidly than production, while production is developing more rapidly than employment' and, consequently, more rapidly than purchasing power. Hence there was growing pauperization, masked by foreign aid. This was the situation existing at the end of the protectorate with which the economic planning of the Tunisian state had to deal.

Agriculture

Agriculture played the largest part in Tunisian economy; the rural population formed 64 per cent. of the whole, while the proportion of agricultural products in the gross internal production was 40 per cent. Although considerable development took place under the protectorate, agriculture was capable of much further expansion.

Land Tenure and Peasantry. Land tenure in Tunisia took three forms: *melk*, or freehold; *habous* (the oriental *waqf*), or religious endowments, administered either by the descendants of the donor—private *habous*—or by a state organization—public *habous*; and, thirdly, tribal common land which belonged to a given ethnic group.

Land legislation was of two kinds; on the one hand Quranic and customary, amended by secular legislation and thus constituting a régime of common law; on the other hand a modern code, instituted in 1885. This was based on the Torrens Act of Australia and applied to properties registered through the decisions of the Mixed Court.

Land reforms introduced by the protectorate tended in the first place to favour the settlement of European colonists, by giving a secure title to acquisitions. Later the protectorate authorities took steps to guard small owners against speculation and to enable the fellah, that is, the peasant who was cultivating land on a big *habous* estate without a legal title, to acquire his holding. These measures made it possible also to divide common lands among the individual members of a tribe.

The application of these laws was very slow. Up to the end of 1957 registration of land and surveying had been completed only for one-quarter of the cultivable area of the Republic. The allotment of *habous* land for the benefit of the occupants had not covered more than a sixth of the total area of such lands. The official allotment of common land had not covered more than a tenth of this category; though most tribes had themselves carried out a semi-official distribution to their members. On the other hand, all lands belonging to the private domain of the state had been distributed or sold, either to colonists or to Tunisians.

European colonists and enterprises held 1,825,000 acres, equal to one-tenth of the total productive area of Tunisia;

these properties, which were for the most part acquired directly from Tunisian owners or as concessions from the state domains, were practically all situated in the most fertile area of the country, the Tell. The greater part of them were in the posses-sion of French settlers and the average size of their holdings was about 750 acres. Italian settlers generally had holdings of only about a tenth of this size, viz. 75 acres each. Their holdings in all amounted to about one-tenth of the total. Many settlers, in addition to their own holdings, rented and worked the lands of their Tunisian neighbours.

The settlers' holdings (as also the estates of the few big Tunisian landowners) amounting in all to about 10,000 farms covering altogether 3,200,000 acres, were exploited according to the best modern practice and with the aid of the latest mechanized instruments. The owners generally farmed their land themselves and employed Tunisian day-labourers. More than 12,000 tractors and 3,000 combine harvesters were in use.

Land Categories and Distribution, 1957

('000 acres)

Tribal common lands		7,410
Habous lands		3,211
State domain:		
Official colonization	803	
Tunisian allotments	1,173	1,976
Melk (freehold) land (1,050 allotted to private colonists)		5,434
Summary		
Total allotted to Tunisians (collectives, *habous*, state domain)		2,347
Total remaining to be allotted		2,717
Total European owned		1,853
Area of registered land		4,693

Note: In the absence of an agricultural census, figures are estimates based on available data.

Two types of agricultural contract, peculiar to Tunisia, are worth mentioning. One is the *enzel*, which makes it possible to acquire the property of a trust (generally *habous*) by simply paying a perpetual annual rent. The other is the *mgharsa* or planting lease. This makes it possible to acquire from the owner the concession of a piece of land for planting with fruit-trees (generally olives); half the land then becomes the freehold of the planter.

Though there were a certain number of big estates generally run by their Tunisian owners on modern lines, the majority of native Tunisian farms were small and cultivated by archaic methods. In the centre and south, where there is a large beduin population, on account of the prevailing drought, the land yielded occasional crops only.

In order to raise the standard of living of these cultivators, measures which were initiated under the protectorate were being further extended. The proper keeping of accounts was being recommended so as to permit them to have the assistance of government agricultural loans; producer co-operatives were being organized in increasing numbers in order to make modern mechanized equipment available; instructors had been trained to improve the methods of cultivation, and olive groves were being planted by the state for their benefit.

Some 10 milliard francs had in the course of the last seven years been advanced by France and invested in ways designed to assist needy peasants. A Fund for the Revival of the Centre and South has recently been created; state loans were to be put at its disposal and its task would be the revival of agriculture in the most afflicted districts.

Since the dryness of the climate was the greatest obstacle to agricultural productivity, a number of water-catchment devices had been and were being built, such as small retaining works for surface water and the boring of artesian wells in the pre-Saharan area. A series of three large barrages had been built in the valleys of the Majarda and its tributaries. This work would provide Tunisia with one-fifth of her needs in electricity, would supply Tunis with drinking water, and would irrigate 125,000 acres of land which were producing cereals but would in future be dedicated to market-gardening and forage crops. Important works had also been undertaken for soil preservation and the prevention of erosion.

Tunisian agriculture was assisted by a Research Institute of which the scientific studies, particularly on cereals, have had a beneficial influence outside as well as within Tunisia; and also by a Zootechnical Institute. There were two agricultural schools, one concerned with the training of engineers; the other with that of inspectors.

Agricultural Products

Tunisia's main natural resources in agriculture are forests, esparto grass, and pasture. The one important forest area is situated in the north-west of the Republic, in Khrumerie; it is formed by cork-trees and deciduous oaks. In other mountainous regions of the north there are wooded areas of scattered pines. A programme of reafforestation was being undertaken and several thousand hectares of coastal dunes had been converted into forest.

Land Use in Tunisia, 1957

(*'ooo acres*)

Total area	31,250
Productive area:	
Forests	2,250
Esparto grass . . .	1,500
Pasture	7,500
Cereals	4,250
Fruit trees and olives .	2,250
Various	500

Esparto grass covers great stretches of the steppes in the centre and south. The collection of this was an appreciable source of income for the beduin population. Hitherto, the entire crop had been exported to Great Britain in its natural form, but a paper-pulp factory was being erected. This region also contains wide pasture lands for sheep and camels; the meagre pasturage could be improved by better management.

The cultivation of cereals was more developed than that of any other crop; 4,250,000 acres were sown and produced 40 per cent. of the agricultural income. Both hard and soft wheat and barley were cultivated. Harvests of 8–12 cwt.[1] per acre could be depended on in the Tell; but those of the centre and south were poor and uncertain. The cereal crop normally exceeds Tunisia's own needs; surpluses were disposed of on the French market while France used to supply Tunisian needs in drought years. An extensive system of mechanized silos provided for the storage of the crop whose price was fixed by the Wheat Office.

The 90,500 acres of vines were almost entirely in European hands; the principal vineyards were around Tunis and on Cape Bon. Wine was exported to Europe and provided 6 per cent. of the agricultural income. The market-gardening and fruit-growing areas were in the same region. There were $2\frac{1}{2}$ million citrus trees and 12 million fruit trees of various kinds. The citrus—oranges, lemons, and pomelos (grape-fruit)—formed an

---

[1] The French hundredweight (quintal) = 100 kilos.

important export to France, as also did early vegetables, particularly artichokes. Almonds were grown principally in the centre and south.

The cultivation of the olive occurs throughout Tunisia, but it is above all concentrated in the coastal plain near Sousse and Sfax. The groves around Sfax, replanted since the protectorate and covering 1 million acres, are the finest in the world. There are estimated to be over 26 million olive trees in Tunisia at present and 500,000 more are being planted annually. The preparation of olive oil is an important industry and source of commerce. But the production of oil is very irregular owing to its dependence on the rains; it varies between 20,000 and 100,000 tons annually and represents 16 per cent. of the agricultural income.

In the oases of the pre-Saharan Shott district there are 2½ million date-palms. The *deglet ennour* date, near Tozeur, is highly esteemed and is the only type exported (3,000–8,000 tons annually).

Average Production of Main Crops
(*Metric tons unless otherwise stated*)

Cork	6,000–7,000
Esparto grass . . .	60,000–100,000
Wheat and barley . . .	10,000–30,000
Wine	22 million galls.
Citrus	30,000–50,000
Other fruit . . .	30,000–50,000
Olives	40,000–80,000
Dates	30,000–40,000

Stock-breeding produced 20 per cent. of the agricultural income; the value of the flocks amounted to 65 milliards and if climatic conditions did not frequently cause losses up to 30 or 40 per cent. the figure would be much higher. The broad-tailed sheep, a speciality of Tunisia, forms the basis of the industry (3 million head in a good year) in the central and southern zones. There is a small camel-breeding industry in the same area.

In the north, cattle (500,000 head) take the place of the sheep. The local breed of cattle are small but well-adapted to the climate. Some settlers cross it with zebu. Around Tunis, there are a few dairy farms, limited by the lack of fodder. The breeding of horses—barbs, sometimes crossed with arabs—and of mules is diminishing. It is impracticable to give an estimate of the meat produced, on account of the great variation in the number of animals from year to year.

Mines and Industry

Tunisia has no coal except some poor quality lignite which was only worth exploitation during the war. Extensive search has not revealed oil in appreciable quantities. The barrages in course of construction will not produce more than 50 million kwh. annually. It was therefore necessary to import coal, and, above all, oil products, in order to provide the energy required. The consumption of electric power, 250 million kwh. in 1957, was increasing at the rate of 10–12 per cent. annually.

Exploration for oil had by 1957 yielded only a supply of natural gas on Cape Bon; this produced 12 million cubic metres annually and supplied the city of Tunis. Imports of coal amounted to 30,000 tons and of petroleum products to 350,000 tons.

Certain other mineral resources, on the other hand, are relatively extensive; they are principally phosphates, iron ore, lead, zinc, and marine salt. Phosphate mines, of which the chief ones are near Gafsa, are abundant; but the phosphates from them have a lower percentage of phosphorus than those from Morocco; the companies concerned have therefore to resort to various processes such as washing, crushing, and the preparation of superphosphates, in order to compete on world markets. The price of the entire North African output was regulated by a Phosphates Office in Paris. The Tunisian output of phosphates amounted to one-tenth of the world consumption; annual exports averaged 2 million tons, worth 6 milliard francs—equal to one-sixth of the total Tunisian exports in 1955. Iron ore is also abundant, particularly along the Algerian frontier; the extent to which it was worked varied with the world demand. In 1957 it was flourishing, about a million tons a year being exported, to a value of 3,785 million francs, forming about one-tenth of the total Tunisian exports for 1955. Lead and zinc are worked in various deposits in the north of the country; here also the output depended on the world demand. In 1955 exports were rated at 2,753 million francs or 7 per cent. of the total. Two large salt pans, one at Tunis, the other at Monastir, produced about 100,000 tons of salt annually, of which four-fifths were exported.

Two types of local industry have been created in Tunisia: processing of local raw materials and processing of imported materials. The former includes the treatment of mineral products, such as the enrichment of phosphates and lead founding;

the preparation of building materials—for example two large cement works which export 200,000 tons of cement as well as supplying local needs—lime kilns, plaster kilns, brick works, and the manufacture of water pipes for plumbing; and the preparation of foodstuffs, flour and semolina mills, macaroni factories, oil presses, preserved fruit factories, fish canning, &c., most of which is used for home consumption. The latter (processing imported materials) included tobacco (of which some however is locally grown), chocolate, jam, woven goods, shoes, chemical products, paint, agricultural products, and building material in metal.

This picture may give the impression that there was a considerable development of industry in Tunisia. There were in fact a number and variety of enterprises; but they were for the most part small, and worked below capacity on account of the limited size of the Tunisian market and the difficulties of getting into the international market. Tunisian industry was not extensive.

Two projects being studied are worth mention. One was that for processing esparto grass for paper-pulp; the other that for exploiting the mineral resources of the marine marshes (*sebkha*) of Zarzis in the south of the country; these include potash, magnesium, hydrochloric acid, &c.

Hopes were also placed in a better exploitation of the fishing industry, which had an annual output of 13,000 tons. The sea off the Tunisian coast, which is shallow on the eastern side, is well stocked with fish; sardines are caught by night fishing with lights; tunny with the crawl and various types with drag nets. Lobsters are fished off the Isle of La Galite; and sponges off Sfax. Factories for the preparation of tinned tunny and sardines already exist; a better organization of the industry should permit its extension.

Labour and Trade Unions

Much French social legislation was introduced into Tunisia under the protectorate. This included the freedom to form unions; collective contracts; the inspection of labour; the regulation of hours of work, with an eight-hour day for women and children; compensation for accidents; paid holidays and family allowances in industry and commerce.

The independent Tunisian Government developed these measures. Hours of work in agricultural occupations were fixed at 2,700 hours per year, with a guaranteed holiday; a system of pensions was introduced for the workers on state enterprises,

and in the mines and docks; family allowances were contrac-
tually extended to certain agricultural enterprises. Here however reform was hampered by the rapid growth of the population and the mass of unemployed. For the same reason it was
impossible to found a system of social security comparable to
that of France, though the working class now received free
medical assistance.

The legal minimum wage was fixed by law, according to the
district. In the Tunis zone, the basic wage for the unskilled
labourer in industry was, in 1957, 72 francs per hour, and in
agriculture 300 francs per day. Though very low, the worker's
purchasing power had slightly increased during the preceding
few years.

The most urgent problem was not that of raising wages but of
finding employment. With the rapid growth of the population,
the number of unemployed was considerable and it was
estimated in 1957 that there were 350,000 men without work;
with their families these amounted to one-third of the population. These unemployed were peasants who could not be supported on the tribal lands and could not find an outlet either in
mechanized modern agriculture or in industry which was little
developed. They had no choice but to live off family charity,
thus lowering the general standard of living, or off the payments
earned in work groups organized by the state. Small as the latter
were in the case of the individual, they nevertheless cost several
milliards annually, a sum which had in the past largely been
provided by France.

The only remedy was the further development of agriculture
and industry, as proposed by the Government; it was however
a very long-term project, and in the meanwhile the population
continued to increase. The prospect was distressing.

Trade unionism had been very active in Tunisia for many
years. A native Tunisian trade union movement developed
beside that of French origin, either in affiliation with metropolitan unions or in autonomous bodies. The union formed by
French officials played an active part in opposing the emancipation of Tunisia and after independence this and other unions of
French origin rapidly lost importance. On the other hand the
Tunisian UGTT took a prominent part in the national struggle;
its able leader, Farhat Hashad, who was considered as the
organizer of Tunisian resistance, was assassinated in 1952 as
part of a French counter-terrorist campaign.

The UGTT was the central Tunisian labour organization
and was composed of ten federated unions—government employees, workers in state enterprises, miners, transport and rail-

way workers, &c. It was directed by a Committee of Administration, backed by a national council, and it was organized in twelve regional unions who were responsible for local activities. It was affiliated to the ICFTU; the latter, with headquarters in America, had given the Tunisian union great assistance. In 1956, membership of the UGTT numbered 182,000. In November 1956 a split occurred when a rival central union was constituted, the UTT. This was far from having the range of the UGTT, though it claimed to have taken 50,000 members from it. It had, however, the backing of the Government which used its influence to unite the two organizations and to direct Tunisian trade unionism towards a constructive corporative activity instead of becoming an instrument of class dissension.

A Tunisian union of Communist sympathies, the *Union des Syndicats de Travailleurs Tunisiens* (USTT) was founded in 1946 and affiliated to the WFTU of Communist obedience. Its members were for the most part European and it was brought to an end in 1956 after the declaration of independence.

Artisans and small shopkeepers with their employees possessed an organization of their own, the *Union Tunisienne de l'Artisanat et du Commerce* (UTAC), as did the small agricultural enterprises in the *Union Nationale des Agriculteurs Tunisiens* (UNAT). These two organizations, like the UGTT and the UTT, were closely linked with the Neo-Destour Party.

French employers, in industry and commerce, had formed unions which were grouped in the *Confederation Générale du Commerce et de l'Industrie*, while a *Confederation Générale de l'Agriculture* embraced the owners of French agricultural enterprises and a few Tunisians. Big economic interests, both Tunisian and French, were represented in the Chambers of Agriculture, Commerce and Mining Enterprises. French and Tunisians had separate Chambers of Commerce, except at Sousse and Sfax where they were mixed.

The Secretariat of State for Social Affairs supervised the carrying out of social legislation.

The Budget and Foreign Aid

The Tunisian budget was shown under two headings. The first consisted of ordinary expenditure which was covered by regular receipts from taxation. For the year 1957–8 the budget under this heading reached the figure of $45\frac{1}{2}$ milliard francs (the Tunisian franc having the same value as the French franc). Indirect taxation was the main source of revenue, as can be seen from the details in the table given below. The second heading concerned expenditure on development which was met from non-recurring sources such as loans, and aid from France and other countries. Its total for 1957–8 could not be fixed until the end of the year on account of the uncertainty concerning foreign aid; for the preceding year it amounted to 13 milliards, provided by France.

Ordinary Budget, 1957–8

(*milliard francs*)

REVENUE			EXPENDITURE		
Direct taxation . . .		8,095	Presidency of the Council .		1,396
Indirect taxation . .		32,798	Foreign services . . .		448
Other dues and taxes .		753	Interior and police . .		5,339
State domains . . .		123	Justice		1,418
Forests, etc. . . .		870	Agriculture . . .		1,583
Various		2,842	Finance . . .		13,862
			Public health . . .		4,143
			National economy . .		457
			Education . . .		7,787
			Public works . . .		4,694
			Town planning . . .		446
			Social affairs . . .		182
			National affairs . . .		2,727
			Unforeseen expenses . .		1,000
		45,481			45,481

This budget was 5½ milliards higher than that of the preceding year.

By February 1958 United States aid to Tunisia totalled about $18 million in cash or kind, and $500,000 in technical assistance. Of this $8 million were used to finance the import of petroleum products ($5·5 million consisting of a grant). Tunisian counterpart funds to the value of $8 million are to be used for financing industrial development loans, and for agricultural development. The remainder of the $18 million United States aid was made up of wheat worth $7·5 million and foodstuffs worth $2,900,000 for children and Algerian refugees.

Foreign Trade

Tunisia was included in the franc area. Tunisia had thus been in monetary union with France, the Tunisian franc being at parity with the French franc. Her former links with French economy and the permanent deficit of her trade balance made it very difficult to withdraw from this area where she had benefited from French financial aid. Hitherto the issuing bank for Tunisia had been a French institution, the *Banque d'Algérie et de Tunisie*; this was under contract to the Tunisian Government to whom it paid dues. In 1957 the Tunisian Government raised the issue of establishing a bank of issue of its own, the *Société Tunisienne de Banque*. This was set up with United States assistance and was to open in July 1958, issuing a new currency of the millième (1 fr.), dirham (100 frs.), and dinar (1,000 frs.).

The banking houses established in Tunisia were for the most part offshoots or branches of the great French banks; but a number of special credit institutes were created by the Tunisian state to assist in economic development; these included a Land Fund for native holdings, a Fund for Trade and the Tunisian Artisanate, and an Agricultural Credit Fund for European farmers.

Tunisia had a customs union with France; this meant that she applied the same tariffs as France to the goods of all other countries. The union was sanctioned by an agreement of 3 June 1955 which laid down two principles. The first stipulated that each of the two countries should apply the same dues and taxes to its own national products and to those of the other country. The second that dues other than customs and fiscal charges must be justified by the services rendered. Subsequent protocols on 28 and 30 December 1955 modified the customs union in favour of Tunisia. For example, they authorized Tunisia to suspend dues on goods necessary for economic development, and to prohibit the entry of goods which might compete with local products (vegetable oils, soap, beer, &c.). They also sanctioned certain practices already customary—the exemption from, or partial suspension of, duty on certain foodstuffs such as butter, rice, and sugar and on certain capital goods such as engines, boring machinery, and agricultural materials. It was, however, expected that negotiations pending in December 1957 would lead to further revision. Tunisian agricultural products, in particular wheat and wine, benefited from the high prices in the French market. Nevertheless the creation of a European free trade area would face Tunisia with a choice and would presumably be taken into consideration in the modification of the economic union with France.

Tunisia's foreign trade was, as has already been mentioned, characterized by a chronic deficit which was balanced by the importation into Tunisia of French investment capital, both governmental and private, which filled a gap of some 20–30 milliards annually. However it was to be noted that the trade deficit applied only to the franc and the dollar areas; Tunisia had a favourable balance of from 1 to 10 milliard francs with the sterling area.

In 1957 there was a remarkable decrease in the franc deficit which was 9·2 milliards as compared with 29 milliards in 1956. This was due to a fall in the demand for imported goods and equipment because of the exodus of Europeans, to a virtual doubling of the export value of agricultural products (partly because of a poor wine harvest in France), and to a reduction in imported foodstuffs.

Tunisia's principal imports and exports have been subject to wide annual variations in the case of agricultural products, on account of the irregularity of the harvests both locally and in France which has remained her principal customer and supplier.

Principal Imports and Exports

(milliard francs)

IMPORTS	1956	1957	EXPORTS	1956	1957
Sugar . . .	4·2	3·8	Olive oil . . .	3·2	7·9
Iron and steel manufac-			Wine . . .	2·8	7·6
tures . . .	4·0	3·1	Raw phosphates .	5·5	5·9
Wheat . . .	4·5	3·0	Iron ore . . .	4·2	4·5
Cotton textiles .	2·6	2·9	Wheat . . .	0·6	3·9
Fuel oil . . .	1·5	2·0	Lead . . .	3·0	2·7
Clothing . . .	1·9	2·0	Superphosphates .	1·5	0·2
Tea . . .	1·6	1·9	Cement . . .	1·0	1·6
Haberdashery, shirts,			Esparto grass .	1·0	1·1
etc. . . .	1·2	1·8			
Machinery . .	1·8	1·7			
All imports . .	68·0	63·4	All exports . .	39·3	54·2

Source: Board of Trade, *Special Register Information Service*, 9 July 1958.

Besides France, the chief countries trading with Tunisia during these years were Italy, Great Britain, Algeria, and the United States as customers, and the United States, Italy, Algeria, Ceylon, and Western Germany as suppliers. Tunisia has concluded trade agreements with Egypt, Yugoslavia, the Soviet Union, Czechoslovakia, Bulgaria, Spain, Switzerland, Denmark, and Western Germany.

Internal trade was largely a matter of the distribution of imported products, and of the exchange of local goods, principally foodstuffs. The expenditure by officials was responsible for a large part of this. The part played in internal trade by a corporation with an ethnic basis is worth note; the people of the island of Jerba possessed thousands of shops throughout north Tunisia which were affiliated with a network of wholesalers. They thus controlled the greater part of the retail trade. A similar role was played in the south by the people of Sfax.

Tourism, the Arts

Possessing a good climate, a variety of Mediterranean and exotic scenery, Muslim local colour, ancient monuments, and excellent roads, Tunisia has possibilities as a country of tourism. It is easy to reach from Italy and from France, being served by regular sea and air services. It has a well organized airport, where several international services meet.

Unfortunately, however, the country was badly equipped for receiving guests, being inadequately supplied with hotels and tourist services. For this reason it has been little visited; in 1957 the creation of a network of hotels was being considered and the Tunisian Government was thinking of making a serious effort to develop tourism.

The main attractions are threefold. Firstly, noteworthy natural scenery, as for example the Gulf of Tunis, the Gulf of Hammamet, the lagoon of Bizerta, the cork forests of Ain Draham, the oases of the south, and above all the island of Jerba whose charm is comparable to that of the islands of the Pacific. Secondly, it has its ancient monuments—the remains of Carthage, the ruins of the Roman cities of Bulla Regia, Dougga, Tuburba Majus, Sbeitla, the Colosseum of al-Djem (the second largest in the world), and the Great Mosque of Kairouan. Thirdly, it has an interesting and picturesque folk life in the suqs of Tunis and Sfax, in the ports of the Sahil, and in Nabeul, a town on Cape Bon, which has interesting potteries.

The Bardo Museum in the outskirts of Tunis has magnificent collections of Roman and Byzantine mosaics and of Carthaginian and Roman statues and jewellery. Roman remains are to be found all over the country and important excavations are carried out by the Department of Antiquities which comes under the Secretariat of State for Education. One room in the Bardo Museum is devoted to Islamic art. The traditional popular arts have been systematically studied by the *Service de l'Artisanat* which comes under the Secretariat of State for Economic Affairs. The modern art-craftsmen model themselves on these collections.

The principal artistic products included carpets and hangings of which there are various regional types. The making of carpets in Kairouan is a family occupation, and they have a world-wide reputation. Glazed pottery is made in Nabeul, about six miles from Tunis. Embroidery is also made at Nabeul and at the nearby Hammamet. Work in iron and embossed copper is carried on in Tunis, Kairouan, Sfax, and elsewhere.

Most of this art work was sold in the local market or through co-operatives, but a small quantity was exported to France.

There was no museum of painting or of modern sculpture, though there was a well-frequented *École des Beaux Arts*, administered by the Department of Education. A number of Tunisian, French, and foreign artists worked in Tunisia, and there were frequent exhibitions of painting.

Tunis possesses a handsome theatre where performances are given by French, Italian and, occasionally, by Egyptian companies; there was also a Tunisian company. An Arab musical society, the Rashidiya, concerned itself with the revival of Andalusian Arab music. The literary section of the *Alliance Française* regularly arranged lectures and other cultural manifestations.[1]

[1] For political developments to the end of November 1958 see Addenda, p. 381 below.

IX

THE UNITED KINGDOM OF LIBYA
(*MAMLAKATU LIBIYA*
AL-MUTTAHIDA)

GEOGRAPHY AND POPULATION

Geography

Geographically speaking, Libya consists of two fertile strips on the African shore of the Mediterranean, and of a vast desert hinterland, sparsely studded with oases. The coast stretches from Tunisia to Egypt. The unity of the country is due to political rather than geographical factors. The western boundary marches with Tunisia and southern Algeria, until it finally reaches French West Africa nearly 700 miles from the Mediterranean. The eastern boundary runs for an equal distance down the meridian of 25° east longitude to Jebel Oweinat, at the junction of Egypt and the Republic of the Sudan, and then follows the Sudan frontier for a further 250 miles to its junction with the boundary of French Equatorial Africa in the foothills of the Erdi region. The Mediterranean coastline of Libya is about 1,200 miles long, though the distance as the crow flies is only 800. The area of the country is some 810,000 square miles, while the fertile coastal strips are nowhere broader than 50 miles. Their continuity is broken round the barren and forbidding Gulf of Sirte; here the desert comes right down to the sea and separates the settled areas of Cyrenaica from those of Tripolitania by a barrier 300 miles wide.[1] In the southern desert the distances between the oases are too great to allow casual movement between them except within the group of oases known as the Fezzan. It has always been a considerable undertaking to go from Cyrenaica to Tripolitania, from the

[1] 'Actually, it is in parts a country of character, or rather, two countries of two characters, for Tripolitania and Cyrenaica are separate, cleft in two by the 650 kilometres of dreary waste round the great bay of Sidra—an abomination of desolation which must be one of the most marked natural and human frontiers in the world' (Elizabeth Monroe, *The Mediterranean in Politics* (London, 1938), pp. 161–2). Miss Monroe's distance is that by road from Misurata to Agedabia. The camel nomad, knowing the water-holes, is not as dismayed as the motorist, and as he is not tied to the roads he makes the distance less. Still it is a most formidable barrier.

coast to one of the oases, or from one oasis to another—indeed much more difficult than from Tripolitania to Tunisia or from Cyrenaica to Egypt.

In terms of climate Libya can be divided into zones roughly parallel with the sea coast. The coastal strip, which varies in width from nothing round the Gulf of Sirte to fifty miles on the Cyrenaican hills, is predominantly well watered and has a warm Mediterranean climate. In it are found the principal towns and villages, and an overwhelming majority of the population. Both rainfall and subsoil water diminish rapidly to the south so that the second zone is too arid for permanent villages though it provides grazing for nomadic tribes who also grow crops of barley in years of good rains. The climate of this zone is more extreme than that of the first, and the *ghibli*, a hot wind from the south, can shrivel plants like a flame. It is, however, the main barley-producing area of the country. The third zone is absolute desert, apart from the four Cyrenaican oasis groups of Jaghbub, Jalo, Marada, and Kufra, and the Fezzan. It has virtually no rain but a typically extreme desert climate. Before the coming of the internal combustion engine, it could only be crossed by camel, and even for the nomad journeys were often made hazardous by parching sandstorms and the great heat. Without the oases, the desert would have been an absolute barrier between the Mediterranean and tropical Africa.

Geographical features break the regularity of the climatic zones in both the northern provinces. The Green Hills (Jabal Akhdar) of Cyrenaica run in an arc parallel to the coast from Dernato south of Benghazi. The seaward escarpment is steep and broken by precipitous gorges while the southern slopes are gradual. Rain is plentiful on the uplands, which rise to 2,000 feet above sea-level, and there is much scrub-oak forest.

Tripolitania also has its line of hills, but these are not so high and have less influence upon the climate. Their eastern end rests on the coast at Homs, whence they rapidly bend inland so that an ever-widening arid plain, the Jefara, separates them from the fertile coastal strip. Their highest points are over 1,000 feet above sea-level and they have the same general pattern as the Cyrenaican hills, a steep northern face and a more gradual southern slope. The upland climate is sufficiently moist for permanent habitation. Olive groves of great antiquity surround the little Berber towns and former Jewish troglodytic settlements. Where the hills merge into the southern desert, the ruins of fortified farms mark the line of the *limes*, the frontier of the Roman Empire.

Communications

In antiquity Libya was both a road along the North African coast and a landfall for seafaring peoples. North–south communications must have been exceedingly difficult in the centuries before the arrival of the camel, but east–west movement was comparatively easy; and the *Tabula Peutingeriana*, an eleventh century copy of a Roman itinerary of the time of Commodus (A.D. 180–92), shows the road from Tunisia to Egypt running much as it does today. There is little evidence of the exact route of the tracks to the south in early times, but geography does not allow much variation and undoubtedly they started from the ports of Oea (Tripoli), Sabratha, Leptis Magna, and Euesperides or Berenice, the modern Benghazi, making for the oases and the tropical regions beyond.

From the sailors' point of view Libya was rather an inhospitable shore. There were many miles of treacherous reef-strewn waters and few good anchorages. But Phoenician and, after them, Greek sailors sought out the harbours and established victualling stations, which afterwards grew into trading posts for the interior and even into colonies. And as Greece and Rome created a demand for African rarities, so the Libyan ports increased in importance. Gold, ivory, ebony, ostrich feathers, and slaves, the wealth of tropical Africa, could most easily reach Europe through Libya. This trade was destined to outlast the exports of olive oil and cereals which were also important in Greek and Roman times. It sustained the oasis-dwellers, the camel owners, the merchants, and even the desert highwaymen, until it was killed for ever by the opening up of West African ports in the nineteenth century. The great explorers, Browne, Clapperton, Nachtigal, and Rohlfs, penetrated to the equatorial regions by the route which their discoveries were to destroy. In the eighteenth century the Fezzan was a wealthy community of slave-owning merchants: the Tuareg, a proud and fierce tribe of desert rovers. Now only the slaves remain to till the fields under the date-palms as poverty-stricken, crop-sharing peasants, for no caravans come to buy their produce; and the Tuareg disdain to practise the arts of peace. The emporia of Tripoli and Benghazi have maintained their trading traditions, but the wealth has vanished. To her Italian conquerors Libya seemed only a *scatalone di sabbia*, or dust-heap.

With the Italian arrival in 1911 a great improvement was made in ports and communications. They provided modern harbour facilities at Tripoli and Benghazi and built a road system of over 6,200 miles. This links both the urban settlements of the coast and the administrative centres of the interior. Even the far oases of the Fezzan and Kufra are connected with the coast by motorable tracks. Although the road system suffered severe damage during the Second World War, it is still more than adequate for the country's economic needs and its maintenance, like that of other public works of the Italian period, puts something of a strain on the modest economy of the country.

There are two small railway systems, centred on Tripoli and Benghazi, with 117 and 99 miles of track respectively.[1] The Tripoli line serves the coastal strip westwards to Zuara (with a planned extension of 25 miles to reach the Tunisian frontier at Pisida) and eastwards to Tagiura (12 miles) with the possibility of an extension of 120 miles to Misurata. Another line runs south to Azizia in the Jefara plain, and it is intended to carry it on to the foot of the hills below Garian. In Cyrenaica a line runs from Benghazi to Barce, 67 miles to the east, the centre of the former Italian agricultural scheme, and another to Solluk, 34 miles to the south.

Communication between the coast and the southern oases is today normally made by motor, and the camel is fighting a losing battle even for the transport of goods. For emergencies, there are airfields in the principal oases.

For external communications by sea, Tripoli is the principal port, and can handle ships of all sizes. Periodical passenger sailings serve Malta, Benghazi, Egypt, France, and Italy; and cargo boats of many registrations call. The harbour of Benghazi, never on the same scale, has not recovered from severe damage during the Second World War. Tobruk is a fine sheltered anchorage, but lacks commercial cargo-handling facilities. The other ports shown on maps are little more than sheltered anchorages for fishing craft.

Idris airport, known during the Fascist régime as Castel Benito, is 12 miles from Tripoli town, and Benina rather more than the same distance from Benghazi. Idris airport is on the international trunk routes of British, French, Italian, and Egyptian airlines. There are also local feeder services, but the so-called Libyan Airways were until the end of 1957 merely agents for various regional airlines.

Strategic Importance

Throughout recorded history Libya's geographical position has given her a certain importance. It was no different at the

---

[1] Both railways suffered severely from war damage. In the opinion of a U.N. expert, the Tripolitanian railway was premature and should be abandoned; he considered that it would also be better to connect Benghazi and Solluk by road.

end of the Second World War and the coming of independence. The United States maintained a strategic base at Wheelus Field on the outskirts of Tripoli. Great Britain had forces of the strength of a brigade divided between Tripolitania and Cyrenaica; and France paid for the maintenance of airfields in the Fezzan.

The friendship of Libya seemed important to the western powers; on the sea, to keep the Mediterranean open; on land to protect an important staging post on the direct route from Britain to East or West Africa; and in the air, as one of the vast chain of American bases round the world which enable her Strategic Air Command to retaliate instantly in case of atomic attack.

Population

The mass of the people of Libya are nomads or peasants of Arab and Berber stock. In Tripolitania perhaps one-quarter of the people have a considerable proportion of Berber blood. In the Fezzan the nomad tribesmen are either Arabs with much Berber blood, or non-Arab Tuareg or Tebu. In Cyrenaica on the other hand, apart from minorities such as Jews and negroids, everyone, whether villager or nomad, is Arab. The Berbers, whose main centres are in south-western Tripolitania, can be distinguished from the Arabs by their less swarthy skins. Many of them have fair hair, blue eyes, and pink cheeks. Their religious sect, the Ibadiya, is more austere in its conventions than most other Islamic sects, enjoining a stricter modesty in women, and a puritan correctness from the men. In this sense it has much in common with the beliefs of the Sanusi by whom, however, as by all Sunni Muslims, they are regarded as heterodox.

There is little trace of former non-Arab conquerors. The Greek and Roman colonists have left only their monuments behind. A few Turkish families are still prominent on the coast of Tripolitania, including members of the former ruling house of the Caramanli.

Since the beginning of the Second World War there have been striking changes in the strength of alien minorities, of which the largest was the Italian. At the outbreak of war there were 44,000 Italians in Tripolitania, of whom about half lived and worked in the towns while the rest were peasant farmers brought to the country under colonization schemes. In Tripolitania, the total number of Italians has not diminished very greatly. On the other hand the whole Italian civilian population of Cyrenaica was evacuated by the Italian Government during the ebb and flow of the desert war. Thus, while there were over 40,000 in 1941, none remained at the end of the war, nor have any appreciable number been allowed to return since.

The Jewish population of Tripolitania has during the last ten years been reduced by emigration, mainly to Israel, from an estimated 25,000 to 7,000; and of Cyrenaica from 4,500 to 400. Those who remain are mostly well-to-do town-dwellers; the majority of the emigrants were needy town-dwellers or peasants who lived in the unique pit-dwellings of the Garian hills. A square shaft, some 30 feet across, was sunk into the ground, and rooms, sometimes in two tiers, were excavated in the sides of the shaft. A sloping entrance tunnel was dug, with the mouth at a little distance from the shaft. The bottom of the pit served as farmyard and drainage pool. At least one cluster of these dwellings included an ancient underground synagogue. They were easily defensible, cheap, and well-insulated against both heat and cold. Their inhabitants spoke Arabic and were outwardly indistinguishable from their Arab and Berber neighbours, some of whom were also troglodytic. They had never been molested during anti-Jewish riots, of which the last, in November 1945, cost 120 lives in less than twenty-four hours.

The census of 1954 gave Tripolitania 746,064 inhabitants in 110,000 square miles of territory; Cyrenaica 291,328 in 350,000, and the Fezzan 54,438 in 220,000 square miles.[1] The area figures in relation to population are, however, misleading, since some 60 per cent. of the people of Tripolitania live in the coastal strip, which is less than 10 per cent. of the area, while 90 per cent. of the Fezzanis live in the comparatively small area of the five actual oases. In Cyrenaica the 255,000 square miles of the southern desert are inhabited by 10,000 persons in four oases.

Eighty per cent. of Tripolitanians live by agriculture and animal-rearing, and of these just under 40 per cent. are nomadic. About the same percentage of Cyrenaicans live in the same way, but all of them are nomadic. There is a much stronger disposition towards settled village life among Berbers than among Arabs.

About one-sixth of the population live in towns, 163,000 in Tripolitania and 58,000 in Cyrenaica. Tripoli, with a population of about 140,000, is nearly three times as large as Benghazi, while the other centres are hardly large enough to be dignified with the name of town; although those on the coast, such as Zuara, Zawia, Misurata, Derna, and Tobruk, are too large to be called villages. Between 1911 and 1940 Tripoli and Benghazi

---

[1] General Assembly, *Official Records*, 10th sess., agenda item 26, p. 5.

increased their Libyan population by more than 60 per cent.; and post-war development has led to a further moderate increase. There are, however, relatively few signs of accelerated urbanization. Although the birth-rate is high at 5·3 per cent. per annum, it is offset by a death-rate of 4·2 per cent.,[1] so the net annual increase is not more than 1·1 per cent.

To complete the ethnic picture, there are insignificant colonies of Maltese and Greek fishermen and traders in Benghazi and Tripoli towns; and of negroids at Misurata and Taourga in Tripolitania and in the southern oases.

HISTORY

In Antiquity

North Africa was first linked to the civilized world—then in the Bronze Age—by Phoenician traders seeking shelter from the storms of the Mediterranean. About 700 B.C., Tripolitania was colonized by their countrymen who founded three cities—Oea, Sabrata, and Leptis—known collectively as the *emporia*. Cyrenaica was first settled by Dorian Greeks, who are said to have founded Cyrene in 631 B.C. Subsequently they built Euesperides (eventually to become Benghazi), Barce, its port of Teuchira, and Apollonia. The five cities, known as the Pentapolis, flourished culturally and commercially and became a part of the empire of Alexander the Great. In 320 B.C. they passed into the hands of his successors in Egypt, the Ptolemies, to whom they were even more closely bound by the marriage to Ptolemy III, in 246 B.C., of Queen Berenice, whose father had made himself independent ruler of Cyrenaica.

Both Tripolitania and Cyrenaica eventually came under the control of Rome. The former was gradually absorbed after the destruction of Carthage in the second Punic War, and the latter was left to Rome by the will of Ptolemy Apion, King of Cyrene in 96 B.C. The two countries were administered separately, Cyrenaica being linked with Crete and Tripolitania becoming the province of Africa Nova, which was finally united with its western neighbour Africa Vetus, by the Emperor Augustus. The Romans occupied Libya for nearly five centuries and brought a prosperity which the country has never since known. They penetrated the Fezzan, far to the south; and went even farther, to places not seen again by Europeans until the nineteenth century. They left aqueducts, cisterns, milestones,

---

[1] U.N. Technical Assistance Mission to Libya, *Report and Recommendations regarding the organization of Vital Statistics Services to Libya*, by M. R. el Shanawany (A/AC. 32/COUNCIL/R. 167; restricted), p. 107.

theatres, and Christian churches, whose ruins still proclaim the greatness of their achievements. They exported corn, olive oil, ivory, gold-dust, and even wild animals for the amphitheatre at Rome. The prosperity of Cyrenaica was checked by a great Jewish rebellion in A.D. 115, but probably Tripolitania was at the height of its glory in the reign of the Emperor Septimius Severus, who was born in Leptis Magna in A.D. 146 and died in York in 211.

The decline of the Empire brought both religious and political discord, and in Tripolitania ended in disaster. In 429 the Roman governor allied himself with King Genseric of the Vandals against the Empress Placidia. Genseric crossed the Straits of Gibraltar, and eventually conquered Tripolitania. His barbaric armies destroyed the civilization which had been built up and put nothing in its place. They were finally expelled by Belisarius, who reconquered Libya for the Byzantine Emperor Justinian. The country, however, never regained its former peace and prosperity, though some of its cities were rebuilt and re-fortified. It remained a shadow of its former self, and was quite unequal to checking the advancing forces of Islam, then mustering in Egypt. •

The Arab Conquest (642) to the Italian Occupation (1911)

In A.D. 642 Arab armies reached Cyrenaica and swept steadily westwards, overwhelming the Byzantine colonies without much difficulty. Libya was controlled first by the Umayyad Caliphs of Damascus, and then by their successors the Abbasids, whose most famous member, Harun al-Rashid, in 800 appointed the Aghlab family as viceroys, with their capital in Tunisia. They remained in power until superseded by the Fatimids, the Shia founders of modern Cairo, whose original capital was Mahdiya in Tunisia. In their turn, the Fatimids appointed the Ziri family as their viceroys in the west; the latter, however, soon rose against their overlords. To punish their bid for independence the Caliph loosed upon them the large and warlike beduin tribes of the Beni Hilal and Beni Sulaim, who completely engulfed Cyrenaica and the greater part of Tripolitania. This second Arab invasion in the eleventh century had much more profound effects than the first on the ethnic composition of Libya and reduced the area to chaos. Tripoli alone of the Libyan cities of antiquity remained an inhabited town. In Cyrenaica, settled life virtually ceased.

During the confusion of the following century the Norman King Roger of Sicily invaded Tripoli, with the intention of extending his empire across the Mediterranean. This brief

European intervention was brought to an end after twelve years by the Almohad rulers of Morocco, who moved east in 1158 in order to put an end to Christian rule in North Africa.

For the next 350 years Tripolitania was ruled from the west, from Tunis and Fez, first by Almohad Caliphs directly, then by their vassals and successors, the Hafsids; while Cyrenaica remained under the influence of Egypt, ruled by the Fatimids and later their successors the Seljuk Turks. As the power of the Hafsids waned, Tripolitania entered an obscure and confused period in her history which Ibn Galbun,[1] the eighteenth-century Tripolitanian historian, dismisses in a few lines.

Spanish expansion in the reign of Ferdinand and Isabella brought renewed European intervention. In 1510 Count Peter of Navarre captured Tripoli in a night attack. The Spaniards added considerably to the fortifications of the city but did not retain it long for themselves. In 1530 the Emperor Charles V granted Tripoli, Malta, and Gozo to the Knights of St. John who had been forced out of Rhodes by the Ottoman Turks. They retained Tripoli, with extreme difficulty, until 1551 when the Turkish Admiral Darghut Pasha seized it for Sulaiman the Magnificent, then at the height of his power. From then until modern times Libya, like Tunisia and Algeria, became a part of the vast Ottoman Empire, which stretched from Iraq to the eastern frontier of Morocco.

The power of the Porte, however, rapidly became little more than titular. In Tripolitania a succession of Janissaries and renegade adventurers from Greece, Italy, and the Mediterranean islands, ruled by force and cunning in the name of the Sultan. They were independent in internal affairs, though paying tribute to Constantinople. In Cyrenaica the Sultan's authority was not acknowledged at all until 1640, when Mohammed Sakesli, a Greek from Chios, and the outstanding ruler of the century in Tripoli, established one of his followers as Bey of Benghazi, and built there a strongly fortified castle. Under these adventurers, privateering, which had always flourished on the Barbary coast, was greatly extended. War which was the legal pretext for these operations was frequently declared and produced reprisals in the form of bombardments of Tripoli. Consulates were established to further trade interests and to conduct diplomatic relations.

Early in the eighteenth century the Caramanli family became hereditary and virtually independent rulers in Tripoli. Ahmed Caramanli (1711–45) secured his position by massacring most of his rivals, both Turkish and Tripolitanian, at a banquet, and

[1] Ettore Rossi, *La Cronaca araba tripolina di Ibn Galbun* (Bologna, 1936), p. 66.

dispatching a large tribute to Constantinople, the property, it was said, of his victims. He was, however, an able ruler who extended his control over the Tripolitanian hills, the Fezzan, and parts of Cyrenaica, and brought an unwonted stability to his conquests. His successors continued his ruthless methods, preying upon the commerce of the smaller maritime powers with great success. The last effective ruler of this house, Yusuf, was a supporter of Napoleon, to whom he rendered services during the Egyptian campaign. On the other hand he came into conflict with the United States when the latter, which had negotiated a treaty to secure the free passage of their shipping, refused a demand for increased 'protection money'. Yusuf declared war by cutting down the flagpole in the American Consulate, on 14 May 1801. This war lasted until 4 June 1805. In 1803 the Americans lost the frigate *Philadelphia* in Tripoli harbour, her captain and crew of 300 being taken prisoner. In 1804 the captured frigate, which was being repaired by the Tripolitanians for their own use, was successfully destroyed in a daring raid by Lieutenant Stephen Decatur. Another remarkable episode of this war was a march from Alexandria of the American Consul in Tripoli, William Eaton (p. 41), with a motley international force of some 400–500 men, including some United States Marines. The object of the expedition was to replace Yusuf by a rival claimant to the throne of Tripoli. The latter's name was Hamed and he and his supporters formed the bulk of the expedition. On arriving at the Gulf of Bomba, the expedition, now in desperate straits, was saved by three American naval vessels with whose aid they succeeded in capturing Derna (13 May 1805) where they were then besieged until peace was declared a month later. This episode was the origin of the line 'from the halls of Montezuma to the shore of Tripoli' in the U.S. Marine Corps ballad, Derna being regarded as a dependency of Tripoli though in fact it lies 1,000 miles farther east than the capital.

Yusuf's maritime activities were henceforth gradually curtailed by the increasingly superior technical qualities of the European navies and by the French seizure of Algiers in 1830 and the British occupation of Malta. Faced with ruin, he abdicated in 1834 and thus precipitated a civil war between his heirs, in which Turkey intervened. In 1835 the Turkish fleet removed the whole Caramanli family, and appointed a new governor, directly responsible to Constantinople. The change was welcomed by the European powers, as promising a more stable government and the end of piracy.

The return of the Turks at this moment was far from popular

in Libya, and made little difference to the chronic unrest prevailing in Cyrenaica. It was soon overshadowed by the rise of a great religious leader who gave a sense of unity, at least to Cyrenaica. In 1843 Sayyid Mohammed Ali el Senussi (Sanusi), grandfather of the present King Idris I, founded the Sanusi sect, to which all the Arabs of Cyrenaica and many in eastern Tripolitania still adhere. He called for a return to the purity and spirituality of Islam at the time of the Prophet Muhammad, finding a ready response from the independent tribesmen of Cyrenaica who for centuries had lacked clear and strong guidance. Sayyid Mohammed Ali had great gifts of organization, and the country was soon covered with a network of lodges (*zawiya*) of the order; half schools, half centres of meditation and work, and wholly fortresses, these had clear analogies in function with the Christian monasteries of the Middle Ages. Like the latter, the *zawiyas* were clearly a by-product of a weak and unpredictable central authority. The analogy must, however, not be carried too far, because celibacy has no place in Islam. These lodges unified the country under the will of the founder and rescued it from the anarchy of centuries. Such activity, although most salutary and impressive in its effect upon the Arabs of Cyrenaica, was not acceptable to the Sublime Porte, and the Sayyid prudently withdrew to the remote oasis of Jaghbub near the Egyptian border. His son, Sayyid Mohammed el Mahdi el Senussi, saw the movement reach the apex of its influence, with over fifty lodges, and sought the fastnesses of Kufra to escape from alien contact and influence. In fact the movement did not increase the difficulties of Turkey in Libya, since after the French had seized Tunis in 1880 it was generally felt that the Sultan's rule was preferable to that of an infidel power. By this time, however, the Porte was in such financial straits that it was unable to take advantage of its fortuitous popularity. Its administration, if congenial, was neither progressive nor efficient. In seventy-five years Libya had thirty-three governors, all except one of whom are held to have enriched themselves at the country's expense. When at last the Young Turks put an end to the tyranny of Abdul Hamid, in 1908, a vigorous effort was made to improve conditions in North Africa. But it was too late. Italy struck before the Empire could be reorganized.

From the Italian Occupation (*1911*) till Independence (*1951*)

On 3 October 1911 the Italians launched an attack on Tripoli; and subsequently landed troops at Derna, Homs, Misurata, and Tobruk. They employed large forces, both naval and military, and met with little opposition, since their invasion was well-timed. Though they had little difficulty in establishing bridgeheads, their progress inland was slow. They had only advanced a dozen miles from their base when the Sultan, alarmed by the threat of war in the Balkans, began to negotiate for peace. In October 1912 he signed the Treaty of Ouchy (or Lausanne) by which he gave up his rights in Libya; he did not, however, recognize Italian sovereignty but by a curious diplomatic device granted the Libyans 'full autonomy'. For their part the Italians had already proclaimed in 1911 their sovereignty as conquerors of the country. By the spring of 1914 they had completed their military occupation, although the Sanusi almost immediately began to attack their outposts in the Fezzan. The outbreak of the First World War weakened Italy's position; and when she joined the Allies she automatically came into direct conflict with Turkey at a time when she could ill spare troops for Africa. The Sanusi, supplied with Turkish and German arms and ammunition, attacked the British in Egypt, while the Tripolitanians turned upon their Italian masters. By 1917 the Italians held only the towns of Homs, Tripoli, Zuara, and the Cyrenaican ports, and were on the verge of losing their new possession altogether.

At the end of the war the Tripolitanian leaders, advised by Abdurrahman Azzam, later first Secretary-General of the Arab League, felt strong enough to proclaim a republic. To counter this the Italians offered to set up locally elected Parliaments in Tripolitania and Cyrenaica, under Italian Governors. For two years the Italian Government negotiated with the Libyans, who continued to press for self-government, finally offering the Amirate of united Libya to Sayyid Idris el Senussi (the present King). The Sayyid's followers had always been the backbone of opposition to Italian rule, and he alone could unite the country. In July 1921 the Italian Government took a decisive step by appointing the dynamic Giuseppe Volpi (later Count Volpi of Misurata) to be Governor of Tripolitania. He proceeded to subdue the Tripolitanians by force of arms, without reference to the liberal and hesitant ministers in Rome. The advent of Fascism a year later strengthened his hand. By vigorous and ruthless action he and his military commander— Graziani—reconquered northern Tripolitania by the end of 1923. Fighting continued intermittently for the next six years, by which time even the Fezzan had been reoccupied. Graziani then passed on to Cyrenaica and reduced it to exhausted quiescence, which he called 'Pax Romana', by the end of 1932. His success was achieved by herding the civilian population into concentration camps and so depriving the Sanusi fighters of supplies and auxiliaries. The subsequent loss of life among human beings and livestock was very heavy. By the time that the 'pacification' was completed, the numbers of the population had been very greatly reduced. The inhumanity of these methods caused a bitterness which outlived the Italian régime.

As soon as the Italian occupation was secure, the Italian Government turned its thoughts to colonization. Count Volpi proposed to grant large concessions of land to wealthy Italians who could develop the resources of the country. Mussolini, however, favoured the establishment of large numbers of peasant proprietors, thinking more of rural overpopulation in Italy than of the economic aspect of the schemes. Libya was to become the 'fourth shore of our sea'. But there were innumerable difficulties and by 1933 it had become clear that if the Government wanted to people North Africa with metropolitan peasants within a reasonable time it would have to do so out of state funds. Accordingly the many small-scale schemes for assisting colonists were finally abandoned, and plans for mass emigration of peasant families were adopted. In 1938 20,000 persons in family groups from the most densely populated rural areas in Italy left Genoa in a blaze of publicity. In 1939 10,000 others left more quietly from Venice. They were settled on the Jefara plain of Tripoli and the Green Hills of Cyrenaica, in small, neat houses, in which everything down to a box of matches was provided before their arrival. The fields were already sown, and the animals in the stalls. The plan provided for hire-purchase of the farm by the peasant tenant who could become his own master after twenty years. The outbreak of the Second World War prevented a third mass migration, and made it impossible to judge the success of the earlier ventures.

When Italy declared war in June 1940, there were large military forces in Libya under the command of Marshal Graziani. With great circumspection they moved to attack the British in Egypt, only to be promptly driven back by General Wavell who captured Benghazi in February 1941 and cut off the retreating mass of the army on the coast road south of the city. Thereafter the war ebbed and flowed over Cyrenaica until, in the autumn of 1942, the British Eighth Army swept the Axis forces out of Libya for ever. On 23 January 1943 the British forces captured Tripoli city and passed rapidly on to link up with the Anglo-American forces in Tunisia. From the beginning of the war Sayyid Idris el Senussi had supported the Allied cause and on his initiative a Libyan Arab Force had been raised in Egypt and trained to fight beside their British allies.

During the several British occupations of Cyrenaica, and the final advance into Tripolitania, British Military Administrations were established. These derived their powers from the Commander-in-Chief of the Middle East Land Forces. Their position, like that of all military administrations, was both curious and difficult. Under the Hague Convention of 1906 they were bound to enforce the laws and methods of administration of the enemy. But in the case of Libya these were entirely Fascist in origin, and were repudiated by the Italian Government set up under Marshal Badoglio in 1944. The Hague Rules had therefore to be liberally interpreted and, even so, it was impossible to remove all traces of twenty years of Fascism. The problem was further complicated by the fact that the future of the former Italian colonies was so obscure that the military administrations appeared likely to continue for several years, and, in fact, lasted longer than such administrations generally do.

In September 1945 the Foreign Ministers of the United States of America, France, Russia, and Great Britain first met to discuss the future of the Italian colonies, upon which they held most divergent views. The Americans wished to place all the territories under United Nations trusteeship (the Byrnes plan). France favoured the return of her colonies to Italy under trusteeship. Russia unexpectedly demanded the trusteeship of Tripolitania for herself; and Great Britain, upholding Mr. Eden's pledge of 1942 that the Sanusi of Cyrenaica should never again come under Italian rule, was opposed to the return of the colonies to Italy. No conclusion was reached, and the matter was left for discussion before the meeting of the Peace Conference in Paris in May 1946. In April 1946 Mr. Bevin, the British Foreign Secretary, announced that Great Britain was in favour of 'the unity and independence of Libya'. He was, however, unable to obtain any support for this policy from the other Foreign Ministers, and by June declared himself to be leaning towards the French view which had remained unchanged. This announcement produced such violent reactions in Tripolitania that the British and Americans were deeply impressed. The latter suggested that the future of the colonies should not be decided until one year after the ratification of the peace treaties, and that meanwhile a Four-Power Commission should investigate the wishes of the inhabitants and report to the Foreign Ministers. This was adopted.

Since Italy, Russia, and France did not ratify the treaties

until September 1947, the temporary military administrations automatically continued until the autumn of 1948. The Four-Power Commission visited the three territories in turn during the spring of 1948 and submitted a report to the Foreign Ministers that summer, which was unanimous only in considering that the Libyans were not yet fitted for independence. In September the Foreign Ministers handed separate and quite different reports to their respective Governments. A decision was therefore not reached and the matter was automatically referred to the Assembly of the United Nations.

The question was first discussed by the Political Committee, at Flushing Meadows in April 1949, where it was suggested that Great Britain should have the trusteeship of Cyrenaica and France of the Fezzan. The future of Tripolitania remained obscure. The French alone proposed to hand it back to the Italians as trustees. The Russians, who had declared themselves in 1948 in favour of the return to Italy of all her colonies, reverted to the Byrnes plan for United Nations trusteeship. After much discussion, during which Count Sforza made an impassioned plea for the return of Tripolitania to Italy, it became clear that the chances of agreement were scanty, since the Latin American bloc opposed all plans ousting Italy entirely from Libya, and the Arab states boycotted all proposals by which she returned. In a desperate effort to end the controversy Mr. Bevin secured the agreement of Count Sforza to a compromise. Tripolitania was to attain independence in ten years, remaining under the existing British rule for three, and reverting to Italian rule for the remaining seven years. In a dramatic midnight session of the General Assembly, the vital Tripolitanian clause failed by one vote to gain the necessary two-thirds majority; this brought down with it the whole compromise plan. Its rejection caused universal rejoicing in the Arab world, and particularly in Tripolitania, where its adoption had produced consternation, demonstrations, and threats of violent opposition.

Six months later, the Political Committee at last settled the fate of the Italian colonies. In the interval, all the powers concerned had abandoned their claims to trusteeship and adopted various methods of establishing an independent and united Libya. The Russians proposed immediate independence, the Italians after six months, the Americans and the British after a period of several years. Finally the Political Committee agreed that independence should become effective 'as soon as possible and in any case not later than 1 January 1952'. Cyrenaica, Tripolitania, and the Fezzan were granted full freedom to determine the form of their union. A United Nations Commissioner was appointed to assist them in framing a constitution. To advise him, an international Council was set up, on which Great Britain, France, Italy, the United States, Egypt, and Pakistan were represented.

The Commissioner, Dr. Adrian Pelt of Holland, arrived in Tripoli in January 1950. Three months later the Council of Libya met for the first time and appointed a committee of twenty-one—seven from each territory—to make plans for the convening of a National Assembly to draw up the constitution. This body, which was finally composed of sixty members, on the basis of equal representation for the three territories, managed to complete its work by the end of 1951, and the independence of the United Kingdom of Libya was proclaimed in December by its first hereditary ruler, Sayyid Mohammed Idris el Senussi.

The Independent Government

The first act of the new state was to hold elections for Parliament. They were not conducted on party lines, except in Tripolitania, where a National Congress Party in opposition to the Sanusi had been organized by Beshir el Saadawi, a returned exile who had held the post of adviser to the King in Saudi Arabia. His party was defeated; riots ensued, in which 17 people were killed and 200 injured; the party was dissolved and Beshir deported. The second general election, held in January 1956, was not contested on party lines but on the grounds of personality and family influence.

Even without organized parliamentary opposition, the task of the King and his ministers was not easy. The three provinces had little in common, and the King's special connexion with Cyrenaica did not help to bind them more closely together. There was a complete absence of educated Libyans to carry on the work of government. Technical assistance could only be expected from the west, but Libya as an Islamic state naturally wished for the closest association with other independent Arab states. The King was the most substantial link between the three provinces, but he was far from young and the succession was in doubt, since he had no son to succeed him. A boy, born in February 1953, lived only for a few hours, and the King's second marriage in June 1955 produced no male heir. The King's brother, Mohammed el Rida, who was heir presumptive, died in 1954, to be succeeded by his second son el Hassan Rida, the present heir presumptive.

During these years of uncertainty the royal family was a

centre of intrigue. Much of it was directed against Ibrahim Shelhi, Controller of the Royal Household, a loyal and able counsellor of many years service. In October 1954 he was assassinated by a young nephew of Queen Fatima. As a result, almost the whole royal family were divested of their titles and privileges, and banished to the Tripolitanian desert oasis of Jadu. Busairi Shelhi, the son of the murdered man, took his father's place, and enjoys much of the same influence and authority.

Two further problems spring from the federal and democratic organization of the state. The King has preferred to reside in Cyrenaica, particularly since an attempt was made on his life during a visit to Tripoli. In theory the Government should alternate between Tripoli and Benghazi, but practical convenience and the expense of moving have caused it to remain principally in Tripoli, thus causing dissatisfaction in Cyrenaica. There has been constant competition between the provinces for money, and between the King and Parliament for authority. Of the second, it is said that insistence on legislation by royal decree has caused the resignation of three Prime Ministers: Mahmud el Muntasser in 1954, Mohammed Sakesli a few weeks later, and Mustapha ben Halim in 1957. The present (December 1957) Prime Minister, Abdul Majid Koobar, has been President of the Chamber of Deputies, with two short intervals as a Minister, since the proclamation of independence. It is, however, easy to make too much of differences between the Throne and Parliament. A measure of direct action by the sovereign may well be essential while the legislature is still immature. The position of King Idris I is extremely difficult. He is driving three unwilling horses in harness, hampered by the activities of some of his family, and harassed by thoughts of the uncertain future. In these circumstances, the faltering or still more the disappearance of the coachman or the bolting of a horse could easily result in the overturning of the coach.

GOVERNMENT AND POLITICAL LIFE

The Constitution

In drafting a framework for a unified Libya the members of the Constituent Assembly had constantly to bear in mind the inescapable fact that the three regions of the country did not want a uniform Government. The Cyrenaicans, almost all nomad Arab tribesmen, were jealous of the settled folk of Tripolitania. They felt that they had borne the burden of the struggle and did not want to share the victory with those who had bowed the knee. The Fezzanese had unhappy memories of the austerity of Sanusi rule in the past, and were strongly attached to their own ruling family of Saif el Nasr. The Tripolitanians felt that as the most populous, prosperous, and progressive province they should not be subject to an unsophisticated minority. These considerations dictated a federal form of government, with King Idris as the only immediate link between the three provinces. It is a tribute to his wisdom and forbearance, and that of his advisers, that the uneasy balance has been held, and that Libya is still a unified if not yet a united, kingdom.

The federal Parliament has a House of Representatives of 55 members, 35 from Tripolitania, 15 from Cyrenaica, and 5 from the Fezzan, all of whom are directly elected; and a Senate of 24. Eight of these are from each province, half elected by the provincial Legislative Councils and half nominated by the King. Each province has its own Legislative Council, of which at least three-quarters are elected, and its Executive Council to advise the provincial governor.

The division of powers between the Federal Parliament and the Provinces follows the normal pattern, with currency, defence, foreign affairs, and higher education as the most important subjects reserved to the former.

Sovereignty is vested in the nation, and the King is Head of the State. He appoints the Prime Minister and, on his advice, nominates and dismisses other ministers. He appoints provincial governors and their executive councils, and senior civil servants. He can delay legislation passed by Parliament, but not veto it. He is in theory a constitutional monarch with the additional power of appointing half the members of the Senate, provincial governors and their councils. In reality he is the pivot of Libyan unity and independence. Without union of the three provinces, as will be seen when the economic problems of the state are discussed, there could be no hope of independence or even of viability; and without the King there is no hope of union. His long leadership of the struggle for independence, his wisdom and experience give him an influence far beyond the terms of the constitution, an influence which he wields boldly to counteract rivalries within the royal house and between the provinces. But it must be admitted that his tendency to cut knots by royal decree, a practice hardly sanctioned by the constitution, has caused his ministers embarrassment and has led to changes of government.

The outstanding defect of the federal system is the consequent heavy financial burden and the dispersal of effort it entails in a country whose resources in wealth and men are scanty.

Justice

The federal system is maintained in the judicial sphere. At the bottom of the pyramid are provincial summary courts, in which a single magistrate tries minor offences. Above these are Courts of First Instance, whose presidents are in some instances Egyptians or Jordanians. Then come the Provincial Courts of Appeal, which are also the Assize Courts. When they sit to hear appeals, there is a president, a vice-president, and three judges. When sitting in assize, the court is formed of three judges sitting with two local notables as assessors. Foreign judges have been called in to form these courts. In 1957 a Libyan, a Briton of Polish origin, an Italian, and a Jordanian formed the Tripolitanian court. There were a Libyan, two Egyptians, and a vacancy owing to the death of an Englishman on the Cyrenaican court. In the Fezzan there was an Egyptian president and Libyan members.

At the federal level there is the Supreme Court, composed in 1957 of a Libyan president, two Libyan members, one American, and one Jordanian. This heard issues between the Federal Government and the Provinces, or between province and province, and appeals from criminal or civil decisions of the lower courts which involved the constitution or its interpretation. Any interested person could appeal to the Supreme Court against any law, procedure, or act, on the grounds that it conflicted with the constitution. It gave final decisions by way of cassation, expressed opinions on constitutional and legislative questions referred to it by the King, and heard election petitions and administrative cases. The legal principles enunciated by the Supreme Court are binding on all lower courts.

The civil and criminal law administered by these courts is based on the law of Egypt, and so derives indirectly from the *Code Napoléon*. The personal affairs of Muslims were regulated until 1954 by the normal Islamic personal law in Sharia courts. These were then amalgamated with the ordinary courts of civil jurisdiction; but the experiment proved unsatisfactory and was under modification. There was no jury system, but particularly in the lower courts, local assessors advised the judge or magistrate on matters of custom and fact. Other than the usual diplomatic and consular exceptions, there was no extraterritoriality, and all foreigners sued and appeared before the normal courts.

The Armed Forces

The armed forces developed from the Sanusi Arab Force of volunteers from Cyrenaica, recruited in Egypt during the Second World War, and at that time staffed with both British and Sanusi officers. At the end of hostilities in Libya the force became a gendarmerie responsible for police and security duties in Cyrenaica under the direction of the British Military Administration. External defence was at that time the responsibility of the occupying power. In July 1956 Great Britain agreed to equip and train a Libyan army. This consisted of three infantry regiments of battalion strength, of which the latest was raised in 1957; an artillery battery; an armoured car squadron; a recruits' basic training centre; and the army headquarters. A Military Academy was opened on 1 October 1957. Two of the regiments were armed and equipped on the normal pattern of the British army, with the addition of machine-guns, mortars, and scout cars. Certain units would also have American arms and equipment in the near future. The budgetary provision for defence in 1957–8 was £L700,000. Gifts of arms have been made by Britain, Turkey, the United States, and Egypt.

The Chief of Staff was a Major-General seconded from the Iraqi army. Beside the main cadre of Libyan officers there were a number of other Iraqi officers either seconded or lent as advisers. A British Military Mission assisted with advice and training.

Also available for defence and internal security were the police forces of the three provinces, of which that of Cyrenaica, over 2,000 strong and well found in small-arms, was a paramilitary body.

Foreign Policy

The principal aim of Libya's foreign policy has been to achieve complete political independence in spite of the dependence of her economy on foreign aid. With the west, Libya has concluded treaties of friendship and assistance—Great Britain (1953), the United States (1954), and France (1955). This last agreement provided for the withdrawal of French troops from the Fezzan; ratification by the French Government was delayed for over a year, during which period Libya insistently pressed for the withdrawal. This finally took place immediately after ratification in December 1956. In 1955 Libya established diplomatic relations with the Soviet Union, but in the following year rejected a Soviet offer of economic aid. While Tunisia and Morocco were still engaged in the struggle for independence, their aspirations were a focus of Libyan sympathies, but the Government naturally looked to the eastern Arab states for support and joined the Arab League in 1953, two years before she became a member of the United Nations. Relations with Egypt were strengthened as the result of the Egyptian military revolution in 1952 and were again promoted by the Israeli attack on Egypt in 1956 and the ensuing Anglo-French expedition to the Suez Canal. On this occasion Libya requested that Great Britain should not use troops from the bases in Libya. At other times, however, Egyptian propaganda and attempted interference in Libyan affairs have caused Libyan-Egyptian relations to deteriorate. While preserving a diplomatically correct attitude towards her neighbour on the east, Libya was politically attracted towards her fellow Maghrib states as soon as their independence was achieved. A treaty of friendship was signed with Tunisia in 1957, which the Libyan Prime Minister described as the 'corner-stone of North African unity'. In 1958 King Idris accepted the resolutions of the Maghrib Unity Conference held at Tangier in April (p. 65); these were presented to him by a deputation composed of Mr. Bahi Ladgham, representing Tunisia, Mr. Mehdi ben Barka, representing Morocco, and Mr. Ferhat Abbas, representing the Algerian FLN. The struggle in the latter country has strongly influenced Tunisian policy towards France; annexed to the Libyan-Tunisian treaty of friendship was a joint declaration calling for the independence of Algeria. In October 1957 an incident on the Libyan-Algerian border which resulted in casualties clouded relations with France for some weeks; but allegations in the French press that Libya was serving as a channel for the smuggling of arms into Algeria did not give rise to serious difficulties between the two Governments. A rapprochement with Turkey, which was marked by an exchange of visits, had as a sequel a substantial gift of arms from Turkey in November 1957. A similar gift of an unspecified quantity was later received from Egypt.

A number of economic and financial questions outstanding between Libya and Italy were settled by an agreement of 2 October 1956,[1] in implementation of a United Nations resolution of 15 December 1950.[2] Italy retained certain buildings for diplomatic, consular, or scholastic purposes, ceding the rest to Libya, which agreed to provide a site for a hospital. Libya guaranteed the property rights of Italians living in the country. Development work on colonization schemes would be

---

[1] *Gazzetta Ufficiale della Repubblica Italiana*, 24 September 1957, suppl.
[2] General Assembly, *Official Records*, 5th sess., suppl. no. 20, Resolution 388(V).

completed within four years after the treaty came into force, at Italy's expense, and colonists would, in general, become full owners of their plots. Italians who had already left Libya, or who had decided to do so during the next four years, might sell their property and transfer their capital, subject to certain restrictions. Details of the financial provisions of the agreement are given on p. 371. An exchange of notes of the same date also provided for the return to Libya of archaeological material removed after 1940.

SOCIAL CONDITIONS

Education

Although Libyans were held by Aziz el Masri to be among the most intelligent peoples of the former Turkish Empire,[1] circumstances combined to restrict their educational opportunities for many centuries. After the occupation in 1911, democratic Italy attempted to carry out a liberal schools policy, but her grasp on the country was too uncertain and with the advent of Fascism, and eventually of complete conquest, the accent was on obedience rather than enlightenment. All schools were closed between 1940 and 1943, and the subsequent military administrations, both French and British, hampered by lack of funds and teachers, had an uphill task in re-creating an educational system for Libyans. But, save among the nomads, so great was the demand for learning that great strides were made, and already in 1950, Dr. Pelt, the United Nations Commissioner in Libya, could report:

> Approximately 26,000 students [in the primary schools] are from the Arab population, about a threefold increase since the Italian occupation. Only a few more than 400 Arab students are in secondary schools in Cyrenaica and Tripolitania.[2]

He further noted that

the school population and the standard of education are both inadequate. The former is far below the average in a normal State, which may be taken as 20% of the population. To raise it to this level, educational facilities would be needed for somewhat more than 200,000 persons. Even if it were assumed that the proportion of the

---

[1] Ronald Storrs, *Orientations* (London, 1937), p. 209, quoting Aziz Ali Bey el Masri: 'He says the people of Baghdad are the most intelligent and really advanced of all. . . . Syrians have more education and polish but less real brain and character. Closely following these come the Tripolitans. . . . After the Tripolitans, he places the people of al-Yaman'.

[2] *Annual Report of the U.N. Commissioner in Libya* (General Assembly, *Official Records*, 5th sess., suppl. 15 (A/1340), para. 188).

school-age population attending school would be relatively low among the nomadic and semi-nomadic group, the number of students for whom education would have to be provided would considerably exceed 100,000.[1]

A determined effort has since been made to meet the deficiency. Foreign teachers have been imported, and the greatest possible number of Libyans recruited. Teacher-training centres have been established, and the number of schools and pupils has increased greatly. By 1955-6 the figures were:

	Schools	Teachers	Pupils
Elementary			
Tripolitania . .	202 (88)	1,238 (310)	39,296 (14,969)
Cyrenaica . .	132 (44)	760 (150)	23,095 (5,809)
Fezzan . . .	45	115	3,500
Secondary			
Tripolitania . .	4 (2)	132	2,532 (120)
Cyrenaica . .	4 (2)	68	764 (42)
Fezzan . . .	—	—	—

Source: Europa Publications, *The Middle East 1958*, p. 309. Figures in parentheses, from reports of the International Commission of Investigation into the Future of the ex-Italian Colonies, show the position in 1947.

The curricula are based on those of Egypt.

In addition to normal schools, technical training goes on apace, at the bench and in the field, wherever new skills are needed. In 1957 there was a commercial and industrial training centre in Cyrenaica with 94 students, a technical and clerical training centre in Tripoli with 300 pupils, and an agricultural centre in each territory.

The needs of higher education had still largely to be met by sending students abroad, but a Libyan University was growing up. In 1957 it had faculties of arts, languages, history, geography, philosophy, social studies, and science. In the autumn of 1957 a faculty of science was opened in Tripoli, and faculties of law and commerce in Benghazi. University education, like that in the lower schools, is free and for some time ahead all graduates will be able to look to teaching or civil service appointments with confidence.

The phenomenal pace of this development might make the quality of the final product suspect, and there is no doubt that standards are still low. But Libyans passionately believe that the opportunity of independence which has come to them after many centuries of alien rule must be seized and made secure. They appreciate that this is only possible through education.

[1] *Annual Report of the U.N. Commissioner in Libya*, para. 190.

A United Nations investigator has stated both the problem and the urgency:

> Education is the core of both economic and social development in Libya. . . . It is to the increase in efficiency through education and training that one must look for much of the initial increase in Libyan productivity. . . . But the extent to which productivity can be raised through technical training is limited by the illiteracy and general lack of education of the people. To make the training programmes effective, formal schooling must also be extended and improved.[1]

It is galling for a proud and independent people to realize that in the last resort their independence rests upon the need of foreign powers for military facilities in their country. The Libyans have no intention of allowing the matter to rest there.

The Press and Broadcasting

Centuries of foreign rule and the lack of even primary education for the vast mass of the people have produced a country with no indigenous literature save the songs and epics of the nomad, the fireside tales of the villager, and some rather self-conscious chronicles and travelogues. The growth of literature depends upon the existence of a reading public. But the emergence of a free press provides the opportunity and, even more important, the opening of local broadcasting stations provides a listening public. It will take more years to teach a significant fraction of the people to read than it does in countries where the written and the spoken word are closer than they are in Arabic; but provided that the broadcasting service avoids pedantry it can capture a hearing at once. Six Arabic periodicals have sprung up in the last few years, but their circulation is very limited. The 'Voice of Libya' broadcasting stations at Tripoli and Benghazi were to open during 1957 with a strength of 5 kilowatts.

Health

The need for education was also at the root of many of the public health problems. Libya is a healthy country. It escapes both the parasitic diseases of the tropics and the afflictions of more highly developed societies, the heart and artery diseases, diabetes, and cancer. Epidemics have been rare. The main preventable ailments are infantile gastro-enteritis, inflammatory diseases of the eye, and tuberculosis.[2] The first was

---

[1] U.N. Mission of Technical Assistance to Libya, *The Economic and Social Development of Libya*, by B. Higgins (A/Ac. 32/TA. 16; restricted), p. 242.

[2] WHO, *Report on the Health Conditions and Health Services in Libya*, by D. K. Lindsay (A/AC./32/TA. 23, Rev. 1).

responsible for an infant mortality of 30 per cent., the second affected 30 per cent. of the population, and fresh tuberculosis was diagnosed each year in one per thousand of the population. The remedies were fundamentally not drugs, but food and instruction in infant management and general hygiene. In fact, as Dr. Pelt said,[1] 'the chief prerequisite in the Libyan public health field is education'. Education was needed to provide doctors and subordinates in the health services, to allow the people to absorb health instruction and to improve their standards of living so that they can carry it out.

The medical service instituted by the Italian Government was beyond the financial capacity of an independent Libya. It was directed principally towards the curing of disease, and had developed a magnificent network of hospitals and dispensaries. These were maintained, and there was 1 hospital bed for every 455 persons. In 1952 there was 1 medical practitioner for 12,000 of the population. Treatment in dispensaries and hospitals was free. As in most Muslim countries, the training of women nurses and health visitors was attended with peculiar difficulty, but a start has been made. The cost of the services in 1957 exceeded £L500,000 a year, and a school milk service even on a modest scale would have added 50 per cent. to this. But it was clear that an expansion of preventive medicine was urgently needed. Ill health was acting as a brake upon the raising of living standards. Yet in turn this expansion depended upon the capacity of the country to staff and pay for it. The absence of the desperate relationship between under-nourishment and disease, common to so many underdeveloped countries, gave Libya a breathing-space to press ahead with that expansion of education and increase in productivity which in time would lessen the incidence of preventable disease.

ECONOMIC CONDITIONS

Agriculture

The traveller who arrives by sea at Tripoli and wanders in the pleasant sunshine through the market-gardens which surround the city, often shaded by date-palms, and cooled by a breeze from the Mediterranean; who sees donkeys and bullocks haul up great skins of water from shallow wells to irrigate luxuriant vegetables and fruits; who is often passed in the narrow mud-walled lanes by strings of donkeys carrying produce to the markets, may well feel he is in a green and

---

[1] *Annual Report of the U. N. Commissioner in Libya,* para. 211.

pleasant land. If he motors east or west along the coastal road, he passes little townships bright with bougainvillea and shaded by palm groves. All is life and bustle, ease and modest wealth. But if he turns inland, after a very few miles the trees thin out and he is in a bare plain, perhaps green with grass and barley in winter, but for the rest of the year hot, dusty, and yellow. Azizia, a township on the northern edge of this plain, has experienced the record shade temperature of 132° F. The contrast with the verdant gardens of the coast, only thirty miles away, is striking; yet this plain is better watered than the vast southern desert.

To form a juster appreciation of the agricultural problems of Libya, it is better to travel by air from Cairo. Then the green and wooded hills of Cyrenaica and Tripolitania and the gardens near the sea take their proper place as tiny incidents in the immensity of the desert. It has been estimated (1951) that of the total area of 434,596,500 acres only about 5 million acres consist of arable land and land under tree crops, and over 2½ million acres are under forests.[1] There are approximately 24½ million acres of productive land in Tripolitania, of which 19·8 million are grazing land; and 9·9 million in Cyrenaica, of which 8·9 million can only be used for grazing and shifting cereal cultivation and 271,700 are covered by forests.[2]

The coastal strip and parts of the Jefara plain of Tripolitania are farmed by village-dwelling peasants, who can rely upon shallow wells in summer and rains in winter to water crops with fair certainty. In the most favoured areas intensive market-gardening is possible and citrus, dates, olives, and almonds are grown. The oases of the southern desert are tilled in the same way, but without benefit of rain and in a much harsher climate. In both areas the land is owned individually, as also in the Tripolitanian hills. The semi-desert south of the hills gives the nomad herdsman a crop of barley when the rains are sufficient, and grazing for his sheep, goats, and camels. It is communally owned by kinship groups (*qabila*) which, in Cyrenaica and southern Tripolitania, still coalesce into the larger tribal unity. The Green Hills of Cyrenaica are also tribally owned.

The main agricultural area of Cyrenaica is the plateau known as the Barce (Barca) plain, which produces cereals, olives, and fruit; the high Jabal of the Cyrene–Derna district is also farmed for cereals but the Cyrenaicans are mainly notable

---

[1] FAO, *Yearbook of Food and Agricultural Statistics*, pt. 1: *Production*.
[2] U.N., Technical Assistance Mission to Libya, *A General Economic Appraisal of Libya* (New York, 1952).

livestock breeders. The Fezzan is entirely desert country except for a few oases of date-palms and irrigated gardens. Barley is the principal cereal crop, and contrary to natural expectations the great seasonal watercourses (wadis) passing through absolute desert south of the hills are the main barley-growing areas. Their beds are several miles wide, and in a normal year they flush two or three times with run-off from rain in the hills. The areas flooded are immediately sown to barley or bulrush millet and, provided that they had a good soaking, will ripen the grain without further water. In Tripolitania barley is also sown on the Jefara plain.

Agricultural methods are simple, but not, as has often been stated, primitive. The wooden nail-plough, drawn by animal, is used for all cultivation. Animal-operated waterlifts are used in the market gardens, and animal-drawn sledges for threshing. This simple mechanization is cheap and suited to the small areas cultivated. Its implements are made and repaired by local craftsmen.

Libyan agriculture is thus of two main types—static farming along the coast, in the desert oases, and the Tripolitanian hills, and animal husbandry and shifting cultivation in the semi-desert and Cyrenaican hills. There is little possible expansion of the former, as most suitable land is already under cultivation. Furthermore the Islamic law of succession tends to cause more and more subdivision of holdings. One date-tree sometimes has seven co-owners; and it is symptomatic that the unit of land measurement is the *gedula*, of 3 square metres. Another result is the prevalence of crop sharing, which enables the land to be farmed by a single tenant, who pays rent in kind to the owners. The owner's share is, however, often greater than that of the tenant, and in the Fezzan the system produced a class of dependent, semi-servile, share-croppers (*jabbad*) who lived almost in bondage to the landlords.

Between 1930 and 1939 large settlements of Italian peasants were planted in favoured parts of the Tripolitanian static farming area and in Cyrenaica on the Barce plain and in some of the hill valleys. The agricultural plans were carefully worked out and appropriate. Over 4,000 farms were laid out, equipped, and occupied, and of these nearly 2,000 in Tripolitania were still occupied by Italian peasants at the end of the Second World War. They produced olives, almonds, wine grapes, and in the wetter regions of Cyrenaica, barley. By careful co-operative organization and rigid authoritarian guidance, these holdings provided a better living for the peasant family than it could have earned in Italy.

There were also a number of earlier land concessions to large capitalists, sited on better land. In Tripolitania they are still worked by their owners, and the great fields of olives and almonds, the spray-irrigated vegetable and forage crops, and the imposing farmsteads show what large-scale methods can achieve on the best land. Unfortunately such land is too rare in Libya for these methods to point the way to progress. Even the second-best land, on to which Italian peasant settlements were forced in the demographic schemes, is not a significant fraction of the country's land resources. But the $3\frac{1}{2}$ million olive trees planted on these concessions and farms, and the experience gained of dry-farming methods and difficulties, are Italy's most important bequest to Libya.

In view of the limited possibilities for industry it is the intention of the independent Government of Libya to make agriculture the basis of a viable national economy. This demands the collection of precise knowledge of conditions, research into possibilities, and education to enable Libyans to demonstrate and to take advantage of potential improvements. Authoritarian regulation is impossible and progress will be slow. A start was made by setting up an Agriculture and Forestry Agency as an auxiliary unit of the Ministry of Finance and Economics, sponsored by the Food and Agriculture Organization of the United Nations in agreement with the Government. It was divided into a research institute, and sections dealing with agricultural production, credit, co-operation and marketing, forestry, and agricultural statistics. It began its work confronted by the inescapable fact that existing methods of Libyan peasant farming would not produce a surplus over the barest of subsistence, except in the most favoured areas of the coastal strip. Elsewhere the peasant was reduced to starvation whenever the rains failed. The tribal or communal right to grazing and water and rains cultivation left management, and consequently production, at their lowest common denominator. In the national interest the peasant must accept the need for a revolution in the use of land. If he does, the techniques of progress are known and have been practised in other comparable areas. Two agricultural experts of the British Military Administration, for example, proposed a reorientation of farming practice which would integrate nomad animal husbandry with static farming. This proposal would have encouraged the fattening in the static farming area of livestock raised by nomads in the semi-desert zone. In conjunction with range control and improvement of the grazing areas it would have added greatly to the animal-carrying capacity of the country and the value of the product, which in existing conditions was fattened after export.[1]

But any plan for the improvement of grazing, for a change in the traditional practice of the peasant, depends on enlisting his co-operation. And as the peasant's attitude towards the land is fundamentally emotional, a reasoned statement, or a scientific demonstration, is not enough. His emotion has to be captured as Sayyid Mohammed Ali Senussi captured his religious feeling 100 years ago. Once this has been done, the planting of forage crops, rotational grazing, afforestation, and the improvement of rainwater catchment schemes, the familiar recipes of the scientist, will be accepted. Perhaps the greatest hope for the improvement of Libyan agriculture lies, not in the impressive array of scientific advice, but in the enthusiasm roused by independence and the steadying influence of the grandson of Sayyid Mohammed Ali.

Finance and the Budget

Finance was perhaps the most formidable problem facing the newly independent state. The adverse climate and inhospitable terrain, the lack of industrial raw materials and sources of power, make Libya one of the poorest countries in the world. Were it not for her strategic position, Libya could not hope to have a viable economy. In 1952 the United Nations expert Benjamin Higgins wrote:

Indeed the economy is deficitary to an extraordinary extent. There are deficits in the budgets of all three Provinces, and of most municipalities; the expected budget surplus of the Federal government will be exhausted by grants-in-aid to the Provinces; there is a deficit in the balance of trade, whether in commodities alone or in goods and services combined, of all three Provinces; this deficit is not met by net receipts from foreign investments, as it might be in an advanced country, but by the grants-in-aid, military expenditures and investment of foreign powers.[2]

It is literally true that without liberal foreign assistance the country cannot command sufficient resources to maintain even its present low standard of living. And had it not been for the importance of Libya's geographical position, the financing of an ambitious federal, parliamentary state would have been impossible.

[1] Robb and Rowland, *Survey of Land Resources in Tripolitania* (British Military Administration, 1945), p. 79. One of the authors is a farmer, and the other a present Director of Grassland Improvement in the Union of South Africa.
[2] U.N. Mission of Technical Assistance to Libya, *The Economic and Social Development of Libya*, p. 6.

As it is, the United States, Great Britain, and France are underwriting Libya's economy, and the Libyan Development Council can plan and execute long-term measures which should eventually enable ordinary revenue to balance expenditure. But these are essentially long-term plans, starting perforce with a great expansion of education, and foreign aid will be needed for many years, unless there is some dramatic discovery of concealed resources, such as oil for which exploration is being actively pursued.

The shape of the budget clearly showed Libya's dependence on foreign aid. For 1956–7 the total estimated revenue was £L8·7 million, and expenditure £L9·2 million; the deficit was made up by external financial assistance, about half being covered by the additional British grant-in-aid described below. Internal revenue amounted to £L3·3 million only (£L2·9 million from customs duties, £L0·3 million from posts and telecommunications, and £L0·08 million from miscellaneous sources). Of the total expenditure of £L9·2 million, about £L2·6 million was allocated to the Federal Government, £L3·9 million to the provinces, and £L2·7 million for economic and social development. This last sum did not include the additional United States aid referred to below.

Foreign Aid

When the new Libyan state was set up it was recognized that it could not become viable without liberal foreign assistance. Most of this came from Great Britain and the United States. Under the Anglo-Libyan Finance Agreement which accompanied the treaty of July 1953, whereby Britain was given rights to military installations and air bases, Libya received £L3·75 million a year, £L1 million for development and the rest for budgetary support. Additional grants towards the budget of £L250,000 in 1956–7 and £L750,000 in 1957–8 were sanctioned when the Libyan Prime Minister visited Britain in June 1956; a new financial agreement with Britain was concluded early in 1958. Under the Libyan-American bases agreement of 9 September 1954 Libya receives $4 million a year for the seven years 1954–60 and thereafter $1 million for the next eleven years; at the same time the United States undertook to give sympathetic consideration to Libya's requirements of additional economic aid for development. This amounted to $3 million in 1954–5, $5 million in 1955–6, and $7 million in 1956–7: at the same time additional military aid and shipments of wheat for relief were given. In the spring of 1957, when Libya welcomed the Eisenhower programme, she was granted $7 million from the $200 million allocated for the programme. Libya has also received contributions for development from Italy, Turkey, and Egypt (£L10,000 a year each) and from France (£L100,000 a year). Under the Franco-Libyan treaty of 1955, but not ratified until the end of 1956, France agreed to make a grant-in-aid of £L350,000 a year and to contribute towards the maintenance of airfields in the Fezzan. In addition, Libya has received United States Point IV aid of about $1·5 million a year, and United Nations technical assistance. She was also to benefit from the Italo-Libyan agreement signed on 2 October 1956 and ratified on 17 August 1957 whereby Italy was to contribute £L1 million for the development and rehabilitation of the former para-statal agricultural enterprises (payable three months after ratification) and a credit of £L1¾ million, in three annual instalments, for Libyan purchases of Italian industrial products.

Banking and Currency

The currency of the country is the Libyan pound, at parity with the pound sterling; it is divided into 100 piastres or 1,000 millièmes. Libya is a member of the sterling area, and the 1951 currency law provided that only 25 per cent. of the cover for the currency should be in non-sterling securities.[1] In 1955 the National Bank of Libya superseded the Libyan Currency Commission as the controlling agency. This Commission, though formally a Libyan body under a Libyan Chairman, had British, French, Italian, and Egyptian members. The Governor and Deputy Governor of the National Bank were to be appointed by royal decree on the submission of the Minister of Finance and with the approval of the Council of Ministers. The five other Directors were to be appointed by the Council of Ministers on the submission of the Minister of Finance. The authorized capital of the bank was £L1 million, and it functioned both as a central and a commercial bank, being banker to the Government, central clearing house, and the agency to implement the Government's monetary and credit policy. It was also the sole bank of issue and operated the control of foreign exchange. As a commercial bank it covered the normal field of operations, in competition with 2 British, 3 Italian, 1 French, 1 Egyptian, and 1 Jordanian bank. To meet the special needs of agricultural credit, the National Agricultural Bank of Libya was set up under a decree of July 1955, although it did not open until 1957.

[1] Law No. 4 of 1952 establishing the Libyan Currency Commission.

Industry and Labour

So far as was known at the end of 1957 Libya possessed no important resources other than agricultural and marine products such as sponges and fish. It has, however, been known for some time that natural gas exists in northern Tripolitania. The discovery of a copious flow of oil by the Mobiloil Company of Canada in the Fezzan has raised hopes of a petroleum industry. There are no other sources of power, and the development of heavy industry is therefore unlikely. Such industry as there is in Tripolitania, which operates Italian plant, concerns itself with the processing of local agricultural and marine products, for example oil pressing, wine making, fish canning, leather tanning, flour, beer, soft drinks, macaroni, shoes, paper, &c. There are two commercial salt works, at Tripoli and Benghazi, capable of producing between 50,000 and 80,000 tons a year, of which most is exportable. They function by the natural evaporation of sea water. Next in importance comes the extraction of olive oil, of which over 1,000 tons a year are made with a further thousand of the second-grade 'sansa' oil. Sponge-fishing, almost entirely carried on by non-resident Greeks, produces over 100 tons of sponges annually, but Libya benefits only to the extent of a modest export duty. In June 1957 a trade agreement with Greece provided for the continuance of Greek sponge-fishing in Libyan waters; in return the Greek authorities are to try to encourage the equally well-established exports of Cyrenaican livestock to Greece. At the same time it was arranged that private Greek capital would co-operate in establishing industries in Libya as well as an airline and a merchant fleet of four vessels.

Local production of consumer goods is considerable. It has been estimated that 'weaving in the old city of Tripoli alone yields an annual income of over $300,000, or some 3 per cent. of the entire national income of Tripolitania'.[1] Leatherwork, carpet and rug weaving, the manufacture of copper and tin ware and of pottery by local craftsmen largely supplies the domestic market and provides attractive mementos for the tourist.

In view of the limited development of industry, and the preponderance of peasant agriculture, it is only in the towns that wage-earning is an important feature of the economy. With a total urban population of little over 200,000, the wage-earning labour force is small. Paid agricultural labourers are virtually non-existent. A wage law of 1955 lays down a minimum of

---

[1] ILO, *Handicraft Occupations in Libya*, by Angel Pappayoannou (1951), p. 12.

25 piastres (5s.) for an eight-hour day, but skill is at a premium and artisans command high rates, comparing favourably for foreign workers with those in their own countries.

Under Italian rule corporative organization had followed Italian workers to the colony, but the Libyans were not included in its benefits. During the war and post-war years of military administration, although the demands of the forces prevented complete stagnation, a succession of droughts reduced the supply of raw materials for processing and the purchasing power of the consumer. There was severe under-employment and wages were at a bare subsistence level. Since independence there has been a great influx of foreign diplomats and technical experts, sufficient in this small labour market to inflate wage rates.

The principal trade union is the Libyan General Workers' Union, affiliated to the ICFTU, with a membership of 6,000 in 1954. The biggest homogeneous body of workers is in the docks; foreign military and air installations employ large numbers.

During the Italian occupation the towns of Tripoli and Benghazi increased their Libyan population by over 60,000 persons. This was due to the demand for unskilled labour created by the enormous construction programme, by the un-settlement of rural life caused by the military pacification of the country and by the displacement of Libyan peasants by Italians in the colonization areas. It led to the creation of large shanty settlements on the town boundaries and overcrowding in the 'old' towns, the predominantly Libyan quarters. Before the last war a start had been made by the Italians on low-cost housing programmes, but work was held up, and the problem still remains. The lure of the town is too constant a feature of countries in which urban occupations offer greater reward than agriculture for the early reversal of this trend to be expected. It is one of the noticeable strains produced by injecting the germ of progress into a traditionalist society.

Economic Development

To supervise and carry out development projects approved by the economic planning committee of the Libyan Government a Libyan Public Development and Stabilization Agency (LPDSA) was set up in 1952 under the chairmanship of the Minister of Finance. It included representatives of the British, French, Italian, Turkish, and Egyptian Governments, with members of various United States missions as observers. It had, however, the additional function of providing a reserve fund

B B

to be used in years of drought, and since a quarter of the annual income was paid to a stabilization fund for famine relief, the amount received for development was not large. United States aid was channelled through three bodies, the Libyan-American Reconstruction Commission (LARC), set up in 1955, the Libyan-American Joint Services (LAJS) to provide technical assistance, and the United States Operations Mission which administered Point IV aid. In 1956 it was found desirable to set up a Development Council to co-ordinate all technical and economic assistance. By 1957 the Council had no power to enforce its recommendations and it was too early to forecast the effect it would have. In the meanwhile the execution of British and United States-financed development programmes has continued. The main aims of the LPDSA programme are the improvement of communications (particularly the construction of a trunk road from the Tripolitanian coast to the Fezzan), flood-control, works and equipment for hospitals and power stations. At the request of the Federal Government it was also asked to plan and supervise the building of a Federal capital and of a large office block in Tripoli. LARC was carrying out an extensive project for soil and water conservation in Cyrenaica and has been constructing dams and dikes on a wide scale. The LAJS has concentrated on agriculture and natural resources, education, health, and sanitation.

A Libyan Finance Corporation was established by the Government in 1953 to make loans for agricultural, industrial, and commercial projects. Its authorized capital is £L1 million, but by 1955 subscriptions amounted to £L160,000 only, of which Italy contributed £L100,000, France £L50,000, and Great Britain £L10,000.

Foreign Trade and Balance of Payments

Libya has a permanent foreign trade deficit. In the first seven post-war years the total value of imports increased by roughly 400 per cent. In 1956 imports totalled £L16·5 million against exports of £L3·9 million. Since 1952, however, foreign aid and expenditure by British and American forces and by oil companies has been sufficient to cover not only the trade deficit but also outgoing payments for invisible transactions, and a favourable balance of payments has been maintained, as is shown in the table at the top of the opposite page.

The import surplus naturally increased with the progress of economic development and general expansion; nevertheless staple foods—especially in years of shortage—and beverages are still among the highest groups of imported commodities.

Balance of Payments, 1952–6

(£L '000)

	1952	1953	1954	1955	1956
Imports	11,566	11,294	11,286	14,282	16,457
Exports	4,363	3,322	3,479	4,340	3,961
Visible balance (adverse) .	−7,203	−7,972	−7,807	−9,942	−12,526
Net invisible income . .	5,820	5,305	2,974	4,239	5,638
Official economic aid . .	2,918	3,121	5,093	8,411	10,074
Surplus . . .	1,435	454	260	2,708	3,186

Source: Libya, Central Statistical Office, *Balance of Payments for the Year 1956.*

In 1956, for example, the imports of tea alone almost equalled in value those of non-electrical machinery and appliances.

The following tables show principal imports and exports for 1954 and 1956 and the direction of Libya's trade.

Principal Exports and Imports

(£L '000)

EXPORTS	1954	1956	IMPORTS	1954	1956
Groundnuts . .	583	818	Wheat meal and flour	651	1,438
Iron and steel scrap .	—	459	Machinery and appli-		
Esparto grass . .	610	403	ances . . .	574	868
Sheep and lambs .	400	307	Tea and maté . .	1,048	865
Wool and other animal			Electrical machinery		
hair . . .	302	241	and appliances .	372	822
Hides and skins . .	223	225	Petroleum and pro-		
Cattle . . .	90	224	ducts . . .	596	757
Sponges . . .	373	188	Cotton fabrics . .	460	752
			Sugar . . .	381	638
			Motor vehicles . .	469	474
All exports . .	3,668	3,805	All imports . .	11,333	16,601

Source: UN, *Yearbook of International Trade and Statistics, 1956,* vol. 1, pp. 366–8.

Direction of Trade, 1956

(£L '000)

Principal Imports		Principal Exports	
United Kingdom . .	4,992	Italy	1,453
Italy	4,969	United Kingdom . .	801
West Germany . .	1,733	Egypt	515
France . . .	996	France	515
Egypt	986	Malta	290
Netherlands . . .	823	West Germany . .	284
United States . .	599	Netherlands . . .	110

Source: Ibid., p. 369.

Libya's chief exports are esparto grass (formerly the biggest item), groundnuts, scrap metal, and sheep and lambs. The reduction in exports of esparto grass, a wild product of south-west Tripolitania, used to make highest grade paper, has been due to a fall in price and the curtailment of purchases by the Esparto Corporation. Production in 1956 was about two-thirds that of 1955. Scrap metal assumed great importance after the war and rose again in 1955 and 1956. Fat-tailed Barbary sheep, mainly from Cyrenaica, are sold to Greece and Egypt. The normal value per head in the post-war period was £L3·5–4·5, although in drought years, when pressure to sell is extreme, the price has fallen to £L1. The wool is of a low grade and is principally used in Europe for making carpets, although there is a flourishing local industry making *barracans*, a blanket-like outer garment. In favourable years barley is exported; in some post-war years it exceeded in value exports of livestock, but in 1956 there was a shortfall in production and it was necessary to distribute United States relief wheat. Tunny fish, sold to Italy, amounted to about 3 per cent. of total exports in 1954.

The Arts, Tourism

The artistic feelings of the people are expressed in their buildings, especially the mosques, and in their woven fabrics. In these their touch is sure; but their choice of Western imports for their own adornment and the embellishment of their houses is often unfortunate. There is a very ancient tradition of domestic architecture, possibly derived from the Romans, which differs from that of the Middle East. The typical house is grouped round a central court, on to which the rooms open. Generally, in the more opulent houses, the centre of the court is occupied by a pool and fountain. The main room, used for receiving guests, has rug-covered couches at either end or along the inner wall, and often raised on a dais. In town houses the central courtyard is still present, though of course much reduced in size, and extends upwards as a shaft to the roof, with upper-storey windows opening inwards on to it. In these houses the decoration of the courtyard is the great opportunity for artistic expression. They are sometimes arcaded, and pillars have been freely borrowed for this purpose from Roman ruins, or the walls are covered with bougainvillea creepers or vines, which are often trained outwards overhead to form a shady bower. Faience tiles are used for ornament and the fish and the hand of Fatima are favourite motifs.

In the mosques it is the austerity of line which pleases, restful after the tortured flamboyance of modern Middle Eastern work. Minarets are squat and sturdy, in keeping with the almost fortress-like appearance of the outside walls. Great use is made of the barrel vault and grouped domes for roofing, and the outer walls often converge slightly upwards, an effect which is helped by massive slanting buttresses. Inside, an effect of extraordinary richness is sometimes given by cut and moulded plaster-work on the ceilings, of which the Caramanli mosque in Tripoli old town is an outstanding example. Undeniably there is great artistic feeling in the design of these buildings.

It is not accident, or the mere influence of the materials, which gives such quiet harmony to the groups of houses in the Berber townships of the Tripolitanian hills. The ensemble of these white cubes, linked at all angles by rectangles of white walls, is often extremely satisfying. Then there is the extraordinary tunnel-town of Ghadames, where the streets run under the houses, with every now and then a blaze of light as the tunnel comes to a courtyard or a pool open to the sky. These things show an instinctive feeling for mass and form, light and shade. The Berber carries himself with as great an air as the Arab, or even greater. No one who has seen a young Tuareg blood dressed in robes stiff with indigo and veiled to the eyes walking with the excessively stately stride of his people, can be blind to the magnificence of the effect.

Bright colours are frowned on by both Arab and Berber for outer garments, but the brilliant lengths of silk woven in Tripoli are freely worn by women in the home. They do not show much fineness, but at least they are honest, strong colours mixed without self-consciousness.

Such things as these, with the historic monuments of the country and its delightful spring climate, are the tourist attractions of Libya. The Italians left behind them a number of well-sited and pleasant hotels. They have been re-equipped and make it possible for visitors to see the Tripolitanian hills (Garian and Jefren), the coastal strip (Zliten, Misurata, and Derna), as well as both capitals and the Greek ruins at Cyrene. The Roman ruins of Leptis Magna and Sabratha are within easy motoring distance of Tripoli.

It is outside the compass of this work to describe the Roman and Greek ruins of Libya, and pamphlets have been published [1] to which the reader is referred. Such works do not, however, do justice to the natural beauty of the ancient cities. The white

[1] D. L. Haynes, *Ancient Tripolitania* (Tripoli, 1946); R. G. Goodchild, *Benghazi, the Story of a City* (Benghazi, 1954).

marble ruins of Sabratha, rising from the sea beach itself and silhouetted against the blue Mediterranean, are a picture that is never forgotten. So is the temple area of Cyrene, hidden on a ledge of a deep valley which plunges headlong to the coast at Apollonia far below. Today its isolation among bare hills evokes in the visitor an awe of the ancient gods.

Besides these, and the old castle and town of Tripoli, there are less-known relics of great interest, beyond the reach of the casual tourist. The Roman *limes* or frontier to the south of the Tripolitanian hills, with its fortified farmhouses; the fourth century A.D. mausolea of Ghirza, decorated with remarkable frescoes in high relief of farming life in Libya and showing no trace of Christian practices; the *wadis* of the Fezzan with their extraordinary profusion of prehistoric implements, can only be visited by well-equipped expeditions accustomed to desert navigation.

ADDENDA

I. DEVELOPMENTS IN 1958: ALGERIA, MOROCCO, TUNISIA

Algeria

The accession to power of General de Gaulle, the prospect of stable French government and of the renewed subordination of army and settlers to the central Government had, by the time of the referendum on 28 September, raised high hopes among many Muslim as well as European Algerians. As regards the political future, General de Gaulle's utterances had remained highly ambiguous; but they gave the impression that he was prepared to concede a large measure of autonomy to a Franco-Muslim Algeria, at some unspecified future date, provided that in the meantime the Muslims had shown by their vote in the referendum and by their behaviour in other respects that they would not ask to secede. Meanwhile he pursued the 'pacification' with renewed vigour. Communiqués which no longer gave the figures of French casualties regularly announced the killing of 300–500 rebels each week; while at the same time the promises of measures favourable to the Muslims were also redoubled. Thus on 3 October 1958 the General announced at Constantine a five-year plan. During this period salaries and allowances would, he said, be raised to the French level; 625,000 acres of land would be distributed to Muslim cultivators; two-thirds of all Muslim children, that is to say about 1¼ million more pupils, would be found places at school; great metallurgical works would be created, using gas and oil from the Sahara, to provide employment for 400,000 workers; and houses would be built to accommodate 1 million people. No indication was given where funds for this operation were to be found. The cost could hardly be less than £2,500–5,000 million; while staffing the new schools would require at least 5,000 new teachers annually at a time when the post-war 'bulge' called for 23,000 more teachers in France itself and many suitable young Algerians were either with the rebels or were refugees. On 23 October he followed this offer with an offer to discuss in Paris the terms of a cease-fire with the representatives of what he called 'the external organization of which we were speaking', i.e. the FLN, to whom he would grant a safe-conduct. The FLN leaders, who had on 27 August constituted themselves a 'Provisional Government of the Algerian Republic', considered that General de Gaulle's policy, in spite of the more courteous language used and the relative willingness to consider them as *interlocuteurs valables*, did not differ in essentials from that of MM. Mollet and Lacoste. While reiterating their willingness to discuss the future of Algeria with the French Government on neutral soil, without preliminary recognition of the

379

principle of independence or other conditions, they refused to proceed to Paris merely to discuss a cease-fire in circumstances which they said would be tantamount to surrender. In Algeria the men of 13 May appeared to be increasingly in control in spite of a directive forbidding the army to interfere in political matters; and the elections of 30 November for the French Assembly, to which Muslim voters were brought in army lorries, were calculated to produce a result corresponding as little to the real opinions of the Muslims as in the case of the previous elections. Under the new Constitution, Algeria with the Sahara was to be represented by 70 deputies of whom 47 had to be citizens of local status (*statut local*) and the remainder of normal civil status (*droit commun*), i.e. Christians and Jews, or Muslims assimilated into the category of Europeans.

In his press conference of 23 October 1958 General de Gaulle gave the French estimate of casualties until that date. These were: rebels killed in fighting, 77,000; French killed in fighting, 7,200 officers and men. Executed by the rebels, or killed in terrorist actions: in Algeria, 10,000 Muslims and 1,500 Europeans; in France, 1,717 Muslims and 75 French. To this must be added killed and wounded in French bombardments of villages and those wounded in the fighting; refugees, who cannot amount to less than 200,000 in Tunisia and Morocco; and detainees, of whose numbers it is only known that 11,000, against whom no charge lay, were said to have been released after 13 May and another 2,000 after the referendum. The number of villagers 'resettled', that is forcibly removed from their villages and established in centres under army supervision, was given in the summer of 1958 as 485,000.

Morocco

The latter half of 1958 was marked in Morocco by a recrudescence of the political crisis which had been obscured rather than removed by the formation of a new Cabinet in May. It was aggravated by symptoms of unrest in two spheres. One was that of the labour unions in Casablanca and was primarily economic in origin, expressing itself in the demand of the left wing of the Istiqlal for a more resolute and socialist-minded Government. The other was in predominantly Berber tribal areas. Anti-Istiqlal or anti-governmental demonstrations took place in the Rif, near the former border of the Spanish and French zones, and a minor attempt at an armed rising at Oulmes in the hills not far from Rabat. The leaders of these demonstrations professed loyalty to the King and there appeared to be a connexion with the movement of the preceding year which had been led by Ahardan and Dr. Khatib. The two latter were arrested, but as things quietened down again were provisionally released. Bombs were exploded outside the office of the Istiqlal paper in Rabat and among the crowd at the Accession Day festivities at Khemisset. External events such as the overthrow of the Iraq monarchy and the sending of British and American troops to the Lebanon and Jordan were a serious challenge to the monarchical principle and to the policy of the leaders of the West. In November the proffered resignation of Abdurrahim Bouabid, Vice-Premier and Minister of Finance and Agriculture, was followed on 22 November by that of the Prime Minister, Ahmed Balafrej; this reopened the governmental crisis. The King in his Speech from the Throne of 18 November made a strong appeal for unity, announced the issue of the long-delayed legislation on political rights, and promised to hasten the holding of the elections whose preparation had taken longer than was anticipated. He warned his people against those who sowed discord; with reference to the economic position he said that it did not 'rain gold and silver' and that the seeds of independence would only mature in the time of the sons and grandsons of the present generation. He stated also that all foreign troops would have to leave, French, Spanish, and American, thus giving his support to a demand for which there had recently been a growing popular clamour. A delegation of discontented tribesmen was received at the Palace and the Minister of Defence, Ahmed Lyazidi, with authority to call on the army for help, was appointed to investigate tribal grievances. Consultations were initiated by the King for the formation of a new Government; Allal al-Fasi was reported to have suggested the formation of a Cabinet with himself as Prime Minister, but it seemed impossible to reconcile the conservative and radical wings of the party and the suggestion was not accepted by the Palace. On 22 November a French lawyer, well known for his friendship with North African Muslim leaders, was killed by a bomb in Rabat. It seemed that this was the work of French counter-terrorists, and was connected with the similar assassination of an Algerian FLN refugee, Ait Ahcene, in Bonn on 5 November. On the other hand, on 5 December a crowd of young Algerians in Casablanca attacked a French officer. When rescued by the police, he had been so badly injured that he died. The Algerians were returning from delivering a protest against an alleged French raid over the frontier near Ujda which resulted in the death of Algerian women and children.

Tunisia

In October and November President Bourguiba endeavoured to mark the independence of Tunisian policy in two directions. On the one hand, on Tunisia's first appearance as a member of the Arab League the Tunisian delegate withdrew after an outspoken protest against Egyptian attempts at subversion in sister Arab states. This led to a propaganda war between the two countries. On the other hand, in view of the slow and limited deliveries of arms by Britain and the United States, the President announced his intention of undertaking negotiations for the purchase of arms from Yugoslavia and Czechoslovakia. This, he said, did not mean that he was throwing himself into the arms of the Communist states, but it did indicate a change of orientation in the direction of a policy of non-engagement.

2. NOTE CONCERNING MUSLIM SLAVES IN MALTA

In 1749 an alleged slave plot led to a trial, 'when nearly all the slaves were condemned to death. They were tortured and executed in batches. Most of the infidels were marched through the streets of Valetta and led to high scaffolds erected in the public squares on which they were birched, branded and finally hanged, beheaded or quartered. Those who consented to be baptized were put to death without further torture. These cruel scenes went on for a whole month, the Knights showing themselves pitiless avengers' (T. Zammit, *History of Malta* (Valetta, 1929), p. 248). Before this event 'the slaves had a great deal of freedom and were even allowed to meet together for their prayers' (ibid. p. 247).

3. CAMOENS' DESCRIPTION OF THE SPANISH SAHARA

Deixámos de Massília a estéril costa,
Onde seu gado os Azenegues pastam,
Gente que as frescas águas nunca gosta
Nem as ervas do campo bem lhe abastam;
A terra nenhum fruto, emfim, disposta,
Onde as aves no ventre o ferro gastam,
Padecendo de tudo extrema inópia,
Que aparta a Barbaria de Etiópia.

We left the sterile coast of Mauritania,
Where the Sanhaja feed their flocks,
A people who never enjoy fresh water,
And whom the grass of the fields inadequately supplies,
A country you may say ill disposed to bear any fruit,
Where the birds consume iron in their bellies,
A land suffering extreme want of everything,
The border between Barbary and Ethiopia.

(*Os Lusiados*, Canto V, st. 6)

A SHORT LIST OF USEFUL BOOKS

1. GENERAL

Benazet, H. *L'Afrique française en danger*. Paris, 1946–8.

Boyer de Latour, P. *Vérités sur l'Afrique du Nord*. Paris, 1956.

Caudel, M. *Les Premières invasions arabes dans l'Afrique du Nord*. Paris, 1900.

Chouraqui, André. *Les Juifs d'Afrique du Nord*. Paris, 1952.

Courtois, C. *Les Vandales et l'Afrique*. Paris, 1955.

Despois, Jean. *L'Afrique du Nord*. Paris, 1949–50.
Handbook, including a bibliography.

Epton, Nina. *Journey Under the Crescent Moon*. London, 1949.
Valuable for the interviews with, and accounts of, nationalist leaders then hardly known outside North Africa.

Fasi, 'Alal al-. *Al-Harakat al-istiqlaliya fi'l Maghrib al-Arabi* (The Independence Movements in the Arab West). Cairo, 1948.
English translation by H. Z. Nuseibeh, *The Independence Movements in Arab North Africa*. Washington, 1954. An account of North African nationalist movements by the President of the Istiqlal Party of Morocco.

Gsell, Stéphane. *Histoire ancienne de l'Afrique du Nord*. 8 vols. Paris 1913–28.
The fullest account of Classical and Carthaginian antiquity.

Fisher, Godfrey. *Barbary Legend*. Oxford, 1957
Sir Godfrey Fisher's book challenges the accepted nineteenth-century point of view on the corsairs and indicates a wealth of sources for further study.

Ibn Khaldun. *Kitab al-ibar wa diwan al-mubtada wa'l khabar fi ayyam al-Arab wa'l Ajam wa'l Berber*. 7 vols. Cairo, 1284/1867 (in Arabic).
Ibn Khaldun was a Tunisian historian of the fourteenth century. Translations: M de Slane, *Histoire des Berbères* (Algiers, 1852–6); Introduction and autobiography, *Les Prolégomènes*, 3 vols. (Paris, 1934).

Juin, Maréchal A. *Le Maghreb en Feu*. Paris, 1957.

Julien, Charles-André. *Histoire de l'Afrique du Nord; Tunisie, Algérie, Maroc*. 2nd ed. Paris, 1952–3.
The best general history from antiquity till the French occupation, with bibliography.

—— *L'Afrique du Nord en marche*. Paris, 1952.
A general account of the growth of nationalism in French North Africa.

Manuel d'art musulman. Vol. 1: *L'Architecture; Tunis, Algérie, Maroc, Espagne, Sicile*. By Georges Marçais. Vol. 2: *Arts plastiques et industriels*. By G. Migeon. 2nd ed. Paris, 1926–7.

383

Mas Latrie, J. M. J. Louis de. *Relations et commerce de l'Afrique septentrionale ou Magreb au moyen âge.* Paris, 1886.

Rouard de Card, E. *Traités de la France avec les pays de l'Afrique du Nord; Algérie, Tunisie, Tripolitanie, Maroc.* Paris, 1906.

Wright, L. B. and J. H. Macleod. *The First Americans in North Africa.* Princeton University Press, 1945.
A very readable account, written from an American point of view.

2. ISLAM IN SPAIN AND SICILY

Amari, Michele. *Storia dei Musulmani di Sicilia.* 2nd ed. 3 vols. Catania, 1930–9.
The standard work.

Castro, Américo. *La Realidad histórica de España.* Mexico City, 1954.
English adaptation by E. L. King, *The Structure of Spanish History.* Princeton, 1954. The author's thesis is that the modern Spaniard and his civilization are the product of an amalgam of Christian, Muslim, and Jewish cultures as developed in Spain.

González Palencia. *Historia de la España musulmana.* Barcelona, 1925.
History and civilization; an excellent summary.

—— *Historia de la literatura arabigo-española.* Barcelona, 1928.

Las Cagigas, Isidro de. *Los Mozárabes.* 2 vols. Madrid, Inst. de Estudios Africanos, 1947–8.

—— *Los Mudéjares.* 2 vols. Madrid, Inst. de Estudios Africanos, 1948–9.
Systematic and scholarly studies of relations between Spanish Muslims and Christians from the Conquest to 1319.

Levy-Provençal, E. *Histoire de l'Espagne musulmane.* New ed. 3 vols. Paris, 1950–3.
This is a scholarly, lucid, and readable work, entirely up to date; but unfortunately it does not go beyond the fall of the Caliphate of Córdoba in 1031. There is also a very fine illustrated Spanish edition, *España musulmana, 711–1031,* trs. by E. García Gomez, published as vols. 4 and 5 of R. Menéndez Pidal, ed., *Historia de España.* Madrid, 1947–56.

Menéndez Pidal, R. *La España del Cid.* 2 vols. Madrid, 1947.
English trs. by H. Sunderland, *The Cid and His Spain.* London, 1934.

3. MOROCCO

Arqués, Enrique. *Tres sultanes a la porfía de un reino (del diario de un cautivo).* Tetuan, 1952.
A colourful account of the court of the Rogui by one who was his captive.

Aubin, Eugène. *Le Maroc d'aujourd'hui.* Paris, 1904.
English trs. *Morocco of Today.* London, 1906. A very clear account of Moroccan government before the occupation.

Becher, Jerónimo. *España y Marruecos; sus relaciones diplomaticas durante el siglo XIX.* Madrid, 1903.
A useful study.

Berque, J. *Structures sociales du Haut-Atlas.* Paris, 1955.

Castellanos, Fr. M. P. *Historia de Marruecos.* 3rd ed. Tangier, 1898.
A general history, old-fashioned, especially interested in Moroccan relations with Spain.

Catroux, Gén. Georges. *Lyautey le Marocain.* Paris, 1952.

Célerier, Jean. *Maroc.* Paris, 1946-8.
Geography.

Chouraqui, A. *La Condition juridique de l'Israélite marocain.* Paris, 1950.

Confluent, Revue Marocaine (Rabat), no. 15, October 1957.
This issue has a useful account of the economic life.

Conrotte, Manuel. *España y los paises musulmanes en el periodo de Floridablanca.* Madrid, 1909.

Forbes, Rosita. *El Raisuni.* London, 1924.
The autobiography of the Sharif Ahmed al-Raisuni, as dictated to Miss Forbes. An illuminating story.

Grandval, Gilbert. *Ma Mission au Maroc.* Paris, 1956.

Guide Bleu. *Maroc.* Paris, 1954.

Harris, W. B. *France, Spain and the Rif.* London, 1927.
A contemporary account of the Rif war by the very well-informed correspondent of *The Times*.

—— *Morocco That Was.* London, 1921.
An entertaining account of the last period of independence.

Lacouture, Jean and Simonne. *Le Maroc à l'épreuve.* Paris, 1958.
A first-rate study of Morocco since independence.

Landau, Rom. *Moroccan Drama, 1900-55.* London, 1956.
A convenient account in a journalistic style of events in Morocco in the period indicated.

Le Tourneau, R. *Fès avant le Protectorat: étude économique et sociale d'une ville de l'Occident musulman.* Paris, 1952.

—— *Naissance du prolétariat marocain.* Paris, 1951.

Maldonado, Eduardo. *El Rogui.* Tetuan, [1950?].
A compilation with much interesting material concerning the end of the nineteenth and the beginning of the twentieth century.

Meakin, Budgett. *The Land of the Moors.* London, 1901.

—— *Life in Morocco.* London, 1905.

—— *The Moorish Empire; Historical Epitome.* London, 1899.
The three books above are simple but well informed.

Milleron, Jacques. *Regards sur l'économie marocaine.* Rabat, Soc. d'Études Écon., Sociales et Statistiques du Maroc, 1954.

Montagne, R. *Les Berbères et le Makhzen dans le sud du Maroc.* Paris, 1930.

Murga, José-Maria de. *Recuerdos marroquíes.* Bilbao, privately printed, [1868?]; reprint, Madrid, 1906.

A most interesting account of the *renegados,* or poor Europeans, captives or otherwise, who had professed Islam. Written by one who shared their life.

Rezette, Robert. *Les Partis politiques marocains.* Paris, 1955.

A lucid, accurate, and detailed account of Moroccan political parties from their origins to 1955.

Ricard, Prosper. *Corpus des tapis marocains.* 4 vols. Paris, 1923–36.

Selous, G. H. *Appointment to Fez.* London, 1956.

Mr. Selous was in the Consular Service in Fez for sixteen years from 1910.

Terrasse, Henri. *L'Art hispano-mauresque des origines au 13ᵉ siècle.* Paris, 1937.

—— *Espagne et l'Islam.* Paris, 1958.

Treats of cultural relations, particularly in the field of art. Fine illustrations.

—— *Histoire du Maroc, des origines à l'établissement du Protectorat français.* 2 vols. Casablanca, 1949–50.

A scholarly general history.

—— *Kasbas berbères de l'Atlas et des oasis.* Paris, 1938.

—— *Maroc, villes impériales.* Grenoble, 1937.

Weisgerber, F. *Au seuil du Maroc moderne.* Rabat, 1947.

An account of Morocco from 1896–1913 as seen by a French doctor.

Westermarck, E. A. *Ritual and Belief in Morocco.* 2 vols. London, 1926.

Writings by Moroccans.

Chraibi, Driss. *Le Passé simple.* Paris, 1955.

A bitter account of the difficulties of a young Moroccan in adjusting a modern education and a traditional background.

Fasi, Allal al-. *Al-Naqd al-Dhati* (Autocriticism). Cairo, 1952.

An interesting exposition of the views of the President of the Istiqlal Party, presented as a basis for discussion by nationalist Moroccans. French translation by Abd al-Kebir al-Fasi serialized in *Istiqlal,* 1957.

Lévy-Provençal, E. *Extraits des historiens arabes du Maroc.* Paris, 1923.

A selection of extracts from the writings (in Arabic) of Arab historians of Morocco. It contains a short annotated bibliography.

Sefriou, Ahmed. *La Boîte à merveilles.* Paris, 1954.

The story of a childhood in old-world Fez.

Bibliographies

Playfair, Sir R. L. and R. Brown, 'A Bibliography of Morocco from the Earliest Times to the End of 1891', Royal Geographical Society, *Supplementary Papers*, vol. 3, 1893.
Since 1923 a monthly roneotyped bibliography has been published by the Bibliothèque Générale de Rabat. A volume (Paris, Larose, 1934) contains those for the years 1923–33. A bibliography with many recent titles is included in Rom Landau's *Moroccan Drama*.

4. FORMER SPANISH PROTECTORATE IN NORTH MOROCCO

Cordero Torres, José-Maria. *Organización del protectorado español en Marruecos*. 2 vols. Madrid, Inst. de Estudios Politicos, 1943.

García Figueras, Tomás. *Marruecos*. Madrid, 1944.

—— and R. de Roda Jimenez. *Economía social de Marruecos, 1950–5*. 3 vols. Madrid, 1950–5.

González, M. *Del Marruecos forestal*. Madrid, 1945.

González Quijano, José. *La Política hidráulica en Marruecos*. Madrid, 1942.

Onieva, S. A. J. *Guía turística de Marruecos*. Madrid, 1947.

Spain, Alta Comisaría de España en Marruecos. *Acción de España en Marruecos*. Madrid, 1948.

—— Inst. Nacional de Estadístico. *Anuario Estadístico de España, 1956*.

—— Dirección General de Plazas y Provincias Africanas and Inst. de Estudios Africanos. *Resúmen Estadístico de Africa Española, 1953–5*. Madrid, 1957.

Tomás Perez, V. *La Economía marroquí*. Madrid, 1954.

Valseca, S. *La Ganadería en nuestro protectorado*. Madrid, 1951.

Valderrama Martínez, F. *Historia de la acción cultural de España en Marruecos*. Tetuan, 1956.

5. TANGIER

Landau, Rom. *Portrait of Tangier*. London, 1952.

Routh, E. M. G. *Tangier; England's Lost Atlantic Outpost*. London, 1912.
A scholarly account of the period of British rule in Tangier.

Stuart, G. H. *The International City of Tangier*. 2nd ed. Stanford, Calif., 1955.

6. IFNI AND THE SPANISH SAHARA

Caro Baroja, Julio. *Estudios Saharianos*. Madrid, Inst. de Estudios Africanos, 1955.

García Figueras, T. *Santa Cruz de Mar Pequeña—Ifni—Sahara.* Madrid, 1941.

Hernández Pacheco, E. and F., and others. *El Sahara Español.* Madrid, Inst. de Estudios Africanos, 1947.

Larrea Palacín, Arcadio de. *Canciones juglarescas de Ifni.* Madrid, 1956.

—— *Canciones populares de Ifni.* Madrid, 1957.

Lodwick, John. *The Forbidden Coast; the Story of a Journey to Río de Oro.* London, 1956.
    A travel book. The author's comments are based on wide reading in Spanish and an unconventional and interesting experience. He gives a vivid picture of the area as he saw it, and his account appears to be the only one existing in English.

Molina Campuzano, Miguel. *Contribución al estudio del censo de población del Sahara Español.* Madrid, 1954.

Monteil, V. 'Notes sur Ifni et les Ait Ba-Amran', Inst. des Hautes Études Marocaines, *Notes et Documents*, 1948, ii. 6–8.

Pérez del Toro, F. *España en el Noroeste de Africa.* Madrid, 1892.

7. ALGERIA

'Algeria', *Encyclopaedia of Islam*, new ed., vol. 1, fasc. 6.

Alleg, H. *The Question*, trs. by John Calder. London, 1958.
    A description of the use of torture in Algeria by a Frenchman to whom it was applied.

Alquier, J-Y. *Nous avons pacifié Tazalt.* Paris, 1957.
    The working of the Special Administrative Services as seen by an officer who was a member of them and believes in their utility.

Annuaire du monde musulman. Paris, 1955.

Aron, Raymond. *La Tragédie algérienne.* Paris, 1957.

Bourdieu, P. *Sociologie de l'Algérie.* Paris, 1958. (Que Sais-je, no. 802.)
    This brief but penetrating analysis of Algerian society is an excellent introduction to the social conditions which underlie the political problem.

Bromberger, Serge. *Les Rebelles algériens.* Paris, 1958.
    A hostile but vivid account of the personalities and personal relations of some of the leading members of the FLN, and of the successful suppression of terrorism in Algiers city. Presumably compiled from Intelligence Service sources.

Brouwer, Desclée de. *L'Algérie ou la guerre des mythes.* Bruges, 1958.
    A thoughtful examination of the Algerian question by a Frenchman who is also a practising Christian.

Capot-Rey, R. *Le Sahara français.* Paris, 1953.

Charles-Roux, F. *France et l'Afrique du Nord avant 1830.* Paris, 1932.

Dronne, Raymond. *La Révolution d'Alger*. Paris, 1958.
An account of the May revolution by a French Deputy who was present for much of the time. Less partial than M. de Sérigny, the writer is more informative about internal disagreements and difficulties.

Egretaud, M. *Réalité de la nation algérienne*. Paris, 1957.

Esquer, G. *Les Commencements d'un empire; la prise d'Alger*. Paris, 1930.

France, Cabinet du Ministre de l'Algérie. *Algérie, 1957*. Algiers, 1957.

—— Groupe d'Étude des Relations Financières entre la Métropole et l'Algérie. *Rapport général*. (Chairman: R. Maspétiol.) Algiers, 1955.

Gaffarel, Paul. *L'Algérie*. Paris, 1883.

Garrot, H. *Histoire générale de l'Algérie*. Algiers, 1910.

Grammont, H. de. *Histoire d'Alger sous la domination turque, 1515–1830*. Paris, 1887.

Guide Bleu. *Algérie, Tunisie*. Paris, 1955.

Haedo, Diego de. *Topografía e historia general de Argel*. Valladolid, 1612; Madrid, 1927.

Initiation à l'Algérie. Paris, 1957.
A work of reference, with bibliography and statistics. Though appearing in 1957, many of the statistics refer to 1954. The different categories of the population are not always distinguished and the general outlook is somewhat 'official'.

Jeanson, C. and F. *L'Algérie hors la loi*. Paris, 1955.

Laugier de Tassy. *Histoire du royaume d'Alger*. Amsterdam, 1725.
English version under title Joseph Morgan, *A Compleat History of the Piratical States of Barbary*. London, 1756.

Martín de la Escalera, Carmen. *Argelia y su destino*. Madrid, 1956.

Masson, P. *Histoire des établissements et du commerce français dans l'Afrique barbaresque, 1560–1793*. Paris, 1903.

Parès, A. J. *Un Toullonais à Alger au 18e siècle*. Paris, 1931.

Pellissier de Reynaud, E. *Annales algériennes*. 3 vols. Paris, 1854.

Saint Germes, J-V. *Économie algérienne*. New ed. Algiers, 1955.
Extremely clear, but throws no light on Arab-French relations.

Schaefer, René. *Révolution en Algérie*. Paris, 1956.

Shaler, W. *Sketches of Algiers*. Boston, 1826.

Shaw, Dr. Thomas. *Travels and Observations relating to Barbary*. Oxford, 1738. (In Pinkerton, *Voyages*, vol. 15, 1814.)

Servan-Schreiber, J-J. *Lieutenant en Algérie*. Paris, 1957.
A critical account of the process of pacification by a left-wing journalist who participated in it in the course of military service.

Soustelle, Jacques. *Aimée et souffrante Algérie.* Paris, 1956.

—— *Le Drame algérien el la décadence français; réponse à Raymond Aron.* Paris, 1957.

Tillion, Germaine. *L'Algérie en 1957.* Paris, 1957.
> English version, trs. by R. Matthews, *Algeria the Realities.* New York, 1958. A well-informed booklet. The conclusions are questionable.

Venture de Paradis, J. M. *Alger au 18e siècle,* ed. by E. Fagnan. Algiers, 1898.
> An interesting account by a French resident in Algiers about 1789.

Novels by Muslims

Chraibi, Driss. *Les Boucs.* Paris, 1955.
> The book deals with Algerian workers in Paris, but the author is Moroccan.

Dib, Mohammed. *La Grande maison.* Paris, 1952.

Feraoun, Mouloud. *Le Fils du pauvre.* Paris, 1954.

—— *La Terre et le sang.* Paris, 1953.

Mammeri, Mouloud. *La Colline oubliée.* Paris, 1952.

Yacine, Kateb. *Nedjma.* Paris, 1956.

Bibliographies

Playfair, Sir R. L. 'A Bibliography of Algeria from the Expedition of Charles V in 1541 to 1887', Royal Geographical Society, *Supplementary Papers,* vol. 2, 1889.

Taillart, C. *L'Algérie dans la littérature français; essai de bibliographie méthodique et raisonée jusqu'à l'année 1924.*

There are also many useful annotated references in G. Fisher, *Barbary Legend,* Oxford, 1957.

8. TUNISIA

Bourguiba, Habib. *La Tunisie et la France.* Paris, 1954.
> A collection of speeches and letters by the leader of the Neo-Destour Party, now President of Tunisia.

Broadley, A. M. *The Last Punic War; Tunis, Past and Present.* 2 vols. Edinburgh, 1882.

Correspondance des Beys de Tunis et des Consuls de France avec la Cour, 1577–1830. Collected by E. Plantet. Paris, 1893.

Demeerseman, A. 'Élites Tunisiennes et Progrès', *Ibla* (Inst. des Belles Lettres Arabes), no. 54, 1951, pp. 125–49.

Despois, Jean. *La Tunisie orientale; Sahel et basse steppe; étude géographique.* 2nd. ed. Algiers, 1955.

Garas, Félix. *Bourguiba et la naissance d'une nation.* Paris, 1956.

Laitman, L. *Tunisia Today.* New York, 1954.

Lépidi, J. 'Situation Démographique de la Tunisie', various articles in *Bull. Éc. et Soc. de la Tunisie* from 1948 to 1953.

Marçais, Georges. *Les Arabes en Berbérie du 11e au 14e siècle.* Constantine, 1913.

—— *La Berbérie musulmane et l'Orient au moyen âge.* Paris, 1946.

Monchicourt, C. *La Région du Haut Tell en Tunisie.* Paris, 1913.

Montéty, H. de. *Les Classes moyennes en Tunisie.* Brussels, INCIDI, 1955.

—— *Femmes de Tunisie.* The Hague, 1958.

—— *Pluralisme ethnique en Tunisie.* Brussels, INCIDI, 1957.

—— 'Les Problèmes agraires en Tunisie', *Notes et Études Documentaires*, no. 2255, 1957.

Vibert, J. 'L'Économie Tunisienne à la Fin de 1955', *Notes et Études Documentaires*, nos. 2216 and 2217, 1956.

Tlatli, Salah eddine. *Tunisie nouvelle.* Tunis, 1957.
    A survey of social and economic conditions; packed with information, and at the same time readable. Expresses the point of view of an enthusiastic supporter of the new régime.

Bibliography

Ashbee, H. S. *A Bibliography of Tunisia.* London, 1889.
    From the earliest times to the end of 1888.

9. LIBYA

Abbott, G. F. *Holy War in Tripoli.* London, 1912.
    An account of the Italian invasion by a correspondent with the Turks.

Ashhab, Mohammed T. I. al-. *Ibrahim Ahmad al-Shelhi.* Cairo, [1956?].
    An account of the life and assassination of I. A. al-Shelhi (in Arabic).

Bérenger-Féraud, L. J. B. *Annales tripolitaines.* Paris, 1927.

Bernet, E. *En Tripolitanie.* Paris, 1912.

Evans-Pritchard, E. E. *The Sanusi of Cyrenaica.* Oxford, 1949.

Graziani, R. *Pace romana in Libia.* Milan, 1937.

Great Britain, Commercial Relations and Exports Dept. *Libya*, by H. H. Thomas. London, HMSO, 1955. (Overseas Economic Surveys.)

Holmboe, Knud. *Desert Encounter; an Adventurous Journey through Italian Africa*, trs. by H. Holbek. London, 1936.

Khalidi, Ismail Raghib. *Constitutional Development in Libya.* Beirut, 1956.

Micacchi, Rodolfo. *La Tripolitania sotto il dominio dei Caramanli, 1709–1835*, ed. A. Airoldi. Rome, 1936.

Moore, M. *The Fourth Shore.* London, 1940.

Tully, R. *Letters during a Ten Years' Residence at the Court of Tripoli, from Originals in Possession of the Family of Richard Tully, Esq., the British Consul.* London, 1957.
    An interesting account.

United Nations, Technical Assistance Mission to Libya. *The Economic and Social Development of Libya*, by Benjamin Higgins. A/AC. 32/TA. 16, 1 July 1952; mimeo.
    This report is not generally available. A condensed version, with the same title, was published in New York in 1953.

Villard, H. S. *Libya, the New Arab Kingdom.* London, 1956.

Bibliographies

Evans-Pritchard, E. E. *A Select Bibliography of Writings on Cyrenaica.* Pts. 1 and 2, reprinted from *African Studies*, September 1945 and September 1946.

Playfair, Sir R. L. 'Bibliography of the Barbary States. Pt. 1: Tripoli and the Cyrenaica', Royal Geographical Society, *Supplementary Papers*, vol. 2, 1899.
    From antiquity to 1888.

INDEX

CC

Frances Greenslade was born in St. Catharines, Ontario, and has since lived in Manitoba, Saskatchewan and BC. She has a BA in English from the University of Winnipeg and an MFA in Creative Writing from UBC. Frances teaches English at Okanagan College in Penticton, BC.

SHELTER

In Northern Canada in the sixties, Jenny and
Maggie are sisters who live with their wild,
imaginative mother and their father in
Duchess Creek. Dad, a logger who knows the
ways of the woods, takes Maggie on camping
trips where he teaches her survival skills and
shelter building. But when he dies in a
logging accident, their mother takes the girls
on camping trips to make them self-
sufficient. However, Mom goes missing after
leaving them with friends while she works at a
logging camp . . . What kind of shelter can
two young girls make then?

FRANCES GREENSLADE

SHELTER

Complete and Unabridged

CHARNWOOD
Leicester

First published in Great Britain in 2011 by
Virago Press, an imprint of
Little, Brown Book Group
London

First Charnwood Edition
published 2012
by arrangement with
Little, Brown Book Group
London

British Library CIP Data

Greenslade, Frances, *1961 –*
Shelter.
1. Canada, Northern- -History- -20th century- -
Fiction.
2. Large type books.
I. Title
813.6–dc23

ISBN 978–1–4448–1299–2

Published by
F. A. Thorpe (Publishing)
Anstey, Leicestershire

Set by Words & Graphics Ltd.
Anstey, Leicestershire
Printed and bound in Great Britain by
T. J. International Ltd., Padstow, Cornwall

This book is printed on acid-free paper

For David, who told me stories.

FOOD

1

Jenny was the one who asked me to write all this down. She wanted me to sort it for her, string it out, bead by bead, an official story, like a rosary she could repeat and count on. But I started writing it for her, too. For Mom, or Irene as other people would call her, since she abandoned a long time ago whatever 'Mom' once meant to her. Even now there was no stopping the guilt that rose up when we thought of her. We did not try to look for our mother. She was gone, like a cat who goes out the back door one night and doesn't return, and you don't know if a coyote got her or a hawk or if she sickened somewhere and couldn't make it home. We let time pass, we waited, trusting her, because she had always been the best of mothers. She's the mother, that's what we said to each other, or we did in the beginning. I don't know who started it.

That's not true. It was me. Jenny said, 'We should look for her.' I said, 'She's the mother.' When I said it, I didn't know the power those few words would take on in our lives. They had the sound of truth, loaded and untouchable. But they became an anchor that dragged us back from our most honest impulses.

★ ★ ★

3

We waited for her to come to get us and she never did.

There was no sign that this would happen. I know people always look for signs. That way they can say, *we're not the type of people things like that happen to*, as if we were, as if we should have seen it coming. But there were no signs. Nothing except my worry, which I think I was born with, if you can be born a worrier — Jenny thinks you can.

Worry was stuffed into the spaces around my heart, like newspaper stuffed in the cracks of a cabin wall, and it choked out the ease that should have been there. I'm old enough now to know that there are people who don't feel dogged by the shadow of disaster, people who think their lives will always be a clean, wide-open plain, the sky blue, the way clearly marked. My anxiety curled me into myself. I couldn't be like Jenny, who was opened up like a sunny day with nothing to do but lie in the grass, feel the warm earth against her back, a breeze, the click of insects in the air. *Soon, later, never* — words not invented. Jenny was *always* and *yes*.

As I say, there was no sign of anything that might go wrong in the small, familiar places that made up our world. The bedroom Jenny and I shared was painted robin's egg blue and the early morning sunlight fell across the wall, turning it luminous, like an eggshell held to the light. I watched how it fell, and after a while tiny shadowed hills rose up and valleys dipped in the textured lines of the wallboard. Morning in that land came slow and slanted with misty light,

4

waking into the glare of day.

Our house in Duchess Creek had a distinctive smell that met me at the front door: boiled turnip, fried bologna, tomato soup, held in the curtains or in the flimsy walls and ceiling or the shreds of newspaper that insulated them. It was a warm house, Mom said, but not built by people who intended to stay. The kitchen cupboards had no doors and the bathroom was separated from the main room by a heavy flowered curtain. Electricity had come to Duchess Creek in 1967, the year I turned seven and Jenny eight. A saggy wire was strung through the trees to our house a few months later. But we had power only occasionally, and only for the lights.

The small electric stove had been dropped off by one of Dad's friends who found it at the dump in Williams Lake. It was never hooked up and Mom never made a fuss about it, though her friend Glenna asked her about twice a week when she was going to get the stove working. Glenna said, 'Hey, aren't you happy we've finally joined the twentieth century?' Mom said that if she wanted to join the twentieth century, she'd move to Vancouver. Glenna laughed and shook her head and said, 'Well, I guess you're not the only one who thinks that way. There's people who like it that Williams Lake is the biggest town for miles and miles in any direction.'

In the Chilcotin, where we lived, there were the Indians, the Chilcotins and the Carriers, who had been here long before the whites came. Their trails and trade routes still criss-crossed the land. And there were the white settlers whose

5

histories were full of stories about pioneering and ranching and road-building. Then there were the late-comers, like our family, the Dillons.

Dad had left Ireland in 1949 for America and ended up in Oregon, then had come north. Others came to avoid marching into wars they didn't believe in, or ways of life they didn't believe in. Some came from cities, with everything they owned packed into their vehicles, looking for a wild place to escape to. They were new pioneers, reinventing themselves following their own designs. Dad had a friend named Teepee Fred and another named Panbread. When I asked Dad what their last names were, he said he'd never bothered to ask.

* * *

Mom didn't care much about the electric stove because she had learned to cook on the woodstove. She cooked out of necessity, not pleasure, and stuck mainly to one-pot stews that she could manage without an oven. We didn't have an electric fridge, either. We had a scratched old icebox where a lonely bottle of milk and a pound of butter resided.

There was a pump in the backyard where we got our water. Someone before us had made plans for indoor plumbing. There was a shower and sink in the bathroom, and a hole in the floor, stuffed with rags, where a pipe came in for a toilet, but none of these worked. We pumped our water and carried it in a five-gallon bucket that sat on the kitchen counter. We had an outhouse, but at night we set a toilet seat over a tin pot and Dad emptied it each morning.

Just at the edge of the bush behind the house, Dad had rigged up a heavy, old claw foot bathtub especially for Mom. Underneath he had dug a hole and in that he'd make a small fire. He ran a hose from the pump to fill the tub. The water heated nicely and Mom sat in there on a cedar rack he'd made so she wouldn't burn herself. Some evenings we'd hear her out there, singing to herself, her voice lifting out of the dark on the steam that rose from behind the screen of fir boughs he'd wound through a piece of fence. Sometimes I sat on a stump beside her, trailing my arm in the hot water. Bats wheeled and dipped above us, just shadows, a movement in the corner of the eye. Stars grew brighter and as thick as clouds of insects while the water cooled. I thought that if she needed any proof that Dad loved her, that bathtub was it.

★ ★ ★

There must have been a time when I sang myself awake, trilling up and down a range of happy notes as a beetle tracked across the window screen and cast a tiny shadow on the wall. But I don't remember it. I can't remember a time when I didn't look at the world and feel apprehension chewing at the edges. It wasn't our mother I worried about, though. I felt lucky to have a mom who took us camping, wasn't afraid of bears, loved to drive the logging roads and what she called the 'wagon trails' that wandered

7

off Highway 20 and into the bush. We found lakes and rotting log cabins and secret little valleys; it felt like we were the first people to find them. Our measure of a good camp was how far from other people it was. 'No one around for miles,' Mom would say, satisfied, when the fire was built. She was the constant in our lives, the certainty and the comfort. It was Dad I worried about.

He had to be approached like an injured bird, tentatively. Too much attention and he would fly off. If he was in the house, he was restless. He would stretch, look around as if he was an outsider, and then I'd feel the sting of disappointment as he went for his jacket by the door.

Sometimes he whistled, made it seem casual, putting his arms into the flannel sleeves. Then he'd go outside, chop wood for a few minutes, like a penance, then disappear into the bush. He'd be gone for hours. Worse days, he'd go to his bedroom and close the door.

I listened with my ear against the wall of my room. If I stood there long enough, I'd hear the squeak of bedsprings as he turned over. I don't know what he did in there. He had no books or radio. I don't think he did anything at all.

When he came back from his working day in the bush, he liked to sleep in the reclining chair by the oil drum that was our woodstove. I wanted him to stay asleep there. If he was asleep, he was with us.

But sometimes he pulled the chair too close to the woodstove. One afternoon, I tried to get him

8

to move it back. 'Don't worry, Maggie,' he said. 'I'm not close enough to melt.' And he fell asleep with his mouth open, occasionally drawing a deep breath that turned to a cough and woke him briefly.

I wasn't afraid that he would melt. I was afraid that the chair would burst suddenly into flames, as the Lutzes' shed roof once did when Helmer got the fire in the garbage bin burning too high.

At the counter, my mother stood slicing deer meat for stew. I watched, waiting for his eyelids to sag, flicker, and drop closed again. Mom peeled an onion, then began to chop. Jenny and I had our Barbies spread on the sunny yellow linoleum. Jenny's Barbie wanted to get married and since we didn't have a Ken, my Barbie had to be the husband. I tucked her blonde hair up under a pair of bikini bottoms. Mom turned to us. Her eyes streamed with tears. For some reason, we found her routine with the onions and the tears very funny. We put our hands over our mouths so we wouldn't wake Dad. Mom never cried. Maybe that's why we found it so improbable that something as ordinary as an onion could have this power over her.

She moved to the woodstove. The sweet smell of onions frying in oil rose up and then Mom dropped the cubes of deer meat into the pot. A pungent, wild blood smell that I didn't like filled the house. But it only lasted a minute, then the meat and onions blended to a rich, sweet fragrance and Mom sprinkled in pepper and reached for a jar of tomatoes.

She struggled with the lid and turned to look

9

at Dad to see if he was awake. She wouldn't wake him. She wouldn't break the spell of all of us being there together by asking him to open a jar. Instead she got out a paring knife, wedged the blade under the rim and gave it a twist.

Smoky fall air spiced the room, drifting in through the kitchen window that was kept open an inch whenever the woodstove was going. The warm yellow linoleum heated my belly as I stretched out on the floor and Mom stood solidly at the counter, her auburn hair curled in a shiny question mark down the back of her favourite navy sweater. She wore her gingham pedal pushers, though it was too cold for them, and well-worn moccasins on her bare feet. Her calves were strong and shapely. Something about the knife and the jar made the easiness radiating through me begin to crumble. Mom had tacked up cloth decorated with brown Betty teapots under the sink to hide the drainpipe and garbage. This became part of my worry, the flimsiness of it. Maybe it meant that we didn't intend to stay, either.

Near the woodstove, black charred spots marred the washed yellow of the floor. Jenny teased me whenever I rushed over to stomp out the embers that popped from the stove when the door was open. Dad would tell her not to bother me about it. 'Mag's like me,' he'd say. 'Safety first.'

Dad worked with Roddy Schwartz on a Mighty Mite sawmill near Roddy's cabin. Roddy had brought the mill in from Prince George on a trailer. It had a Volkswagen engine that ran two saw blades along the logs and could cut almost any tree they hauled out. They usually spent a few days felling and limbing trees, then skidded them out to where the mill was assembled. Dad didn't like the skidding, because they couldn't afford a proper skidder. Instead they had an old farm tractor with a chain that they wrapped around the logs to pull them out of the bush. Dad worried about the logs snagging on something and the tractor doing a wheelie.

I had listened to him talking to Mom about the work one evening when they were sitting out on the porch.

'I don't trust Roddy when he's hungover,' he'd said. 'He gets sloppy like. Says I'm bitching at him. Like an old woman, he says. Claims he knows the mill inside out, could do it with his eyes closed. I keep telling him, it doesn't matter how many times you've done it. You let your guard down, one of those boards'll take your fingers off so fast you won't know what hit you.'

'Oh, Patrick,' Mom shuddered. 'Don't even say that.'

'I know, but he's a law unto to himself. Cocky bastard, that's what gets me. These are thirty foot trees we're fooling with.'

'Don't remind me.'

'You don't need to worry about me.' Dad raised his voice a little when he saw me standing at the screen door. 'Mr. Safety,' he said, and winked at me.

It was Dad's nickname. It wasn't just our family who called him that. His friends did too, irritated by his careful checking and rechecking

11

of his guns, his gear, his methodical testing of brakes before descending the Hill to Bella Coola. The Hill had an 18 percent grade and a reputation for turning drivers' legs to rubber. The local habit was to fuel up with liquor before making the attempt. But Dad was disgusted by that.

'You can't rush Mr. Safety,' his friends teased, lighting another cigarette to wait while he put an air gauge to each tire in turn.

★ ★ ★

Now as he slept in his reclining chair by the stove, I went over to hold my hand flat against the green vinyl. It was almost too hot to touch. I didn't know which I wanted more: to have him stay asleep and with us or to have him wake up and get out of harm's way. I stood behind his chair watching the whorl of his red hair quiver as he breathed. At the crown where the hair parted, a little patch of ruddy scalp showed.

I pulled a kitchen chair over to the counter and got down the biggest glass I could find. Then I scooped water into it from the bucket and, as Mom watched me, took a little sip. I carried the tall glass of water over to the chair where Dad slept and I stood on guard.

A few minutes passed calmly as I pretended to be interested in the top of Dad's head. Suddenly he drew one of his deep ragged breaths and his whole body went stiff, then jerky, with his hands pawing the air and choking sounds rising from his throat.

'Mom!' I called as she dropped her knife and whirled.

'Patrick, wake up,' she said. She knelt by his knees and took hold of his hands. He cried out then, making the most un-Dad-like sound I'd ever heard. Like a baby. Like a cornered animal.

'Patrick!' Mom said again, then, 'Give me your water, Maggie.'

I handed her the glass and she brought it to Dad's lips. 'Take a sip, Patrick. Have a drink. It's nice and cold. There you go, there you go.'

He opened his eyes and coughed as he swallowed.

Mom said, 'It's okay now, girls, he just had a terror.'

'I had a terror,' Dad said. That's what they called them, these fits of Dad's. Apparently, his father had had them too — seizures of fear that took possession of his whole body when he was on the edge of sleep. He drank down the water and shook himself awake. His messy red curls were damp with sweat.

'Don't look so worried, Mag,' he said and pulled me onto his lap. 'Nothing's going to happen to me. I'm Mr. Safety, remember?'

Dad smelled of tobacco and woodsmoke and the outdoor tang of fall leaves. I began counting the freckles on his arms.

'Do you think I have as many freckles on my arms as there are stars in the sky?' he asked.

'Maybe more,' I said. It was what I always said and it was what he always asked. As long as I was counting his freckles, he was my captive.

13

Nothing bad had happened. It was only a terror. Still I worried.

★   ★   ★

As I walked to the school bus each morning, shuffling my boots along in the fresh snow to make my own trail, Jenny already a powder blue beacon by the power pole at the highway, I worried about leaving Mom at home alone, about the wild way she swung the axe when she was splitting kindling and the way Dad nagged her to be careful. One of these days she was going to chop off her own foot, he said. And when we got off the bus at the end of the day, just before we rounded the final bend by the bent pine tree and our little house came into view, I worried that I'd see it engulfed in flames, or already a smoking heap. And each time it stood blandly, paint peeling to grey, smoke rising from the chimney pipe, I felt my tight muscles loosen and I broke into a run.

We were a normal family; that's our story. Our days were full of riverbanks and gravel roads, bicycles and grasshoppers. But you think a thing, you open a door. You invite tragedy in. That's what my worry taught me.

2

There were families in Duchess Creek who knew trouble like their own skin. Things went wrong for these families as a matter of course, and they were the subject of kitchen table conversations over the pouring of coffee and the dipping of biscuits, The Lutzes were one of those families. They lived a couple of miles from our place in a half-built house with plastic stapled over the windows and tarps on the roof to keep the rain out.

'It always comes in threes.' Glenna was having tea with my mother at the kitchen table. Her spoon rang against her cup, punctuating the authority of this remark. She let it sink in. Glenna worked at the nursing station in Duchess Creek, so she had the inside story on most of the tragedies in the area. 'First the twins, then Peggy's cancer treatments, and now this.'

'Poor Mickey,' Mom said.

Mickey Lutz was my best friend in Duchess Creek. Mom would let me go to their house for sleepovers only if Helmer was away on one of his hunting trips with his buddies. 'On a tear,' was what Mom called it. The house smelled like baby piss and sour milk. Dirty dishtowels hardened into place littered the living room, and balled-up socks, chewed baby toys, and drifts of dog hair. The Lutzes had a little white and brown dog named Trixie. Trixie was going grey around the mouth, like an old man, but she was so faithful she would run alongside Mickey and me on our bikes, limping to keep up. When we stopped, she'd curl up in the gravel on the side of the road, exhausted. But as soon as we made a move again, she'd force herself up on her rickety old legs and start running.

The bed Mickey and I slept in was always coated with white dog hair, and I would try to discreetly brush it off before I got in. Once, before bed, Peggy gave me an orange that smelled like a dirty sock. When I peeled it, the segments were dried out. I ate it anyway, because Mickey was eating hers and didn't seem to notice. For breakfast we had crackers and orange pop.

'The Lutzes all came in together,' Glenna continued. 'Just showed up at the nursing station like a pack of wolves with their injured. Helmer was hanging off Peggy's shoulder, poor thing; she could barely hold him up, and him dragging this bloody foot across the floor. Little Mickey had the baby.'

When Glenna came for coffee, she would bring her own packets of Sweet'N Low. She bought them in big boxes at the co-op in Williams Lake. It allowed her to count calories, so she said. It seemed to be her only gesture towards trying to lose weight. She tore open the Sweet'N Low packets as Mom refilled her cup and then, two at once, poured the powder into her coffee. She stirred, staring into her cup, giving Mom time to ask the questions to which she'd have the answers.

'Poor Peggy,' said Mom. 'How did he do it?'

'He was hunting.'

They both laughed at this. I knew it was because Helmer's idea of hunting was sitting on the tailgate of his truck in the sun, drinking beer and waiting for game to wander by. 'You know Helmer,' Glenna said, 'if there's trouble, he'll find it. He forgot the rifle was loaded? Who knows? Took off the whole big toe and part of the next two.'

Their heads moved left to right, slowly, in unison. It was pity, sincere, but with just a hint of self-satisfaction. I don't think it's fair to call their talk gossip, though. If they could have, they would have set Helmer up with a regular paying job. Driving truck would suit him, Mom said, doing deliveries town to town, up and down Highway 20, something not too challenging that would keep him out of the house and Peggy and the kids in groceries.

Still, there was always that underlying confidence that things like this couldn't happen to us. Glenna and Mom had husbands who knew better than to carry around their rifles with the safety off. They themselves knew better than to stay home pregnant with twins, like Peggy had, well past the due date.

'I don't know why she didn't get him to drive her to Williams Lake,' Glenna still said every time she came to visit, though it had happened months ago now and she'd heard all of Helmer's excuses. I'd heard Mom say Glenna kept talking about it because she felt guilty since one of the babies died on her shift, and Peggy herself had nearly bled to death in the nursing station and had to be rushed to the Williams Lake hospital.

As for the cancer, the talk was that Peggy had never taken good care of herself. She spent too much time inside, she didn't get enough fresh air. They didn't eat properly either. Everyone knew that when Helmer got his welfare cheque, Peggy would stock up on TV dinners. I'd seen her myself in the store, wearing that defiantly ashamed face as she stacked the counter with the flat boxes. Then when the money ran out, the Lutzes lived on Wonderbread and jam.

'He's a dead weight around Peggy's neck,' Glenna said, stirring. 'She'd be better off without him. Best thing that could happen to that family, Helmer isn't paying attention, gets airborne out over the canyon.'

'He's got horseshoes up the whazoo, that guy,' Mom said. 'He should be dead by now.'

'He should be dead three times over. Listen to us. I take it back, God,' Glenna called to the kitchen ceiling.

'Yeah, well,' muttered Mom. 'More coffee?' She glanced at me and Jenny playing checkers in the patch of sunlight by the woodstove. I suppose Mom thought that her conversations with Glenna were part of our education.

★ ★ ★

Mickey stayed with us the night her mother lost one of the twins. She stayed with us again when her mom found out she had cancer and had to fly to Vancouver for treatments. And she stayed

18

with us the night after her dad shot off half his foot with his 30.30. Mom had bought the new *McCall's* magazine and Mickey and I sat cross-legged on the bed cutting out the Betsy dolls. I could hear Mom at the kitchen counter, getting down pans, then the crash as they all slid to the floor.

'Sorry!' she called, to no one in particular. She began to hum 'Sweet Caroline.' Something else clattered to the floor.

She was making meatloaf following a recipe that allowed her to use the roasting pan on top of the woodstove. Mickey's and my feet were dusted with breadcrumbs from running through the kitchen looking for scissors and tape. Mom called to me to bring her a piece of toilet paper — she had grated her finger along with the carrots.

'Let's pretend I'm the dad,' said Mickey when I came back. She said it like 'lepretend,' which irritated me. She wasn't a baby. She should speak properly.

'Lepretend I just bought a new truck. Like it?' She drove her paper doll along the edge of my bedspread.

'What colour is it?' I asked.

'It's red,' she said.

Her games bored me, but I played along because I knew that this was the Lutz family story about how one twin died.

Helmer didn't drive to Williams Lake that night because he didn't think his truck would make it. He always kept a couple of cans of transmission fluid in the back so he could top it

19

up every few miles, all the while complaining about how he needed a new truck.

Mom had fumed about it for days when she'd heard.

'Slouching around with his guilty, hangdog look,' she said. Hangdog was the word Mom used to describe the kind of men who treated their families so badly in the privacy of their own homes that when they went out, they couldn't look anyone in the eye. Especially other women. Guilty conscience, that was the hangdog look.

'Lazy son-of-a-bitch,' Mom had said. 'Cowardly, lazy son-of-a-bitch. Blames it on his truck.'

Dad had laughed.

'What?' Mom demanded.

'Oh nothing, nothing,' he'd said, smiling.

'Tell me what's so funny then. You think losing a baby and almost dying yourself is funny?' She was really mad. 'She'd be better off without him. At least then she could keep the welfare cheque for herself and the kids. He's useless. Like a baby, only he's bigger and he eats more.'

★   ★   ★

'Lepretend you're the mom and you're going to have a baby,' said Mickey.

Mickey always wanted to play these improved-version-of-reality games. Even though they bored me, usually I said, 'Okay and my baby is the next king of the empire and we have to protect him from the kidnappers who are hiding in the hills nearby.' And that way we were both happy. But not today. Today I made my Betsy doll say, 'I

20

don't feel so good. I think I'm going to have my baby.'

'I'll drive you to the hospital,' Mickey's doll said.

'No thanks. I have my own truck,' I said. I couldn't help myself.

Mickey stared at me, at a loss for a minute.

'My truck's not new,' I said. 'But it works fine.'

'Let's go outside and play,' said Mickey.

That night, lying with Mickey's feet near my head and Jenny whistle-snoring in the next bed, I listened as the coyotes started yipping. One began it, a full-voiced, forsaken wail, long and high. Then others took it up, and the dogs from the nearby Indian reserve joined in, their unburdening ringing in the night.

At the other end of my bed, Mickey was crying. I could hear her, though she tried to stifle it.

I felt sorry for Mickey. But more than that, I was glad I was not her.

3

Nights when I couldn't sleep, when I worried about the fire in the woodstove and whether it would get too hot and set the roof on fire and we'd lose everything like the families whose kids had to come to school wearing their neighbours' too-big and too-small cast-offs, I would tiptoe to our bedroom door and peek out.

'I'm thirsty,' I'd say. And if Mom or Dad nodded, I padded across the warm floor, past the stove, brushing my hand across the back of Dad's chair as I went. I couldn't keep glasses of water on the dresser. Mom had an obsessive knowledge of the habits of mice. She knew, for instance, that though they only needed tiny amounts of water to survive, they did need water, and so each night before bed she made sure that cups and glasses were tipped bottoms up and the water bucket was covered with a board. One time, she had wakened to the sound of something rustling through the wastebasket and found a mouse going after the hardened flour and salt play-dough that Jenny and I had been rolling into cakes in the shower stall, then dropped in there. She slapped a piece of cardboard over the top of the basket and woke the whole house as she carried it out to the front yard, dumped it and smashed at the mouse with a shovel, her nightgown flapping in the moonlight. Dad, in his pyjama bottoms, stood at

22

the door laughing sleepily. 'Just let it go,' he called.

Her obsession worked to my advantage, since it meant I had to stand at the counter and drink down the whole glass of water, dry the glass and return it, bottom up, to the cupboard. That meant I could linger within the safety of Dad lightly snoring in his chair and the snap of Mom's game of solitaire on the table.

Sometimes I would find Mom and Dad playing cards together, with the table pulled close to the woodstove and the kerosene lantern burning between them. I'd drink my water and watch them, absorbed in their hands, shifting cards, teasing each other. Those rare nights I was content to go back to bed and listen to their muffled game and the sporadic victory shout from Mom, followed by Dad's low laughter.

But usually, if I couldn't sleep after the drink of water, I followed up with a tiptoed trip to the tin pot in the bathroom, shivering in my nightgown, because the bathroom never warmed up. Sometimes Dad noticed and said, 'Can't sleep?' and he pushed himself out of his chair and came to sit on the edge of my bed with me. He'd tuck the blankets close around my chin. 'Imagine we're out in the bush and we're building a lean-to shelter,' he'd say. 'We're setting some long sticks and fir boughs against the ridgepole. The clouds are building up for a good, hard storm, but we have to be patient. We want to be able to build a fire in front of the lean-to that's protected from the wind. One branch after another, weaving them into each other so they hold together. Make a nice, firm mat against the wind. You keep laying down the boughs, Maggie, and I'll make the fire. Then you gather up some leaves to put inside so it'll be nice and soft. Here comes the rain. We're just in time.'

I was glad to be in my bed then, and I could feel myself drift into the safety of sleep.

★   ★   ★

In the late summer and fall Dad would take me into the woods almost every weekend. Jenny never came on these outings and I never wondered why. She was off with her friends, playing Barbies or riding bikes down to the river for picnics and to play house in the forts they built. I figured she wouldn't have wanted to come. Dad and I never went very far, maybe an hour or so from home at most. Sometimes we went fishing in one of the small lakes. If there was an abandoned canoe or rowboat on shore, and often there was, we took that out, cast into the green softness of the early morning, mist rising up, the plop of a fish going for a fly. Once we built a raft ourselves, spent most of the day at it, cutting poles and lashing them to two floater logs. Then we paddled across the lake to an island where we made a fire and stayed until the moon rose. Sometimes we looked for mushrooms or berries and we brought a feed home to Mom and Jenny. But my favourite thing was when Dad showed me how to build a shelter for real. He knew how to make lean-tos, teepee style shelters, or natural shelters that already provided protection from the elements, like an overhanging rock that formed a cave and just needed some insulating leaves tucked into it for added warmth.

'I want to show you the place I found, Maggie,' he said one Sunday when I was nine.

Little lakes dotted the land around Duchess Creek, and roads led to many of them. Some of the roads were logging roads. Some had been made by homesteaders who'd put up cabins in the woods, made a go of it for a while, hand-logging or doing odd jobs, then moved on and left the cabins to the raccoons and the mice, shells of hand-chinked logs and caved-in roofs, mouldy newspapers, dusty shelves and canning jars. I liked to imagine what these cabins would be like at night, with the wind whistling through the empty window spaces and the dust kicking up where the door used to be and moonlight falling on rusted bedsprings.

It was fall. Dad kept the window open a crack; a sharp tangy breeze freshened the cab. As we followed the rutted road deeper into the woods, we slowed and the sun on the windshield warmed my face. The truck bounced over rocks and tree roots, rocking me to sleepiness.

'Warm in here, eh?' Dad said. He wore his blue flannel jacket; his red hair curled over the collar. 'Hold the wheel for me?'

I scooted over and held on while he took off his jacket. The steering wheel jerked like something alive in my hands.

'You want to drive?'

'Yes, please.'

Dad gripped the wheel again then braked to a stop as I crawled under his arm to sit in the little triangle of seat between his legs. He put his hand over mine on the gearshift and helped me find first. We lurched forward then stalled.

'That's okay,' he said. 'Try again, Maggie.'

Once we were riding along in second I relaxed a little into Dad's warm chest. His freckled arms, and his scent of sweat and tobacco, made a protective circle around me.

I drove until the track petered out into grass, then Dad took over again. The woods closed around us, a lit tunnel of yellow, orange and red. Aspen leaves whipped the truck windows and caught in the mirrors; trees scraped along our sides; a branch with brilliant yellow leaves caught in the windshield wipers and fluttered there like a butterfly trying to free itself. Then the canopy of trees opened into a clearing by a small turquoise lake and Dad parked the truck. A peeling, overturned rowboat lay half-hidden in reeds.

'Here we are.'

We got out. A crisp wind rippled across the lake, sending up a faint song from the reeds and grasses.

'See this tree?' Dad said. It was a big old gnarly fir with a solid branch that curved out from the trunk about eight feet up. 'I'll show you how to make a double lean-to shelter from this tree. You go find a long sturdy branch, one that'll go from the crook here to about here.'

I went off into the bush. Leaves dropped from

above like large snowflakes, sailing gently down to land on the spongy forest floor. I stood and watched them, the whole woods gently raining dying leaves. Underfoot, the ground felt hollow, a shell of earth covered in dead leaves and fragrant burnt orange pine needles. Below, the tunnelled homes of insects, ants and beetles, then below that, the hollowed bones of animals, layer upon layer, then rock then coal.

I picked up a branch. It felt hollow in my hands and when I cracked it against the side of a tree it flew into pieces. Deeper in, I came across a tangle of deadfall. I took up an aspen limb, thick enough, and pulled it from the tangle. It was about twelve feet long, still greenish, not brittle. A high wind rose and shivered through the trees. I turned and looked for the lake. Through the leaves, sun glinted on water.

When I got back, Dad was sitting on the hood of the truck smoking, his red curls fluttering like the fall leaves.

'Good job, Maggie,' he said. 'That's perfect.' He jumped down from the truck, put out his cigarette and put the butt back in the package.

'A lean-to is one of the easiest shelters to build. But this one has an extra wall,' Dad said. 'We don't need it to be very big, so we'll put the ridgepole right about here. Now what are you going to look for?'

'The sun. Face the door east for the morning sun.'

'That's right. You want that warmth to hit you as early as possible.' Dad set the ridgepole tightly into the V of the tree. 'But we're going to make it a little more to south so we can look out at the lake. Now what else?'

'Make sure there's no overhanging dead branches and we're not near any landslide danger.'

'Anything like that around here?'

'No.'

'Right. This is a perfect little spot at the edge of this clearing here. The bush behind us, the lake in front, but not too close. We don't want animals stumbling over us on their way to get a drink.'

Dad placed one of the branches he had gathered against the ridgepole. 'It doesn't matter if they stick up,' he said. 'It makes it stronger.' We worked quietly in the autumn sun, laying branches to make the walls of the shelter. After a while, a cold wind blew up and drummed at our bare hands and faces. When I went to get more branches, I squatted for a minute against the lee side of a pine out of the wind, the sun on my face and the sweet warm spice of bark and forest rising up around me.

I couldn't wait to be done the shelter and climb inside away from the wind. But Dad was methodical and, even though we were only building the shelter for this afternoon, he would make sure it was near perfect.

'Know why I came to this country?' he said, as we worked.

'You'd had enough of Ireland.'

'Yes, but I could have stayed in the States. I got a job logging in Oregon. I made pretty good money. For Christmas I went to Portland to spend some of it. In a little bar I heard a musician named Pete Seeger, singing about the draft. I'd read in the paper that they were going to call up fifty thousand young men for the army. That was the Korean conflict. I didn't leave Ireland to get caught up in someone else's war.

'When I went back to work, I met a fellow who told me his grandfather had been a chief of one of the great tribes near Bella Coola. They were like the kings and queens of the land back then. So much wealth, they gave it away just to show how wealthy they were. But the government came along and outlawed all that, their language, their religion, their old songs and dances. I told him it was just like in Ireland.

'His mother had married into the Ulkatcho band. He said if I went almost straight north of where we were in Oregon, and just kept going, I'd find the place where he grew up. There was a network of trails the people had made over hundreds of years, from Bella Coola to Williams Lake, and they moved along those trails following the food and the seasons. You never had to go hungry as long as you knew what you were doing. As long as you had your freedom, you could find game, berries, fish. It was a land of plenty. Make your way to the coast and you've got nature's grocery, free for the taking: cockles and clams and salmon. So I came. I listened and I watched. That's how you learn to do it.'

When he felt satisfied that the pine bough walls would repel a light rain and heavy dew, if not a downpour, he said, 'Let's try her out.' We backed into the opening, one of us on either side

29

of the supporting tree, until just our heads were poking out.

'If you ever get lost, this is what you do first. You build yourself a little shelter. Don't forget.'

I couldn't forget. He told me the same thing every time we went into the bush.

'And oh, I almost forgot.' He took a bottle of Orange Crush from inside his jacket and handed it to me. Then he brought out a beer for himself. He fished deeper in his inside pocket and brought out a package wrapped in a dishcloth. 'Then you eat your chocolate biscuits.'

★   ★   ★

Some people believe that a person knows when he's going to die. Even if he's not sick, even if death comes out of nowhere like a deer on the highway. I don't know about that. But sometimes I think about it when I remember this afternoon with my father.

The pop chilled me, but I drank it, shivering, because he'd brought it for me. Dad cracked open his beer and had a few slow sips as we watched the lake rippling in the wind. He said, 'You know, Maggie, I'm not fond of talking. You know that, don't you? Nothing I think about seems worth saying when I think twice about it. Your mother doesn't understand that.'

He took a sip of beer and smiled at me. The right fish bait to use, the name of the bird trilling an unfamiliar song, these were the things Dad usually told me. I didn't know if I was supposed to say anything or not.

30

'You know on a sunny afternoon when we sit outside against the house and the sun is warming us? I look at her and she looks lit up. Her skin, her hair and everything. And then I feel it. Like a little fish flipping on the bottom of the boat. It makes me want to celebrate. I want to get a cold beer and forget about the rest of the day. Make a toast, to her.

'And if I could just spit it out, the way I see her. But I never do. The words just don't seem good enough. And when I go and get a beer, I spoil everything. You know that look she gets?'

He took a long swallow.

'She never says anything, bless her. I can tell she's trying to keep the smile on her face. And I know I'm going to spoil everything, but I can't help myself. Now why is that?'

Did he want me to answer? I held the Orange Crush to my lips, took a gulp, and studied the backwash as it foamed into the bottle.

'My father, your grandfather, he was the same. No, he was worse. I swore I'd never become a drunk like him. And I never did. I'm my own kind of drunk.'

He tipped the neck of his beer at me, and said 'cheers.' I clinked my Orange Crush bottle into his, the way we always did.

* * *

I had never seen Dad drunk like Helmer, laughing loudly at jokes that weren't that funny, then turning weepy, then suddenly mean and the other men trying to calm him down. My mother

31

hated that maudlin weakness in a man and I suppose if Dad had been that kind of drunk, she wouldn't have married him. 'It goes from funny to pitiful to mean pretty quick,' she said.

But there were those nights when Mom went to bed without him, after her low, pleading voice came through our bedroom wall and his turned insistent: 'I'm just enjoying myself here, Irene.' I could hear Mom's anger in the slam of a dresser drawer, the rattle of hangers in her closet. I wondered what kept him sitting there by the stove all by himself, sometimes singing 'Goodnight Irene' softly. His shaky whispery voice made me smile, but it didn't have that effect on Mom.

When he started in on his Irish songs it made Mom cry. Once I heard her say, 'You remind me of my dad.' I didn't see why his singing would make her cry. I was mad at her for leaving him alone and for being angry at him. Why wouldn't she sing with him and have fun, like he wanted?

And there was the day when Dad, his friend Panbread and Mom were playing darts against the side of the house. I could hear Dad teasing Mom about something. Next thing I knew, Mom was telling Jenny and me to get our shoes on because we were going for a walk. She went in the house to get us some apples for the road and baseball caps to keep the sun off.

Dad called after her, 'Aw, come on Irene, finish the game at least.'

I heard Panbread say, 'Let her go, Pat. That's women for you.' Then they both laughed, too hard and too long, and I was glad that Mom was in the house and couldn't hear them.

Mom set a blistering pace through the woods, then slowed as we picked our way up a dry creekbed. I stopped so often to pick up smooth rocks that Jenny was way ahead of me, out of sight, and Mom was a long way past her. The sun burned down on the creekbed. I caught glimpses of hummingbirds hovering over orange Indian paintbrush. A woodpecker drummed against a tree. The sun, the hollow drumming reverberating through the firs, the soft clacking of my running shoes against stones wrapped me in a cocoon. Some part of me was looking down at myself, moving along the creek. A narrow trickle of water wove its way through the stones. When the tips of my running shoes turned dark from the water, I raised my eyes and there were trembling Saskatoon bushes, bright white daisies and turquoise sky. I felt as if I had wakened from a dream.

Then I heard Mom calling me. 'Ma-ggie!' the two-note fee-bee, like a chickadee. 'Ma-ggie! Come on. We're over here.'

I followed a skinny deer path through the brush and over a little rise. There was Mom, up to her neck in a clear green-blue lake. Jenny was jumping up and down with excitement in the mud, naked except for her baseball cap, her long red hair sticking out from under it.

'Guess what?' Mom called.

'What?'

'It's not deep!' and she threw her arms up and burst splashing from the water like a jumping fish. It was only waist-deep on Mom who was

33

naked too, her clothes dumped in the grass beside Jenny.

'Hurry up!' Jenny yelled at me, and laughed as she ran into the water with her baseball cap still on.

I remember that sweet, bone-tired exhaustion we got from playing in the water for hours. We had to duck under the water to escape the horseflies. We held contests: chasing each other in the shallows, our hands in the mud pushing us along; who could stay sitting upright on a floating log the longest; who could hold her breath longer; who could spring out of the water and into the air higher. We dried off on a big boulder in the sun, with the warm stone under our cheeks, then back into the water again to cool off, yelling at Mom to watch from where she was lying on our clothes in the grass, her smooth hip curved into her waist and one brown-nippled breast resting against the other.

By the time we dragged ourselves within sight of home that evening, the summer sky had darkened to purple. Our legs felt like rubber from the long walk and we couldn't stop giggling, because we were all tired and scratching in fits at ourselves. Along with mosquito bites, we'd got some kind of swimmer's itch from the lake.

'We'll have to have baths,' Mom said. 'Then we'll put some calamine lotion on.'

Jenny led the way to the front step. 'Dad,' she said, and stopped. She'd nearly stepped on him. He was curled up on the grass at the foot of the steps with a toppled kitchen chair beside him.

'Go in the house,' Mom said.

'Is he all right?' Jenny asked.

'Go on in the house, Jenny, Maggie. Go on!'

Jenny and I went inside, but we stood near the door and watched.

Mom had him half off the ground, hauling on him to get him up. But he slipped through her arms and slumped back to the grass.

'For Christ's sake, Patrick! Come in the house.'

It was one of the few times I heard my mother swear and it scared me. Though we only went to church at Easter and Christmas, she considered herself a good Catholic and God-related curses were strictly forbidden in our house.

'What's the problem, Irene?' my dad said, suddenly awake.

'Get in the house. Go to bed.'

'Calm down, calm down. I was just getting some air.' He shook free of her and waltzed into the house, winking at Jenny and me as he went by.

Mom let him go. She sat on the step, her back to us.

'I'm itchy,' Jenny said after a few minutes.

Mom pushed herself up and went to pump water for our bath.

4

One morning in June, when I was ten, Mom called Jenny and me to the door to watch the Indians from Duchess Creek Reserve heading to Potato Mountain, where they'd camp and harvest wild potatoes.

'Used to be a lot more of them,' Mom said, leaned against the door, watching. 'Big caravans, like you'd imagine crossing the desert. When I was a kid they used to take the trail right behind our cabin. When my dad saw them headed to Potato Mountain, he'd get antsy. He wanted to go up there, too. The Indians used to move around more back then, for fishing and hunting.'

It still seemed like a lot of people to me, more than I ever saw when we rode our bikes around the reserve. Where had they all come from? They had their horses loaded down with packs and tools and bedding. Some of the horses had five-gallon cans strapped to their backs. These were to bring back the potatoes they would dig. A long string of dogs trotted along behind the horses. A team pulled a Bennett-wagon, made from the frame of an old car, with old folks and kids riding in it, some of them holding even littler babies.

When Mom raised her hand to wave, a woman left the group and came walking up the driveway. She was about Mom's age, with long hair as shiny black as a crow's wing and wearing a purple-flowered print dress over her pants. Even with the pants, I could see her legs were thin and a little bowed. But she walked like I imagined a ballerina would walk, graceful, her toes touching down first, lightly, on the gravel.

'Agnes,' Mom acknowledged.

'Brought your moccasins,' the woman said. She had a soft whispery voice and a way of cocking her head, like she was shy. Jenny, sitting next to me, pinched my arm as a warning. When I looked up at Agnes's face, I gasped. Her lip had a mashed gap in it that joined her nose in what looked like an open wound. She smiled at Jenny and me kindly and I felt my face flush in embarrassment for reacting.

'You remembered,' my mother said. She took the moccasins from Agnes, a large pair made of soft moosehide, beaded with blue and orange and white beads. Dad's birthday was coming. 'Get my purse, Maggie.'

I realized that Agnes was the woman Glenna sometimes talked about. 'I feel so sorry for the poor thing,' I'd heard her say. 'She says no one will marry her because of the harelip. And you know she's probably right.'

Mom never agreed with Glenna about Agnes. 'I think she does all right. There's something about that woman that's made of steel.'

I'd also overheard Glenna talking to my mom about the time Agnes came to the nursing station with bruises on her face. 'And with that harelip. What a mess!' The man who had promised to marry Agnes had done it. My mother called it rape, a word I didn't know then, and she and

Glenna had argued about the word. 'But can you call it rape?' Glenna asked, and my mother had gotten angry.

As for me, I had not understood how something so minor as a harelip, which I had pictured as a kind of soft mustache, could have such an impact, and I thought this was something maybe peculiar to Indian men, this dislike of hair, like some of the other traits that they were supposed to have, like never allowing themselves to be rushed, or spending money as fast as they got it.

I brought the purse back and handed it to Mom, deliberately looking in Agnes's face to let her know I wasn't bothered.

'Bring back potatoes for you girls,' she said, as if she was telling us a secret, and she smiled again.

'Thank you,' Jenny and I said.

We watched her go. Her long hair swung gently down her back as she picked her way carefully along the road to rejoin the caravan.

'Some years Dad would get up to Potato Mountain,' Mom said then. 'He went looking for cattle but he stayed to race horses.' She rarely talked about her parents. Her mom had died when she was little, and her dad wanted to be a cowboy, not a father, that's what she said. 'Mom went with him once. They joined the Indians camping one night. She said she'd never seen so many wildflowers as she did in the meadows they passed through on the ride up: Indian paintbrush and yellow balsamroot and blue mountain lupines covering the hills. And then at the top, the blankets of white potato flowers. She only went that once, but she talked about it as if she'd gone every year. She would say, 'I remember that mountain covered in little white flowers.'' Mom made her voice wistful, teasing: ''And the berries. So many you couldn't pick them all. Dik. That's what the Indians called them. We ate dik and wild potatoes, this big, the size of my thumbnail, and deer meat cooked over the fire. And at night the stars were so thick. As thick as the white flowers covering the hills. We slept outside under the stars. I say slept. The music and singing and dancing all night, who could sleep? You couldn't imagine all the stars.' And then when she got fed up with us, with the snow, and being trapped in the cabin all day, she used to say, 'I wish I could go to Potato Mountain. I want to see those wild flowers one more time before I die.''

'And did she?' I asked.

'No, she never did get back up that mountain.'

'I wish I could go to Potato Mountain,' Jenny said. 'Instead of going to school. All those kids are skipping the end of school. Lucky ducks.'

'I don't think I'd like it now. I used to want to go,' Mom said, still watching the caravan, the horses' hooves sending up little puffs of dust. 'Too much drinking now, from what I've heard.' She looked away and to the house, then added, 'That might not be true. That's just what people say.'

* * *

39

That night I had a dream that Mom, Jenny and I were getting ready to go up Potato Mountain. We were outside packing the car, even though in real life you couldn't get up the mountain in a car. We came in and out of the house with our suitcases and blankets while Dad sat in his green vinyl chair by the stove.

'Isn't Dad coming?' I asked Mom.

'No, he's not strong enough. He'd never make it up that mountain.'

I felt so sorry for him. Mom was right; he was only a little boy and he'd hold us all back. I looked at him sleeping in the chair. Then it hit me: he was not sleeping at all — he was dead. The shock of it woke me up.

A bright half moon shone in our bedroom window, washing our bedspreads with ghostly blue light. Our clotheshorse cast the shadow of a hunched old woman on the wall. I listened to Jenny's gentle breathing and felt my own heartbeat clipping raggedly along. I sat up and looked at my sister for signs that she was actually awake. My feet touched the cold linoleum. Even in summer, our floor was cold at night. I bent over Jenny and she mumbled a bit then went back to snoring. She really was asleep. She'd be mad at me if I woke her up. I had the uneasy feeling that someone was outside watching me and so I forced myself to look out the window.

I thought of Agnes and her harelip and imagined her walking gracefully in the moonlight, along the road to Potato Mountain. Shadows crisscrossed the grass and driveway.

Something black darted across the yard, a bat probably. No wind at all, not a shiver.

I went to Mom and Dad's room and stood at the door. It was open about a foot and I listened to them breathe, Dad making a choppy, whistling sound. He was fine. I turned sideways and slipped into the room without a sound. On the dresser, Dad's jackknife gleamed in the moonlight. He kept it in his pocket all the time, pearl-handled and decorated with a moose and the words Beautiful British Columbia printed on it. He used it to cut twine, thread, fingernails, fruit. I picked it up and held it in my hand, and then took it into my room. I sat down on my bed and opened the blade. I turned it and watched it glint. I looked for something to test its sharpness. I didn't think it would cut the doubled edge of the sheet's hem, but when I ran the blade along it, it sliced through the fabric easily. Mom would be annoyed. When I went to snap it closed, the blade sliced my finger. A dark drop of blood spread on the sheet. I had to pad through the dark of the house to the bathroom for a piece of toilet paper to wrap my finger in. I fell asleep holding the knife in my hand.

When I woke up, Dad had already gone to the sawmill. I fished around in my blankets for his knife. I found it near the bottom of the bed, twisted in the sheets.

'Isn't that funny,' I heard Mom say from her bedroom as Jenny and I were eating breakfast.

'What?' Jenny called.

'Oh, your dad was looking for his jackknife this morning and he couldn't find it anywhere and here it is on the dresser, where he always leaves it.'

'Weird,' said Jenny, bent to her cornflakes. After a minute she raised her head and looked at me.

I felt guilty then, but it was nothing like the guilt I felt later, when we suddenly became a family like the Lutzes, our grief unfolding at the nurses' station for everyone to see. I pictured Dad that morning, looking for his knife and not finding it in its usual place, checking and re-checking the dresser-top, his pants pockets from yesterday. How many times that morning had he thrust his hand in his pocket to finger the smooth imitation pearl and not found it there?

* * *

I was the one who saw Roddy's truck at the nurses' station as we went by on the school bus that afternoon. Both cab doors were wide open and I thought of saying something to Jenny, but she was laughing with her friend Josie, and the two of them always made fun of anything I said. So instead, after we got off the bus, I yelled, 'Race you' and ran up the road ahead of Jenny with the worry boiling into panic.

'Why is Roddy's truck at the nurses' station?' I burst out as soon as I saw Mom. So in a way, it was me who brought the bad news.

'What?' I could see her fear was instant.

'The cab doors were open.'

'Stay here.' She grabbed the station wagon

keys from the hook near the door. 'I'll be back in a few minutes.'

'Mom? What's going on?' Jenny asked, trailing into the house.

'You two stay here. I'm going to the nurses' station.'

'Why?' said Jenny, but Mom was already out the door. We watched her drive off, dust flying up as she turned onto the highway.

★ ★ ★

Jenny says I didn't speak at all after Dad died. I don't remember not speaking, though I remember Mom crouched in front of me, holding my shoulders, looking into my face. 'Say something, Maggie,' she begged. I wanted to, for her sake. But what did she want me to say? I understood now how Dad had felt. There was absolutely nothing in my mind that seemed important enough to put into words. I heard Mom in the bedroom whispering with Glenna. Their whispers went on and on, crescendoed into anger, then fell back almost to silence, a soft mumbling like chickens settling in their roosts at night. What could they possibly have to say so much about?

I remember physical sensations — smell, hunger, heat and cold. I sat in Dad's green vinyl chair by the woodstove and I smelled him. Sawdust. Tobacco. Motor oil. Sweat. And something else. Warm, musty, spicy. Not really spicy. Not musty either. Like the top of his head, a familiar skin tang. I could smell it too if I went into Mom and Dad's room and stood there.

Women came with casseroles and tubs of stewed rhubarb and home-canned salmon and I watched them bend to try and find room in the icebox. I watched their strong legs — a hot spell had settled into the Chilcotin and the women wore the first shorts of the season. Their legs were rosy from the weeding they'd done under the noon sun. How could legs hold you up without you even having to think about it? But somehow there was something in your brain that kept them working and it could let go all of a sudden too, like Jenny's and Mom's had that afternoon when we found out what happened to Dad.

Mom had barely been able to stay standing when Glenna and Ron brought her through the door, each one holding her up by an elbow.

'Mom?' Jenny had said, then without even hearing a word, she folded like a lawn chair whose old aluminum legs have finally given out. Mothers don't have to be held up between two people unless the worst thing you've imagined as you sat staring out the window, waiting for the station wagon to appear at the end of your road, has actually happened.

'There's been an accident, girls,' Glenna said.

I hated her for saying it. I hated her instantly and ever after, the sight of her and her self-satisfied sympathy, as if she had immunity, and her a nurse who should know better.

'Is Dad dead?' Jenny managed through her tears.

Mom said simply, 'Yes.'

They say that when you get food poisoning, you'll never again eat the last thing you ate before getting sick, even if it was something else that poisoned you. I had the feeling that Dad died because I'd taken his jackknife. Later, I would learn that a pile of logs had rolled loose and knocked him flying. I would learn that Roddy had carried him like a baby into the nurses' station. Why this detail? Why 'like a baby'? But that's what people said, and so it made it hard to blame Roddy; people could go on liking Roddy if they wanted and not hate him for living when Mr. Safety had died.

The wake went on for four days, during which time a constant stream of food flowed into our little house. A big aluminum coffee pot bubbled on the stove. Someone's white coffee mugs were arranged in a row on the counter. Glenna even brought her Sweet'N Low. I watched her set out a little margarine tub of packets beside the mugs. I watched her tear them, two at a time, shaking the powder into her mug as the candle for Dad burned beside his photo. Her routine, at least, would not be broken, not even by the death of her best friend's husband. She was counting calories.

When there was no more room in the icebox, someone got the idea to dump ice into the unused shower and store the food there. Mom grumbled about this after everyone had gone home for the night. The ice had melted and she had to try to find room in the icebox for the pots of potato salad and plates of Nanaimo bars.

'Why all this eating?' I heard her saying to herself.

That's what I wanted to know, too. But I realized the food wasn't really for us. It gave each person who walked through the door something to say. 'I brought a rhubarb pie,' was something at least. 'Is there any room in the icebox?' was something else and 'I'll make another pot of coffee' was something else again. And so the talk went on and the ache and the anger and the fear burned like the candle, endlessly.

Dad himself was nowhere to be seen, except in the framed photo that sat on top of a tall shelf that Glenna and Ron had brought over. I heard some adults whisper that there would be no viewing of his body because of the heat, and another corrected authoritatively that it was really because of the accident. I didn't know what either of these things meant.

★ ★ ★

After the funeral, as the reality of Dad's death descended, Jenny's grief gathered and built like a summer storm. Her crying spells piled on top of each other, majestic and furious, then died to small, helpless sobs as her body collapsed on her bed, beyond the ability of her mind to call it back together and stand and walk. Jenny's grief drew people to her. Glenna and the other women brought cups of chicken noodle soup to her bed and later came out with the cup saying, 'She took a little more than half,' or,

46

'She barely touched it.'

For me, where Dad had been there was a hole now, gaping with the memory of him. I couldn't find a way to put it into words. But each night Jenny talked to Mom, who sat with us until Jenny wore herself out with questions.

'Are we going to be poor now?' Jenny asked. 'Like the families who have to wear other people's hand-me-downs?'

'No, sweetie, that's not going to happen.'

'Did Dad love me?'

'Of course he loved you, don't be silly.'

'Why did he always take Maggie to the woods and not me?'

'Oh, Jenny. I don't think he ever knew you wanted to go. He thought you preferred girly things. He brought you Barbies from Williams Lake, didn't he?'

'Maggie's more of a tomboy, I guess. No offence, Mag.'

In this way, her storm began to calm.

After a few days, two of Jenny's friends came and took her outside. They would sit on a blanket in the sun with their Barbies, dressing them up in different outfits and combing their hair with little pink combs and brushes. They went on picnics, with their lunch in a cloth sack. I watched them disappear into the trees, three sets of legs pale against the rich green of the woods, their ponytails swinging softly down their backs. Hours later I saw them reappear on the road, coming from the other direction, blurry in the heat haze rising from the highway.

After the hot spell, the rain came. The noise of it woke me early one morning, the hollow ping ping on the stovepipe and a gentle steady pattering on the roof like small pebbles were falling. It picked up force as I lay there listening, until it hammered down in a roar of water. Mom got up to close her window, then went out to the kitchen and closed those windows, too.

Jenny opened her eyes and lay there blinking at me. I pictured the rain soaking the road, the patchy lawn around our house, our vegetable garden, and the scented, springy earth beneath the spruce outside our window. The roaring abated a little, like an engine gearing down, then rose and rose and rose to a thunder of water, as if the sky had cracked wide open and an ocean of rain poured on Duchess Creek.

I felt the creep of worry. A steady dribble of roof run-off twisted in a finger-sized stream across our bedroom window. It wasn't that. Mom clattered in the kitchen and the leak trickling in by the stovepipe drummed into an aluminum pot. It wasn't that, either.

After breakfast I put on my rubber boots and went outside to crouch under the limbs of the spruce. The rain continued, a steady slanting volley.

'In a pinch, you can always find natural shelter,' Dad had told me the fall day we'd built the lean-to by the lake.

'Like under the spruce tree at home,' I'd said.

'That's right. If you just need something

temporary, there's almost always something you can use. But you might as well build yourself a shelter. It helps you think, keeps you from panicking until you're found.'

A puddle seeped into the thick bed of needles under the spruce and crept closer to my rubber boots. If I was going to camp under here, I would need to dig a trench to catch the runoff and a trough to carry it away. I realized that what I was worried about was the lean-to by the lake that Dad and I had built the fall before. I hoped it was still standing. And if someone was in it, I hoped the rain was not seeping in through the branches.

★   ★   ★

After the rain started, we were left alone with our grief like a family in quarantine. For a time, even Glenna seemed to be avoiding my mother.

'If this rain keeps up, I'm going to have get up there and fix that leak,' Mom said as she made lunch in the dull light of another rainy afternoon.

'Why don't you ask Glenna to get Ron to do it for you?' Jenny said.

Mom looked at her for a minute, thinking. 'I guess I've never really fit in in Duchess Creek,' she said. She didn't seem regretful or upset. She spoke as if this was a fact she'd only just learned. 'I was more at home on the ranches where my dad worked. I could go into the hills for hours and never see anyone. I even preferred the coast, where I didn't know anyone. Though I hated the rain,' she continued, to herself, it seemed, more than to Jenny.

Late in the afternoon, the sun came out and shone on the puddles and brightened the leaves and grass. Mom got the wooden ladder from under the front porch and asked me to hold it for her as she climbed onto the roof.

'Maggie, Jenny you've got to come up here,' she called, as she looked out over the land. 'Jenny, you hold the ladder for Maggie.'

I scrambled onto the wet roof where Mom was straddling the ridgepole. She held out her hand and guided me up to sit facing her, one leg on each side of the roof.

'Look how far you can see.' She pointed with her hammer out beyond the glistening highway and across the meadows that ran down to the valley. I was still not talking and I knew Mom was doing her best to unlock whatever had a hold over me.

'Things look different from up here, don't you think?'

I smiled at her. Jenny climbed up and joined us.

We watched as a white pick-up truck slowed and took the turn at our driveway. I could see into the box: a cage with chickens in it, a stack of two-by-fours, some buckets. The truck stopped below us and the door opened and a blonde woman in overalls and a white T-shirt got out.

'Need any help up there?' she called. 'I saw you from the road.'

'Know anything about roofing?' Mom yelled.

Her head appeared above the eavestrough. She

had long braids and bangs cut evenly across her forehead. 'Is there room for me? It looks like a party up here.'

It turned out that the woman, whose name was Rita, knew quite a bit about roofing, and a lot of other useful things, too. I liked the way she helped without taking over. She showed Jenny and me how to place the shingles we'd found in the shed and then watched as Mom nailed them into place. After that job was done, Mom made coffee and they sat on the damp step in the sun and drank it. Mom leaned back against the warm wall of the house like she always did and I saw her relax. Rita talked about the deer that had been eating from her garden, a young one who came by herself. No tin plates or bars of soap could keep her away.

'I finally just planted some lettuce and spinach for her,' Rita laughed. 'She seems to know that's her part of the garden. She doesn't eat from the main one anymore.' I wanted to ask if she'd given her a name, but I didn't. The sun lit Rita's pale bangs; the sharp smell of coffee and rank mud rose up from under the step.

'Does she have a name?' Jenny asked.

'A name?' Rita turned to Mom. Her eyes shone very green, like cats' eyes, and they were lazy, too, like a sleepy cat. 'Yes I have. I have given her a name. And the name I have given her is Fond. I call her Fond.'

'Fawned?' said Mom. 'Like pawned?'

'Sure. Like pond. Fond. F-O-N-D, because she's a fawn and I'm fond of her, you know.'

I liked Rita.

Later that night, Mom came to our bedroom. Jenny was already sleeping and Mom whispered to me. 'You know Rita lives out on Nakenitses Road all by herself. She has a nice little place with a house and sheds and a small barn. She keeps chickens and she delivers the mail. I was there once, a long time ago. She can fix anything. She fixes her own truck. She built her shed and her barn. She doesn't really need anybody.'

When I didn't say anything, Mom smiled and kissed my forehead. 'I'll tell you a little secret.' She waited again. She smoothed my eyebrows. 'I hope Rita will be my friend. That's my secret. I like the way she can take care of herself, don't you?'

I nodded. Mom tucked the blanket up under my chin and I let her, though the night was warm.

'I have a present for you,' she said. And she uncurled my hand and in it placed Dad's jackknife. 'I want you to be able to take care of yourself, too.'

I should have said something then. She left the room. I wanted to call her back. She had never mentioned the sharp cut in the hem of my sheet or the stain my bleeding finger had left. Yet she must have seen them both and wondered. Maybe she was waiting for me to admit that I was the one who had taken the knife and left Mr. Safety vulnerable.

5

I rode my bike down to Bull Canyon, where I could sit on a ledge of land overlooking the Chilcotin River. On the bank, wild roses were in bloom; pine needles baked in the sun. The river hurried past, turquoise and swift with mountain run-off. I took up a pine branch perfect for a walking stick, dug Dad's knife from my pocket and began to shave off the bark. Aspens trembled in the slightest breeze and the stink of cow parsnip floated past. The air shivered with the whir of hummingbird wings. No one here. But it seemed like someone was, someone high in a tree watching or hidden just out of sight around the bend, listening. It was the feeling I always had in the woods, not troubling, but teasing.

I was sleepy, listening to the river. I sat down, leaning against a crumbling pine log and stretched out my legs in the sun. Again I had that cocooned feeling, moving away from myself and observing from a distance. The air thickened and grew very still and then the aspen leaves began to shiver and turn like little hands waving. A twig cracked and I sat up. A little girl, about three feet tall, stood looking at me. She had a face of bark and hair of lichen, decorated with yellow balsamroot flowers. She wore a skirt of purple harebells. Her feet and hands were twigs.

'Who are you?' Her voice was funny, not child, not adult either.

'Maggie,' I said.

'Where do you come from?'

'From up the road.'

'Up the road.' She laughed. 'What tribe do you belong to?'

'I don't have a tribe,' I said. 'I have a mother and a sister.'

'No tribe? But you must have a tribe. Who keeps you safe at night? Who does the hunting?'

'My father is dead.'

'Dead, is he? Maggie's father is dead. Would you like to belong to our tribe? You have to climb through a hole in the curved tree to get to our land. Follow me. I'll show you. Can you run fast?'

She smelled of pine pitch and wild roses and her twig feet barely scratched the earth as she ran. I followed, dodging trees and leaping deadfall. She disappeared and then I heard her voice, a chatter shivering through the trees. 'This way!' Her head came down from the crook of a gnarled pine. 'I'm a fast runner, aren't I? I'll help you up.'

I reached for her twig fingers and they closed around mine.

'Shut your eyes and when you open them again you'll be in our territory.'

I did as she said.

Soft blue-flowered hills, bathed in lemon light, rolled away to the edges of dusky blue mountains. Down in a shady valley, a jade-green river sparkled in the light. Smoke rose from fires beside the river and small figures moved near them. Across the lemon hills, herds of mountain

54

sheep ran, turning as one like a flock of birds.

'Let's go swimming. Our river is so sweet and cool. I have ten sisters and they'll play with us.' The twig girl ran through the field of blue flowers, trailing a shadow of a path that undulated in the wind, leading me down to the river flats.

'Oh dead, dead, dead,' she sang. 'Maggie's father's dead!'

Her sisters were twig-girls, too, their dresses made of different wildflowers, orange Indian paintbrush, yellow buttercup, blue forget-me-not, white violet, blue chicory, purple foxglove, and the prettiest, on a tiny little girl, delicate red columbine that drooped below her knees.

'Swimming! Swimming!' they shouted to me and dropped their dresses in the grass. I stripped off my shorts and jumped in after them. Cool water closed around me like a skin. The heat of the pinewoods slipped away.

The girls gathered in a circle in the river. One threw a white hollow bone to another and they sang, tossing it around the circle:

Maggie's father, hair of red
Right as rain when he went to bed
Went to work, so they said
Now Maggie's dad is dead dead dead!

'Join in, Maggie!' they called. The water splashed and rolled off my skin, the drops travelling down my fingers, my arms, spilling down my sides and the twig arms of the girls sprayed glistening droplets through the air.

55

Maggie Dillon out to play
Fell asleep on a sunny day
Knock knock knock. Go away!
Maggie isn't dead today.

We swam and I dove with my eyes open, parting tall weeds with my hands and gliding by, watching the sun cut through water and shine on the deep rocks and glimmering sand bottom. I shot back to the surface and swallowed great gulps of air and the girls sang until the sinking sun turned the water red-orange.

I climbed out and sat on a rock. I watched the water bead on my legs. As the hills shadowed and changed, I felt a sudden chill pass over me. Night must be beautiful here, the hills bathed in moonlight, but I wouldn't wait for it; it was too lonely and I felt cold now.

'I have to go home,' I told the twig girl.

'I guess you do,' she replied.

I pulled on my shorts and took her hand. When I opened my eyes I was standing by my bike near the side of the road. The sun had not yet begun to set and it was still hot. My walking stick was peeled clean and lying on the ground. I picked it up. I felt for my pocketknife. Still there, nestled in my pocket, smooth and cool. Beneath my shorts, though, my underpants were cool and wet with river water and the bottom of my T-shirt was damp.

I felt very hungry. I wanted hot deer stew, salted tomatoes, a whole saskatoon berry pie. I fastened my walking stick onto my handlebars

56

with a shoelace and hopped on the bike. My legs burned as I rode towards home.

★   ★   ★

I felt hungry all the time then, a constant gnawing in the pit of my stomach. Two things filled me the longest: our neighbour Mrs. Erickson's homemade bread, which she brought over to our house two loaves at a time, wrapped in dish towels, and the mountain potatoes Agnes brought back for us.

Agnes came up our road one day in July. She was carrying a burlap sack. I sat on the step and watched her come. She stopped in front of me, then opened the sack and let me look inside. The fresh earth smell of the potatoes wafted out.

Agnes smiled at me. 'Take you with me next year,' she promised.

Next year seemed a very long time away, but I did feel a small thrill at the thought.

'Your grandpa used to go,' she said. 'My grandpa and him were friends. Used to round up the wild horses together, take them up Potato Mountain for the races.' She stood there and we looked out at the road as if we might see them riding by.

'Ask your mom to take you to the bush,' she said. 'You'll start to feel better.' She held my gaze for a minute, then Mom came out on the porch.

'Agnes,' she said.

'Irene. Heard about what happened to your man.' They disappeared into the house and shut the door and the low chicken mumblings began again.

That night Mom boiled some wild potatoes and put a pat of butter on them and salt and pepper. We ate them along with a jar of salmon someone had brought and early green beans from Glenna's garden.

'We're going camping,' Mom announced. 'Get out of this quiet house. It's driving me crazy. We'll leave in the morning. I have a place I want to show you girls.'

Over and over I have dreamed of that meal, the crisp green beans, the salty, oily salmon, and the sweet little potatoes hot with butter. My grandma had wanted to see the wildflowers of Potato Mountain again and I want to eat that simple meal again, with my mother and sister around the table.

6

'We're hitting the Freedom Road,' Jenny said as she carried her sleeping bag past me to the car. It was something we said whenever we went west on Highway 20. The night before, Mom had begun packing for our camping trip and Jenny was trying to get me excited. Freedom Road was the name the locals had given the highway in the 1950s when they had chopped the route from the coast to the interior, without the help of government, so they could get out with their own vehicles. 'Or die trying,' Mom said. The steep drop to the valley was sometimes called Courage Hill. Like Dad had, Mom scoffed at the idea of fortifying herself with alcohol to drive it. 'People think liquor makes them better drivers. Idiots. It just makes them care a bit less about going over the edge.'

It had rained during the night and when we got out on the highway, Mom opened her window. A fresh rain scent drifted in; the road steamed in the morning sunshine. 'Pour me some tea, please,' she said to Jenny, who sat beside her in the passenger seat. I was in the back. These were our usual places. Dad had rarely come with us when Mom took us camping. He had hardly been in the station wagon at all. It was Mom's car, and ours, a tan-and-white 1963 Chevy Impala with creamy white seats and brown dashboard and trim.

Mom loved the car. She kept the seats clean and had a little garbage can on the hump that she emptied, along with the ashtray if it had been used, each time we stopped at a gas station. She kept good tires on the vehicle, checked her own oil and fluids and wrote her oil changes in the owner's manual, which she kept neatly tucked into the glove compartment. 'But it's a car,' she'd say. 'And cars are made for driving. I'm not going to baby it.' That meant she would take it down most any road where we had enough clearance and there were no sharp rocks that could pierce a tire.

Driving like this, the three of us, it felt like nothing had changed. Jenny poured the tea from the thermos and I settled into my job, which was to watch for wildlife. I didn't have to be so vigilant at this time of day; dusk was when the deer came out and grazed the open spaces along the highway. Mom's strong hands held the steering wheel. Jenny leaned into a pillow propped against the door. A sense of safety filled the car. I think we all felt it. Nothing could go wrong and there was no such thing as trouble coming in threes.

'Roll me a cigarette, sweetie,' said Mom.

I smelled the spicy tobacco as Jenny opened the pouch, then the sulfur flare of the match as she held it for Mom. Mom only smoked when she drove or when we were camping, and only hand-rolled cigarettes. Sweet, light smoke perfumed the air like incense, like every other trip we'd taken in the safety of that station wagon, with Mom at the wheel.

When we entered the Redstone Indian Reserve we could see the mountains in the distance ahead.

'I want to stop,' I said. My voice sounded rusty and odd even to me.

Mom's eyes met mine in the rearview mirror. Jenny whirled in her seat and put her arms out, as if to hug me. 'Maggie, you're alive!' she said.

'This is near where Dad took me last fall,' I said.

'Okay.' Mom said it almost cautiously, as if the spell of ordinariness could break again at any minute. 'Where do you want to stop, Maggie?'

'The road's just past here.'

Mom slowed the station wagon and made the turn. The track cut straight and flat through a meadow, then entered the woods, the way I remembered. The trees grew thicker, their branches tangled above us.

'Are you sure, Maggie?'

'This is it,' I said.

For a moment, when we came out in the clearing by the lake, I was disoriented. The water was in the right place, but everything else looked different: green reeds piercing the surface of the water, grass grown up where there hadn't been grass before, trees leafed out and obscuring the entrances to the paths. But then I saw our lean-to, tucked into the shade of some aspens with the entrance facing the lake.

'There it is,' I said, and I jumped out of the car. Mom and Jenny followed, stretching and yawning. Someone had made a fire pit in front of the lean-to with a circle of rocks. Charred logs, mostly burnt, lay in the pit.

'Did you and Dad find this?' Mom asked.

'We built it,' I said.

'You built it? What's it for?'

'You sit in it,' I said, leading the way. 'It's a shelter. We built lots of different ones. We can all fit in if we squish.' I backed in feet first, leaving my head and shoulders in the opening, then Jenny followed. Mom wriggled her hips to squeeze between us. She was as supple as a girl; the muscles in her thighs showed when she moved, even through her blue jeans. Her forearms, too, exposed to the sun beneath her rolled-up shirtsleeves, were tanned, freckled and muscled. She wasn't afraid of anything, either; anyone could see that.

The sun shone full on our three heads poking from the opening. Mom rested her forehead on her arms and closed her eyes. The lake lay dead calm, the only movement made by clouds of insects moving in unison above the reeds. In the warm sunshine, Mom was soon asleep. Like Dad had said, the way the sun landed on her hair, she was lit up. Jenny traced a stick through the sandy soil, writing her own name in curlicue letters. I watched for horseflies looking to land on Mom's bare arms and flicked them away when they did. The lean-to seemed even more solid than the day Dad and I had built it, and I wondered if someone had reinforced it, made it more waterproof. The ground underneath me felt dry, even after a night of rain. Maybe someone had even spent a night in it.

'Dad never took me out to build things,' Jenny

whispered. Her voice was matter-of-fact; I didn't hear any bitterness in it.

'Maybe he thought you wouldn't like it. I'm the tomboy, remember?'

On the lake, we caught sight of a heron standing near the shore.

'Yeah,' she said. 'I guess that was it.'

★ ★ ★

After Mom's nap she drove us back to the highway, then west. 'Rocks!' I warned, and Mom swerved the car just as a small avalanche came tumbling down the rock face beside the road. One pinged off the bumper.

'It's like Maggie has ESP,' Jenny said. 'She knows things are going to happen before they do.'

This wasn't new. Jenny liked to say this about me. It gave her the creeps, she said.

'She just pays attention,' Mom said, trying to nip Jenny's Maggie-is-weird theme in the bud. Jenny could warm to it, and she sounded so persuasive that I started to believe it myself and didn't even mind hearing her say it. But I did pay attention and I couldn't relax, like Jenny did, her bare feet up on the dashboard, or sometimes sticking out the window in the breeze.

We began the precipitous descent down the Hill, the famous 18 percent grade. Mom pumped the brakes so they wouldn't get too hot, but even so we could smell the linings. On the north side of the road the rock face rose up sharply, but on the south a clipped ledge crumbled then dropped, tumbling thousands of feet through jack pine and rock to the bottom of the canyon. When I had the guts to look over, I saw only empty space and treetops. Were there rusted-out bodies of cars down there, those whose brakes had failed or whose owners had bitten off more than they could chew and lost their nerve for just a second? I pictured them, sailing out into clear blue sky, then the moment of pure wonder before they dropped, bounced, once, twice, and rolled, over and over to the canyon floor.

★ ★ ★

It was dusk when we got to the fir forest, the place Mom wanted to show us. Usually, Jenny and I were boisterous as we settled into a new campsite, abandoning the gear we hauled from the car to run off and explore. Tonight was different. The fir trees around us were giant and unmoving. A thick carpet of moss and needles spread out cleanly beneath them. It was very quiet, very still and the slam of our car doors echoed unnaturally. Even though it was evening, the air felt warm, heavy with the rich piney fragrance of the forest.

'This looks like a good place to put the tent,' said Mom, walking off a square in a flat area among several large firs. Jenny and I stood beside the car, watching her. She looked up. 'Do you like it?'

Jenny asked, 'Did you used to come here with Dad?'

64

'No, I found this place myself. Quite a long time ago. Before I even met him. This is an old forest. You can feel it. Bring the tent, girls.'

Jenny and I lugged the heavy canvas tent from the station wagon as Mom laid out the poles and began fitting them together. I liked the familiar oil smell that rose from the canvas as we unfolded it. Mom moved confidently; she knew exactly what she was doing here.

Even before we had the tent all unfolded, we knew where the door was by the patch in the canvas over a hole from a hot ember. 'There's the patch,' said Jenny. 'Which way do you want to face?'

'The sun will be coming up over here. Let's face that way,' said Mom.

She had to turn the flashlight on before we were finished. Pale light still washed the sky above the trees, but didn't reach the forest floor where we clattered around with our supper dishes and frying pan.

'I could make a fire,' said Mom. 'But it's so warm, maybe we should just make our wieners on the Coleman stove?'

When we didn't answer she got the stove from the car and began pumping it up. I put our lawn chairs in a semi-circle and Jenny lit two candles in mason jars and set them in the crook of a rotted log. We sat mesmerized by the barely moving candle flames and listened to Mom stir the beans and wieners in the frying pan as the stove hissed gently. She handed us the steaming plates then closed the valve on the stove and the blue flames died.

Our human noises barely made a ripple before the quiet folded in again, like a thick liquid we were moving through.

'Sure is still,' said Jenny, bending her head back to look up at the treetops.

'No coffee for me tonight,' Mom said. 'I'm beat. There's a creek over that way, girls. We'll find it after we eat.'

The wieners and beans were smoky and delicious. My eyes followed the progress of a beetle making his way up the side of one of the mason jars as we ate.

'Look at that,' Jenny said, reaching for my arm. 'It's pitch black over there.'

When we were done, Mom picked up the wash basin and led the way into the dark with the flashlight. Just a few yards from camp a sandy bank sloped down. We could hear the creek before we saw it, the gentle trickle of slow water flowing over rocks. Mom splashed her face and neck and ran her wet hands over her hair. Jenny and I did the same. Then Mom plunged the basin into the water and let it fill. We stood on the sandy bank watching the creek flowing in the dark.

'What are those little lights in the water?' Jenny said.

'Where?' Mom and I said together.

'Look. Watch carefully. There.'

'It's starlight!' said Mom. We turned to the open sky above the creek, where a wide path of stars fuzzed the night sky.

I still remember the feeling of falling asleep that night, sunk deliciously into my sleeping bag like I had no bones, like our tent was floating in a still, warm sea, the baked canvas smell enveloping us like a cocoon. Some time in the night I woke to the sound of an owls low hoot. Owls were supposed to be harbingers of death, but even that didn't disturb me. Its call was clear and reassuring. I didn't move my sleep-heavy limbs but let the peace of this place and the soft breathing of my sister and my mother on either side of me carry me back to sleep.

★ ★ ★

Bees darted among the wild raspberry bushes as Jenny and I filled our pails in the sunny clearing by the creek after breakfast. The raspberries were firm and juicy; we raced to see who could fill her pail fastest. When we were done, we sat by the creek eating them one by one.

'Have you ever heard of Chiwid?' Jenny asked.

'The old lady who lives outside?'

'Yeah. People see her all over the place, camping out. They say she doesn't sleep in a tent or anything. Even in the winter. What she does is she makes a little fire in a hole in the ground, then she scrapes out all the ashes and she sleeps in there. The heat keeps her warm till morning. Pretty good idea.'

'I've seen her,' I said.

'You have not,' said Jenny.

'I saw her once when I was with Dad. She had all these bundles of stuff she was carrying alongside the road. Dad said he'd offer her a ride but she didn't like strangers, especially if they were white. He said if we stopped she'd run away.'

'Cool,' said Jenny. 'I heard she has a lot of money and she hides it all over the place, like in swamps and stuff. I bet there's some hidden around here.'

'I doubt it. Where would she get money?'

'Josie's grandpa knows her and he says she gets money from somewhere. She hardly needs any, living out like that, so she hides it. Josie said maybe she gets the money from her husband because he feels bad for what he did to her.' She looked at me as she said this, as if she wasn't sure she would tell me what it was he did. She put a handful of berries in her mouth.

'She doesn't have a husband,' I said. 'Dad said she's on her own, even though she's an old lady. Some people say she's part coyote, that's what Dad said.'

'Maybe she is. But she used to have a husband. She used to be normal. Live in a normal house and stuff.'

I couldn't hold back anymore. 'So what happened?'

Jenny looked at me intently and hugged herself. 'This is true. You can ask anyone. But don't ask Mom because she'd kill me for telling you.'

'Okay,' I said, but now I wasn't sure if I wanted to hear it.

'Her husband was really mean. Josie said she heard her grandpa talk about him. He once saw Chiwid's husband take a harness and whip a horse with the metal bit, in the head and everything, till the horse kicked him in the stomach. He thought it was funny. He didn't care who saw. Sometimes he'd say he was going to shoot Chiwid. He'd hold the rifle to her stomach and then their kids had to go running off to get help.'

'She has kids?'

'She used to, a long time ago. Like I said, she used to have a normal life. Anyway, one time her husband was so mad he took a chain, one of those big ones for logging, and he beat her with it. She was beautiful, too. Well, she's old now, but once she was beautiful. Some people say he was jealous. He didn't like how other men looked at her and that's why he did it. He choked her with that chain and almost killed her. That's when she ran away and she never went back to living with people. It is like she's a coyote, because she's spooked like that. She's afraid to come near people now.'

'What about her kids?' I said.

'I don't know,' said Jenny.

Dad had said that Chiwid was happy. 'She likes sleeping out,' he'd said. 'Some people say she's a bit crazy, but she's right as rain. She's lived this long. She must know what she's doing.'

Mom had come down to the creek. She slipped out of her shorts and T-shirt and waded into the water. I put down my berry pail. A chickadee was singing on the other side of the creek.

Jenny took off her runners and tossed them, one by one, beside a stand of willow. 'Let's go wading,' she said, pulling me up by the arm.

Mom sat on a rock with her feet in the water, and as the sun grew hotter, Jenny and I stretched out and let the cool current bubble over us. I thought of Chiwid alone in the bush sleeping in her little warm spot in the ground. I couldn't decide if I pitied her or envied her.

★　★　★

Night dropped again as suddenly as it had the evening before, and with it the light breeze that had been sifting through the firs fell calm. Mom built a fire, her rustlings and twig-snapping echoing in that strange silence. Worn out, Jenny and I drew our legs up in the lawn chairs with a shared blanket over our knees and watched the heat curl bark into orange embers that leapt into flame, grew and twisted.

'What a perfect day,' said Mom, settling into her own lawn chair.

'Are you ever afraid?' Jenny asked her.

'Afraid of what?'

'Anything. Like bears or wolves or cougars.'

'I'm more afraid of humans,' said Mom.

'What humans?' asked Jenny.

'None in particular,' she said. 'There just seems to be more to fear from humans than from any of those animals. Humans are unpredictable.'

After we lost her, I tried to put together a list of the important things Mom told us: Never make big decisions late at night. Don't touch the sides of the tent when it's raining. Never lean on a stove because you never know when it might be hot. Don't drink from a creek if you don't know what's upstream. Humans are unpredictable.

★ ★ ★

A sound outside the tent woke me. At first I thought it was the wind coming up. Then I recognized the low hum of an engine and the soft crunch of tires, moving slowly towards our camp. Mom was still out by the fire. I heard her push her lawn chair back and saw her shadow on the tent as she stood. I held my breath. It seemed to me that if I didn't let on that I was awake, I would not have to be a part of whatever happened next, or even that it would not happen.

The vehicle stopped and a door opened, then closed with a soft click.

'You nearly scared the life out of me, coming in here with your headlights off like that,' said Mom quietly.

A man's low voice answered her. 'You knew it would be me, didn't you? Who else knows this road in the pitch dark?'

'What, have you been following me?'

The words alarmed me, but there was a teasing tone to her voice. She wasn't scared of this man.

I heard the chairs scrape again and then the mumble of their voices wove into the gurgle of the creek. I wanted to get up and look out at them. I thought about lifting the door flap. But I was too close to sleep. I woke again later to the sound of a high wind moaning through the tops of the firs. I tucked my blankets closer. Mom's soft laughter sounded below the wind. She was still out by the fire. The man's voice murmured, deep and soft. The fire snapped. I felt cold. When I sat up, Mom was beside me, her body curled warmly between Jenny and me.

★　★　★

I was the first one up and out in the chilly morning. The bright blue sky promised a nice day. Sun filtered through the feathery fir branches. No high wind, only the gentle swaying of the wild rose bushes near the creek. A squirrel scurried along the ground and flew up a tree trunk. Behind the tent, I scanned the earth for tire tracks. I couldn't see any. Our car still sat on the road, the windshield winking in the sun, and I felt as if I had dreamed the night visitor.

After breakfast, Mom sat sipping her coffee from a blue enamel cup. She closed her eyes as she drank, then tilted her face a little to the sunlight streaming through the fir trees.

Jenny laid two battered tablespoons on the ground between us. 'Guess what these are for?'

'Cereal?'

'We already ate. Guess again.'

'We're going to make something?'

'No — we're going to look for something,' Jenny corrected. 'Chiwid's treasure.'

'Using spoons.'

'We don't have any shovels. Anyway, she wouldn't have to bury it very deep.'

Mom smiled and tilted her head towards us.

'Chiwid's treasure?'

'She must have some,' Jenny said. 'Don't you think so, Mom?'

'I suppose she would. I'm not sure she'd bury it, though.'

'So no one would steal it. It makes sense. She knows the bush like nobody else. She wouldn't carry it around. That would be too dangerous.'

'And heavy,' I said. 'What are we going to do if we find some?'

Jenny's face fell for a moment, then she brightened again. 'I know. We'll add some money to it — just a bit. And we can write her a note saying we found your money, but we're not going to steal it. So maybe she'll start to trust people again.'

'That's a nice idea, Jen,' Mom said sleepily, and closed her eyes again.

'Why do you want her to trust people?'

'Let's just dig,' said Jenny.

The day warmed as the sun's angle widened and lit the pink fireweed along the creek edge and the scrub aspens and tangle of salmonberry bushes growing in over the logged clearings. We dug in the springy fir-needled soil, beside unusually shaped trees and deadfall that we thought would make landmarks for Chiwid's memory. Some distance away, Mom crouched, in her baseball cap, picking berries. She had found a patch of ripe wild strawberries, late for the time of year, and she ate as she picked, humming happily.

I kept looking for an opportunity to ask Jenny if she'd heard the night visitor. But I didn't want

Jenny to dig into it in her usual fearless, reckless way. Jenny could ask so many questions she'd make herself cry with the answers. I never did that. If I could picture an answer I didn't want, I wouldn't even ask.

Mom had hummed yesterday, too, I told myself. Camping with Jenny and me made her happy. But that distant soft pleasure I saw in her as she foraged in among the radiant pink feathers of fireweed and shafts of sunlight — that was something else, I knew. It was not a gift given to her by Jenny or me.

7

Back at home a few days later, Mom bent to sip her coffee and Rita bent to sip hers, the two heads nodding in unison in the shade of the spruce tree. Then Mom leaned back the way she did when she savoured her coffee, the tang of spruce, the perfect warmth of the day. Rita turned to her and smiled.

Their conversations differed from the ones Mom had with Glenna — less actual talking, more pensive sipping, bouncing of bare crossed legs, watching of swaying grasses and patterns of summer light through the trees.

Rita liked to talk about her projects. She had built a three-compartment composter that could break down almost anything — bread, bones, paper, pasta, along with the usual potato peels and coffee grounds.

'No rodents, not a one. There's no smell if you do it right.'

Mom nodded and smiled. They sipped, in unison.

'I could make one for you,' Rita said.

Mom's snort caught on her mouthful of coffee and she jerked forward to spit it in the dust. They both broke into giggles and had to set their cups on the ground.

They often broke into helpless laughter that way, set off by almost nothing, and they laughed till their eyes ran with tears. I sat on the step making cigarettes with a little black machine Rita had brought. For every twenty-five cigarettes I made for her, she'd promised to pay me twenty-five cents. I liked the fresh smell of the tobacco when I opened the tin and spread a line of it along the paper in the rubber holder.

A car came slowly up the driveway, an old maroon Mercury Monterey with the back window missing. It stopped a small distance away and Agnes got out. She walked slowly towards us with her careful, elegant gait.

'Agnes.' Mom smiled, wiping her eyes.

'Irene.'

'Have you met Rita?'

Both women nodded. Mom went in the house to get coffee for Agnes.

'You're the one who lives without a man out Nakenitses Road,' Agnes said.

'That's right.'

Mom came out with a mug and handed it to Agnes.

'I have something you better come look at,' Agnes told Mom and pointed with her chin towards the car. The three women walked out to the car. I understood that I was not meant to come. They bent over the back seat and Rita straightened and shook her head, but she was smiling. They spoke for a couple of minutes, but I couldn't hear what they were saying. Then Agnes lifted a cardboard box out of the back and handed it to Mom. They walked slowly back to the house, all of them now looking at me. Mom put the box down in front of me. Inside it was a little white and orange kitten curled up on an old towel.

'That one's the runt,' said Agnes. 'Other ones, five other ones, won't let her near the mother. She needs to be fed.'

Mom asked me, 'Do you want a kitten to take care of?'

'Really?'

'Feed her with an eye dropper,' Agnes said. 'Give her goat's milk.' She brought a jar out of her pocket and handed it to me. The milk was still warm.

I named her Cinnamon, because of the orangey patches on her head and back. She lapped goat's milk from the dropper with her tiny pink tongue, then fell asleep on my chest, her little paws kneading me in her dreams. Cinnamon purred like a tractor, that's what Rita said. I liked to take her under the spruce boughs and watch her bat around spruce cones and test her claws on the tree roots. She didn't wander. She ventured out in a small circle around me, returning to me every few minutes, climbing onto my legs. She liked me to hold her on my chest, with her paws and head resting on my shoulder so that she could observe from a safe height.

'That kitten is more dog than cat,' Jenny said. 'The way she follows you around. That's not normal cat behaviour.'

It was true that when I walked in the bush, Cinnamon hopped along behind me, sometimes stopping to sniff the ground or cackle at a bird, but always running to catch up with me again. She didn't go out unless I did. Mom had warned me about coyotes and eagles that would be attracted by Cinnamon's snowy white fur. When school started in September, I left her each morning sleeping safely on my bed. But I worried that she could get out the kitchen window that Mom left open a crack. Or that as Mom went about her day, she might leave the door ajar and Cinnamon could slip out.

'I'll be careful,' Mom said each morning as she kissed me goodbye at the door.

★   ★   ★

Jenny and I walked up the driveway after school, with the early fall chill taking the summer edge off the afternoon sunshine. The yellow aspen leaves flickered like lights against the turquoise sky, like the day Dad and I had built the lean-to by the lake. A familiar ache spread out from my centre. Sometimes it felt like it slowed my whole body down — I couldn't run as fast as normal, and my feet felt leaden. It would grow if I couldn't find a way to stop it.

Jenny chattered about the oil pastel drawing of a deer she'd done in art class and how she'd tried to get the shading right for the ears. 'Ears are hard,' she announced, getting no response from me.

Our house appeared beyond the big spruce tree. The front door was closed; a pot with a lid on it sat on the step, a wet newspaper beside it, covered in a pile of potato peelings. Mom liked to peel potatoes on the step. I opened the door, dropped my books and went to my room where I expected to see Cinnamon stretching her legs and yawning at my arrival. She wasn't there.

'Cinnamon?' I bent and looked under the bed where she sometimes curled herself up on a triangle of bedspread that touched the floor.

'Mom!' I heard Jenny call. She came to our bedroom doorway. 'Where's Mom?'

'Is she lying down?'

'No. She's not in the house. Maybe she's in the shed.' Jenny headed back outside. I heard her calling.

I followed her out, calling for Cinnamon. She always greeted me when I came home; she was always here. Jenny stood by the shed and screamed 'Mom!' at the top of her voice. Just then Cinnamon came bounding out of the woods past the edge of the vegetable garden. She ran right to me and I picked her up and buried my face in her fur. I realized I was crying, my tears wetting her soft fur, and she licked at my hand with her rough tongue.

Mom was right behind her, tripping through the underbrush and bursting out of the trees like someone who had been lost and has at last blundered on home.

'Mom!' Jenny shouted. 'What are you doing? We didn't know where you were — we came home from school and you were gone.' She ran to Mom and threw her arms around her and now Jenny was crying, too.

'Girls, girls, relax,' Mom said. 'I was just out for a walk in the bush. I lost track of time. I'm sorry.'

But something seemed odd about it, about

her. She came in the house, picking burrs from her shirt and laughing as she drew Jenny close.

'I'm sorry about the cat, Maggie. She followed me. She was with me the whole time. Are you two hungry? I'm starving.'

Her eyes shone and she was flushed and giddy, her skin mottled with red, not just on her face, but down her neck and chest, into the white skin beyond the soft V of her flannel shirt.

'But what were you doing?' Jenny persisted.

'I just needed to get out of the house for a while, so I went for a walk. Cinnamon must have slipped out when I opened the door, and I didn't notice. But after a while I saw her following me.' Mom got out bowls and the chocolate syrup. 'Time for our reward!' she said brightly.

'You bought ice cream?' Jenny said.

Mom pulled a small carton from the icebox. She scooped a large curl of vanilla into each bowl, then broke bits of graham cracker over the tops. She set them on the table and let us pour our own chocolate sauce.

I watched Mom as she ate her ice cream. She was absorbed, not noticing my eyes on her. She licked her spoon slowly, thoughtfully, then she got up and went to get the pot of potatoes from the step. She bent and took another pot from the icebox and carried it to the stove. Then she stretched her arms over her head, a long, deep stretch, and said, 'I'm going to take a nap before supper.'

I was mad at her about letting Cinnamon out, but what bothered me more was the distance that seemed to have opened up between us. It seemed as if, for now, she was not really my mother, but some beautiful woman with flushed skin going to have a nap in my mother's bedroom.

8

When I remember the first fall without Dad, I think I can see that a change was coming. I should have been expecting the second thing, known it was building from the grey days when we came home from school and found Mom lying on top of the blankets on the bed, Cinnamon stretched innocently alongside her. But I could never have guessed where it would come from.

It was not the normal thing for Jenny to have to make supper. She tried to percolate along cheerfully, as if she didn't mind, as if she liked it, liked to experiment with things she found in old spice jars under the sink, improvise a spaghetti sauce from the jars of stewed tomatoes that neighbours had brought. When we sat down to eat, she would not allow a gloomy silence; she described the things she drew in coloured chalk on the board at school for Halloween, Thanksgiving, Remembrance Day.

'We each used a whole orange chalk on the pumpkins, right down to the nubbins. The nubbins, I tell ya!' Jenny's science teacher that year had a verbal tic and punctuated his sentences with 'I tell ya.' It made Mom laugh the first time Jenny mimicked him, so she used it often.

★ ★ ★

Jenny had real friends and sometimes spent the night at their houses. I had Mickey, who I didn't even like most of the time, and who couldn't spell at all, not even words like 'don't,' which she spelt 'donet,' or 'when,' which appeared variously as 'wen' or 'wan.' This bothered me enough to make me think we could never be real friends.

I pretended to be sick some school mornings that fall and Mom pretended to believe me. These were usually the days after the nightmares I'd started to have about Cinnamon. In the dream I came home and she was gone. Her absence was thick and sharp and it was the sound of my own wailing that woke me. In the morning, I couldn't bear to leave Cinnamon knowing I would have to worry all day about whether Mom was paying proper attention. I held her in my lap in Dad's chair by the fire and smoothed her fur. Mom let me stay home and brought me a salted boiled egg and a cup of weak sugared tea. After school, Jenny squeezed herself into the chair with me and tickled me until I fell out.

Rita came over on a cold Saturday in early November to help Mom split the wood that Glenna's husband Ron had brought. Then the house smelled of coffee and tobacco and the light changed, like there was a spark of something warmer in the air, and Mom seemed to wake up. Rita put a Carole King 8-track on in her truck and kept the doors open while they chopped and we stacked.

They both sang along to 'I Feel the Earth Move.' They synchronized their movements, two axe-wielding dancers matching rhythms until someone's axe stuck and threw them off. That night, Rita stayed over. I listened to their low voices rising and falling in the kitchen. When I came out of our room for a glass of water, the conversation stopped.

'Can't sleep?' Mom said, and they waited while I filled my glass and stood drinking. Back in my room, I heard them start again.

'I feel like a teenager,' Mom said.

'Do I make you feel like a teenager?' Rita asked, and they burst into laughter.

Jenny was listening, too, and smiled. We both liked Mom's mood better when Rita was around. In the morning, she was still there, teasing Mom while they made breakfast together.

'Those eggs are all cooked the same,' she said.

'I know,' said Mom.

'Why'd you ask me how I wanted them, then?'

'I was hopeful. But I always break the yokes.'

'Next time, I'll do the eggs.'

After that, Rita came more often, always bringing something — fresh eggs, deer sausages, a moose roast, a bottle of her homemade berry wine. Mom brightened, and Jenny didn't have to pretend to be happy. Rita and Mom stayed up drinking wine. I fell asleep listening to the hum of their voices, talking, talking. Late in the night, the clatter of the stove being stoked woke me and then their soft laughter and the squeak of the bedroom door was reassuring.

Jenny teased them about their pyjama parties. 'You two *are* like a couple of teenagers.'

84

We drove the three and a half hours to Rita's farm on Nakenitses Road for a few days over Christmas, with Cinnamon sleeping peacefully on the rumbling floor of the station wagon. We pretended not to notice that Dad wasn't with us. We pretended not to miss the game he played, tapping the roof on Christmas Eve, Jenny and I imagining it was reindeer hooves. We pretended not to care that the selection of the Christmas tree from the bush and digging it out and chopping it down was mostly carried out by Mom and Rita, who warmed themselves with a flask of peppermint schnapps and giggled and cursed their way through the ritual with none of the proper solemnity or democracy, no standing and considering with us in respectful silence, no fire in the snow nearby.

Christmas night I'd always felt a sadness I couldn't explain. Maybe it came from Mom and Dad who I could see tried their best to make our little family everything we needed. But there was an absence even then, of something I had never understood. I missed it because they missed it, their links to their families broken or missing. This year, without Dad, it was worse. I couldn't help resenting Rita a little for not being Dad and for trying to keep us from noticing he was gone. In my head I repeated *Dad is dead, Dad is dead.* Feeling the pain of it — properly feeling it burn and squeeze in my gut — was almost a relief.

Rita roasted one of her own ducks for Christmas dinner and, after she opened a bottle of her homemade wine, she placed a glass each in front of Jenny and me.

'Special occasion,' she said. 'It's not very strong.'

'It's good,' said Jenny, trying to hide a slight shudder as she swallowed. I liked the taste of it. After a couple more sips, Jenny said, 'Why didn't you get married, Rita?'

'Jennifer!' Mom said.

'I just wondered.'

'It's okay,' Rita said. 'I didn't think getting married would make my life better. I wanted to be independent.'

'Like Chiwid?'

'Not quite like Chiwid, no. Maybe I didn't want to end up like Chiwid. You want to be careful you don't marry someone who's going to crush your spirit.'

'Let's hope you can aim a little higher than just not crushing your spirit,' Mom put in.

'Hear, hear!' said Rita, and they clinked glasses.

On Boxing Day, we put on snowshoes and headed out in the deep snow behind Rita's place. I led the way because I could walk along on top of the crusted snow, sometimes not breaking through for a long time. In the wide-open meadow below the mountain, sun glinting on the blue expanse of snow, I forgot that they were behind me. It was just me and some chubby little winter birds feeding on frozen berries from the scrubby branches poking through the snow. I felt detached from my body, as if it were some amazing machine that lifted my knees, one after the other. Then everything disappeared except the snow and the webbed sinew of my snowshoes, forward, forward, forward and the reassuring pounding of my heart — *not dead, not dead, not dead.*

★ ★ ★

The next day, just before we were to head home, a snowstorm blew in, plugging the road and Rita's driveway with wide drifts. I was happy to be stranded, but Jenny wanted to get back to her friends, and even Mom seemed restless. That night, as the wind peppered snow against the windows in a frenzy, and the little house shook with the storm, I heard Mom's and Rita's voices rise in the living room.

Rita said loudly, 'Well I don't understand what you object to.'

'It's nothing. I can't explain it, Rita. Just quit — I don't know what. I don't even know what I'm trying to say. I'm just grouchy. I want to sleep in my own bed.'

'Fine. I understand that. I'm just trying to be a good friend.'

'You're a great friend, okay? You always come to my rescue and you're Rita my saviour, is that what you want to hear?'

It was quiet for a minute.

'No, not really,' Rita said. 'I don't really want to hear that at all.'

More quiet, but now the wind screamed around the eaves of the house, like a human voice, rising and falling in moans. I pictured the meadow, the snow belting it in whirlwinds and the winter birds huddled in the pines for shelter, and I wondered if Chiwid was sleeping out tonight or safe in someone's house with the fire stoked up red-hot. That was what they said about Chiwid, that she was warm outside, but when she was coaxed in by people who couldn't stand the thought of her out in forty below weather, she always felt cold. She'd been responsible for nearly burning down the cabins of a few people when she over-stoked their stoves, trying to get warm.

'Listen to that wind,' Rita said. 'I'll try and get the tractor out tomorrow to clear the driveway.'

★　★　★

In spring, Mom announced she had got a summer job baking for a fly-in fishing camp. We would be based at the camp owners' beautiful log cabin on Dultso Lake about two hours west on Highway 20, just the three of us. Float planes would arrive every other day to take the baking into camp. The owners had agreed to let Mom start after the school year ended. Mom wasn't much of a baker, but they told her they had their regular recipes she could follow. Rita knew the owners, who were mostly concerned about getting someone they could trust to look after their house while they were away at the camp. In the past, their teenage daughter had done it, but she had moved to Vancouver.

Jenny calls Dultso Lake the best place we ever lived. I call it the last place we ever lived. I find it

88

hard to call nights playing another family's Scrabble game with Cinnamon sleeping warmly on someone else's blanket our 'best.' For the first time, we lived in a house with a TV. A giant antenna extended up the side of the cabin and we could get shows from the U.S., like *The Partridge Family*. The TV was run, like all the other electric appliances in the house, by a generator that hummed through the day. At night, when Mom shut it off, the quiet flooded back into the house like the rightful owner.

Beside the TV was a shelf stacked with Yahtzee, Monopoly, Life, checkers. There was a hi-fi in a dark wood cabinet with a sliding door that enclosed someone else's records: Elvis, the Beatles, the Bells, Conway Twitty. Jenny played Sonny and Cher's 'I Got You Babe' so many times that summer that even now I can't hear the song without expecting the crackles and static of that album. On quiet afternoons, while Mom's bread was baking and Jenny sat out on the dock reading, I leafed through these records, wondering about the family who had picked them out.

I developed an intense dislike for the album *Conway Twitty*. The cover pictured a grinning Conway Twitty in a red shirt with a smoothed-back hairdo. His songs had titles like 'I'll Have Another Cup of Coffee' (then I'll go) and 'Guess My Eyes Were Bigger than My Heart.' I think for me this album came to personify everything about this stupid, fortunate family with this oversized house by the lake, equipped with everything their hearts desired. This was not a family who had their wounded or dead dragged out into the public eye at the Duchess Creek nursing station. The worst things that had happened to them could be made into maudlin songs that you could sing along with. Or so I believed that summer, with a hatred burning in the pit of my stomach that puzzled even me. Sometimes I took out the Twitty album just to stare at it and enjoy hating the fortunate family.

★　★　★

Most days, I went walking in the bush around the lake, sometimes only coming home in time for supper. Cinnamon came with me, hopping along in her curious way over fallen logs and tree roots. When I stopped, she stopped, finding a patch of sunlight to sit in, her paws neatly together as she watched me. Sun lit the longer hairs on her fur in a halo around her. Sometimes the two of us nestled against the warm side of a rock and slept.

One day when we were out walking, a high wind came up, sifting through the treetops and making the big trees sway and creak eerily. I was headed for the crescent of sandy beach I'd found on the west side of the lake. If it started to rain, I could build a shelter there for Cinnamon and me. I turned to let her catch up, but she wasn't there. A sudden scuffle of leaves and branches came from about thirty feet away and then a short yowl. I ran back to see the flash of her white fur streaking through the woods, some small animal chasing her.

'Cinnamon!' I called sharply. What good was

that going to do? I followed the scuffling until I couldn't hear it anymore and I had to stop and listen. Nothing but the rush of wind like a waterfall through the spruce and the trees swaying.

'Cinn-a-mon!' I called in the singsong voice she would recognize. I walked and called, then stopped and listened. I couldn't hear anything but the wind.

What an idiot I was to let her get so far behind me. What was I thinking?

I think about two hours passed before I started to cry. I didn't know what to do. She could have gone in any direction. Dad used to tell me that if you were lost, you shouldn't let yourself cry. Or if you had to, you should sit down on a rock and cry until you were done, then wipe your eyes and nose and take ten deep breaths until you were calm again. Crying could lead to panic and you didn't want to panic. I sat down on a log and called her name a few more times, then I wiped my nose on my T-shirt and decided that the best thing to do would be to go back to where I'd seen her last and call her. If she still didn't come, I would go home and get Mom and Jenny to help me look. There was still a lot of light left before night fell.

When I thought that I might not find her, I sobbed until I was mad at myself. I wiped my eyes again and took the ten deep breaths, then stood up. The creaking trees sounded like plaintive meows, and so did the little peeps of birds sneaking through below the moan of the wind once in a while.

Back at the spot I'd seen her last, I busied myself by building a small teepee shelter, big enough only for a cat. I didn't really think she would use it, but I needed to mark the spot with something and I needed to keep busy as I waited. I found sticks to use for poles and I set them into place, stopping every few minutes to call her again. When it was done, I called once more, then walked home.

Jenny was standing on the deck, looking out. 'Maggie, where have you been?' she yelled. 'Mom's been worried about you. Maggie? What's wrong?'

'I lost Cinnamon,' I burst out, and Jenny came running and put her arms around me.

'Don't worry,' she said. 'We'll find her.' She patted my back. 'We'll find her, Maggie. She'll come home. That cat loves you like crazy. She'll come home.'

They had already eaten supper, so while I picked at the potato salad and ham Jenny put out for me, Mom scurried around collecting things to take with us on the search. 'We'll take a flashlight because it gets dark earlier in the bush. Jenny, get that box of catfood. We can shake it when we call her. We'll need jackets; it's getting chilly already.' Mom put her hand on the back of my neck. 'You know, I wouldn't be surprised if she comes back before we're even ready to go.'

But she didn't. As we headed back into the woods, I felt so sick with worry I thought I would throw up.

'That little cat knows where home is,' Mom said, glancing sideways at me.

But I wasn't so sure. If she did, why would she always follow me so closely? Maybe being taken away from her mother so early meant that she didn't have all the proper cat instincts.

That evening, as we made circles out from the teepee and back again, crossing paths with each other, our three voices singsonging through the woods, Jenny rattling the box of cat food as she called, I believed that I was protected by their love and this would not be my second bad thing. As it got dark, I sank down on a log and stared into the dense woods, sure that any minute now I would see her hopping through the woods toward me. After a while Mom came and took my arm and helped me up. 'I bet she'll come home tonight. She could be there right now, for all we know.' But she wasn't.

I don't think I slept. I think it was the first time in my life that I stayed awake all night, listening for scratching at the door, drifting and then starting awake again to listen to the house groan and the wind hum through the TV antenna. As soon as light showed through the skylight, I got up, grabbed an apple and one of the sweet buns Mom had set on the counter, and left the house. The morning was still and cold, a grey light washing the sky. A heavy dew lay on the trees and grass. Little creatures skittered into the underbrush as I made my way back to the teepee. I sat on a log. I was conscious of being cold and shoved my hands into my pockets. My voice sounded out of place as I called her. I listened. Then I thought I heard a tiny meow. I stood up and called again. I heard it again, a tiny, tinny meow. I walked maybe fifty feet into the woods, following the sound. It was louder now. 'Cinn-a-mon!'

And there it was again, very close. I looked up. Way up, high in a tree, she perched on a branch, looking down at me and crying. 'On my god, Cinnamon, you crazy nut.' I laughed at her, ecstatically, crazily relieved.

The tree she had got up was a tall skinny spruce with no lower branches, no footholds until about twenty feet up the trunk. I didn't think I could possibly get up there. I tried a few times, clutching with my arms and trying to get a toehold on the bark, but it was futile. Another spruce, only a few feet away, had plenty of sturdy limbs. I hoisted myself into it and hauled myself up, calling softly, 'Don't worry, Cinnamon. I'll get you out of there. Good kitty.'

But at about twenty feet, I couldn't climb any higher. The branches were too small, and even if they could have held me, the trunk was now too far from the one Cinnamon was in. I considered going home to get Mom. But I just couldn't stand the thought of leaving her there, so I stayed in the tree. 'Mom will come looking for me,' I told her. 'Don't worry. She knows where to find me and she'll get you down.'

After about an hour, the sun started to come up in the distance and I felt a bit warmer. A little while later I heard the screen door slam and then I heard, very faintly, Mom calling 'Ma-ggie!' I knew that we would not have long to wait. I heard the screen door slam again. It was either Mom going back in or Jenny coming out. I stood up on a thick branch so I could see them coming.

Maybe ten minutes later I saw a flash of colour through the trees. 'I told ya, I told ya!' I sang to Cinnamon. 'Mom! Jenny! I'm way up here.'

★　★　★

We told and retold the story of rescuing Cinnamon like a legend, to ourselves or whoever came to visit. Mom had wrapped the tree trunk with her jacket and used it like a sling to shimmy up the bare trunk, finding footholds on the slightest swellings and scars. When she reached the branches, she climbed quickly to where Cinnamon stood eagerly, rubbing her back against the tree. I've heard that mothers can perform incredible feats of strength when their children are in danger — lift a car off a leg or fight a cougar. My mother's feat that morning, climbing the unclimbable tree, descending with the scared cat clinging to her shoulder, proved that she would do anything for me.

9

When the end of August came, we had to leave the well-equipped house in Dultso Lake, the records and games and the foreign smell of someone else's life. I wasn't sad to go, but Jenny grew anxious as the time approached.

'Where are we going to go?' she asked at least three times a day, sometimes asking me, sometimes Mom.

'First we're going to camp,' Mom said. 'We haven't really had a holiday this summer. We'll find a nice spot and settle in for a couple of weeks.'

'I don't want to camp,' Jenny said. 'It'll be too cold. I want to go home.'

'Well,' Mom said, then smiled tightly. She didn't say what we all knew — that we had no home anymore. She had given up the house in Duchess Creek because she didn't want to pay the rent on it for the summer, and we had left our most important possessions in a shed at Rita's. Anyhow, there was no work for her in Duchess Creek, and she needed work.

'Will I be able to go back to my old school?' Jenny wanted to know.

'We'll see,' Mom said.

'"We'll see" means no,' Jenny muttered.

★   ★   ★

In a way I suppose I blamed Jenny for what happened next. All through the bright cooling days of an Indian summer, our gypsy life — sleeping out, fishing for trout in the river, frying them crackling in a cast iron pan over the fire, even learning to shoot with Dad's 30.30 and, once, helping to bring hay off a field for pay — was soured by Jenny's constant questions about school. Mom grew tired of trying to reassure her, and the lightness went out of our adventure. We drove the dusty back roads in silence, each of us occupied with our own worries.

Once September came and school had started, Jenny became sullen and stayed in the station wagon all day with Cinnamon, reading and rereading old Archie comics, chewing her nails to ragged nubs and staring out the window while Mom and I fished or made camp. About the second week in September, Mom drove down the Nakenitses Road to Rita's, and Rita came out on the porch and hugged each of us tightly and made a fuss over how much Cinnamon had grown.

There was a school at Nakenitses Lake, but Jenny didn't want to go to it. 'I want to go to my own school,' Jenny demanded. 'Why should I start school here and be the stupid new girl if we aren't even going to stay? Then I'll just have to do it over again somewhere else.'

I didn't want to go to school at all, and at first Mom, distracted and irritable, let it go. She left us with Rita some days and went off in the car, returning late. I watched for the station wagon headlights swinging into the driveway and sweeping across the living-room wall. Rita didn't like it when Mom was gone, I could tell. She grew testy and tried to play the parent with us, which she hadn't done before. 'Don't you think you should clean that litter box?' or 'You better turn on the lamp or you'll ruin your eyes.' One evening after Mom had been gone all day, I was doing the dishes and broke a glass trying to get the milk ring out of the bottom. I cut myself, only a little, but blood seeped into the hot water. It looked like a lot and Rita, who was drying, snapped, 'Oh for Christ's sake. Now what?'

'It's nothing,' I said. 'It's just a cut.' I put the two pieces of the glass in the garbage, feeling my face flush with shame. It was all I could do to stand there at the sink.

'I'll finish them up,' said Jenny, coming up beside me. I felt tears well up in gratitude. I dried my hands and went to the bathroom to get a strip of toilet paper. I sat on the couch with my hand wrapped and stared out the window, trying not to cry. The dishes clattered in the awkward silence.

'It's only a glass, guys,' Rita finally said. 'We'll live, right? Will we all live?' She looked over at me and I nodded, trying to smile.

★　★　★

That night we were in bed when Mom got back. I don't know what time it was, but I'd had long enough to imagine the various horrible accidents that could have befallen her. She came into the

98

room and kissed Jenny and me on our foreheads. 'Sleep tight, my sweets,' she said, and relief coursed through me.

I had drifted to sleep when Mom and Rita's voices woke me.

'I think you should send them to school,' Rita said. 'At least Jennifer. She's thirteen — she's at that age when she just wants to belong. You're a conformist at thirteen.'

'When I was her age my mother had already died and I was only three years away from being pregnant with her.'

'What does that have to do with anything?'

Silence.

'Have you been drinking?' Rita asked.

' 'Have you been drinking?' What are you, my mother?'

'Well, it seems like you could use a mother.'

'Ha. I've been managing just fine for many, many years. If anyone is going to remember what it was like to be thirteen, it's me.'

'I'm just giving you my opinion as your friend.'

'Rita, I'm tired.'

'Here's an idea — come home earlier. It's not like I don't worry.'

'I appreciate what you do for us, I really do.'

'I'm afraid you don't get it, Irene.'

★   ★   ★

Jenny and I started school in Nakenitses Lake the next Monday. I was in grade six and in a room together with the grade four and five kids, and Jenny was in grade eight and in with the sevens and nines. Because the fall weather had turned warm, the teacher had us outside collecting leaves for a project. After school I wandered far along a creek and out to the lake, looking for more leaves. At Rita's, I used the iron to press yellow aspen leaves, red maple, the heart-shaped cottonwood and paper birch between two sheets of wax paper. I labelled them with name and habitat. I got the project back on Friday, A+.

Mom wasn't there when I got home. I waited on the porch, the leaf project in my lap, until Rita called me in and wordlessly placed bowls of canned spaghetti on the table. Jenny read at the table as we ate, and Rita didn't tell her not to.

I kept the leaf project beside my bed all through the night, woke up to touch it, check the colour of the light coming in the window and listen.

When Mom drove up on Saturday afternoon, I was sitting on the porch waiting. But when she kissed me lightly, I was too overcome with relief to show her my project.

'Did you miss me?' she said on her way in, as if being gone all night was nothing.

Jenny came out a minute later and the two of us sat and listened to the argument going on inside.

'What am I, your babysitter?' Rita shouted.

'You're my friend.' Mom's voice, calmer, but still insistent.

'And what does that mean to you?'

'What does it mean to *you*?' Now her volume

rose, too. 'You've got some rigid formula of debits and credits and every time you do something for me I feel as if you're waiting to see if I fill in the matching thing on the ledger. I'm always just a little in the red with you.'

'A little?'

'See. This is pointless.' Mom came outside, letting the screen door slam behind her. The three of us sat there gloomily. Through the trees, the afternoon light shadowed the mountains. We had nowhere to go — the porch, the car, that was it, the safe zones. I picked up Cinnamon and went and sat in the car. Its smells and warmth cocooned me in familiarity. I might sleep in it if Mom would let me. That way I wouldn't have to worry about her slipping out of my sight.

* * *

Sometime in the middle of the night the car door jerked open and a blast of cold air rushed in. Mom began throwing in blankets and pillows. Jenny climbed in on top of them, groggy with sleep, her eyes barely open. The two of us sat in a stupor as Mom made several agitated trips in and out of the house, piling armloads of our possessions into the back of the station wagon. She slammed the hatch and got into the driver's seat, all without a word to us. Then she started the car, revved the engine for a minute, and drove out onto Nakenitses Road, ribboning out in front of us in the moonlight. I don't know how long it was — maybe twenty minutes, half an hour — before Jenny spoke. 'Why was Rita crying?'

'Never mind, honey.' Her tone said that was the end of it.

Rita crying was such a bizarre and improbable thing that I couldn't even imagine what it would look like. A long time later I asked Jenny about it. She told me Rita had sat in a kitchen chair with her face in her hands and cried like her heart was broken.

★   ★   ★

We drove all night. I woke up once when the car stopped and saw Mom outside, leaning against the car smoking a cigarette. The northern lights sent fingers of green light creeping, retreating, shooting up into the night sky. Cinnamon sighed and stretched in the nest of blankets, then settled herself again. Mom climbed back in and put her hands on the wheel. For a moment I felt intensely happy. Everything I had was in this car and safe.

10

The Edwards' place in Williams Lake smelled of old hamburger grease with an undertone of mothballs. This was not the scent of a happy house. I could sniff some tragedy — large or small, I didn't know — hanging in the close air. I wondered what it was. It may have had to do with the husband, Ted, who sat in the kitchen in his wheelchair, using a bent spoon to dunk his teabag in a stained white mug. He smiled crookedly at us as we came in.

I disliked Mrs. Edwards instantly, with her straw blonde hair and her runny eye. She was not like my mother or Rita, women who took charge, did what needed to be done, enjoyed their competence. Mrs. Edwards seemed helpless, trapped, a woman who wrung her hands and wept and moaned — I could see that right away. I could tell by the dingy house, lit by fixtures dimmed with drifts of insect bodies inside the glass globes, the TV on in the corner, dusty drapes drawn against the brilliance of a fall morning.

Our mother's need to find a viable solution to whatever problem plagued her must have been strong, because she blinded herself to what was obvious even to an eleven year-old: Mrs. Edwards was not a happy woman and she would be no use to two unhappy girls.

Our mother took us into a bedroom with two

twin beds covered in matching blue bedspreads with a synthetic sheen to them. I expected a puff of dust to rise up when I sat on one. Later, when I had had a lot of time to reflect on every object in the house, every plastic, pretend-crocheted doily and scented, fake flower-decorated toilet roll cover, I thought that even the bedspreads spoke of Mrs. Edwards' unhappiness and helplessness. Only a person who had no idea how to be comfortable and happy in the world would pick such a slippery, staticky, uncomfortable fabric to adorn a guest's bed.

'You're going to billet for a while with the Edwards,' Mom told us, as Jenny and I sat side by side on one of the beds, frightened by the look on her face.

'What does billet mean?' Jenny asked.

'You're going to stay here,' Mom said. 'The Edwards are old friends of your dad's. They're good people. They'll take care of you while I go cook in the logging camps.'

'I don't want to stay here,' Jenny said.

'Neither do I,' I said. 'We can come with you. We won't be any trouble. I know how to take care of myself.'

'I know you do,' Mom said. 'But they don't allow kids. Those are the rules. We need money.'

'Why can't you get a job here in town? Why can't you be a secretary or something? Why couldn't we go back to Duchess Creek? Glenna could get you a job in the nurses' station.'

'Stop it right now,' Mom said. 'This is the best I can do. Let's just hope it won't be for long.'

'How long?' I asked.

'Let's hope not too long.'

'How long?' Jenny said. Her voice cracked and she started to cry.

'Stop it,' Mom said sharply. 'There's nothing I can do. The Edwards are good people. You'll be able to go to school here.'

Good people. Never trust someone described as a 'good' person. I know now that 'good' means that they won't murder you, throw you out into the snow or let you starve. But also that there are obvious shortcomings and you're going to find out what they are pretty damn quick. Those were the kind of people our mother left us with.

Jenny pulled her knees up under her chin and cried softly into the circle of her arms. She was like an island on the slippery bedspread. I knew she would be of no more help to me in persuading our mother to collapse with regret, then drive us to the nearest campground where Mom would boil up some coffee, lean back in her lawn chair, gazing up, then Jenny and I would ask her for spoons to dig for Chiwid's treasure by the river.

★ ★ ★

Mom led me outside to the car. I remember the feeling of my small hand in hers. She was still my protector that day. If I held on to her hand, I didn't think she would let me go. I didn't think she would be able to. But at the car she shook free of me, and there was nothing I could do.

105

'Maggie,' she said. 'I know Jenny's the older one, but I'm going to rely on you. You were right when you said you know how to take care of yourself. I don't have to worry about you.'

She must have meant it as a compliment, a way to get me to look at myself as something other than a helpless child. But when she said it, smiling at me softly, her face open like a wish, it felt more like a recognition of a weakness I had, a thing I'd always have to live with, like a harelip.

'Okay,' I said because I couldn't say anything else. Mom began to unpack the car. I picked up Cinnamon from the back seat and carried her into the hamburger-smelling house. Mom followed with our pillows and suitcases.

'What's that?' Mrs. Edwards said.

'What?' Mom said.

'Is that a cat?'

I slipped quickly into the bedroom and dropped Cinnamon to the floor, as if I could hide her.

'No, no,' Mrs. Edwards said. 'We can't have cats. I'm very allergic.'

'Beatrice, please,' Mom said. She pulled the bedroom door closed and I heard their voices going back and forth.

Jenny raised her head to look at me. Behind her on the wall above the bed hung an embroidered picture of two hands clasped together, praying. I picked up Cinnamon and she curled two soft white paws over my shoulder and clung to me like a baby. I buried my nose in her blanket-scented fur. She began to purr, deep contented trills. Cinnamon could be happy anywhere, as long as she was with me.

When Mom came into the room, I could tell by the look on her face that she had lost.

'I'm sorry, Maggie,' she said. 'I promise I'll take good care of her.'

That was the second time I saw Mom cry. Tears filled her eyes and ran down her cheeks leaving tracks across her brown freckles. Some brief understanding of her situation flickered in my brain, just for a moment, and I wanted to say something to make her feel better, maybe tell her that Cinnamon wasn't a city cat anyway, but a lump had risen up from my heart and was choking me, and I couldn't say it.

Neither Jenny nor I said a word about this being our second thing. To acknowledge it openly would be to acknowledge that the third thing was still to come.

* * *

I had once seen a house demolished, a little shack of a house in Duchess Creek where an old man had lived until he died. The shack was razed to be replaced by a bigger, solid log house, the kind that wants to look rustic even though it's brand new. Jenny and I had watched from the road as the backhoe bit into the roof and pulled down the walls like they were cardboard. Faded flowered curtains, still on the rod, clung to the tines of the backhoe as it came up for another round, then the curtains and rod were folded into the dust of the ruins and disappeared. With my unpacked suitcase on the bed in front of me, I felt like that house, a tumult of dust and disorder, nothing where it should be, nothing left standing.

11

I can't say that Mom was wrong about my being able to look after myself. I soon recognized Bea Edwards for the ticking time bomb that she was. Only three weeks into our stay, I learned that what could set her off was unpredictable. It was my job to set the table each night. Sometimes Ted didn't come home until after supper, when one of his drinking buddies dropped him off and pushed him up the plywood ramp to the door. He could do it himself, unless he'd had a few.

One night I thought I might save time by finding out if he'd be home. 'Should I set a place for Ted?' I asked Bea, as I took down the plates.

'How should I know?' she snapped.

But this was nothing. This was just normal Bea impatience. It was later, when we were washing up the supper dishes and I tucked Ted's clean, unused plate in with our three dirty ones that Bea exploded. Her soapy hands shot up from the hot dishwater and tore the steaming eyeglasses from her face. She hurled the glasses across the kitchen, where they skittered against the refrigerator grill, and she screamed, 'Do I have so little to do around here? Do I? Do I?' Her pale eyes popped wetly in the midst of the red blur that was her face. 'Now I'm washing clean dishes! I'm washing dishes that haven't even been used! Is that how you do things at your house? Here!' She began clumsily scooping clean plates and saucers and bowls and cups from the cupboards and piling them haphazardly beside the sink. She didn't stop until she had cleared every last dish from every shelf.

I stood back, my hands knotted tightly in front of me. I watched as her face swelled, grew redder and redder, the veins throbbing at her temples. She might literally explode, I thought. But instead she went limp as a wet dishrag and with a choked sob hissed, 'Wash them.' She left the kitchen, the door swinging in her wake. And so I did.

★   ★   ★

One day not too long after Bea's explosion, I was wandering around town after school, killing time until Jenny was done volleyball practice. Jenny liked the novelty of living in a town. She'd bought herself a paisley wallet at Stedman's and tucked the money Mom had given her into it. After school, when she wasn't playing volleyball, she went to the Tastee-Freez with her friends. She had an easy charm that I didn't and acted as the buffer between Bea and me. Up ahead, the doors of the Maple Leaf Hotel swung open and Ted rolled out into the sun. Ted had a way of wheeling his chair that I wouldn't have expected from a man who couldn't walk. There was a vigour to it, the way his hands gripped the wheels, pushed off strongly. He was not feeble, Ted, and it seemed like he wanted anyone who saw him to know it. He had broad shoulders, a straight back and large, lean hands. He had silver-grey hair, lots of it for a man his age, I thought, although I didn't really know how old he was. He went to the barber once a week for a trim. Ted wore the same kind of flannel shirts and blue jeans as my dad had worn, so that made me like him a little.

He stopped when he saw me and waited till I caught up to him.

'Hello, Maggie.'

I thought I might do a good deed, not for Ted, but for Bea, by delivering him home for supper. Or maybe the good deed was really for myself.

'How was school?' Ted asked.

'Fine,' I said. He set off again, wheeling along the road with me beside him.

'How do you like Williams Lake?'

'It's fine,' I said.

He laughed. 'You like the bush better, don't you? You're like your dad.'

It pleased me so much to be told that I was like my dad that for a minute, I just walked along smiling.

'If you push me, I can show you a good place,' Ted said. The Edwards' place wasn't far from the hotel, but we wheeled right past their street. 'We can't go over the railroad tracks in this thing, so we have to take the long way. You're not in a hurry, are you?'

I thought of Bea. 'No,' I said.

At the end of Oliver Street I helped push him along to the highway. A small fear took hold of me. What if I lost control of the chair? What if he went wheeling down the highway towards Vancouver? But Ted said, 'Here we go! Hang a right. You got a licence to drive this thing, Maggie?' I laughed and felt a lightness rise in me, the giddiness of adventure.

I pushed Ted with difficulty down a narrow trail bumpy with tree roots and fir needles. Scent rose up as we crunched over them. No wind, but a warmed air, a different air, gently wrapped me. Something invisible inhabited the long shadows and winked from the silver spiderwebs running from wild rose to birch. The knot of worry that had been twisting my gut since Mom left us loosened. My shoulders relaxed.

'Pretty place, isn't it?' Ted said. 'You keep heading up the river that way, you'll get to the Fraser.' We could not get very far with the chair. So I parked him and sat down, leaning against a tree.

He took out his tobacco and began tamping it into the bowl of his pipe. I must have been looking at Ted in a funny way, because he said, 'I can tell you how I ended up in this chair. Most people are curious and I don't mind.' A crow began to squawk and fuss on a high branch above us and the birch leaves trembled. A swallow hovered and dove at the crow and Ted and I laughed. He lit a match, drew the flame into the pipe and a cloud of sweet-scented smoke curled into the air.

'I was working with an outfit north of here, logging a steep hillside. We lived in tents, rough and ready. It was a gyppo show. That's what they call a small outfit. That can be okay if guys know what they're doing. If they're careful and they get along. But from the get-go, I never liked the way the hook tender did things. He was the boss, but he was strung tighter than a fiddle and he wasn't happy unless everybody was going in three different directions at once. I was planning to quit as soon as I could.

'That day I had a bad feeling. It was hot, stinking hot. We woke up to heat and it stoked up to a furnace as the morning went on, sun blazing down on the hillside. Everyone was tetchy, but that joker of a hook tender poked and screamed, jumped on one foot. I sometimes wondered if he was all there.

'Three of us choker setters were on the crew that day, me, old Jim, and a greenhorn we called Dewy, because he had this soft white face he washed with special soap every morning. We were down in a ravine, attaching the choker and climbing back up in that inferno to get clear. It was exhausting. We decided to take turns, give each other a rest. It's Dewy's turn and he's walking down a steep log. His cork boots got caught up on the bits of loose bark and he lost his gription. Tumbled head over heels and winds up upside down, on his head, out cold. Jim and me climbed down to him and pulled him out, gave him a drink of water and he went back to work. That's what you did.

'The day before, some men were standing on a stump watching the logs being yarded. No one saw the haulback catch on the roots of a big old stump. The stump broke loose and came thundering down the mountain, heading straight for these guys standing there, mouths open. It hit the ground about fifteen feet in front of them and flew up and over their heads. Barely cleared them. We teased them about the shave they got that day. But those things can happen, even in the best-run show.'

Ted held another match to his pipe and the ripe cherry smell floated on the air. 'At lunch I sat on a stump. I was soaked with sweat, not a dry spot on me — even my socks were sopping. The bugs were out, I was itching from the dust and bark that stuck to me. I thought about walking off the job, right then and there. That's how sure I was that something was going to go wrong. It was Friday anyway and I was going home for the weekend, and I'd already decided I wasn't coming back. This old-timer, Jim, he'd been a faller, was mostly deaf now. All morning he grumbled about this being the worst job he'd ever been on and hadn't he paid his dues? This fella was comical, Jim. He had no front teeth. He had dentures but he didn't wear them on the job. I suppose he thought he'd break them or swallow them while he was working or something. He was skinny, too, but still muscled like a racehorse. He knocked over his coffee at lunch. That was the last straw for him. He let out a blue streak of curses from his toothless old mouth. I said to him, 'Jimbo, why don't you and me just bunch it and head on home?''

'So did you?' I asked.

Ted looked off through the lace of leaves and sunlight and was silent for so long I thought I'd asked the wrong thing.

Finally he said, 'No. No we didn't leave. We did what you do, which is to finish the job. It's funny, when I think about it now, how sometimes the good lessons you learned can sink you.

'We were close to done for the day. I kept thinking about the ice-cold beer I was going to drink when we got to town. Jim was at the top of the ravine, Dewy was down below, and I was standing clear. The whistle blew and all of a sudden I heard a snap, like a giant guitar string busting. There was a shout, some curse I won't repeat, and guys diving left and right. I saw Jim's head coming up like an old hound dog sniffing the air. I shouted 'Jim!' at the top of my lungs and he looked at me and I saw the change in his eyes as he understood and he made a move, digging in as if to run, then the cable came whipping through the air and carried him right off the hill.'

'Oh no!' I said. 'Did he die?'

'Oh yes, he died all right.' Ted's pipe had gone out and he sucked deeply on it, twice, then held it in his big hand on his lap. The sun had sunk behind the hills and the air felt chilly now, the light gone flat and lonely among the trees. But I hadn't yet heard how Ted ended up in the wheelchair.

'Poor old Jim deserved better,' he said. 'We wrapped him up to bring him home. But then, when we got back to camp, what with all the confusion, we had to wait for our cheques. I couldn't stand it. I wanted to go. Finally I made up an excuse, I got paid in cash and I got out of there as fast I could. I got a lift to town where my truck was parked and I had a cold beer and supper. Then I felt, well Maggie, I'm ashamed to say it, but I felt glad it wasn't me. I was just glad to be alive. Really glad. And I wanted to go home.

'I headed out. It was getting dark, but that time of year it never does get entirely dark. And then the moon came up and the road ran out ahead of me shining like a river. Gosh I was happy. What a beautiful night. Then I thought I heard that snapping sound again, of the line right there in my truck. I thought that was strange. I shook my head and I opened the window to get some fresh air. Bugs flew at my windshield and I saw them coming at my headlights like a gentle rain. Then I heard it again, that crazy whipping snickety-snack. And there in front of me in the headlights I saw someone running along the road. Right in the middle. So I slowed a bit and this runner came alongside my open window and yelled something. I saw his face and it was Jim with that big toothless mouth. 'What?' I yelled back and then I heard him, clear as a bell, 'Wake up!'

'I opened my eyes. Right in front of me was the grill of a truck, no headlights on. In the split second it took for me to figure out that it was parked on the side of the road, I jammed on the brakes, then I slammed right into it.

'Old Jim saved my life, yelling at me just like I'd yelled at him on the hillside. The truck I hit was loaded with a big load of logs, and the driver had pulled off to have a nap. The cops said the tracks showed I had been driving on the shoulder for nearly a mile. The hood of my truck accordioned under his and then the two trucks went slowly over, the weight of the logs carrying us. My truck ended up in the air, clamped onto his grill. I don't remember any of that. I was in a coma for seven days and when I woke up, I was in a hospital bed in Williams Lake and I'd never have to work as a logger again.' Ted laughed quietly. 'That's it. That's the story.'

I pushed Ted's wheelchair through the chilly dusk back along the trail, across the highway and up the Edwards' street, even when Ted could have rolled it himself. Bea and Jenny were clearing away the supper dishes when we came in bringing a drift of fall air into the steamed house. Jenny looked up in a combination of surprise and relief. Then she arranged her mouth into a tight-lipped line and tried hard not to smile. Bea said nothing, didn't meet our eyes, just disappeared into the kitchen. Ted hung up his coat and wheeled over to the table where his bare plate sat staring up between fork and knife.

'I'll get your food,' said Jenny. I should have helped, but I didn't want to go in there. I went to the bathroom and washed my hands. Then I took my place at the table and began to eat. Jenny sat and watched, smiling a little now.

I waited for the slams and crashes of Bea's rage to reverberate off the kitchen walls and come ringing through the house. But I heard only the rush of water filling the sink, the sucking of the dish detergent bottle and the clink of silverware against glass.

Jenny passed me an envelope across the table. 'This came today.' Jenny & Maggie was written

in Mom's handwriting in pencil on the envelope.
I took out the letter, a single thick sheet torn
from a sketchbook.

Dear Girls,
    I hope you like Williams Lake and are
having fun living in a town for a change. I've
sent some money to the Edwards to cover
your expenses, so if you need anything, just
ask Mrs. Edwards. You can buy yourselves a
treat now and then, too. Don't go crazy,
though! All is well here. Bye for now.
                                          Love Mom

There was nothing in the letter, nothing about
when she was coming back, or where she was, or
where Cinnamon was. My eyes filled with tears
but I kept eating. I wouldn't cry in front of Ted.
I thought of him instead, out on the lonely road
with old Jim running alongside him.
    'I think I'm going to try and get a job,' Jenny
said. 'I saw a sign at Frank's. I could be a
waitress or a cook. Couldn't I?'
    'Sure you could,' Ted said.
    'I'd have to arrange it around volleyball
practices, though. The Duchess Creek team is
coming to our school to play us. Cool, eh?'
    I heard her, but I was out on that road, with
the night insects flitting around in the headlights
of a truck lifted right off the ground.

12

If I walked to the end of Yorston Street, where the Edwards' house was, I could see the lake, and the smoky blue hills beyond it. I sat out there sometimes and waited for the moon to come up. I thought that wherever Mom was, she'd be looking at the same moon.

A path wound from the end of the street down to the stampede grounds. I always cut through there on my way to school, though it took me longer. Mornings, leaving the Edwards' house, the fresh air was a balm, the nowhere between house and school a sanctuary of dirt, weeds and wind. I took my time. Escape ran through my mind like a melody. I picked up snatches without really noticing. Kicking a clod of dried manure, I thought horses would be perfect for packing gear through this country, covering some distance. I never thought of a destination, except back. I could picture her smiling when she saw us, trying not to, trying to hide how proud she would be that we had done it, we had found her.

When I tried to fit Cinnamon into the picture of Mom working in a logging camp, the uneasiness I carried constantly billowed up in my body and I thought I might vomit or my legs give way. A cat in a logging camp wouldn't last long. She would be dragged off by a coyote or, with her white fur, picked from the night by an owl or a hawk.

At school, Mrs. Wallace, the teacher of the split grade six and seven class, had decided that I was an exemplary student, and she had taken to reading out my descriptive paragraphs to the rest of the class and singling me out for special jobs like writing on the chalkboard. It must not have occurred to her that this would make my classmates even more suspicious than they already were of the new girl who carried her books in a paper bag and whose running shoes were stained with mud and grass.

The other student she often singled out was a Carrier boy named Vern George. He was in the seventh grade. Vern kept his head down. He had white North Star running shoes with blue stripes, but one of his laces was a piece of twine. This intrigued me. Mrs. Wallace liked to ask him, 'Vern, are we keeping you awake?' but no one laughed, the way they did when she said the same thing to Marv Dressler, the class clown. Vern smiled mildly at her. When she changed the seating arrangement so that my desk was beside his, I saw that he kept a book tucked inside his textbook. His head was down because he was reading, not frightened like I thought.

One day I was sitting on the school steps after the dismissal bell, carving a small branch with Dad's knife. I was waiting for Jenny, because we were planning to walk to Stedman's together. I had pared off the bark and was trying to carve my initials into the smooth, peeled wood when Vern came out, carrying an armful of library books. I looked up at him and then turned back to my stick.

'What are you doing?' he said.

I jumped.

He laughed, something I had never seen him do. 'I scared you.'

'No you didn't.'

'Can I see?'

I handed him the stick. 'I just started it.'

He turned it over in his hands. 'Cool.' And he handed it back and walked down the steps and off the schoolyard. I went back to carving the stick, but lifted my eyes every now and then to watch as he disappeared at the end of the street, his arm tucked around the library books.

When Jenny came we went to Stedman's, where she bought navy knee socks and I bought grey wool work socks, then I left her at her new job at Frank's Chicken and Pizza.

At the Edwards' house, I let myself in and was surprised to find that Bea wasn't home, though the TV was on, *The Flintstones* theme song drifting from the living room. In the two months or so that we'd been here, I had never seen Bea leave the house, though she must have gone out to get groceries while we were at school. The door to her bedroom was ajar. In there was a dainty roll-top desk she called a 'secretary.' When Ted asked her where some paper was, her answer was almost always, 'In the secretary.' It was where she sat to pay bills, and if Mom had written a letter to the Edwards, that was where it would be. Maybe she had explained herself more to them.

I wondered if I had time to look through Bea's desk before she came back. Their bedroom was

121

at the back of the house so I couldn't watch for her coming out the window, but I thought I would hear her come up the steps. I got a glass of milk and a cookie, took a bite then put it on the coffee table in front of the TV. If I heard her coming, I'd scoot out to the couch and she'd never know.

The Edwards' bedroom smelled of Yardley lavender powder and the menthol liniment Ted used. The bed had been made, the nubby white spread pulled tight and tucked under the pillows neatly. Why go to the trouble when you're only going to get back in it later? The desk was closed and my eye fell on the little keyhole. I hoped she hadn't locked it. But no, Bea Edwards had no secrets worth locking up. I stopped to listen, but I heard only Fred Flintstone's 'Yabba dabba do!' and Barney's chortle. There were some bills in one compartment. I leafed through them quickly. In another, there were a few envelopes and on one of them, the Edwards' address in Mom's handwriting. But the letter inside was even briefer than the one to us: 'Here's the amount we agreed on. Thanks for helping us out. Irene.' I checked the front of the envelope. No return address, but over the postage stamp there was a red post office stamp that said Kleena Kleene. I put the envelope back, closed the desk and went to the couch to watch the rest of *The Flintstones*.

Out the window, I saw it was snowing, just a few light flakes straggling down, and there was Bea, coming up the sidewalk wearing her short, black fur-topped boots and a yellow woollen tam with a pompom on it. I felt a tinge of pity for her and the bland life she led.

By the time Jenny got home, there was enough snow to soak her canvas running shoes. A sharp wind had begun to sweep across town and snow eddied around the yellow porchlight. Jenny burst through the front door, gasping. 'My feet are icicles!' She kicked off her shoes and stood in her knee socks, shivering over the heat register.

'Maybe school will be cancelled tomorrow,' I said.

'We can always hope.'

Bea called from the kitchen, 'It'll be gone by morning.'

'Three feet of snow on the ground in two hours and she thinks it'll be gone by morning,' Jenny said to Ted.

'There's not three feet of snow,' Bea called.

'Come and see for yourself.' Jenny pulled the curtain wide as Bea came out of the kitchen, and she huffed in surprise to find the front steps buried. Jenny poked her in the side with her finger. 'Told you,' she said.

Bea actually laughed. 'That's not three feet, that's drifted, that's all.'

But the wind whinnied and flung snow against the window screens all night and by morning the streets of Williams Lake were plugged, the snow was still falling, and no one was going anywhere.

I tried to read one of Jenny's Nancy Drew books, *The Mystery of the 99 Steps*, but I kept drifting into sleep. I wanted to be outside.

Jenny sat with five bottles of nail polish lined up beside her on her bedspread. She started with frosty brown, carefully painted each fingernail, then blew them dry and surveyed them. 'It matches my hair, don't you think?' She was happy as long as I made some kind of noise of agreement. She reached for the nail polish remover and dipped a Q-tip into the bottle.

'Jenny, you're asphyxiating me,' I said.

'I didn't ask you to sit in here with me.'

I left the book on the bed and went to the basement. There was a spot between the dryer and the furnace where a heating duct ended in a vent that could be opened. I opened it and sat on an old scrap of carpet with a blanket around my shoulders. Warm air blasted down on me. The small window above the dryer was drifted over and I listened as the wind whistled through the cracks and the snow shifted, piling into a peak against the glass.

I wondered if the shelter Dad and I built could still be standing. In extreme weather, Dad said, it's best to hole up and wait it out. People can die of fear, Dad told me. Once, when he was working up north, a man he knew drove his truck off a remote road in a snowstorm and got bogged down in several feet of snow in a wide ditch. There was no way he could budge and the weather was so bad, he knew he couldn't expect anyone to come along to help. Huddled in the cab of the truck, sheltered from the wind by the ditch and snow, he should have been safe. The man told Dad later that he started to worry that he was going to starve. He had visions of hot turkey dinners, gravy, warm apple pie. After about three hours in the truck, cold, but not freezing, he left the shelter of the cab and set out walking in an irrational search for food. He lost all his toes and fingers, his face was scarred by frostbite, and he nearly died.

'The last thing you need to worry about is starving,' Dad had said. 'It's not fun to be hungry, but it'll take a long time before you have to worry about dying from it. Shelter first, then water, fire and food.'

*   *   *

The snowstorm raged and Beatrice's anxiety festered and bubbled in the confines of the house. She went from room to room picking things up and muttering, sometimes about the fact that Mom's monthly payment was late. I pictured her day while we were away at school and wondered how she filled it. I could only see her in a dim cavern of smelly vacuum cleaner, dirty blue carpet, freezer-burned meat, mugs of Nescafé coffee, a stack of *National Geographics*.

It used to be, when we were storm-stayed, Mom dropped her normal routine and we played games of rummy, drank sugary tea and roasted pieces of meat at the open door of the woodstove. We lit the lantern early in the afternoon; it was us against the elements and I loved the sound of the wind battering the house.

Beatrice had started in at breakfast, saying to Ted, 'The bills aren't going to wait. I hope she didn't forget to send it.'

Ted said, 'She's not going to forget. Quit fretting about it.' And he winked at me.

'Bea,' Jenny said, catching the wink. 'Always buzzing about something.' Bea gave her a sharp look, but a smile played around her lips. I kept shovelling my corn flakes in, thinking it was amazing the things Jenny could get away with.

I came up from the basement around one o'clock, the time the mail usually arrived. I was putting my boots and jacket on near the door when Bea pushed past me, opened the door and reached her hand out into the cold, fishing in the mailbox.

'It didn't come again today,' she announced.

'Of course it didn't come today. No mail came today,' I said. But I couldn't manage the same light, teasing tone as Jenny had.

Bea turned on me. 'Don't get smart with me, Margaret Dillon. If you think I do this for the good of my health, you've got another think coming.'

Jenny had looked up from her reading. I could see her measuring how much magic her charm could work. She looked at me, then back at Bea and said, 'Oh, Bea. Be honest. You'd keep us for free just for the pleasure of our company.'

'One of you, I would,' Bea said, and stalked away from the door.

Jenny's eyes locked on mine with an expression that was a combination of warning and apology. She had tried; I should too. I couldn't. What mechanism did Jenny use to sit there pleasantly like that? It was missing in me. I put my mittens on and left the house.

I wore a pair of snow boots that I had found in the basement a few days earlier. They were army green with thick felt liners. I'd tried them on down there by the furnace. They were too big, but I could wear two pairs of woollen socks inside them.

'Can I borrow these?' I'd asked Ted, dropping them on the living-room floor in front of him.

'Borrow them? You can have them. They're no good to me anymore.'

I clumped along down the middle of the street, through the deep, powdery snow, pleased at how warm my feet were. A neighbour was out on his snowmobile, sending up a spray of snow in his wake, right in the middle of town. The storm shut down the normal order of things. If someone had to be rushed to the hospital or someone else was out of bread, no one could do anything about it.

I had stuffed my pockets with cookies, matches, a short stub of candle, my jackknife and a wad of toilet paper. I didn't bring water because I had nothing to carry it in. Dad had told me that out in the bush, people often lose their common sense. In fear, they follow stupid advice they heard somewhere, like rubbing snow on frostbitten skin or sucking the poison out of a snakebite. Across the deserted highway, with the wind snatching my breath from me, I walked face first into the storm. I thought that Dad would understand I wasn't leaving shelter, but looking for it.

I crossed the tracks and followed the river north. My hands were cold at first, but as I swung my arms, they warmed up so that they were almost hot. My face flushed warm against the biting air and snowflakes melted as they touched my skin. In the fresh snow, my footsteps went deep and I had to lift my legs high to step again. There was a smell to the snow that I loved, dry and metallic, like the taste of a smooth grey rock.

In the open grassy areas, I was pummelled by the wind. At a tall stand of cottonwoods I headed off the trail and into the bush. The trees had snow stuck to one side of their trunks. The forest was deep white, soft and quiet, except for the sound of my own sharp breathing and my pants brushing together as I walked. A few yards in, I stopped. I stood still, held my breath and listened. Nothing. No wind, no birds, no traffic noise. The snow still fell and I watched the flakes coming down, sometimes in clumps, and I thought I could hear them making a tiny muffled tinkling.

Farther along, I saw some tracks that had been lightly covered in snow. There was a fallen tree leaned against a huge fir stump and I climbed up and sat on the stump. I wasn't cold at all; if I had food, I could walk for days. People do it, people who know the bush. I could do it, too, if I learned to trap.

I climbed down and began to walk again, confidently. The brush beneath the snow had thickened and I struggled to lift my heavy boots through it. A sense of doubt crept over me and all at once I didn't know which way to go. I looked up at the sky, but everything was white, no sign of where the sun was. I thought I should retrace my steps while I could still see them. The wind was gusting stronger and already the snow was smoothing over the tracks I'd made. Just about the moment that thought hit me, I realized my hands were cold because I hadn't been moving very fast. I turned and picked my way along what I thought was my trail, but the pattern began to dissolve in front of me. Dips and indentations that looked like a trail stopped, and then nothing looked like a trail, and there was just the quiet expanse of white, dipping and rising over deadfall.

I stopped and whirred my arms around like helicopter blades, then shook out my hands to get rid of the numbness. I knew I hadn't come too far off the river trail and if I kept calm, I should be able to find my way back. The wind had been coming from behind me, so I headed into it. I tried to walk more quickly to keep warm, stumbling over hidden deadfall and brush.

Then the wind shifted and seemed to be coming from all directions and the trees looked thicker and the terrain unfamiliar, deadfall everywhere crisscrossing at knee level, almost impassable. I stopped again and listened, and this time, below the sound of the wind hissing, I heard a crunching, like an animal digging. I turned slowly in the direction of the sound and as I did, a head popped up from behind a mound of snow.

'Hey!' I called, at the same moment he saw me.

Vern George was kneeling in the packed snow at the entrance to a cave he was digging out with his mittened hands.

'Hi,' I said.

'Hi,' he answered. He kept digging and I watched him for a minute.

'That's a good cave,' I said. I struggled over to him, and bent down to get a look inside.

'I built a better one last year,' he said, without looking up. 'Better snow.'

'This snow is dry,' I said.

He didn't answer.

'Do you know how far the trail is?' I asked.

Vern stood up and brushed the snow off his knees. 'Are you lost?' He smiled and the sweetness of it startled me again.

'Not really. Maybe a bit. I've only been in this woods a few times, and there was no snow then.'

'A bit lost.' He smiled again and so did I, in spite of myself. 'Well, it's a ways,' he said.

I beat my arms against my sides, trying to pump blood into my hands. 'Which way? My hands are freezing.'

'It's twenty below,' he said, watching my face for a reaction. I kept my eyes on his. 'We better make a fire.'

'I've got matches.'

'If you collect some wood, I'll make a pit.'

I went off, flailing my arms against the cold and broke dead branches and dry fir boughs from standing trees. When I came back with a big armload of wood, Vern had dug a nice firepit in the snow, a few feet in front of the entrance to his cave. I broke up some little twigs and made a teepee. Vern held a lit match to it and we fed it the fir boughs, then bigger pieces, till the fire was

130

roaring and I could take my mitts off and hold my hands close to the flames.

Vern stood by the fire and, slipping off one boot at a time, held his feet to the heat.

'Where do you live?' he asked.

'In town,' I said. 'Where do you live?'

'With my uncle, at the trailer park up the road.'

'Where are your parents?'

He shrugged and I thought it was a shrug that meant he wouldn't say, not that he didn't know.

'Me and my sister billet at these people's house in town. My mom works in logging camps.'

'She does?'

'As a cook,' I added, feeling like a liar. 'Do you know where Kleena Kleene is?'

'Yeah, it's on the way to Bella Coola. Is that where she works?'

I shrugged.

'Where's your dad?'

'He died last year.'

'I can dry your mitts,' Vern said, picking up a long, forked stick out of what was left of the woodpile. I handed them over and he put one on each fork and held it above the flames. In a few minutes, steam rose from them.

'I'm going to try the cave,' he said. He poked the branch with my mitts into the ground so that they hung near the fire. I watched him crawl in, feet first.

'How is it?' I asked.

'It's great,' he grinned. 'Warm. You can come in if you want. There's room.'

I edged in. There wasn't much room, but we weren't touching the walls.

'If we had to spend the night, we'd have to close the entrance in better,' Vern said.

'And maybe make the walls thicker,' I said. 'In case it gets even colder.'

'We'd need to find something to melt snow in for water. We could make fir needle tea.'

'We'd want to find some food,' I said. 'If we had to stay a few days.'

'If our plane went down, way back in the wilderness. No towns around for hundreds of miles.'

'Then we'd have to build something more permanent. We wouldn't be able to walk out till spring. We could use pieces of the plane for things. Like a stove.'

The stick holding my mittens shifted and they bent a little too close to the fire.

'I have to get my mitts,' I told Vern and I crawled out. He followed me.

'Want me to take you back now?' he said.

'Sure.'

We dumped snow on the fire and Vern marked his cave with a long branch. When we got back to town, it was almost dark.

'Bye,' I said.

'Bye,' he answered.

When I got home my face was stiff with cold and my thighs were stinging between where my jacket ended and my boots began.

'Holy moly, it's a Mag-sicle!' Jenny called as I came in the door. 'Twenty-five below and she's out for a stroll.'

132

Bea hurried to the door and helped me take my boots off. 'You could freeze to death out there, you really could,' she said. 'I'll bring you some tea.' I knelt by the heat register, thawing my limbs. Bea's kindness was as unpredictable as her rage. I accepted it, always wary.

'Where'd you hike to?' Ted asked.

'Up the river, the way you showed me.'

'Come and play a game of Canasta with me. I'm about ready to go out of my gourd with boredom here.'

We sat at the table and Ted shuffled the cards. Bea brought the teapot and cups.

'Your dad liked to hike around the bush, too,' Ted said. 'He'd go out in any weather. I met him back before he knew your mother. I was working as a faller with an outfit around Bella Coola and he came on as a bucker. Right away I could tell he was a good one. You see a lot of sunshine loggers come and go. They come in, big plans, big talkers, work harder than they need to right off the hop, something to prove, and then they peter out. A little bad weather, they're grumbling and whining. But your dad was steady. Hard-working, quiet, nothing showy. He had a feeling for the bush. You could see the ease he had there.'

Ted beat me twice, then he sat back in his chair and fell asleep.

★　★　★

That night as Jenny and I lay in bed in the dark with the wind still humming outside, I said, 'Do you think Mom is really a cook in logging camps?'

Jenny didn't say anything for a minute. 'I don't know.'

'She never liked to cook. And it's winter. Do they even have logging camps in winter?'

Jenny didn't answer and I turned towards the wall and pulled my blankets up.

A little while later I heard Jenny crying, trying to stifle her sobs in her pillow.

13

Three days later, after streets had been ploughed, sidewalks cleared, cars jump-started and windows scraped, I arrived home from school and found an envelope on the dresser addressed to us in Mom's hand. I held it to the light, smelled it, picking up a faint musty odour. Maybe this would be the letter telling us when she would come to get us and where we would go. Jenny hoped Mom would rent us a house in Williams Lake, or even an apartment in the building near Safeway. I wanted to go somewhere else, far from here. I couldn't wait for Jenny to get back from work, so I opened the letter. A twenty-dollar bill fell out. I held the letter to my nose, too. Nothing familiar.

Dear girls,
    The $20 is for Maggie's birthday. I can't believe you're 12! I hope you'll buy something practical like new jeans. You needed them in the summer. You would like it here. The other night when the moon was full, a whole pack of wolves sat on a hill above the lake and sang all night long. One night I even saw a wolf down at the lake. He was crossing the ice and so was I. Jenny, I'll send you some $$ before Christmas. I hope you like Williams Lake. Be good!
                                                Love Mom

You need practice to be able to handle disappointment, and I didn't have enough of it yet. I lay down on my bed and tried to breathe past the crushing heaviness on my chest. For some reason, I thought of Vern, pictured his lean brown hand as he held the lit match to our teepee of sticks. A flicker of comfort flared deep in my chest and was gone again.

It took about fifteen minutes for the disappointment to brew into anger.

'Do you have any scraps of denim?' I asked Bea. She was lying on the couch with her glasses resting precariously on her forehead. An open *National Geographic* lay across her chest. I didn't care if she was sleeping. Today I didn't fear her wrath.

She opened her eyes. 'Denim? What for?'

'I need it to patch my jeans.'

'I think I have some.' She pushed herself upright with a groan. I would never get old the way she was, I thought. 'Would you like embroidery thread?'

Bea found the denim and a sewing case with twelve colours of bright embroidery thread, still in their paper wrappers.

'This shows you how to do different stitches,' she said, handing me an old book.

From the denim, I cut out oval patches for the knees of my jeans and over the next few days, I stitched my own design: a campfire of orange and yellow flames, brown logs and white stars of snowflakes falling above it. Bea came by once in a while to watch over my shoulder, even saying once, 'You picked that up pretty quickly.' As I stitched, my anger flared and sputtered and flared again, and finally formed into a kind of plan. If she wouldn't come back to us, then we had to go and find her.

This time, I found the outside envelope from Mom's letter by accident. It was lying in the kitchen garbage can and it caught my eye as I threw some orange peels in. I smoothed it and looked closely. Again there was the cancelled stamp from Kleena Kleene, but nothing else.

The first day I wore my jeans with the new patches to school, I went and sat on the swing next to Vern at recess.

'You going anywhere for Christmas?' he asked.

'No. You?'

'Maybe. I might go see my mom.'

'Cool. Where does she live?'

'Nistsun Lake. Know where that is?'

I nodded. We swung in lazy half circles, our feet on the frozen ground.

'What's that on your knee?' he asked, leaning over. He didn't say anything, just tapped my knee twice with his finger and, as the bell rang, headed back to school.

After school I had two things to do. I walked over to the bank and opened an account. My first deposit was twenty dollars. Next, I went to the Esso station on the highway. Inside, there was a man on his knees arranging quarts of oil on a shelf.

'Are you the manager?' I asked.

'Who's asking?'

'Me. I'm looking for a job. I can pump gas and work the cash register and I know how to check oil and top up radiators.'

'Hand me that box, will you?' He gestured to a box on the counter and I lifted it down for him.

He took a jackknife from his shirt pocket and slit open the top. 'Can I trust you?'

'I billet in town here and I'm very responsible,' I said.

'How old are you?'

'I'm thirteen,' I lied.

He pushed himself to his feet. He had a round paunch under his Esso shirt. He stuck out his hand. 'I'm Bob,' he said and we shook. 'I could use some help over Christmas. How about I try you out? I'll give you two weeks to show me what you can do.'

'Two weeks is great!' I nodded. 'I can start today if you want.'

Bob looked around the store. It smelled of motor oil and chocolate bars. 'Don't you have to let someone know where you are?'

'I can phone.'

Just then the gas bell rang. Bob looked out at the pumps where a long Chrysler had just pulled up.

'Okay,' he said. 'You can start with this guy. He'll only get a couple dollars of gas but he'll want his oil checked, windshields washed, front and rear, and he might even ask you to check the air in his tires.'

★ ★ ★

Vern's uncle worked for the highways and stopped at the gas station about twice a week.

The first time I met him, I was filling up his tank and peered over the edge of his truck into the back. He had some bags of sand, a large folded-up tarp, rope, axes in a bucket, a shovel, a spare tire and a large wooden box locked with a latch and padlock.

'You're Maggie, aren't you?' he said, as he climbed out of the cab. Two long braids hung down the front of his plaid jacket, tapering to neat, skinny ends.

'Yes.'

'I'm Leslie. Uncle Leslie, Vern's uncle. He's told me about you.'

I smiled and hung up the nozzle and tightened the gas cap.

'Want me to check your oil?'

'Good idea,' he said. 'He says you come from Duchess Creek.'

I nodded.

'Come up to the trailer sometime for dinner. I'm a good cook.'

'Okay,' I said. I checked the dipstick. 'You're down about half a quart.'

★ ★ ★

Now that I was earning my own money, I started buying some of my own food. I used the excuse that I didn't want to inconvenience Bea when I got home from work after suppertime. I stopped at Safeway and picked up canned stew, instant mashed potatoes, tins of devilled ham, and oranges. As I put the food in my basket, I liked to imagine that I was outfitting for a wilderness trip. I would need some packets of instant oatmeal and some sugar and tea. But I wouldn't buy those just yet because Bea would ask questions.

At the checkout one day someone behind me said, 'Real potatoes are just about as fast.' It was Uncle Leslie. He had a cart full: a big bag of flour, oats, potatoes, onions, fresh carrots, tomatoes.

'You were going to come for supper. I guess I've got to give you a day. How about tomorrow?'

'Okay,' I said.

'Come with Vern after school. Make sure you ask Mrs. Edwards first.'

The next day it was snowing as Vern and I walked up the hill to the trailer park. Big flakes floated in the air, caught on the wind, and seemed not to land at all.

'Uncle Leslie thinks you must be homesick,' Vern said. 'He's making deer stew.'

'Really?' I said, so eagerly I felt embarrassed. I tried to reclaim a casual tone. 'Yeah, we used to have deer stew a lot.'

'Ever go hunting?'

'Not really. Not with a gun, I mean. You?'

'Yeah. But I don't really like it. I mean I like everything but the killing part. And that's supposed to be the point, right?'

The trailer was a neat white one with a bay window on one end. There was a cedar porch with two wooden loungers on it, dusted in snow.

'Come on in,' said Uncle Leslie when Vern opened the door. 'Leave your boots there and I'll give you a pair of moccasins to wear. The floor gets a bit cold.'

The trailer smelled of stew and a hint of wood smoke. A stack of wood was piled beside a black woodstove.

'Will these fit?' Uncle Leslie held a moccasin next to my foot. 'Looks about right.'

I put them on. 'Perfect,' I said. 'Thank you.'

The only trailers I'd been in were the kind you pulled behind a car. This one seemed bigger than the Edwards' house.

Uncle Leslie made three mugs of hot chocolate from some packets and water from a kettle that was steaming on the little woodstove. Then he washed the spoon, dried it and put it away. I caught a glimpse of the inside of his cupboard, neatly loaded with food, boxes on one shelf, cans on another, jars of canned fruit and salmon on another. A pair of oven mitts hung on a rack by the stove, along with a ladle, spatula, slotted spoon, long fork and different-sized frying pans in a row. The knives were ranged in a block of wood on the counter, from large to small, and beside that were big jars of flour, rice, sugar, tea and coffee, all neatly labelled. On a dishtowel spread on the counter, various sizes of jars and lids, washed and with their labels removed, sat drying. On the window ledge above the sink were four potted plants. I recognized one as parsley. My eyes went to the drawers alongside the fridge. I was tempted to look inside them. The neatness, all the order and organization, was as appealing here as it was claustrophobic and repulsive at the Edwards's.

Uncle Leslie sat with us as we drank our hot chocolate. He got up once to stoke the stove.

'I got this deer we're about to eat right around Duchess Creek in the fall,' he said.

I nodded and we sipped.

'Well, no rest for the wicked.' He stood and carried his dirty cup to the sink.

Vern and I played cards as the smell of baking buns filled the trailer. A pungent scent of deer stew wafted up each time Uncle Leslie opened the lid of the pot. I glanced over at him, clad in an apron, with his braids tucked inside his shirt. He whistled and rattled pots and pans busily. Something sweet floated below the savoury smells.

When supper was almost ready, he called Vern to set the table.

'I'll help,' I said.

'Okay, because it's a lot of work,' Vern said, smiling.

Uncle Leslie set down the pot of stew, a steaming dish of spinach, roasted potatoes, a basket of fresh buns and a saucer of butter.

'Uncle Leslie thinks you eat too much junk,' Vern said.

'Girls your age need iron,' Uncle Leslie said. 'Now take spinach, for instance. There's lots of iron in that.'

'My mom used to make stinging nettle,' I said.

'Oh yeah, that's even better. Takes a bit of work to get it, though.'

'I used my Dad's work gloves.'

'Then you need to boil it twice to get the sting out.'

'Mrs. Edwards won't eat any of that kind of thing. 'Weeds,' she says. 'They could be poisonous.''

Uncle Leslie laughed at my imitation of her voice.

'Sure,' said Vern. 'You'll wind up dead and then who's going to take out the garbage?'

When we were done the stew, Leslie put bowls of apple crumble and vanilla ice cream down in front of us. 'I wonder what you two sound like when you imitate me,' he said.

14

When the money from Mom stopped coming, we didn't know for three months. For some reason Bea had decided to keep it to herself. I can't decide now what motivated her, if she had gotten used to having us there, or if the money had become less important now that Jenny and I both had jobs. Maybe it was compassion, who knows. Stranger things have happened.

The last letter had come just before Jenny's fourteenth birthday in May. Mom wrote that she hadn't been feeling well. She didn't say where she was or what she was doing. The envelope, which I had taken from the mailbox myself, was addressed in someone else's handwriting — small, tight writing that I took to belong to a man. I couldn't make out the cancellation over the stamp, but it didn't look like it said Kleena Kleene.

I can't say it worried us that Mom wasn't feeling well. It barely registered. We took it as a thing you say as a little tidbit of news in a letter that tries to be intimate, but is really hiding something. Namely, that she wasn't coming back yet, but wouldn't say why.

Jenny pocketed the twenty dollars Mom sent. For her birthday party, she and her friends Tracy and Lila went to see *The Poseidon Adventure* at the Starlight Drive-in with Tracy's brother.

Ted and I were playing Canasta at the table

when they came home, wound up, playing a game where they would only speak lines from the movie.

'Hard left!' Jenny said and steered Lila into our bedroom.

'You're going the wrong way, dammit!' Tracy said.

'That's our only chance!'

'Sail yourselves into the kitchen and have some cake,' Bea called.

'She's right. That's the way out!'

They gave Ted and me a blow-by-blow of the plot as they ate the cake at the table, then they disappeared into our bedroom to drink orange pop. Later, when Jenny was giggling uncontrollably as I got ready for bed, I learned they had spiked the pop with lemon gin that Tracy's brother had given them.

★ ★ ★

By summer, Bea had things to worry about other than money. One night about an hour or so after suppertime, I arrived home from the gas station. A couple of neighbour boys squealed and hopped in and out of the sprinkler sweeping across the dry patch of sunlit lawn in front of their house. The sprinkler cast a rainbow in the air, and behind it, a man sat on the step smoking and watching the boys. He lifted his hand to wave at me and I lifted mine in return. It was a hot evening and Bea had the screen door open and a fan going in the living room, the stale hamburger grease smell floating out into the street. I didn't want to go into the hot house. I would have some supper, then go for a hike down to the river before dark.

'You're finally home!' Bea said as soon as I stepped inside.

The clean plates were still on the table.

'I was at work,' I said. 'I'm not late.'

'Did I say you were late?' She advanced towards me, waving her dishtowel wildly. I stepped backwards; I was familiar with the winding-up Bea. She would begin shrieking any minute, and she did. 'Go find Ted! I can't think what in God's name he thinks he's doing. It's not like I don't have supper on the table at the same time every night. If anyone notices, I try to provide a routine around here. Like you give a damn. You show up whenever you damn well please . . . '

Bea didn't need to tell me where to look. I walked towards the Maple Leaf Hotel, where Ted spent his days in the cave-like dimness of the smelly, windowless pub. I passed Francie's Famous Bakery, which always radiated the smell of fresh bread and reminded me of the summer in the log house at Dultso Lake. And I passed the three drunk men who hung out on the sidewalk in front of the liquor store and called me sweetheart when they asked for money.

I was still half a block from the pub when I saw him, slumped in his wheelchair by the side of the road. I assumed he was drunk, although he rarely showed any visible signs of drunkenness. Once in a while he fell asleep in the pub and the owner, Mr. MacNeil, phoned the house

146

for me to come and get him.

'Ted!' I called.

He didn't respond. When I got close, I saw he was running with sweat. A drop of it was poised on the end of his nose, ready to fall. His eyes were only half-open.

'Ted!' I said and shook his shoulder. He winced. The drop of sweat landed on his shirt front.

'Mag,' he whispered. 'Better take me home.'

★ ★ ★

Ted had stomach cancer.

'I told him what it would lead to,' I heard Bea say to her sister on the phone. 'You don't pour that much alcohol into your system without some kind of consequence.' Then she started to cry, tried to poke her Kleenex up under her glasses, had to take them off. 'They have him on morphine — for the pain.' She said it pitifully, lingering on the word 'morphine.'

But Bea rose to her trouble; it enlivened her. She shredded apple and made it into puree for Ted. She boiled up beef bones, added a hash of cabbage and carrots and carried it to his hospital room in a Thermos. 'They give him broth made from powder,' she said disdainfully. 'How is that supposed to make you healthy?'

She brought him fresh pyjamas and a stack of *National Geographics*, left them with him for a few days, then exchanged them for new ones. There was no evidence that Ted read them. He mostly kept the tiny TV a few inches from his face, and dozed in and out with the ebb and flow of morphine. But Ted reading them was not the point; Bea needed to be the model bereft wife. For her efforts, she received tender pats on the arm from the nurses at the hospital, as well as sympathetic noises from the grocery store clerk and her sister's late night phone calls. Her life finally had purpose.

★ ★ ★

I believed that my worry was a jinx. I had never saved anyone with it. Quite the opposite, it seemed that, one by one, those I cared about were slipping under the spell of my worry and being carried away. And so I was determined not to worry about Ted.

I went to see him after school. He was awake and playing solitaire on the table pulled up to his chest.

'Mag!' he said. 'Sit down. I've got sweet bugger-all to do here.'

'Want to play Canasta?'

'Get the other deck out of the drawer.'

Ted shuffled the cards and began dealing. He looked different in the hospital bed, smaller, and older. The light blue gown tied loosely around his neck emphasized his bony collarbone, the pale blue veins of his neck and the almost translucent skin of the hollow at his throat. He had lost about thirty pounds, according to Bea's phone reports, and he was in constant pain. But today he was awake, at least.

We played, cards snapping quietly on the

table. Ted shifted his position gingerly every few minutes and I saw his face twist with pain. He tried to hide it.

After a while, he said, 'I can tell you what I know about your dad if you like.'

I nodded.

'I met Patrick in about 1957, I think it was. He told me he came to the U.S. from Northern Ireland when he was twenty. There was some bad feeling between his father and him. His father was a drinker, I understand, and he could get pretty mean when he tied one on. Didn't work much. Sounds like they were hand to mouth, most of the time. When Patrick got old enough, he joined the RUC. Do you know what that is?'

'Dad said he was a policeman once.'

'That's right. The Royal Ulster Constabulary. A kind of police force and border patrol combined. The pay was good, but there were very few Catholics. Patrick's dad was livid when he found out. They were Catholic, of course.' Ted paused and laid down two more eights to make his first Canasta. 'I got lucky there,' he said.

'My mother's family is Irish, too,' he went on. 'We've got long memories, the Irish do, and we know how to hold a grudge like nobody else. I don't know where exactly your dad lived, but his father thought joining the RUC was a cop-out. Said they'd never accept Patrick, being Catholic. Patrick could do a funny send-up of him, with his Irish accent. 'You're after turning soup-taker, me own son. Never thought I'd live to see the day. Colluding with the filthy prods.'

149

Well, I can't do it justice.

'But the thing is, Patrick said, his father was right. The little songs at first, then the taunts. One of his partners started each shift by saluting: 'For God and Ulster.' One day Patrick found something nasty scrawled on his locker. He wouldn't tell anyone about it, and for damn sure not his father. So he took his next paycheque and bought a ticket to the United States. Left without saying goodbye to anyone. He couldn't bear to tell his mother. I imagine he felt bad about that to the day he died. I suppose your mother would know that story. After he'd met your mother, he told me they had that in common: they were both orphans.'

Ted had started a meld of queens, so I threw down a three of clubs to block him from taking the discard pile. I knew Dad had come from Ireland; he had a lilt in his voice that his friends teased him about. But he rarely talked about it.

'Living in such a sensible place as this, it's hard to imagine the bitterness back there. Families turning against their own. And that was in the good times. Now, well, your dad didn't live to see Bloody Sunday. What am I going to discard here? What's going to do the least damage?' He threw down a nine of hearts and I took the pile.

He picked up Dad's story again. 'In New York, he met up with a guy going to Oregon. Patrick went along. That's where he learned to log.'

Ted exhaled a long slow sigh and I thought he was about to tell me something I wouldn't want to hear. My stomach contracted in readiness. But

150

he reached for the buzzer to call the nurse instead and then sat back against his pillow and closed his eyes. He let his cards fall on the table, face up; I pushed back my chair and went for the door just as the nurse was coming in.

Ted whispered he was sorry and I sat with him for half an hour, as he sank into the relief of the morphine. Then I put the decks away in the drawer and slipped out.

15

That fall, as Ted lay dying in the hospital with tubes poking out of him, Vern and I built a tree fort in the bush. Vern found scrap lumber around the trailer court and I brought hammers, nails and a saw from the Edwards' basement. We built a platform between three aspens. Each time we went there and sat back in the lemony light of the fragrant trees surveying our work, we thought of something new to add: a wall to lean against, a window, a rope ladder, then a real ladder. We didn't need a roof because the leaves of the aspens formed a golden canopy that flapped around us like tiny flags in the breeze. In the sun, the leaves flipped and tossed patterns of light on the rough floor of our fort. Even in the slushy fall rain, we were protected; the wet flakes pattered a rising and falling song against the leaves. Eventually, if we stayed long enough, we would get wet, but it was worth it to be inside that sound.

'If you were blind,' said Vern, 'I bet you could learn the names of trees just by listening to how they sound in the wind.'

An eagle hovered, then landed on a fir snag near our fort. He was a regular. Vern and I had watched him a few times.

'My grandma says that if you call someone's name when an eagle is near, that person will hear you, wherever they are.'

'Ted!' I called.

Vern joined me. 'Ted! Ted! Ted!'

The eagle lifted his giant wings and rose with a rush of air. We watched as he cruised towards the hill where the hospital was. Vern and I grinned at each other.

* * *

When the leaves had all gone from our fort, we hammered planks into place for a partial roof to keep the wind off. We still went after school when I didn't have to work, and put our backs to the wall where we could catch the last of the sun.

'How's Ted?' Vern asked one Friday.

'Hanging on. Or so says Beatrice.' I drawled her name. I had no real idea how Ted was. He was doped up now most of the time I visited, which Bea said was because they'd upped his dose of morphine.

'Do you know how to braid?'

'Sure. I braid Jenny's hair sometimes.'

'I want to braid my hair.'

'It's almost long enough. We can practise with some twigs.' I pulled out my pocket knife. 'We need three skinny twigs.'

'What about practising on you?'

I met Vern's eyes. He was smiling. 'My hair isn't long enough,' I said, smiling back.

He slipped down the rope ladder that we still used even though we'd built the sturdy wooden one, and found three small green shoots. He scrambled back up into the fort.

'Okay, it's really easy.' I set the twigs on the

boards in front of me. 'You cross this one over the middle one. Then this one over that one. Then you just keep going.' My fingers moved down the twigs till they were braided into a coarse braid.

'We need something smaller.'

We untied the shoelaces from both of Vern's runners and one of mine and I showed Vern how to make a nice, even braid. I untied it and he practised with the shoelaces till he had the method down.

'This is a cinch,' he said. 'But can you do it in my hair?'

'Barely,' I said. 'Your hair really needs to get a little longer.'

Vern fished in his jeans pocket and pulled out a fine, black comb. He handed it to me. I positioned him in front of me and set the comb gently into his hair. Ravens cawed raucously from the woods and burst out of the trees in a fury of black wings, fighting over something.

I lifted the comb and started at his forehead, working gently.

'Your hair is thick.'

'Yeah.'

As I smoothed Vern's hair, the warmth of his back heated my legs where he rested against me. A shampoo scent wafted from him.

'Stop moving,' I said, and held his shoulder. It was warm and solid.

'Ever think about going to see your mom?'

'My mom? I think about it,' I said. 'I don't know where she is right now.'

'I thought she was cooking in a logging camp

near Kleena Kleene.'

'I don't think she's there anymore. She'll write to us soon and tell us where she is.'

'I think I'll go see my mom,' Vern said. 'I'm free to go whenever I want.'

I divided his smoothed hair into three and began braiding, pulling it close to keep it tight.

'Is it working?' he asked.

I laughed. 'It'll be short, but it'll be a braid.'

We heard a high whistle above us and Vern pointed to the eagle, cruising in on a wide circle. It landed on top of the fir snag and looked out over the trees as if it were deliberately ignoring us. Vern twisted around to meet my eyes and he was smiling.

'Hey, quit moving. I'm not done,' I said.

'That's a good sign, you know,' he said. 'I think it means it's good that I'm braiding my hair in the Indian way.'

'Give me your shoelace,' I said.

'My shoelace?'

'I need to tie it.'

He handed it over and I tied his braid.

'Cool.' He swung his head and touched the braid gently. 'I hope it stays in.'

'Braid it when your hair's wet. That's what Jenny does.'

We watched the eagle lift off and ride a thermal high above the trees. I thought that this eagle could also be a sign for me, but I didn't mention it to Vern. Maybe it was a sign that Ted was getting better. Or maybe my mother had heard me say her name. Maybe she had been cutting onions in some makeshift shack of a kitchen, and her eyes had begun to run with tears. Maybe at that moment the knife had stopped, resting against the cutting board, and she had looked up, listening for my voice. But then I remembered that 'Mom' was not her real name. If I called to her, I would have to call her Irene.

'I'm going to hitch to my mom's place tonight,' Vern said suddenly. 'Do you want to come?'

'Tonight? Bea won't let me go, I know that.'

'So don't ask her. I'm not telling Uncle Leslie. I'll just go.'

'I don't know,' I said. I was worried about leaving Ted, but I didn't want to be worried. I was not supposed to be worrying. 'Not the best hitchhiking time of year.'

'True. Well, I might go,' he said. 'I'll have to see.'

* * *

On Monday, Vern was at school. He hadn't hitched anywhere after all. But having the plan was important, I knew that. My birthday was a few days away. I had hoped a letter might come from Mom, but nothing did and even Bea let that pass without comment. Jenny baked a chocolate cake and drew a big '13' on it in yellow icing. She studded the cake with thirteen yellow candles. I blew out the candles in the kitchen with the lights off and then Bea flicked on the fluorescent light above the sink, put her hands on her hips and sighed, 'Well!'

'Open your present,' Jenny said, clapping.

Unwrapping it, I felt a wave of nausea; this moment was not right, could not be right without Mom and we all knew it.

'Moccasins,' I said. 'Thanks.' They were fur-trimmed slippers, with a shimmery flower beaded on each one. I held them to my nose and smelled the smoky tanned hide.

'Do you like them? Vern's uncle got them for us from a lady on the reserve,' Jenny said.

'They're great,' I said. And I meant it, but I couldn't keep that disappointed sound out of my voice.

'Cake!' said Jenny. 'Who wants ice cream?'

★   ★   ★

Two days later I was at the gas station, my parka hood laced tight around my face against the cold wind. I filled Mrs. Gustafson's truck, peering over the edge of the box as I usually did — two bags of sand, spare tire, a length of chain. I saw Jenny hurrying across the highway towards me with her nylon-stockinged legs and white runners, her coat tossed on unbuttoned over her Frank's Chicken and Pizza uniform.

Her face was red with the cold. 'Ted's dead,' she said and I couldn't believe that we both smirked at the rhyme. 'No, but he is, Mag, he died about an hour ago. Bea wants us to come home.'

I tightened the gas cap on Mrs. Gustafson's truck. Jenny and I looked at each other for what seemed like a long time. 'I'll come home after work,' I finally said.

'You sure?'

I nodded.

'Okay, then. I'm going to go home now.' She wrapped her coat tighter around herself and turned to walk away. She hesitated. 'You . . . you know. Be careful or whatever.'

'What?'

'I don't know.' She looked around the gas station. 'Don't light any matches or anything.' Then she ran off, the wind gusting so hard, it made a part in the back of her thick, dark red curls as she leaned against it.

I took the twenty Mrs. Gustafson handed me, rang it into the cash register and brought her back the change. Standing on the pump island with the wind whipping at me, I watched the wheels of her truck as she drove away.

★ ★ ★

After the funeral, Jenny said, 'That was our third thing. And it's not that bad. I mean, I'm sorry he's dead but I'm not that sorry. I didn't know him enough to be that sorry. Well, you did I guess, so it's worse for you. But my point is, our third thing is an easy one. And now we're free and clear.'

She waited for me to say something. We were in our room taking off our good clothes. Beatrice had bought us both black skirts and sweaters and leotards. They had not been washed yet, and the new smell mingled with the sweat that flowed from being corralled in a

158

church hall, surrounded by strangers who seemed to think we wanted their sympathy.

'We should look for her,' Jenny said.

'She's the mother. She should look for us.' I said it without thinking, but later I thought I must have been saving it up for a long time for it to have come out like that.

Jenny said, 'For a girl, you're sure an asshole.'

16

That spring, as the meltwater trilled from the eaves and the smell of wet, bare earth rose on the night air, I sat doing my social studies homework on the bed. Bea was in the kitchen, on the phone with her sister.

'It's not the money now,' I heard her say. 'I've got enough from Ted's pension. But we haven't heard a thing for months. It's like she's dropped off the face of the earth.'

A silence.

'I don't know anyone who knows her. It was Patrick that Ted knew. I'm not a mother, but . . . ' Her voice dropped to a murmur, which was followed by another long silence.

The meltwater ran from the eaves, making a prolonged note. My blue pencil crayon scratched a low accompaniment as I coloured Hudson Bay on my map of Canada. Eventually all the snow would melt, and the note would change then die out.

Bea's voice rose. 'It may be that. Anything could have happened, I suppose.' Dropped again, too low to hear. Then: 'It's not like that up here. Not if you don't want to be found.'

Bea could talk for hours. She'd circle around and around and alight on fruitless little thoughts, like the bee of Jenny's nickname. I turned on the radio Jenny had bought for herself. Elton John was singing 'Crocodile Rock' and I turned it up.

A couple of minutes later I heard the clump, clump of each of Jenny's shoe as she kicked them off at the front door. She opened the bedroom door and brought the fresh spring air in with her. And something else. The skunky scent of pot smoke.

She tossed her books on her bed, then threw back her head and launched into the la-la-la-la-las.

'Where were you?' I demanded.

A quick knock on the door and Bea came in. She would do that, knock, but not give us time to answer before she barged in.

'Where were you?' Bea's tone was more playful than mine.

'I was out with Brian. We went to Rudy Johnson Bridge and watched the ice floating by on the river.' She was glowing, her cheeks a fiery red.

'Crazy,' said Bea, wiping her weepy eye. 'Watching ice melt. Not exactly my idea of a great date.'

'I didn't say we were watching it melt,' Jenny laughed. 'I'm freezing, though. I want a hot bath.'

'Oh my! Freezing for love,' said Bea and let her eyelashes flutter and rolled her eyes heavenward. 'I'll run it for you.'

I was surprised she didn't comment on the scent in the room. Could she really not have noticed it?

'I hope you're not forgetting about your homework,' I said after Bea had gone. 'It's nine thirty.'

'What are you, my mother now?'

I hated the sound of my own voice, the tight, needy worry. But Brian was a liability to me, to my plan. If I had thought about it then as I do now, I would have realized that Jenny being happy was a liability. I could not have her behave as if our lives were normal, as if we weren't the people adults felt sorry for and for whom voices dropped to cluck and murmur over. I didn't want their sympathy, but I needed Jenny to be aware of herself as an object of pity. Self-pity is supposed to come naturally to fifteen-year-olds. But it didn't to Jenny. Jenny was sunny; she was sweet; she was happy.

⋆   ⋆   ⋆

Vern and I were out on the highway, heading west. The moon was a pale wafer, brightening by degrees in the dusky sky. Before us, the road opened up, spun out to the horizon, a flat, dun ribbon cut through dry brown fields. Spring in the Chilcotin and everything was still brown, waiting. It might rain. It might rain tonight. A bank of clouds was piling up, purple on grey on navy blue.

We walked, Vern with a small duffel bag slung on his shoulder like a hobo. I had nothing — only my soft blue and black flannel jacket, pockets stuffed with Kleenex, Dad's pearl-handled jackknife, four Fig Newtons and some wooden matches. Frog song filled the air, rising and falling in waves. All along the road, their chorus rose up, then dropped as they heard our

162

footsteps crunching in the gravel. As we passed they took it up again, trilling high and urgent and joyful.

I didn't care that only two cars had passed us in an hour. I didn't care that as the first one drew closer, we hesitated over who should stick their arm out or if we both should and whether the thumb really needed to be crooked into a hook like we were trying to catch a car instead of signal it. We both broke down laughing and I nearly peed myself and had to run for the cover of some bushes. The next one, a pickup loaded down with hay, slowed before we'd even recovered from the first. The driver, wedged in tight with three other passengers in the cab, lifted his hands from the wheel in apology and drove on.

A giddiness had risen in my chest, like the frog song. I was happy. Happy that my running shoes were crunching along this wide-open road beside Vern, happy that my jacket was warm, that dew was settling on the fields and a pungent smell of spring perfumed the dusk.

My shoulder bumped Vern's. 'Sorry,' I said.

'Watch where you're going, will ya!' he said. 'Do you want to get me killed? Look at this traffic screaming by! It's a death race out here.'

Just then a pair of headlights bobbed over a rise and we broke down laughing again.

'No, come on Maggie, get serious,' said Vern. He dug out his flashlight, straightened and watched the approaching vehicle. 'We need a ride or we'll never get to Nistsun tonight.' I fell in behind him and we both stuck out our arms, then he turned to assess my hitchhiking form. He nodded approval, faced the approaching lights again. At the same moment, both our thumbs popped up.

The car sped towards us, kicking up gravel. 'Do they see us?' I asked. Vern shook his flashlight; the light kept cutting out. Only a murky wash of daylight remained. I edged over to the grass, afraid of being creamed. The car swerved violently to the side of the road and slid to a stop just past us. Led Zeppelin's 'Rock and Roll' blared from the open windows. As the dust settled, a pale-faced boy with a shaggy blonde haircut draped himself out the passenger-side window. He dangled his arms against the dirty door panel. 'Hey, you guys need a ride, man?'

'Yeah,' said Vern, stepping forward.

'Where you going?'

'Nistsun Lake.'

'Nistsun?' The pale boy exploded into giggles. 'Shit. You got a ways to go.'

The driver leaned over and called, 'We're going as far as Duchess Creek.' Vern and I bent to look at him. He took a long swig from a mickey of rye, sat back and wiped his mouth. 'I think,' he added. They both broke up giggling again. The mention of Duchess Creek made my heart leap. But I wasn't going anywhere with those guys.

'You can clear a space in the back there,' the driver said when he caught his breath. The car was a black Mustang fastback, the backseat littered with 8-track cassettes, balled up clothes and blankets and crumpled chip bags.

Vern looked at me.

'I think I'd rather walk,' I said, and I didn't whisper it.

That set the pale one off again. His laughter turned to coughing and choking and he slapped the dashboard. The driver hesitated, unsure if he should be insulted or not, then started laughing himself. He had a high-pitched girlish giggle and Vern and I couldn't help laughing, too.

'She's honest!' howled the pale one. 'You gotta give her that! She's honest!'

'You sure?' asked the driver, putting it into gear. 'It's a long walk . . . '

Vern waved them off.

'You sure? Last chance!' the pale one shouted out the window as they fishtailed off down the road.

Vern put the flashlight under his chin. It lit up his face. 'Margaret, Margaret,' he said, in a pretty good imitation of Beatrice. 'You're such a rude girl. That was a minty-cool car, too.'

We heard a low rumbling and thought another car was approaching. But it died down a bit, then grew louder and closer.

'Thunder!' we both said at the same time. I looked up and the white face of the moon was half-hidden by boiling clouds.

'We're gonna get wet,' Vern sang quietly.

Thunder split the air with a terrifying crack. A quick white flash lit up Vern and me and the ribbon of road. He grabbed my arm.

'Come on. Let's walk faster,' he said.

I laughed. 'What's that going to help?'

'The faster we walk, the less drops can hit us.'

'That's not true. If anything, it's just the opposite.'

'Let's just hurry,' he said.

'You're scared!'

The thunder rumbled again, then exploded right overhead, shaking the ground. Vern screamed and started running down the road. I was laughing so hard I could barely keep up. His scream trailed behind him and as big drops of rain began to fall, he flailed his arms theatrically.

'Whose idea was this anyway?' I shouted.

'Who was too good to take our one and only ride?' Vern shouted back.

'A little rain isn't going to kill us.'

'Maybe not. But I'm worried about getting hit by lightning.' Vern was loping along the road sideways now, in big scissor strides. 'If we were in that car, we wouldn't have to worry. Rubber tires.'

'We wouldn't have to worry because we'd be in the ditch! Nice and low.'

I caught up to Vern and we slowed to a walk. The rain bucketing down chilled us through. Beyond the roadside all we could see was thick, murky blackness. We had no idea how far we were from any kind of shelter. If we could find a fir tree, with low drooping branches, it would be dry enough under there. And we could put some boughs on the ground to sit on, in case the rain ran in. But we'd have to worry about the lightning. I couldn't see getting a fire going in this downpour. Right now a gas station or a restaurant sounded a lot more appealing. Vern and I walked closer and closer together till we were bumping elbows and apologizing repeatedly.

The thunder was moving away from us when I heard another rumbling.

'I think this time it's a car,' I said.

Sure enough, we could see the points of light, far away and blurred through the rain.

'They won't see us,' Vern said, but he flicked his flashlight on anyway and pointed it in that direction. It cut out, he shook it, it came back on, flickering wanly. The car came towards us slowly. Round headlights. High. A truck. It drove along cautiously. The flashlight cut out again and when Vern shook it, it wouldn't come back on.

'Great,' he said.

'It's a truck,' I said out loud. We waved our arms as it came closer.

'Ford,' said Vern. 'That's Uncle Leslie's truck.'

'Oh.' As it pulled up beside us, I asked him, 'Are you in trouble?'

Vern laughed.

Uncle Leslie leaned over and rolled down the steaming passenger window. 'Well, if it isn't two drowned rats.'

I looked at Vern. I was secretly overjoyed to see Uncle Leslie. Vern pulled open the door.

'Want to sit in the middle?' he asked me.

'Sure, okay,' I said, trying to keep the enthusiasm out of my voice.

'I better turn some heat on, eh?' said Uncle Leslie. 'You two are about as wet as you can get. I'm going to have to wring my truck out tomorrow.'

Vern slammed the door and we were inside.

The heat was blowing and the radio played 'Heartaches by the Number.' A big shiver overtook me.

Uncle Leslie shook his head, back and forth, as he made a wide U-turn on the road.

'Anytime you want to go to Nistsun Lake, I'll take you. But not tonight.' Then he said to me, 'Beatrice called. Well, first your sister did, then Bea got on the line. She's not too happy with you.' He laughed. 'That there is what you call an understatement.'

I nodded, but didn't say anything. I just wanted to ride along in the truck, the wipers slicing the rain across the windshield, fiddle on the radio moaning in time.

We drove east, the rain still coming down hard, back to Williams Lake.

Uncle Leslie pulled up in front of his trailer. A yellow bug light burned outside. He said to me, 'I have a little piece of advice for you. Gained over years of experience. Phone home and tell Bea you're safe and you're going to camp out on the couch here tonight. I'll take you home in the morning. She'll still be mad tomorrow, but not like she is tonight.'

He held his hand on the key in the ignition and looked at me.

'Thanks,' I said and smiled. He switched off the truck and killed the lights.

'Okay, let's go find some towels.'

I dripped a puddle on the kitchen linoleum as I made the phone call. Jenny answered.

'Mag, you're dead,' she said simply.

'Don't exaggerate,' I said.

'No, Bea, I told you! Put that butcher knife away! What did you say, Maggie?'

'Jenny, tell her I'm going to stay at Vern's. His uncle will bring me home in the morning.'

'You don't want to talk to her?' Jenny asked sweetly.

'No.'

'Well, she doesn't want to talk to you either. She's too busy sharpening her axe.' I heard Bea say something in the background. I couldn't help smiling. I knew this was Jenny's way of telling me it was okay.

'You're crazy,' I told her. That was my way of thanking her.

It was dim in the trailer, just a warm orange glow cast from the coloured globes of a pole lamp by the couch. I found a rag under the sink and wiped up the puddle I had made. Uncle Leslie handed me a fluffy yellow towel, a pair of Vern's jeans, a soft flannel shirt and wool socks.

'You can use the bathroom,' he said.

In the bathroom, I stripped off my clothes and rubbed my chilled body with the towel. I could feel the welcome heat returning, more intense the way it is after you've been wet and cold. I rubbed my hair and put on the warm, dry clothes. In the living room, Vern sat wringing out his skinny, wet braid. Uncle Leslie brought us hot chocolate studded with mini marshmallows. We all gazed through the window of the woodstove at the crackling fire inside. I suppose that our night had been ruined, our adventure scuttled, and maybe Vern was angry, but he didn't look it. He blew on his hot chocolate and

169

took a sip. I thought that I would have to keep it secret that this had been the perfect end to a perfect day and I hadn't felt so happy in a long, long time.

Uncle Leslie spoke calmly. 'It's hard not to have your mother with you. That's the way it is with some families. Lots of different reasons. It's not easy for you. A father gone, that's different. We learn to live with that. But your mother, that's a kind of ache that won't go away. I know how that is.'

He sipped his hot chocolate. 'You have to be strong for yourself. Talk to her in your mind. Tell her how you feel. Don't think it's because of something you did. It never is.'

Vern and I both watched the fire and sipped our hot chocolate. The silence was not awkward. After a while, Uncle Leslie said, 'Get many rides?'

'The only one who stopped, Maggie turned down.'

'Why was that?'

'The guy was drunk,' I said. 'I wasn't getting in that car.'

'Good for you! Good for you!'

'She said, 'I'd rather walk.' So polite, right to his face.' Vern tossed his head back and laughed.

'You'll go far, Maggie,' Uncle Leslie said, draining the last of his hot chocolate and getting up. I wasn't sure what he meant, but his words stayed with me and I would summon them sometimes, later, when I felt the need of them.

★   ★   ★

We did go to visit Vern's mother, Jolene. It was in May, about a month after our hitchhiking fiasco. Vern invited me to go along, one night when I was at his place for supper and we were doing dishes afterward.

'We're going to Nistsun Lake next weekend,' he said. 'Do you want to come?'

'To see your mom?'

'You'd like her. She's nice.'

'I'll have to trade shifts with someone.'

'And make sure Beatrice says it's okay,' Uncle Leslie said, coming into the kitchen.

We headed out on a sunny Saturday morning. At Duchess Creek Uncle Leslie said, 'Your old stomping grounds, eh Maggie? We'll stop and get some cold drinks here.'

'Maggie Dillon,' Uncle Leslie said to the man behind the counter as he handed me my Orange Crush. 'She used to live in Duchess Creek.'

'That right?' said the man. 'Me and my wife just bought the place. We lived in Quesnel before this.'

We got back in the truck and we drove right by the driveway of our old house. The yard looked overgrown and deserted.

'Do you know where Kleena Kleene is?' I asked.

'It's about two hours up the road. But there isn't much to it. I'll point it out to you.'

Later, when Uncle Leslie slowed and said, 'That's Kleena Kleene,' all I saw was an old log house close to the road with a post office sign on the wall. There were no more houses, just rail fence stretching all along the gravel road, beyond

171

that the forest, then mountains. I wanted to say something to Uncle Leslie, but I was embarrassed. How could I not know where my own mother was? It seemed to me that the adults we knew kept quiet because they understood something that Jenny and I didn't want to admit — that Mom didn't want to be found.

★ ★ ★

When we got to Vern's mother's house on the reserve, she opened the door and pulled Vern to her.

'Hey,' she said, rocking him back and forth in her arms. She looked at Uncle Leslie and me over Vern's shoulder and smiled, but I could see her eyes tearing up. 'You've got a braid,' she said, touching it gently. 'You're getting so big. You're as big as me already.'

Actually, he was bigger. Jolene was a small, delicate woman and young, younger than my mother. Everything about her was slim and compact, like a doll. As she hugged Vern, I noticed her slender fingers and her perfect fingernails, painted a rosy pink. When she released him, I saw her face — small, heart-shaped with skin as smooth as cream. Her black hair was cut in a pixie style and her eyebrows were perfectly arched and thin. She wore frosted pink lipstick to match her nails and a pink and white gingham blouse, tied at the waist above slim white jeans.

Jenny would have loved the look of Jolene. Even her feet. Dainty little bare feet in open-toe pink slippers. I was in my navy blue and black flannel jacket, patched Lee jeans and dirty runners.

Jolene ushered us in. I started to take off my runners.

'Oh, no! Don't worry about that,' she said. 'Your feet'll be black. This place gets like Grand Central Station.'

Vern and I sat on the couch as Jolene poured coffee for Uncle Leslie. A man came out from one of the bedrooms. He was a big white man, over six feet and muscular, wearing a tight black muscle shirt with faded print on the front that read Jim's Towing above a picture of a cartoon woman wearing a bikini.

'Lester!' he boomed.

'Jim,' Uncle Leslie acknowledged. I could tell right away he didn't like the man.

'Coffee?' Jim scoffed. 'It's four o'clock in the goddamn afternoon. Way past Miller time.'

'Watch your language,' Jolene said pertly and gestured towards Vern and me.

'What'd I say? Christ! I gotta watch my language in my own house now?'

Jolene carried a tray over and set it in front of Vern and me — on it were pickles and buns with salted meat in them. Vern's leg bounced in impatience. Then his cousins came in and crowded around the couch.

'Come and see my car,' one of them said.

We all tramped across the reserve to the edge of the bush where a car sat on several stout logs. Three girls joined us, one about my age and the other two younger. Sharman, the owner, pulled

173

off a canvas tarp. The Beaumont was sleek and gold. It had no tires and no roof, so it gave the illusion of a boat, waiting for the water to rise. Sharman climbed in behind the wheel. 'You two get in the front,' he said to Vern and me. Everyone else climbed in the back or perched on the hood.

'It's going to be cool when it's done. Look at the upholstery. It's like factory,' Sharman said.

'Cool,' said Vern. 'Where'd you get it?'

'Guy over at Redstone.'

We relaxed into the car, the afternoon sun heating us. I leaned my head back against the seat and closed my eyes. A dog barked and some kids shouted and voices murmured in the car. I wondered why Vern didn't live here. He'd never told me the reason. His mother seemed nice and she lived in a house with two or three bedrooms.

A boy named Lawrence, Sharman's younger brother, said, 'We have to come back tonight when it's dark and see if we can see the ghost.'

'What ghost?' said Vern.

'Don't you know about the ghost?' said Lawrence. 'Man, you've been away too long.'

'Tell him about the ghost,' said Sharman, and some of the other kids said, 'Yeah, tell the story.'

'I don't like that story,' said the littlest one and one of the girls said, 'Don't worry, Normie. I won't let it get you.'

'My uncle told me about this story,' Lawrence began. 'It happened before I was born. Not too long before, though. Lots of people on the reserve still remember. There was these two brothers. One was real handsome — tall, slim,

174

muscular. He wore a white silk scarf tied at his neck and a cowboy hat. Had cheekbones like a woman. He was a charmer, could tell jokes that'd make anybody forget the bad stuff they were worried about. All the women loved him. His name was Louis.

'His brother, Henry, was pretty much the opposite, kind of a porky fella, but good hearted and real quiet, real shy. He played guitar like some kind of Spanish angel. People say when Henry played, the animals all stopped what they were doing, moose held their heads up listening, owls stopped hooting and eagles lost the field mice they were hunting and everything just stood still. Which is all well and good but he couldn't do much else. He wasn't no hunter and he wasn't no cowboy either. And of course Louis was both. And a logger. Louis excelled at any kind of physical work you could throw his way. He was the best rider, never broke a bone, and he was a crack shot. He could bag a deer with a .22, just perfect aim and pow, down. Louis was the kind of guy that women wanted for a husband.'

'I don't like the next part,' little Normie said.

'Shhh.'

'Sit still. Quit rocking the car!'

'Now, Louis had a girlfriend,' Lawrence resumed. 'The prettiest girl this side of Williams Lake, and probably all the other sides, too. I never saw her, but I heard she had lo-ng hair as black as a raven's wing, right to her ass.' Everyone laughed. 'And her eyes sparkled like summer stars and she had a step as light as a fawn. Her name was Etoile, which, in case you don't know, means star in French. They say her mother was a Métis from the Prairies and she gave her that pretty name the moment she saw her sparkling eyes. Etoile and Louis weren't exactly married but they lived together like husband and wife in Louis's little cabin in the bush. It was just over there. If you walk in about half a mile, you can find the stone foundation in the grass. The stones have been blackened by fire, but that comes later.'

'No! Don't tell that part!' wailed Normie.

'That comes later, Normie. You can plug your ears.'

'Tell me when it's coming, okay?'

'Shh!'

'Louis left Etoile alone for long stretches when he went off to work. He loved her, there's no doubt about that. But he couldn't stay put for long. He liked to be off, being praised for climbing the tallest spar-tree, or rounding up the most wild horses, or guiding tourists on the best bear hunt. That was Louis. So Etoile stayed alone and sometimes when Henry had nowhere else to go, he visited with her and he played that angelic Spanish guitar. That didn't bother Louis any. He was glad Etoile had the company.

'One winter when the snow was deeper than this car, deeper than the roof of that house over there, and Louis was out looking for horses to bring back to someone's ranch, Henry put on some snowshoes and strapped on his guitar and hiked out to see how Etoile was getting on. That was hard going, seeing's how he was kind of porky, as I said. But he worried about her, maybe the way Louis should have. They say Henry had to dig down in the snow to get to Etoile's door. She was okay in there. She'd bagged herself a deer and she had a good stew going on the stove, though her woodpile was getting low.

'Some people say that Etoile fell in love with Henry, plain and simple, even though he was kinda porky and couldn't hunt worth a damn. Some say that that night while he played his guitar, the northern lights came down and touched that little cabin and enchanted the two of them. That cabin wasn't very big. They ate the deer stew and Henry played by the fire and the wind raged outside and jack pines in the woods split like thunder in that cold winter night. You can imagine what else happened,' said Lawrence, and everyone laughed again.

'The next day, Louis came through that deep snow on a half-wild cayuse and dug down through the snow to get to the door, a little worried since he hadn't been home in over three weeks. Henry and Etoile didn't hear a thing. They were still sleeping off their night and when Louis pushed in the door he found them in bed, in each other's arms.

'Nobody knows exactly what was said and who said it. But Etoile gathered up her things and got on the half-wild cayuse and rode away and nobody ever saw either her or the horse again. As for the brothers, Louis opened up the first bottle in the case of whisky he'd brought home and they drank that. By the time they reached the bottom of that bottle, Louis was laughing a little. And halfway through the second bottle, he said, 'What the hell!' But by the third both Louis and Henry were in tears and they cried and cried that they'd lost the best girl this side of Williams Lake.

'They slept a couple of days, didn't eat at all. And they began to drink again. Everything outside was as still as death, the storm over, the snow settling heavy in the woods. Something evil crept into that cabin. When Henry passed out, Louis eyed him and fingered his hunting knife and thought about how he'd do it, how he'd pierce that fat flesh and find a vein to open. Then he shook himself and took another drink and when he passed out, Henry woke up and watched his brother and hated every slick thing about him, every curve of his muscles, every long black eyelash, each strong-boned finger. He eyed Louis's rifle and thought about where he'd bury him. That night, blind drunk, hate as thick as greenwood smoke filling up the cabin, the brothers made a pact.'

'Plug your ears, Normie,' said the girl beside him.

'Oh, no!' Normie cried and slapped his hands over his ears.

'They made a suicide pact. Each one would aim their rifle at the other's neck and when they counted to ten, they'd shoot the other dead. They could barely stand up. They stood only about five feet apart, swaying and leaning. They took aim and started to count. At four, Henry said, 'Wait, wait, I got my safety on.' So they started over.

178

'They got to three and Louis said, 'Wait. Are we shooting at ten, or just after?'

''What's the difference?' Henry said.

''Big difference,' said Louis. 'One of us is dead, the other one's still standing there holding his gun like a dick.'

''Okay, we shoot at ten. Right at ten. Say it, then POW.'

''Say it, *then* pow?'

''Yeah, say ten, then shoot.'

''Ten then pow.'

''Ten then pow. Right. Got it?'

'They started counting again. This time there were no mistakes, except at the last second, Louis lost his nerve and knocked the barrel of his brother's gun away. His own went off. He shot Henry dead. Henry's bullet hit Louis in the left shin. Louis passed out. In the morning, he woke up and found his brother still dead. He put him in the bed and covered him up, then he set that cabin on fire, burned it to the ground.'

Everyone in the Beaumont was quiet. 'Holy shit,' I said. 'Is this a true story?'

'Can I unplug my ears?' Normie sang out. The girl took his hands and lifted them away from his head.

'It's true,' said Sharman, and everyone nodded.

'Louis took off deep into the bush and lived as a hermit for a while. Then one winter someone came across a camp he'd made and found him hanging from a tree, frozen solid. But he haunts the bush out here. You can hear moaning and whisky bottles rattling and smell the fire

179

sometimes. And when the northern lights are out, you can hear music, that Spanish angel music that Henry played on his guitar.'

'I know what happened to the girl,' the oldest girl spoke. 'My aunt was married to her cousin. She said Etoile hitchhiked all the way down the coast to Mexico. She ended up in a town as far south as you can go and still be in Mexico. A family of Germans took pity on her and took her in. Their daughter had just died in childbirth and so they gave the baby to Etoile to raise. Eventually, she became just like a mother to that child.'

Twilight had fallen and the air had turned cold. 'I'm hungry,' said Vern.

'Come back later tonight,' said Lawrence. 'We might hear the ghost.'

★　★　★

For supper Jolene had made roast beef and scalloped potatoes and peas. She put the food on the table using dishcloths to keep from burning her hands. I watched her, and when she caught me staring, she smiled at me. Jolene talked, mostly to Uncle Leslie, about people they knew. Then she turned to Vern. 'So how did you two, a boy and a girl, become friends?'

'You really gotta ask?' said Jim, leering. 'I mean I can put two and two together and get four, even if you can't. A teenage boy, a pretty girl . . . '

I flushed red and hated Jim.

'It's not like that,' Vern said sharply. 'We're

friends for the same reasons any two people are friends.'

'Oh, well,' Jim began.

'Leslie says you come from Duchess Creek,' Jolene said to me, before Jim could say more.

I nodded.

'I have friends in Duchess Creek.' Jolene began to tell a story of some people and the dog they had that had to be put down.

'They don't want to hear that,' said Jim.

'Yes we do,' said Vern.

'Can't you shut up?' Jolene said to Jim. 'This is my son and my house. Why don't you go get drunk somewhere else?'

'Oh, so now it's your house.'

'I'm going to have to get going soon,' said Uncle Leslie. 'It's getting dark.'

'You going to turn into a pumpkin?' Jolene went to the kitchen and got a beer out of the fridge, then sat at the table sipping it, her plate of food untouched. While we ate the chocolate cake she'd made for dessert, she opened another beer and smoked two cigarettes, pressing the butts into her cold scalloped potatoes.

After supper we sat outside and more people gathered. Vern and I threw a Frisbee for the dog.

'Where are those kids sleeping tonight?' Uncle Leslie asked Jolene.

'Vern can be a gentleman and give Maggie his room,' Jolene said. 'He can sleep on the couch.'

'No,' Uncle Leslie said, and I could see he was mad. 'He won't get any sleep there and you know it.'

Jolene looked angry, too. 'Well, we can set up

the cot in my room.'

'Put the cot in with Vern,' Uncle Leslie said. 'Is that okay with you, Maggie?'

'Yeah, it's fine,' I said quickly.

'They're fourteen,' Jolene began.

'It's okay,' Vern interrupted. 'We can put the cot in there. It's no big deal.'

'There's a man who knows what he wants,' said Jim.

'Shut the fuck up,' said Uncle Leslie. It was the first time I'd ever heard him swear.

'All right,' Jolene said and she closed her eyes and took a long drink of her beer.

'Hey,' Vern said, taking me by the arm. 'Let's go see the ghost.'

We walked with Sharman and Lawrence and little Normie back to the edge of the bush.

'Jim's a fucking asshole,' Sharman said. 'I wouldn't let anybody treat my mother that way.'

Vern looked at the ground and didn't say anything.

'Don't go any closer,' Lawrence said. 'This is close enough. Now we just have to wait.'

A light breeze was blowing and we watched the trees as the evening turned deeper blue.

'He's a freeloader, too,' Sharman continued. 'Mr. Big White Guy. Smashed up his tow truck on a drunk one night and now he lives off a little Indian woman's welfare cheques in her house on the reserve. If you were bigger I guess you'd paste him, eh?'

'Yeah,' said Vern. Then, 'But she likes him. I don't get why she likes him.'

'Shh. Hear that?' Lawrence cocked his head.

Something was rustling, moving through the trees. Not far away, an owl hooted.

'Means a death is coming soon,' Lawrence whispered.

We stood perfectly still and listened.

'Look!' Lawrence whispered suddenly. Through the trees we could see something white moving.

'Let's go back,' Normie said.

'Shh, you'll scare him off.'

The white disappeared and we sat and waited till the night dew made the ground damp.

When we got back, Uncle Leslie had gone. Vern's mother was sitting on the kitchen counter holding two halves of a broken plate. Her face was loose, her features like a blurred photograph. Jim had been saying something, but stopped when we came in and said instead, 'You can take it or leave it, but I see the big picture.'

'The big picture,' Jolene mocked, then she burst out laughing. 'Come and see your old mother, son!'

'You're not old,' Vern said.

'You're such a good boy. You know just the right things to say.'

I said goodnight and slipped away to Vern's room just as Jolene said, 'You'll always be my son. You know I love you, my son. Leslie thinks he knows better because he's my big brother but you belong with your mother.'

'Boys don't want to hear that,' Jim said.

'It's okay whatever she says,' said Vern.

Jim laughed hard at that. I could still hear him when I closed the door. The room was crowded with boxes of clothes, an ironing board, a drying rack, shelves of fabric and an old sewing machine. The blankets had been turned back on the bed. Moonlight flooded the room and I sat on the bed watching it cast silver light on the homemade quilt. Who made this quilt? Who took the time to cut these floral pieces and set them in this pattern, four narrow strips surrounding a square? The back was soft flannel. I held it to my nose. Some dim memory fought its way to the surface, something from when I was little and my mother gave me her mother's quilt for my bed in Duchess Creek.

I climbed between the sheets with my flannel shirt still on and lay there, listening to the din in the kitchen. A few minutes later, Vern came in.

He undressed and got into the cot in the dark. We could hear the voices rising in the kitchen, then harsh bursts of laughter.

'Do you like my mom?' Vern asked through the darkness.

'She's pretty. And she's nice.'

'I'm going to paste that jerk, Jim. She'd be way nicer if he wasn't around. Uncle Leslie can't stand him.'

We heard a thud in the kitchen and shouts. Outside a band of coyotes took up barking at the moon.

'Do you believe about the ghost?' Vern asked.

'Do you?'

'Maybe. But there's more than just that kind of ghost. Spirits. Good ones. You might not see them, but they're there.'

'Like angels?'

'Same thing,' Vern said. 'We've all got one on each shoulder.'

'Really?'

'Sure. Maybe an animal spirit or maybe an old one who died a long time ago.'

More thudding came from the kitchen and the voices grew louder, shouting. There was no more laughter. My heart was racing.

'Do you hear that?' Vern asked.

'Yeah.'

'No, not the yelling. Listen. Outside. Drums.'

As soon as he said it, I heard the drumming, like a heartbeat carried on the spring night. I shivered. I could feel the beat in my chest slow to match it. From the kitchen came the smashing of glass. Vern put on his pants in the moonlight and went out.

I listened, but the only thing I could follow was the drums. After a few minutes he came back and got into bed.

'She sometimes throws things when she gets mad,' he said. Then he giggled. 'My mom's small but she can throw a scare into that asshole when she gets going.'

★ ★ ★

In the morning there was no broken glass anywhere and Jolene made us bacon and eggs and toast with homemade blackberry jam for breakfast.

185

17

Months passed and still no word came from Mom. I was ashamed of her silence, what it meant. Jenny and I walked down to the lake, and swam with all the other kids and their families. When Lila and Tracy showed up, they all smeared themselves with Hawaiian Tropic coconut oil and smoked menthol cigarettes, practising their elegant exhales. I munched Freezies. We said nothing about her.

The stampede came to town. Teepees and tents and trailers moved in and all day dust billowed, bands played, and the announcers voice drummed up the crowd, rising and falling over the loudspeakers. I could smell the pungent odour of horses and cattle manure coming in the bedroom window. At night music and shouts sailed out over the town from Squaw Hall, the open-air dance hall on the stampede grounds. At the end of the street where the Edwards' house was, I sat in the grass and looked down at the lights strung above the hall and heard the crash of beer bottles being thrown over the walls. One night when a band called the Saddle-ites was playing, Jenny and her friends decided to go dancing. They were all underage but no one asked questions.

Later, they snuck back in the house shaken but giddy.

'I can't believe that guy grabbed my ass,' Tracy

186

kept saying. 'Next time I'm gonna get juiced before we go in there.'

'No way José,' said Lila. 'You won't catch me going back there. Sickos grabbing your tits. I was ready to paste somebody.'

'It was mental, Mag,' Jenny said. 'People fighting and throwing beer bottles, broken glass and beer all over the dance floor. And the band just kept playing.'

* * *

I hiked the river valley with Vern, past the hoodoos and cliffs, then Vern went west to Nistsun for a while and I stayed, pumping gas for tourists on the highway. I went to rummage sales on the weekend and bought an old canvas tent that I set up in the backyard. Jenny and her friends hot-knifed hash in Beatrice's kitchen late at night with the windows open, crickets chirping and the summer breeze carrying away the smell. They giggled and made elaborate, salty snacks, BLTs and tuna melts, and I came into the kitchen at one in the morning, drawn by the aroma while Bea slept.

How could Mom not come? How could she not send word? I sometimes thought of Vern's mother and her sewing room. Once, Jolene was that mother who dreamed up patterns out of colourful bits of cloth and bent over her sewing machine to make quilts for the people she loved. Who was she now? Girlfriend to an asshole whom she almost seemed to hate. Maybe our mother had become someone known only as

Irene, a pretty redhead with muscled thighs and work-strong hands.

Beatrice was worse than useless. She no longer threw her glasses across the room in frustration; Ted's death had freed her and she seemed almost happy. But she continued to fry sausages and boil potatoes, check the mailbox, refrain from comment — loudly. Comment was called for now, but now she failed to make it. I blamed her for not doing something to find our mother. I hated her for her silence. I could see she was embarrassed for us. I hated her for that. All around us piled up this impenetrable silence about the thing most important of all.

Sometimes I wanted to accost some stranger and demand, 'Where is my mother?' Or a teacher or a policeman. 'Do you know where my mother is? Can you help me find her?' Why did I stay silent?

* * *

When Vern came back, I told him I had a plan to find my mother. I made him swear not to tell anyone, not even Uncle Leslie.

We were on our backs in the tree fort, watching the aspen leaves flapping back to front like hands waving against the turquoise of the sky.

'When will you leave?' he asked.

'I have to convince Jenny first.'

I was waiting for the right moment to tell her. I found it a week later when she finally broke up with Brian. I don't know why it took her so long — the guy was dumber than a bag of hammers. But Jenny had a soft spot for sad sacks and Brian was that in spades. Nothing he did turned out right: he drank too much, his father was mean, he smashed up his car, he lost his job (several times), there was talk that he had even fathered a child by a girl down near Lillooet and she was demanding money from him. Jenny rose to that kind of tragic story; she wanted to be his saviour. He did thoughtless things. He left her stranded at parties while he took off drunk in somebody else's car. He flirted with other girls. Still, Jenny had some notion of loyalty that couldn't be fazed by such minor transgressions.

But one cooking-hot Saturday night I was sitting outside on the front step when Jenny came marching up the sidewalk, strands of sweaty hair plastered to her face and neck, the bottoms of her white jeans and her runners coated in dust, and her face flushed bright red.

'What's up?' I said.

She looked at me. I knew this look. Her eyes were on fire. I could see the anger sparking off her.

'I can't speak right now,' she said, and she went inside. Sometime later I found her on her bed, a pillow held tight in her arms as she stared up at the ceiling. She was listening to Supertramp on her record player. *Crime of the Century* was Jenny's favourite album. Usually she listened repeatedly to 'Dreamer,' but tonight it was 'Bloody Well Right.'

When the song finished, she put it on again. I

stretched out on my own bed and listened with her.

After a while she spoke. 'You know, when people are drunk they do stupid things. I don't like it, but I can understand it. Brian's done a lot of stupid things. But he crossed the evil line tonight.'

I waited a bit. 'What did he do?'

'Oh, Maggie, you don't even want to know. It'll bother you even more than it does me, knowing how you feel about cats.'

'Cats?'

'I know. I don't even like cats all that much, but there's no excuse for what he did. Just being cruel for no reason.'

'Don't tell me,' I said.

'I won't. But I begged him not to do it, all of them, but him especially, I begged him. And right then I realized that he doesn't care what I think. He really doesn't. He's just a selfish, stupid, conceited idiot. A great big evil asshole.'

I had to let her think she was the first to notice his true nature, so I bit my tongue. But I saw my opening.

'We should leave here. We need to look for Mom,' I said.

'She's the mother. That's what you said. She should look for us.'

'I know I said that, but maybe I was wrong. We can't just stay here and wait forever. I have a plan.'

'You have a plan?' Jenny said. 'And in this plan, what do I have to do?'

'You drive,' I said.

190

'One slight problem. You know I don't have my driver's licence, right?'

'You can get your beginner's now. By your next birthday, we'll be legal.'

'There's the small matter of a car.'

'I'll get the car. That'll be my job. I've already got most of the camping equipment we'll need.'

'Hell of a plan.'

'Shut up. I don't see you coming up with anything better.'

Jenny's face clouded and her lip began to quiver. I felt bad so I said, 'How about we go on a test run? Next weekend.'

'With whose car?'

'Not with a car. We'll hitch. We'll just head out. Like Chiwid. Hit the Freedom Road.'

Jenny smiled. 'Sometimes I like you.'

*　　*　　*

We left after work late one afternoon. I met Jenny at Frank's Chicken and Pizza. She was dressed in her wide-legged white Wranglers and a peach top that laced at the front.

'For Christ's sake, Jenny. Nobody hitchhikes looking like that.'

'I wanted to look presentable,' she said.

'Take this,' I said, and helped her heft her pack onto her back.

'Are you kidding, Maggie? This thing weighs a ton.'

We got our first ride quickly, from Jenny's friend, Ron.

'I'm not really going anywhere,' he said. 'But

191

I'll take you out of town.' When his Ted Nugent 8-track looped around to start over again, he said, 'How about here?'

We walked as the sun went down. Cars swerved carefully around us when they saw our outstretched arms, and kept on going. The evening was mild, good for walking, but our gear was heavy.

'I've got to rest,' Jenny said, and she dropped her pack and sleeping bag to the ground. She sat down on top of it. I put my pack down beside her and sat, too. We leaned back-to-back against each other and listened to insects trill from the roadsides.

Each time we saw a car approaching, Jenny jumped up and stood with her thumb out.

The car that finally slowed was a newer white Pinto. A middle-aged, ordinary-looking man with short hair and a sea-green leisure suit was driving. He smiled and said we were in luck — he could take us as far as we wanted; he was going all the way to Vancouver. It looked like a good ride to me. We threw our gear in the back and Jenny scurried in beside it.

That meant I had the front. But when I went to get in, the man's hand was there, palm up, where I was supposed to sit. My left foot was already in the car. For a moment I was confused, but only for a moment, because when our eyes met, I saw the grin, the steady stare, and I knew.

'Jenny,' I said evenly. 'Get out of the car.'

'What?' she began, but I had already reached over her and yanked my pack out onto the gravel. She tumbled out after it, dragging her backpack. I slammed the door so hard the little Pinto shook before it buzzed off down the highway.

'You fucking scumbag!' I screamed after him as he pulled away.

'Maggie!' Jenny stared at me like I'd lost my mind.

My legs gave way and I sat down on my pack again. My hands were shaking, so I squeezed them between my knees.

Jenny just stared at me, opening her mouth to speak, then stopping, till she finally said, 'Why did you do that?'

The look on her face was so ridiculous that I started to laugh. 'I'll tell you why I did that!' I said. 'I didn't like his stinking looks!'

After I'd told her what had happened, she said, 'Oh Maggie. This was a bad idea. We're girls. Hitchhiking is dangerous for girls. I mean, I know you act like a boy, but — newsflash — you're a girl. Sorry. You did get your period, remember?' She put her arm around my shoulders and pulled me to her. 'Maggie-girl, let's just sleep here somewhere.' And for once I was happy to let her act like my big sister.

Down a little grass track below the highway we found a trail that in our pale flashlight beam seemed to head into a field and peter off to nowhere. We spread out our tent in the long dry grass beside it, laid our sleeping bags on top and pulled the corners of the tent up so they covered our feet.

Across the meadow, we could see the orange-lit windows of a cabin. Once in a while we heard traffic slide past on the highway above us. We'd positioned our heads beside a mound of earth for a little wind protection and put the packs on either side of us.

'Remember Mom used to say you should never sleep on a path because ghosts will walk over you and keep you awake all night?' Jenny said.

'We aren't on a path.'

'Well, we're very close to one. What if there were three ghosts walking side by side? Or what if a phantom wagon came through here?'

I closed my eyes on the stars and settled deeper into the sleeping bag on the hard ground. A truck geared down on the road. I thought about Chiwid, digging a bed in the earth, settling in, letting the snow drift over her so that she seemed part of the land. I was so tired, but every time I started to slip into sleep, I felt the pressure of feet trying to get by — soft moccasins, the bony hooves of deer, stiff leather boots and paws.

I woke to find it had turned cold and that a heavy dew had settled over everything, including our sleeping bags. I tried to pull the tent further over us, but it was wet, too. My feet were cold and my nose was like ice. I drifted back into sleep, woke to check the sky for signs of morning. When dark finally began to turn milky silver I saw a grey mist hanging over the field. I closed my eyes and when I opened them next, a ragged coyote stepped calmly out of the mist. He sat on the path and watched me. Then he ambled off, disappearing into grey.

As soon as the sun burned through the fog, it

194

was too hot to sleep. I kicked off my sleeping bag, covered my face with my hands to keep the sun off and tried to fall asleep again. But I could hear ranchers out starting engines and rattling around. I sat up. My eyelids felt like sandpaper. Below us, a truck slowly wound its way through the pasture. It might be coming this way. I shook Jenny's shoulder and she yawned and stretched.

'I had such nice dreams,' she said.

Breakfast was bread, cheese sliced thin with my jackknife and an apple each, washed down with swigs of already-stale water from a plastic canteen.

Jenny balanced her diary on one knee and scribbled in it as she ate. 'Want to hear my poem?' she asked as I was rewrapping the cheese.

'All right.'

She cleared her throat. 'Here we are on the freedom road, and there's not a cloud in the sky. We're carrying a heavy load, but we're going to fly.'

'Huh. Not bad. It even kind of rhymes.'

'Kind of? It does rhyme. That's why I changed 'road to freedom' to 'freedom road.' I couldn't think of a word to rhyme with freedom.'

Jenny closed her diary and tucked it back into her pack.

'Not the greatest camping spot,' she said.

'This was just a practice run. Next time we'll find something better.'

'Like a campground?' she said. 'I'd at least like to swim.'

A cowboy from Quesnel gave us a ride back to

Williams Lake, the sun burning in through the windshield. Nestled in the hills, I saw a deserted log cabin chinked with white plaster between the squared, weathered grey logs. There were deserted cabins like that all over the Chilcotin. They were solid, cured by the sun and wind. I didn't see why we couldn't move into one, fix up the roof, put glass in the windows and live off the land, me, Jenny, Mom and Cinnamon.

18

'I wonder if I could live like Chiwid does.'

Vern didn't say anything.

'You know Chiwid, right?' I asked.

'Yeah, I do.' I could tell he was thinking. 'You couldn't do it,' he said. 'I just mean, I couldn't do it either. People say she's left her body. She's a spirit now. What happened to her, it was too much. She survived but she's free of her body. Do you get it?'

'I think so.'

'She's a spirit walking around in a human body. But she doesn't really need the body. That's how she survives. Out in the winter, twenty below, and no fire. Some people say she's an animal spirit. My aunty heard this screaming one night. They were camped near Eagle Lake and they heard this crazy howling in the hills above camp, kind of like a cougar, but scarier. They all got their guns ready. Aunty said the next day they went up there and they found Chiwid and her little camp. Chiwid was smiling. She's always like that.'

We stretched out on the sun-warm boards. Aspen leaves like plump green hearts shivered in the summer breeze. I closed my eyes and could still see the dappled pattern of sun and leaf and blood against my eyelids. Beside me, Vern's skin had a familiar, clean smell — soap and sun. I breathed it in. I opened my eyes. He'd crossed his warm brown arms over his white T-shirt. A small indentation at the top of his ribs dipped and rose with his breathing.

'So you're going to leave,' he said.

'That's the plan.'

He took my hand and held it to his chest and his heart padded against my palm as if I could catch his heartbeat.

'Mom was good at finding lost things,' I said. 'Funny, eh? Jenny lost her Barbie doll once when we were out camping. She was only wearing her bathing suit.'

'Jenny?'

'No, Barbie.'

'So she was worried she might catch her death?'

'She really was. She was just young. I don't remember how old, maybe eight or nine. Mom said, 'Start at the beginning. Retrace your steps. Tell me everything you did with her.' And while Mom closed her eyes and listened, Jenny went through it step by step. 'I got her out of the tent after breakfast. She climbed a mountain and rescued Stick Man, who broke his leg because his horse got spooked by a bear and bucked him off. Then we had lunch. Then she married Stick Man. She went swimming in the creek, then she was sunbathing.''

'Barbie?' Vern said.

'Yeah. And Mom said, 'That's where you'll find her' and sure enough, there she was, sunbathing in the mud by the creek. Under the stars.'

'So you're going to retrace your steps,' said Vern.

'That's the plan.'

* * *

It didn't take long for Jenny to meet another boy. His name was John. This one was different from the others. I liked him, and that made me nervous. He played three instruments, drums, piano and saxophone, not only in the school band, but also in the country and cover bands that played at weddings and community dances. Jenny said he stayed up all night composing his own songs. He had unsettling blue eyes and a gaze like an X-ray. When he looked at me, I squirmed.

Also, Jenny had started to worry about what would happen to Bea without us. I sensed my plan unravelling. As she was getting ready to go out with John one evening, Jenny said, 'You should get out yourself more, Bea. Why don't you ever go to the Elks Hall?' She blew delicately on her freshly painted nails.

'What would I go to the Elks Hall for?' Bea said.

'I don't know. Dancing? Maybe for fun? Do you even know that word, Bea? Fun is not washing dishes, not doing laundry, not even watching TV — well, except for *Get Smart*.'

Bea laughed and waved Jenny away with one hand and wiped her weepy eye with the other. 'I don't like drinking and those smoky places bother my eyes. And dancing with some smelly drunk is not fun to me.'

Jenny smiled, her nail polish wand poised for the second coat. 'Okay. I can see that. But what is fun to you? You're not so old. You've still got lots of time. Who wants to waste away in this little house in Nowheres-ville, B.C.?'

'Shh, Jenny!' Bea said, as if her boring life was a well-kept secret and someone listening might be offended.

'So what is your idea of fun?'

'Oh, I don't know.'

'See, it's been so long since you've had any, you forget what it is.'

'Well,' she said hesitantly, 'I do like to bowl.'

Jenny threw her hands up dramatically. 'You like to bowl? You like to bowl?' Jenny looked at me, where I sat silently, impatiently, leafing through a *National Geographic*. 'Bea likes to bowl. For heaven's sakes, Bea — that's so simple. You can bowl right here in Williams Lake. I thought you were going to say you liked going to art galleries or something and we'd have to ship you off to Paris or New York.'

Bea took off her glasses and rubbed her eye harder, laughing.

'What else is fun to you?'

'Oh, I don't know. I thought once I'd like to go on a cruise.'

'That can be done,' Jenny said. 'Do you have any money?'

'That's not a polite question. But since you ask, I have enough to get by. But who would I go with?'

'You don't need to go with anybody. That's

why you go on a cruise — to meet eligible men.'

'It's no fun going alone,' Bea said.

'You live alone. I'd say going on a cruise alone is a heck of a lot more fun than being here alone.'

'I don't live alone.' Bea looked at Jenny strangely.

I shot Jenny a murderous stare, silently pleading, shut-up, shut-up, shut-up.

Jenny looked at me with stupid alarmed bird eyes, her mouth clamped shut, 'I meant, you're alone, like not with a husband or anything.'

Bea nodded at that and it was okay again. 'I would like to swim in the Caribbean Sea. I've seen photographs of that white sand and turquoise water. They say it's like bath water. I read about that in the *National Geographic*. Have you seen that, Margaret?'

I looked up, startled, because she never included me in their conversations.

'Yeah. I think so.'

'That would be something. You can put on those scuba diving outfits and get right down under the water.'

It was more enthusiasm than she'd shown for anything, ever, around us.

'They've got fish, all kinds of colours, really different from what's around here.' Bea waved her arm in the general direction of the kitchen.

★ ★ ★

Through the heat of August, Jenny and John went for long walks down to Scout Island and around the lake. He wore no shirt. His jeans hung loosely around his hip bones and his chest was lean and tanned. When it cooled off in the evening, he put on his flannel shirt with the sleeves rolled up and the buttons undone. I suppose I had a crush on him. One night he sat on the front step with me while Jenny was inside getting dressed.

'Hear those crickets?' he asked. 'When I'm old, I'll dream about that sound every winter. I'll want just one more summer, so I can hear them again. Winter makes you old. I want to live in a place where I can walk around all year with no shirt on, feeling the wind on my skin.'

Talk of wind on his skin made me shiver. He was sitting so close, I could feel the heat from his body.

'Would you like that?'

'Pardon?'

'Where would you live where you could be what you really are?'

'I don't know.'

'I mean, there must be a place where Maggie Dillon would be so comfortable in her skin she wouldn't care what anybody else said or what clothes she wore.'

'There would be crickets,' I blurted.

He laughed. 'I like that. I want crickets, too. I wonder if there are crickets in Mexico.'

Jenny came out. When she looked at John her face softened. He smiled. There was something between them that made me jealous. It made me think that as long as John was in Williams Lake, I would not get Jenny to leave.

WATER

19

By September, John was gone. He'd taken his saxophone and the clothes on his back. That was the story around town. I heard it from Bob in the gas station when John's parents had pulled away after stopping to fill their tank. People said it with a touch of wonder and admiration.

He didn't tell Jenny he was leaving, but he mailed her a thick letter. I wanted so badly to read it, but after she'd read it through, she took it out to the backyard and set it on fire. I watched her.

'He asked me to burn it,' she told me. She didn't cry and at first she seemed proud that she'd been the one he singled out. He entrusted her with the secret of where he'd gone and why. School had started again and she rose to the sacrifice her loyalty required. But after school, she started closing herself in the bedroom with the window open, smoking cigarette after cigarette.

Bea could smell the smoke, of course, but she didn't say anything. She wouldn't risk upsetting Jenny, who could do nothing wrong in her eyes, or so I thought.

Some days, Jenny asked me to phone Frank's Chicken and Pizza to tell them she wouldn't be able to come to work. They were tolerant with her — everybody liked Jenny — but I worried she would lose her job.

One night, I heard Bea call, 'Who used all the hot water?' I had my homework spread out on the dining-room table, and she came to the doorway of the kitchen and glowered at me.

'It wasn't me,' I said.

Half an hour later, Jenny emerged from the bathroom, steaming and red like a boiled tomato. She slammed the bedroom door behind her. She was in a mood. These moods had become frequent.

I heard a strange thumping sound. I put down my pen and went to the door to listen. What was she doing in there? I opened the door a crack. Jenny was in a T-shirt and underwear, doing jumping jacks. Her breasts bounced with each jump.

'Close the door,' she said.

I did. The sound continued.

I went back to my homework. I pictured John stripping off her T-shirt. I pictured him pulling her against his bare chest. He said, 'Maggie Dillon, where would you live where you could walk around all year with no shirt on?'

I couldn't concentrate on my homework. The jumping had stopped.

'Jenny?' I said, opening the door carefully.

She was on the bed with a black look on her face, holding a bottle of cod liver oil. 'Have you ever tasted this stuff?'

'Why are you drinking cod liver oil?'

'You don't drink it. You are so dense sometimes, Maggie. Other times, you're quite bright. But I can't believe you haven't figured it out yet. We do share a room.'

'It's about John, isn't it?' Suddenly I knew. 'You're going to run away to be with him, aren't you?'

'Have you been watching soap operas with Bea? I'm not 'running away' with John, as you put it. Or any other way you want to say it. Don't worry, I'm stuck here. Really stuck. Fuck it,' she said to the cod liver oil, and she reached for her smokes and lit one up.

'Don't you care if Bea finds out?'

'Finds out what? That I'm pregnant?'

'What? Jenny, what? Jenny, no.'

She laughed. She laughed until she cried. Then she threw up in our little tin garbage pail.

20

'Are you going to tell him?'

'Who?'

'John.'

'No.'

'I think he'd want to know.'

'What would you know about it, Maggie? You are so naive, you don't even know how naive you are. Anyway, what would I do, write to him at P.O. Box Wherever the Hell You Are?'

Jenny didn't intend to tell Bea, either. I don't know what her plan was, but it didn't include throwing herself on Bea's mercy. That was my idea.

I was convinced Bea would do anything for Jenny. I told Jenny how it would go.

'She'll need to sit down. She'll collapse on the couch. She'll be kind of shocked at first. Her mouth might hang open and she'll stare at you like a raccoon in a flashlight beam. She'll take off her glasses and rub her weepy eye. She might even start to cry and say how disappointed she is in you. Like, oh, Jenny how could you let this happen? And what about your future and how will you finish school. But then she'll pull herself together. She'll say something like, 'What's done is done. There's no use crying over spilt milk. The cat's out of the bag. The roosters have come home to roost. The ship has sailed.''

By this time Jenny was laughing. I think I had

already persuaded her.

'Bea's lonely, Jenny. Who has she got but us? This'll give her something to do.'

She was about two and a half months along when she told Bea. It was a rainy night in October. Jenny had come home from work, had a hot bath and put on her pyjamas. Bea had made hot chocolate, so it seemed like she was open to mercy.

Jenny came into the bedroom. 'Will you tell her with me?'

'Me? Why do you want me there?'

'You're my sister. You're all I have.' She teared up so I couldn't say no, even though I thought it was a bad idea.

Bea had a look of fear in her face when Jenny and I both sat down on the couch. It was rare for me to sit in the living room. Jenny said, 'Could we turn the TV off? I have something I need to tell you.'

Bea's face went pale right away. I don't know what she was expecting. 'All right,' she said, and got up and did it.

Jenny had rehearsed a little speech. She had tried it out on me and I thought it was pretty good. She started, 'You've been really good to us, Maggie and me. And I hope, well, I hope . . .'

She was floundering. Bea just gaped at her, a frown creasing her forehead.

Jenny was supposed to say something about hoping we hadn't been too much trouble and that she'd made a bad mistake and then ask for forgiveness. But it came out differently. 'You're going to be surprised,' she said. 'It looks like I'm pregnant.' Her tone seemed almost gleeful.

Bea did look shocked. Her mouth did kind of fall open. 'It looks like?' she said. 'Are you or not?'

'I am,' said Jenny. She started to cry.

'Oh don't turn on the water works with me,' Bea said, deadly calm. 'If you think that's going to work with me you've got another think coming. Who is it? Is it that John? I knew there was something fishy with him. I had a bad feeling when he took off like that.'

'He doesn't know anything about it,' Jenny said.

'I will not have this house turned into the talk of the town. Everybody thinking we're just running wild over here, that I'm keeping a pair of sluts, no men to look after them. I want you out of my house.'

It was my turn for my mouth to fall open. She ran on. 'I've lived in this town for sixteen years. We're respectable people. Poor Ted will be turning over in his grave.'

'Shut up!' I shouted. I stood up. I wanted to slap her.

'No, you shut up. This is my house and you'll do what I say. I can see I've been far too lax. I felt sorry for you. And all the while *this* has been going on behind my back. I must be the laughingstock. I want her out of my house.'

Poor Jenny started to sob and ran to her room.

I shouted, 'This is 1974, you cow!'

'Don't say another word,' Bea said, calm again. 'Don't say another word to me. You go to your room, I don't want to see either of your faces. Go!' She screamed the last word so hard the house shook.

Except for Jenny's heartbroken sobs, the house fell quiet. My mouth had gone dry, but I wouldn't leave our room to get water. I wasn't scared so much as shaken. I couldn't believe my instincts had been so wrong.

After a while, I heard Bea on the phone. She would be calling her sister.

I could not think of a single thing to say. Jenny got up, went to her dresser drawer and took out the letters from Mom. As she read through each one, she sobbed even harder.

'I shouldn't have called her a cow,' I finally said.

'What?'

'I called Bea a cow. I shouldn't have done that.'

Bea swung the door wide.

'I found a place she can go,' she said to me, as if Jenny wasn't there. 'She can stay there until she has the baby. They'll arrange the adoption.'

Jenny kept her head down and said nothing.

'Where is it?' I asked.

'It's in Vancouver. It's a home for unwed mothers. Run by the nuns. Maybe they'll knock some sense into her head.'

'What about school?' I said.

'What about it? She should have thought about that before she went running around. Now she's made her bed.'

'Do I have any choice?' Jenny finally said.

'No,' said Bea and left the room.

Jenny and I stayed awake most of the night. I couldn't stand to see her so broken, but we had little to say to each other. Outside, the rain fell steadily. Winter coming on. We couldn't escape to the woods or the tree fort. There was nowhere to go. My mind kept going to Chiwid. She was out there dug in under a tree, trying to stay dry.

Bea bought a ticket for Jenny the next day. The day after that, she would get on the bus to Vancouver. I went to Stedman's and bought her a travel toothbrush and soap holder and a box of stationery, printed in pink gingham and scented like strawberries.

'I'll write to you every day,' Jenny said, as she climbed on the bus. I watched her go. I had managed to keep myself from asking her the question that had been hounding me for three days: what's going to happen to me?

21

Dear Maggie,

Here I am in Our Lady of Perpetual Help Home. Lots of pregnant girls here (obviously). I'm the only one who isn't showing, which makes me wonder what I'm doing here. All they talk about is 'relinquishing' or 'keeping' and their due dates, and if they're carrying high or low, whatever the hell that means, but it's supposed to tell you if you have a boy or girl, but who fricking cares since almost everyone is 'relinquishing' anyway, which means putting it up for adoption, though some are still 'undecided.' Kind of like the dating game, bachelor number one, bachelor number two or bachelor number three. Except sadder.

If you ask me they're pretty obsessed about the whole thing. Some girls are even knitting stuff, like little hats and blankets. Remember when we used to play house with our Barbies? It's kind of like that, except no Barbies. I just want to get it over with.

But in case you're worried about me, there are no bars on the windows or anything and the food is pretty good. I have a nice room, too, all to myself. There's a bed (obviously), a dresser, a bedside table with a ceramic ballerina lamp on it, and a desk in front of the window that looks out onto the back lawn and gardens. It's pretty decent, even in the rain. It hasn't stopped raining since I got here, which was exactly twenty-five and a half hours ago. I know that because I didn't really sleep last night and I could hear the rain all night long, that and a sound like wind, which I figured out today is actually traffic. This house is in a nice neighbourhood, though. I was surprised when the nun who picked me up at the bus depot drove up to this big old house surrounded by trees. It's like a mansion, actually. You might like it. But don't go getting any ideas. If I have to get a freaky, disgusting stomach like these other girls, that's my punishment.

Oh yeah, you might ask yourself why I have a desk in my room. Homework. Yes, they have classes here. The nuns teach them. I met the English teacher today. She's a nun, but really young and she doesn't wear a habit. She's a writer. Her name is Sister Anne. She said we'll be doing lots of creative writing in class. So I plan to work on my poems.

Also, I guess the idea of Our Lady of Perpetual Help is that you've made this mistake but you're supposed to learn from it and learn to make better decisions and improve yourself. Which is where typing comes in. Maggie, if you want to learn a skill, which you do if you don't want to be a DRAIN ON THE SYSTEM, you can't go wrong with typing. Apparently, if you can type, you'll always have a MARKETABLE SKILL. Do you think Mom could type? I don't think so, but I doubt there's a big demand for it around Williams Lake anyway. I could be wrong, though, since I am only an unfortunate girl who made a BAD DECISION.

Try not to worry, Maggie. I don't know what the point is of telling you that, but actually I'm okay here and it's better than staying with the double-crossing Beatrice Edwards. Actually, it's probably worse for you right now. Did you apologize for calling her a cow yet? Tell her, 'I'm sorry that you're a cow.' Please don't run away or anything stupid like that. I need to know you're in the same place I left you.

Love XXOO Jenny

P.S. We are allowed to make phone calls out, but only collect calls.

Bea didn't speak to me for several days, and I kept away from her. I went to school, went to work and wore a path from my bedroom to the bathroom and back. I kept my door closed and Bea kept the TV up loud, as if I wasn't there.

The snow had started. I tried to think of where else I could go. There were people Mom and Dad used to know who lived in tents all winter long, usually while they were building their cabins. They had special stoves and fitted the stovepipe through a canvas opening in the tent. They kept a hole open in the ice to get water. But if you couldn't keep in a wood supply, you'd freeze. I remember spending a few days in the fall with one family so Mom and Dad could help them with the wood. The two kids ran around wearing only shirts, no jackets. Mom said they were used to it and they weren't cold.

At the gas station, Bob was more cheerful than usual. When Vern came in, Bob said, 'Hey Chief! How's it hanging?' which bugged me. 'Chief' was the same thing he called the man who came in selling salmon and smelling of alcohol. Outside, I asked Vern if it bothered him. He said, 'Maggie, if I got my shorts in a knot every time some dickhead called me Chief or Tonto, I'd have really knotty shorts.'

When Vern had gone, Bob looked up and said, 'How's life treating you, Maggie?'

'Fine,' I said.

One day he asked, 'How's that sister of yours? I haven't seen her around lately. I hear she's not at Frank's anymore. Frank said that's a big loss. The customers really liked her.'

I thought about making some excuse. Bob was a gossip. In fact I think some of the customers preferred that I pump their gas because if Bob got going, they could be there half an hour. But something made me not give a shit. I was tired, and besides that, I just wanted to tell somebody.

'Jenny's in Vancouver,' I said.

He gave an exaggerated recoil and so I knew that he already knew. News got around that town. I had only told Vern, but of course she'd

216

taken the bus, people had seen her, and they could put two and two together.

But Bob wanted me to tell it. 'What's she doing there?'

'She's in a home for unwed mothers. Beatrice sent her there.'

Bob shook his head, looking at the floor. I suppose he hadn't expected me to tell him the truth.

'I'll tell you what I think. Can I tell you what I think, Maggie? I mean, I know it's none of my business, but if you want the opinion of someone who's been around the block a few times, I'll give it to you.'

I smiled.

'You want it?'

'Yes,' I said. He was my boss. What else could I say?

'My thinking is, where the hell is that woman's head at? Beatrice Edwards, I mean. This is 1974.'

'That's exactly what I said.'

'This isn't the dark ages we're living in. We're not some backwater town here. Where does she get off sending that poor girl to Vancouver? Her friends are here. And just so you know, Frank feels the same way.'

I smiled at him.

'Ah, shit. You can't keep a secret in this town,' he said.

Dear Maggie,
   Today I made an ashtray. We do crafts here. I'll keep it so when we get our own

house, we'll at least have an ashtray. Most of the girls smoke. They're allowed, which is weird, don't you think, considering all the other things we're not allowed to do, including 'loitering' in the front yard. We are allowed to sit out in the backyard if it's nice, which as far as I can tell is never.

I have a social worker. She asked me all kinds of questions about our family and wrote the answers on a clipboard and wouldn't look at me for some reason, and seemed pretty bored. (She looked at her watch twice.) But then she suddenly put the clip board aside and gave me this 'poor you' kind of look which really bugged me — she has these glasses with big thick frames and she's got a huge, wide mouth, she looks like some kind of bug — and then she said, 'Well, in some ways it's easier for you. Your choice is clear. You don't need to spend a lot of time worrying about your options because clearly you have no support and no means of keeping a child.'

Which may be true, but still.

'You don't seem too upset,' she said and sat there looking at me with her stupid bug eyes. I shrugged, which I assume was the wrong thing to do. I think she wanted me to cry. She had a box of Kleenex sitting in the middle of the table. Which also seemed wrong. Sort of like 'Everyone cries, you're not so special, so get it over with.' I think they could at least have the courtesy to put the Kleenex away and then take it out if you do cry, because you feel like some kind of cold fish if you don't cry. I have too much time to think, don't you think? Though they do try to fill up our idle hands with 'activities.' Typing, for example. One girl here can type 80 words per minute, that's 80 wpm, like a speed limit. She'll be able to go anywhere, apparently. She wants to be a legal secretary. Who wants to be a legal secretary? Well, this girl does and she'll win some award for Most Improved Typist, aka MIT. Which I, too, could aspire to! Sister Anne says in this very dry voice that typing is useful for writing papers in university, too. She says I should try to learn it, since I want to be a writer. I might type you a letter, except it probably won't be done until I'm ready to pop.

Miss Bug Eyes wants to know who the father is. I said I didn't know. Her pen stopped in mid-air. She was waiting to write something down. I figure there must be an 'unknown' box to check off. She did not like my answer. I said I had a couple of different boyfriends and I didn't know their last names. She knew I was lying.

She said, 'The father's family is your only chance.'

'Chance of what?' I said.

'Of keeping the baby.'

'I'm relinquishing,' I said. She kept her big lips pursed tight and wrote it down on her clipboard.

I don't want them to go looking for him. If

anyone comes around, promise me you won't say anything. I have a good reason, but it's nobody's business.

Hi again,

It's Wednesday. Last night I talked to a girl who I'll call Ginger, because that's her name, ha ha. She's called Ginger because she has red hair. So she said she'd call me Ginger #2. I told her I didn't like the bodily function sound of it, so she came up with Ginger-B, which I like. She has a bit of an English accent. She lived in England until she was ten, then her parents divorced and she came here with her mom. They were living with her aunt and uncle. The uncle was a real creepo and was always giving her the hairy eyeball. Her mom knew it, but never did anything, because she didn't want to upset her sister. Creeps come in many different types, right? But he was a special type of creep.

They had these parties all the time, even on school nights. The music was so loud the floorboards under her bed vibrated. The uncle had some fabulous stereo system he was awfully proud of. That's how she put it. Awfully proud. I love the way she talks. She says trousers instead of pants. Funny eh?

Sometimes a record would skip for an hour. She says you haven't lived till you've heard 'Break on Through to the Other Side' skipping for a whole hour. 'You ever listen to people getting drunk?' she asked me 'It

220

could be quite interesting if it wasn't so goddamn pathetic. First they're all jolly and oh, the larks and the raucous laughter over who the hell knows what, but everything, apparently, is very, very funny when you drink, until it isn't. Then comes the snarking and the shouting and the personal attacks. Then things start to crash around. There are eerie moments of silence. You wonder if someone has cut someone else's throat and is suddenly aghast and sober. Once, my uncle took after his best mate with a hatchet. I saw it with my own eyes; the sound of splintering wood got me out of bed finally. Sometimes I put tissue in my ears, but that's almost worse, not knowing what's coming.' She said her house in England was in a quiet village and the only thing that ever disturbed her sleep was the peacocks shrieking. Her dad was nice too, and she missed him. Makes you wonder what happened.

Anyhow, one night Ginger snuck out of the uncle's house and broke into a shed on the school grounds. She brought a blanket and slept in there for a week, until one morning the janitor found her. The principal called the uncle's house and she got in a shitload of trouble. The uncle said, 'If you're so high and mighty that you can't sleep in my house, then you can bloody well find somewhere else to live.' Her mom told the principal that Ginger had been acting up since the divorce and it was nothing serious. Then she actually put her hands together like she was begging her and said, Please dear, don't rock the boat.

About a week later there was another party. Do you know the Cream song, 'White Room'? She said she can't hear it now without being sick. I mean really vomiting. It was playing when her uncle pushed her door open. He had to push hard enough to break the lock. He grabbed her by the throat, lifted her out of bed and threw her across the room. Ginger said she can't figure out how no one heard. He picked her up and threw her again and again. She hit the dresser and the window and door. She remembers slamming into the wall between songs. She said someone had to have heard it, but no one came.

Another song started. 'The album was *Wheels of Fire*, if you're interested,' she said. 'Kind of a bluesy feel to it. Before I left his house, I took a candle and melted patches in the vinyl. Then I put it back in the sleeve. Should give him a nice surprise next time he listens to it.' He raped her for the length of time it took to play the whole album. 'Slapping and punching, that's what gets him off. You don't even want to know the details.' I think I really don't. She said nothing was so disgusting as the smell of him. 'I've tried to name it, I don't know why,' she said. 'Beer breath and fish that's gone off. But then there's something that's only itself, as rank and rotten as he is.'

I didn't want to believe her, but I could tell she wasn't lying. Some girls here do lie, which you can also tell, but I don't blame them. Everybody has their reasons. I think maybe if I was Ginger, I would lie. She says everybody's afraid of her uncle, but she's not anymore. He's a pathetic lowlife pig, she said, and then we chanted it, pathetic lowlife pig, pathetic lowlife pig.

She doesn't know where her mom is right now, if she's still living there or if she's found another place. And she doesn't know where her mom was the whole time that night, which obviously really bothers her.

But here's the weirdo part. She wants to keep the baby. She said she once had a kitten and her mom wouldn't let her keep it in the house because it scratched the furniture, and she had to put the kitten outside and it got sick and died. I don't know what that has to do with anything, but she says no one is going to take the baby away from her. She's not a stupid girl at all — she's really intelligent — but I don't see how she plans to take care of it.

Also, she hasn't told the social worker or the nuns about the uncle. She says they suspect something, partly because she came in here looking like she'd been run over. But she doesn't want to tell because she thinks they might take the baby away if they know. And, she said she can just picture her uncle waiting for the axe to fall. 'He'll never know when I might strike and ruin his pitiful excuse for a life. It seems like a kind of justice.'

Well, sorry for the el-depressing story, but I wanted you to know that even though I make the nuns sound strict, they're actually more like angels. They call Mother Mary 'Our Lady' and they say, 'Our Lady was once a mother in trouble, too.' Kind of beautiful when you think about it.

What kind of person spends her days feeding pregnant girls chicken for supper and putting pretty little soaps in the bathroom and ceramic ballerina lamps in the bedroom to make a lonely girl feel better? I would never say anything too snarky about that kind of person. It's not their fault I ended up here.

Love xxxooo Jenny

Bea must have heard the talk around town. She had begun to speak to me, with a ridiculous courtesy that she had never used before.

'I'm making tea. Would you like a cup?' was the first thing she said. I was so startled I turned her down before I even thought about it, then realized I did want some. I made myself wait about an hour, then went and made my own cup. I wanted her to think that nothing she did could rattle me.

'Your dinner's still warm in the oven,' she said another night when I got home from the gas station and was brushing snow from my gasoline-scented jacket. She had asked me to leave my jacket at the back door by the basement, so it didn't stink up the front closet, and that night she took it from me and carried it out there herself, as if it was something she always did, and as if keeping my dinner warm in the oven was our usual routine. It was spaghetti, an exotic food to Bea and usually when we'd had it, it was Jenny who had made it. Bea had even made meatballs and, as I ate in silence at the table while Bea watched *Mary Tyler Moore*, I knew that she had spent a portion of her day mixing up the ground beef and egg and breadcrumbs.

When a letter from Jenny came, she left it at the end of my bed. One afternoon, I found my clothes from the dryer all neatly folded, too, along with another strawberry-scented envelope from Jenny.

Dear Maggie,
    Today Ginger and I put on wedding rings and went out walking. Believe it or not, there is a box of fake wedding rings in the TV room, and when you go out, you slip one on, kind of like a charm to protect your dignity. I chose a tasteful gold band, but Ginger went for a glass rock the size of a pea, nestled between two red rubies. There is also a closet full of maternity clothes. I'm not that desperate yet, but you should see my boobs. I know, Mom would say that's crude. It's what twelve year-old boys say, etc, etc. So tits then, I mean breasts, whatever you want to call them! The girls here trade bras all the

time, because their tits are always changing size, and I now have a hot pink C-cup. In the peach top I got for my birthday, I actually have cleavage. And with my white Wranglers (I can't do up the zipper, so I safety pin it and hide it under my shirt) I look killer diller, if I do say so myself. But I wore a raincoat to hide my *shapely* figure when I went out, since the nuns get on our case if we dress 'provocatively.' Ginger is showing but she manages to look killer even pregnant. She wore black leotards and a tartan dress that is actually a blouse but is long enough on her — barely. Did you know that when you're pregnant you feel very — shall we say? — amorous. Or at least I do. Don't tell anyone, because I'm probably a sicko to say so.

The sun came out while we were walking down Granville Street and everything shone. The streets and sidewalks started to steam. There are stores here that have flowers and vegetables out on tables on the sidewalks. This might be a nice place to live if the sun came out a little more often and if I hadn't made a BAD DECISION.

Ginger and I stopped at one store to look at the flowers. A man came out — Italian, I think. In his elegant accent he said, 'Did you two lovely girls bring this sunshine?' Then he said, 'It must be my lucky day, two beautiful redheads at my store at the same time. You wait here, I have something for you.' He went inside and came back with two big bouquets of flowers. 'I usually keep these for my wife, but today they're for you.'

So now I have a vase of flowers in my room. There are some white roses and something yellow that smells fantastic. This room is painted soft pink with white trim. I actually like it. There's a green homemade quilt on the bed and the little bedside lamp with a ceramic ballerina for the base. I think I told you.

The rest of the house is nice, but a little dark, with a lot of polished wood and blue carpets and then there's the rain. I'm trying to be optimistic, but to tell you the truth, when you go out, the light is grey, the pavement's grey, the buildings are grey, the pigeons, even, are grey — it's kind of a downer. I wash out my socks and underwear and hang them to dry on the radiator, but they're still damp the next morning. There is a leak in the English classroom ceiling and during the whole class we hear the drip-drop-drip-drop into a pan on the floor. Sister Anne says this must be symbolic, though she's not sure of what, and that the person who comes up with the most convincing symbol gets bonus marks. I say it's the passage of time. It sounds like a clock, and there we sit, waiting.

The most depressing thing, though, is all these girls sitting around playing cards, listening to Tony Orlando and Dawn, discussing due dates and eating snacks, which they buy with their 'pocket money.' The nuns have all these funny expressions. 'Pocket money' can be earned by doing chores — folding sheets, polishing floors, cutting vegetables for dinner. The girls buy cheezies, pretzels and hickory sticks, my personal favourite. I think I'm addicted. I wander down to the laundry room to fold sheets, but I'm really thinking of hickory sticks.

Some of the girls are waiting for their boy-friends to show up, marry them, and carry them off to a four-bedroom house in the suburbs where their days will be spent bliss-fully Ajaxing the bathtub. Speaking of symbolism, 'Tie a Yellow Ribbon Round the Ole Oak Tree,' which I've now heard about fifty million times, no guff — listen to the lyrics, except it's the girls who are in prison. That's not exactly true. Sometimes this place feels like a hideout.

I'm always chilled from the rain. Luckily there is a bathtub down the hall. I soak in there every night after supper. I'm probably going to get fat. I know what you're thinking. Don't even say it.

Sister Anne had us writing poems today. We had to start with the words 'something changed.' Everybody was teasing her: 'Subtle, Sister.' I was surprised, though, by what came out. Sister read it over my shoulder when it was done and gave me a little thumbs up. She was actually kind of choked up, I could see it. Well, I shouldn't get your hopes up too much. It's just a poem. (which doesn't have to rhyme, by the way)

Something changed
When night after night
I tried to sleep
But waited
Maybe I would hear your car door slam
Maybe your footsteps in the hall
Maybe you would wake me up
Singing Sweet Caroline
Like you did when we were little
And thunderstorms were the scariest thing
Something changed
When night after night
You didn't come.

I realized something the other day. I used to cry when I thought about Mom. I kind of even liked it, the crying I mean. I always had this idea that Mom could see me, and she would feel bad for breaking my heart and she would come. Now I can't even cry, which is probably for the best, because if I did, I don't know what would happen. I'm starting to show, which makes it feel more real. I guess this is my real third thing.

Dear Maggie,
I now have a psychiatrist, as well as a social worker. I went to see Miss Bug Eyes today and a man was sitting there with her. Bug Eyes said, 'Jennifer, I'm concerned.' Apparently she's concerned that I don't seem to understand the serious situation I'm in (translation: I haven't bawled in her office

and used up her Kleenexes). So she brought in the big guns, as Ted used to say. Dr. Ruskins.

Before I go any further I have to tell you about Robert. That's right, Robert Ruskins is his name. Cute, eh? And I'm supposed to call him Robert, not Dr. Ruskins. Speaking of cute . . . He has this soft blonde curly hair and killer green eyes, like a cat, and a voice like the guy in the band America, the one who sings 'A Horse with No Name.' I asked him if he's American, but he's not, he's from Ontario. I guess that explains the accent. How do I know his hair is soft, you ask? I don't, but I can imagine.

Once Bug Eyes had left the room, he told me he wasn't interested in judging me. He doesn't believe in God, doesn't even believe in marriage and thinks 'sex is a normal healthy part of an adult life.' Ha! I couldn't help telling him that everyone blames the boy. That's what I said. I just blurted it out, then I wasn't sure I really wanted to continue the thought. He said, 'You mean you had sex willingly. You wanted to.' He said it like a statement, not a question.

'Yes,' I said.

'And you're feeling guilty about that.'

I said, 'I guess I am, now that you mention it.' And he laughed. Nice laugh. I continued, 'Some of the girls here have been attacked or raped. One girl even told me that she didn't actually have sex at all.'

Swear to God, Maggie, this is true. She

claims she's still a virgin. I think she thinks the sperm just sort of crawled up her leg.

The doctor, I mean *Robert*, smiled at me and said, 'You're a perfectly normal, healthy young woman and healthy young women like sex just like healthy young men do. People will say all sorts of things to alleviate their guilt. Only some of it is true. As good as these dear Sisters are here, they serve their mercy with a heavy helping of guilt.'

I liked the way he said that. He could be a writer. That line could be from a Bob Dylan song: *They serve their mercy with a heavy helping, a heavy, heavy helping . . . of guilt.*

Anyways, he kept saying 'sex' as if it was no big deal. Then he offered me a cup of coffee, and I don't even like coffee, but I said yes because it made it like two adults having a normal conversation. I know. I'm not an idiot. He's probably just really good at his job, that's what you're thinking, but I couldn't see the harm in it. And did I mention he's cute? Did I mention I noticed his eyes lingering on my hot pink C-cup running over when I leaned to put my coffee cup down? Maybe he's bored, too. Maybe he daydreams about long-legged pregnant gals who have a normal appreciation of sex. And what else do I have to do all day, besides sit around talking about my due date and knitting booties? (No! I will not knit booties!)

As relaxed as I felt with him, I'm not going

to tell him the father's name. I see Robert
again on Friday.

Love xxoo *Jenny*

P.S. I told you about The Girl who got Pregnant Without Having Sex. Now I will tell you
the story of the Prettiest Babies Get Sold to
Rich People. This is true, too. I know
because all the girls say it's true. But I'll let
you be the judge.

The story goes that if you see someone
taking Polaroid snaps of your baby, you
should be worried. I didn't even know that
we get to see our babies after they're born,
but apparently we do. Anyhow, if you have a
cute baby, especially a blonde one, especially
a boy, or one with blue eyes, and you want
to keep it, dream on. Even if you already
decided to keep it and signed the papers,
etc. They will tell you that the baby is sick.
Then they'll tell you it died. But really it got
Sold to Rich People who can't have their
own baby. And that's how the nuns keep
this place going. How else could they afford
to keep this big mansion and feed all these
girls year after year? Not to mention the
nice fresh soaps in the bathroom all the
time. They don't have jobs. Makes you
think.

I asked Ginger if she believes it and she
said these girls have too much time on their
hands. But . . . she didn't say no. Believe it
or not . . .

P.P.S. (this means post-post, in case you didn't know) Do you think I could call you collect at the gas station? You work by yourself on Saturday afternoon, right? We (which actually means you, sorry) could pay Bob back. But you know I'll repay you someday when I'm a rich poet. Ha ha.

22

On Saturday afternoon Jenny called the gas station collect.

'Holy shit, Mag, I can't believe how glad I am to talk to you. You're not going to get into trouble, are you?'

'No, I'll pay for it. Bob likes me. He thinks Bea's a hag for sending you away.'

'He knows?'

'I didn't tell him. It seems like half the town knows. I never even knew so many people around here knew our names. Vern told me Uncle Leslie heard some ladies in the grocery store talking about it. They think Bea went too far.'

Jenny didn't say anything.

'Are you there?'

'Yeah, I'm here.'

'It's kind of ironic, don't you think?'

'Yeah, I guess.'

'What's wrong?'

'What isn't? I guess I just don't like the idea of it. Everybody talking about me.'

'Well, not everybody. I exaggerated. I just thought you'd be glad that Bea's plan backfired.'

'Yeah, score one for pathetic me. I really just want this to be over. Sorry, Mag. I don't mean to be such a downer.'

'I guess you've got a right, Jenny.'

'You're not mad at me, are you?'

'What are you talking about?'

'It's been bugging me. I screwed up your plan. I know how you worry and now you've got this to worry about.'

'But you'll be back in a few months.'

'Yeah, that's right.'

She was quiet. I tried to think of something to say. 'It snowed here.'

'Yeah? It's raining here. Do you have a minute or two? I mean, there's no one waiting for gas or pickle chips or something.'

'No. It's dead today.'

'Do you think I should tell John? This will sound weird. Promise me you won't tell anyone.'

'I won't,' I said but I felt my stomach flip.

'I don't know why I say that. Who are you going to tell?'

'What is it?'

'It's about John. The reason he left town. It wasn't because he wanted to see the world. In that letter that he wrote to me? The one I burned?'

'Yeah.'

'He told me he left because he's homosexual. Weird, eh? I mean you wouldn't think it somehow. I don't know a lot about sex or anything, but it sure seemed to me like he liked it. But maybe I forced him.'

'You didn't force him, Jenny. You can't force a guy to have sex.'

'But are you shocked?'

'I'm kind of shocked, yeah. He didn't seem homosexual to me.'

235

There were about five seconds of silence on the phone and then Jenny and I both broke down laughing.

When she could catch her breath, she said, 'Because you're the expert. You should meet Dr. Robert. But it's not funny, really. John said he didn't think he could ever be himself in Williams Lake. So even if I wanted him to come to my rescue and marry me, which I don't, that probably wouldn't work out too well.'

'It's not — it hasn't crossed your mind, has it? In your letters you sounded pretty sure.'

'I've got to go, Maggie — my time's up. No, don't worry, I'm fine. I just have way too much time on my hands. I'll write to you tonight. DON'T worry, okay?'

'Okay.'

She hung up.

But I think we both knew how pointless it was for her to tell me not to worry. As soon as I put the phone down I felt the heaviness in my stomach rising up and tightening around my chest. Her letters had sounded like the Jenny I knew, always sunny, always righting herself, like a good canoe riding rough water. But on the phone I could hear some dark thing crouched on its haunches, calling her. She was having a hard time hanging on.

The bell rang for the gas pumps. I looked out and saw Uncle Leslie's green truck in the falling snow. The afternoon light was almost gone. He waved at me and as I went towards him, I wanted to say, 'Help.'

Dear Maggie,

I don't have the same memories of Dad as you do. I always thought he saw you as kind of like a son (no offence). But me he didn't get. Maybe because I was too girly. (I don't think I'm too girly, but you do. Really, I'm just a girl.)

I remember when we were little — I doubt you'd remember — we went to visit a friend of Dad's. It was way out in the bush on a very rough road. We had fun getting there. There was a tree across the road at one point and Mom and Dad had to get out and move it. They were laughing and teasing each other and I held you in my lap. How old was I? Five? Six? I don't know exactly. Old enough to remember it.

The cabin was one room, smoky and dirty. Frying pan full of grease on the woodstove, flies on dirty dishes on a wooden box. Dirty clothes in the corner. There was no running water or bathroom. There were too many mosquitoes to leave us outside. I know because Mom tried, put us on a smelly blanket under a tree and we were attacked instantly. We both cried and she brought us in. The bed you and I sat on smelled like piss and body odour.

After a while, a few empty beer bottles had been set on the floor by the woodstove, and the man, I forget his name, took Dad out to show him something. Something they had been talking about, I don't know what. When they left, the man picked up the sack of beer and took it with him.

Mom yelled after him, 'Are you worried I'm going to drink it all while you're gone?'

And his voice came back, 'You might just, Irene. You might just.'

'Jesus Christ,' Mom said. I remember being surprised because it meant she was really, really mad. She'd only use the God curses if she was super-mad. I had no idea what had upset her so much. She paced the cabin, breathing heavily like she was out of breath. When I asked her what she was doing, she said, 'Trying to calm down.'

Then I spit up on the bed. I mean I barfed. All over the bed. I don't know why. The man had given us some bread and jam. Maybe it was that.

Mom said, 'Oh, for Christ's sake! Leave me in this shithole with the kids. I guess I deserve it.'

And I started to cry. She picked us up, one under each arm and carried us out to the car and she held me and said, 'Don't cry. You're my peach. You're my beautiful, beautiful girl. You didn't do anything wrong. Don't cry.'

I barfed some more, I think. Then she told me she was going to look for something for my stomach. I saw her come out of the cabin with the blankets bunched up and she shook them out and threw them over a bush. After a while she came out again and brought me a cup of weak tea.

'I'm not squeamish but that's a filthy cabin,' she said. 'I boiled the water good and long. It'll make you feel better.'

I slept a bit and some time later, I heard the car start. Mom was in the driver's seat. She drove, saying nothing, and Dad sang songs. Remember those pretty Irish songs he knew? There was the one about the belle of Belfast city — 'I'll tell me Ma when I go home' — Dad reversed the words and sang, 'The girls won't leave the boys alone.' And the one he called the fake Irish lullaby. 'Too-ra-loo-ra-loo-ra, hush now don't you cry.'

I fell asleep again and woke up when the car stopped. I barfed some more and Dad looked over the seat at me. He was holding you. His lips were curled in a nasty kind of disgust. The look on his face made me cry. Mom was leaning in the back door and said, 'Aren't you going to help me?' Before he could answer, she slammed the car door and went in the house. Dad said, 'She's your daughter.' Mom didn't hear him, but I did. He carried you in the house and left me there. I remember I felt sorry for myself, lying there in my own vomit all alone in the dark. I felt like it was a test. Would he come back and get me? I didn't wait long, but it was Mom, not him, who came with a towel and a blanket and rough, angry movements. It stuck with me, Maggie. I'd seen this secret side of Dad and he knew I had. Any time we were alone together after that, there was that secret.

Well, I was thinking about him because I was thinking about fathers. One of the girls here, she's kind of funny, but also mean and mad, she tells the Tony Orlando and Dawn girls, 'If you think any fuzzy-dicked guy cares half a crap about your babies, you're so far gone there's no coming back.'

That makes the girls go quiet, but after she's gone they say things like, 'She's just bitter. Who would want her? I can't imagine what her baby's going to look like. She won't have to worry about her baby getting sold to rich people.'

Maybe it's true, though. Girls have the babies and girls love the babies. A guy like John, he's a decent guy, but he doesn't want to know he's a father.

Hi again,

It's about one a.m. and I can't sleep. Since I was awake anyway, I thought I'd get up and write to you. It's raining again and if you didn't know, you might think something was burning, the rain hisses and crackles like that. I'm sitting at my desk and I put the quilt around my legs because the radiator is cold. The ballerina lamp is on. When we get our house, I'm going to buy a ballerina lamp.

I felt the baby move tonight. It felt like a butterfly swimming around in my belly. It started when I went to bed and I was lying still. At first I thought a bug had crawled across my stomach and I tried to brush it off. Then I realized what it was. It went on for about an hour, Maggie, like she was playing in there. It was so cool. You might be wondering why I say 'she.' As I was lying there I sort of felt like she was talking to me. Not really talking, but you know. And she's a girl. For sure. Bet you any money. Well, I have a 50/50 chance of being right — ha ha.

Today I went to Mass. We don't have to go, it's optional. Sister Anne said she noticed that I don't go, even though I checked off 'Catholic' on the intake form. I told her Mom is Catholic, but she was pretty easygoing about it. Sister laughed, but she said if I wanted to, I could go. She said maybe I'd feel closer to Mom if I did. So I thought what the hell. Ha ha.

Do you remember that little church in Duchess Creek that was so cold in the winter? I remember lying on the wooden pew, so I must have been little. It smelled like mothballs. And I was playing with Mom's purse, opening and closing it because it made a nice snap. And a smell of spearmint gum came from it.

The priest here told the girls we should say the rosary every night and one of the prayers should be the Act of Contrition. I doubt you'd remember it. The first part goes, 'Oh my God, I am heartily sorry for having offended Thee.' I remembered it. I always thought of it as an exclamation, Oh My God! Kind of like Sweet Jesus! Or Bugger it! I am heartily sorry. And then it goes on about the pains of hell and whatnot.

I thought I didn't feel sorry at all, just sorry for myself, maybe. Definitely not for offending God. But right now, I do feel kind of sorry. And if I offended anyone, it's *her*, the baby. She needs me to protect her and I act like I don't even care about her.

Don't you think we're kind of a bad design? Human beings, I mean. If there is a god, he was a little too casual or absent-minded or something. He should have thought to make sure we had maturity before we were able to reproduce, especially since, according to my biology class, human beings nurture their young longer than any other species. Like about eighteen years, Sister Rosa said, and everyone in the class gasps, as if we didn't know — most of us aren't even that old yet. But then I couldn't help thinking about Mom and us. So I put up my hand and I said, 'But not all mothers do it the way it's supposed to be done and yet those off-spring still survive.'

'Meaning?' said Sister Rosa. (She's this tall, thin nun, all business, no nonsense, cat's-eye glasses, pixie haircut, and the way she speaks makes you think she's on a tight schedule and she wants her answers the same, pronto.)

'Meaning some mothers leave their off-spring to fend for themselves sooner, kick them out of the house at sixteen, or even leave them in a basket on the hospital steps.'

'Point taken. The community takes over, then. Without the human community, the baby in the basket would starve to death.'

'But the sixteen-year-old wouldn't. Or even

the twelve-year-old.'

'I get where you're going with this, Dillon.' (She calls us by our last names.) Which was funny, because I didn't even know. She said something about instinct and the debate in biology about which behaviours we could attribute to instinct. But I wasn't thinking about that. I was thinking about how when Dad died, it was like a flood that comes sweeping in and knocks you down. And you think you'll just drop dead right on the spot. But you don't.

Which brings me to my recurring dream. I've been dreaming about tidal waves. I don't know where my brain got the idea of tidal waves, but I must have heard it somewhere. They do happen on the BC coast. I think I remember Mom talking about one once and how the village had to move to higher ground.

Anyhow, I dream that a big wave has risen up from the ocean and surged through the city, everything's floating, cars and trees, and it rises up right up the steps of Our Lady of Perpetual Help Home for Unwed Mothers, and it sloshes in under the door, and keeps coming, washes across the polished hardwood floor of the foyer and laps at the stairs, one by one. I pull my blankets up so they won't touch the floor, but pretty soon the water has risen so high the bed becomes unmoored and floats free. Night before last, the whole house listed and I had to hold on to the table leg to keep from washing out the window. Symbolism. If I knew what the table leg symbolized, maybe I would know what to do.

To tell you the truth, I'm starting to regret that I came here. I'm homesick, and I don't even know for what. Not for Bea's house or our crummy little bedroom there, but it's just this feeling of loneliness. Sometimes I think this feeling will never leave me. And I wonder if she feels it, wherever she is. She must think we're okay. If she knew we weren't okay, she would come back. We've been wrong, Maggie, up to now, to do nothing. We need to let her know we're not old enough to be away from our mother yet. I don't know anyone here in Vancouver and I'm surrounded by people who want something from me. They're taking my blood and asking me questions about sex and writing down the answers and staring at me sadly with these eyes that try to appear non-judgmental, but are really just dripping with judgment. I can almost hear their private thoughts: dopey girl, I never would have, your bad choices, your type, your age bracket, your prospects, your failure to plan. Failure to plan is planning to fail. (Do you like that one? I find it catchy.)

I only came here because I didn't have time to make any other decision. I thought I owed it to Beatrice, because I had so disappointed her. But what can she do to me? Shame me to death? Do people die of shame?

244

I will leave you with that deep philosophical question now while I go to bed and dream of floating out the window.

Love xxoo Jenny

Dear Maggie,

Sorry for that downer letter I wrote last night. I think I was trying to avoid going to sleep because I hate mornings the most. I wake up and it's all still true and I just want not to wake up, which I can do by not going to bed, if you get my drift.

Are you sitting down? Probably, since you're reading this. You should sit down, so you won't fall down. Don't be mad at me, please don't think I'm a spacey, dopey girl, I've given this a lot of thought and I've decided that I'm not relinquishing after all. I'm keeping.

What in the seven circles of hell??? (I just imagined you saying that, like Ted used to, so I wrote in your part so I'd feel like you were here with me.)

So far I've only told Ginger and she's thrilled and thinks we can get an apartment together, but I told her no, I couldn't live in the city. I want to go home, wherever that is, somewhere up there with you and the coyotes and chickadees. No, I haven't figured out a plan yet, since as I said before I don't think there's a big demand for typists in the Chilcotin, but the pioneer women managed with all their babies. I told Ginger she could come and live with us. I hope you don't

245

mind. You'd like her. She won't anyway, so no harm in asking.

If Robert can stop looking at my boobs long enough today, I'll tell him. I have this feeling everyone is going to be disappointed in me all over again. More later.

Hi again,

Like I suspected, no one is exactly cheering my decision. Dr. Robert said, 'Can I ask what made you change your mind?' I said, 'Mother's instinct.' He looked at me rather stupidly, I thought. (That's Ginger's expression.) He couldn't think of anything to say for quite a long uncomfortable time. He tents his fingers when he's thinking. He wrote something down. Finally, to rescue him, I said, 'You wouldn't understand it because you're a man.'

'True,' he said. Ha ha. But still nothing. And then, 'So mother's instinct, you say. And you see that as . . . ?'

'As the reason I want to keep my baby.'

'I'd like to explore that a little further.' And blah blah blah, it wouldn't interest you. But after a while, he said, 'And in terms of a plan.'

I have learned that his statements are meant to be questions. So I told him I didn't exactly have a plan yet but that I had about five months left to figure it out.

'These are big choices, Jenny. Big for anyone, very big for a fifteen-year-old girl.'

'I'm aware of that.'

I was impressed by my own voice, very firm, very sure. The funny thing is that I feel so much better now that I've decided. She was the table leg. All along.

Please write to me and, keeping in mind I'm not going to change my mind about this, tell me what you think.

Love xxoo Jenny

23

I did write to Jenny. It wasn't my finest moment. She didn't keep the letter, thank God. She ignored most of what I had to say, which included, if I remember right, the phrase 'give your head a shake.' But she kept what she could use. That meant taking my advice about talking to Sister Anne, who I saw as my sensible ally.

Sister Anne surprised me by not trying to talk her out of it. I expected more from her, a persuasive argument. But instead she told Jenny, 'Inform yourself.' And this became Jenny's motto.

Then Jenny changed her mind about John and wrote to him care of his parents' house in Williams Lake. She made it clear that the only thing she really needed from him was money. She said she would pay him back. John got the letter eventually. He was in Northern California, picking fruit, washing dishes and playing saxophone and piano in bands wherever he could find them. The first cheque he sent was for $200. 'Don't say you'll pay me back,' he wrote. 'I don't want you to.'

Sister Anne also took Jenny to write the test for her beginner's licence, and then she took her out for drives in the evening. Jenny told me she practised parallel parking down in the shipping yards, between some big containers.

'I drove down Granville today!' she wrote in

one letter and drew a little happy face beside it.

You can't die of shame, Jenny. If you could, I'd be dead. Christmas was coming and what I should have done was go to Vancouver to be with my sister. Bea was taking the bus to White Rock to spend the holiday with her sister.

'If you want to come along with me on the bus, I'll buy you a ticket,' she said. 'The home will allow visitors for Christmas.' I didn't ask her how she knew.

'No,' I said. 'I'll stay here. They need me at the gas station.' Not true, of course. I was just too mad at Jenny for deciding to keep the baby to make the sacrifice of riding a bus for twelve hours with Bea. And also too worried. I carried around the constant hope that Mom would pull up in front of Bea's house with her grin and her strong legs and her kiss. My fourteenth birthday had passed without word from her. But Christmas seemed like a time when she might come. We needed her now more than ever and if there was such a thing as mother's instinct, maybe she would know. I was afraid to be away and miss her. She could slip away again, not knowing that we weren't okay.

'Suit yourself,' Beatrice said and went about pulling her little white suitcase out from under the bed, wiping the dust off it and folding clothes I'd never seen her wear in a neat pile on the couch. Beatrice had two sets of clothes she wore all the time, navy stretch slacks and an off-white cardigan or grey stretch slacks and a green cardigan. But it turned out she had a closet full of other things: pastel pantsuits and crêpe blouses with bows and paisley scarves. She talked to herself as she packed. She had started doing that soon after Jenny left, little things like, 'It could use dry cleaning.' And 'Where did I leave my umbrella?' It irritated me, but then everything she did irritated me, even the condiments she kept in the fridge but never used. Ancient relishes, mint sauce and HP Sauce — they must eventually go bad, like after three years. She put her suitcase by the door two days before her departure.

I should try to think of something kind to say. I should be more generous, but I was happy to see her go. Having someone else's house to yourself is not the same as having your own. Still, a stifling cloud of rage and unspoken accusations lifted from me the moment she was down the steps. I made hot chocolate and watched *Get Smart* with my feet on the coffee table. I smoked a stale cigarette, one of Jenny's. There was no alcohol in the house. I thought briefly that it might be fun to get some, then I decided it would involve talking to people, so I dropped the idea.

All the snow had melted over the previous week. Everyone who had come through the gas station said something about it being a green Christmas. But I didn't mind. I didn't want it to feel like Christmas at all. Then the morning after Bea left, Christmas Eve, it started to snow, so light that three customers in a row said, 'Is that snow?' and I said yes, as if I was the authority. By noon, when the flakes were coming down like apple blossoms, I had to listen to every second person say that they guessed it would be a white Christmas after all.

I kept expecting Mom to drive in. Every crunch of tires on the gravel made me look up. Why I thought she would come to that gas station where I happened to be working, I don't know. I suppose I thought someone would have told her.

Bob closed up at three o'clock and I walked back to the house through the falling snow. It was sticky enough to make a snowman. I had a pork chop to fry up and I made instant mashed potatoes and a can of creamed corn to go with it. Dark already, the snow coming down steadily, I felt like I was being buried. I turned on Bea's silver Christmas tree on top of the TV, although I hated it, both its chintzy falseness and the fact that she put it on top of the TV. It just reinforced how pathetic her life was, the TV the centre of her world. Jenny once asked Mom why we didn't have a TV and Mom said, 'You mean overlooking the fact that we don't have a fridge or a dryer either? We could have a TV, if it was important enough to us.'

But I liked the coloured light that Bea's tree threw. Not a fire, but a memory of a fire, Christmas Eve playing cards by the light of the lantern and Mom bringing us a plate of biscuits with fresh cream and blackberry jam. Where did she get the cream? What plans did she make for the day, following some dream she had for all of us together on Christmas Eve? The woodsmoke perfume. Snow angels later, all four of us, Dad giggling. Looking up at the stars, the night so clear and cold. I don't know how old I was, but even then I knew to hold on to it. I understood how fragile it was.

I looked out the window at the quiet street. Fallen snow had turned the neighbours' cars into weird tall shapes. More was falling, and it blurred under a porchlight like a cloud of insects hovering.

I went to the phone and dialled information. 'I'm looking for Our Lady of Perpetual Help in Vancouver,' I said.

'I'm sorry? What is the name you're looking for?' said the operator.

'Our Lady of Perpetual Help. That's the name.'

'Hold on please. There's an Our Lady of Perpetual Help church. Is that the number you want?'

'No.'

'I'm sorry miss, that's the only number I have. Merry Christmas,' said the operator.

Bea's backyard was a bowl of deep snow capped by sky thick with reflected light. It was only a city backyard and Christmas was all wrong but I couldn't help seeing how beautiful it was. I put on my parka and went out the door. I found the snow shovel and began a pile right in the middle of the yard. Music floated from a neighbour's house. I hoped they didn't know Bea was away and that they wouldn't see me, alone out there. I piled and packed, piled and packed, took off my parka and worked in my sweatshirt. I stopped to make hot chocolate, sat on the back step and drank it, thinking of

Vern, who had gone to his Mom's for the holidays.

Voices on the street, happy shouts and car doors slamming. Then the commotion of revved engine and spinning tires and shouted directions. 'Straighten your wheels. Okay, put her in reverse. Give her some juice. Again.' Then quiet, deep, even here. It must be late.

I began to dig a tunnel into the pile. After a while, I got the flashlight and went to the shed for a smaller shovel. Sweeping the dark corners with the flashlight beam, I saw her travelling fast, too fast on a snow-plugged road, her muscular hands gripping the wheel, headlights cutting through thick falling snow. She'd like a cigarette. There'd be no one there to roll it for her and you couldn't stop on a road like that or you'd get stuck for sure. Her thermos of tea would be between her legs, the tea only lukewarm by now.

I locked the shed. If anything came down the street, I'd hear it. But nothing was moving. Not even out on the highway.

★　★　★

It was early morning, not yet light, by the time I finished the snow cave. I found a candle, stuck it on a little snow shelf inside and lit it. It was better in here. Christmas day had come. No one in the world knew how my arms ached, or how pale the light of the candle was against snow crystal walls.

I wonder now how deep a person's grief can

253

go. Jenny never mentioned that Christmas, not in the letters she wrote afterwards, not ever. But I wonder if leaving her alone there like I did altered her, and if it led to what came later.

24

There should be different words for giving birth than the ones we have. 'Giving' should at least be 'undertaking' or 'undergoing.' I remember in church how the priest said, 'Mary bore Jesus,' and I always thought of it as 'bored.' But now that I know what 'bore' means, and now that I've seen what Jenny went through, it's a much better word than the passive 'the baby was born,' like it's as easy as growing fingernails.

Sister Anne said if men gave birth there would be different words, and we thought of some, sitting around the card table playing Scrabble and waiting for Jenny to come back from the hospital. I had left school three weeks early to be with her. Sister Anne had a visitor's room beside her own where she let me stay. We came up with 'disgorge,' 'disburden,' 'unship' and, my favourite, 'disembogue,' which we found in the thesaurus. It means a pouring forth of waters.

Jenny was sleeping like the dead when I left her, the baby, a girl, as Jenny had predicted, sleeping peacefully in a little plastic bassinet beside her bed. Jenny had just had time to name her before she passed out. Sunshine. That's her name. I thought it was too hippy at first, but it's the kind of thing Jenny would think of. It's what she should have been named herself. 'We'll call her Sunny,' she said, closed her eyes and was gone, abandoning herself to sweet relief from the drugs, the blood, the panic and the forceps.

★ ★ ★

When Jenny came back to Our Lady of Perpetual Help with Sunny, she didn't behave the way I expected. I had pictured a soft-eyed, red-haired Madonna, cooing over her baby and gazing lovingly down at her. Instead, she was nervous and irritable.

'I'm so tired,' she kept saying. 'I just want to sleep.' She claimed she hadn't slept an unbroken hour in the hospital, and because of her complaining, they let her go early.

'They don't want someone messing up their schedules. Honestly, the nurses think if you don't wake up at seven a.m. raring to go, you're a negligent mother. They should try sleeping in a room with three other girls all snoring and crying and moaning like ghosts. And then they kept threatening to give her the sugar water if I didn't nurse her often enough. And they were yacking about bonding and whatnot. You can tell they're just waiting for me to fuck up so they can say I told you so.'

'No one thinks you're going to fuck up,' I told her. Sunny was asleep on her chest in the upstairs nursery and I was keeping her company. The idea was that I would stay with Jenny and, as her primary support, learn how to help her with the baby and then we'd go home together. 'Home' was another story.

'Oh yes. They do think I will fuck up,' said Jenny, 'and they already have a list of people who want my baby. Look how beautiful she is.' She moved her arm aside to let me see Sunny's face. She was beautiful. She had a fuzz of pale hair, an angelic, heart-shaped face and perfect little lips that moved in her sleep. But Jenny's voice was angry.

'Do you know I actually prayed for an ugly baby? I prayed it on my rosary. I asked Our Lady of Perpetual Help for it and look what I got. I'm being punished.'

'Jenny, that's ridiculous. She's beautiful because you're beautiful. She's even got your green eyes. What did you expect? A pig nose and three eyes?'

'Very funny.' She laid her head back against the rocking chair and closed her eyes. In a moment, her mouth dropped open and she started to snore lightly. I lifted Sunny gently off her chest, but Jenny woke with a start.

'Where are you taking her?'

'I'm just putting her in her bassinet so you can sleep.'

'That's another thing. Why is her bassinet set off to the side like that? And why does it have that strip of tape on it?'

'I don't know. Maybe it's because she's a newborn. Why don't you go to your room and nap for a while? She's sleeping now. They say you should sleep when she does.'

'Will you watch her?'

'If you want. But you know there's always someone here.'

She snorted drily. 'That's what I'm worried about.'

'I'll watch her,' I promised.

That night with Jenny in her room trying to sleep, I asked Sister Anne, 'Is it true that there's a waiting list for Jenny's baby?'

'No, Maggie, it's not true. Her decision will be respected. We'll do everything we can to help her be successful.'

'But who decides if she's successful?'

'She'll be fine. It's always hard at first and not just for the young mothers. She's doing fine.'

I believed her, but Jenny's fears didn't seem unfounded. She was in a place, after all, where babies were regularly given up for adoption. The mothers were watched, helped for sure, but also watched. I trusted the nuns more than the social workers. We knew kids in Williams Lake who were in foster homes because they'd been taken away from their families by social workers. Mostly Indian kids, but not only.

And Jenny was not doing fine, no matter how much I wanted to believe her behaviour was normal for a new mother. She told me things that she wanted me to keep between her and me. 'A girl came to my room last night,' she said, one morning. 'She had long black braids and she was wearing a long white nightgown. It was soaked in the front. When I turned on the light, I could see that it was soaked with blood.'

'You were dreaming.'

'I wasn't dreaming, Maggie, I talked to her. She even knew my name. She had been at Our Lady of Perpetual Help. She told me that her baby had been chosen, and now mine was chosen, and that I better protect her. Her baby was taken away from her because she hemorrhaged and she was too weak to care for her. She was warning me.'

'That's weird, Jenny.'

'I know. But this place is weird, you've got to admit that. The stories that go around. There's got to be some truth to them.'

'Not really. They're just a bunch of worries. You're becoming a worrier like me.'

'It wasn't a dream, Maggie, I'm telling you. I wasn't even asleep. I don't sleep. I can't.'

The detail in Jenny's dream unnerved me and I spoke to Ginger about it. Ginger had a room on the third floor, down the hall from the nursery. She'd had her baby, a curly headed boy she named Jamie. She was breast-feeding him when I came to her door. She seemed older than Jenny, and completely at ease as a mother.

'Where does she get this stuff?' I asked her. 'Where would she have heard it?

'Get her to talk to Dr. Robert.'

'She won't. She swears me to secrecy about all this stuff. Maybe *I* should talk to Dr. Robert.'

'I don't think so. You can't betray her trust.'

So I kept quiet, too. But it didn't matter. Dr. Robert figured it out by himself.

'He wants to know why I didn't name the baby Irene,' Jenny said to me one evening after she'd seen him.

'What do you mean? Just out of the blue, he asked you that?'

'He thinks there's something wrong with me.

As a mother. I know it.'

'Because you didn't name her Irene?'

'He knows about Mom.'

'What about her?'

Jenny laughed, this dry laugh she had developed that was nothing like her real, happy laugh. It was sarcastic and full of bitterness and although I was trying to be mature and helpful, it hurt me. It was a 'you are a naive idiot' kind of laugh.

'I'm not following,' I said, with just an edge of impatience.

'I told him way too much about myself. And Ginger's in on it, too. I confided in her. I saw a file in his lap with Ginger's name on it. Everything I told her is in there.'

'You're scaring me, Jenny.'

She laughed again. 'That's good. You need to be scared. You need to get a grip on what's happening here.'

Two days later Sister Anne ushered me into the room that served as Dr. Robert's office. He looked up and smiled at me, but it was not an easy, genuine smile. It was the pained and crooked, trying-to-be-sympathetic smile of someone about to deliver bad news. He danced around with some small talk, presumably meant to put me ease but didn't. Then he said, 'Have you ever heard of the baby blues?'

I shook my head.

'Women get a little weepy and emotional after the baby is born. It's normal. Happens to seven out of ten women and usually lasts a week or so. We thought that's what Jenny was experiencing.'

He smiled the pained smile again. I looked at Sister Anne, who was frowning. I believe she had more respect for my intelligence than Dr. Robert did.

'It turns out that what Jenny's experiencing is a bit more severe. It's known as postpartum psychosis. Now I know that's a scary name.'

I stared at him. It wasn't scary yet, since I didn't know what it meant, but when he said that, I swallowed drily.

'We don't know a lot about what causes it, but we do know how to treat it. That's the good news.' He paused. I waited for the inevitable other half, the bad news. I thought he looked — gleeful. He was percolating with the scientific details he wanted to discuss.

'Now, is there any history of mental illness in your family?'

'I don't know.'

'Any alcoholism?'

'No. I mean I don't think so.' I thought of Dad, his quiet spells.

Dr. Robert sat back and met Sister Anne's eyes.

'This line of inquiry . . . ' began Sister Anne.

'I'm trying to get a picture of the family's mental health. We know that postpartum psychosis often occurs when there's a family history of mental illness.'

'Maggie's father died when she was ten. She's now fourteen.' Sister Anne said my age a little pointedly, but Dr. Robert didn't seem to notice.

'And how did he die?'

'Logging accident.'

'And your mother?'

'How did she die?' I said.

'Did she die?'

'I don't know. Hasn't Jenny told you all this already? What are you going to do to her?'

'Okay,' Dr. Robert smiled again. 'I guess we're getting ahead of ourselves. Jenny will need to go back to the hospital. We'll be able to watch her there, and treat her of course.'

It may have been the only thing they could do for her, it may have been the right thing, but it was also the worst thing. It was just what Jenny feared.

25

Even if Jenny hadn't asked me to, I probably would have gone looking for Mom. There was nothing I could help by staying. I couldn't soothe her agitation or persuade her that her fears weren't real. Besides, nearly everything she said had some ring of truth to it, and even as I spoke the words to dismiss it, my gut churned with the slim possibility that she was right. People were watching her, 'observing,' as she put it. They could take Sunny away; it's not as if it hadn't happened before. Bad things happened to people all the time. They could happen to us. They came in threes. I knew it. Jenny knew it.

But I didn't believe, as Jenny did, that her being held in hospital, given various doses of drugs, some that made her inconsolably sad, others that made her stony and blank, had anything to do with Mom's disappearance. No one knew where she was, and, furthermore, everyone seemed to take it as a given that she was somewhere she didn't want to be found. I guess there was no law against deserting your children. It was a crime only to us. And it happened gradually, like winter coming, the way you don't put your bike away until one day it's buried in snow and you realize that the days of bare legs and lung-burning speed are gone and you don't really believe they'll be back.

To an outsider, it was almost like she planned it.

★ ★ ★

'I want you to go,' Jenny said to me one evening. It was June. Outside, sunlight and long shadows spilled across the green hospital lawn. Blue hydrangeas glowed with the last light. Sister Anne and I had walked over from Our Lady of Perpetual Help, through the smells of cedar and ocean air. I had told Sister Anne I was leaving.

'I think it's best, Maggie. There's nothing you can do here. Jenny's in good hands. We'll take care of both of them. I promise I'll visit her every day. She's a gutsy girl. She and Sunny can come back and stay with us once Jenny's able.'

So I had been prepared to tell Jenny. But she beat me to it.

'You have to look for her. She needs to know what's going on. They won't let me out of here until we find her.'

I took a breath. I was about to protest. The psychiatrist had warned me not to 'indulge her delusions.' But I was tired of fighting.

'I'll try,' I promised.

'They won't let me nurse Sunny,' she said, and the tears welled up and ran down her cheeks.

'I know, Jenny.'

'It's because of the drugs. It's for her own safety.'

'I know. But she likes the bottle. She's getting chubby.'

'Do you think so? You don't think she'll be

damaged? Sometimes an hour or two goes by and I realize I haven't thought of her at all. It's like I forget I even have a baby.'

'You're a good mother, Jenny. Look at you. You're in the hospital, you're sick and still you're worried about being a good mother. That's the sign right there that you are.'

'Maybe the same thing is happening to me as happened to Mom.'

'No.'

She cried then and all through the rest of visiting hours, even when Sister Anne brought Sunny in from the nursery and Jenny gave her a bottle and Sunny clutched her finger and gurgled happily. A little baby girl trying to soothe her girl of a mother. Then Jenny fell asleep with Sunny on her chest and the tears continued to soak Jenny's hair.

Sister Anne and I took Sunny back to the nursery, then on our way out we spoke to the nurse about the crying.

'It's not an exact science,' the nurse said. 'The doctors try to get the dose right. It might take another week or so. She'll improve gradually. It takes time.'

* * *

Jenny had given me some of the money that John had sent. He had also offered to buy her a car, but that was no help to me yet. I made a list of people I could trust. It was a short list: John, Vern, Uncle Leslie. Vern had got some summer work with his other uncle near Bella Coola. John was still in California. Uncle Leslie never knew my mother, so I couldn't picture myself asking him for help.

That night I listened to the low rumble of traffic from Granville Street and I tried to pretend it was a river, the Chilcotin in early summer, rushing along with the sun glinting off it. I dipped a tin pot in the flow; it spilled onto my legs. An eagle whistled. I realized that I couldn't wait to get away, from Vancouver, from Williams Lake, and from the storm of worry that boiled and thundered in the heart of me.

26

A chickadee sang fee-bee below the raucous cry of a raven. A waxwing chirruped high and thin and a woodpecker hammered a nearby tree. Early morning, fresh and cool, and the bush was a jungle of sounds. The sunlight held just the soft breath of the heat it would bring later. I had only what I needed: matches, a tin cooking pot, a flask of water, some teabags, packages of Tang, a loaf of bread, a jar of peanut butter, some fishing line and hooks, a coil of rope, a sleeping bag and Dad's jackknife.

I went down to the creek and scooped a pot of water. There was no breeze and I easily rekindled last night's fire and settled the pot between two stones to boil water for tea. I had a handful of strawberries the size of my baby fingernail that I'd collected yesterday. I ate them for breakfast. They were so tart and delicious. I felt the stirrings of the same deep peace I'd felt last night by the fire, watching the constellations take shape in the night sky, the Big Dipper, Orion, Cassiopeia, Perseus. Peace seemed wrong; I felt guilty for feeling it. Still it came again with the familiarity of morning sounds. My mother had disappeared, my sister was in a mental hospital and I was sitting in the shade of an aspen, heating a pot of creek water for tea.

I had a sleeping bag, the pot, a mug and cutlery set, and a backpack to carry it all. I had money tucked away so that I could buy more food at the store in Duchess Creek. I had decided, like Chiwid, to walk and sleep out. The first day out of Williams Lake, I kept expecting someone to come after me. I didn't want them to. Mom would not be found by asking someone to lead me to her. I'd have to sneak up on her, like the man in the fir forest that night, who slipped in with the headlights off, leaving her no place to run.

After breakfast, I packed up my things, doused the fire and scattered the rocks and set out again. I was following the road. As the day began to heat up, I found the creek again and soaked my hair and shirt, let my feet cool in the fast running water. I knew the names of things out here: Canada mint, stinging nettle and horsetail by the water. Nodding onion on a sunny slope, the pale purple flower bending gently. Mallow, lamb's quarters — you can make a salad from the fresh young leaves. Yarrow for tea. Salsify, plantain, thistle, all along the roadside. You can eat the leaves and stems. Strawberries, you have to have the eye for them, the three leaves low to the ground, the tiny ruby berries. Last year's rosehips, shrivelled, but still good to chew or put in tea.

I made camp that evening near a path leading to a swampy lake. In the night I started awake and reached out for something familiar. Sand under my fingers, pebbles, twigs, the night very dark. I listened for what had wakened me. Nothing. Maybe that. That silence — not a breath, not a peep, not a stir. A quiet so soft and full I wanted to stay awake for it.

The smallest breeze rose and, on it, the scent of woodsmoke. I remembered then that I had dreamed of fire, carried on the wind, racing across the treetops. I was running with the animals, deer and raccoons and squirrels and long-legged birds, fleeing to the creek with flames thundering overhead.

And then from the woods, a single deep call, an owl. A few seconds later, an answer from another direction.

Not everything can be a sign. They're just signalling each other, calling out their territory. They don't know anything about me or my disappeared mother or how she loved the quiet of the night and sought out the lonely places.

But the worry crept into the calm of the night and down deep where I kept my darkest fears. Like the silence, there was nothing I could name, nothing that took shape, not yet, but worry billowed and gnawed, grew, and then came the drift of smoke again. That was something to latch onto, a forest fire nearby maybe, or someone camping. Which was worse? Mom feared humans more than bears or wolves or storms. 'Which humans?' Jenny had asked. None in particular. Humans are unpredictable.

Leaves shivered now, softly. Nothing else, though I listened until my heartbeat galloped in my ears. I rolled to the precipice of sleep and jerked awake several times, sweating, sniffing the air, listening. When I woke to daylight, snow was gently floating down through the trees. I blew a flake from my arm. It wasn't snow, but ash, falling from the sky. Through the aspen leaves the sun was an orange smear, obscured by smoke. A breeze had picked up in the night and blew in ash and the heavy smell of pinesmoke. Somewhere north of here, the forest was on fire.

★   ★   ★

I walked through the day. Helicopters cut the quiet, flying north. A man in a big silver car pulled alongside me. His window whirred down and he offered me a ride. 'No, thanks anyway,' I said. Hundreds of birds rose from the telephone wire like a cloud, and turned all at once, sweeping across the road, turned again, and wheeled the other way, across the open meadow. Vehicles went by, some with an acknowledging wave of the hand. Some stopped to ask, 'You all right?' or 'Can I help you any?' But I didn't take any rides. I had lunch on a rock, the sun beating down on me, insect sound filling the roadside.

In the late afternoon, a truck came towards me and stopped on the other side of the road.

'We've got to stop meeting like this.' Uncle Leslie smiled broadly through his open window. 'I was just to Bella Coola. Smoke bothering you?'

'No. A little,' I said.

'Where you headed?'

I couldn't answer, didn't know how to answer. I had not so much lied to him about my mother as neglected to tell him the whole story. The truth embarrassed me; it seemed to reflect badly on Jenny and me. The pain was a river I rode; I could not plant my feet in it or it would knock me down.

'I can take you to Duchess Creek,' he said when I didn't answer.

'That's out of your way.'

'Maggie,' he said. Just that, but the tenderness in it took me by surprise and something broke in me. Standing there in the falling ash at the side of the road, my knees gave and I sank to the gravel. I began to cry, first like a baby and then like some kind of injured animal and I couldn't catch my breath and almost toppled over into the dirt from the weight of my backpack. Leslie caught my arm, saying, 'Okay now, it's all right now. Let me help you.'

He took my pack and put it in the truck then guided me into the cab and closed the door behind me.

I choked on air, and tears and snot streamed down my face. Leslie sifted through the glove compartment and found some serviettes and handed them to me, saying, 'That's all I have.' I wiped and choked, wiped and choked. He took my hand and held it, tight.

'It's all right now,' he repeated, over and over.

His solid grasp steadied me. Slowly, slowly I returned to firs and aspen, the road ahead, hazy sky.

We drove west.

'Not to Duchess Creek,' I said.

'Find a place to camp?'

I nodded. Closed my eyes.

We drove into the canyon south of the river on a lonely road. The land opened up to undulating

271

grassland, an eerie wind slicing paths through the soft grass. Prairie birds wheeled and scolded. Hoodoos cut in sandstone climbed the other side of the river. Leslie pulled in where a log cabin had been abandoned. Its doorway, missing the door, gaped in shadow. Brambles poked up through the porch floorboards.

'The cabin's no good now, but I like the spot,' he said. 'The smoke isn't as bad over here.'

I nodded. The river was a swift silty green and cool air rose from it.

'It might get a little bit chilly tonight. How're you set up?'

'I've got a good sleeping bag,' I said.

'I put my tarp up on the back of the truck and sleep under there. Got a bit of foam for a mattress.' He went about rigging it up and set his propane stove on the tailgate.

'Tea or hot chocolate?' he asked.

'Either is good.'

I sat by the river. Suddenly I was so tired. This was Mom's favourite time, the space between day and night when the breeze, if there was one, died down, the sky deepened with green-tinged clarity and the clatter of day hushed. When we were at a lake, she liked to make her after-supper coffee over the fire and take it down to the beach to sit and listen to the water slap softly against the shore.

Leslie brought me a mug of hot chocolate and sat beside me. We drank in silence, watching the river. After a while, he heated up some beans over a little fire. We ate while the night darkened.

'Tell you a story,' said Leslie. 'How Vern came to live with me.'

He'd been out to Nistsun to visit his sister and her son. He didn't like the white man Jolene was living with. 'I've never liked any of them, truth be told. Superior sons of bitches. But this one was real bad. Violent. Vern had had to call my brother William one night when this piss-ant held the butt of a shotgun against Jolene's stomach. Poor little guy came running over to William's house in his underwear, yelling his head off, William said. I couldn't get that picture out of my head. I went to pay them a visit. Thought to talk some sense into Jolene and get her to turf the guy, with our help of course. What did she see in these guys? I just don't know. What did she see in herself that made her think she didn't deserve better?

'I stayed at William's place that first night. I was tired from the road and I couldn't stomach seeing the white guy when I was tired. I was sleeping in the screened porch. It was the longest day of the year. As I said, I was tired from the drive but I couldn't sleep. Beyond the pines I saw the mountains white capped and shadowed by cloud. I remember I watched the moon rise over the mountain and fill the clouds with silver light. I heard howling and wondered if it was a wolf. Something was knocking against the side of the porch in the wind. Next thing I knew, I found myself standing outside Jolene's house in the moonlight. A small blue bird flung itself against the bedroom window again and again. It was trapped inside. I moved to the living-room window and looked in. In the middle of the floor, a wolf was bent over a deer carcass, tearing chunks from her ribcage. The doe's neck stretched towards me and she opened her eyes and looked at me — not afraid but so soft and pitiful.

'I saw a shovel leaning against the step and hefted it, ready to smash the window. Then I woke up in the bed in William's porch. My heart was going ninety miles an hour. The moon had gone down again and so had the wind.

'I got up and went inside the house. I wanted to ask William what he thought about the dream, but he was asleep. So I put on my pants and shoes and I walked across the reserve to Jolene's house. I had no idea what time it was, but the reserve was quiet so I knew it must be late. She lived up close to the bush — you remember — and as I got closer, a long, lonely howl played out somewhere nearby in the hills and this time it really was a wolf. It sounded so forlorn, I felt a chill. I could see light from the living-room window spilling out on the dirt in front of Jolene's house. I heard shouting, a scream, maybe Jolene. A few vehicles were parked out front. I had a hell of a dread of what I would find. It was just like my dream. There was the shovel, leaning against the step, and I picked it up. I didn't stop to look in the window or knock, I just walked right in.

'Jeez, they were surprised. He had some other guy by the hair. White guys, both of them. Some others were half passed out at the table.

'"I'll scalp ya, swear to god you try that again,

274

you fuck.' That was him, pardon my language. I remember the way he talked. There was nothing good in him, nothing. I held the shovel up, ready to swing. Their mouths dropped open. 'What the hell are you doing here?' Jolene said. I must have looked like a ghost. 'I'm taking the boy,' I said. No one tried to stop me. No one said anything.

'I still remember carrying him in my arms down the road. He woke up and said my name then fell back to sleep. Little Vern. God, I loved him. That wolf took up again and some others joined in and they howled us all the way home. He slept that night in the porch, curled up beside me. I worried for Jolene, but I knew I'd done what I could for her by taking her son out of there.'

Uncle Leslie leaned over and put a few more sticks on the fire.

'I tried to protect him. He missed his mom, but I couldn't let him go back there. Sometimes I wondered if I had the right. I still don't know.'

After a while I said, 'Jenny had her baby. She named her Sunny. She's keeping her.' I told him about the nuns and Jenny's paranoia and her visions of girls with bloody nightgowns and baby-stealers. 'Jenny needs Mom. She's just a girl and I don't know what to do for her. She needs her mother.'

'And you're looking for her?'

'Yes,' I said, and he didn't ask me anything more.

Uncle Leslie put out the fire and I tucked my sleeping bag alongside a boulder near the truck.

'You're going to be okay there?' he asked.

'Yeah. As long as it doesn't rain.'

'It won't rain tonight. You sleep well, then, Maggie. If you need anything, anything at all, just call out. I'm not a heavy sleeper.'

'Okay. Uncle Leslie?'

'Hmm?'

'Thank you.'

'You're like my own niece. Sleep well.'

★   ★   ★

I thought I would be able to sleep. I wasn't afraid and I wasn't cold, at least not at first. The stars were bright in spite of the smoke; the rhythmic rushing of the river drowned out any other night sounds, except the higher pitch of crickets singing from the grass. But my mind ticked and twitched at the edge of sleep. I had a picture of Uncle Leslie carrying little Vern through the wolf howls. I saw the little body curled into the protective arms of the bigger one. Then it was me carrying Cinnamon, her tiny body warming me. Each time I opened my eyes, the moon was a little higher and the air a little colder. Something large was down at the river, splashing and huffing. I was cold now. I got up and went to the tailgate of the truck. Just stood there.

'Cold?' Leslie said, as if he'd been awake the whole time too.

'Yes.'

'Come in here, then.'

Leslie made room for me beside him and I

crawled in with my sleeping bag, firewood and lawn chairs on one side of me and Uncle Leslie on the other.

'Go to sleep,' he said and his arms folded over me like I was a little girl.

27

Smoke from the forest fire had settled over the region. There was no wind and the sun hung above the trees, a pale orange disc. Leslie stopped at the end of the driveway of our old house in Duchess Creek.

'Doesn't look like anyone's living there,' he said, and we laughed. The porch had caved in on one side and the window of Jenny's and my room was broken. The hydro wire looked to be sagging almost to the ground.

I lifted my knapsack and got out.

'I'll make a few inquiries, if it's okay with you,' Leslie said.

I nodded, set off down the driveway. When I looked back, he was still sitting there. He waved and put the truck into gear.

★ ★ ★

I left my pack near the spruce tree. What had once been a scraggly front yard had been returned to the wild. Deer scat nestled in tufts of grass here and there. They grazed here, on the wild rose bushes. The roof that Mom and Rita and I had once fixed was missing shingles; those that were left had rotted in the heat and cold of the seasons.

It wasn't a house built by people who meant to stay, as Mom used to say.

The door was unlocked. Inside, the house still smelled of old wallboard and mouldering insulation. But our family's smell was gone. The house had been scavenged of almost everything. The Formica table and chairs were gone; so was Dad's green chair and the beds in our room. The only thing left was the woodstove and Mom and Dad's bed. I pushed open the bedroom door. A film of dust coated the mattress. On Mom's side, a blood stain the size of a quarter. Spiders had stuck the folds of the curtains together with their webs; they crackled as I parted them to look out the window.

And then I caught a whiff of her lipstick, the briefest breath of that drugstore cosmetic-counter sweetness. I raised my head to breathe it in deep. Then the acrid scent of the forest fire billowed in on the breeze. Except there was no breeze. I turned to see if I had left the door open. I hadn't.

I swear she was there. I know that sounds crazy, but it felt as though she'd taken my hand in hers. It felt so good, I started to cry again and I heard her voice, telling me to shush now, Maggie-girl. I sat on the bed and it stayed with me, that feeling of her being there with me. I thought of phoning Jenny to tell her, but I thought, what would that do, two of us off our rockers and hearing things?

I slept that night in that haunted house. I know that sounds crazy, too, but I wanted her to come back. Any minute she would be real, her footsteps crunching in the driveway.

But in the morning it was Agnes who came, in

a sky blue cotton dress dotted with red flowers and wearing jeans underneath it, just like she used to.

She said she had wondered if she'd ever see me again and then she swallowed hard and her eyes glistened. 'I'm getting so old, I cry when I'm happy now,' she said. She wiped tears from her cheeks.

'You're not old,' I said and hugged her. She felt thin in my arms and she held on after I went to pull away. Her chest heaved with the effort of not crying. It felt strange, me comforting her as if she was a child. But I wasn't comforting her, really. I was thanking her, though I couldn't say the words.

'I'm canning fish,' she said, ducking her head to try and hide new tears. 'Come over and help me.'

We drove over to her house, and I watched her graceful gait, maybe a little tentative and pained as she climbed the steps, though she wouldn't be forty yet.

'I've got a touch of arthritis,' she said, feeling my eyes on her. 'I'm too young for that!'

In the house, she put the kettle on. 'Have you come to make an honest woman of me?'

'Honest woman?'

'How many years ago did I promise to take you to Potato Mountain?'

'Four or five.'

'Let's go tomorrow then,' she said. 'We'll have to put together a few things. We can take some of this fish.'

'I don't want to mess up your plans.'

'You're not going to believe the flowers we'll see up there. This is the time of year to go.'

'Really, Agnes? Are you sure?'

Agnes started to laugh. She picked up the teapot and carried it to the sink and she stood there looking out the window, her shoulders shaking.

'Do you have a sleeping bag?' she said, still looking out the window.

'Yes.'

'Good.' She wiped her eyes and turned to me again. 'We'll just take one little bag each. Sleeping bags. Some food, some water. Matches. A little tarp. Who did I lend that tarp to? Oh, you're going to love it up there. I haven't been in three or four years, I don't know why. You just forget how much you need to go.'

* * *

When we got to the end of the road in the cool morning, a horse stood waiting, tethered to a fence. She flicked her tail and whinnied softly when she saw us.

Agnes patted her nose and fed her an apple. 'This is Linda. She'll carry our gear for us. You can ride her for a while if you want. Gotta watch the steep parts, though.'

I shook my head. We left the sunshine and headed into the shade of the trees. We walked in single file, the horse snuffing her breaths and her tail swishing softly. We passed a big old pine and stopped to stare up at the deep fissures of its orange bark. The purple of Jacob's ladder pushed through ferns. Grasses poked from rock and, in breaks in the shade, patches of yellow balsamroot glowed in the morning sun. We climbed and the pines grew smaller, the aspens brushier and the meadow opened up, green and awash with flowers. The sun poured down, lighting the Indian paintbrush, the balsamroot and silver skeletons of pines, twisting amid the grass.

Agnes stopped to rest on a rock beside the trail. Warm now, I took off my jacket and looked out across the valley and the snow still lying on the mountaintops, white blending to ragged white cloud. But above us, farther up the trail that wound through the meadow, the sky was friendly, unforgettable turquoise brightened by sunlight, and the mountain was softened and gentle. Wild onion tanged the air. Agnes named the plants for me: violet, speedwell, buttercup, saskatoon, kinnikinnick, saxifrage, meadow rue, foxglove, columbine, strawberry, arnica, forget-me-not, soopollalie.

Soopollalie, soopollalie.

'We make Indian ice cream from that one,' Agnes said. 'The berries whip up like soap suds. That's the name, I guess.'

A spell had been cast, or had one been broken? Here on the mountain, the sun pouring down, birdsong, wild onion and pine, among familiar flowers, things I could name and words I understood.

We had lunch on the mountaintop, looking out across the valley and the lake below. Later, settled around the fire in our little camp, Agnes told me the story she knew.

'I met your mother in Williams Lake when we were teenagers. Her mother had died — I don't know when — she was little, I guess. Her father was a cowboy. He came up from the States somewhere, didn't know a thing about ranching — that's what people said. But he was a fast learner. My dad and him worked some ranches together. He came to love that life, I guess. But he never knew quite what to do with Irene. Especially when she grew to a teenager. She was a little wild, you know. And beautiful. You know that. Her dad sent her to high school in Williams Lake and she didn't see much of him after that. I know, because holiday time everybody went home, but Irene stayed, and if there was no car at home, I stayed, too, with my old aunty. She was kind of dotty, sat in a chair in her room all day long, looking out that window at the mountains to the west. I suppose she was homesick, too, come to think of it. I made her meals, brought them to her on a tray. It was lonely sometimes.

'It was a Friday after school. Irene was walking behind me. I knew she was there. That was a holiday weekend, Thanksgiving, a long weekend. You didn't like those too much if you couldn't go home. 'You have beautiful hair,' I heard her say. I didn't turn around right away. What if she was talking to somebody else? But I knew it was me she was talking to. I was older than her — we weren't in the same grade. She ran to catch up with me. 'You have beautiful hair,' she said again. 'Do you do use something special on it?' I told her it was eggs. She looked at me with this funny look, like she thought I was kidding. Then she burst out laughing. I just stared at her, and then I started laughing too. My god, we laughed. Laughed till we cried. What was so damn funny, I don't know.

'But I invited her to my aunty's house in town. We made a big turkey dinner for just the three of us. My old aunty ate like a bird, just a bit of white meat and a tablespoon of mashed potatoes. So really, it was just for your mom and me. We made the stuffing, we made a mountain of potatoes, turnips, cranberry sauce, cauliflower with the cheese sauce. Pumpkin pie and whipped cream. Spent my aunty's money on all those groceries. We put a white tablecloth on the table and used my aunty's good dishes. We had to wash them first, they hadn't been used for so long — you know, the gravy boat, the platters, she had all of that. I don't know what possessed us, just the two of us and all that trouble, all that food. We were at it the whole day and night. We were still doing dishes after midnight. But, boy, we sure had fun. Your mom, she had that spirit in her — just up and do something, just because.'

'I remember,' I said.

'We stayed friends after that. But we didn't run with the same bunch. Irene was in with a drinking crowd. Not that she did much of that herself. But she tolerated it. I couldn't stand to be around it. Look what it did to so many of our people. Just wrecked them. Wrecked plenty of whites, too, but there's more of them, so you don't notice so much.'

The fire had burned down so I put on more wood and poked it to life again.

'Can I ask you something, Agnes?'

'Yes, you can.'

'Was my dad a drinker?'

'I didn't know your dad too well.' She stared into the fire and I thought that was the end of it. She took up a stick and rearranged the embers so the fire flared and lit up her face.

'Some men think if they don't do anything bad, you know, like beating the wife or kids or yelling at them, where's the harm? Some men just open that bottle and in they go. They disappear. Maybe that's worse. Maybe harder for the women.'

We sat in silence. The fire popped and spit bright embers on the ground and we stomped out the big ones.

'Your mother didn't finish high school. She didn't like living in town. She took off halfway through grade eleven. I heard she went to Bella Coola, got a job in a restaurant or motel or something. She was only sixteen or so. She met a man there.'

I felt my stomach tighten.

'Name of Emil Deschamps. Métis fellow from the Prairies. He had a fishing boat and she got a job fishing with him.' Agnes laughed. 'Imagine that. That's going to go one of two ways. I guess they fell in love. I guess maybe Emil was in love with her when he asked her to go out on his boat. I saw him once in Duchess Creek on his way through to Williams Lake or somewhere. Irene told me who he was. He was a handsome man, shiny black hair, curly, kind of tall, nice smile. Had a big old car. Maybe a Pontiac.'

'Was Mom with him then?'

'Not at that time, no. But she told me they took that boat out and went to the most beautiful places, islands and beaches. She told me I would love to see it. She told me we should go sometime and I thought I might, she made it sound so good. But I didn't. She didn't either, as far as I know. She was married to Patrick. She had little Jenny. That would have been 1959, because my dad died that year. Irene loved being a mother.'

I looked up at the sky and there was the riot of stars that my grandmother had missed so much.

I spoke slowly. 'She did love being a mother, didn't she?'

'She told me so, Maggie.'

'Well then I don't understand.'

'No,' said Agnes.

'I'm looking for her. I'm out here looking for her. Jenny needs her. But I don't really want to find her. I know that's a terrible thing to say. But what would it mean if we found her, alive somewhere, living her life?'

'No,' said Agnes again.

A star shot across the sky just above the trees. I breathed in quickly. Then another followed, a brightness disappearing.

'You need to go see Rita,' said Agnes.

28

Uncle Leslie was waiting for us when we got back to Agnes's house.

'I found her car,' he said.

'Come on in,' said Agnes, and we went inside where she made tea. She brought out biscuits and homemade jam and we sat at the kitchen table.

'I asked around about your mom,' Uncle Leslie began again. 'A fellow over here said, 'That lady with the red hair that drove the Chevy station wagon?' He said he knew a guy who bought the car about three years ago. Over near Dultso. So I drove over to see him. He said he bought it from a man, dark-haired guy, maybe Japanese, he said. Told him the car had been well cared-for by his wife. And it was. Still in beautiful shape. I bought it from him.'

Agnes started to laugh.

'You what?' I said.

'You in need of another car?' Agnes said.

'I bought it for you, Maggie. You're going to need a car, you and Jenny and the baby. You can't be hitchhiking around the countryside with a baby.'

'Uncle Leslie, I . . . '

'No, don't say anything. I don't want to hear it. By rights the car is yours. And I got it for a song.'

I called Jenny from Agnes's house. She sounded so much better, the worry that clutched my stomach uncoiled a little.

'She's a happy baby,' Jenny said.

'Like her name.'

'It makes it easier for me. Sister Anne got us a stroller. Ginger calls it a pram. We've been out walking. The roses are all in bloom. But I can't wait to come home.'

I swallowed. What did she mean?

'Mag?'

'Yeah, I know, Jenny. Hey, you won't believe this.' And I told her about the car.

'That old car,' Jenny said. 'I loved that car.'

Driving in that car with Mom always felt like escaping. We hit the road with no one to answer to. We were unaccountable and unaccounted for. There were strings of days when even Dad wouldn't know where to find us. Powdered milk and canned meat, no toilets, no beds or doors.

I used to pity the people we passed along the way, especially the women. I pitied Mrs. Duncan yawning behind the counter at the Nakenitses Lake store. As I paid for my Orange Crush, I could feel in her eyes that she wanted to escape, too. Sometimes I said to Mom, 'Do you think she's jealous?'

'Sure she is. Who wouldn't be?' she always said and I wonder now if she was serious. I should ask Jenny, but at the time, I believed her.

We napped under the sheltering branches of giant spruce trees and made tea from rosehips and spruce needles, and sweetened it with honey. Mom kept some one-gallon glass jugs in the car and she knew where there were springs grown round with graceful willow. We knelt in the thick moss and caught the water in the jugs as it bubbled out. We swam naked in remote lakes and creeks. We sunbathed on warm rock, like wood nymphs, Mom said. Sometimes she called Jenny and me 'the little people.'

'Who are the little people?' Jenny asked.

'They're the secret ones who live in an underground world that can only be entered at the water's edge. They like it if you leave them little gifts of candy and cloth.' Sometimes she gave us a bright kerchief to tie to a branch near the water.

'But you don't want to get too friendly with them,' she warned. 'If you do, they'll steal you away to live with them for seven years.'

And then, when we returned to the car, there was the sunbaked vinyl smell of it, the warmth, like a nest.

Uncle Leslie brought the car over to Agnes's. I wanted to be happy to see it, but any trip we made now in the station wagon would not be an escape. A net of memory was tightening around me.

FIRE

29

The yard was the same as I remembered it — chickens scattered as we drove in. The grass was as green as it would get all season. In the shade of a row of crab apple trees, Rita looked up from digging and rested her foot on her shovel. I thought her mouth fell open a little when she saw the car. I waved and Uncle Leslie cut the engine. My stomach twisted.

I got out of the car.

'I'll come back in a while,' he said, and I almost laughed. Was he scared of Rita, too?

As he pulled out of the driveway, Rita ran her hand through her hair then thrust the shovel into the earth and came towards me.

'Aunt Rita,' I said, before I thought about how it would sound.

She breathed in sharply. 'Margaret,' she said. She stood there in the sun, dumbfounded and flustered. I thought to hug her but I was waiting to see which emotion her clouded face would settle on.

'It's been a long time,' I said into the awkwardness.

She laughed drily. 'Bit of an understatement.'

'Who's your driver?' she asked, but she was looking over at the shovel sticking up in the dirt.

I had the urge to back up slowly, the way you're supposed to if you meet a bear, throw something down to distract her, run.

'He's from Williams Lake.'

'Does he have a name?'

'Leslie. Leslie George.'

'I guess I could use a break. Would you like some coffee?' she said, finally turning her head to me.

Inside, the house was the same. The woodstove that separated the kitchen and living-room areas, kindling neatly stacked in a box beside it, the same big old dining room table cluttered with mail and newspapers, where Jenny and I had done our homework, the sagging couch, the braided rug. So much had changed for Jenny and me, but Rita had settled into her life a long time ago. I envied that. Change would be an irritant to Rita now, and I was bringing it, like a cold wind funnelling up the valley.

Rita went to the kitchen cupboard and took down the coffee tin.

'Where are you staying?' she asked.

'I'm camping.'

She hesitated, just a second too long. 'Stay here.'

'I don't want to be any trouble.'

'Oh for god sakes.' She rattled the coffee pot on the stove. 'I meant for the night, not forever.'

'I know,' I said. No excuse came readily to mind and there was no turning back. The last time I'd seen Rita, we'd left in a hurry in the middle of the night. She had not forgotten.

We took our coffee mugs and sat in lawn chairs on the porch. The boards had that soft silver sheen I remembered. I had sat here watching for Mom and brushing my fingers back and forth along the grain of the weathered wood.

A clumsy silence wrapped us. Rita looked out at the road, I looked at her. Her mouth seemed tighter and the skin around her eyes and neck looser. Her fine blonde hair was shorter, but cut in the same plain way, straight bangs, the rest just grazing her shoulders. I tried to remember the way she had been, the face that had drawn Mom to her — a wide-open frankness and a crease of mischief around the eyes.

'Where are you living?' Rita asked.

'Williams Lake. But Jenny's in Vancouver.' I was about to blurt it all out, but Rita cut me off.

'Good for you.' Her voice was flat, just a semi-tone off a taunt. 'How long have you been there?'

'Let's see. I guess it's about three years.'

She looked surprised. Was it possible that she knew nothing about where we'd been since we left her? I decided not to tell her about Jenny right away. Maybe I wouldn't tell her at all.

'I've got some horses since you were here last. Would you like to see them?'

'Okay.'

'Listen Margaret,' she said. 'I can't stand the polite chit-chat. You came here for a reason, and soon enough I'll find out what it is. But for now, let's cut the crap and go see some horses.'

Ten deep breaths, I heard Dad say, to keep from panicking in a survival situation. I breathed deeply.

Rita took an apple from her jacket and handed it to me. 'Last year's,' she said. 'They'll take it.'

And so we walked down to the corral and I fed the horses and they nuzzled their soft noses against me.

When Uncle Leslie came back, I told him I'd stay a couple of days. He nodded to Rita and she nodded back. As he drove away again, she said, 'Family friend?'

'My friend,' I said, and it was only then that it dawned on me that Rita was waiting for me to tell her about Mom as much as I was waiting for her to do the same for me.

I helped Rita finish transplanting some lilacs, while the afternoon sun brightened the snow that still held high in the mountains across the lake. Then she said, 'I've got about two cords of wood to stack. When's the last time you did any hard work?'

'It's been a while.'

'Then I'm doing you a favour.'

We bent and tossed, bent and tossed and I remembered those fall days after Dad died, Rita and Mom stacking wood and singing. I had the feeling I was walking backwards through our lives and that I would knock up against something suddenly that would make sense.

Later, we fried a chicken and ate that with mashed potatoes and peas.

'Everything on the table is grown here,' Rita said.

'Good for you,' I said, in the same tone she'd used with me. And she smiled.

When the light began to fade, uneasiness seeped back into my body. The day had been nice and I was afraid of the talk that was to come. After the dishes, we went out to the porch again.

'I love this time of day,' Rita said. 'My muscles are aching, so I know I've done something. And there's the moon rising. It's so peaceful. I think about the work I did, what I'll do tomorrow. I wouldn't change it, you know.'

'I want to have a farm someday.'

'You do?'

'Yeah. With Jenny and her baby. My niece.'

'Huh,' she said. 'Jenny had a baby?'

'Yeah.'

'Huh.'

Some bats dived in the dark, and the dog lifted his head to look up then settled back into sleep. The lighted house cast a glow into the yard.

'Maggie,' Rita said. It was the first time she had called me Maggie in a long time. 'You might as well tell me why you came and get it over with.'

I considered ways to begin. But there was really only one question. 'Do you know where my mother is?'

'No. Where?' said Rita.

'No. It's a real question. I want to know if you know where she is.'

'Why on earth would I know where your mother is?'

I didn't answer. Agnes had said I should come to see Rita and I hadn't thought about asking why.

'You were best friends.'

'Were we? Oh god, Maggie, this is so

unpleasant. What's to be gained by dredging it up?'

'What's to be gained?' I felt my face burn. 'Maybe you didn't understand my question.'

'Maybe I didn't.'

We sat there, the house, the porch, the moon, the trees, and I burned and she burned and my heart beat furiously and I thought of leaving, on foot if I had to, then thought how ridiculous it would be to replay that scene.

After a few minutes, I calmed enough to think of a new tack. 'Why did you and Mom fight that night? Why did we leave?'

Rita didn't speak and when I looked over at her, she appeared to be crying. 'Christ I need a scotch,' she said. She got up, and went into the house and came back with a large glass.

'The problem is I'm going to come out looking badly in this. No way around it.' She sipped the scotch. 'Forgive me if I'm not too enthused about dragging myself through the mud.'

I almost said, 'I'm not asking about you.' People who live alone become selfish, I thought. Bea was selfish in the same way, even though she wasn't exactly alone. Maybe it was because Bea and Rita had no children. Mothers give and bend, even when they get nothing in return. At least, that's the way it's supposed to be.

'What do you remember about that night?' Rita said, after another swallow of scotch. 'What did Irene tell you?'

I was momentarily confused. Irene, the woman who was my mother.

'I was sleeping in the car that night.'

'I'd forgotten that.'

'You and Mom fought earlier in the day.'

'She'd been out all night. I hadn't had a moment's sleep. I was worried sick. I mean the gall of it just sent me. You might not want to hear this, Maggie, but it was so irresponsible. She's a mother and she's got two little girls and she's off gallivanting all night. The only reason she could get away with it was because she trusted me to cover for her. And she was just so smug, coming home in the middle of the afternoon with her clothes all wrinkled. I could smell the stink of that man on her.'

I felt like I'd been punched. 'That can't be right.'

'Damn right. It wasn't right.'

'Who was he?'

Rita sipped her scotch and stared out at the night. The silence yawned. A bird called in the woods, and another answered.

'Who was the man?'

'She was pretending, that's what she was doing. And she was cowardly. I couldn't forgive her.'

'Rita, who was the man?'

She didn't answer.

I got up from my chair and went inside. In the bathroom I splashed cold water on my face. Rita's anger had smouldered all this time and I was poking it back to life. Whoever the man was, he was getting Mom's attention, and Rita wasn't.

I settled back into my chair. The bottle of scotch was now sitting beside Rita's lawn chair.

'I loved her,' she said.

'What?'

'You heard me.'

'You mean, like . . . '

'Yes like that.'

'I . . . '

'Maybe you've never heard of such a thing. Well, it's more common than you think. I'm just a normal woman who loved a woman, who just happens to be your mother.'

I couldn't have said anything if I'd tried.

'I told her that night. That's why she ran. But she knew long before that. She just pretended she didn't. It was more convenient.'

I didn't know what to say. My head was buzzing like the bugs crowding around the porch light. Rita sat there sullenly nursing her scotch. She was still angry, after all this time.

'But did you see her again?' I finally asked.

'She sent me a letter. A fucking letter. Not even a page long. I opened it, hoping maybe she had come to her senses. She would apologize. But no, it was excuses, 'if I understood et cetera, et cetera.' Why bother? Why bother to write someone that kind of letter? Why bother to read it? Waste of paper. Today, when you drove into the yard, I thought for a minute that it was her, at last. Pathetic.'

She was drunk now and I supposed it would all come out, all the bile. Maybe it would be good for her.

'I'm going to tell you something you don't seem to know,' I said.

'All right.'

I had scared her a little. I could hear it in her voice.

'The last time we saw Mom was the day after we left here.'

'What do you mean?'

'That night you fought. We drove away. We went to Williams Lake and she left us there.'

'With your father's friends.'

'That's right. The Edwards. We haven't seen her since. She sent some letters, some money, but then even that stopped. For all I know she's dead.'

Rita seemed suddenly sober. She shook her head. 'That's not possible.' She stared at me as if I'd take it back. When I said nothing, she got up and lurched inside. I could hear her through the screen door, in the washroom, vomiting.

Minutes passed. I began to feel a chill in the night air.

I went inside and put the kettle on. Muffled noises came from the bathroom. In the cupboard I found a box of tea. I warmed the pot and dropped in the bags. When she still didn't come out, I went to the door and knocked. 'Are you okay?' I said. 'I'm making tea.'

'Thanks,' I heard. I went to get the kettle. Several more minutes passed before she came out.

She lowered herself into a chair at the table and I put the tea in front of her. She inhaled the steam, her hands wrapped around the mug. I sipped mine and could think of nothing to say.

'Maggie,' she finally began. 'I didn't know.'

'But you know more than you're saying.'

'Yes, you're right. I do.'

It was my turn to be scared.

Her hands shook as she lifted the mug to sip the tea. 'She came to see me one more time. It was January. I'd got the letter in October and then she showed up one day in January. It was stinking cold. Deep snow. The roads were in no shape. I hadn't even cleared my driveway. She was driving a pickup truck. She didn't have the station wagon any more. She said she'd sold it. The truck wasn't that good, that's why I remember. I was worried about her driving around the freezing countryside in that hunk of junk. The battery was for shit. I gave her jumper cables. Well anyway,' Rita waved her hand. 'She was pregnant, Maggie.'

Something happened next, but how can I tell it? Something, nothing, I don't remember. I believe I did nothing. I believe I sat. Some storm raged inside me, lightning, treetops exploding in flame. The cage of my body somehow contained it.

'She asked me to take in you girls,' said Rita. 'She said it would be temporary, but she'd left you too long at the Edwards. She didn't know them well and she'd never meant it to be that long. She offered to pay me. I said no. Or wait. Let me think now for a minute. What I said was, 'Am I just your pal who helps you out whenever you have an emergency? Is that all I'm good for?' And she said, 'I don't know why I imagined you would help me. You're a selfish woman. A selfish, lonely, bitter woman and that's what you'll always be.' If I'm remembering right.'

'But why did she have to leave us?' My voice was someone else's. It hovered high above my body and drilled and drilled like a woodpecker and I had the strangest feeling, my body a shaking whirling blizzard, and I thought of Jenny — that maybe that was what it was like for her now.

Rita said, 'His name was Emil. She said he needed her.'

'What about us? We needed her,' I said. It croaked out of me like the squawk of broken bird.

I found myself out on the Nakenitses Lake Road, howling. It was getting light in the east. I was suddenly just there on the road, walking hard and howling. I don't know how I got there but I had covered quite a bit of ground. I saw headlights coming towards me. A woman picked me up, not Rita. She had a blanket and she wrapped me and she spoke softly. She was kind. I don't know who she was. Still don't. She took me back to Rita's and Rita thanked her. Rita put me in her own bed. She gave me hot milk and she sat with me while I drank it. Then she turned off the light and left me.

30

What I couldn't get over when I listened to the story Rita told me the next day, what I can't get over still, is that she would know this at all, and we wouldn't. How could a stranger come into our mother's life and, after just a few months, know more about her than her own children? I had this image of Mom as a lake, with Jenny and me bobbing around on her surface, never dreaming, never even wondering about the green depths beneath us.

Rita had brought me a cup of tea when I woke up and said, 'Breakfast is on the table.' We ate in silence. When we were done, she said, 'After you're cleaned up, come on outside.'

I could hear the ring of the axe as I stepped onto the porch. She was splitting wood. I joined her at the woodpile and she handed me a pair of gloves, then looked across the meadow at the mountains and said, 'It's beautiful, isn't it? I often think how lucky I am to have this piece of land, and when I wake up in the morning the most complicated thing I have to do is split up a pile a wood. Did you know I used to live in the city? I was a teacher.'

'You?' I said.

'You're shocked, I see.' She drove the axe into the chopping block and took off her gloves. 'Well, I don't blame you. Obviously, I'm not doing it anymore. But yes, I went to Teachers'

304

College in Saskatchewan. Then I taught up north for a year and I hated every minute of it. So I applied for another teaching job in Vancouver and I got it. It was such a change from northern Saskatchewan, and at first I liked it. I went out to plays and movies and I spent a lot of time at the library.

'But then I started to miss the north. I read books about it. I read this one book called *Driftwood Valley*. I'll lend it to you if you want. It's about a woman and her husband who go into the wilderness in British Columbia. Just north of here. And they build a cabin and live there. I decided I wanted to do that. Without the husband. I could see my life, ten years, twenty years of it day after day and only the summers to do what I wanted. I realized I didn't really like kids. It just infuriated me how little sense they made. No offence. But you're not really a kid anymore. I wanted to get away. I wanted to be left alone.'

'Why did you become a teacher in the first place?' I asked.

'Survival. I had to survive. It was that or get married and there was no way I was going to do that.' She put her gloves back on. 'I found this place for sale. It came with the mail delivery job. It seemed made for me. Come on Maggie, help me stack this pile. I've had the night to sleep on it and I've decided to tell you everything I know. You and Jenny have been fending for yourselves all this time — you're old enough to know.'

We worked through the morning, as the sun beat down on us, growing hotter as it rose

305

overhead. Dust and bark chips clung to the glaze of sweat on our arms. I tried to focus on stacking, fitting each log neatly into the pile, and not on the image I kept getting of Mom sitting in a cabin somewhere feeding lunch to a baby, a baby who would be about three years old.

Then I latched on instead to what Rita had said about the crappy old truck with the bad battery. Maybe she had had an accident. Maybe she'd gone off the road, been buried in snow and never found. Or maybe the truck had stalled out somewhere in the middle of nowhere. She'd been driving to us, after she left Rita, and when she couldn't get the truck going, she'd broken the golden rule of survival: leaving the shelter of the truck and trying to walk out.

I stopped to drink the mug of water Rita brought. The more I thought about it, the more sense it made. I wanted to tell Rita to forget about telling me what she knew. I wanted to call Uncle Leslie and get the hell out of there, go back to Jenny and tell her a story that would protect her, instead of destroying her.

★　★　★

'I know we must seem old to you,' Rita said. We were eating our lunch in the shade on the porch. Rita had poured herself a glass of berry wine. 'I'm a bit older, but your Mom is only, what, thirty-two?'

'If she's still alive,' I said.

'What do you mean?'

'She could be dead. For all we know.'

306

'Don't even think it, Maggie. Don't think the worst.'

I wanted to say, 'That's not the worst.' But I didn't.

'My point is, when Irene got pregnant with Jenny she was sixteen.'

'Jenny is sixteen.'

'That's right and you see how young she is, and probably scared.'

'She's in the hospital.'

'With the baby?'

'She had the baby a month ago.'

'So why is she still in the hospital? Don't play guessing games with me, Maggie. I'm trying my best.'

I told Rita what had happened to Jenny and after she heard it, she said, 'So. It's even more important that I tell you.'

She refilled her glass. 'You need to know about Emil. I'm not going to hide anything from you, but you'll have to be patient, Maggie. I'm going to tell it in my own time, the way I remember her telling me. She told me once that she wanted to tell you girls someday, when you were old enough. I think that ship has sailed.' This is what Rita told me.

*　*　*

Irene had met Emil in Bella Coola. After she quit school in Williams Lake, she headed west until she couldn't go any farther. She got a job in a café. She didn't know anyone. The cloud in Bella Coola was depressing, hanging low like smoke in

307

the valley if there was no wind. To Irene, coming from the dry sunny plateau, it seemed like there was always something coming from the sky, rain or snow or just the feeling of rain sometimes. Sometimes the east wind howled down there like they'd all be swept out to sea. She was probably lonely.

Emil came in for lunch every day. He was from the Prairies and must not have known very many people himself. He always came in alone. He always had the same thing, the homemade soup and a grilled cheese sandwich and a pot of tea. They had this routine, where she'd say *the usual?* And he'd say *the usual*. It was a little game they played.

Emil talked to her, but his talk was a bit odd, it didn't seem ordinary and yet in some ways, it was dead ordinary. He'd comment on what she was wearing, even when she rarely wore anything other than flannel shirts and jeans. He'd comment on the folds of the shirt, for instance, the way the fabric fell softly from her shoulders, maybe the pattern of the plaid. He'd notice the way the cheese melted in his sandwich and spilled over the bread. When she brought him his order he'd point that out. And he'd say, *This is the best sandwich ever. I think you are the queen of grilled cheese sandwiches.* The queen of grilled cheese sandwiches, of all things. But she was sixteen and his oddness appealed to her. That and the fact that he was so interested in everything she did.

He told her about the places he went in his boat, the *Elsa*. A white-shell beach with old totem poles hiding in the trees. You could pick clams and mussels and feed yourself on salmonberries and trout. *When the tide is out, the table is set*, that was the expression he used. Old Indian villages, no one there in the summer, just the ravens and bears and once in a while a cougar. That appealed to her.

Of course when Irene told Rita the stories, Rita thought Emil was long gone out of the picture. She'd been out on a boat around there once, and had often thought of going back. But it had scared her a bit, the ocean. She didn't think she was the coastal type.

Irene didn't know anything about boats or the ocean either. She didn't know a clam from a mussel.

What she liked about Emil was that he was kind. She talked about his eyes. How soft and kind they were, his long eyelashes. He was older than her by about ten years, in his mid-twenties. At first, she didn't think of him romantically. But she liked his stories and the intensity of him. He wasn't like anyone she'd ever met. *Come and visit me on the Elsa*, Emil said one day. And one day she went.

They walked down to the dock where he was moored. He had restored the boat himself. It struck her that it looked fresh, like it hadn't been out on the water much, painted white with a fresh blue stripe and *Elsa* lettered on the hull. He kept herbs in clay pots on the deck and she noticed that. She noticed his clothes drying on a line. Maybe she fell in love with the boat first.

Emil told her he had first seen the boat for sale

at the dock in Bella Coola — it was a thirty-five-foot gillnetter, in need of repair. Someone had brought it up from Steveston and then run out of money. But Emil's father was a carpenter and he'd worked at that himself for a few years. He liked that kind of work. So he'd bought it and done the repairs, then added his own touches. He'd built a cabin behind the wheelhouse. He'd made a narrow table and shelves and polished the wood to a gleam. Everything had a place. There was a little oil stove and a row of four green mugs hanging on hooks. She fixated on the mugs for some reason. They were translucent green, the colour of seawater, and every time she used one she thought how ordinary and beautiful they were. She loved the compact order of that little boat, and she imagined how it would be, bobbing in the ocean at night, snug in the cabin, drinking tea from a sea-green mug.

The cabin smelled of turpentine. He was an artist. On the shelves, held in place by a thick strip of elastic, were tubes of oil paints, brushes, and palette knives. His art was fastened to every available space. He painted recognizable things like cedar trees, totem poles, birds, but some were just triangles and squares of light and shadow.

How did you end up here? she asked him that first day. He said it was a long story, asked her how much time she had. *I better make tea*, he said and that was the start. She was giddy with the attention he showed her, tucked away in the cabin of his boat with the rain pecking the windows and a man making tea for her. What had she known up until then? Cowboys her age who wanted to rope her like one of their calves and grab her tits.

★ ★ ★

I could see what Rita was doing. She was trying to build my sympathy for Mom for something else that was coming, and that worried me. She had relaxed into the story; she was enjoying it. We were facing west, and she kept raising her eyes and gazing out towards the mountains, as if she was watching it unfold over there. I thought about lying side-by-side with Vern in our tree fort and I missed him intensely.

★ ★ ★

Irene said that Emil was gentle and slow in all his movements. He had long slender legs and arms, long brown fingers. He was graceful, always touching things, stroking them. He liked textures, noticed them in a way most people don't. She figured that was the artist in him. He made tea, not from teabags, but with leaves measured from a tin, poured the water over it, gave it a stir, timed it steeping. Sugar, milk from a can. He peeled an orange and put the segments on a plate. It became one of the things she loved, watching him make tea for her.

He gave her a pillow and helped her tuck it behind her back. She could sense his desire, but

311

said she ignored it. She was flattered by his attention.

Emil told her he had inherited money from his aunt, lots of it, not that there was much left by the time she met him. He'd gone to New York, to art galleries, art shows, talks, coffee houses. He'd travelled, gone to Europe to see the masters. He was admitted to art school in Toronto on the strength of his work.

Art school changed his life. When he returned to the Prairies, the landscape felt claustrophobic. He had the feeling all that sky was closing in on him. He began to have what he called visions. Weird visions, like dreams, but they happened when he was awake — intense and very real. He had a recurring one he told Irene about. Birds of prey were following him, hawks and falcons and eagles. He saw them everywhere, perched on fences, store roofs, signposts, in the tree outside his bedroom window. He'd done a series of drawings of them and he showed her. Two whole sketchbooks full.

He had another aunt who lived in Bella Coola and he came out to visit her, to get away from the Prairies and the visions.

That's when he decided to buy the boat.

Irene's visits to his boat became a regular routine and, eventually, he asked her to go out on the boat with him. He said he wanted to fish and he needed a partner. This was a pretence and they both knew it. But the idea of bobbing in the ocean with Emil looking after her was too appealing to resist. Irene had been on her own for quite a while already by then. Her dad had

312

left her to go to school in Williams Lake while he was out cowboying around the countryside. He seemed to think she could take care of herself. Which was probably true. He didn't even know she'd gone to Bella Coola and it was a long time after that when she found out he'd died of a heart attack way out in the woods, looking for horses.

Anyway, one day in the café, Irene was serving a group of men, and after Emil left, they started to talk about him. They didn't seem to care if she overheard, in fact she thought maybe their talk was partly for her benefit:

He knows fuck-all about fishing.

He's from the Prairies. He knows prairie chickens and deer.

His boat looks good.

Sure it does, he's a carpenter. Not a fisherman.

I don't think he cares much if he catches anything or not.

He'll get himself drowned.

Long as he doesn't take anyone down with him.

It should have made her uneasy, but being sixteen going on seventeen, she just thought they didn't understand Emil. He wasn't just looking for fish; he was looking for experiences. He was an artist.

They went out the first time in June. They didn't take the nets and gear. Emil said he wanted Irene to get used to the *Elsa*, learn how to use the tide charts, all of that.

The cliffs rise straight up from the water out

313

there and they stretch down into the water just as far, like there are two worlds, and you're in between them. Irene had to surrender to the mountains and the bald eagles and the wind, and to Emil. That started to dawn on her as she watched him steering the *Elsa* — she was in his hands.

Everything about this world was unfamiliar to her. The words *galley* and *deck* and *dinghy* and *bunk*. Emil on the bunk in his blue jeans and bare feet, eating a plate of fish that they'd caught with handlines off the boat, and watching her. It was so intimate, to see his feet. She had never seen his bare feet. And the way the boat was called 'she.' The engine was called *Vivian*. Emil would say, *I better tend to Vivian*. And he'd go down below and start her up and then chuff, chuff, chuff, off they went up the inlets. Irene found out later that Vivian was the engine make, and not a name he'd made up.

A couple of days out, Emil came up behind her on the deck, pulled her close and kissed her neck. She had a moment of fear, but it burned off in the heat of his touch.

★　★　★

Rita stopped.

'What?' I said. I almost shouted it.

'I need a little break.'

'Now?'

'I'm going to get some crackers. The wine's going right to my head.'

I had been thinking that Mom then had not

314

been much older than I was now, and that Vern was gentle like Emil. And that Rita's voice had grown tender as she talked and I supposed she missed Mom, missed staying up through the night with her, talking and giggling over the things they'd done when they were younger.

When she came back outside, carrying a few crackers, she said, 'Let's walk. I can't sit the way I used to. I must be getting old.'

'You're not old.'

'No. But telling this story makes me feel ancient.'

So we headed across the meadow. The sun wasn't as intense now, and the heat felt comfortable on my shoulders. Rita kept her head down, as if she was considering where to start again. We wound through a few scrub trees then into deeper shade.

'Let's just say Emil was a kind and gentle lover, too,' she finally began again. 'I give the guy credit. He had studied it. Read books about it.'

'There are books?'

'Sure. And he was very patient. They didn't even make love that first day when he kissed her. Or the next. It was a few days later, I don't know how many. I guess he wanted her to want it as much as he did.'

* * *

So he'd do things like take her clothes off, slowly, piece by piece, but stay fully dressed himself. And then maybe he'd trace her body with his fingers. He'd take a smooth stone and

315

place it at the hollow of her throat, find the places of her pulse with it and let her feel how warm the stone would get. He made sure she was comfortable on the bunk and he did charcoal drawings of her. She grew to love his eyes on her. He was systematic about winning her over. And she was the one finally who knocked him down on the bunk one day and made him take his pants off.

Life on the *Elsa* was sweet. They put in at little bays and took the dinghy ashore to explore. They swam in warm tidal pools at night with trails of shining phosphorescence dripping from their bodies. Every few days they looked for a mooring where they could find fresh water to wash off the salt that dusted their skin and caked their hair. Irene had had no idea how salty the ocean really was.

They had their daily domestic tasks, crab traps to drop over the side, dishwater to heat on the Coleman stove on deck. But Emil wouldn't let Irene play the housewife. He snatched a shirt from her hand when she went to wash it one day. *Don't do that*, he said. *Why?* she asked. *That's not what you are to me.*

★   ★   ★

'I like him for that,' Rita said.

I did, too. I could see myself in Mom's place. Nothing to worry about and all the time in the world.

★   ★   ★

One morning, Emil ran them into a little white shell beach. They anchored the *Elsa* in deep water, and took the dinghy in. The terrain can be rough going as soon as you try to go inland. It's rainforest, lush as it gets, like a tropical jungle. They bushwhacked through thickets of wild roses and devil's club as tall as Irene, leaves as big as her head, and spiky stems. The only sound, other than the ocean, was the ravens heckling them. Before they saw it, she could hear the rumble of a waterfall, then feel the coolness.

She said it was like an Eden, the water tumbling straight down from the mountains and at the bottom, a series of pools. She couldn't wait to strip off her salt-stiff clothes. She and Emil stood naked under the cascade of water. It was very cold but it washed the salt away. Afterwards they lay on the warm rocks and Emil fell asleep in the sun.

When he woke, he said, *Do you see that?*

He pointed through the trees at a pole with a bird carved into it, his hooked beak overlooking the forest and beach beyond. Irene noticed boxes in the spruce trees that she hadn't seen until she looked carefully. They were tied with strips of cedar, and some had come loose and were flapping in the breeze.

What is it? she asked him.

They're graves. The dead are tied into trees with their possessions. If you walk through there, you can find copper bracelets, necklaces, maybe some skulls.

She wouldn't touch any of it.

He said, No. *You shouldn't take what belongs to the dead. The ravens are watching.*

Seems like you've been here before, she said.

I like it here. It's peaceful.

It was peaceful. Still beyond still. Even the ravens had left them.

Emil suddenly jumped up, said *I'll be back in a while.* Before Irene could ask any questions, he was gone.

She wasn't worried. She lay in the sun daydreaming, listening to the water spill over the rocks. She slept a little. When she woke up, she passed the time as she waited for Emil by looking for nice stones in the stream.

She kept looking over to the beaked pole and the graves like clusters of nests in the trees. She wanted to go search for bracelets in the grass, not to take them, but just to see proof that someone had been there once, led a life from start to finish there. But she wouldn't go alone.

Two ravens came back and talked to her, back and forth, know-it-all remarks, like ravens do. *All alone? All alone. Where did he go? He took off. He took off.* They laughed about it, she swore they did.

The afternoon wore on and still Emil didn't come back. She began to get annoyed. The ravens cackled: *Scared? Scared?* Then she heard movement in the brush, branches cracking, and she saw a large shape slip among the trees. Emil had warned her about bears, but this moved too swiftly and smoothly to be a bear.

She called out. *Emil! I don't like your jokes.* She thought he was playing a game with her.

But the shape moved past her and the sound trailed off.

She shouted his name over and over, scared now, and the ravens seemed to mock her openly. Finally, in the distance she heard, *I'm coming!* Then she felt the pounding of his feet approaching.

He appeared through the trees, two lovely trout hanging from his hand.

Of course she was so relieved she cried.

And he said, all innocence, *Was I gone too long?* Like he had no idea.

Let's just go, she said.

I want to make a fire on the beach to roast the trout.

She said no. She wanted to go back to the boat.

It was the first time he'd seen her angry and Emil, apparently, didn't like anger. He never got angry himself, didn't have it in him. When he saw it in her, he turned away, like he was embarrassed for her.

They rowed back to the *Elsa* and Emil cleaned the fish and fried it up. But Irene was uneasy. It was partly the place. From a distance, the totem pole looked menacing. The beak seemed like a warning. Later, when they'd eaten the trout, Emil presented Irene with a bowl of red huckleberries. And then it was hard to stay mad at him. She told him she'd been scared and she told him about the shape she'd seen in the trees.

When he didn't seem surprised, she left it alone. It was night by then. The tide was out, and a stink rose up from the mud flats and it drifted over to the boat. She was glad not to be on shore. The *Elsa* seemed like a haven of safety against the dark forest and mountains rising up out there. She missed her mother, even though Emil was there, sitting on the deck, smoking, leaning against the cabin window. It occurred to her how little she knew about him and how utterly she depended on him out there.'

★   ★   ★

Rita stopped talking for a minute as she scrambled up the side of a large boulder and patted it. 'Come and join me. I love sitting here. This time of day, the sun slants through here and warms it up.'

I climbed up and sat beside her.

'I once found a crab claw on top of this rock. Strange, eh? It was just the end part. I kept it. I've always meant to ask someone how a crab claw could end up on a rock in the interior of BC, a couple hundred miles from the ocean.'

'A bird?'

'That's probably it.'

★   ★   ★

The way Irene described Emil, he sounded soft. Like the stroke of an eyelash. He would never mean any harm. But after the trip to the waterfall, she started to sense that there was something dark that had power over him. It came in spells, and when it came, it took him away from her.

If the water turned rough, they'd have to wait it out somewhere. One day, they'd anchored in a sheltered bight out of the worst of the weather, but the cliffs were too steep to allow them to go ashore. A couple of days passed and they ran out of fresh water. They didn't even have enough to make their morning coffee. So they decided to make a run for a nearby bay they saw on the charts.

After some hard going, they ran in and dropped anchor at another white shell beach. It was an Indian village — she could tell by the thick white midden, discarded shells of generations of families living in the same place. There wasn't much left of the village itself, just a leaning totem pole and the remains of some houses near the shore. But at the edge of the beach, almost overgrown by salmonberry bushes and stinging nettle, they saw a house that was still standing. They took their water jugs and coffeepot and two crabs they had caught and rowed over.

They had to beat down the nettles with their oars to get to the door that was watched over by a carved post of a big-beaked bird with outstretched wings. Inside, the house was empty. A low bench ran around the room. A few cooking pots hung on the walls. There was an opening along the roof rafters for smoke to escape and a stone fireplace in the middle of the floor. No sign of anyone, but Irene felt uneasy. She felt a presence, like they were being watched. It could have been that the village wasn't abandoned, just not being used right then. Maybe it was a winter village and the people were out fishing for the summer.

Still, it was good to be on dry land and out of the rain. They got some water from a stream coming off the mountain and Emil went looking for wood dry enough to make a fire. He was gone a long time and she started to worry. But finally he came back and they built the fire and made coffee and cooked the crabs.

They fell asleep on the floor near the fire. When Irene woke up, the fire was out and Emil was gone. She could see pale light through the roof hole and she could hear the surf rushing into the beach. She had been dreaming about drums and a dancer wearing a mask that opened up to reveal another mask inside it. Once she was awake, she could still hear the drumming. She went to the door and looked out. No sign of Emil. But the dinghy had been carried out into the water and was slamming up against the rocks, making a knocking sound. She had to wade out and tow it back up the beach.

Mist hung in the trees. It burned off through the morning while Irene sat on the beach and waited for Emil. She didn't have matches, Emil had them, so she couldn't even make coffee. As the tide went out, she realized they had miscalculated and brought the *Elsa* in too close to shore. She was caught in a little pool, while around her the bay emptied out. There was nothing Irene could do about it, so she dug clams for lunch with a spoon.

You get a real sense of time passing when you're sitting on a beach waiting. The weather had calmed. The *Elsa* sat squat and helpless and behind her nothing moved out on the ocean. After a while, Irene got up and fought her way through the nettles to the edge of the forest to have a look, but it was so thick with brambles she didn't go any further. She slept a little and when she woke it was late afternoon and the tide had begun to slop back in.

She couldn't stand the sense of waiting around, being helpless. She wanted Emil to come back and find her, a vision of self-sufficiency, cooking clams on the beach. Barely noticed he was gone.

When the tide was full, she thought she should row out to the *Elsa* and try to move her to deeper water. She had never started the engine herself. It was a one-cylinder gas engine with a flywheel that had to be cranked. It could be tricky if you weren't used to it.

She took the coffeepot full of water, rowed back and climbed aboard. She was burning to do this right. First she had to turn on the magneto switch. Then, open the petcock and figure out where the cycle of the engine was: on intake or compression. You had to turn it until it was on intake; you'd hear the suction noise. Then you poured a little gas into the petcock. Stick the starting bar in the flywheel, give it a crank. The first time she did it, she forgot to close the petcock and gas blew all over the place. So she had to clean it up and try it all over again. She cranked and cranked, but she couldn't get Vivian to spark for her.

She felt helpless, bobbing in the chop, miles

from anywhere with no sign of Emil and a boat she couldn't operate. Rock cliffs on one side, a wall of forest in front of her and a rough sea out beyond the shelter of the bay. She wouldn't let herself panic. She started the Coleman stove that they used on the deck when the weather was nice, and she boiled her clams and made coffee. But she vowed to pay more attention to what Emil was doing to the engine.

* * *

Rita swallowed and had a hard time getting the next words out. 'She had learned something and she told me she never forgot it. She said she tried to teach you girls, too.'

She seemed to be struggling to keep from crying.

'What was it?' I asked.

'She wouldn't ever put herself in someone else's hands like that again.' Tears ran down the side of Rita's nose and she brushed them away. 'You should never do that. End up at someone else's mercy. She knows it. I know it. You have to look out for your own safety.' She breathed deeply. 'I think you probably understand this, Maggie. You, me, Irene, we're all a bit like that. We protect ourselves. You even more than your mother. You can take that as a compliment. But it makes us difficult to live with. Irene decided that from then on, whenever they went to shore, she'd make sure she had everything she needed — matches, a knife, and food.'

It grew dark and the tide went out again. She heard something big splashing around out near the cliffs. An owl called. You know what the owl call is supposed to mean, right? It's just silly superstition, but try to convince yourself of that when you're grounded in a tide pool in the dark, with just a mast light and an oil lantern.

The owl call made her think suddenly that she should be out there looking for him. He must be cold and hungry. Maybe she should have gone looking hours before. It hadn't even occurred to her.

She couldn't see anything on the beach now. She considered slopping through the shallow water in her rubber boots to the shore. She could take the big flashlight and try to signal him. But her anger returned and instead she went below deck and crawled into the bunk. She didn't expect to sleep, but when she next opened her eyes, an orange light was flickering on the porthole.

When she went up on the deck, she saw a bonfire burning on the beach. She climbed down the ladder and into the dinghy. She couldn't call out to him. She didn't know what to say or what she would find. The tide was coming in and light was starting to show over the trees. It was near dawn. When she pulled the dinghy onto the beach, he didn't get up from where he sat by the fire. He looked strange and distant. Her first thought was that he was mad at her. Maybe she really didn't understand how things worked out there. There was something she was supposed to have done, and she missed it and now he would take her back to Bella Coola and drop her off.

She said his name. She asked him if he was all right.

He didn't answer. A shiver ran through her. She really didn't know much about him at all, and she was out there in her rubber boots and pyjamas with only a flannel jacket over top.

Let's go, she said. *Put out the fire. Let's go back to the boat.*

He looked behind him at the woods as if he had been followed.

What is it? she said. Finally, he stood up and began to walk to the dinghy. She kicked some sand into the fire and hopped into the dinghy and, since he was making no effort to move, she took the oars and rowed them back.

He was covered in bleeding scratches and deeper cuts. Leaves and bits of bark and twigs were tangled in his thick curls and his shirt was ripped to shreds. When she saw the state he was in, she forgot her anger and her fear. She helped him take his shirt off and she boiled water and tried to wash his cuts. But he turned away from her. He wouldn't let her pull out the thorns and nettles that had made burning rashes on his skin. So she made him tea and a can of beans. He ate without looking at her.

What happened? she kept asking. He finished the food and lay down, turned his back to her and fell asleep.

★　★　★

326

'It's getting chilly. Let's go back.'

'What?' I said.

'Back to the house. The sun's gone,' Rita said.

'Oh, I thought Irene said that.'

We jumped down off the boulder and headed back through the woods to Rita's.

'I have some deer sausage,' she said. 'We can have that with potatoes.'

We ate on the porch, watching the light disappear behind the snow-topped mountains. We didn't talk much; I was still out on Emil's boat, waiting to hear what had happened to him. I only wanted things to turn out well if I could think of this Irene as someone who was not my mother. I wanted everything to be okay with Emil; I didn't want him to drop her off in Bella Coola. They might be out there still, roasting fish on the beach and chugging into civilization only to grub up and get gas.

It seemed to me that Rita could do that, separate the Irene she knew from this girl she was telling me about. She wasn't angry as she told the story. There was no jealousy or bitterness in her voice.

'It took several days before Emil was anything close to his old self,' Rita began again.

★   ★   ★

It was as if he'd been under a spell, and one morning it lifted. They were drinking their tea in the silence that Irene had stopped trying to fight when he said, *I'm sorry. I know I had no business leaving you like that.*

327

Then he told her in a rush all the things he loved about her: the noise she made when she sipped her tea, her strong hands, the way she frowned when she was concentrating. He took her hands and kissed her neck and repeated that he was sorry, he didn't know what he had been thinking. She was the best thing that had ever happened to him. He promised to do better. And Irene was relieved. He was the Emil she loved again. She assumed it had been an aberration and she forgave him.

They ran into Namu for gas and grub. That night was behind them. Nothing had happened. They slipped down the ladder to swim in the sea. They gathered sea urchins and dug clams, tried drying seaweed and sprinkling it on their eggs in the morning. Emil's cuts healed. They made love with the hatch open and the stars shining on them.

But in the evenings, he told her bits and pieces of the most fantastic story.

You should know, he said. *I don't want to scare you, but you may have noticed the birds following us. They've been following me since Winnipeg.*

That's what he said.

Just when I think I've escaped them, they come back. I'm not saying they're the same birds.

Irene had noticed the birds, too. Had they been there all along? And he'd say, *There are things we don't understand, things that happen that we can't explain rationally.* Irene knew that to be true. He'd say, *You don't think I'm crazy,*

328

do you? She said no. She began to watch the cormorants that hung around the *Elsa* and the bald eagles that gazed down on them from the branches of spruce trees. But she also noticed that Emil's eyes had a bright restless sheen she hadn't seen before.

The other morning in the old village house, he said one evening, *I heard them. They were outside, but I knew it wouldn't be long before they figured out how to get in. I waited until they were in the trees by the beach and I ducked out of the house and ran for it. That's how I got all cut up. It wasn't that I was deserting you.* It was important to him that she understood that. *It's me they're looking for.*

He told her he managed to evade them for a while. But when he had to stop and catch his breath, he heard them in the tops of the cedars, their wings beating the air. They were screaming down at him.

He warned her that she'd find it a little hard to believe what happened next. He saw a huge feather lying on a rock. It wasn't an eagle feather, or a hawk's; it was about two feet long. He thought it might be an offering of some kind, or maybe some kind of protection. So he picked it up.

I would never trust anyone else with this story. I'm not making this up.

And Irene saw that he believed every word of what he told her.

He lowered his voice to a whisper. *When I picked up the feather, I became a bird. A giant one, about the size of a human. I lifted on these* huge wings and I rose above the tops of the cedars and I just kept going. I broke through the low cloud. The sun was shining up there, but the world beneath had disappeared, the ocean, the forest, everything was gone. Then I saw mountains, snow-topped, almost silver and I found myself landing at the foot of one, in front of a large black bird who was surrounded by other, smaller birds. How did you get here? he asked. His voice was weird, like a crackly radio.

I picked up a feather, I said.

You're lying.

I'm not.

Where is it then? Give it to me.

I don't know where it went. I must have dropped it.

You're lying.

I don't know what happened to it.

That's what you always say, isn't it?

No.

It's never your fault, is it?

Then Emil told Irene there was something he had never told her, never told anyone at all. He needed to tell her. The bird knew it. He didn't know how, but he knew.

Irene wasn't afraid of what he would say. All she wanted then was to be worthy of whatever secret he told her.

The bird said, I know all about your brother and what you said and what you didn't. You told yourself it wasn't really lying if you didn't tell everything. Humans don't know how to lie. You could learn a lot from us birds. We don't feel guilty. You start to feel so guilty, you erase all *the benefit you got from lying in the first place.*

The bird offered Emil a deal. He'd keep Emil's secret if Emil kept his. The bird's secret was that place. He called it his kingdom. He said Emil had to find the feather he'd dropped and bury it. Not just shallowly either. He wanted it at least three feet underground. Emil said he would do it. Next thing he knew he was lying on the forest floor again. He looked for the feather. He must have looked for hours, until it was too dark to see. Then he came back to the beach and lit the fire.

So you never found it? Irene asked.

Emil said no. But he thought maybe it was a trick. Maybe the bird already had the feather. He probably got a good laugh at his expense.

Irene said that in spite of how crazy the story sounded, she believed him. Or she didn't believe exactly what he had said, but she believed the essence of what he had told her, that he had had some strange encounter. And she was nervous about the fact that he hadn't found the feather like the bird asked. She thought this would haunt Emil. She asked him if he thought they should go back and look for it.

He said no. He thought it was best to stay away from there.

★   ★   ★

'What about the brother?' I asked.

★   ★   ★

331

Irene didn't push it, and for a while it seemed as if Emil had forgotten about it. One afternoon, a wind kicked up. It looked as though it might blow for days and they needed to find shelter before it really blew up. But they'd left it a bit too late, I guess.

The *Elsa* pounded into giant waves that broke over the deck. The chart showed a bay ahead, but all they could see, when they cleared a bit of window, was a choppy foaming white sea. The wind kept pushing them back and little by little the *Elsa* had edged close to the high cliffs. They had to worry about not only the cliffs, but what might be near them, under the water. Irene steered while Emil poked his head out and shouted directions.

They were being hammered by the wind, not making any headway. The cliffs were drawing closer. Emil thought they might be smartest to try and tie up to a deadhead rising straight up out of the water. He went out on deck with a pole and tried to keep the *Elsa* from smashing into the rocks. It was a terrifying couple of hours. Irene could hear things scraping the hull. Rocks or submerged trees or something else, she didn't know. Water crashed over the *Elsa* and she dipped and plunged like she might go down for good. Finally, out of the storm, a bigger fishing boat came alongside. They tossed them a rope and towed the *Elsa* in behind the shelter of a kelp bed.

The water suddenly flattened out. She said it was the strangest thing to see. Emil told her he'd heard that the Indians used to slide their dugout canoes up on top of these kelp islands when the water was too rough. They even built fires on them and rode out the storms there.

The fishermen told Emil there was a good chance they'd damaged the *Elsa*'s propeller or cracked the hull since there were mountain peaks of rock under the water where they'd been tied up. He went below to check, but could see no sign of cracks. The fishermen said they'd let someone know to check on them when the weather let up.

That night, with the waves crashing into the kelp bed and the storm lashing rain against the portholes, Emil handed Irene a photograph of a boy, about her age.

That's my brother, he said. *That picture was taken in high school. He was beautiful.*

Irene agreed. He had thick black hair like Emil's, and dark spirited eyes. His smile was a grin, all confidence.

His name was Edward and he was a year older than Emil. Everybody loved him. He was always happy, a practical joker. He had a beautiful voice, sang in the church and school choirs. Most people didn't know that he had a mean side. Emil said he may have been the only one who knew about that.

Socially, Edward was at ease in a way Emil never was. He liked people, he knew how to like them. He hated how nervous Emil was. What did he have to be nervous about? Sometimes, after they'd been somewhere together, he'd just open a valve and let all his hate pour out on Emil. Why couldn't Emil ever say the right thing? Didn't he realize he insulted people? He was embarrassed to be seen with Emil. He said that often. He told Emil he should go live like a hermit in the bush since he couldn't learn how to act properly in public. He'd rage and roar like a wildfire you couldn't stop until finally he'd start to sputter out.

Emil said that everything Edward said was more or less true so he didn't know how he could defend himself. He didn't even try.

But one day after school had ended for the year, they went out to a bush party. Everyone got drunk, Emil included. Edward didn't say anything to him that night as they were walking home and Emil was relieved. The next day they went fishing, just the two of them. They went down to a bridge over a creek near their house. They drank some beer to take the edge off the night before. But Emil knew there was something coming. There was always something coming.

His brother had this way of clearing his throat before he spoke. It was a kind of warning. And he finally heard it, the throat clearing. Edward was good at finding Emil's most vulnerable places. Some people are like that. Siblings maybe most of all.

You were an embarrassment. That much he remembered, but that was nothing new. *That girl you were chatting up thought you were an idiot. I saw her laughing it up with her girlfriends after you walked away.*

He'd heard worse before, but Emil liked the girl and that day, he'd had enough. He shoved

Edward so hard in the chest, he went down on the bridge on his back. His head hit something, hard, and he kind of bounced back up. He was surprised. Emil had never fought back.

Edward sat there rattled for a few minutes while Emil brought in his line. The day was ruined. He was going home. Edward caught up to him and said, *So you do know how to defend yourself.* His voice was a little slurred. Emil thought he'd bitten his tongue when he hit the bridge.

That night Edward didn't come down for supper. He told their mother he had a headache and wasn't feeling well. He stayed up there all night. When Emil went to bed, he thought Edward was pretending to sleep so he wouldn't have to talk to him. Edward wouldn't apologize — he never had — but something might have to change, now that Emil had stood up to him.

When he woke up the next morning, he turned over and saw Edward still sleeping. It was late and he wondered what kind of game Edward was playing. But something made him uneasy. Maybe he was too still, or maybe it was too odd, Edward sleeping in on a beautiful Sunday morning when he usually met his friends in the park for rugby. He went to Edward's bed and leaned over him to get a look at his face. His skin was the colour of ashes. He put his hand on his arm to nudge him. He was cold.

★ ★ ★

'Oh my god,' I said.

'Yeah,' said Rita. 'He called for his mother. She came running. When the doctor got there, he focused on that headache Edward had complained of. Emil didn't even know if his brother really had a headache or if it was just something he told his mother. But the doctor went from there. He asked about what Edward had been doing the day before and Emil told about the party on Friday night, told about the fishing, and the beer they'd had to drink. He just didn't tell about the way he'd shoved him so hard he'd slammed his head into the bridge.'

'Poor Emil,' I said.

The stars had come out. Rita carried our plates into the kitchen and put the kettle on to make tea. I stepped off the porch to get a better look at the sky. I could see Cassiopeia above the house. I wondered if Mom was out on the *Elsa* again with Emil, looking at these same constellations. Maybe they'd both been lost at sea. It could have been an accident. But I couldn't go from the last time Rita had seen her to an accident on the *Elsa* without a lot of time in between that I couldn't account for.

'I'm almost at the end of what I know, of what she told me,' Rita said when she came back with steaming mugs.

★　★　★

When the weather calmed, Emil went underwater to look at the propeller. Sure enough, a blade had been sheared off. They hailed a passing boat

336

and were towed into Namu.

The wharf was busy with boats coming and going. That was 1958, the year of the record salmon run. Seine boats were coming in loaded down with all this fish. People made their fortunes that year. The village stank of fish. Boats were tied to the float six deep. At night the tires that kept the boats off the dock creaked and rocked, the wind rang through the rigging, and voices carried across the water. Irene wanted to leave as soon as possible. But Emil seemed in no hurry. He struck up conversations with the fishermen and drank beer and tinkered with the boat while he waited for the propeller. He said he planned to get in on the salmon run and needed to refit the boat for it. Not wanting to feel like a prisoner to his plans, Irene went for long walks along trails in the bush, picking berries.

One day she came back to the *Elsa* after a walk and he was gone. He had left his tools on the deck, along with an opened, warm bottle of beer. She expected him back any minute. She thought he had gone to the store to pick up something for the boat. But night fell and the noise of the wharf rose and floated over to where she made her coffee on the Coleman and tried not to worry.

Days passed. In spite of her best efforts to keep busy, to pretend not to be bothered, her anxiety grew. She couldn't eat, could barely sleep, and in the mornings, she threw up.

There was a doctor at the cannery in Namu. Irene sat outside the office for two hours and watched people come and go. Finally, she made herself go in. The doctor was a white-haired man, kindly. She told him she thought she was pregnant. He asked her some questions and examined her. He said a blood test would confirm it, but he was pretty close to sure already and by the time he got the test results back, she'd already know herself.

He called her *dear*. He said *Dear, who are you living with here?*

Irene was afraid to tell him.

He said he wasn't there to judge her. He was seventy-five years old, something like that, and he'd seen it all. But he told her she was going to have to start looking after herself. She was too thin. He wanted her to put on a good twenty or thirty pounds. He told her she'd be okay to work for a few months, so she might look in at the cannery. He said, *You think about yourself and that child you're carrying. That's all you need to worry about now.*

She didn't do anything right away, but as the days turned into two weeks, she realized that Emil might never come back. Her first job was mopping the floor of the cannery. But after a couple of weeks, when they could barely keep up with the volume of fish coming in, she moved to filling tins.

Each night, she returned to the *Elsa*, made supper on the little stove and wondered when Emil would come walking back up the wharf. The weather was turning and she knew she wouldn't be able to tolerate the boat all winter long. She was dying for a hot bath. At the end of the day, her hands and feet were so cold, she had to boil hot water and soak them before she could get to sleep.

★　★　★

'Was it Jenny?' I said. 'Was she the baby?'

'Let me finish, Maggie,' Rita said. Then more softly, 'Okay? But I wonder if you can guess what happened next.'

★　★　★

Irene was making good money at the cannery. She decided to look for a decent place to live. On her next payday, she went to the general store and bought some dishes, pots, a cast iron frying pan, some towels.

She had put on a few pounds, but she wasn't showing.

There was a redheaded man working at the cannery. His name was Patrick and he was as sweet as peaches. The older Indian ladies Irene worked with liked to tease him. They called him Salmonberry. He even blushed like one, they said. He'd made friends with some of the Chinese men who worked on the cutter. One of their parents ran a Chinese restaurant in town. At lunch break one day, while they sat outside catching the sun before it disappeared for the winter, Patrick invited Irene to come with him to the restaurant that evening. She hesitated about ten seconds, maybe fifteen. Not only had she not eaten in a restaurant for several months, and

339

never in a Chinese one, she liked Patrick. When he smiled, her heart skipped a beat. Later, when the Indian ladies saw them together, they nudged each other and said, *Two salmonberries. They belong together.*

★ ★ ★

Rita stopped. We had both heard an owl calling, very close by.

I had been trying not to let Rita see I was crying. I didn't want her to soften it for me. I wanted to know. But my breath had caught and I had to wipe the string of snot hanging from my nose.

'I often hear owls here,' she said.

'I know.'

'It's just a superstition.'

'I know.'

'I'll get you something for that runny nose.'

The night was clear. It was getting late, but pale purple light still showed in the west.

Two salmonberries. That was the story Mom and Dad told Jenny and me. Jenny was born in May 1959. So there was no way there could be another baby. It was Jenny. And Dad was not Jenny's father. Emil, poor, romantic, beautiful Emil was Jenny's father. I couldn't imagine telling her.

Rita handed me a roll of toilet paper and a glass of water.

'Thank you,' I said.

'I hope I haven't been mistaken, telling you all this,' she said. 'It can't be wrong to tell the truth, can it? I've always believed that.'

'Will you tell me about Dad? After they met.'

'I think you've heard most of it.'

★ ★ ★

She didn't tell Patrick everything right away. She told him she was living on a friend's boat, but looking for a place for the winter. He told her there was a nice little room for rent in the house he was living in. After they ate their chow mein, they walked over to see it. It was on the top floor and had a window overlooking a creek. There was a bed, a hotplate, and best of all, a private bathroom with a bathtub. Irene was so excited, she told Patrick she wanted to meet the landlady right away. She rented it to her that evening.

That weekend she packed her things into a child's wagon that one of the fishermen lent her, and she hauled them up to the house. She left the *Elsa* shut up against the weather as best as she could. She considered leaving a note for Emil, but when she tried to write it, nothing would come. If he wanted to find her, she would be easy enough to find. The rest was so obvious, it didn't need to be said.

She waited until October to tell Patrick she was pregnant. By that time, she had a sense of how he might react. She told him during lunch break at work. That way she didn't have to answer a whole lot of questions. He was too nice to reject her outright. He was surprised, she could see that, but his only question was, *What will you do if he comes back?*

She said, *I'll keep doing what I'm doing.*
That night after work as they walked home from the cannery, he asked her to marry him.

★   ★   ★

'And, as you know, she said yes.' Rita stretched her arms over her head. 'Too much sitting.'

I was relieved to know that Dad had known. I didn't want to think of him being fooled. I didn't want to think there had been that secret between them all those years.

'The rainy season had started on the coast, so they went to Williams Lake shortly after. Irene was glad to be back to sunshine. Patrick got a logging job and he was away quite a bit. But he was there when she had the baby. When Jenny was born, Patrick said, *Another salmonberry.* Irene told me that was when she knew she loved him.'

Rita went in the house. She was gone for quite a while. When she came back she had two glasses and the berry wine. She poured some for each of us and raised hers.

'To . . . ' she began, but then she choked up. We clinked our glasses and sat looking out at the night and wondering where she was.

31

When Mom's station wagon pulled into Rita's yard Saturday morning, it was Vern who was driving it.

'Who's that?' Rita asked, her voice teasing, as he stepped out of the car and smiled at me.

'Vern!' I almost ran to him.

'Uncle Leslie had to go clear a rockslide somewhere. He asked me to pick you up.'

'You got your driver's licence,' I said.

'More or less.'

Rita gave us the lunch she had packed and made me promise to call her.

'I will,' I said, but as I waved and smiled, I felt relieved to drive out of her yard.

'You look pretty comfortable behind the wheel,' I said to Vern.

'Thanks.'

'How long have you been driving?'

'About two weeks. I had to get to work.'

'How come you're not at work now?'

'I've got a few days till they need me again.'

He also looked good, in his white T-shirt and worn corduroys. His skin had darkened from working outside and the muscles of his forearms were taut as he held the wheel.

'When do you have to be back?'

'Next week,' he said.

We drove the Nakenitses Road with dust flying up behind us and a cooling breeze from the open windows. Vern put the radio on and the rhythm of the road made me sleepy. When we got to the stop sign at the crossroads, I said, 'Let's go to Bella Coola.'

'What's in Bella Coola?'

'Maybe someone who knows about Mom.'

'I'm game,' said Vern.

'Really?'

'Sure.'

'Should you ask Uncle Leslie?'

'I know what he'll say. So not asking will save time.'

'Will he ream you out?'

'Doubt it. Unless we don't come back. Just jokin'.'

'I've heard the road's kind of hairy.'

'The Freedom Road,' said Vern.

'Have you been on it?'

'Oh yeah. On it, up it, down it.' Vern giggled.

'Are you nervous?'

He started to sing the first few lines of 'I've Been Everywhere.' He giggled some more and so did I. 'No, not nervous at all.'

'Maybe we should stop and eat lunch first.'

'Good idea.'

Vern pulled the car to the side of the road and we got out. The sun was hot so we made our way down the ditch to a rail fence that was shaded by fragrant pines. Perched on the fence, we ate the egg sandwiches Rita had made for us. Something large was walking down the highway, coming our way.

'I hope it's not a bear,' Vern said.

'Are you afraid of bears?'

'I have an average, normal fear of bears.'

'Lightning, bears ... I wonder what else you're afraid of. Look, they're horses.'

'Phew,' said Vern.

Two horses walked single file and riderless along the side of the road, heads down, as if they'd been travelling all day and were getting tired. One was a bay and the other was a beautiful brown and white pinto. They were sleek, well cared for horses with combed tails. They stopped parallel to us and observed us, then munched some grass, and moved on.

Across the road in the distance, mountains rose up blue and snow-topped and a small blue lake interrupted the green of the meadow. Vern noticed it at the same moment I did.

'It's probably full of weeds.'

'But it looks so tempting.'

We straddled the rail fence and ran for it. As we got close, our feet sank in the boggy ground.

'It's mucky,' Vern said.

'Yeah, but the water looks nice.'

'I dare you.'

'What'll you give me if I go in?' I said.

He laughed as he took hold of my shoulders. 'My admiration?'

'No way,' I said and grabbed him around the waist. We struggled into the shallows and then we both went down.

'It's cold!' Vern yelped.

'I'm wet,' I said, pushing myself onto my hands and knees.

'That was the idea.'

'Your idea,' I said and tackled him again.

Reeking of muck, and snuffing boggy water, we struggled out of the lake and picked our way through the meadow and back to the car.

'That was refreshing,' said Vern.

'I have a change of clothes.' I smiled at him. 'Do you?'

'I have my dirty laundry I was taking to Uncle Leslie's. You won't mind if I put on my dirty work jeans?'

'Go right ahead.' I laughed.

Vern and I changed on opposite sides of the car. It felt good to stand for a minute with the sun on my bare damp skin and to know that I was with Vern, driving west as far as we could go. I looked over and he was looking at me.

* * *

We left the plateau at the same place a large roadside sign read, Chains must be carried by ALL vehicles.

'Does that mean us?' I said.

'It's just in winter. Chill out, Maggie. Vern George is at the wheel.'

Another sign, just after the other but bigger: Steep grade ahead. Test your brakes.

Vern looked at me. He made an elaborate show of pumping the brakes. 'Brakes — functioning. Gas tank — on half. Oil — present, as far as I know. Everything's copacetic.'

The blue mountains that lay ahead were wilder, more remote than the ones we were used to. The snow on their tops was such a vibrant white, they looked pretend, like a magical land

346

lay at the end of the road.

'No turning back now,' Vern said.

To the south, the mountains repeated themselves to the limit of our sight. There seemed to be no habitation in there, no roads, no towns. The forest thickened, spruce and firs with shreds of black moss caught in their branches, interspersed with ponds and bogs. A small black bear was eating by the roadside. Vern looked at me pointedly, but didn't comment. A light rain began to dot the dusty windshield. We had begun our descent.

Along the roadside, wild roses bloomed luxuriantly and we cracked the windows to catch their scent and the hint of rain. We crawled along. The edge of the road, which dropped off into trees and canyon, was less than a car width away. The road was built for escape, a way to get out when the rain and the mountains were getting to you. It must not have seemed necessary to have two lanes. Maybe the road builders had ploughed through in a frenzy, not thinking about the traffic that would eventually have to travel back in.

A pickup truck was approaching.

'Oh boy,' said Vern.

'Just stay on the inside,' I said.

'Don't worry. I'm not going anywhere near that edge.'

Vern tucked in close to the mountainside to let him pass. The truck was thick with mud, and the driver waved and went on, leaving us alone again. Moments later, we drove into the rain.

'Shit,' said Vern under his breath. Then, 'Fear

not, Maggie! Vern George is in control.'

'I'm not afraid,' I said.

'Good, because you shouldn't be afraid. What's there to be afraid of?' He kept his eyes straight ahead as he talked, and his knuckles were pale with tension on the steering wheel. 'Besides the fact that we're sliding down an eighteen percent grade, five feet from plunging into the abyss? I'm not afraid either. It's all downhill. Nothing to it.'

I smiled at him, though he didn't see it. I had the strangest feeling, not fear, but surrender, like the road was swallowing us, our tires barely clinging to earth. I was grateful to Vern, in this car, in the rain, him cracking jokes.

Our windshield wipers moaned as the downpour came full force. The road became a slime of mud. The tires slid more than rolled. Vern pumped the brakes and steered to the inside. There was no need to touch the gas pedal. He did everything he could to slow us down for the curves.

'Smells funny,' I said.

'It's the brakes.'

'Should we stop?'

Vern laughed weakly. 'I don't think we can.'

There was nowhere to stop anyway, and if we did stop in that mud, we might not get going again.

It was hard to tell how many feet deep the canyon was, maybe a thousand, and how many rusted-out car bodies might be at the bottom.

'How deep is this mud?' Vern asked.

We were creeping along so slowly, I opened

the door to check. We were about six inches deep in thick sticky ooze, being sucked downhill by gravity. 'Deep enough,' I said.

We could see the height we were at, hills and mountain-tops at eye level. We went down and down, and then the road spit us out into a broad green valley with trees towering over us and the mountains so close. Vern pulled over and dropped his head to the steering wheel.

'Holy shit, I wish I had a smoke right now,' he said.

He began to giggle. Then we both giggled ridiculously till tears streamed down our faces and the adrenalin had been evenly shaken throughout our bodies.

'I don't ever want to drive that road again,' said Vern. He looked out the window. 'This looks like a pretty good place to live, right? We can just stay here forever.'

We had driven back into sun. Vapour rose from the road. Everything looked incredibly green and vibrant and I didn't want the day to end.

We drove along Highway 20, looking for a good road. When we found one that looked promising we took it. Deeper into the woods, the land rose up and closed in around us.

'Bear shit,' said Vern, pointing ahead of us. 'We're not alone.'

We stopped beside a scree that left a little room for us to pull off the road. A stream ran beside the road, and there looked to be a path leading into the forest.

'Want to see where that goes?' I asked Vern.

'Looks like up this mountain.'

'We might find berries.'

'And the source of the stream. Maybe hot springs.'

We set out, the path quickly disappearing among the thick trees. We kept going, climbing gradually and steadily. Moss and rock and huckleberry bushes, their delicate leaves catching the sunlight. I tried a berry but it wasn't ripe enough yet. The trees thinned and the wind picked up. Coming out onto rock, there were just a few scrubby trees to break the wind. We had been breathing heavily with the effort of climbing and when we stopped, I had the feeling someone was watching us. We sat looking down on the tops of trees, as the wind swept over the rock. Animal paths wound through the bushes.

'There's something eerie about this place,' Vern said.

'Maybe it's the wind.'

'Yeah, maybe. Let's get out of it.'

Back down in the trees, the wind seemed to grow even stronger, but it was high in the treetops, which were beginning to sway wildly. We weren't paying a lot of attention to retracing our steps and we found ourselves walking in swampy ground with tall ferns growing from rotting, moss-covered stumps. Through the wind, I thought I heard a voice call out a single word.

'This terrain isn't familiar,' said Vern.

'Did you hear that?'

'What?'

'It sounded like someone calling.'

We both stopped to listen. Nothing. As we began walking again, I heard it again, a two-syllable word that sounded a lot like my name.

'I heard it that time,' Vern said.

'What did it sound like to you?'

'A woman's voice, calling someone.'

'Yeah.' I tried to shake the feeling of anxiety that had overtaken me. Who would be looking for me? Who would know I was here?

Suddenly a shape burst out of the trees from behind us and streaked off leaving a wake of shaking underbrush.

'Jesus Christ,' said Vern, his hand to his heart.

'I think it was a dog.'

'How could you tell?'

'I just got a glimpse of the tail.'

Then in front of us appeared a woman in a raggedy leather jacket, jeans and rubber boots. A rifle hung from a strap over her shoulder.

'You better get in out of this wind,' she said. 'Storm's coming. You never know what trees might come down.'

Vern and I were so surprised we both just stared at her.

'Just looking for Laddie, my dog.'

'He ran by us,' I said.

'Chasing something,' she said. 'There was a small plane went down in here a few days ago. Wreckage still hasn't been found, but I saw it come down. Did you come across anything?'

Vern and I shook our heads.

'If you do, come and let me know. I'm camped

down the road about a mile. You'll see it. Blue tent.'

'Sure,' Vern said.

'Some government people on the plane, the RCMP said.'

A gust of wind piled into the woods and the treetops bent to their limits.

'Better get inside,' she warned us again and disappeared into the trees.

'The road's got to be close,' Vern said. We hurried ahead, and he was right.

The car was nowhere in sight at the spot where we came out, but we were pretty sure we were too far south.

'That way?' I said, and Vern nodded.

After about five minutes, we could see the scree piled at the bottom of the mountain.

'Thank god,' said Vern.

Once we were safe in the car, Vern said, 'That was kind of weird.'

'She didn't look like the official search party.'

He turned on the car and cranked the heat. 'For a minute there, I thought someone was calling your name.'

'Really?' I crawled over the seat to get my sleeping bag.

'Cold?' said Vern. He helped me spread the sleeping bag. There was something in his manner, some restraint that I recognized in myself.

'You?' I said.

He nodded and I spread the sleeping bag to cover both of us. The wind hammered the car and whistled at the windows. There was too much to say, so we said nothing.

Vern put his cool hand at the back of my neck. I turned to him. He pulled me close and I felt his warm lips on my neck. Then he cupped my face in his hands very tenderly and kissed me. Like sliding down that mountain road, the surrender.

The windows fogged over. The car had stalled. Vern shut it off. His hands travelled from my neck to my shoulders, down my arms to my hands, which he held for a moment. Then he slid his fingers up under my shirt and cupped each breast gently. He fell against me with a moan. Ignoring the buttons, he pulled the flannel shirt over my head and halfway off my arms. His mouth moved down my neck and his tongue touched one nipple. I breathed in sharply. Vern made a noise like a small animal, pressed his hips against me and bucked and shuddered in my arms.

We lay there like that, damp and hot under the sleeping bag, as dusk dimmed outside the fogged windows.

'Maggie,' Vern said.

'Yeah?'

'I've been wanting to touch you so bad. I'm sorry if I . . . '

'No. Me too. I'm glad. I mean I liked it.'

He cleared a patch on the windshield and through it we saw a sliver of moon showing over the ridge.

We put the back seat down and made pillows from our clothes and pulled the sleeping bag over us. Vern fell asleep right away. But I lay there listening to two coyotes barking close by and I worried. I couldn't see how I would tell Jenny that Dad was not her dad, that we were only half-sisters and that Mom had a life we never knew about. I couldn't think of a way to soften it. I decided I wouldn't even try to tell her over the phone. I'd wait to see her in person, and even then, I'd wait. But when I thought of telling her in person that meant I had to think about where we would be, where we would live and whether I'd have to quit school or not.

★ ★ ★

Whispering. 'Maggie.' Louder. 'Maggie!'

I struggled to open my eyes.

Vern was bending over me, his voice thick with sleep.

'What?'

'You were dreaming. Are you okay?'

'Mom was calling me. I heard her. Just like today — *Ma-ggie*. She was standing there, holding Cinnamon and calling me. But when I got closer, it was that old lady from the woods and she was pointing her rifle at me.'

'You're crying. Don't cry.' Vern put his arm under me and pulled me to him. 'Don't cry. Maybe we'll find her. Maybe she's in Bella Coola.'

What would he think of me if I told him that the absence I felt right then like a hole scooped out of my stomach was not for my mother, but for my white and orange cat with her soft little chin and her purr like a tractor.

32

Bella Coola lay drenched and grey in the late morning light. Rain soaked a small white church, a faded totem pole and the paint-peeling houses of the reserve. We found a store and I went in and bought a can of beans, a loaf of bread, and a few barely ripe bananas. An older man was at the till. As he put my groceries in a paper bag, I said, 'Do you know a Deschamps in town?'

'Alice Deschamps? I know just about every-body, darling. There might be a few names I forget now and then, but not too often.'

'Older woman, from the Prairies?'

'That's her. Her house is the red brick-sided one over by the river.'

'Thanks.'

We found the red house by the river. It was small and neat, with fake brick siding, sheltered by lilacs and with catmint and daisies drooping in the rain around the front step. I knocked at the screen door. No answer. I knocked again. The front drapes were drawn, but I thought I saw them move gently. Just beyond the edges of trimmed lawn, a dense forest of cedars and firs towered. I knocked once more, then went back to the car where Vern and I sat, ate our lunch and waited.

When no one came after a couple of hours, we drove down to the docks. Rain pitted the water and soaked the cedars. Moss ate at the old silvered wood of a rotting pier. Blue, green, grey, greyish green, greenish blue, bluish grey. Only the orange, rusted tin roofs of the cannery buildings and the docked boats with blue and yellow and red trim interrupted the monochromatic landscape. A man in a pickup truck pulled over by the side of the road and sat with the engine idling. The cannery roof slanted at the same angle as the deep green mountain behind it and the snow-covered far blue mountains behind that. This was the end of the road. To go any farther, we'd have to get in a boat and wind our way along the river, through cloud-shrouded mountains and out to the ocean.

Vern and I decided to make phone calls. Vern called Uncle Leslie, but there was no answer. I called Sister Anne.

'She's out of the hospital, Maggie. She's staying here for now with Sunny. They're both doing very well.'

'So she's better?'

'She's much better. They're monitoring her medication, but she's been clear-headed. She's taking good care of little Sunny. Do you want her to call you?'

'I'm in Bella Coola,' I said. 'She could call me at the pay phone, I guess.'

I gave her the number and we arranged for Jenny to call at five o'clock. The rest of the day, as Vern and I took muddy back roads and poked around dripping rainforest and fast-flowing creeks, I thought about what I could say to her.

But at five o'clock when the phone rang right on time, I didn't need to say anything.

'Maggie, you wouldn't believe how cool Sunny is. She's got these serious brown eyes and she's always watching everything. The nuns say she has an old soul. They don't think she'll give me any trouble. I'm so glad I named her Sunny — it's perfect for her. And she smiled at me the other day, I forget what day that was, when she was feeding. And she's growing like crazy. You've gotta see her. We've been out in the stroller. I'm starting to like Vancouver. You can just walk to the store and buy flowers and all kinds of fruit. What are you doing in Bella Coola?'

'Wow, Jenny, you sound really good,' I said.

'I feel so much better. That was pretty weird for a while there, eh? You must have been freaked out. But this is the best thing that ever happened to me. I mean, not the freaking out part, but Sunny. When I think I almost gave her up, it makes me cry. I look at her and I just start bawling my head off, thinking what an awful thing that would have been. She'd never have known her mother.'

'That's great, Jenny. So, I'll call Sister Anne again in a few days, okay?'

'Wait. What have you found out about Mom?'

I hesitated. 'I told you about the car.'

'Yeah.'

'Not too much more yet. But there's someone in Bella Coola who might know something. That's why I'm here.'

'Maggie?'

'Yeah?'

'Now that I'm a mother, I can't believe she'd

357

just walk away. I hope you know what I'm getting at.'

'I think so.'

'Okay. Well, see you soon then. You won't believe how big Sunny's getting.'

'I can't wait to see her.' I hung up. I was glad that I had not said anything to disturb Jenny's joy.

★   ★   ★

The next day, while Vern went to the docks to try some fishing, I walked over to the red house and knocked again. This time, when the curtains moved, I saw a cat poke her head around the fabric, her little white paws clinging to the window ledge. She looked at me furtively and disappeared. I tapped the window with my fingers. I wanted a good look at her face, but it couldn't be a coincidence. It was Cinnamon.

I pounded on the door. No one answered. I felt the tears rising. My cat. Who was this woman who had my cat? I went around the house and tried the back door. I thought of looking for a screwdriver, popping the lock. I even checked the windows, after first making sure no neighbours were watching me. Then I sat on the step and waited until I got too chilled and wet to sit there any longer.

Vern and I had made a little camp down a logging road that night. We built a fire in the evening and watched the sky finally clear above the woodsmoke and trees. When I stood to stretch, Vern stood too and took my hands. I moved into him and felt him stiffen against me. He unzipped my jeans and slipped his hand inside. When my knees gave a little he caught me by the small of the back. It was glorious to be standing by the fire with the stars shining on us, the lonely road, the fragrance of the towering cedars and Vern's hands moving over my body.

'Don't worry,' he whispered. 'I know we can't go too far.'

And so I didn't worry. We opened the back door of the station wagon and stretched out on the sleeping bag, our heads hanging out to look up at the stars. Our skin was as moist as the air and dimpled with the pleasure of fingertips mapping muscle curve and nipple and smooth line of dark hair on belly.

33

'Cinnamon,' I said and bent to pat her. She was sitting tight at the door when it opened.

'What did you call her?' the woman said.

'Cinnamon. Isn't that her name?'

She studied me, 'I didn't name her. My nephew gave her to me. She's an old cat.'

'She's not that old. She'd be about five. She's my cat. I named her Cinnamon.'

'Who are you?'

'My name is Maggie.'

'I don't know you.'

'Margaret Dillon.'

'I'm sorry, no. I don't know the name. Who are you looking for?'

'I'm looking for Emil.'

She studied me again. 'You better come in then. Sit. You can move those buckets. I've been out picking berries.'

She looked nervous. She wiped her hands on her apron. 'Would you like some tea?'

'Please,' I answered. When her back was to me, I said, 'Is he still alive?'

She turned to me abruptly. 'You're going to have to tell me who you are.'

'My sister is Emil's daughter.'

★   ★   ★

360

Alice, Emil's aunt, piled the counter with potatoes, onions, carrots, and celery as I sipped my tea slowly, waiting.

'I'm making fish soup. I could use some help.' So, while she cleaned and cut up the salmon, I chopped the vegetables. Cinnamon came and sat patiently waiting for her share of the fish trimmings. Alice made up a small plate and handed it to me. I set the plate on the floor, smoothed Cinnamon's fur and watched her eat.

'She was the runt of the litter,' I said. 'I had to feed her goat's milk with an eye dropper to keep her alive. She was just tiny. I got her just after my dad died. My mother is Irene.'

I could feel Alice stir at the name.

'Do you know her?' I asked. I handed over the chopped celery and she put it in the soup.

'I know the name. I never met her. I didn't know she had children.'

'I haven't seen her in three years.'

Again Alice bristled, then sighed.

'Emil is my brother's son. He's artistic, always was. Grew up kind of a quiet boy, very serious. Not like his brother. I think that was hard for him. Edward was everyone's favourite. He died suddenly when they were teenagers and Emil never really got over that.

'I always had a soft spot for Emil as a boy. He used to climb into my lap and sit watching the world. That was when he was really little. But I didn't really know him as an adult until I moved out here. He came out to visit me and he ended up buying a boat. I understand he met Irene around that time. I didn't see him again for many years. A couple of years ago now, late summer, he showed up at my door in the middle of the night with the cat. Your Cinnamon — I just call her Puss.' She looked at me apologetically. 'Emil didn't tell me her name. He was in no state.'

He had been thin and wild-eyed, barely recognizable. He had only come to ask her to take the cat. He had not even spent the night, only left the cat after making her promise she would take care of her and then he had gone. It was months more before she learned where the cat came from and the story it was a part of.

Alice promised me she would tell me all she knew. But she said it was a story that should be told in safety and that she wanted me to spend the night and the next day with her. I said I would.

I walked down to the dock to find Vern and we drove back to Alice's house together.

'You sure, Maggie?' he said.

'I'm sure,' I said.

'I'll come round here tomorrow afternoon.' He had a hold of my hand and seemed reluctant to let go. 'Sleep well,' he said and leaned over to hug me. 'It'll be just me and the bears tonight.'

★ ★ ★

All that evening, Alice and I kneaded dough, rolled out pie crusts and cleaned berries.

Alice told me she had left Manitoba in 1955.

'I ran away,' she said.

'Ran away from what?'

'My husband. I had inherited some money from my sister. She knew what was going on in our house and when she died she left money to me and to Emil. I didn't actually have the money yet, but I couldn't wait. I had enough for a bus ticket to Calgary. Then I hitchhiked. I wanted to go somewhere my husband would never have heard of. I got a ride from a logger who was heading to Bella Coola. He told me about this road that had been pushed through a couple of years before. Told me it was called the Freedom Road. And that convinced me that it was the place for me. Mind you when we drove that road, I didn't think I'd live to enjoy my freedom.'

'I know what you mean.'

'Oh, it's nothing now compared to what it was.'

Before bed, the counter was laden with fresh buns and berry pies.

'You need to get some sleep,' Alice said.

I had waited this long and I would have to wait some more. I could hear the river from the spare bedroom where Alice had made up the bed for me. The room was chilly and I pulled up the extra blanket. I heard the rain coming down hard again. Vern would be listening to the steady rhythm on the station wagon roof. In the middle of the night I woke hot and tangled in the sheets, dreaming that Vern was touching me. A sweet ache spread from my centre out to my limbs, my fingers, my toes. I tried to open my eyes, to remember where I was, but I was held on that warm, soft edge of sleep. There was a sound, familiar and comforting, in the room. It was

Cinnamon, purring beside me, her warm body curled against my back.

★ ★ ★

In the morning, we didn't eat breakfast. Alice gave me a cup of weak tea. She led me to the edge of her property and into the bush. We followed a muddy path through the trees to the rocky river's edge, then down along the riverbank until we saw smoke rising from a fire on a strip of pebbly beach. Two young women were tending a fire. They smiled at me as we approached. Not far from the fire was a shelter made of a frame of bent branches covered with blankets and canvas. The rain had stopped in the night and the mountains and sky were bright-washed blue. The river tumbled cold and clear over rocks. One of the young women dipped a pot into the flow and scooped the fresh water into a barrel. She did this several times. Cedar smoke scented the air. The other woman gave me a flannel nightgown to put on and asked me if I was wearing any jewelry. I wasn't. The women and Alice put theirs on a bench beside the fire.

When everything was ready, we went into the shelter. Blankets were pulled down over the door. The darkness was total. Water hissed and a blanket of steam enveloped us. My heart slowed. My eyes closed. The heat burned the surface of my skin, then seeped still deeper into my bones and loosened them.

A story rose in the darkness, a story of a man

who lived in the shelter of a burden so huge he was impervious to ordinary fear. He wasn't afraid of grizzlies or cougars, lightning strikes or snowstorms or the birds of prey that made their nests in the trees beside his cabin. Sometimes when his aunt took the motorboat up the inlet and hiked in to see him, she found him outside his cabin in the clearing, his hands red with cold as he sat in the drizzling rain drawing birds in charcoal on damp cardboard.

She stoked his fire and made him soup and pan-bannock and stayed to make sure he ate it. He had been scraped clean — there was nothing more for loss to scavenge from him. Guilt had spread in him like rampant stinging nettle and choked out every other thing so that he no longer felt it like other people did, because he had no other feeling to compare it to. It was only because of this that he could live at all.

This is a sad story. Don't think about approaching him gently like a wild, cornered animal. Don't think about holding out a hand to him. This will not be allowed.

★ ★ ★

After some time, we emerged into the sunlight, splashed ourselves with river water from the barrel and listened to the birds scolding each other as they built their nests in the trees on the far bank.

When we went back inside, the rocks hissed, steam rose and the heat deepened. Hooves rushed past outside and thunder rumbled.

365

Stories peopled the dark.

A woman named Irene in a cabin in the bush with the snow just melting and the Solomon's seal blooming under the trees and the tender turquoise broken shells of hatched birds' eggs cushioned in the moss. Irene, our mother, who had beautiful red hair and legs as shapely as a fawn, labouring in childbirth with only a man who loved her and a self-help book several years old. The sun shone on the cabin floor and moved up the walls, then the shadows lengthened and the windows darkened and the fire popped and crackled, the water boiled again, steam rose and still she laboured and the baby refused to come.

He offered to carry her to the truck and she spat at him and called him an idiot. But he'd read about that. How mothers could turn ugly that way. It didn't stop him from trying to massage her with olive oil, which didn't stop her from slapping his head and telling him to get away from her.

The story, you have to understand, is told by a man who loved our mother to the woman who was his protector who told it to me to protect him. But I suppose that most of it is true. When he could see the crown of the baby's head, Emil held a mirror for Irene to see and when the head refused to budge any further, Emil tried to help it out. Irene was worn out from pushing so long and couldn't do much more. It was dark outside. An owl hooted at the window and Emil felt he was being taunted. Sometime after midnight, Emil finally pulled the baby out. He was a boy and he was blue. At the same moment, from somewhere deep within our mother's body, blood began to flow in a torrent. Emil had never seen a torrent of blood like that.

It gushed onto the floor while Irene lay spent and asking for a blanket. Emil didn't know whether to tend to the baby or Irene. He stuffed towels between Irene's legs and tried to get the baby to breathe. The books said you weren't supposed to spank the baby, but in desperation he did it anyway. It didn't help. So he put the baby in the basket they had prepared for him and he turned to Irene and the blood.

She had stopped asking for the blanket but he tucked it around her anyway and kissed her forehead. The colour of her skin was like the inside of a mussel shell, luminous gray-purple. The towels were soaked through and there were no more, and when he tried to look, the blood just gurgled out, a viscous gelatinous purply red. He thought of cold water, to stop the bleeding, but he had only hot water.

The owl was hooting and Irene was still and cold to the touch, her breathing barely discernible. So he ran outside to the woods and found some snow and scooped it into a clean pot and carried it back into the steaming, bloody house. He kissed her again but by then she was dead. The cat, Cinnamon, hunched in the chair by the stove.

He spent part of the night in the rank-smelling bloody house while the fire cooled. Then as dawn came, he carried the cat outside in his arms, took a can of gasoline and splashed it on the front door, on the walls, at the four corners of the cabin and he lit it. He stood in the trees and watched it burn to the ground with both Irene and the baby inside. He himself disappeared with the cat and was not seen for a long time. When he surfaced, he was not a man anyone who had once known him would recognize. His aunt Alice saw the ghost of him that one night when he brought her the cat. Then she did not see him again until she heard the rumour of the black-bearded rake of a man living in the bush drawing birds on cardboard. She knew it must be him and she went to find him.

The heat had laid me out flat on the ground. A baby wailed. Snot streamed from me and into the cool mud under my cheek. The light, when I crawled out of the heat, stung my eyes. Sun and turquoise sky. Steam billowed from my body as a woman rinsed me with cold river water.

We ate salty salmon soup and buttery rolls. Berry pie. Sweet tea. Birds hopped from branch to branch, chattering, working on their nests.

'There's a piece of land up the valley,' Alice said. 'Emil has the deed for it. He told me it's in a safety deposit box somewhere. He meant it for Irene. I think he will want Jenny to have it now.'

The fire snapped and smoked with the rich scent of cedar. We watched the shadows change; sunlight striped the ferns and fallen trees. And then it was time to go back.

★ ★ ★

In the morning, when the sun came over the mountains, Vern and I packed up the station wagon and drove out of the valley. We saw two bears, three deer, and wild roses blooming everywhere. I held Cinnamon, who watched out the window, alternately meowing and purring, then climbed into the back and curled up on the floorboards in the same place she used to. Alice had insisted I take her. 'She's all I have of her to give you,' she said.

I closed my eyes and slept. I dreamed of Mom, and in the dream I was cradling her in my arms.

Acknowledgements

I wrote the first draft of *Shelter* in 1992, five years after my mother died, and shortly after I'd met my husband, David. David told me stories of his childhood, some of which took place in the Chilcotin where he had lived for a short time on a wilderness ranch about an hour from Williams Lake. The first summer after we met, we travelled Highway 20 and the back roads between Williams Lake and Bella Coola in David's indestructible Volkswagen Scirocco, and it was on that trip that the two sisters, Maggie and Jenny, and their missing mother, began to haunt my imagination.

I finished the novel a year or so later and sent it to a publisher, where it was rejected. So I put it away and began work on other things. But a few years after I became a mother myself, Maggie and Jenny's story drew me again and I began rewriting it completely.

I mention this because there are people I would like to thank who supported me in various ways through those first drafts in the early '90s: Jay Draper and Barbara Johnston; Allan MacDougall of Raincoast Books; and my colleagues at UBC where I was finishing my MFA.

For the current *Shelter*, I owe thanks to the Saskatchewan Arts Board for initial financial assistance, I am grateful to Okanagan College for supporting the research and writing of the manuscript. My talented colleagues in the Okanagan College English department inspire and sustain me. Anne Cossentine, Deborah Cutt and Surandar Dasanjh in the Penticton campus library went out of their way to chase down microfilm of newspapers from the 1960s and '70s, as well as any obscure articles I needed. Stan Chung talked to me about growing up in Williams Lake in the 1970s and I consulted his book of essays, *Global Citizen*. Sage Birchwater's beautiful book, *Chiwid*, gave me insight into the people of the region, as well as the inspiration for the fictional Chiwid in *Shelter*. Mr. Birchwater also met with me and answered my questions about the Chilcotin area during the 1970s.

While researching the novel, I stayed at Bracewell's Lodge in Tatlayoko Lake twice. My thanks to Connie for making me welcome. The hike from the lodge up Potato Mountain in June is unforgettable. My generous hiking companions on the second trip were Al, Jesse, Jack, Lynn and Maggie, our guide. They named the wildflowers for me as we climbed.

The Cowboy Museum in Williams Lake provided historical details. Gaines McMartin answered my questions about logging. My father-in-law, Dan Joyce, was an invaluable source of information about fishing and boating on the BC coast. He told me stories of fishing in the 1950s, and read parts of the draft and corrected details.

Although I have tried to incorporate all the

information that I received, any inaccuracies are mine. People who live in the region will notice that I have fictionalized most of the smaller place names, out of respect for the people whose histories are intertwined with the names.

Thanks to my very good friend Rozanne Haddad for inviting me to stay with her at Nimpo Lake, where she worked one summer as a baker for a fly-in fishing camp. Her effervescent personality helped introduce me to a side of the Chilcotin I wouldn't have seen otherwise. In the novel I've given a tip of the hat to Fred (whose last name I still don't know), who drove me to Bella Coola on the Freedom Road and showed me 'the good place' that I've tried to re-create here.

I want to thank the Naramata Centre, where I stayed on several occasions during the writing of the manuscript. The peaceful setting beside Okanagan Lake allowed me quiet, uninterrupted working hours. Melanie Murray and I shared manuscript drafts while staying at Naramata. Anne McDonald encouraged me at various stages along the way. I appreciate their ongoing interest and support.

Denise Bukowski is not only an indefatigable agent, she also offered advice on my initial rewrites, advice that I took, and that strengthened the novel considerably. I thank Louise Dennys for her enthusiastic response to the manuscript. My editor at Random House Canada, Anne Collins, seemed from the start imbued with the spirit of *Shelter*; her editorial suggestions were both insightful and exacting.

Thank you to Angelika Glover for fine and careful copy-editing.

I am so grateful for the unflagging encouragement that comes from my family, siblings Anne, Mary, Pat, Barbie and Neil. My father, Arthur Greenslade, died before *Shelter* was published, but he never failed to ask me, each time we talked, 'How's the writing going?' As I write this, David is in the kitchen cleaning up the breakfast dishes and my son, Khal, is playing a tune on the harmonica in the living room. Having them in my life gives me the joy and sense of security that make my writing possible. I thank them deeply.

We do hope that you have enjoyed reading this large print book.

Did you know that all of our titles are available for purchase?

We publish a wide range of high quality large print books including:
Romances, Mysteries, Classics
General Fiction
Non Fiction and Westerns

Special interest titles available in large print are:
The Little Oxford Dictionary
Music Book
Song Book
Hymn Book
Service Book

Also available from us courtesy of Oxford University Press:
Young Readers' Dictionary
(large print edition)
Young Readers' Thesaurus
(large print edition)

For further information or a free brochure, please contact us at:
Ulverscroft Large Print Books Ltd.,
The Green, Bradgate Road, Anstey,
Leicester, LE7 7FU, England.
Tel: (00 44) **0116 236 4325**
Fax: (00 44) **0116 234 0205**

THE UNCOUPLING

Meg Wolitzer

A strange, formidable wind blows into Stellar Plains, New Jersey, where Dory and Robby Lang teach at Eleanor Roosevelt High School. Dory is suddenly and inexplicably repelled by her husband's touch, whilst back at school, life imitates art. The new drama teacher's end-of-term play is Aristophanes' *Lysistrata*, in which women withhold sexual privileges from their menfolk in order to end the Peloponnesian War. And all across town, there's a quiet battle between the sexes: relationships end abruptly and marital issues erupt. Women continue to be claimed by the spell — from Bev Cutler, the overweight guidance counsellor to Leanne Bannerjee, the sexy school psychologist — even the Langs' teenage daughter, Willa, is affected — until everything comes to a climax on the first night of *Lysistrata* . . .

THE MIDWIFE OF VENICE

Roberta Rich

Hannah Levi is famed throughout Venice for her skills as a midwife, but as a Jew, the law forbids her from attending a Christian woman. However, when the Conte di Padovani appears at her door in the dead of night to demand her services, Hannah's compassion is sorely tested. And with a handsome reward for her services, she could ransom back her imprisoned husband. But if she fails in her endeavours to save mother and child, will she be able to save herself, let alone her husband?